Dedication

I believe everything in life happens for a reason. I also believe in life we always have doubts, as far as what we can accomplish and if we can reach a certain goal. I have been fortunate to have some very special people in my life that have always supported me, guided me, and inspired me to never give up and always have given me confidence to reach new heights. It has made all the difference in my life. I hope everyone reading this understands the special gift they have and the ability they have to support, guide, inspire, and build confidence in others.

I have been very fortunate throughout my life!

I was raised by the greatest parents (Gene and Adrienne) that have ever lived. My father's favorite saying is "EGBAR (Everything is Going to Be All Right)", and my mother's favorite saying is "The Sky is the Limit". I think it is evident from those two sayings what kind of people they are. I thank them and dedicate this book to them for supporting and guiding me throughout the years to make me the person I am today.

When I was 16 years old, I began dating my wife-to-be. Lori and I married when we were each 22 years young. At the time, I did not realize how blessed I was for God gave me the opportunity to share the rest of my life with such a remarkable person. Over the years, Lori and I have become closer than I ever thought possible. When we were 24, we had our first child and by the time we were 30, we had four beautiful daughters. Over the years she has taught me about life, true friendship, caring for others, and true sacrifice. Lori and I have a special bond that has lasted the test of time. And there is no doubt, we have had our share of challenges to face over the years, but with Lori, these challenges have been minor bumps in the road. I thank her for all her understanding, support, and guidance throughout the years, especially in this latest journey that has forced me to spend much less time with her and our children, than normal. Yes, that journey is this book. I appreciate all her support and sacrifice through this trying time and for taking the ball with all the pieces that I have been unable to handle over this journey. I would like to tell both her and the girls: Thank you for your understanding during this journey. To Nicole, Ashley, Britney, and Danielle, I am 100% complete with the book…No more Chapters! I would like to dedicate this book to Lori and the girls, and I promise that I will be there more for each and everyone of you. Slumber nights are back!

Lastly, Lori, I want to let you know that you are my inspiration every day and I appreciate the positive difference that you make for me, the girls, and all the other people that you touch.

I always thank God for blessing me with my angel. That angel is you, Lori!

About the Authors...

Brad Brown, Rich Niemiec, and Joe Trezzo founded TUSC in 1988. In addition to TUSC's corporate office in the Chicago suburb of Lombard, Illinois, the founders have since expanded the company with offices in suburban Denver (Lakewood) and Detroit (Farmington Hills). Brad, Rich, and Joe are all members in the Entrepreneur Hall of Fame.

 TUSC is a full-service consulting company specializing in Oracle providing senior-level expertise for the analysis, design, development, implementation, and support of information systems. TUSC is on the Inc. 500 list of the fastest-growing private firms in America for 1997 and 1998, and is recognized as an industry leader within and outside of the Oracle community.

TUSC attributes its success to its "adapt and overcome philosophy" grounded in the traits of an uncommon leader: integrity, moral courage, physical courage, self control, enthusiasm, knowledge, initiative, respect, tact, loyalty, and unselfishness. The members of TUSC believe that it is always better to give than it is to receive, the TUSC-authored books are TUSC's way of sharing its knowledge with other professionals in the Oracle community. If you have any comments about the material covered in this book, or would like to share some of your tips, feel free to drop the author an e-mail at trezzoj@tusc.com. Or, visit our home Web page at www.tusc.com. Our Web site features downloadable technical papers, additional tips, white papers, and links to other sources of Oracle information.

Joe Trezzo

Joe is the author of this book. He has been designing, developing, deploying, administering, and managing Oracle-based systems since 1985 (version 4). Joe is a certified Oracle DBA, an accomplished author, having served as Editor-In-Chief of *Exploring Oracle DBMS* magazine, and a VIP presenter at international conferences. He has presented papers at the last 12 international Oracle conferences, earning Top 10 honors the last five years.

Brad Brown

Brad Brown is the author of *Oracle Application Server Web Toolkit Reference* published by Oracle Press. Brad has been working with management information systems for more than 15 years, including the last 12 years with a focus on Oracle. He is recognized worldwide as a leading Oracle author and is involved with numerous organizations, having served as president and membership chair of the Rocky Mountain Oracle Users Group and Executive Editor of *Exploring Oracle DBMS* magazine.

Rich Niemiec

Rich is the author of *Oracle Performance Tuning Tips & Techniques* published by Oracle Press. He is recognized by his colleagues as an expert in the industry, having delivered the top presentation at international Oracle user groups, and having served as Executive Vice President of the International Oracle Users Group-Americas, President of the Midwest Oracle Users Group, Executive Editor of *Select* magazine, and Editor-In-Chief of *Exploring Oracle DBMS* magazine. He was the 1998 Chris Wooldridge Award winner.

Contents

FOREWORD xvii
ACKNOWLEDGMENTS xix
INTRODUCTION xxiii

1 Reviewing PL/SQL Growth and Setting the Stage (Developer and DBA) 1
   Reflect on the PL/SQL Past 2
   Identify the PL/SQL Version 4
   Realize the PL/SQL Location Transformation 8
   Review the Major PL/SQL Version Enhancements 8
   Look Ahead to the PL/SQL Future 12
   Understand the Database Testing Environment Used for the Book 14
   Review the Example Database 15
   Identify the Role of the Developer Versus DBA in the PL/SQL World 22
   Summary 24

2 Maximizing PL/SQL Development with the Power of SQL
    (Developer and DBA) 27
   Understand the Role of SQL in PL/SQL and Other Products 29
   Review Critical SQL Concepts 31
      Understand the Deceptive NULL Value in Oracle 31
      Understand the Hidden Details of SYSDATE and DATE Columns
        in Oracle 40
      Understand the Usefulness of ROWNUM in Oracle 45
      Understand the Power of ROWID in Oracle 48
   Explore the Power of the SQL Language and Functions 51
      Date Functions 51
      Character Functions 54
   Highlight Helpful SQL*Plus Commands and Concepts 61
      Utilize SQL*Plus Startup Files 61
      Execution of Stored PL/SQL Objects in SQL*Plus 63
      Expand the DESCRIBE Command 63
      Expand SQL*Plus Variables into PL/SQL 64
      Understand the HOST Command 65
      Define the SQL Buffer 65
      Detail the TIMING Command 68
      Commit Transactions in SQL*Plus 69
      Use the SET Options 69
      Use the USER Variable 71
   Summary 72
   Tips Review 72

3 Establishing PL/SQL Coding Standards (Developer and DBA) 75
   Develop Descriptive Filenames 77
   Differentiate Case to Increase Visual Distinction 80
   Use Meaningful Variable Names to Signify Scope and Type 82
   Integrate White Space to Increase Readability 84

Integrate PL/SQL Program Unit Level and Inline Documentation 87
Incorporate Various Conventions to Aid PL/SQL Development 89
Develop an Audit Trail/Version Control of Stored PL/SQL Code
    in the Database 89
Summary 94
Tips Review 94

4 Defining Standard PL/SQL Coding Techniques (Developer and DBA) 97
Learn Your Application Development Schema 99
Understand Your Application Development and Deployment
    Environment 105
Know the Database and Product Versions You Are Working with 107
Use Variable Type Casting to Shield PL/SQL Code from Schema
    Changes (%TYPE and %ROWTYPE) 108
Default PL/SQL Variables to Eliminate Hidden Problem Conditions 111
Take Special Care When Dealing with NULL and DATE Values 113
Use Booleans to Reduce Coding Errors and to Simplify
    Conditional Tests 119
Use DBMS_OUTPUT.PUT_LINE Effectively 121
Use Explicit Cursors Versus Implicit Cursors 125
Use CURSOR FOR LOOPs to Reduce Coding and Margin for Error 128
Implement PL/SQL Records to Limit Local Variables and Improve
    Maintainability 131
Implement PL/SQL Tables of Records to Improve Performance
    and Provide a Temporary Storage Table 134
Use Parameters in Explicit Cursors to Improve Readability 139
Implement Cursor Variables for Similar Queries with Different
    Data Sources 141
Use PL/SQL VARCHAR2 Data Type to Search and Manipulate
    LONG Database Columns 145
Ensure PL/SQL Variable Names Do Not Mimic Column Names 148
Specify Table Columns with INSERT Statements 149
Use Synonyms for Portability of PL/SQL Code 150
Use a Database Table to Make Program Units Dynamically
    Adjustable 152
Use ROWID to Improve Transaction Processing Performance 155
Use FOR UPDATE to LOCK Records for Transaction Processing 157
Choose Large Rollback Segments When Processing Large
    Transaction Sets 163
Use a Counter to Limit Size of Transactions per COMMIT 166
Develop a Monitoring Facility for Long-running Processes 169
Summary 173
Tips Review 173

5 Defining Standard PL/SQL Program Unit Techniques
    (Developer and DBA) 181
Understand the Advantages of Stored PL/SQL Program Units 184
Locate Stored PL/SQL Program Units Components Correctly 185
    Package Specification 185
    Package Body 187
    Procedures 189

Functions 189
Database Triggers 190
Declare a Program Unit within a Program Unit 190
Understand Variable Location Declaration Scope 191
Encapsulate PL/SQL Logic for Error Handling 193
Store Source Code for Stored Program Units in Flat Files 195
Implement Stored PL/SQL Packages 196
Understand Features of PL/SQL Packages 196
Modularize Code with PL/SQL Packages 197
Create Session-Wide Global Variables and Elements
with Package Specifications 198
Implement Version Reporting in PL/SQL Packages 202
Separate Package Specification and Body 204
Make Stored PL/SQL Program Unit Compilation Easy 207
Limit PL/SQL Functions to a Single RETURN Statement 215
Use Functions to Simplify Complex or Common SQL Statement Logic 216
Implement Packaged Inline Functions 219
Use Database Triggers to Enforce Data Integrity 221
Use Database Triggers to Create Audit Logs for Data Manipulation 225
Avoid Mutating Tables (ORA-04091) in Database Triggers 227
Overload Procedures and Functions to Make Calls More Flexible 232
Provide Default Parameter Values When Possible 233
Use Named-Notation for Parameters 235
Use PL/SQL Tables as Parameters to Pass Data to Program Units 237
Provide Labels for All END Statements 238
Encrypt Stored PL/SQL Program Unit Source Code 239
Use PL/SQL Tables to Build a Custom Error Stack 242
Use RAISE_APPLICATION_ERROR and User-Defined Exceptions to
Supplement Error Handling 244
Create a Standard User-Defined Exception to Communicate
Program Unit Failure 245
Create a Generic Error Handler to Log Errors 250
Summary 253
Tips Review 253

6 Exploring the Expansive PL/SQL Language Commands **259**
Build Flexibility into the Declaration Section 261
Use Constants for Flexibility 262
Expand Default Values by Using Functions 263
Ease Maintenance by Using %ROWTYPE and %TYPE 264
Understand the NOT NULL Attribute 266
Name Anonymous Blocks to Enable Unique Variable Naming 268
Expand LABEL Usage for LOOPs to Allow More Control 269
Use PL/SQL Cursor Flexibility 270
Use Column Aliases in Cursors 270
Check the %ROWCOUNT Cursor Attribute 271
Understand the %FOUND Cursor Attribute 272
Use IF Statement to the Fullest 274
Use the ELSIF Component of the IF Statement 277
Use of the NULL Command 278
Control All Transaction Logic Before a PL/SQL Program Unit
Completes 279
Enable the Use of Literal Single Quotes in Literal Strings 280

Beware of Multiple Line Comments 281
Examine the Differences Between SQL and PL/SQL 282
Expand the Standard Operand Capabilities 283
    Expand the BETWEEN Operand Usage 283
    Expand the LIKE Operand Usage 286
    Expand the IN Operand Usage 289
Build a Numeric Function Arsenal 290
    Use MOD for Controlling Feedback 290
Use CEIL and FLOOR for Forced Rounding 292
    Manipulate Numbers with ROUND/TRUNC/SIGN/ABS 293
Build a Character Function Arsenal 296
    Modify Character Strings with INITCAP/LOWER/UPPER 296
    Format and Convert Character Strings with RPAD/LPAD/CHR/TO_CHAR ... 297
    Process Character Strings with INSTR/LENGTH/LTRIM/RTRIM 300
    Transform Character Strings with REPLACE/TRANSLATE 301
Build a Date Function Arsenal 303
Make Data Type Conversion Easy by Using the Conversion Functions 305
    Convert Dates and Numbers with TO_CHAR 306
    Convert Character Strings to Dates with TO_DATE 308
    Convert Character Strings to Numbers with TO_NUMBER 308
    Ensure NULL Values Are Handled as Expected with NVL 310
Summary 310
Tips Review 311

7 Maximizing PL/SQL By Optimizing SQL (Developer and DBA) 315
Understand the Value of SQL Performance Tuning 318
Understand Oracle Index Use 319
    Create an Application Index Listing 324
    Examine RULE-Based versus COST-Based Optimization 325
Pinpoint Problem SQL Statements 327
    User Information/Feedback 328
    V$SQLAREA View 328
    Session TRACE Statistics 332
Establish a Developer Tuning Methodology 335
    Optimize in SQL*Plus 337
    Use TRACE/TKPROF 344
    Use Explain Plan 344
Establish the Developer Tuning Checklist 346
    Execute Statements Twice to Get True Timings 347
    Beware of Index Suppression 348
    Ensure the Leading Column of a Concatenated Index is Used 353
    Watch Adding Indexes 355
    Improve Subquery Execution 359
    Beware of the Optimizer and
        Distribution of Data 361
    Understand UPDATE/DELETE (SELECT First) 363
    Force the Driving Table 364
    Use Hints to After the Plan 366
    Watch Out for Database Links 369
    Limit Dynamic SQL Statements 369
    Fine-Tune Web-Based Application SQL Statements 371
    Modify NOT EQUAL Operators to Use an Index 371

Determine Selectivity of a SQL Statement 372
Cache Small Tables in Memory 372
Use the Most Selective Index When Multiple Indexes
Can Be Used 373
Understand the Overhead Associated with Large Transactions 374
Summary 374
Tips Review 374

8 Maximizing PL/SQL by Optimizing PL/SQL (Developer and DBA) **379**
Identify the Ranking of PL/SQL Tuning Impact 381
Create a PL/SQL Performance Testing Environment 384
Use DBMS_APPLICATION_INFO for Real Time Monitoring 388
Log Timing Information in a Database Table 391
Reduce PL/SQL Program Unit Iterations and Iteration Time 394
Use PL/SQL Tables to Improve Performance 396
Use ROWID for Iterative Processing 403
Reduce the Calls to SYSDATE 405
Standardize on Data Types, IF Statement Order, and PLS_INTEGER 407
Ensure the Same Data Types in Comparison Operations 408
Order IF Conditions Based on the Frequency of the Condition 410
Use the PLS_INTEGER PL/SQL Data Type for Integer Operations 411
Reduce the Use of the MOD Function 413
Understand the PL/SQL Engine Handling of Bind Variables 415
Use Explicit versus Implicit Cursors 419
Find Similar SQL Statements and SQL NOT Using Bind Variables 420
Store PL/SQL Program Units in the Database 422
Review Added PL/SQL Performance Related Considerations 423
Increase the Shared Pool to Increase Performance 424
Identify PL/SQL Objects that Need to Be Pinned 424
Pin/Cache PL/SQL Objects 424
Modify the sql.bsq File to Reduce Data Dictionary
Fragmentation 425
Execute PL/SQL Program Units on the Server-Side 425
Use Temporary Database Tables for Increased Performance 425
Integrate a User Tracking Mechanism to Pinpoint Execution
Location 426
Create a Timing and Tracing Mechanism to Turn On/Off
Conditionally 426
Use Rollback Segments When Processing Large
Transaction Sets 427
Limit the Use of Dynamic SQL 427
Learn the Oracle Supplied PL/SQL Packages That Assist
in Performance Tuning 428
Summary 428
Tips Review 429

9 Examining DBA-Related PL/SQL Issues (DBA) **433**
Review the Creation of the PL/SQL Components 435
Examine the Change of Source Code Storage with PL/SQL 436
Review the PL/SQL Source Code Storage Size 437
Build a Solid Security Model for PL/SQL Objects 439

Explore the Oracle Supplied Packages for the DBA 441
Know When to Encrypt PL/SQL Source Code 442
Understand the PL/SQL Versus SQL Engine 444
Evaluate Impact Analysis at a Detailed Level 444
Pinpoint Invalid PL/SQL Objects 450
Identify Disabled Database Triggers 452
Review PL/SQL Related init.ora Parameters 453
Monitor the Shared Pool Use to Determine Optimization 459
Monitor Memory and Use of PL/SQL Program Units 463
Monitor PL/SQL Related Information with the V$ Views 468
    Monitor the Library Cache (V$LIBRARY_CACHE) 468
    Monitor the Dictionary Cache (V$ROWCACHE) 469
    Evaluate I/O per User (V$SESS_IO) 470
    Evaluate Each User's Resource Consumption (V$SESSTAT) 471
    Highlight Open Cursors per User (V$OPEN_CURSOR) 472
    Identify Current Session SQL Execution (V$SQLTEXT) 473
    Determine Object Access at a Point in Time (V$ACCESS) 474
    Pinpoint Lock Contention (V$LOCK) 475
    Monitor Rollback Segment Use (V$ROLLSTAT
       and V$TRANSACTION) 476
Build a DBA Monitoring System with DBMS_JOB, DBMS_PIPE,
    and DBMS_ALERT 477
Pin PL/SQL Objects and Cursors 478
Provide Experienced Developers with Additional Access 484
    Provide Developers with READ Privilege on Oracle
       Supplied PL/SQL Files 485
    Provide Experienced Developers with SELECT Privilege
       on Selected V$ Views 485
Learn PL/SQL Yourself to Take Your DBA Skills to the Next Level 487
Summary 488
Tips Review 489

10 **Unlocking PL/SQL Security (Developer and DBA)** **493**
Establish Security for an Oracle Environment 495
    Provide Oracle System Privileges 496
    Provide Application Object Privileges 502
Understand Security for Creation of Stored PL/SQL Objects 504
    Grant Necessary System Privilege
       to Create PL/SQL Stored Objects 505
    Grant Necessary Object Privilege to Create PL/SQL
       Stored Objects 506
    Grant Necessary Privilege for Users
       to Execute PL/SQL Stored Objects 508
    Understand Early Binding 509
Understand Oracle Supplied PL/SQL Package Privileges 511
Ensure Application Portability Through the Use of PUBLIC Synonyms 511
Review System and Object Privileges in Your System 512
Lock Application Account After Production 517
Additional PL/SQL Related Security 518
    Permission for Web-Based Applications 518
    Encrypt Source Code 518
    Limit SQL*Plus Access 519

Provide Forms Security on Login 519
Provide Additional Security with Database Triggers 520
New PL/SQL Security Feature in Oracle8i 520
Summary 520
Tips Review 521

11 Exploring the Oracle Supplied PL/SQL Packages (Developer and DBA) **523**
Understand the Scope of the Oracle Supplied Packages 525
Explore the Structure of Oracle Supplied Packages 525
View the Script Files at the Operating System 528
Create the Oracle Supplied Packages 531
Execute the Oracle Supplied Packages 533
Identify the Oracle Supplied Packages in Your System 534
Provide a Detailed Reference of the Oracle Supplied Packages 538
Summary 557
Tips Review 557

12 Understanding the Power of the Oracle Supplied PL/SQL Packages
(Developer and DBA) **559**
Build an Alert System into Your Environment (DBMS_ALERT) 561
Register Sessions 561
Signal an Alert 562
Wait for Alerts 562
Remove User Session from Registry 563
Raise an Alert When Inventory Reaches the Reorder Point 563
Possible Uses of DBMS_ALERT 565
Create an Application Registration and Asynchronous Communication
Vehicle (DBMS_APPLICATION_INFO) 566
Register or Log Session Information 566
Change Only the Action Column Value 569
Read the Current Setting of the Action and Module Columns 570
Set and Read Additional Information in V$SESSION 571
Possible Uses of DBMS_APPLICATION_INFO 572
Compile and Analyze Objects (DBMS_DDL) 573
Compile an Object 573
Analyze an Object 574
Possible Uses of DBMS_DDL 575
Use the Oracle Job Scheduler (DBMS_JOB) 575
Modify the init.ora Parameters 576
View the Job Queue and Jobs Executing 577
Submit a Job (DBMS_JOB.SUBMIT) 579
Modify a Submitted Job 581
Remove a Submitted Job from the Job Queue 581
Disable a Submitted Job and Keep in the Job Queue 582
Execute a Submitted Job in the Job Queue Immediately 583
Possible Uses of DBMS_JOB 583
Provide an Easy Debugging Facility (DBMS_OUTPUT) 584
Possible Uses of DBMS_OUTPUT 586
Create an Asynchronous Message Facility (DBMS_PIPE) 586
Create a Pipe 587
Remove a Pipe 588

Package a Piped Message 589
Send a Piped Message 590
Process Mixed Data Types When Reading a Piped Message 591
Flush the Contents of the Current Message Buffer 591
Receive a Piped Message 591
Unpack and Read a Piped Message 592
Manage Pipes 593
Example of DBMS_PIPE Being Implemented in a
    Database Trigger 593
Example of DBMS_PIPE to Monitor Long-running Processes 594
Possible Uses of DBMS_PIPE 596
Enhance Session Control and Identification (DBMS_SESSION) 597
Work with Roles via IS_ROLE_ENABLED and SET_ROLE 598
Modify NLS Parameters via SET_NLS 601
Conditionally Turning on TRACE via SET_SQL_TRACE 602
Reset the State of All Package Values via RESET_PACKAGE 603
Free Unused Session Memory via
    FREE_UNUSED_USER_MEMORY 605
Possible Uses of DBMS_SESSION 607
Control the Caching of PL/SQL Objects (DBMS_SHARED_POOL) 608
Pin PL/SQL Objects 608
Unpin PL/SQL Objects 610
Identify Candidates for Pinning 611
Possible Uses of DBMS_SHARED_POOL 612
Retrieve Free Space Information (DBMS_SPACE) 613
List Space Not Used for Objects 613
Listing Free Blocks for Objects 613
Possible Uses of DBMS_SPACE 615
Extend PL/SQL by Dynamically Creating SQL and PL/SQL
    (DBMS_SQL) 615
Execute DML and DDL Statements 616
Execute SQL SELECT Statements 619
Execute PL/SQL Blocks and Stored Code 623
DBMS_SQL Error Processing 626
Possible Uses of DBMS_SQL 628
Turn on the TRACE Facility for Any Session (DBMS_SYSTEM) 628
Possible Uses of DBMS_SYSTEM 630
Specify the Rollback Segment
    to Use for Large Processing (DBMS_TRANSACTION) 631
Possible Uses of DBMS_TRANSACTION 633
Expand the PL/SQL Language with a Set of Utilities (DBMS_UTILITY) 634
Computing Statistics via ANALYZE_DATABASE and
    ANALYZE_SCHEMA 634
Compile Objects via COMPILE_SCHEMA 636
Process Errors via FORMAT_ERROR_STACK and
    FORMAT_CALL_STACK 637
Integrate Timing Routines to Monitor PL/SQL Performance via
    GET_TIME 640
Possible Uses of DBMS_UTILITY 642
Read and Write Server-Side Operating System Files (UTL_FILE) 642
INIT.ORA Parameter 643
Declare the File Handle/Identifier 644

Open a File 645
Read from a File 646
Write to a File 646
Closing a File 647
Handle Exceptions 647
Example of a Procedure to Load a Data File and Search
    the File for a Character String 648
Possible Uses of UTL_FILE 654
Pause Execution for a Specified Amount of Time (DBMS_LOCK) 655
Possible Uses of DBMS_LOCK.SLEEP 656
Summary 656
Tips Review 657

13 **Taking Advantage of the PL/SQL Data Dictionary (Developer and DBA)** **663**
Execute catalog.sql and catproc.sql when Re-creating a Database 665
Automate the SQL Files Executed upon Database Creation 667
Understand Oracle Filenaming Conventions 669
Modify the sql.bsq File for Optimal Storage and Speed 670
Automate the Process of Checking Space Fragmentation 673
Know the Contents of the PL/SQL Data Dictionary 675
Provide Correct Access to the PL/SQL Data Dictionary 678
Determine Access on Stored PL/SQL Program Units 681
Build Online Help for All PL/SQL Data Dictionary Information 682
View Object Creation and Modification Timestamps 684
Verify All PL/SQL Objects Are Valid upon Creation or Modification 685
Re-create PL/SQL Source Code from the Database 687
Provide Capability to Enable/Disable Database Triggers 692
Provide a Facility to Identify All Stored PL/SQL Object Errors 694
Develop Search Engines for the PL/SQL Object Source Code 696
Develop an Impact Analysis Facility for Database Objects 698
Determine the Object Size Loaded into Memory 700
Use Dynamic SQL on the Data Dictionary to Build DDL Scripts 701
Summary 703
Tips Review 704

14 **Exploring PL/SQL Product Integration (Developer and DBA)** **707**
Review the Evolution of PL/SQL Product Integration 709
Understand the Integration of PL/SQL in the Product Set 711
Understand and Use the Built-in PL/SQL Packages
    in Oracle Developer 719
Determine the Best Location for PL/SQL Source Code 725
Understand PL/SQL Program Unit Name Resolution 727
Share Variables Between Forms 728
Use Explicit Cursors Versus Implicit Cursors 732
Build Communication Between Forms and Stored PL/SQL
    Program Units 734
Check the Database Error When Responding to a Form Error 738
Use the On-Error Trigger to Capture Interface Errors in Forms 739
Use KEY-Triggers to Centralize Code 746
Base a Form Block on a Stored Procedure 748
Summary 752
Tips Review 752

15 Understanding the Critical Role of
PL/SQL in the Web (Developer and DBA) **755**
Understanding Cartridges and the PL/SQL Cartridge 758
Explaining How URLs Execute Applications 758
Identifying the Underlying Operation When Referencing URLs 760
Detailing the PL/SQL Web Toolkit 761
Outlining the Components of the PL/SQL Web Toolkit 761
Creating HTML Tags not Located in the PL/SQL Web Toolkit 763
Building Web Pages with PL/SQL Packages 763
Outlining PL/SQL Toolkit Considerations 764
Debugging Parameters Passed into PL/SQL Procedures 765
Writing Oracle PL/SQL for the Web 765
Using Templates for Code Generation 765
Using WebAlchemy to Convert HTML to PL/SQL 766
Setting Standards When Writing PL/SQL for the Web 766
Accessing Stored Procedures 767
Understanding Transaction Life 767
Viewing HTML Output from SQL*Plus 768
Showing the Source Code of a Stored PL/SQL Program Unit 768
Testing Procedures with Default Values 768
Reviewing Locking in a Web Environment 769
Highlighting the Best Uses of Transaction Services 770
Maintaining State with Optimistic Locking 770
Preventing Nontransactions 771
Creating a Less than Optimistic Locking Strategy 771
Using a Last_Update_Date Column Locking Strategy 771
Using the OWA_OPT_LOCK Package 772
Including Functional Objects 772
Adding Functional Objects not Supported by the
PL/SQL Toolkit 772
Including Graphics 773
Including Sound 773
Understanding the Quality of MIDI Sound Files 773
Reviewing Java 774
Reviewing JavaScript 775
Reviewing Form Objects 775
Understanding the PL/SQL Agent Usage of Environment Variables 780
Passing Parameters to PL/SQL 780
Getting Parameters from the Web Browser to
the PL/SQL Agent 780
Passing Parameters Using an HTML Form 781
Providing Default Parameter Values 782
Handling Multivalued Parameters 784
Understanding Overloading Procedures 787
Understanding the PL/SQL Agent Error Handling 788
Handling Application Errors 789
Handling System Errors 790
Integrating Error Pages 791
Summary 792
Tips Review 792

16 New PL/SQL Related Features in Oracle 8 and Oracle 8i
(Developer and DBA) 795
Learn the New Features of a Release Prior to Deployment 798
New PL/SQL Commands and Concepts 798
    DDL Commands, Dynamic SQL, and
      PL/SQL Made Easier and Faster with
      EXECUTE IMMEDIATE 799
    Bulk Binds with the FORALL Statement 801
    RETURNING Clause of DML Statements 802
    NOCOPY Parameter Option 803
    External Procedure Calls 803
    Serially Reusable Packages 803
    Autonomous Transactions 805
    Data Dictionary Changes 806
    New Database Triggers 807
    PL/SQL Backward Compatibility 810
Performance Improvements 811
Oracle Supplied Packages 812
    Advanced Queuing (DBMS_AQ and DBMS_AQADM) 814
    Large Object Support (DBMS_LOB) 815
    Random Number Generator (DBMS_RANDOM) 816
    Block Repair Facility (DBMS_REPAIR) 817
    Process ROWIDs (DBMS_ROWID) 819
    Probe Facility 821
Extended Security Methodology 824
    Stored PL/SQL Program Unit Execution 825
    Enhanced Schema Security 827
    Addition of Schema Profiles 829
    Password Management Facility 831
Support for Large Object (LOB) Data Types 831
New Objects Types and Concepts 834
    Standard Definitions and New Object Terms 835
    Support of Collections 836
    Support of Object Data Types 838
Database Limitations 839
New SQL-Related Enhancements 840
    ROWID Changes 840
    Function-based Indexes 841
    NO_INDEX hint 842
Index-Organized Tables 843
    Drop Column Command 843
Expanded Web Integration into Oracle 844
    Web Development Products (JDeveloper
      and Oracle Developer) 844
    Oracle Developer and Web-Enabling 845
    Integration of Java with SQL (SQLJ and JDBC) 846
Additional Features of Oracle 8.0 and Oracle 8.1 847
Summary 848
Tips Review 848

A The Example Database (Developer and DBA) 853

B PL/SQL Quick Reference (Developer and DBA) 881
   SCHEMA-LEVEL UNITS 882
   TYPES 884
   DECLARATIONS 886
   CURSORS 886
   BUILT-INS 887
   STATEMENTS 890
   DML AND QUERIES 891
   DDL 892
   INVOCATION FROM SQL*PLUS 893
   QUICK TROUBLESHOOTING 893
   LITERALS 894
   MISCELLANEOUS 894
   EXTERNAL PROCEDURES 895
   PRAGMAS 896

C PL/SQL Data Dictionary Reference (Developer and DBA) 899
   Main PL/SQL Data Dictionary Views 900
   View Name: USER_ARGUMENTS (ALL_ARGUMENTS) 900
   View Name: USER_DEPENDENCIES (ALL_DEPENDENCIES, DBA_DEPENDENCIES) . 901
   View Name: USER_ERRORS (ALL_ERRORS, DBA_ERRORS) 902
   View Name: USER_JOBS (DBA_JOBS) 902
   View Name: DBA_JOBS_RUNNING 903
   View Name: USER_OBJECTS (ALL_OBJECTS, DBA_OBJECTS) 903
   View Name: USER_OBJECT_SIZE (DBA_OBJECT_SIZE) 904
   View Name: USER_SOURCE (ALL_SOURCE, DBA_SOURCE) 905
   View Name: USER_TRIGGERS (ALL_TRIGGERS, DBA_TRIGGERS) 905
   View Name: USER_TRIGGER_COLS (ALL_TRIGGER_COLS, DBA_TRIGGER_COLS) . 906

   Index 907

Foreword

C ritical business decisions are often dependent on solving complex problems—fast. At Oracle Support, we recognize that the fastest way to solve many problems is to provide our customers—many of them technical professionals with years of experience—with accurate, comprehensive information before a problem or question occurs. To that end, we have put emphasis over the years on making information accessible to our customers through our premiere electronic database, MetaLink.

For many years, support meant placing a call to a service representative—even if it was just to verify a solution, obtain the latest patch set, or confirm the correct configuration for your site—and for many years, this model worked. As our customer base 'exploded' and became more experienced, and as more IT professionals turned towards the Web for information and answers to their problems and questions, Oracle saw that we needed to provide more *pro-active information* to our customers. In 1997, MetaLink was born out of the structure of the knowledge database used by our own people to solve complex problems every day. Today, MetaLink is available in 72 countries, serving over 180,000 customers. Over 6500 Web sites 'hit' MetaLink every day, initiating over 400,000 downloads of information. As you can see, I am a big fan of pro-active 'tips and techniques' getting in the hands of our customers.

It is, therefore, my pleasure to introduce *Oracle PL/SQL Tips & Techniques*, by Joseph Trezzo, as another example of getting you, the experienced PL/SQL developers and DBAs, the information needed to solve a problem and answer a question, quickly. I will recommend this book to my own support staff around the world. I am proud to recommend it to you.

Randy Baker
Executive Vice President——Oracle Support Services
Oracle Corporation

Acknowledgments

A long time ago, my father told me "Life is a learning experience". I have learned the validity of this statement time and time again. Every time I think I know something, I look back a year later and realize how little I knew and how much I have learned. This book has convinced me again, not only in the technical learning and growth, but also in terms of the vast team of talented people that take part in creating a book like this. I had a great team that assisted in the success of this book, as well as many other people that have impacted me over the years to help me get to where I am today. I will attempt to mention and thank everyone who has played a part in this success. The vast team is mentioned in no particular order of significance to the book. I believe in the statement Rich Niemiec constantly expresses, "Each person plays a piece of the puzzle to make the complete picture, some pieces are bigger than others, but without any one piece, the picture would not be complete."

I have two tremendous partners and friends, Brad Brown and Rich Niemiec, whom I have had the honor of working with over the last ten years in building TUSC, a company built on the highest level of character. They have educated me on technology, business, and life. They have been there 24 hours a day, 7 days a week. They are two very special people in my life who have elevated my confidence and vision, well beyond my wildest dreams. I thank both of them for all their confidence in me and for helping me over the years, especially over the long journey of creating this book. To Kristen Brown and Regina Niemiec, I want to thank them for the never-ending support that they have provided my two mentors and for standing by each of us and TUSC through the years. You are two very special people that deserve the best.

There are six people at TUSC that deserve a tremendous amount of credit for not only helping TUSC grow over the years and making TUSC what it is today, but especially for supporting TUSC and everyone at TUSC over the last year and a half while I was entrenched in this book. This great team includes Tony Catalano, Dave Kaufman, Bill Lewkow, Burk Sherva, Jake Van der Vort, and Dave Ventura. A special "Thank you" to each of you for your dedication, commitment, and unselfish contributions to TUSC.

I had a tremendously gifted team that assisted me in creating this book. This talented TUSC team assisted in writing several original draft versions or portions of chapters; the team includes Brad Brown (Chapter 15), Pat Callahan (Chapter 4, Chapter 5, Chapter 12, and the Example Database), Tony Catalano (Chapter 14), Bob Taylor (Chapter 4, Chapter 5, and Chapter 12), Joe Tseng (Chapter 3), Jake Van der Vort (Chapter 9), and Dave Ventura (Chapter 16). To Rich Niemiec for providing valuable insight into Chapter 7 and Chapter 8 on performance tuning, and for many other chapters in this book. To Jeff Spicer for providing the PL/SQL Quick Reference from Oracle. For many detailed facts in the book, I contacted a technical support team internally at TUSC that included Brad Brown, Pat Callahan, Tony Catalano, Deb Dudek, Rich Niemiec, Randy Swanson, Bob Taylor, Jake Van der Vort, and Dave Ventura. To Dennis Pieniazek for assisting in the detailed review of the code examples in several of the chapters. To Dan Martino for creating the draft version of a PL/SQL tools review chapter that was left on the editing floor due to space limitations. To Rich Niemiec and Brad Brown for educating me on each stage in the book process and providing me the roadmap to success.

To Randy Baker for his dedication to technology and the accomplishments he has made at Oracle to advance the open dissemination of information with the creation of MetaLink, as well as his kind words in support of this book in the foreword. To Eyal Aronoff, a good friend who is an icon in the Oracle world and a technology leader, for his kind words in the quote in the front of this book. To Ian Abramson and IOUG-A for their support over the years and for the kind words on the back cover.

To my solid technical review team at Oracle, who has provided the in-depth technical reviews of every chapter and educated me on many of the new features of Oracle 8i. This Oracle team from the Oracle PL/SQL Development Languages and Object Relational Technologies Department included Ajay Sethi (Senior Member of Technical Staff), James Mallory (Principal Member of Technical Staff), and Chandrasekharan Iyer (Principal Member of Technical Staff). Thank you each for your time and to Ajay for coordinating this effort.

To Scott Rogers, Assistant Publisher and Editor-in-Chief, and Brandon Nordin, Publisher, at Osborne/McGraw-Hill, who believed in TUSC from the beginning. To the incredible team of people at Osborne/McGraw-Hill that was extremely patient and understanding throughout the entire book process. This team helped bring this book to the next level. This team included Jeremy Judson (Acquisitions Editor), Mark Karmendy (Project Editor), Monika Faltiss (Assistant Editor), Marcia Baker (Copy Editor), John Gildersleeve (Proofreader), Richard Shrout (Indexer), Jani Beckwith (Series Design), Liz Pauw (Computer Designer), and Marlene Vasilieff.

To Jennifer Galloway, TUSC Technical Writer, who was instrumental in the entire book process. Jennifer was a pleasure to work with and her extremely positive attitude will bring her to great heights in life. She was extremely flexible, dedicated, and committed to the success of this book at all hours. She single-handedly took this book to the next level with her attention to detail.

To Sheila Reiter, one of the first TUSC employees, she has been at TUSC since the beginning and helped TUSC get to where it is today. To Barb, my Executive Administrative Assistant, who wears more hats than I do and makes everything happen. To the entire team at TUSC, I would love to detail the piece of the puzzle each team member makes up, but can only mention by name because of space limitations. A special thanks to the TUSC Team for affording me the time to create this book: Lynn Agans, Brian Anderson, Dianna Anderson, Joel Anonick, Diane Ansah, Greg Bogode, Brad Brown, Mike Butler, Pat Callahan, Alain Campos, Tony Catalano, Holly Clawson, Judy Corley, Janet Dahmen, Jennifer Deletzke, Susan DiFabio, Doug Dikun, Deb Dudek, Barb Dully, Brett Feldmann, Robin Fingerson, David Fornalsky, Jennifer Galloway, Craig Gauthier, Deb Gollnick, Chelsea Graylin, Mark Greenhalgh, John Gregory, Steve Hamilton, Georganna Hathaway, Scott Heaton, Mike Holder, Mohammad Jamal, Ray Jensen, Dave Kaufman, Lori Kelley, Prabhjot Khurana, Andrea Kummer, Jean Kuzniar, Felix Lacap, Ron Lemanske, Bill Lewkow, Larry Linnemeyer, Antonia Lopez, Matt Malcheski, Dan Martino, Sean McGuire, Michael McIntyre, James Michel, Kevin Morgan, Paul Murray, Arjun Murthy, Kent Nichols, Rich Niemiec, Karen O'Donoghue, Mike O'Mara, Mark Pelzel, Allen Peterson, James Pianki, Dennis Pieniazek, Nadica Podgurski, Amy Prevatt, Heidi Ratini, Bob Reczek, Sheila Reiter, Mark Riedel, Kathleen Rinker, Chris Rizzo, Kim Ross, Chad Scott, Larrel Scott, Kevin Sheahan, Burk Sherva, Avi Smith, Rick Snyder, Tim Somero, Chi Son, Jack Stein, Kathy Sumpter, Randy Swanson, Linda Talacki, Jennifer Taylor, Bob Taylor, Chris Thoman, Cheryl Thomas, John Thompson, Don Tornquist, Joe Tseng, Jake Van der Vort, Vince Vazquez, Dave Ventura, Jon Vincenzo, Jack Wachtler, John Wagner, Jim Walsh, Kim Washington, Chuck Wisely, Dan Wittry, Tom Wood, and Bob Yingst.

Refer to the dedication for the acknowledgment of my parents, my wife, and children. To my two sisters, Gina and Chrissy, that have endured the many years of distant hockey games, to our ever-increasing friendship, and for always being there for me. I appreciate all the sacrifices that both of you have made for me over the years.

To Phyllis Lanzarotta, my mother-in-law, who has always been there for Lori and me throughout the years. Lori has become the type of person she is today because of her mother's caring and generous nature. To my father-in-law, who is a light shining down on us now, for all his support and assistance through the years; it is unfortunate that he is not able to share in our good fortune. Lori and I miss him dearly.

To the rest of my close, one-of-a-kind family: Kelly and Lance Agne, John Athans, Joe Dougherty Jr., Jody Lanzarotta, and Joey Lanzarotta.

To some very special people in my life that have made an impact on my life over the years, either personally or professionally: Mike and Vicki Albrecht, Michael Ault, Jason Bennett, John Beresniewicz, Billy Breslan, Mickey Breslan, J. Birney and Julia Brown, Anna Buffardi, John and Ann Cashman, John and Denise Clinnin, Mike and Laura Dalton, Ann DiBrita, Chandra Dorsey, Joe Dougherty Sr., Tom Drew, Mark and Ann Marie Dubler, Lisa Elliot, Larry Ellison, Mike and Linda Fergus, James Fitzgerald, Fred Garfield, Tony and Linda Granato, Wendell and Angie Griess, Mike Harrold, Mike Henderson, Chris Insley, Ken Jacobs, Roland Knight, Dave Krienes, Ray Lane, Gary and Brenda Lange, Betty Lanzarotta, Ingolf and Eileen Magnus, Scott and Michelle Metz, Bob and Jennifer Miller, Bob Miner, Tony Miner, Tim Moyers, John Murphy, Sandra Niemiec, Tracy and Anita Nixon, Dave Noss, Tim Parenti, Clark Penn, Mark Prieksat, Frank and Lisa Provenzano, Greg Pucka, Mark and Annie Rathjen, Cheryl Rouland, Tom Schill, George and Val Schnepf, Joe Schnepf, Tim and Lisa Schossow, Greg and Donna Stankiewicz, Scott and Christine Stuth, Kathi Suchy, Mark and Beata Thompson, Connie and Frankie Trezza, Boomer Trezzo, Mary Trezzo, Dave Wallace, Kenny Weber, Kurt and Nicolette Wehrle, Steve Wilkinson, Dan Zajac, and all TUSC clients. Lastly, for anyone that I forgot to mention, I sincerely apologize.

To Scott Urman and Steve Feuerstein, who have written several PL/SQL books that have helped me and countless others learn the PL/SQL language. And to the many other authors who have sacrificed greatly to educate us all to make us better.

Introduction

B y sharing your knowledge, you contribute to the aspiration of wisdom and excellence, within yourself and others. I am a firm believer in the following statement, "When you die, everything you do for yourself dies with you; everything you do for others, lives on and is immortal." Take the time to think about the relevance of this statement and the impact you have on others' lives. This book is one more way of sharing the knowledge and a combination of my 14 years of Oracle experience along with the experience of the PL/SQL experts at TUSC to create an all-encompassing PL/SQL best practices, and tips and techniques repository. This book is packed with example techniques and source code critical to **all Developers and DBAs** to use when developing, testing, deploying, and maintaining Oracle-based applications.

As this incredible journey comes to a close, I believe I am running out of things to say. I have spent the last year and a half working two jobs, working at TUSC, and writing this book. The initial thought of writing a 300-400 page book did not seem to be too difficult…WOW, was I wrong! Now, with over 900 pages and after many long, hard days and nights, I realize that writing a book is a much higher mountain to climb than ever imaginable.

My original thought was that I know Oracle pretty well; I have been working with the product since 1985 with Oracle version 4. Over the years I have been a developer, a DBA, and often times have been both. I have seen the Oracle product evolve from a very simple product to an unimaginable suite of products, and I can no longer recall some of the product's names. It is absolutely amazing to consider the growth and accomplishments by Oracle, and the future that still lies ahead. It is a tribute to Larry Ellison and the team he has assembled.

I created this book in an attempt to take all that I have learned over the years along with the knowledge of an incredible group of technically gifted individuals, and create what I call a masterpiece. This book is a PL/SQL conglomeration of tips, techniques, and reference material. It contains a unique approach to presenting information relating to PL/SQL. The book is both developer- and DBA-centric.

This book is not intended to teach you PL/SQL. It is intended to educate Oracle developers and DBAs on the complete PL/SQL world. I use the term "world" and this is a very accurate term. PL/SQL has been at the heart of Oracle since version 6, and continues to grow and branch into every facet of the Oracle products as seen in the major advances in Oracle 8i. This book covers the world of PL/SQL and will catapult developers and DBAs to the next level and expose the full picture and breadth of PL/SQL. Many books on the market educate on certain pieces of the PL/SQL world. This book covers all pieces of the language by providing best practices and proven techniques to deploy in your environment, many of which were learned through trial and error, many of which lead me on small journeys. I can remember one journey in the book that I have to mention. It is called the "five-hour journey"...I told Lori, my wife, I had five hours to complete a chapter. Unfortunately, this five hours continued for over a week and became a one-hundred-hour journey. That is the only unfortunate part of writing a book, when you test something and something unexpected happens, you originally think you did something wrong, and then hours later you determine that the particular area of PL/SQL works differently than you expected or what you believed it to be. I went on many journeys throughout the book and now that it is over, I am glad I went on each journey; I have learned much more than I ever thought I would in writing this book. I also am a realist and know that there is so much more to learn especially with the Oracle 8 and Oracle 8i product.

Structure of the Book

The book contains two main types of information, namely, tips and techniques, and reference information. Most of the chapters in the book are centered on tips and techniques, whereas some of the chapters are more reference oriented. I have included reference material where I thought it was important to have a reference to add to your PL/SQL arsenal to remember an expansive area or to add awareness on a topic. Other chapters that are more reference-based center around new features or areas of Oracle.

All chapters contain several topics that focus on a specific area of the PL/SQL language with explanations of each topic and why the tip or technique is important, with example code segments heavily integrated throughout the book to illustrate each area. Each of the chapters are organized in the following format:

- **Title**   The title of the chapter describes the overall content of the chapter with the target audience of the chapter following the title in parenthesis. The target will be Developer, DBA, or Developer and DBA.

- **Introduction**   There is a brief introduction to every chapter outlining the components of the chapter; the goal of the chapter; and a list of the tips, techniques, or topics covered in the chapter.

■ **Tip/Technique/Topic**   Each section contains the following structure: the title of each section is the actual tip, technique, or topic covered. The first portion of each section explains why the tip, technique, or topic is important or useful. Last, each section provides an example or examples of code segments to illustrate the tip, technique, or topic. Therefore, each section is structured in the format of *What, Why,* and *How.* Also, you can use the tab you see on the outer margin of each page as a quick thumb-through reference to locate the main tip on that page.

■ **Interspersed Tips**   Throughout each chapter, additional tips or important information is highlighted through TIP designations.

■ **Summary**   Each chapter completes with a brief summary section.

■ **Tips Review**   Each chapter ends with a summary of the TIPs interspersed throughout the chapter. Some chapters are more heavily tip oriented and are based on the chapter coverage.

Additional detail related to the book content is provided in the following:

■ **Audience Focus**   This book is designed for developers and DBAs. As I outline in Chapter 1, the responsibilities of these two roles continue to become blurred as many overlap. Therefore, I believe both developers and DBAs should read the entire book to gain a true understanding of the entire scope of the PL/SQL world. I also believe each will gain a valuable appreciation for each other's role in making sure the team is successful.

■ **Example Database**   An Example database is outlined in Chapter 1 and Appendix A; it is the basis for every example in the book, with the exception of Chapter 15 and a small number of code segments where the use of the Example database was limited. I am a firm believer in being able to learn through doing. This Example database can be created in your environment to enable each section and code example to be tested, modified, and expanded.

■ **Code Segment Examples**   All code segment examples contain a filename that enables the file to be located easier. The code segment files are named with the standard naming convention of each file beginning with the chapter number followed by an underscore (_) and the number of the script within the chapter. Therefore, the fifth script in Chapter 9 would be 9_5.sql. The output from the execution of most scripts is also provided.

■ **Code Segment Standards**   All code segments follow the standard conventions defined in Chapter 3; however, throughout the book, some example code segments only conform to a subset of the standards because of space limitations.

- **Code Segment Detail** Many of the code segments contain extra detail illustrating more than one tip or technique; therefore, when reading this book, review each code segment in detail to receive the full benefit of each code segment. Many of the code segments are generic in nature and can be used in your environment with little or no modification.

- **Oracle Version Coverage** The book covers Oracle through version 8.1 (8i). Several Oracle 8.0 and Oracle 8.1 designations are interspersed throughout the book, with a specific focus on the new PL/SQL related features in Chapter 16. If the PL/SQL features prior to Oracle 8.0 are known, then learning the new features in Oracle 8.0 and Oracle 8.1 is straightforward.

Chapter Overview

The following is brief chapter summary to provide a high-level description of each chapter content. In addition, certain areas are highlighted per chapter.

Chapter 1: Reviewing PL/SQL Growth and Setting the Stage (Developer and DBA)

The goal of this chapter is to review the PL/SQL language history and set the stage for the content of this book. The new features in the PL/SQL versions, Example database (including ER diagram), and an outline of my view of role responsibility between a developer and DBA are provided.

Chapter 2: Maximizing PL/SQL Development with the Power of SQL (Developer and DBA)

The goal of this chapter is *not* to cover the basics of SQL, but rather to target areas of the SQL language to assist in the refinement of your SQL knowledge and development, thus advancing your capabilities to the next level.

Chapter 3: Establishing PL/SQL Coding Standards (Developer and DBA)

A PL/SQL Development Foundation, which is established in Chapters 3–5, is comprised of three components: PL/SQL Coding Standards, Standard PL/SQL Language Coding Techniques, and Standard PL/SQL Program Unit Coding Techniques. This chapter concentrates on establishing PL/SQL coding standards. A stored PL/SQL program unit source code archiving mechanism is introduced in this chapter.

Chapter 4: Defining Standard PL/SQL Coding Techniques (Developer and DBA)

The goal of this chapter is to define standard PL/SQL coding techniques to help a developer be more effective in PL/SQL development. This chapter is the second component to the PL/SQL Development Foundation. Several data dictionary scripts are provided to assist a developer in learning an application environment, as well as a technique of updating an entire table during production hours without affecting production users.

Chapter 5: Defining Standard PL/SQL Program Unit Techniques (Developer and DBA)

The goal of this chapter is to define standard PL/SQL program unit coding techniques to help a developer be more effective in PL/SQL development. This chapter is the third and final component to the PL/SQL Development Foundation. Stored PL/SQL program unit compilation is explained in detail and a procedure is provided to solve the nightmare of INVALID objects, and the advantages of packages are highlighted. The necessity of separately compiling package specification and package body program units is identified, and a generic error handler is defined.

Chapter 6: Exploring the Expansive PL/SQL Language Commands (Developer)

The goal of this chapter is to highlight the PL/SQL language commands and the power built into the language to ensure developers are using the language to the fullest.

Chapter 7: Maximizing PL/SQL by Optimizing SQL (Developer and DBA)

The goal of this chapter is to provide basic to intermediate aspects of SQL tuning to enable developers to embrace the responsibility of performance tuning from a SQL perspective. This combined with the next chapter will help developers to optimize PL/SQL source code.

Chapter 8: Maximizing PL/SQL by Optimizing PL/SQL (Developer and DBA)

The goal of this chapter is to cover a variety of areas that play a part in the overall performance improvements of PL/SQL program units. Developers must embrace the responsibility of performance tuning from a PL/SQL perspective. This combined with the previous chapter will help developers to optimize PL/SQL source code. There is a table at the beginning of the chapter that identifies each performance tuning area covered in the chapter, the impact rating, and the role responsible for the area.

Chapter 9: Examining DBA-Related PL/SQL Issues (DBA)

The goal of this chapter is to highlight and examine several of the PL/SQL areas that can seriously affect the DBA's responsibilities. A procedure is provided that creates a multi-level dependency map of any object, either top-down or bottom-up, as well as several V$ view scripts that pinpoint important PL/SQL-related information.

Chapter 10: Unlocking PL/SQL Security (Developer and DBA)

The goal of this chapter is to highlight the various security issues related to Oracle systems and outline techniques to ensure that necessary security measures are established to secure your environment. Stored PL/SQL program unit security requirements are detailed.

Chapter 11: Exploring the Oracle Supplied PL/SQL Packages (Developer and DBA)

The goal of this chapter is to outline the Oracle supplied PL/SQL packages and to build a reference framework of these packages that can be combined with Chapter 12 to ensure that this Oracle gift is used effectively.

Chapter 12: Understanding the Power of the Oracle Supplied PL/SQL Packages (Developer and DBA)

The goal of this chapter is to expand the understanding of the Oracle supplied PL/SQL packages through a set of examples demonstrating the power of these packages.

Chapter 13: Taking Advantage of the PL/SQL Data Dictionary (Developer and DBA)

The goal of this chapter is to examine several areas relating to the data dictionary with specific emphasis on the creation of the PL/SQL data dictionary, the storage allocation of the dictionary, and an arsenal of scripts that highlight the key PL/SQL-related views.

Chapter 14: Exploring PL/SQL Product Integration (Developer and DBA)

The goal of this chapter is to highlight the integration of PL/SQL in development products and outline the expansive realm of PL/SQL in the client-side and sever-side architecture. The PL/SQL Engine is explored in detail to explain the true operation of this powerful component in the Oracle architecture, along with a review of location dependency of PL/SQL program units.

Chapter 15: Understanding the Critical Role of PL/SQL in the Web (Developer and DBA)

The goal of this chapter is to introduce you to the integral role of PL/SQL in Oracle's Web product, namely Oracle Application Server. The chapter provides details on the various areas of this technology to jump-start your knowledge in the development and deployment of PL/SQL on the Web.

Chapter 16: New PL/SQL Related Features in Oracle 8 and Oracle 8i (Developer and DBA)

The goal of this chapter is to provide awareness of the changes in Oracle 8.0 and Oracle 8.1 (8i) with specific emphasis placed on the new PL/SQL features.

Appendix A: The Example Database

This appendix contains the complete example database used throughout the book for most examples. These three scripts, namely, plsqlusr.sql, plsqlobj.sql, and plsqlsyn.sql, can be downloaded from the Osborne/McGraw-Hill Web site (www.osborne.com) or the TUSC Web site (www.tusc.com).

Appendix B: PL/SQL Quick Reference

This appendix is a PL/SQL Quick Reference that covers Oracle 8.0 and Oracle 8.1 (8i). The tear-out card you'll find at the front of the book is an abridged version of this appendix.

Appendix C: PL/SQL Data Dictionary Reference

This appendix contains a list of the main PL/SQL data dictionary views for Oracle 8.1 (8i), along with a brief description on the content, the usage of the view content, and the differences with Oracle 8.0 and Oracle 8.1.

References

The following is a list of sources that I referenced throughout this journey. Thank you to each of the authors of these books and documents.

- www.tusc.com
- www.osborne.com
- *Oracle Application Server Web Toolkit Reference* (Oracle Press), Brad Brown
- *Oracle Performance Tuning Tips & Techniques* (Oracle Press), Rich Niemiec
- *Oracle8 PL/SQL Programming* (Oracle Press), Scott Urman
- Complete Oracle Manual Set for Oracle7.3, Oracle8.0, Oracle8i
- Bullet Proof Manager Seminars, Krestcom Productions, Inc.
- *Oracle PL/SQL Programming* (O'Reilly), Steve Feuerstein
- *Oracle Built-in Packages* (O'Reilly), Steve Feuerstein, Charles Dye & John Beresniewicz
- *Oracle PL/SQL Language Pocket Reference* (O'Reilly), Steve Feuerstein, Bill Pribyl & Chip Dawes

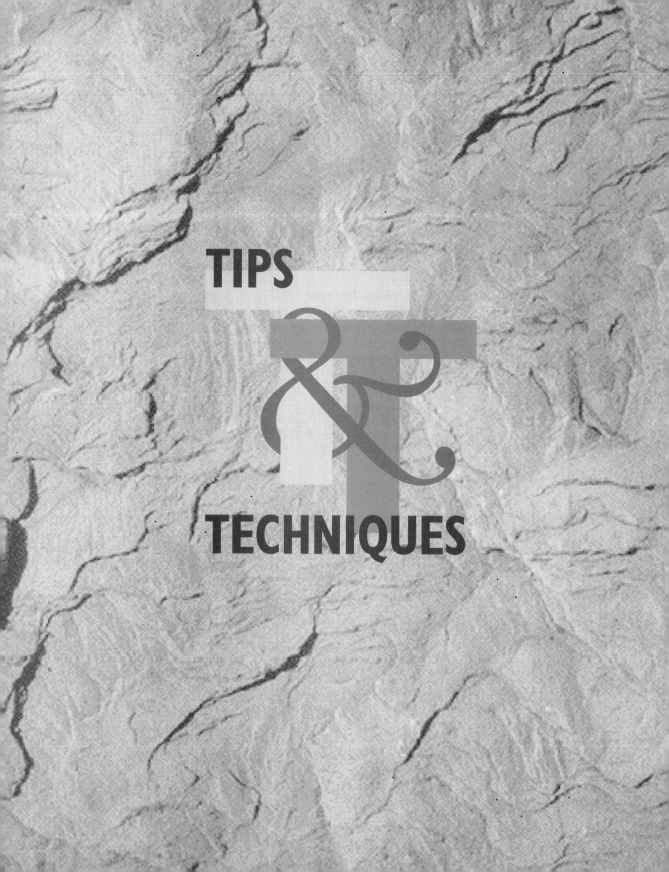

TIPS

&

TECHNIQUES

CHAPTER
1

Reviewing PL/SQL
Growth and Setting the
Stage (Developer
and DBA)

A constant battle is being waged to stay ahead of the curve in application systems development. Your company strives to keep up with technology as it continues to accelerate and forge ahead into the twenty-first century. What does the future hold or, more important, are we positioned for the future? It is extremely important to analyze the past while attempting to answer this question and predict the future. Understanding the history of the PL/SQL language and its tremendous growth over the years, as well as its future in the Oracle architecture, is also extremely important.

This chapter reviews the PL/SQL language throughout its growth and identifies some of the new features. The PL/SQL language has become a full-fledged, procedural programming language that is central to the Oracle database and toolset. The future of PL/SQL in the Oracle architecture is also reviewed. The goal of this chapter is to review the PL/SQL language history and set the stage for the content of this book.

After reviewing PL/SQL's past, present, and future, this chapter finishes with sections that set the stage for this PL/SQL tips and techniques book.

The topics are covered in the following sections:

- Reflect on the PL/SQL past
- Identify the PL/SQL version
- Realize the PL/SQL location transformation
- Review the major PL/SQL version enhancements
- Look ahead to the PL/SQL future
- Understand the database testing environment used for the book
- Review the example database
- Identify the role of the developer versus DBA in the PL/SQL world

Reflect on the PL/SQL Past

Whatever happened to the days when programming was simple, basic, with minimal complexity? I remember when I started in Oracle in 1985, my first job, fresh out of college, and I entered the doors of my first company to begin my career. I sat down at a desk and stared at these two large black binders with the Oracle name staring back at me. Without knowing it, Oracle was about to become an important and constant part of my life. At the time, I did not consider the Oracle product simple, but reflecting back now, I am amazed that it was possible to develop applications that performed any complexity. Think of it. Back then, when you bought Oracle, you got it all—the database, the screen interface (IAF, which was made up of two modules, namely IAG for developing and generating the screens and IAP for running the screens), the report interface (RPT), and the 3GL program interface (Pro Languages). As far as developing screens, it was a manual character process of answering questions, modifying the code in an editor, and drawing the screen lines and boxes with characters (*t, q,* and so forth). Only five triggers were available in a screen (post-change, pre- and post-insert, update, and delete). This was Oracle version 4. The Internet did not exist and my first PC was a top-of-the-line 286 with 1M of RAM and a 20M hard disk.

Oracle has truly grown up since then and the complexity of the database and toolset has experienced several evolutions over the years. Oracle has continued to fulfill their motto of Scalability, Availability, and Portability. This has catapulted them over the years into the lead and dominance of the database arena, with minimal competition.

When Oracle rewrote 70 percent of the kernel progressing from Oracle version 5 to version 6, they introduced the PL/SQL language, version 1.0. This language has become the standard foundation of Oracle with PL/SQL integration into the database, as well as the development product set. Originally, the PL/SQL language was used primarily as a replacement of the cryptic step trigger method of logic development in Forms (namely, SQL*Forms 3.0) and to add some procedural logic in SQL*Plus.

Oracle expanded the role of PL/SQL with the introduction of Oracle7; this language became the core foundation for the database kernel and all product sets. Oracle7 introduced version 2.0 of the PL/SQL Engine. With each incremental release of Oracle7 versions came the introduction of a new version of the PL/SQL Engine on the server-side (PL/SQL incremented the second digit of the version to correspond to the second digit of the Oracle7 version). When Oracle8 was released, they changed their versioning schema to an engine version mirroring the database version. Therefore, Oracle version 8.0.4 of the database includes PL/SQL version 8.0.4. The following table shows the server-side version of Oracle and the corresponding versions of PL/SQL.

Oracle Database Version	PL/SQL Version
6.x	1.0
7.0	2.0
7.1	2.1
7.2	2.2
7.3	2.3
8.0	8.0
8.1	8.1

Reflecting on the PL/SQL Past

With each new version came new enhanced features to increase the capability of the PL/SQL language, enabling it to become the de facto Oracle database procedural language that is the foundation for all products. A quick overview of the new features for each version is highlighted later in this chapter.

So far, I have concentrated on the server-side and the PL/SQL Engine version on this side. However, Oracle has extended the PL/SQL language architecture and integrated a separate PL/SQL Engine in many of the product toolsets such as Oracle Developer (Forms, Reports, and Graphics), Oracle Designer, Oracle Discoverer, and Oracle Application Server. This product integration enables the front-end interfaces to process some of the PL/SQL parsing and execution tasks without communication to the server side database (PL/SQL Engine). This works well in theory, but Oracle had a problem with keeping the PL/SQL Engines for each product on a consistent level. At one point, the database was up to PL/SQL version 2.3 and the Forms PL/SQL Engine was still only supporting PL/SQL version 1.1. This caused a problem because many of the new features that were introduced from 1.1 to 2.3 were available on the server-side and not on the client-side. Workarounds existed, but it caused extra complexity and confusion for developers.

Today, Oracle has upgraded the PL/SQL Engines in each product to ensure consistent feature capability at any level of PL/SQL programming.

Figure 1-1 displays the method of execution for PL/SQL blocks. Oracle Designer, Oracle Developer, Oracle Discoverer, and Oracle Application Server all contain their own PL/SQL Engines. A PL/SQL Engine also exists in the Oracle kernel. If possible, the PL/SQL Engine on the client will execute a PL/SQL block. SQL statements are passed to the server for execution. If a stored PL/SQL program unit is called, then the call is passed to the server-side PL/SQL Engine and executed on the server.

Note that SQL*Plus, Oracle Programmer (the Pro*Languages) and third-party Oracle products that support PL/SQL do not contain their own integrated PL/SQL Engines. These products must pass all PL/SQL source code to the server-side PL/SQL Engine for processing. Refer to Chapter 14 for a detailed explanation of PL/SQL Engine execution.

Identify the PL/SQL Version

So many PL/SQL versions have been released in the past three years that it is very difficult to remember what was available in which version. Obviously, if you are on the most recent version of PL/SQL, all features are available. Many companies support multiple database instances and applications, so finding a company where all database instances are on a consistent Oracle version is rare. Companies typically upgrade one database instance and application at a time. The first upgrade is the most important to ensure all unknown issues are identified and addressed for the next database instance and application. If you are in consulting, you are constantly faced with this particular

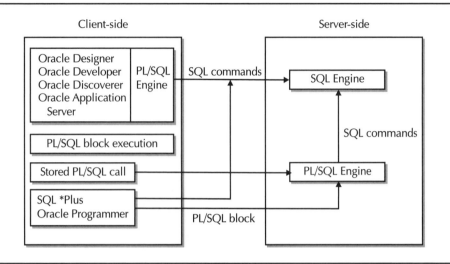

FIGURE 1-1. *General diagram depicting the PL/SQL Engine integration and execution in the database server and product toolset*

challenge because all companies have different strategies for upgrading versions. I currently know of companies that have production applications deployed on versions as low as version 6 of Oracle, others on Oracle 8.1, and still others on Oracle7 (7.0, 7.1, 7.2, and 7.3).

It is important to know the version of each product you are working with. You need to know the server-side and client-side tools because they may differ.

To determine the database PL/SQL version, the following two methods are outlined.

   1. Log into SQL*Plus and note the version of PL/SQL, as shown in the following example:

Oracle 7.3 example:

```
SQL*Plus: Release 3.3.4.0.0 - Production on Fri Oct 16 11:07:47 1998
Copyright (c) Oracle Corporation 1979, 1996.  All rights reserved.

Connected to:
Personal Oracle7 Release 7.3.2.1.1 - Production Release
With the distributed and replication options
PL/SQL Release 2.3.2.0.0 - Production

SQL>
```

Oracle 8.0 example:

```
SQL*Plus: Release 3.3.4.0.0 - Production on Fri Oct 16 11:26:44 1998
Copyright (c) Oracle Corporation 1979, 1996.  All rights reserved.

Connected to:
Oracle8 Enterprise Edition Release 8.0.4.0.0 - Production
With the Partitioning and Objects options
PL/SQL Release 8.0.4.0.0 - Production

SQL>
```

Oracle 8.1 example:

```
SQL*Plus: Release 3.3.4.0.0 - Production on Fri Jul 17 10:22:41 1999
Copyright (c) Oracle Corporation 1979, 1996.  All rights reserved.

Connected to:
Oracle8i Enterprise Edition Release 8.1.5.0.0 - Production
With the Partitioning and Java options
PL/SQL Release 8.1.5.0.0 - Production

SQL>
```

2. While in SQL*Plus, execute the following query:

```
SELECT *
FROM   product_component_version;
```

Oracle 7.3 example:

PRODUCT	VERSION	STATUS
CORE	3.5.4.0.0	Production
NLSRTL	3.2.4.0.0	Production
PL/SQL	2.3.2.0.0	Production
Personal Oracle7	7.3.2.1.1	Production Release
TNS for 32-bit Windows:	2.3.4.0.0	Production

Oracle 8.0 example:

PRODUCT	VERSION	STATUS
CORE	4.0.4.0.0	Production

```
NLSRTL                           3.3.1.0.0   Production
Oracle8 Enterprise Edition       8.0.4.0.0   Production
PL/SQL                           8.0.4.0.0   Production
TNS for 32-bit Windows:          8.0.4.0.0   Production
```

Oracle 8.1 example:

```
PRODUCT                          VERSION     STATUS
-------------------------------  ----------  ----------
CORE                             8.1.5.0.0   Production
NLSRTL                           3.4.0.0.0   Production
Oracle8i Enterprise Edition      8.1.5.0.0   Production
PL/SQL                           8.1.5.0.0   Production
TNS for 32-bit Windows:          8.1.5.0.0   Production
```

To determine the Forms PL/SQL version, under the Form Builder Help/About Form Builder menu, a list of all the versions of the products is in use for the current product as illustrated in Figure 1-2.

The same method used to determine the version of PL/SQL in Forms can be administered to determine the PL/SQL version in most other Oracle products.

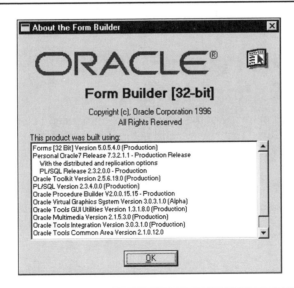

FIGURE 1-2.   *Help window displaying the PL/SQL versions (server-side and client-side) and other component versions used in this Forms version*

Realize the PL/SQL Location Transformation

With the release of Oracle7 came the capability of storing PL/SQL source code modules (PL/SQL objects) in the database. The four types of PL/SQL program units that could be stored in the database were packages, procedures, functions, and database triggers. This database storage capability started the location transformation of PL/SQL source code into the database. This movement has now become a standard. Many advantages exist in storing PL/SQL code in the database, including performance improvements, security improvements, ease of maintenance, and the list goes on. These advantages are covered more in Chapters 5, 8, 9, 10, and 13.

What does this transformation mean in terms of the architecture of an Oracle application? Think about the size of the PL/SQL source code in your applications. You are housing more of your application source code in the database, rather than at the product or operating system level. The PL/SQL logic in many products is reduced to calls that execute stored PL/SQL program units. In addition, these stored PL/SQL program units are already compiled.

This has been the direction of Oracle for some time, evidenced in many of their product sets that store information in the database. This transformation will continue, as evidenced by Oracle's upcoming products, continuing the movement of code and information into the database.

Review the Major PL/SQL Version Enhancements

This section focuses on many of the new features introduced in each version of PL/SQL and can be used as a reference to determine if something is available in your version of PL/SQL.

PL/SQL version 1.0:

- Introduction of PL/SQL
- Basic PL/SQL language with anonymous blocks

PL/SQL version 2.0:

- Stored PL/SQL program units (packages, procedures, functions, database triggers)

- Data Dictionary views for storage of stored PL/SQL program units
- Character (CHAR) changed to fixed length to support ANSI standard
- User defined composite Types: Tables and Records
- Many Oracle supplied packages

PL/SQL version 2.1:

- More than one of the same type of database trigger on a table
- In-line functions (PL/SQL functions callable in SQL)
- User defined subtypes
- PL/SQL subtype
- DBMS_SQL package
- Several Oracle supplied packages expanded
- RESTRICT_REFERENCES pragma

PL/SQL version 2.2:

- Cursor variables (REF CURSORS)
- User defined constrained subtypes
- WRAP facility (also used by Oracle to WRAP their supplied package bodies)
- DBMS_JOB package
- Data Dictionary DBMS_JOB views to store job information
- Several Oracle supplied packages expanded

PL/SQL version 2.3:

- Database triggers can be compiled
- Cursor variables enhancements (unconstrained)

Reviewing Major PL/SQL Version Enhancements

- Remote object dependency signature method
- PL/SQL tables expanded (tables of records; attributes to manipulate PL/SQL tables)
- PLS_INTEGER data type
- UTL_FILE package
- DBMS_APPLICATION_INFO package
- Several Oracle supplied packages expanded
- Full support for subqueries (FROM clauses)

PL/SQL version 8.0:

- External calls to 3GL programs
- Support for new object data types and methods (Objects, NLS, LOBS, Collections)
- Database trigger expansion (INSTEAD OF)
- REF INTO on INSERT, UPDATE, and DELETE statements
- RETURNING clause on INSERT, UPDATE, and DELETE
- SERIALLY_REUSABLE pragma
- Nested table support
- REF object type
- VARRAYs support
- Tracing and debugging capabilities expanded
- Advanced Queueing support
- Large object support
- DBMS_IOT package
- DBMS_LOB package
- DBMS_ROWID package
- DBMS_AQ package
- DBMS_AQADM packages

- DBMS_RANDOM package
- DBMS_DEFER package
- DBMS_DEFER_SYS package
- DBMS_DEFER_QUERY package
- UTL_REF package
- Several Oracle supplied packages expanded

PL/SQL version 8.1:

- Stored PL/SQL program unit AUTHID option
- EXECUTE IMMEDIATE statement (replaces DBMS_SQL)
- FORALL statement
- NOCOPY parameter for stored PL/SQL program units
- AUTONOMOUS_TRANSACTION pragma
- Eight new database triggers (beyond database table definition)
- Data Dictionary expansion to support new types
- Several internal PL/SQL Engine performance improvements
- DBMS_DEBUG package
- DBMS_LOGMNR package
- DBMS_OLAP package
- DBMS_ORACLE_TRACE_USER package
- DBMS_PROFILER package
- DBMS_REPAIR package
- DBMS_RLS package
- DBMS_SPACE_ADMIN package
- DBMS_STATS package
- DBMS_TRACE package
- DBMS_TTS package

- UTL_COLL package

- Several Oracle supplied packages expanded

Look Ahead to the PL/SQL Future

PL/SQL has become a full-fledged programming language that is the foundation for Oracle's database and product set; therefore, PL/SQL will be around for a long time. Oracle has committed to integrate Java into the Oracle core foundation, enabling the development in Java to assist in the advancement of Oracle into the Internet and the Network Computing Architecture. Java takes a significant leap forward in Oracle 8i, enabling development to be performed in Java and PL/SQL.

Oracle has stated its continued commitment to PL/SQL, as evidenced in the following statements taken from one of Oracle's white papers on Oracle8:

"We are committed to further build on PL/SQL's strength as a tightly integrated, easy-to-use, efficient, and scaleable application development solution in the Oracle environment."

"We intend to build on our inherent strengths and continue to make PL/SQL the language of choice for SQL programmers."

Oracle will continue to expand the functionality and performance of PL/SQL to continue its effectiveness and role in Oracle's architecture. This is evidenced in the major expansion of PL/SQL with Oracle releases 8.0 and 8.1. PL/SQL is integrated into the kernel and Oracle's main development products. PL/SQL has been proven to be a capable and efficient language. Most, if not all, companies developing in Oracle are tied to PL/SQL or have a major investment in PL/SQL from both the standpoint of the volume of already developed PL/SQL source code in existing applications and staff with a core competency in PL/SQL.

As Oracle continues into the future, improvements will continue in the PL/SQL language as Oracle continues to improve performance, reduce memory requirements, and expand the language capabilities. Some of these improvements that are introduced in Oracle 8.1 are highlighted in the following:

- Faster execution of PL/SQL functions (the standard package character and math functions)

- The PL/SQL Engine will be coupled tighter with the SQL Engine

- Code generation optimization improvements

- PL/SQL remote call procedure (RPC) performance improved
- Stored PL/SQL subprogram calls optimized
- Reduction of memory for PL/SQL execution per user
- Improved error and exception handling
- Support of PL/SQL APIs

As for Java, Oracle has committed to making Java an integral part of the Oracle environment. Java will be integrated into the Oracle database architecture in a similar manner to PL/SQL and become an alternative development environment to PL/SQL. Java and PL/SQL will coexist and interoperate in the database. Java will be tightly coupled with the Oracle database, having a Java Virtual Machine (VM) integrated in the database. The Java VM includes JDBC drivers and SQLJ translators, enabling Oracle to support JDBC and SQLJ code. Oracle will allow the creation of Java stored procedures and database triggers. Oracle provides the capability to embed SQL in Java through SQLJ and will extend both PL/SQL and Java to enable calls to each other's stored objects with transparent execution. Therefore, if you decide to go forward implementing just Java, no need exists to rewrite current business logic and rules written in PL/SQL; these can be called "as is" from within Java.

Oracle's JDeveloper product enables Java development in JDBC or SQLJ code to assist in the development of Java-based interfaces to the Oracle database.

Java appears to be the way of the future, but it is still not proven. PL/SQL is a proven language, and it is here to stay. Oracle will continue to enhance and improve the PL/SQL development language, and to integrate and exploit the Java language and capabilities. Both have advantages and disadvantages you must weigh to determine where to make your investment. My recommendation at this time would be to continue to develop in PL/SQL and to start examining the Java language and its capabilities. As Java continues to become a viable programming language, use Java where it makes sense in your environment. If you stay with PL/SQL for a long time or go full force into Java as your programming standard, your current and future investment in PL/SQL will not be lost because PL/SQL stored objects can always be called from Java. Keep an eye on this evolving playing field and time will tell when, or if, you should change.

My recommendation any time regarding technology is "Never be on the bleeding edge, unless you have time and money to waste or a very strong business need. Typically, by the time you work through all the problems and/or bugs or come up with workarounds, the next version is available and many, if not all, the problems you encountered are corrected. Once there is stability, assured from talking to peers in the industry and not from what you read in trade magazines, then take the next step. You will save a tremendous amount of time, money, frustration, and pain."

Looking Ahead to the PL/SQL Future

Understand the Database Testing Environment Used for the Book

The testing of most of the examples in the book were executed under three different environments to ensure cross-version correctness and to enable cross-version differences to be highlighted in examples. The example database outlined in the next section was created under all three environments for testing. These environments are outlined in the following tables:

Environment 1:

Product	Version
Microsoft Windows 95	4.00.950.B
Personal Oracle7	7.3.2.1.1
PL/SQL	2.3.4.0.0
SQL*Plus	3.3.4.0.0
Oracle Developer: Forms (PL/SQL)	5.0.5.4.0 (2.3.4.0.0)

Environment 2:

Product	Version
Windows NT	Server 4.0 Service Pack 3
Oracle8 Enterprise Edition	8.0.4.0.0
PL/SQL	8.0.4.0.0
SQL*Plus	3.3.4.0.0
Oracle Developer: Forms (PL/SQL)	5.0.5.4.0 (2.3.4.0.0)

Environment 3:

Product	Version
Windows NT	Server 4.0 Service Pack 3
Oracle8i Enterprise Edition	8.1.5.0.0
PL/SQL	8.1.5.0.0

Product	Version
SQL*Plus	3.3.4.0.0
Oracle Developer: Forms (PL/SQL)	5.0.5.4.0 (2.3.4.0.0)

Review the Example Database

Most of the examples shown throughout this book refer to a common database, which provides the capability to re-create each example on your own system. There are a couple of examples throughout the book that do not use the example database due to the unique conditions or the nature of the example (Chapter 15 examples do not use the example database). The example database is created from three SQL scripts as outlined in the following table.

SQL File	Description of Contents
plsqlusr.sql	Contains the creation of the PLSQL_USER user account with privileges to execute the plsqlobj.sql script
plsqlobj.sql	Contains the creation of all tables, sequences, indexes, constraints, as well as the data insert statements to populate the example database
plsqlsyn.sql	Contains the creation of all synonyms for the example tables

No special storage parameters are specified on the objects, so the objects by default will be created in the SYSTEM tablespace and with the default storage for the SYSTEM tablespace. These scripts can be modified to change the PLSQL_USER account to a default tablespace for the creation of the objects and/or to include a storage section to the object creations. If you are unfamiliar with these operations or do not have the necessary privilege, contact your DBA. If at any time, your example objects become unusable from your manipulation and you want to start over, you can drop the PLSQL_USER user and re-execute the three scripts again. The drop user command is shown in the following:

```
DROP USER plsql_user CASCADE;
```

Figure 1-3 provides an entity relationship (ER) diagram to depict the relationships between the tables in the example database.

The scripts outlined in the preceding table are included for reference and can be downloaded from the Osborne McGraw-Hill Web site (www.osborne.com) or the TUSC Web site (www.tusc.com). The plsqlusr.sql script is shown in its entirety, where-

Reviewing the Example Database

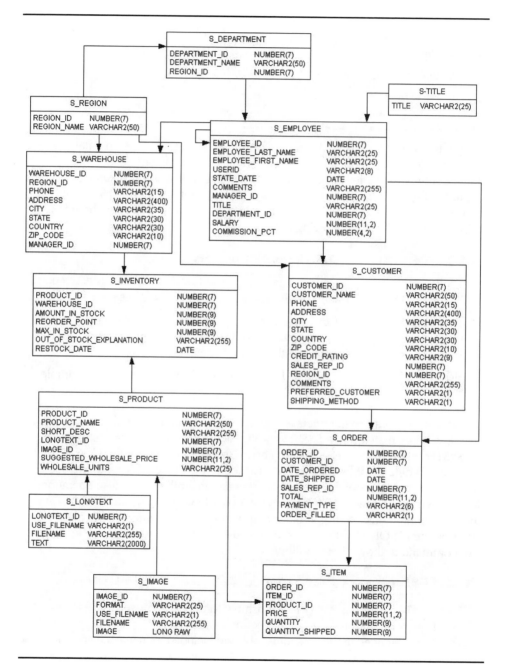

FIGURE 1-3. *ER diagram of the example database*

as the contents of the plsqlobj.sql script has been limited in this chapter to only the table definitions and content comments. The plsqlsyn.sql script is not shown below. The three scripts can be found in their entirety in Appendix A of this book.

File: plsqlusr.sql

```
- Program:      plsqlusr.sql
- Creation:     09/01/97
- Created By:   TUSC
- Description: Creates the PL/SQL user named plsql_user to allow
-              for the plsqlobj.sql script to be executed.  This
-              script needs to be executed under a user with DBA
-              privileges.

SPOOL plsqlusr.log

CREATE USER plsql_user IDENTIFIED BY plsql_user;
GRANT CONNECT, RESOURCE TO plsql_user;

SPOOL OFF
```

File: plsqlobj.sql

```
- Program:      plsqlobj.sql
- Creation:     09/01/97
- Created By:   TUSC
- Description: Creates the sequences, tables, constraints, and
-              inserts the example data for the PL/SQL Tips and
-              Techniques Book.

SET ECHO OFF
SET FEEDBACK 1
SET TERMOUT ON

SPOOL plsqlobj.log

- *******************************************************************
- Creates sequence numbers for use in example database.
-
-    Sequence Number        Table
-    -----------------      --------
-    s_customer_id          s_customer
-    s_department_id        s_department
-    s_employee_id          s_employee
-    s_image_id             s_image
-    s_longtext_id          s_longtext
```

```
-    s_order_id           s_order
-    s_product_id         s_product
-    s_region_id          s_region
-    s_warehouse_id       s_warehouse
- ***************************************************************
- ***************************************************************
- Creates tables and constraints for use in example database.
-
-    Table
-    -------
-    s_customer
-    s_department
-    s_employee
-    s_image
-    s_inventory
-    s_item
-    s_longtext
-    s_order
-    s_product
-    s_region
-    s_title
-    s_warehouse
- ***************************************************************
CREATE TABLE s_customer
(customer_id          NUMBER(7)
                      CONSTRAINT s_customer_id_nn NOT NULL,
 customer_name        VARCHAR2(50)
                      CONSTRAINT s_customer_name_nn NOT NULL,
 phone                VARCHAR2(15),
 address              VARCHAR2(400),
 city                 VARCHAR2(35),
 state                VARCHAR2(30),
 country              VARCHAR2(30),
 zip_code             VARCHAR2(10),
 credit_rating        VARCHAR2(9),
 sales_rep_id         NUMBER(7),
 region_id            NUMBER(7),
 comments             VARCHAR2(255),
 preferred_customer   VARCHAR2(1) DEFAULT 'N' NOT NULL,
 shipping_method      VARCHAR2(1) DEFAULT 'M' NOT NULL,
 CONSTRAINT s_customer_pref_cust CHECK
    (preferred_customer IN ('Y', 'N')),
 CONSTRAINT s_customer_ship_method CHECK
    (shipping_method IN ('M', 'F', 'U')),
 CONSTRAINT s_customer_id_pk PRIMARY KEY (customer_id),
 CONSTRAINT s_customer_credit_rating_ck CHECK
    (credit_rating IN ('EXCELLENT', GOOD', 'POOR')));
```

```
CREATE TABLE s_department
(department_id    NUMBER(7)
                  CONSTRAINT s_department_id_nn NOT NULL,
 department_name VARCHAR2(50)
                  CONSTRAINT s_department_name_nn NOT NULL,
 region_id        NUMBER(7),
 CONSTRAINT s_department_id_pk PRIMARY KEY (department_id),
 CONSTRAINT s_department_name_region_id_uk UNIQUE
    (department_name, region_id));

CREATE TABLE s_employee
(employee_id         NUMBER(7)
                     CONSTRAINT s_employee_id_nn NOT NULL,
 employee_last_name  VARCHAR2(25)
                     CONSTRAINT s_employee_last_name_nn NOT NULL,
 employee_first_name VARCHAR2(25),
 userid              VARCHAR2(8),
 start_date          DATE,
 comments            VARCHAR2(255),
 manager_id          NUMBER(7),
 title               VARCHAR2(25),
 department_id       NUMBER(7),
 salary              NUMBER(11, 2),
 commission_pct      NUMBER(4, 2),
 CONSTRAINT s_employee_id_pk PRIMARY KEY (employee_id),
 CONSTRAINT s_employee_userid_uk UNIQUE (userid),
 CONSTRAINT s_employee_commission_pct_ck CHECK
    (commission_pct IN (10, 12.5, 15, 7.5, 20)));

CREATE TABLE s_image
(image_id      NUMBER(7)   CONSTRAINT s_image_id_nn NOT NULL,
 format        VARCHAR2(25),
 use_filename  VARCHAR2(1),
 filename      VARCHAR2(255),
 image         LONG RAW,
 CONSTRAINT s_image_id_pk PRIMARY KEY (image_id),
 CONSTRAINT s_image_format_ck CHECK
    (format IN ('JFIFF', 'JTIFF')),
 CONSTRAINT s_image_use_filename_ck CHECK
    (use_filename IN ('Y', 'N')));

CREATE TABLE s_inventory
(product_id     NUMBER(7)
                CONSTRAINT s_inventory_product_id_nn NOT NULL,
 warehouse_id   NUMBER(7)
                CONSTRAINT s_inventory_warehouse_id_nn NOT NULL,
 amount_in_stock NUMBER(9),
 reorder_point  NUMBER(9),
```

```
max_in_stock        NUMBER(9),
out_of_stock_explanation VARCHAR2(255),
restock_date        DATE,
CONSTRAINT s_inventory_prod_id_whse_id_pk PRIMARY KEY
    (product_id, warehouse_id));

CREATE TABLE s_item
(order_id            NUMBER(7)
                    CONSTRAINT s_item_order_id_nn NOT NULL,
 item_id            NUMBER(7)
                    CONSTRAINT s_item_id_nn NOT NULL,
 product_id         NUMBER(7)
                    CONSTRAINT s_item_product_id_nn NOT NULL,
 price              NUMBER(11, 2),
 quantity           NUMBER(9),
 quantity_shipped   NUMBER(9),
 CONSTRAINT s_item_order_id_item_id_pk PRIMARY KEY
    (order_id, item_id),
 CONSTRAINT s_item_order_id_product_id_uk UNIQUE
    (order_id, product_id));

CREATE TABLE s_longtext
(longtext_id   NUMBER(7) CONSTRAINT s_longtext_id_nn NOT NULL,
 use_filename  VARCHAR2(1),
 filename      VARCHAR2(255),
 text          VARCHAR2(2000),
 CONSTRAINT s_longtext_id_pk PRIMARY KEY (longtext_id),
 CONSTRAINT s_longtext_use_filename_ck CHECK
    (use_filename in ('Y', 'N')));

CREATE TABLE s_order
(order_id       NUMBER(7)      CONSTRAINT s_order_id_nn NOT NULL,
 customer_id    NUMBER(7)
                CONSTRAINT s_order_customer_id_nn NOT NULL,
 date_ordered   DATE,
 date_shipped   DATE,
 sales_rep_id   NUMBER(7),
 total          NUMBER(11, 2),
 payment_type   VARCHAR2(6),
 order_filled   VARCHAR2(1),
 CONSTRAINT s_order_id_pk PRIMARY KEY (order_id),
 CONSTRAINT s_order_payment_type_ck CHECK
    (payment_type IN ('CASH', 'CREDIT')),
 CONSTRAINT s_order_order_filled_ck CHECK
    (order_filled IN ('Y', 'N')));

CREATE TABLE s_product
(product_id        NUMBER(7)
```

```
                     CONSTRAINT s_product_id_nn NOT NULL,
product_name      VARCHAR2(50)
                     CONSTRAINT s_product_name_nn NOT NULL,
short_desc        VARCHAR2(255),
longtext_id       NUMBER(7),
image_id          NUMBER(7),
suggested_wholesale_price NUMBER(11, 2),
wholesale_units VARCHAR2(25),
CONSTRAINT s_product_id_pk PRIMARY KEY (product_id),
CONSTRAINT s_product_name_uk UNIQUE (product_name));

CREATE TABLE s_region
(region_id      NUMBER(7)     CONSTRAINT s_region_id_nn NOT NULL,
 region_name   VARCHAR2(50) CONSTRAINT s_region_name_nn NOT NULL,
 CONSTRAINT s_region_id_pk PRIMARY KEY (region_id),
 CONSTRAINT s_region_name_uk UNIQUE (region_name));

CREATE TABLE s_title
(title VARCHAR2(25)
 CONSTRAINT s_title_nn NOT NULL,
 CONSTRAINT s_title_pk PRIMARY KEY (title));

CREATE TABLE s_warehouse
(warehouse_id NUMBER(7)      CONSTRAINT s_warehouse_id_nn NOT NULL,
 region_id      NUMBER(7)
               CONSTRAINT s_warehouse_region_id_nn NOT NULL,
 phone         VARCHAR2(15),
 address       VARCHAR2(400),
 city          VARCHAR2(35),
 state         VARCHAR2(30),
 country       VARCHAR2(30),
 zip_code      VARCHAR2(10),
 manager_id    NUMBER(7),
 CONSTRAINT s_warehouse_id_pk PRIMARY KEY (warehouse_id));
- ****************************************************************

- ****************************************************************
- Inserts data into each table for use in example database.
-
-    Table            Record Count
-    ---------------  ------------
-    s_customer       15
-    s_department     12
-    s_employee       25
-    s_image          19
-    s_inventory      114
-    s_item           62
-    s_longtext       34
```

Reviewing the Example Database

```
-      s_order          16
-      s_product        33
-      s_region          5
-      s_title           8
-      s_warehouse       5
- **************************************************************
- **************************************************************
- Alters tables and adds foreign key constraints for use in
- example database.
-
- Foreign Key Table/Column    Primary Key Table/Column Referenced
- ---------------------------------------------------------------
- s_department/region_id      s_region/region_id
- s_employee/manager_id       s_employee/employee_id
- s_employee/department_id    s_department/department_id
- s_employee/title            s_title/title
- s_customer/sales_rep_id     s_employee/employee_id
- s_customer/region_id        s_region/region_id
- s_order/customer_id         s_customer/customer_id
- s_order/sales_rep_id        s_employee/employee_id
- s_product/image_id          s_image/image_id
- s_product/longtext_id       s_longtext/longtext_id
- s_item/order_id             s_order/order_id
- s_item/product_id           s_product/product_id
- s_warehouse/manager_id      s_employee/employee_id
- s_warehouse/region_id       s_region/region_id
- s_inventory/product_id      s_product/product_id
- s_inventory/warehouse_id    s_warehouse/warehouse_id
- **************************************************************

COMMIT;

SPOOL OFF
```

Identify the Role of the Developer Versus DBA in the PL/SQL World

Over the years, I have given many Oracle-related presentations at the developer and DBA level. To learn the audience knowledge and role (developer or DBA) and to ensure I present at the proper level, I ask the following three questions:

- How many people are developers?

- How many people are DBAs?

- How many people are both developers and DBAs?

The overwhelming majority of people in the Oracle World categorize their role and responsibility in their company as both a developer and DBA. The line between an Oracle developer and DBA has evolved over the years, thus becoming somewhat blurred. To be an expert in either role, you must spend the majority of your time in that role because the Oracle products are so massive and ever changing at such a rapid pace.

A developer should concentrate on development. Certain traditional DBA responsibilities can and should be assisted by a developer. Some of these PL/SQL-related responsibilities deal with optimizing source code, SQL and PL/SQL logic, knowing rollback segments for large transaction executions, understanding stored PL/SQL subprogram security, and knowing the Oracle supplied packages.

A DBA should concentrate on the many database administration responsibilities, including configuration management, schema management, performance tuning (system, application, and operating system), security, and many more. This is a full-time responsibility and should be treated as such.

Developers and DBAs should work together as a team. I know this is a hard concept for some, but without each communicating and ensuring everything is in sync from creation to development to deployment to maintenance of a system, the system is destined to fail.

I think it is crucial to identify the responsibilities of each role in the development of any successful application. The following is a list of some of the responsibilities that exist when developing and using PL/SQL in your environment. The list contains my recommended responsible party for each responsibility (Developer & DBA means a responsibility of both roles, or areas exist within the responsibility that should be performed by each role):

Responsibility	Role Responsible
Knowing the SQL language	Developer and DBA
Knowing the basics of the PL/SQL language	Developer and DBA
Knowing the details of the PL/SQL language	Developer
Knowing the Oracle supplied/DBMS packages	Developer and DBA
Knowing the PL/SQL data dictionary views	Developer and DBA
Knowing the Object data dictionary views	Developer and DBA
Knowing the V$ views	DBA
Knowing PL/SQL security	Developer and DBA
Knowing PL/SQL modulation and storage	Developer and DBA
Creating PL/SQL objects	Developer and DBA

Identifying the Role of the Developer Versus DBA

Responsibility	Role Responsible
Creating tables/indexes/objects	DBA
Application performance tuning	Developer and DBA
Database performance tuning	DBA
Database configuration and sizing	DBA

The preceding list is not all-inclusive, but it offers some advice to identifying resource allocation and role responsibilities. Typically, when the responsibilities include both the developer and DBA, each has ownership of certain aspects of the responsibility. The following are two examples:

- Knowing PL/SQL Security: The developer needs to know how stored PL/SQL security works to architect the structure of the PL/SQL code, whereas the DBA needs to know how stored PL/SQL security works to provide the proper privileges in the development, test, and production environments.

- Knowing the Oracle Supplied/DBMS Packages: The developer needs to know the packages Oracle has provided for use in PL/SQL development to make programming easier, whereas the DBA needs to know the packages Oracle has provided for use in administration of PL/SQL and the database.

This responsibility and role matrix serves as a guideline. This matrix may change, depending on the customer and environment configuration.

Each chapter in this book includes an identification to whom the chapter applies—a developer, a DBA, or both. Remember, this is a recommended responsibility designation of chapters, and you should not be discouraged or limited to the chapters that apply only directly to your role.

Your role can and may change in time. Don't ever limit your thirst for knowledge. My background began as a developer in Oracle version 4 and then continued as a developer/wanna-be DBA in version 5, followed by a DBA in version 6, and now a developer and DBA in version 7 and 8.

Summary

This chapter reviewed the PL/SQL language history, the future of PL/SQL, and the role PL/SQL will play in the evolving Oracle architecture. The major PL/SQL version features were highlighted and methods of identifying the version currently implemented. The PL/SQL version is important to know to determine if certain features are available. The chapter included a look at the example database used in this book for most examples. Refer to Appendix A for complete details of the example database. The chapter ended with a responsibilities and role matrix guideline for developers and DBAs.

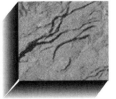

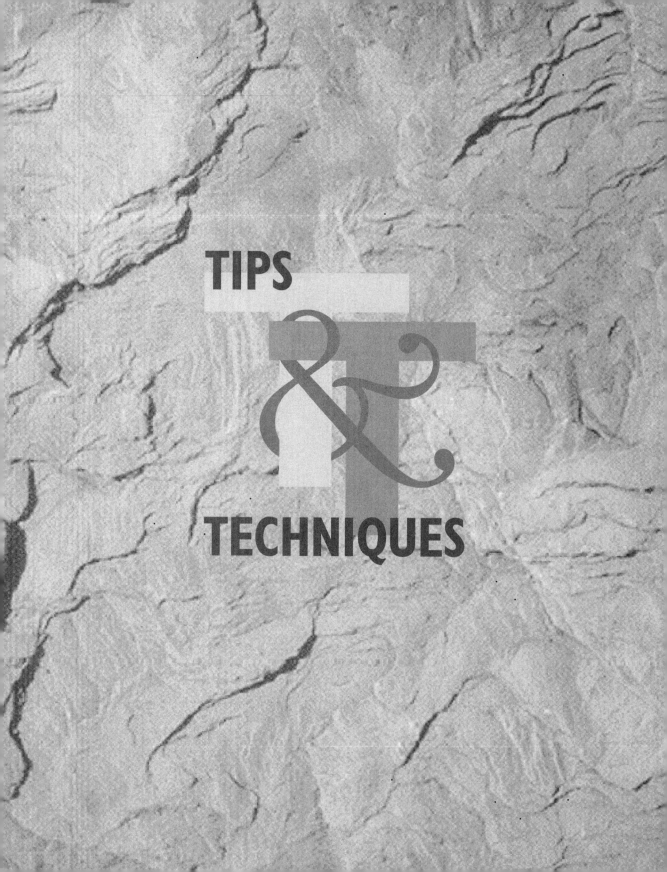

TIPS
&
TECHNIQUES

CHAPTER
2

Maximizing PL/SQL
Development with the
Power of SQL
(Developer and DBA)

S QL is the most important key to becoming proficient in any facet of the Oracle
RDBMS. A person starting in Oracle must first learn and become proficient in
the SQL language. It is essential to build a solid foundation for their future career
development and success in the Oracle realm. SQL is the most important language
to learn as a first step. SQL is an essential component of the products that interface
to the database. Therefore, once SQL has been mastered, the products that interface
to Oracle, including Oracle's and third party products, are much easier to learn.
SQL is used in all Oracle products, including SQL*Plus, PL/SQL, Oracle Developer,
Oracle Designer, Oracle Discoverer, and Oracle Application Server.

At this point ask yourself, "Do I feel 100 percent comfortable in SQL?" If the
answer is Yes, then set aside your ego and ask yourself this question again. I cannot
stress how important the SQL language is to your success in Oracle. Even if you are
convinced you possess a thorough knowledge of SQL, I still recommend reviewing
the SQL language reference for a refresher. I periodically review the SQL language
reference to ensure that I have not forgotten any commands I have not used in a
long time and to increase my awareness of new command functionality added with
new versions.

I strongly urge learning the intricacies of the SQL language prior to advancing in
this book and in your Oracle education. The philosophy of building a foundation of
knowledge is similar to building a house: If a solid foundation is built first, the
house is constructed with greater ease, is stable for the future years to come, and
can support future expansion easier.

The goal of this chapter is *not* to cover the basics of SQL, but rather to target
areas of the SQL language to assist in the refinement of your SQL knowledge and
development, thus advancing your capabilities to the next level. Developers and
DBAs spend a tremendous amount of time in SQL*Plus to review and process
information about an application or database. I am an advocate of also knowing
SQL*Plus commands and the environment in detail to increase your efficiency and
capability in this powerful development product.

Because SQL and SQL*Plus knowledge are extremely important to both
developers and DBAs, the focus of this chapter is on SQL and SQL*Plus tips and
techniques. Even if you think you know all the capabilities of SQL and SQL*Plus,
review this chapter to make sure you know these areas of importance. This chapter
contains the following:

- Understand the role of SQL in PL/SQL and other products
- Review critical SQL concepts
  - Understand the deceptive NULL value in Oracle
  - Understand the hidden details of SYSDATE and DATE columns
    in Oracle
  - Understand the usefulness of ROWNUM in Oracle

- Understand the power of ROWID in Oracle
- Explore the power of the SQL language and functions
  - Date functions
  - Character functions
    - CHR function
    - DECODE function
    - TRANSLATE function
    - INSTR function
    - LTRIM/RTRIM/REPLACE functions
- Highlight helpful SQL*Plus commands and concepts
  - Use SQL*Plus startup files
  - Execute stored PL/SQL objects in SQL*Plus
  - Expand the DESCRIBE command
  - Expand SQL*Plus variables into PL/SQL
  - Understand the HOST command
  - Define the SQL buffer
  - Detail the TIMING command
  - Commit transactions in SQL*Plus
  - Use the SET options
  - Use the USER variable

Understand the Role of SQL in PL/SQL and Other Products

SQL is the component of the PL/SQL language for retrieving and manipulating data in the Oracle RDBMS. The SQL language performs the database interaction and interfacing, while the PL/SQL language allows for the manipulation of the information with procedural capabilities.

The goal is to use each piece of the PL/SQL language to the fullest. Many different methods of solving a problem exist and there are many methods of coding with the PL/SQL language to accomplish the task at hand. Ensure the code you develop is not only accurate and functional, but also efficient and standardized.

Understanding the Role of SQL in PL/SQL

When developing in PL/SQL, a developer is faced with deciding where to perform certain business logic, at the SQL level when retrieving the data or after the data has been retrieved from the database at the PL/SQL level. This decision of where to place logic is typically made based on the environment configuration and the developer's knowledge of the SQL and PL/SQL language. By knowing SQL and PL/SQL, the developer can better determine what will be more efficient and effective.

Many of the functions (numeric and character) available in SQL are also available in PL/SQL. Functions available in SQL that are unavailable in PL/SQL can typically be accomplished within the PL/SQL language. The following illustrates this fact.

File: 2_1.sql (SQL example of DECODE function)

```
SELECT customer_name, DECODE(preferred_customer, 'N', 'NO', 'YES')
FROM    s_customer
ORDER BY preferred_customer, customer_name;
```

File: 2_2.sql (PL/SQL example of same logic not using the DECODE function)

```
SET SERVEROUTPUT ON SIZE 1000000
DECLARE
   CURSOR cur_customers is
      SELECT customer_name, preferred_customer
      FROM    s_customer
      ORDER BY preferred_customer, customer_name;
   lv_customer_txt  s_customer.customer_name%TYPE;
   lv_preferred_txt VARCHAR2(3);
BEGIN
   OPEN cur_customers;
   DBMS_OUTPUT.PUT_LINE('Customer(Preferred)');
   DBMS_OUTPUT.PUT_LINE('------------------------------');
   LOOP
      FETCH cur_customers INTO lv_customer_txt, lv_preferred_txt;
      IF lv_preferred_txt = 'N' THEN
         lv_preferred_txt := 'NO';
      ELSE
         lv_preferred_txt := 'YES';
      END IF;
      DBMS_OUTPUT.PUT_LINE(lv_customer_txt || '(' ||
         lv_preferred_txt || ')');
      EXIT WHEN cur_customers%NOTFOUND;
   END LOOP;
   CLOSE cur_customers;
END;
/
```

As shown in the two preceding code segments, the SQL DECODE function can be used to eliminate PL/SQL logic. This is a basic example, but as the complexity increases, SQL functions are often more effective and concise than performing everything in PL/SQL.

The most important language to learn is SQL. The second most important language to learn is PL/SQL. By gaining a core competency in these languages, a developer can advance into Forms, Reports, Application Server, or most other products, and the possibilities become limitless. Granted, the developer needs to become proficient in the front-end product to build the interface, but the core functionality and complex logic will be developed using embedded PL/SQL.

Review Critical SQL Concepts

SQL is a powerful language, but some of the intricacies of the language are not always apparent on the surface. These intricacies require an in-depth understanding to ensure they are taken into consideration so the results of the code developed are accurate. If these intricacies are not considered, some deep hidden problems can lurk in your systems. These intricacies are explored in detail in this section to ensure a full understanding exists for all developers and DBAs. The areas covered include the following:

- NULL Values

- SYSDATE and DATE Columns

- ROWNUM Column

- ROWID Column

Understand the Deceptive NULL Value in Oracle

A thorough understanding of NULL values in Oracle can eliminate inaccurate retrieval and manipulation of data. The following statement is a simple way to define a NULL value.

"NULL is not equal to anything, not even itself."

The following three rules apply to NULL values and may dissolve some of the confusion that often lies hidden with deceptive NULL values.

- When a column that contains NULL values is used in a predicate clause that contains a "not equal" operand (!= or <>), records with a NULL value in the column being compared will not be retrieved, unless NULL values are accounted for.

■ When a column that contains NULL values is used in a group function, the records with a NULL value in the column being calculated are not used in the group function, unless NULL values are accounted for.

■ When a column that contains NULL values is used in an arithmetic operation, the resulting value of the arithmetic operation will be NULL, unless NULL values are accounted for.

The following subsections concentrate on examining these three rules through several examples to ensure these intricacies of NULL values are being handled in the manner you desire.

Using Columns with NULL Values in a Predicate Clause

Retrieving records by a column that can contain NULL values must be treated with care. Columns used in a predicate clause that contain NULL values must be treated differently than columns that do not allow NULL values. The following script can be used to display all the columns in a table and specify the columns that can contain NULL values.

File: 2_3.sql

```
column nullable format a10 heading 'NULL|ALLOWED?'
SELECT table_name, column_name,
       DECODE(nullable, 'N', 'NO', 'YES') nullable
FROM   all_tab_columns
WHERE  table_name = UPPER('&table_name');
```

Output (2_3.sql: entered table_name=s_customer)

TABLE_NAME	COLUMN_NAME	NULL ALLOWED?
S_CUSTOMER	CUSTOMER_ID	NO
S_CUSTOMER	CUSTOMER_NAME	NO
S_CUSTOMER	PHONE	YES
S_CUSTOMER	ADDRESS	YES
S_CUSTOMER	CITY	YES
S_CUSTOMER	STATE	YES
S_CUSTOMER	COUNTRY	YES
S_CUSTOMER	ZIP_CODE	YES

The s_customer table contains 15 columns (only eight of the columns are shown here). Of the eight columns displayed, only two do not allow NULL values.

Of the 15 records in the s_customer table, three of the records contain a value for the zip_code column and 12 of the records contain a NULL value for the zip_code column. The following query displays all the records in the s_customer table to show the zip_code column values:

File: 2_4.sql

```
SELECT customer_id, customer_name, zip_code
FROM    s_customer
ORDER BY zip_code;
```

Output (2_4.sql)

```
CUSTOMER_ID CUSTOMER_NAME                       ZIP_CODE
----------- ----------------------------------- -------
        214 OJIBWAY RETAIL                      14202
        213 BIG JOHN'S SPORTS EMPORIUM          94117
        204 WOMANSPORT                          98101
        201 UNISPORTS
        202 SIMMS ATHLETICS
        206 SPORTIQUE
        208 MUENCH SPORTS
        210 FUTBOL SONORA
        215 SPORTA RUSSIA
        212 HAMADA SPORT
        211 KUHN'S SPORTS
        209 BEISBOL SI!
        207 SWEET ROCK SPORTS
        205 KAM'S SPORTING GOODS
        203 DELHI SPORTS
15 rows selected.
```

TIP
When a query orders by a column with NULL values, the records with a NULL value in the order column are retrieved after all records with a non-NULL value. If you want NULL values to be retrieved first and keep the list in ascending order, you can change the ORDER BY clause in the previous example to the following:

```
ORDER BY NVL(zip_code, '1111111111')
```

or

```
ORDER BY DECODE(zip_code, NULL, 'A', 'B'), zip_code
```

The following query displays the records in the s_customer table where the zip_code column equals 94117, followed by the records in the s_customer table where the zip_code is not equal to 94117:

File: 2_5.sql

```
SELECT customer_id, customer_name, zip_code
FROM   s_customer
WHERE  zip_code = '94117';
```

Output (2_5.sql)

```
CUSTOMER_ID CUSTOMER_NAME                        ZIP_CODE
----------- ------------------------------------ --------
        213 BIG JOHN'S SPORTS EMPORIUM           94117
```

File: 2_6.sql

```
SELECT customer_id, customer_name, zip_code
FROM   s_customer
WHERE  zip_code != '94117';
```

Output (2_6.sql)

```
CUSTOMER_ID CUSTOMER_NAME                        ZIP_CODE
----------- ------------------------------------ --------
        204 WOMANSPORT                           98101
        214 OJIBWAY RETAIL                       14202
```

The first query returns one record as expected; therefore, the second query should have returned 14 records. The preceding example (2_6.sql) illustrated that NULL is not equal to anything and, therefore, cannot be returned in this type of query. To ensure all records that do not meet the NOT EQUAL (!=) condition (including NULL values) are retrieved, the predicate clause must be changed to one of the following (both queries will return the 14 records):

Reviewing Critical SQL Concepts

Predicate 1 (using the NVL function)

```
WHERE  NVL(zip_code, 'XX') != '94117'
```

Predicate 2 (using an OR condition and comparing to NULL)

```
WHERE  zip_code != '94117'
OR     zip_code IS NULL
```

The NVL function treats the value of a column as the value specified in the NVL function if the column value is NULL. Thus, in the previous example, "XX" is not equal to 94117 for the records where the zip_code is NULL The OR condition with the IS NULL includes the records containing a zip_code that are NULL.

The preceding example highlights the solutions to deploy when NULL value columns exist in predicate clauses. This problem extends to the comparison of one NULL value column to another NULL value column as well. The following example demonstrates this comparison.

First, we need to create a temporary table. The following statement creates a table called s_customer_temp that duplicates the s_customer table.

File: 2_7.sql

```
CREATE TABLE s_customer_temp AS
SELECT *
FROM   s_customer;
```

If we join the s_customer and s_customer_temp tables by the customer_id as the following illustrates, we return all 15 records.

File: 2_8.sql

```
SELECT a.customer_id, a.customer_name, a.zip_code
FROM   s_customer a, s_customer_temp b
WHERE  a.customer_id = b.customer_id;
```

If the query is modified to also join on the zip_code column, the result set will be different as the following displays.

File: 2_9.sql

```
SELECT a.customer_id, a.customer_name, a.zip_code
FROM   s_customer a, s_customer_temp b
```

```
WHERE   a.customer_id = b.customer_id
AND     a.zip_code    = b.zip_code;
```

Output (2_9.sql)

```
CUSTOMER_ID CUSTOMER_NAME                           ZIP_CODE
----------- ------------------------------------    --------
        204 WOMANSPORT                              98101
        213 BIG JOHN'S SPORTS EMPORIUM              94117
        214 OJIBWAY RETAIL                          14202
```

On the surface, it would appear the result should be all 15 records, as in the previous query, because the zip_code fields of both tables are the same for each of the customer records. Remember, NULL values are not equal to anything, not even another NULL value. To keep the same predicate conditions and retrieve all 15 records, the predicate clause with the zip_code column would need to be changed to the following:

Predicate

```
AND    NVL(a.zip_code, 'XX') = NVL(b.zip_code, 'XX')
```

Using Columns with NULL Values in Arithmetic Operations

NULL values can be extremely deceiving during arithmetic operations and should be treated with care. The general rule when manipulating columns that can contain NULL values is "Always use the NVL function on the column and default a NULL value to a zero (0) to ensure proper arithmetic calculations." The following queries and updates applied against the s_employee table illustrate this important rule.

The s_employee table has a column named commission_pct and is set to a commission percentage for certain employees and to NULL for other employees. The example will be limited to the employee_id of 17. The following query displays the salary and commission percentage for this employee.

File: 2_10.sql

```
SELECT employee_id, employee_last_name last_name,
       employee_first_name first_name, salary, commission_pct
FROM   s_employee
WHERE  employee_id = 17;
```

Output (2_10.sql)

```
EMPLOYEE_ID LAST_NAME   FIRST_NAME   SALARY COMMISSION_PCT
----------- ----------  -----------  ------ --------------
         17 SMITH       GEORGE          940
```

If the commission percentage for this employee were to be incremented by ten percent, the following update would be executed to accomplish this task:

File: 2_11.sql

```
UPDATE s_employee
SET    commission_pct = commission_pct + 10
WHERE  employee_id = 17;
```

Output (2_10.sql—repeat from previous)

```
EMPLOYEE_ID LAST_NAME   FIRST_NAME   SALARY COMMISSION_PCT
----------- ----------  -----------  ------ --------------
         17 SMITH       GEORGE          940
```

As evidenced, when this employee is queried after the update, the commission_pct was still equal to NULL because a NULL plus any value is NULL. A NULL value is not treated as a zero (0).

TIP

*As a rule, always re-query records you manipulate through a SQL statement in SQL*Plus to ensure the operation was completed properly prior to committing.*

The developer must specify NULL values be treated as zero (0) by using the following NVL function as illustrated in the following.

File: 2_12.sql

```
UPDATE s_employee
SET    commission_pct = NVL(commission_pct,0) + 10
WHERE  employee_id = 17;
```

Output (2_10.sql—repeat from previous)

```
EMPLOYEE_ID LAST_NAME   FIRST_NAME   SALARY COMMISSION_PCT
----------- ----------  -----------  ------ --------------
         17 SMITH        GEORGE          940             10
```

The end result is the employee with employee_id of 17 is updated properly when the NVL function is used.

TIP
Use the NVL function if you desire to treat a NULL value as zero (0). The preceding examples are valid for this condition. If you want to increase the commission percentage of those employees who were already receiving a commission, then you would not want to use the NVL function.

Using Columns with NULL Values in Group By Functions

Records that contain columns with NULL values that are used in a GROUP BY operation are not included in the GROUP BY functions when it relates to arithmetic functions. If you want these records to be included in the GROUP BY function, then use the NVL function again. A general guideline for GROUP BY functions does not exist because it always depends on the company's configuration and design (is it desired to include or exclude the records with NULL values ?). The following example highlights the differences of including and not including the NULL column records in GROUP BY functions.

File: 2_13.sql

```
SELECT employee_id, commission_pct
FROM   s_employee
WHERE  commission_pct IS NOT NULL;
```

Output (2_13.sql)

```
EMPLOYEE_ID COMMISSION_PCT
----------- --------------
         11             10
         12           12.5
         13             10
         14             15
         15           17.5
```

There are 25 employee records, but only 5 employees have a commission percentage.

File: 2_14.sql (average *not* counting employees without commission)

```
SELECT AVG(commission_pct)
FROM   s_employee;
```

Output (2_14.sql)

```
AVG(COMMISSION_PCT)
-------------------
                 13
```

The sum of the five records is 65; therefore, the average commission percentage is 13 (65/5). But the question is "Do we want to include the other 20 employees to determine the average of all employees?" This depends on the company and the application, but developers must know the answer to this question to make the correct coding decision. If you need to include the NULL value records, the following query ensures all employees are included in the equation.

File: 2_15.sql (average counting employees without commission)

```
SELECT AVG(NVL(commission_pct,0))
FROM   s_employee;
```

Output (2_15.sql)

```
AVG(COMMISSION_PCT)
-------------------
                2.6
```

The total of the 25 records is 65; therefore, the average is 2.6 (65/25), which is quite a different result.

Remember, NULL values are misleading on the surface and can lead to unwarranted result sets when retrieving or updating records. Use the NVL function or IS NULL functions to ensure proper results with columns that could be NULL. If a column is defined as NOT NULL in the table creation definition or as a constraint, then the NVL and/or IS NULL functions are not necessary. As a rule, it is typically better to always use this functioning to ensure NULL values are treated as expected and to eliminate the potential for problems. In addition, it eliminates any problems that can arise if the constraint of NOT NULL is some day turned off.

Reviewing Critical SQL Concepts

Understand the Hidden Details of SYSDATE and DATE Columns in Oracle

A thorough understanding of the SYSDATE variable and DATE defined columns in Oracle eliminates inaccurate retrieval and manipulation of data. The following statement is a simple way to remember DATE values.

"SYSDATE and DATE defined columns contain date and time components."

SYSDATE is a predefined Oracle variable commonly used to time stamp records as they are inserted or updated. SYSDATE is composed of both the date and time, therefore, when used to set a column in the database that is of data type DATE, the date and time are both stored, NOT just the date. By default, Oracle only displays the date portion of a column with a data type of DATE when retrieved (assuming the default nls_date_format of DD-MON-YY). This often leads to misleading and/or inaccurate results returned from the database. This section explores the DATE data type and SYSDATE characteristics and provides details of how the DATE intricacies should be handled to ensure a consistent and accurate system.

The query that follows illustrates the typical and expanded method of displaying the column values of a database column that has been defined as a DATE:

File: 2_16.sql

```
SELECT  employee_id, employee_last_name last_name,
        employee_first_name first_name, start_date,
        TO_CHAR(start_date, 'DD-MON-YY HH24:MI:SS') start_date1
FROM    s_employee
WHERE   employee_id < 6;
```

Output (2_16.sql)

```
EMPLOYEE_ID LAST_NAME       FIRST_NAME START_DAT START_DATE1
----------- --------------- ---------- --------- -------------------
          1 VELASQUEZ       CARMEN     03-MAR-90 03-MAR-90 08:30:00
          2 NGAO            LADORIS    08-MAR-90 08-MAR-90 00:00:00
          3 NAGAYAMA        MIDORI     17-JUN-91 17-JUN-91 00:00:00
          4 QUICK-TO-SEE    MARK       07-APR-90 07-APR-90 00:00:00
          5 ROPEBURN        AUDRY      04-MAR-90 04-MAR-90 00:00:00
```

Notice the difference in the dates returned. The first retrieval of the start_date column was selected as is; the second start_date column was retrieved using the

TO_CHAR function with a format mask to display the date and time portion of the column. The second date illustrates employee_id 1 has a start time of 08:30:00, whereas all other employees have a start time of midnight or 00:00:00. The "HH24" in the format mask specifies the hours to be returned based on a 24-hour time system, the "MI" specifies the minutes, and the "SS" specifies the seconds.

Typically, the date portion of a DATE column is the only desired information to display and manipulate; therefore, the column is selected with no formatting. In the case that the time portion is desired, the TO_CHAR function can be used to display this information.

If the time portion of the DATE column is not needed, then do not store this information. Even if the time portion is needed, I strongly recommend storing the time in a separate column. When a DATE column is used in the predicate clause and the time portion is stored in the DATE column, the results can be inaccurate and often hard to detect. This is shown in the following query:

File: 2_17.sql

```
SELECT  employee_id, employee_last_name last_name,
        employee_first_name first_name, start_date,
        TO_CHAR(start_date, 'DD-MON-YY HH24:MI:SS') start_date1
FROM    s_employee
WHERE   employee_id < 6
AND     start_date = '03-MAR-90';
```

Output (2_17.sql)

```
no rows selected
```

The preceding query should have returned the record for employee_id 1. Because the column included a time of 08:30:00 rather than 00:00:00 (analogous to not storing the time), it was not returned. To retrieve the employee_id 1, the query would have to be changed to eliminate the time portion of the DATE column with the TRUNC function as shown in the following example:

File: 2_18.sql

```
SELECT  employee_id, employee_last_name last_name,
        employee_first_name first_name, start_date,
        TO_CHAR(start_date, 'DD-MON-YY HH24:MI:SS') start_date1
FROM    s_employee
WHERE   employee_id < 6
AND     TRUNC(start_date) = '03-MAR-90';
```

Reviewing Critical SQL Concepts

Output (2_18.sql)

```
EMPLOYEE_ID LAST_NAME   FIRST_NAME START_DAT START_DATE1
----------- ----------  ---------- --------- -------------------
          1 VELASQUEZ   CARMEN     03-MAR-90 03-MAR-90 08:30:00
```

The TRUNC function, when used on DATE columns, truncates the time portion of the column. Therefore, the records matching the date specified are returned. This also applies when using the BETWEEN and other DATE comparison operators. If the time value is equal to 00:00:00, the TRUNC is not necessary, as shown in the following example:

Output (2_17.sql—repeat from previous with start-date = '08-MAR-90)

```
EMPLOYEE_ID LAST_NAME   FIRST_NAME START_DAT START_DATE1
----------- ----------  ---------- --------- -------------------
          2 NGAO        LADORIS    08-MAR-90 08-MAR-90 00:00:00
```

The SYSDATE variable available in Oracle can be used for setting the date and time and is set to the current system date and time. This is displayed by querying the SYSDATE variable from the dual table as shown in the following example:

File: 2_19.sql

```
SELECT SYSDATE, TO_CHAR(SYSDATE, 'DD-MON-YY HH24:MI:SS')
FROM   dual;
```

Output (2_19.sql)

```
SYSDATE   TO_CHAR(SYSDATE,'DD-MON-YY HH24:MI:SS')
--------- ---------------------------------------
17-MAR-98 17-MAR-98 07:27:03
```

The SYSDATE variable is often used to time stamp records. If used without truncating the time portion, problems of displaying column values could arise with DATE columns as shown in the previous examples. The following update and queries provide examples of the SYSDATE usage problem:

File: 2_20.sql (SYSDATE = 17-MAR-98)

```
UPDATE s_employee
SET    start_date = SYSDATE
WHERE  employee_id < 6;
```

Output (2_20.sql)

```
5 rows updated.
```

File: 2_21.sql

```
SELECT  employee_id, employee_last_name last_name,
        employee_first_name first_name, start_date,
        TO_CHAR(start_date, 'DD-MON-YY HH24:MI:SS') start_date1
FROM    s_employee
WHERE   employee_id < 6
AND     start_date = '17-MAR-98';
```

Output (2_21.sql)

```
no rows selected
```

File: 2_22.sql

```
SELECT  employee_id, employee_last_name last_name,
        employee_first_name first_name, start_date,
        TO_CHAR(start_date, 'DD-MON-YY HH24:MI:SS') start_date1
FROM    s_employee
WHERE   employee_id < 6
AND     TRUNC(start_date) = '17-MAR-98';
```

Output (2_22.sql)

```
EMPLOYEE_ID LAST_NAME     FIRST_NAME START_DAT START_DATE1
----------- ------------- ---------- --------- -------------------
          1 VELASQUEZ     CARMEN     17-MAR-98 17-MAR-98 07:27:47
          2 NGAO          LADORIS    17-MAR-98 17-MAR-98 07:27:47
          3 NAGAYAMA      MIDORI     17-MAR-98 17-MAR-98 07:27:47
          4 QUICK-TO-SEE  MARK       17-MAR-98 17-MAR-98 07:27:47
          5 ROPEBURN      AUDRY      17-MAR-98 17-MAR-98 07:27:47
```

Notice the query (2_21.sql) that did not TRUNCate the start_date column did not return any records. To eliminate this problem with SYSDATE, the time can be TRUNCated during the update and will set the time value to 00:00:00, thus eliminating the need to use the TRUNCate function in queries for retrieval based on DATE columns. This is shown in the following update and query.

File: 2_23.sql (SYSDATE = 17-MAR-98)

```
UPDATE s_employee
SET    start_date = TRUNC(SYSDATE)
WHERE  employee_id < 6;
```

Output (2_23.sql)

```
5 rows updated.
```

File: 2_21.sql

```
SELECT employee_id, employee_last_name last_name,
       employee_first_name first_name, start_date,
       TO_CHAR(start_date, 'DD-MON-YY HH24:MI:SS') start_date1
FROM   s_employee
WHERE  employee_id < 6
AND    start_date = '17-MAR-98';
```

Output (2_21.sql)

```
EMPLOYEE_ID LAST_NAME     FIRST_NAME START_DAT START_DATE1
----------- ------------- ---------- --------- ------------------
          1 VELASQUEZ     CARMEN     17-MAR-98 17-MAR-98 00:00:00
          2 NGAO          LADORIS    17-MAR-98 17-MAR-98 00:00:00
          3 NAGAYAMA      MIDORI     17-MAR-98 17-MAR-98 00:00:00
          4 QUICK-TO-SEE  MARK       17-MAR-98 17-MAR-98 00:00:00
          5 ROPEBURN      AUDRY      17-MAR-98 17-MAR-98 00:00:00
```

As noted in Chapter 7 on SQL tuning, if the TRUNC or TO_CHAR function is used in the predicate clause and the columns these functions are used on are indexed, then the index will be unusable by Oracle. Remember this when using these functions or any other functions.

Several problems are introduced into your system if a consistent approach is not deployed in your systems regarding DATE columns. I recommend the following guidelines when using DATE columns in applications.

■ Never store the time value in a DATE column. Therefore, when using SYSDATE, always use the TRUNC function. This eliminates the need to use the TRUNC or TO_CHAR function in the predicate clause when querying by DATE columns.

■ If the time is necessary to capture, then store this value in an additional column defined as VARCHAR2(8) (example: 13:45:23) and update this column during timestamping. Therefore, the time value would still be stored and available, and the DATE column problems would be eliminated.

The previous guidelines eliminate the date and time dilemma that could lead to misleading and false results. If your current system contains this problem, it is not too late to deploy these guidelines. These guidelines can be integrated in your system by first modifying all locations where SYSDATE is being used to timestamp records (change references of SYSDATE to TRUNC(SYSDATE)) and then modifying the existing DATE column values to eliminate the time value.

The existing data can be modified by an update of each of the DATE columns as shown next.

File: 2_24.sql

```
UPDATE s_employee
SET    start_date = trunc(start_date);
```

DATE columns are then much easier to work with and the correct information is retrieved consistently.

TIP
An approach to ensuring that the time portion of all DATE columns is stripped off of dates, is to create database triggers on the tables that contain DATE columns to perform the time stripping function. This would protect your system from any DATE entry and ensure proper handling of all DATEs.

Understand the Usefulness of ROWNUM in Oracle

Oracle supplies a pseudo column named ROWNUM that is not stored in the database, but is available for every record retrieved from the database. The ROWNUM column changes every time a query is executed and is assigned to the result records one by one sequentially. Therefore, the ROWNUM for the first record received is 1, the second record is 2, and so on for every record returned. The ROWNUM can be used to provide a counter for records or limit a result set. The following query illustrates the use of ROWNUM to provide a counter for each record.

File: 2_25.sql

```
SELECT ROWNUM, customer_name
FROM    s_customer;
```

Output (2_25.sql)

```
ROWNUM     CUSTOMER_NAME
---------  ---------------------------
        1  UNISPORTS
        2  SIMMS ATHELETICS
        3  DELHI SPORTS
        4  WOMANSPORT
        5  KAM'S SPORTING GOODS
        6  SPORTIQUE
        7  SWEET ROCK SPORTS
        8  MUENCH SPORTS
        9  BEISBOL SI!
       10  FUTBOL SONORA
       11  KUHN'S SPORTS
       12  HAMADA SPORT
       13  BIG JOHN'S SPORTS EMPORIUM
       14  OJIBWAY RETAIL
       15  SPORTA RUSSIA
15 rows selected.
```

The following query limits the number of records returned to five:

File: 2_26.sql

```
SELECT ROWNUM, customer_name
FROM    s_customer
WHERE   ROWNUM < 6;
```

Output (2_26.sql)

```
ROWNUM     CUSTOMER_NAME
---------  ---------------------
        1  UNISPORTS
        2  SIMMS ATHELETICS
        3  DELHI SPORTS
        4  WOMANSPORT
        5  KAM'S SPORTING GOODS
```

The ROWNUM column can only be used to limit the records, therefore, only the less than (<) or less than and equal to (<=) operators can be used. It assigns the ROWNUM to a record as it is being retrieved. Therefore it does not apply to records that are never retrieved. This would be the case if other operators were used as the following illustrates:

File: 2_27.sql

```
SELECT  ROWNUM, customer_name
FROM    s_customer
WHERE   ROWNUM > 6;
```

Output (2_27.sql)

```
no rows selected
```

Because the ROWNUM is assigned upon retrieval, it is assigned prior to any sorting. If used with sorting criteria (that is, ORDER BY) the ROWNUM will not necessarily correspond to the sorting order. This is illustrated in the following query:

File: 2_28.sql

```
SELECT  ROWNUM, customer_name
FROM    s_customer
WHERE   ROWNUM < 6
ORDER BY customer_name;
```

Output (2_28.sql)

```
    ROWNUM CUSTOMER_NAME
---------- --------------------
         3 DELHI SPORTS
         5 KAM'S SPORTING GOODS
         2 SIMMS ATHELETICS
         1 UNISPORTS
         4 WOMANSPORT
```

The ROWNUM can also be used to update a table and to add a sequential number to each record. If a column named customer_id2 of datatype NUMBER(7) was added to the s_customer table, then the following update can be performed to uniquely number each record.

File: 2_29.sql

```
UPDATE s_customer
SET    customer_id2 = ROWNUM;
```

As illustrated in this section, the ROWNUM is a valuable pseudo column Oracle provides to add to the arsenal of tools to use when querying the database.

Understand the Power of ROWID in Oracle

The ROWID is a column that is part of every record in the database. It represents the physical location of the record in the database and is the fastest method of retrieving records (even faster than the use of an index). Like the ROWNUM pseudo column, the ROWID is a pseudo column and does not take any space in the database. The ROWID does not change per query like the ROWNUM.

The ROWID column should *never* be hardcoded because the ROWID of a row will change when database reorganizations are performed.

Although the content and format the ROWID has changed from Oracle7 to Oracle8, it still serves the same purpose and function as in prior releases of Oracle. This column should still be used to optimize your SQL manipulation and to serve as a means for uniquely identifying records when possible.

When a DESCribe is performed on any table in the database, the ROWID will not display as a column, but is a part of every record. Remember, the ROWID changes when certain operations are performed (that is, export and import). The following query displays the ROWID for five of the records in the s_customer table.

File: 2_30.sql (Oracle7)

```
SELECT ROWID, customer_id
FROM   s_customer
WHERE  ROWNUM < 6;
```

Output (2_30.sql)

```
ROWID                 CUSTOMER_ID
------------------    -----------
00000D6C.0000.0001            201
00000D6C.0001.0001            202
00000D6C.0002.0001            203
00000D6C.0003.0001            204
00000D6C.0004.0001            205
```

The ROWID is in hexadecimal format and an explanation of the ROWID content (Oracle7) follows:

"00000D6C"	Identifies the block ID
"0000"	Identifies the record number in the block
"0001"	Identifies the data file number

The following query is file 2_30.sql executed against an Oracle8 database.

Output (2_30.sql—Oracle8: repeat from previous)

```
ROWID                   CUSTOMER_ID
------------------      -----------
AAACLmAACAAAAPSAAA          201
AAACLmAACAAAAPSAAB          202
AAACLmAACAAAAPSAAC          203
AAACLmAACAAAAPSAAD          204
AAACLmAACAAAAPSAAE          205
```

An explanation of the ROWID content (Oracle8) follows:

"AAACLm"	Identifies the object ID
"AAC"	Identifies the data file number
"AAAAPS"	Identifies the block ID
"AAA"	Identifies the record number in the block

There are times when data is being loaded into a table and, in the process and usually by mistake, duplicate information is loaded. When this happens, the easiest method of deleting the duplicate records is by using the ROWID to identify each record uniquely. An example follows that illustrates the usage of the ROWID in this scenario.

The next five steps outline the scenario and then illustrate the usage of the ROWID to delete duplicate records.

1. A duplicated s_customer table is created named s_customer_temp (table and records)

2. The records are then duplicated in the s_customer_temp table

3. The records in the s_customer_temp table are displayed

Reviewing Critical SQL Concepts

4. The duplicate records are deleted using the ROWID

5. The records in the s_customer_temp table are displayed

Step 1—File: 2_31.sql (only first five records)

```
CREATE TABLE s_customer_temp AS
SELECT customer_id
FROM   s_customer
WHERE  ROWNUM < 6;
```

Step 2—File: 2_32.sql

```
INSERT INTO s_customer_temp
SELECT *
FROM   s_customer_temp;
```

Step 3—File: 2_33.sql

```
SELECT ROWID, customer_id
FROM   s_customer_temp;
```

Output (2_33.SQL)

```
ROWID                CUSTOMER_ID
-------------------  -----------
00005756.0000.0006           201
00005756.0001.0006           202
00005756.0002.0006           203
00005756.0003.0006           204
00005756.0004.0006           205
00005757.0000.0006           201
00005757.0001.0006           202
00005757.0002.0006           203
00005757.0003.0006           204
00005757.0004.0006           205
10 rows selected.
```

Step 4—File: 2_34.sql

```
DELETE FROM s_customer_temp a
WHERE  ROWID !=
(SELECT MAX(ROWID)
```

```
FROM    s_customer_temp
WHERE   customer_id = a.customer_id);
```

Output (2_34.sql)

```
5 rows deleted.
```

Step 5—File: 2_33.sql (repeat from previous)

```
SELECT ROWID, customer_id
FROM   s_customer_temp;
```

Output (2_33.sql)

```
ROWID                 CUSTOMER_ID
------------------    -----------
00005756.0000.0006            201
00005756.0001.0006            202
00005756.0002.0006            203
00005756.0003.0006            204
00005756.0004.0006            205
```

The ROWID format changes in Oracle8 for support of the new features, however, the ROWID provides the same functionality. Refer to Chapter 8 for further information on the use of the ROWID for optimizing PL/SQL.

Explore the Power of the SQL Language and Functions

The SQL language is extremely powerful with a wide range of functions that offer developers and DBAs a wide range of flexibility and capability. The true power is realized by combining and nesting these powerful functions. This section highlights several of these SQL functions that can be used in SQL statements to add a new dimension, and capability when writing SQL statements. Many of these functions are also available in the PL/SQL language as well, but understanding the features are available in SQL provides the developer with the ability to determine the best location to use these functions.

Date Functions

Oracle provides a robust set of DATE functions that can be used to alter columns returned from the database, as well as to limit the data returned. Oracle provides a

DATE data type that stores both the date and time. Depending on the desired results, the appropriate DATE function(s) can be used. Several of these DATE functions are demonstrated in the examples below to provide a framework for understanding the power included in this function set.

Example I

If you need to manipulate dates to return information for a given quarter, you can use the ADD_MONTHS and LAST_DAY functions to return the data for the desired quarter with the user inputting the starting month and year for the quarter as the following illustrates.

File: 2_35.sql

```
SET ECHO OFF
PROMPT Input Date prompts for the beginning month and year of the
PROMPT quarter in the format of mmyyyy.
PROMPT
SET ECHO ON
SELECT  employee_last_name, start_date
FROM    s_employee
WHERE   start_date BETWEEN TO_DATE('01' ||
                                   '&&input_date','DDMMYYYY')
AND     LAST_DAY(ADD_MONTHS(TO_DATE('01' ||
                                   '&&input_date','DDMMYYYY'),2)));
UNDEFINE input_date
```

If the value entered for the INPUT_DATE prompt was 011991, then the date range used would be '01-JAN-91' and '31-MAR-91'. The combination of the ADD_MONTHS and LAST_DAY functions made this quarterly calculation possible.

TIP
The double ampersand "&&" sets a variable for the entire session or until it is undefined. The previous example includes the command to undefine a variable set in SQL*Plus. If only one ampersand "&" were used instead of the "&&", the input_date variable would prompt the user twice because the single ampersand only sets the variable for one occurrence.

To verify the dates in SQL*Plus, they can be tested by SELECTing from the dual table as the following illustrates.

File: 2_36.sql

```
SELECT TO_DATE('01' || '&&input_date','DDMMYYYY') start_date,
       LAST_DAY(ADD_MONTHS(TO_DATE('01' ||
       '&&input_date','DDMMYYYY'),2)) end_date
FROM   DUAL;
```

Output (2_36.sql: entered input_date=011991)

```
START_DAT END_DATE
--------- ---------
01-JAN-91 31-MAR-91

1 row selected.
```

TIP
*The ADD_MONTHS function can accept negative
numbers to return a previous month.*

Example 2

If you need to determine the number of distinct months between two dates, you can
use the MONTHS_BETWEEN function combined with the TO_CHAR and TO_DATE
functions, as the following will demonstrate.

File: 2_37.sql

```
SELECT MONTHS_BETWEEN(TO_DATE(TO_CHAR(TO_DATE('&date1'),
       'mmyyyy'), 'mmyyyy'),
       TO_DATE(TO_CHAR(TO_DATE('&date2'), 'mmyyyy'),
       'mmyyyy')) Diff_Date
FROM   DUAL;
```

Output (2_37.sql: entered date1=13-jan-98 and date2=24-dec-95)

```
DIFF_DATE
----------
        25

1 row selected.
```

In the preceding example, the extra TO_CHAR and TO_DATE are necessary to convert the dates to the first of the month for each month to return an integer. If these two functions were eliminated, the result would have included a fraction.

When working with DATE columns, the SQL DATE functions should be examined. They contain a variety of helpful routines and formats.

Character Functions

Oracle provides a robust set of character functions to manipulate character strings. Depending on the desired results, the appropriate character function(s) can be used. Several of these character functions are demonstrated to provide a framework for understanding the power included in this function set.

CHR Function

The CHR function allows for control characters to be embedded into SQL commands. This is helpful when creating flatfiles (ASCII data files) or varying output and the need for Tabs or Linefeeds is necessary. The following example shows the method of integrating control characters in SQL commands to format the output.

File: 2_38.sql

```
SELECT 'Line 1' || CHR(10) || 'Line 2' ||
       CHR(9) || 'Line 2-1' || CHR(9) ||
       'Line 2-2' || CHR(10) || 'Line 3' threelines
FROM   DUAL;
```

Output (2_38.sql)

```
THREELINES
-------------------------------------------------
Line 1
Line 2   Line 2-1        Line 2-2
Line 3
```

The control character ASCII equivalent must be known and can be looked up in an ASCII chart. In the preceding example, an ASCII '9' is a Tab and an ASCII '10' is a Linefeed.

DECODE Function

The DECODE function is not available in the PL/SQL language; however, the DECODE functionality can be realized by using nested PL/SQL IF statements. The

DECODE is a powerful function that provides IF logic in SQL statements as demonstrated in the following examples:

Example 1

If you need a list of customers and you wanted to highlight the preferred customers, you could return YES or NO for the preferred_customer column of the s_customer table instead of Y or N.

File: 2_39.sql

```
SELECT customer_id, customer_name,
       DECODE(preferred_customer, 'Y', 'Yes', 'No') preferred
FROM   s_customer
ORDER BY preferred_customer, customer_name;
```

Output (2_39.sql)

```
CUSTOMER_ID CUSTOMER_NAME                          PREFERRED
----------- ------------------------------------- ---------
        209 BEISBOL SI!                            No
        213 BIG JOHN'S SPORTS EMPORIUM             No
        215 SPORTA RUSSIA                          No
        206 SPORTIQUE                              No
        207 SWEET ROCK SPORTS                      No
        203 DELHI SPORTS                           Yes
        205 KAM'S SPORTING GOODS                   Yes
        202 SIMMS ATHELETICS                       Yes
```

Example 2

If a preferred customer rating system was developed based on the following table, nesting DECODE statements can be used to return the rating.

Preferred_Customer	Credit_Rating	Customer Rating
Y	EXCELLENT	A
N	EXCELLENT	B
Y	GOOD	B
N	GOOD	C
Y	POOR	C
N	POOR	F

File: 2_40.sql

```
SELECT customer_id, customer_name, preferred_customer,
       credit_rating,
       DECODE(preferred_customer, 'Y',
       DECODE(credit_rating, 'EXCELLENT', 'A', 'GOOD', 'B', 'C'),
       DECODE(credit_rating, 'EXCELLENT', 'B', 'GOOD', 'C', 'F'))
FROM   s_customer;
```

Output (2_40.sql)

```
CUSTOMER_ID CUSTOMER_NAME                          P CREDIT_RA D
----------- ------------------------------------- - --------- -
        201 UNISPORTS                             Y EXCELLENT A
        202 SIMMS ATHELETICS                      Y POOR      C
        203 DELHI SPORTS                          Y GOOD      B
        204 WOMANSPORT                            Y EXCELLENT A
        205 KAM'S SPORTING GOODS                  Y EXCELLENT A
        206 SPORTIQUE                             N EXCELLENT B
        207 SWEET ROCK SPORTS                     N GOOD      C
        208 MUENCH SPORTS                         N GOOD      C
        209 BEISBOL SI!                           N EXCELLENT B
        210 FUTBOL SONORA                         N EXCELLENT B
        211 KUHN'S SPORTS                         N EXCELLENT B
        212 HAMADA SPORT                          N EXCELLENT B
        213 BIG JOHN'S SPORTS EMPORIUM            N EXCELLENT B
        214 OJIBWAY RETAIL                        N POOR      F
        215 SPORTA RUSSIA                         N POOR      F

15 rows selected.
```

Example 3

If you wanted to see this report horizontally displayed versus vertically with only the counts of customers per customer rating, you could use the DECODE function to change the resultant record set by using GROUP BY functions to sum values. The first example shows the vertical query and the second example shows the horizontal query.

File: 2_41.sql

```
SELECT credit_rating, COUNT(*)
FROM   s_customer
GROUP BY credit_rating;
```

Output (2_41.sql)

```
CREDIT_RA    COUNT(*)
---------  ----------
EXCELLENT           9
GOOD                3
POOR                3
```

File: 2_42.sql

```
SELECT  SUM(DECODE(credit_rating, 'EXCELLENT', 1, 0)) EXCELLENT,
        SUM(DECODE(credit_rating, 'GOOD', 1, 0)) GOOD,
        SUM(DECODE(credit_rating, 'POOR', 1, 0)) POOR
FROM    s_customer;
```

Output (2_42.sql)

```
 EXCELLENT        GOOD        POOR
----------  ----------  ----------
         9           3           3
```

For the second query, you have to know the possible values for the credit_rating column. This becomes helpful if the value column is an amount and you want to sum the amount per value. Instead of the sum adding one for a match, you could be specifying a column value to sum.

TRANSLATE Function

The TRANSLATE function can be used to verify the use of a consistent format by first, converting the value, then verifying the converted value follows a consistent format. The following query illustrates the functionality of the TRANSLATE function by converting numbers 1-9 to an *X*.

File: 2_43.sql

```
SELECT  TRANSLATE('555-143-3344', '1234567890','XXXXXXXXXX') phone
FROM    dual;
```

Output (2_43.sql)

```
PHONE
------------
XXX-XXX-XXXX
```

The TRANSLATE function is a single character replacement and changes all occurrences in the string with the character replacement specified. For every character listed in the "change from" set (1,2,3,4,5,6,7,8,9,0), a corresponding character must be listed in the "change to" set (X,X,X,X,X,X,X,X,X,X). If a character should remain unchanged, the character should not be included in the "change from" set. The following example retrieves only the customers with a valid phone number format of "X-XXX-XXX-XXXX".

File: 2_44.sql

```
SELECT customer_id, customer_name,
       TRANSLATE(phone, '1234567890','XXXXXXXXXX') phone
FROM   s_customer
WHERE  TRANSLATE(phone, '1234567890','XXXXXXXXXX') =
       'X-XXX-XXX-XXXX';
```

Output (2_44.sql)

```
CUSTOMER_ID CUSTOMER_NAME                          PHONE
----------- -------------------------------------- ---------------
        204 WOMANSPORT                             X-XXX-XXX-XXXX
        213 BIG JOHN'S SPORTS EMPORIUM             X-XXX-XXX-XXXX
        214 OJIBWAY RETAIL                         X-XXX-XXX-XXXX
```

INSTR Function

The INSTRing function is invaluable when searching a character string for a character set. The function returns a number of the position where the start of the character set was found within the character string searched. The following example illustrates how the extension of a filename could be removed from the string. The string is searched to find the "." separating the filename and extension with a SUBSTRing function used to specify the range of the string to parse out. The DECODE and LENGTH functions are needed to handle filenames that do not have an extension.

File: 2_45.sql

```
SELECT filename, SUBSTR(filename, 1,
       DECODE(INSTR(filename, '.') -1, -1, LENGTH(filename),
       INSTR(filename, '.') -1)) new_filename
FROM   s_image;
```

Output (2_45.sql)

```
FILENAME                 NEW_FILENAME
-------------------      ------------
bunboot.tif              bunboot
aceboot.tif              aceboot
proboot.tif              proboot
pucbat.tif               pucbat
winbat                   winbat
```

LTRIM/RTRIM/REPLACE Functions

The LTRIM function strips characters from the left side of a character string. The RTRIM function strips characters from the right side of a character string. These functions are often used when reading and parsing data files by trimming spaces from the left and right side of a string. The following example illustrates the deceiving operation of these TRIM functions.

File: 2_46.sql

```
SELECT LTRIM('ABCBCA12345', 'ABC')
FROM   DUAL;
```

Output (2_46.sql)

```
LTRIM
-----
12345
```

The TRIM functions remove all characters from the specified side (left or right) that are in the string of characters listed in the function, character by character. The previous example not only strips "ABC" from the left side, it also strips off all characters from the left side until the character does not show up in the TRIM character list. Therefore, it checks the *A* to see if it is in the list to strip, then the *B*, then the *C*, then the *B*, and so forth, until a character is not found in the character list.

The following example is a common error when using OPS$ accounts. OPS$ accounts enable users to use operating system usernames and passwords to log into Oracle. If a user account "PLSQL_USER" exists in UNIX, then an Oracle account can be added as "OPS$PLSQL_USER" (the Oracle password can be set to anything because authentication is performed on the UNIX password and a user is not required to enter an Oracle password when logging into Oracle). If this scenario is set up, when you log into the PLSQL_USER UNIX account, you can connect to Oracle by using "/" for the username and password. Oracle authenticates the user by verifying the UNIX account exists in Oracle. This is extremely useful when using captive logins by creating script files that log users into Oracle immediately upon UNIX login. In this case, the username and password are set to "/", which eliminates the need to hardcode a username and password.

In this type of environment, when OPS$ accounts are deployed, and new and updated records are stamped with the Oracle username that made the change, it is important to handle the "OPS$" string that precedes the Oracle username. The natural approach is to strip the 'OPS$' off to show the user. This can be incorrectly coded, if the following logic is used.

File: 2_47.sql

```
SELECT LTRIM('OPS$SPORANO', 'OPS$')
FROM   DUAL;
```

Output (2_47.sql)

```
LTRI
----
RANO
```

To strip only the 'OPS$' off, the REPLACE function can be used as the following illustrates.

File: 2_48.sql

```
SELECT REPLACE('OPS$SPORANO', 'OPS$')
FROM   DUAL;
```

Output (2_48.sql)

```
REPLACE
-------
SPORANO
```

TIP
*The prefix of OPS$ added to each Oracle username to
link the Oracle account to the operating system
account can be changed to anything desired by setting
the init.ora parameter 'os_authent_prefix'. A common
value to set this parameter value to is blank in the
init.ora, as the following illustrates:*

```
os_authent_prefix= ""
```

The preceding setting allows the Oracle username to be set to the UNIX
username without a prefix. This eliminates some of the confusion introduced with
the 'OPS$' prefix.

Highlight Helpful SQL*Plus Commands and Concepts

SQL*Plus is a tool where most developers spend a great deal of time developing and
testing application source code. The more knowledgeable you are in SQL*Plus, the
more efficient you will become in developing and testing. This section outlines
helpful tips and techniques to use when using SQL*Plus.

Utilize SQL*Plus Startup Files

When starting SQL*Plus, two possible startup files are executed. These files can be
used to set up the SQL*Plus environment or set up default conditions that are
always used by a user in SQL*Plus. These files serve the same purpose as startup
files executed during login to UNIX-based systems or any other operating system.

The two files are the glogin.sql and login.sql. The SQL*Plus and SQL commands
contained in glogin.sql are executed upon successful login to SQL*Plus. The
glogin.sql file is located in the same directory as the SQL*Plus directory under the
main Oracle home location (under Oracle7.3 on Windows95, it is located in
ORACLE_HOME\plus33). This is the first file executed and will be executed for all
SQL*Plus sessions. The login.sql file is used to customize individual user
preferences and is executed after the glogin.sql file has been executed. Oracle will
use the login.sql file located in the current user's working directory, if one exists,

when logging into SQL*Plus. Settings that are set in the glogin.sql file are overwritten if also set in the login.sql file. Two examples follow:

- Changing the default editor
- Changing the default date format

```
DEFINE_EDITOR=c:\pfe\pfe32.exe
ALTER SESSION SET nls_date_format='mm/dd/yyyy';
```

For the ALTER SESSION command to be executed by all users logging into SQL*Plus, each user must have "ALTER SESSION" privilege which is a privilege granted to the connect role by default.

Disclaimer: The date format in the previous example is helpful for displaying the four-digit year by default when DATE values are returned in SQL*Plus. It does not solve the Year 2000 compliance issue.

When a user logs into SQL*Plus and edits a file with the EDIT command, the default editor used after the previous setting will be PFE (Programmer's File Editor - a third-party Windows editor). When a user logs into SQL*Plus and queries any DATE column, the format is changed for the session to display in a different format as shown in the following example.

File: 2_49.sql

```
SELECT SYSDATE
FROM   dual;
```

Output (2_49.sql)

```
SYSDATE
----------
10/20/1998
```

The following is a login.sql file I use on a regular basis. The comment lines are provided to explain each command.

File: 2_50.sql

```
-- Displays the literal text 'LOGIN Execution' to the screen
PROMPT LOGIN Execution
-- Changes the default SQL*Plus editor
DEFINE_EDITOR=c:\pfe\pfe32.exe
-- Changes the default Oracle DATE display
```

```
ALTER SESSION SET nls_date_format='mm/dd/yyyy';
-- Changes the default temporary file to edit
SET EDITFILE "PLUSTEMP.SQL"
-- Sets feedback to display the number of records returned if > 1
SET FEEDBACK 1
-- Sets the size of the page to 23, which will only display the
-- title and column headers every 23 records of output
SET PAGESIZE 23
-- Sets pause on, so scrolling will pause every page
SET PAUSE ON
-- Sets the pause message to say 'More...'
SET PAUSE "More..."
-- Enables DBMS_OUTPUT so all DBMS_OUTPUT.PUT_LINE statements will
-- display in SQL*Plus (the buffer is set to the maximum and
-- wrapping will not break words)
SET SERVEROUTPUT ON SIZE 1000000 format WORD_WRAPPED
-- Sets timing on, so every SQL statement executed returns a timing
SET TIMING ON
```

Execution of Stored PL/SQL Objects in SQL*Plus

When you are in SQL*Plus and you wish to execute a stored PL/SQL object, two methods can accomplish this execution, as the following illustrates:

```
SQL> SET SERVEROUTPUT ON
SQL> EXECUTE DBMS_OUTPUT.PUT_LINE('Hello')
Hello

PL/SQL procedure successfully completed.
```

or

```
SQL> SET SERVEROUTPUT ON
SQL> BEGIN
  2    DBMS_OUTPUT.PUT_LINE('Hello');
  3    END;
  4  /
Hello

PL/SQL procedure successfully completed.
```

Expand the DESCRIBE Command

The DESCRIBE command in SQL*Plus is not limited to displaying the definitions of tables. It also lists attributes about stored PL/SQL objects as the following illustrates:

```
SQL> DESC DBMS_OUTPUT.PUT_LINE
PROCEDURE dbms_output.put_line
 Argument Name                      Type              In/Out Default?
 ------------------------------     --------------    ------ --------
 A                                  VARCHAR2          IN

PROCEDURE dbms_output.put_line
 Argument Name                      Type              In/Out Default?
 ------------------------------     --------------    ------ --------
 A                                  NUMBER            IN

PROCEDURE dbms_output.put_line
 Argument Name                      Type              In/Out Default?
 ------------------------------     --------------    ------ --------
 A                                  DATE              IN
```

In describing the DBMS_OUTPUT.PUT_LINE procedure, we see the procedure is overloaded and can accept character, numeric, or date values.

Expand SQL*Plus Variables into PL/SQL

When using SQL*Plus for testing, you can reference variables set in SQL*Plus for use in PL/SQL code or use the ampersand variables syntax of SQL*Plus to prompt the user for input as illustrated in the following example:

```
SQL> SET SERVEROUTPUT ON
SQL> DEFINE var1=Hello
SQL> BEGIN
  2      DBMS_OUTPUT.PUT_LINE('&VAR1');
  3  END;
  4  /
old   2:      DBMS_OUTPUT.PUT_LINE('&VAR1');
new   2:      DBMS_OUTPUT.PUT_LINE('Hello');
Hello

PL/SQL procedure successfully completed.

SQL> BEGIN
  2      DBMS_OUTPUT.PUT_LINE('&input_var');
  3  END;
  4  /
Enter value for input_var: Hello Again
old   2:      DBMS_OUTPUT.PUT_LINE('&input_var');
new   2:      DBMS_OUTPUT.PUT_LINE('Hello Again');
Hello Again

PL/SQL procedure successfully completed.
```

Understand the HOST Command

If you are in SQL*Plus and need to retrieve information outside of SQL*Plus, you can branch out to the operating system from within SQL*Plus and suspend the current activity. When doing this, all SQL*Plus settings and the SQL buffer will remain intact. The command to branch to the operating system is HOST. In UNIX and VMS, additional commands will branch to the operating system and are "!" and "$", respectively. Once at the operating system, you can enter operating system commands. To return to the suspended SQL*Plus session, you must enter the operating system command that would typically log you out of your operating system session. If you desire to only execute one operating system command, this can be accomplished by issuing the HOST command and preceding this command with the operating system command, as the following illustrates:

```
SQL> HOST dir/w
```

The preceding method of executing an operating system command results in immediately returning you to SQL*Plus.

Define the SQL Buffer

SQL*Plus commands are not buffered in the SQL buffer. Only the most recent SQL or PL/SQL statement is buffered. Therefore, SQL*Plus commands must be re-entered for every session. This can be demonstrated by typing the LIST command in SQL*Plus after executing a SQL*Plus command.

When saving the SQL buffer to an operating system file, use the SAVE command followed by a filename. If the file exists and you wish to overwrite it, you can issue the SAVE command with the REPLACE argument. Not as commonly known is the capability to append to an existing file with the SAVE command and APPEND argument. This command is illustrated in the following example:

```
SQL> SELECT * FROM dual;

D
-
X

SQL> SAVE test1.sql
Created file test1.sql
SQL> SELECT 'T' FROM dual;

'
-
T
```

Highlighting SQL*Plus Commands

```
SQL> SAVE test1.sql
File "test1.sql" already exists.
Use another name or "SAVE filename REPLACE".
SQL> SAVE test1.sql APPEND
Appended file to test1.sql
SQL> EDIT test1.sql
```

When issuing the last command from the preceding example, the editor will be opened with the test1.sql file contents displayed as illustrated below.

```
SELECT * FROM dual;
SELECT 'T' FROM dual;
```

The SQL*Plus attributes can also be saved to an operating system file. The command to save the SQL*Plus attributes is the STORE SET command. The same arguments are available with the STORE SET command and the command functions the same as the SAVE command for the SQL buffer. The STORE SET command logs all SET options to a specified file. This file can be executed in another session to set the session with the same attributes, by executing the operating system file with the START or @ command. The following is an example of saving these settings:

```
SQL> STORE SET test1a.sql
```

The test1a.sql file can then be opened and the following contents would appear:

```
set appinfo ON
set appinfo "SQL*Plus"
set arraysize 15
set autocommit OFF
set autoprint OFF
set autotrace OFF
set blockterminator "."
set closecursor OFF
set cmdsep OFF
set colsep " "
set compatibility NATIVE
set concat "."
set copycommit 0
set copytypecheck ON
set crt ""
set define "&"
set echo OFF
set editfile "afiedt.buf"
set embedded OFF
```

```
set escape OFF
set feedback 6
set flagger OFF
set flush ON
set heading ON
set headsep "|"
set linesize 80
set long 80
set longchunksize 80
set maxdata 60000
set newpage 1
set null ""
set numformat ""
set numwidth 10
set pagesize 55
set pause ON
set pause ""
set recsep WRAP
set recsepchar " "
set serveroutput ON size 2000 format WORD_WRAPPED
set shiftinout invisible
set showmode OFF
set sqlcase MIXED
set sqlcontinue "> "
set sqlnumber ON
set sqlprefix "#"
set sqlprompt "SQL> "
set sqlterminator ";"
set suffix "SQL"
set tab ON
set termout ON
set time OFF
set timing OFF
set trimout ON
set trimspool OFF
set underline "-"
set verify ON
set wrap ON
```

TIP
*The STORE SET command is very helpful when you have changed many of the settings in a SQL*Plus session with the SET command and you want to retain these settings for later use.*

Highlighting SQL*Plus Commands

Detail the TIMING Command

If you want to time certain portions of a SQL*Plus session, use the TIMING command. This command allows for multiple timers to be set, therefore, you can have several timers tracking certain events at once. The timers are set in succession and you can see how many timers you have active. However, you can only see one timer at a time, namely, the timer last started. Once you stop the last timer, then you will see the previous timer in the sequence. When a timer has stopped, the time is displayed along with the name of the timer, if you specified a name. The following example illustrates this technique (note that the comments in parentheses below have been added for clarification only and are not actually displayed when executing these commands):

```
SQL> timing
no timing elements in use (no timers started yet)
SQL> timing start
SQL> timing start time1
SQL> timing start time2
SQL> timing
3 timing elements in use (3 timers have been started, two named)
SQL> timing show
timing for: time2
 real: 7190
SQL> timing show time1
timing for: time2 (although time1 desired, can only see last time)
 real: 13780
SQL> timing stop
timing for: time2
 real: 18840
SQL> timing
2 timing elements in use
SQL> timing show
timing for: time1
 real: 33450
SQL> timing stop
timing for: time1
 real: 37190
SQL> timing show
 real: 47240
SQL> timing stop
 real: 50760
SQL> timing
no timing elements in use
```

Notice, the time is in thousands of seconds. To get the number of seconds, you must divide the number returned by 1,000.

Commit Transactions in SQL*Plus

DDL commands are explicit operations in SQL*Plus; therefore, an implicit commit takes place once a DDL statement is successfully completed. DML commands are operations that can be backed out or rolled back to the previous commit point (assuming the default of the SQL*Plus AUTOCOMMIT option is unchanged and is set to OFF). Changing the AUTOCOMMIT option to ON is highly discouraged because SQL*Plus DML operations should be queried to ensure correctness prior to committing the transaction.

By default, when you exit SQL*Plus, an implicit commit is performed and all uncommitted transactions will be committed.

TIP
*Anytime ad hoc UPDATES or DELETES are performed in SQL*Plus, the information updated or deleted should be queried prior to committing the transaction to ensure the operation is completed as desired. This is highly recommended as a safeguard. Once a COMMIT is performed, there is no going back.*

Use the SET Options

A long list of SET options is available in SQL*Plus. Review these options and determine if any of these options can be set to help you or other users in SQL*Plus sessions. If you determine something would be good for all users who log into SQL*Plus, then place the SET command in the glogin.sql file as outlined in a preceding section in this chapter. If you determine something would be good for only yourself, then place the SET command in the login.sql file as outlined in the preceding section. If you want to see the list of SET options and their settings at any time, the SHOW ALL command can be issued in SQL*Plus.

A few useful SET options are shown in the following examples:

```
SQL> SET TIME ON
09:50:32 SQL> SET TIMING ON
09:51:14 SQL> SELECT COUNT(*)
09:51:22   2  FROM  s_customer;

  COUNT(*)
----------
        15


real: 50
09:51:28 SQL> SET AUTOTRACE ON
```

```
09:54:24 SQL> /

  COUNT(*)
----------
        15

real: 440

Execution Plan
----------------------------------------------------------
   0      SELECT STATEMENT Optimizer=CHOOSE
   1    0   SORT (AGGREGATE)
   2    1     TABLE ACCESS (FULL) OF 'S_CUSTOMER'

Statistics
----------------------------------------------------------
        0  recursive calls
        2  db block gets
        2  consistent gets
        0  physical reads
        0  redo size
      185  bytes sent via SQL*Net to client
      270  bytes received via SQL*Net from client
        3  SQL*Net roundtrips to/from client
        0  sorts (memory)
        0  sorts (disk)
        1  rows processed
10:03:02 SQL> SET SQLPROMPT 'INST 1> '
10:03:19 INST 1>
```

The SET TIME command changes the prompt to precede the prompt with the time down to the second. The SET TIMING command turns a stop watch timer on, which displays the elapsed time for any SQL statement executed (must be divided by 1,000 to view the seconds). The SET AUTOTRACE command turns on an automatic tracing facility for every SQL statement executed that includes an EXPLAIN PLAN and statistics of the SQL operation. The SET AUTOTRACE command is discussed in more detail in Chapter 7. The SET SQLPROMPT command enables you to change the SQL*Plus command prompt. If working with multiple instances, set the SQL prompt to the name of the instance that you log into. The technique to perform this is shown in the following example:

```
SQL> COLUMN instance NEW_VALUE _instance
SQL> SELECT instance_name instance
```

```
 2  FROM   v$instance;

INSTANCE
----------------
devd

 real: 9500
SQL> SET SQLPROMPT "&_instance> "
devd>
```

The COLUMN, SELECT, and SET commands in the preceding example can be added to the glogin.sql file to have the instance name automatically be set to the instance that you log into. The previous example was executed under 8.0.4 and all users would have to be given SELECT privilege on the V$INSTANCE view by SYS as shown in the following:

```
GRANT SELECT ON v_$instance TO PUBLIC;
```

TIP

When working in an environment with multiple instances, it is very easy to lose track of the instance that you are logged into. One good method to eliminate the potential for performing a critical modification in the wrong instance is to change the SQL prompt automatically in the glogin.sql file.

If spaces are needed in the SET SQLPROMPT command, the string must be enclosed in single or double quotes.

Use the USER Variable

When you log into any Oracle product, Oracle sets the USER variable with the username of the current session. This variable can be referenced in SQL and PL/SQL. In SQL*Plus, the USER variable can be viewed using the following methods:

```
SQL> SHOW USER
user is "PLSQL_USER"
SQL> SELECT USER FROM DUAL;

USER
------------------------------
PLSQL_USER
```

Summary

In this chapter, we began by outlining the critical role SQL knowledge plays in learning and using the PL/SQL language to the fullest. We then covered the importance of the PL/SQL language to advance in the Oracle realm. The chapter focused on some valuable segments of the SQL language that are important to know in detail, followed by some valuable SQL functions. Finally, the chapter covered some useful SQL*Plus techniques not readily known to developers and DBAs to assist in their efficiency and effectiveness in SQL*Plus.

TIPS

REVIEW

Tips Review

- When a query orders by a column with NULL values, the records with a NULL value in the order column are retrieved after all records with a non-NULL value. If you want NULL values to be retrieved first and keep the list in ascending order, you can change the ORDER BY clause with a DECODE function.

- Use the NVL function if you desire to treat a NULL value as zero (0).

- One approach to ensuring that the time portion of all DATE columns is stripped off of dates is to create database triggers on the tables that contain DATE columns to perform the time stripping function. This would protect your system from any DATE entry and ensure proper handling of all DATEs.

- The double ampersand "&&" sets a variable for the entire SQL*Plus session or until it is undefined. If only one ampersand "&" were used instead of the "&&", the variable would prompt the user twice because the single ampersand only sets the variable for one occurrence.

- The ADD_MONTHS function can accept negative numbers to return a previous month.

- The prefix of OPS$ added to each Oracle username to link the Oracle account to the operating system account can be changed to anything desired by setting the init.ora parameter 'os_authent_prefix'. A common value to set this parameter value to is blank in the init.ora.

- The STORE SET command is very helpful when you have changed many of the settings in a SQL*Plus session with the SET command and you want to retain these settings for later use.

■ Anytime ad hoc UPDATEs or DELETEs are performed in SQL*Plus, the information updated or deleted should be queried prior to committing the transaction to ensure the operation is completed as desired. This is highly recommended as a safeguard. Once a COMMIT is performed, there is no going back.

■ When working in an environment with multiple instances, it is very easy to lose track of the instance that you are logged into. One good method to eliminate the potential for performing a critical modification in the wrong instance is to change the SQL prompt automatically in the glogin.sql file.

Tips Review

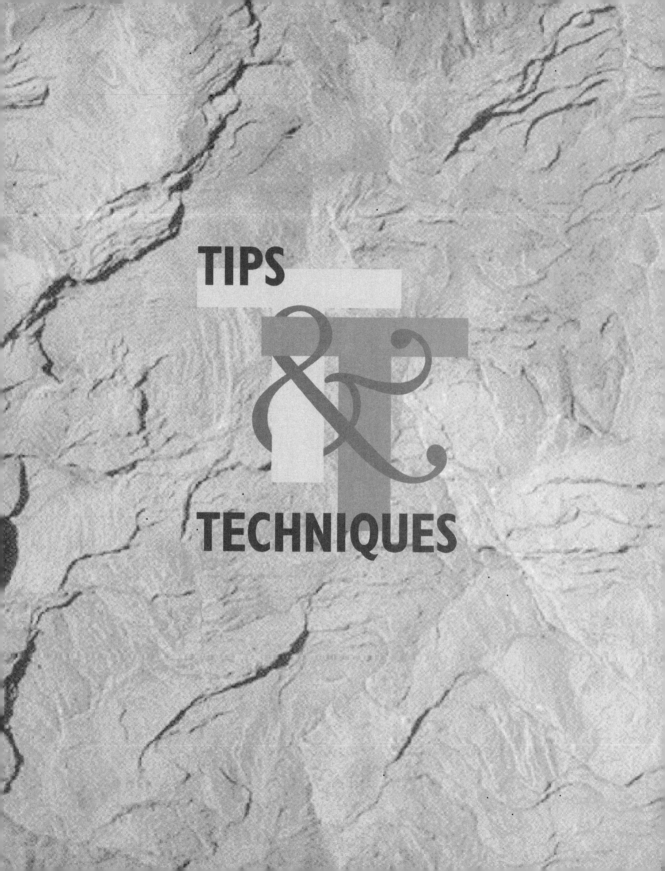

TIPS
&
TECHNIQUES

CHAPTER
3

Establishing PL/SQL
Coding Standards
(Developer and DBA)

One of the most important components of any application development environment is establishing a Development Foundation. Every language has unique characteristics, and PL/SQL is no different. A PL/SQL Development Foundation, which is established in the next three chapters, is comprised of three components: PL/SQL Coding Standards, Standard PL/SQL Language Coding Techniques, and Standard PL/SQL Program Unit Coding Techniques. This chapter concentrates on establishing PL/SQL Coding Standards.

A consistent coding standard for PL/SQL development must be created and enforced to ensure readability, maintainability, and efficiency. Defining a coding standard is usually a monumental task because most developers become set in their ways early in their careers. Defining a coding standard collectively becomes nearly impossible. The ideal situation is to develop standards collectively because this involves input from all team members and becomes more easily accepted. If this is not possible in your environment, someone should be tasked with this critical responsibility.

Once the standard is defined, some resistance will always occur to conform to the new standard, because the standard will not be the coding style to which everyone is accustomed. The benefits become evident once the standard has been adopted and developers start creating new source code, and begin to read and modify other developer's source code.

Once coding standards are defined, they must be documented and enforced. A coding standard becomes increasingly important as the number of developers and number of systems increase. Coding standards increase readability and maintenance, which is extremely beneficial to both the current and future development staff.

Coding standards should meet the following criteria:

- Provide a consistent guideline to follow
- Address the major components of the language
- Ensure they are simple to follow and understand
- Allow flexibility and creativity
- Not inhibit speed of development

If these criteria are not met, the standard will never be adopted. Remember that coding standards should not hinder developers' ability to program fast, but they should create a natural set of standards that allow for streamlined development.

One method of ensuring standards are followed is to integrate a mechanism into the deployment process that provides reviews of coding standard adherence. This responsibility is a natural extension of the Quality Assurance (QA) team. It can be the QA team's responsibility to correct any non-conformity of the defined standards prior to deployment, and ensure standards are enforced by re-educating the development staff on the importance of standards compliance.

The goal of this chapter is to define a set of PL/SQL coding standards. These coding standards are used throughout this book to ensure a consistent format of source code is presented. This coding standard is by no means meant to mandate an industry standard, but is a standard that has been developed with the help of many experienced PL/SQL developers, and one that we have found to be extremely effective in PL/SQL development environments. If you are in an environment that does not have PL/SQL coding standards in place, there is no better time to develop a standard than NOW! Feel free to adopt these standards or a modified version into your environment.

The following is a set of PL/SQL coding standards that cover the basic areas.

- Develop descriptive filenames

- Differentiate case to increase visual distinction

- Use meaningful variable names to signify scope and type

- Integrate white space to increase readability

- Integrate PL/SQL program unit level and inline documentation

- Incorporate various conventions to aid PL/SQL development

- Develop an audit trail/version control of stored PL/SQL code in the database

Develop Descriptive Filenames

PL/SQL source code should reside in operating system files to provide easy development and maintenance. Each time developers create a new file, they should take the same care in naming that file as they do in naming variables in programs. The filename should be an abbreviated description of the source code. This filenaming approach becomes invaluable as the number of PL/SQL modules continues to increase. Ensuring the filenames are truly descriptive makes locating source code modules much easier when they are needed.

A common naming convention limits all filename prefixes to a maximum length of eight characters and extensions to a maximum length of three characters to ensure portability between all operating systems. When defining standards, consider the big picture. Particularly in filenaming conventions, remember the platform may change over time and adhering to the lowest common denominator is the best standard. Avoid using the underscore "_" because the number of characters is limited. A package containing modules to manipulate employee information might be found in the files *empupd.pkh* (contains package specification/header) and *empupd.pkb* (contains the package body). As a rule, always separate the package specification from the package body. This separation creates major advantages during compilation of packages (this is reviewed in detail in Chapter 5). Remember:

- The package specification and package body are compiled separately

- Package specification variable, procedure, and function declarations are global to a session

- References to public (global) package procedures and functions is accomplished through the reference to the package specification definition

- When the package body is modified, the package body must be recompiled; the package specification does not have to be recompiled unless it, too, is modified

- When a stored PL/SQL program unit is recompiled, all stored PL/SQL program units referencing that program unit become INVALID and must be recompiled

Because the package specification is separated from the package body and modifications are typically performed to the package body contents, the package specification (contains public objects) does not need to be recompiled. The stored PL/SQL program units that reference any public objects in that package will not become INVALID. By following this standard approach you will save a tremendous amount of time and pain.

Each package specification, package body, procedure, function, and database trigger should be placed in a separate file. The file should identify the type of PL/SQL program unit contained in the file. This can be accomplished through a standard filenaming convention. Use the prefix of the filename to describe the source code contents and the extension to signify the type of PL/SQL program unit. The following table outlines the extension standard to follow:

PL/SQL Source Code Type	Extension	Example
Package Specification/Header	pkh	empupd.pkh
Package Body	pkb	empupd.pkb
Procedure	prc	empsal.prc

PL/SQL Source Code Type	Extension	Example
Function	fnc	empterm.fnc
Trigger	trg	updemp.trg
SQL Script	sql	crsource.sql

TIP
Use filenames with a prefix of eight characters or less and use an extension of three characters or less. Because filename lengths are not consistent across all platforms, choosing the lowest common denominator is best.

The location of the PL/SQL source code files must also be considered. One of the following two methods can be deployed in your development environment.

- **Method One**   Store all PL/SQL source files in one directory under a main application directory named *source.* This method is usually deployed successfully when the number of PL/SQL source files is limited.

- **Method Two**   Store each type of PL/SQL source file in a separate directory under the main application directory named *packs, procs, funcs, trigs,* and *sql.* In this method, the package specification and package body are stored in the same directory. In a production environment, a central *source* directory is usually the approach for the PL/SQL source code files.

If your environment encrypts the PL/SQL source code (WRAP utility) for production implementation, then a standard filenaming convention for WRAPped files must be created for your environment. The preceding standard naming conventions table would change to the following to support encrypted files:

PL/SQL Source Code Type	Extension	Example	Extension Wrapped	Example Wrapped
Package Specification/Header	ph	empupd.ph	phw	empupd.phw
Package Body	pb	empupd.pb	pbw	empupd.pbw
Procedure	pr	empsal.pr	prw	empsal.prw

Developing Descriptive Filenames

PL/SQL Source Code Type	Extension	Example	Extension Wrapped	Example Wrapped
Function	fn	empterm.fn	fnw	empterm.fnw
Trigger	trg	updemp.trg	N/A	N/A
SQL Script	sql	crsource.sql	N/A	N/A

Notice the Triggers and SQL script files have N/A (Not Applicable) signified for the wrap extension for the two files because the WRAP utility only WRAPs packages, procedures, and functions.

If the preceding method is deployed, then the only files that should be copied to the production system and deployed are the WRAPped versions of the PL/SQL source code. These should be WRAPped on the development system and stored in a directory under the source code directories.

The standard method of WRAPping packages is to WRAP the package body, keeping the package specification unWRAPped. The specification contains global declarations of the package contents. This is the portion of the package to which calling PL/SQL program units refers, whereas the body contains the actual program unit source code, and, thus, the logic that may need to be hidden. The WRAP utility is described in more detail in Chapter 5.

Oracle supplies a set of PL/SQL built-in packages that greatly enhance the PL/SQL language. These supplied packages have a filenaming convention that places all package specifications in filenames with a prefix of dbms*xxxx*, where *xxxx* is the package content description and the extension is .sql. The package specifications are not WRAPped. The corresponding package bodies are typically WRAPped and placed in filenames with a prefix of prvt*xxxx*, where *xxxx* is the package content description that matches the package specification file and the extension is .plb.

Differentiate Case to Increase Visual Distinction

The PL/SQL language is not case-sensitive (identical to the SQL language), so commands and arguments can be either uppercase or lowercase. A recommended standard is to program all PL/SQL language commands, SQL commands, PL/SQL reserved words, SQL reserved words, and supplied Oracle packages in UPPERCASE and all other PL/SQL source code in lowercase, such as user-defined package names, variables, and so forth. An example of this standard is illustrated here:

File: 3_1.sql

```
DECLARE
   CURSOR cur_orders IS
      SELECT order_id, customer_id, total
      FROM   s_order;
BEGIN
   FOR lv_order_rec IN cur_orders LOOP
      DBMS_OUTPUT.PUT_LINE('Order Id: ' ||
         TO_CHAR(lv_order_rec.order_id) || ' Customer Id: ' ||
         TO_CHAR(lv_order_rec.customer_id) || ' Total: ' ||
         TO_CHAR(lv_order_rec.total));
   END LOOP;
END;
/
```

TIP
Ensure SQL and PL/SQL reserved words are not used for any object creation in your database. In addition, do not use PL/SQL reserved words in your PL/SQL source code to name any variables or other module components. This causes confusion when debugging PL/SQL source code and extra coding to work around this issue. The following example illustrates this situation and two workarounds.

File: 3_2.sql

```
DECLARE
   lv_class_txt  VARCHAR2(18);
   lv_count_num  NUMBER;
BEGIN
   -- The following SELECT executes without error in SQL*Plus
   -- (without the INTO clause), however in PL/SQL it results
   -- in the error below. The reason for the error is that 'count'
   -- is a SQL reserved word.
```

```
    SELECT class, count
    INTO   lv_class_txt, lv_count_num
    FROM   v$waitstat a
    WHERE  ROWNUM < 2;
END;
/

DECLARE
*
ERROR at line 1:
ORA-00937: not a single-group group function
ORA-06512: at line 5
```

To execute the preceding script, the user must have SELECT privilege on the V_$WAITSTAT view. The work-around for the error received in the preceding example is to change the reference to the count column to:

- a.count (preceding the column with the table name or table name alias)

- "COUNT" (change the reference to uppercase and enclose the column in double quotes)

Either change eliminates the error.

Use Meaningful Variable Names to Signify Scope and Type

A standardized convention for the naming of PL/SQL code variables is beneficial for any database application and becomes an absolute necessity as the number of developers and program units increases. By establishing a standard for naming variables, code becomes easier to read and write because objects are more easily understood in the context of the code. Perhaps the biggest advantage, especially in a large project involving many developers, is that a properly designed naming convention helps identify the variable definition location. Consider the following recommendations as a guideline:

Variable Category	Rule	Examples
Program unit or block local variables	Prefix with lv_	lv_hire_date
Package global variables (defined in the package specification/header)	Prefix with pvg_	pvg_hire_date

Variable Category	Rule	Examples
Package variables (defined in the package body)	Prefix with pv_	pv_hire_date
Procedure or Function parameter variable	Prefix with p_	p_input_date

The preceding recommendations concentrate on the scope of the variable. This is valuable to determine the scope of the variable without searching through the source code for the definition location.

The next level of recommended variable-naming convention signifies the type of variable in the name. This set is shown in the following table:

Variable Category	Rule	Examples
Cursor Names	Prefix with cur_	cur_employee_info
User Defined Data Types	Prefix with type_	type_year_month
Character Variables	Suffix with _txt	lv_state_txt pv_zip_code_txt
Numeric Variables	Suffix with _num	lv_account_num pv_trans_num pv_zip_code_num
Date Variables	Suffix with _date	lv_hire_date pv_hire_date
Boolean Variables	Suffix with _bln	lv_comp_bln
Record Variables	Suffix with _rec	lv_customer_rec
Table Variables	Suffix with _table	lv_product_table
Exception Variables	Suffix with _excep	lv_employee_excep

In addition to variable names containing the scope and type of the variable, they should describe the use of the variable. They should be descriptive in nature and common sense should be used. The use of variables abc and xyz in the program is much harder to figure out, whereas, lv_ar_total_num and pv_employee_txt are much easier to determine because they are descriptive by name. Longer variable names increase the number of keystrokes needed, but the benefit of the description is invaluable. I recommend making all variables completely lowercase. I find mixing case between words is easier than mixing case within words. The following code illustrates several variable examples.

Signifying Scope and Type

```
CREATE OR REPLACE PACKAGE employee_update IS
   pvg_emp_start_date   DATE;
   pvg_employee_rec     s_employee%ROWTYPE;
   pvg_order_num        s_order.order_id%TYPE;

CREATE OR REPLACE PACKAGE BODY employee_update IS
   pv_order_total_num       s_order.total%TYPE;
   pv_payment_type_txt      s_order.payment_type%TYPE;
   pv_order_count_num       NUMBER(5);
   pv_order_count_num1      pv_order_count_num%TYPE;

CREATE OR REPLACE PROCEDURE employee_update_comp
   (p_employee_num NUMBER) IS
   CURSOR cur_employee IS
      SELECT employee_id, employee_last_name
      FROM   s_employee;
   TYPE type_employee_table IS TABLE OF s_employee%ROWTYPE
      INDEX BY BINARY_INTEGER;
   lv_employee_rec            cur_employee%ROWTYPE;
   lv_emp_table               type_employee_table;
   lv_employee_sal_num        s_employee.salary%TYPE;
   lv_employee_commission_num s_employee.commission_pct%TYPE;
   lv_salary_adjust_num       NUMBER;
   lv_comp_bln                BOOLEAN;
   lv_salary_excep            EXCEPTION;
```

Integrate White Space to Increase Readability

When it comes to writing code, two of the most underused keyboard keys are the carriage return and the space bar. The day is over when 20-megabyte hard drives are the norm and every bit of space is precious. With the drive capacities increasing daily, accompanied by constant disk-drive price reductions, there is no need to bleed code dry of every unessential character. Modern programming languages are free-form and do not make requirements for code appearance or format. Developers should employ common sense when it comes to indentation and the usage of free space. PL/SQL is no exception. As a free-form language, indentation and word spacing should both flow freely. There is no overhead in having blank lines or indentation within PL/SQL programs. As such, there is no excuse for PL/SQL code that is all left-justified and crammed together as one continuous block of text.

TIP
*Ample use of blank lines increases code readability
by creating logical blocks that are easily visible to
the human eye.*

Consider the following PL/SQL code.

File: 3_3.sql

```
DECLARE
CURSOR cur_employee IS SELECT employee_id, commission_pct FROM
s_employee;
lv_employee_rec cur_employee%ROWTYPE;
CURSOR cur_customer IS SELECT customer_name
FROM s_customer WHERE sales_rep_id = lv_employee_rec.employee_id;
BEGIN
OPEN cur_employee;
LOOP
FETCH cur_employee INTO lv_employee_rec;
EXIT WHEN cur_employee%NOTFOUND;
IF lv_employee_rec.commission_pct > 10 THEN
FOR lv_customer_rec IN cur_customer LOOP
DBMS_OUTPUT.PUT_LINE(lv_customer_rec.customer_name);
END LOOP;
END IF;
END LOOP;
CLOSE cur_employee;
END;
```

The preceding segment of code is performing two distinct operations: retrieving sales representatives with commission greater than 10 percent and then displaying all customer accounts for that sales representative. Following and determining the logical separations and flow of the PL/SQL code is difficult.

To get maximum readability from your code, try using the following guidelines:

■ Use blank lines to modularize code into sections that are no more than 20 lines long. These blank lines are like magnets for the eye, drawing the reader to the next section without the need for detailed reading.

■ Use three blank spaces for each line within a conditional statement or any control structure to show ownership of those lines by the conditional. Increase the indention by three spaces for each nested conditional or control.

Increasing Readability

■ Use multiple blank spaces to left-align items within the various sections of a DML statement. This includes left alignment and separate lines of the main sections of DML statements, as well as alignment of operands in the predicate (where) clause.

■ Use three blank spaces to show the logical relationship of cursor definitions or user-defined data types that have been split across multiple lines. This extends for any command line that must extend beyond one line.

When you use these four guidelines, the PL/SQL code previously shown becomes much more readable, as the following illustrates here:

File: 3_4.sql

```
DECLARE
   CURSOR cur_employee IS
      SELECT employee_id, commission_pct
      FROM   s_employee;

      lv_employee_rec cur_employee%ROWTYPE;

   CURSOR cur_customer IS
      SELECT customer_name
      FROM   s_customer
      WHERE  sales_rep_id = lv_employee_rec.employee_id;

BEGIN
   OPEN cur_employee;

   LOOP
      FETCH cur_employee INTO lv_employee_rec;
      EXIT WHEN cur_employee%NOTFOUND;

      IF lv_employee_rec.commission_pct > 10 THEN

         FOR lv_customer_rec IN cur_customer LOOP
            DBMS_OUTPUT.PUT_LINE(lv_customer_rec.customer_name);
         END LOOP;

      END IF;

   END LOOP;
   CLOSE cur_employee;
END;
```

Increasing Readability

Integrate PL/SQL Program Unit Level and Inline Documentation

The maintenance of code is a less desirable activity than new development for most developers. When it comes to creating and writing any sizable piece of code, developers would almost always prefer starting from scratch over having to understand and then modify someone else's code. Anyone who's been in this industry for any length of time knows this: You play it cool in status meetings, letting everyone think you are way ahead of schedule when, in fact, you are frantically rewriting major portions of code that were so poorly documented by your predecessor, because you thought starting over was best. Are the rewrites always necessary? Probably not, but if you have to spend ten hours deciphering a piece of code, why not spend the same amount of time coding it again? Documentation is one way we can alleviate the trepidation developers feel when it comes to taking over the code written by someone else. There are two components to proper documentation: module documentation and inline documentation.

- **Module documentation** This is high-level documentation written for a package, procedure, or function. This should appear at the beginning of the source code file and contain, at bare minimum, the following sections: The creator and creation date, a brief description of the module, calling syntax including argument list description, return values, and revision history (dates of modification, developer name of modifier, and overview of modifications). A technical section may be included to provide more detailed information that may not be readily obvious from the code itself, such as the algorithm or assumptions upon which the module is based.

- **Inline documentation** This is helpful comments actually integrated within the source code of a module. The purpose of this type of documentation is simple—to clarify what is happening in the code. This type of documentation can be useful when linking together the beginning and end of a cursor loop or conditional test (especially if they span multiple pages), tracking the individual lines affected by a module revision, recording assumptions that were made, specifying the purpose of a section of code, and documenting work-arounds for a bug or strange behavior. Another use for inline documentation is to section off parts of code to bring a greater degree of readability. This can be accomplished by using a line of hyphens (-) to accentuate the separation.

Comments should be viewed as an essential component, but common sense should be used when commenting code. Comments are also valuable to track version modifications and to provide an audit trail for modifications. There are two methods of adding comments, namely, the '--' for single-line comments and '/*' (start comment) and '*/' (end comment) for multiline comments. I recommend using the two hyphens as a standard to limit the possibility of error. I have seen developers comment out a large portion of source code logic and then have seen a follow-up developer place logic in the middle of that source code. Because the source code logic was placed between a multiline comment section, it will never make it in production.

Remember, any comments inserted in the operating system file that creates the stored PL/SQL program unit will only be stored in the database upon creation if the comment is after the CREATE statement and prior to the END statement of the PL/SQL program unit. Any comments prior to or after these commands will not be stored in the database upon creation, so a conscious decision should be made in terms of the location of your module comments.

Each procedure, function, and trigger should be placed in a separate file, and therefore the comments in each of these files are specific to one PL/SQL program unit. Because packages contain two components (a package specification and package body), containing multiple procedures and functions, and are typically separated into two files (the package specification and package body), packages need to be commented differently.

The package specification should contain a description of the overall content and purpose of the package, followed by specific comments to public variables and general information for each procedure and function contained in the package. These general comments should describe the overall purpose of the procedure or function and any details related to the input and output of each. These comments should not contain all details of the interworkings of the procedures and functions. This should be included in the package body.

The package body should provide specific documentation to private package variables and for each procedure and function more specific details on the contents from a development standpoint. In addition, inline documentation should be included as necessary in the package body.

The easiest way to remember how to document the package specification versus package body is stated below:

- Document the package specification by remembering the package specification purpose: to provide the means for calling the detailed contents of the package body. Therefore, the documentation should provide the purpose of the package procedures and functions, as well as the input and output information.

- Document the package body by remembering the package body purpose: to provide the detail logic and functionality of each procedure and function that processes the input and provides output to the calling program units.

Integrating Documentation

The documentation should describe the detailed logic and functionality of the source code, to enable the code to be understood by other developers so modifications can be made more easily.

An example of the effective use of module and inline documentation is illustrated in the source code provided in the section "Develop an Audit Trail/Version Control of Stored PL/SQL Code in the Database" later in this chapter.

Incorporate Various Conventions to Aid PL/SQL Development

A variety of other standards make development and deployment much easier. The following is a quick list of conventions to aid PL/SQL development, by incorporating into the PL/SQL coding standardization process:

- At the end of any PL/SQL program unit (package, procedure, function, and trigger), follow the END command with the name of the program unit.

- In the source code files that create the stored PL/SQL modules, use the CREATE OR REPLACE command versus the CREATE command (the REPLACE allows for the replacement of a stored PL/SQL program unit without an explicit DROP and CREATE).

- At the end of the source code files place a "/" character to allow for a stored PL/SQL program unit creation or modification to be executed when the file is referenced in SQL*Plus (*@filename* or *START filename*).

Develop an Audit Trail/Version Control of Stored PL/SQL Code in the Database

It is imperative to ensure that your development adopts a version control system. The version control system should be deployed at the operating system level. I would recommend utilizing a true version control product such as PVCS or other product to ensure that your development is properly versioned and maintained. This becomes increasingly important when you are in a large development environment. When there are multiple developers, there needs to be a mechanism to ensure only one developer is modifying a program at a time.

In addition to using a version control system at the operating system level, it is possible to build your own source code version control for stored PL/SQL program units within the database, adding another layer of version protection.

Developing an Audit Trail/Version Control

The following steps can be implemented in your system to build a mechanism that will automatically log versions of source code stored in the database view DBA_SOURCE to a backup table. This backup table is an added measure of ensuring proper source code versioning.

The general steps are as follows:

1. Create a database source code log table (source_log).

2. Create a procedure (log_source) to compare the modification date (last_ddl_time) in the DBA_OBJECTS view for all stored PL/SQL program units (package specifications, package bodies, procedures, and functions) to the source_log table modification date (last_ddl_time). If the modification dates do not match, then a copy of the source code, from the view DBA_SOURCE for that object, is made to the source_log table with the date and time stamped for the copy.

3. Submit the procedure to execute using the DBMS_JOB package, and specify the interval at which you wish to execute the log_source procedure.

Pay particular attention to the source code in this section: it demonstrates all of the coding standards outlined earlier in this chapter.

The source_log table is created with the following script under user PLSQL_USER.

File: 3_5.sql

```
-- Program: 3_5.sql
-- Created: 05/20/98
-- Created By: Joe Trezzo (TUSC)

-- Description: This script creates the source_log table, an index
--              on the table, a PUBLIC synonym on the table and
--              select and insert access on the table.

SPOOL 3_5.log
CREATE TABLE source_log
(backup_date     DATE,
 backup_time     VARCHAR2(6),
 last_ddl_time   DATE,
 owner           VARCHAR2(30),
 name            VARCHAR2(30),
 type            VARCHAR2(12),
 line            NUMBER,
 text            VARCHAR2(2000)); -- For Oracle8 change 2000 to 4000

CREATE INDEX source_log_idx1 ON source_log
  (last_ddl_time, owner, name);
```

```
CREATE PUBLIC SYNONYM source_log FOR source_log;

GRANT SELECT,INSERT ON source_log to PUBLIC;


SPOOL OFF
```

The table in the preceeding example can be created under any user that has the ability to create tables, indexes, and synonyms. I would strongly recommend adding a storage clause on the table and index creation. These objects will grow based on the amount of PL/SQL stored source code in your database, and the number of revisions that are made to the stored source code.

Remember that source code for all stored PL/SQL program units is inserted into the database every time a revision is made (if the PL/SQL program unit existed, the previous source code is deleted and replaced with the new version of source code). I do not log the SYS and SYSTEM stored PL/SQL program units in the backup method outlined here, since this can be re-created from the Oracle installation script files if necessary. To give you an idea of the size of the standard Oracle stored PL/SQL program unit code: On a Windows 95 Personal Oracle copy of Oracle 7.3, there were 34,700 lines of source code for all SYS and SYSTEM PL/SQL stored source code modules.

The log_source procedure was created with the following script under user PLSQL_USER (in order to execute the following procedure, the PLSQL_USER was directly granted SELECT privilege on the DBA_OBJECTS and DBA_SOURCE views).

File: 3_6.sql

```
-- Program: 3_6.sql (logsrc.prc)
-- Created: 05/12/98
-- Created By: Joe Trezzo (TUSC)

-- Description:  This procedure is used to create backup versions
--               of the stored PL/SQL source code. It can be
--               executed on demand by executing the log_source
--               procedure in SQL*Plus or at a regular interval by
--               setting up the execution of this procedure in
--               DBMS_JOB. In order for this to work, the SQL
--               script 3_5.sql must be executed under the schema
--               that the source_log table should reside. This
--               procedure can be executed under the owner of
--               the source_log table by granting SELECT privilege
--               to the dba_objects and dba_source views from SYS.
--               This script also creates a public synonym and
--               grants access to all users. The procedure only
--               selects new or updated source code and does not
```

Developing an Audit Trail/Version Control

```
--                    pull SYS or SYSTEM.

-- Syntax:      log_source
-- Parameters: None

-- Table(s) Selected: dba_objects, dba_source, source_log
-- Table(s) Updated:  source_log

-- Modified: 07/01/98
-- Modified By: Joe Trezzo (TUSC)

-- Modification: Added the display of the count of records
--               inserted.

CREATE OR REPLACE PROCEDURE log_source IS

   -- Selects all new source code records
   CURSOR cur_source_code IS
      SELECT TRUNC(SYSDATE) log_date,
             TO_CHAR(SYSDATE, 'HH24MISS') log_time,
             obj.last_ddl_time last_ddl_time, obj.owner owner,
             src.name name, src.type type,
             src.line line, src.text text
      FROM   dba_source src, dba_objects obj
      WHERE  src.owner = obj.owner
      AND    src.name  = obj.object_name
      AND    src.type  = obj.object_type
      AND    obj.owner NOT IN ('SYS', 'SYSTEM')
      AND    NOT EXISTS
      (SELECT 'X'
      FROM    SOURCE_LOG
      WHERE   last_ddl_time = obj.last_ddl_time
      AND     owner         = obj.owner
      AND     name          = obj.object_name
      AND     type          = obj.object_type);

   lv_records_updated_num PLS_INTEGER :=0; -- # of records inserted

BEGIN
   -- Every new line of source code found is inserted
   FOR lv_source_rec IN cur_source_code LOOP
      INSERT INTO source_log
         (backup_date, backup_time, last_ddl_time,
          owner, name, type, line, text)
      VALUES
         (lv_source_rec.log_date, lv_source_rec.log_time,
          lv_source_rec.last_ddl_time, lv_source_rec.owner,
          lv_source_rec.name, lv_source_rec.type,
```

```
            lv_source_rec.line, lv_source_rec.text);

    lv_records_updated_num := lv_records_updated_num + 1;
  END LOOP;

  DBMS_OUTPUT.PUT_LINE('Number of New Source Records: ' ||
                    TO_CHAR(lv_records_updated_num));

  COMMIT;
  EXCEPTION
    WHEN OTHERS THEN
        ROLLBACK; -- Any problems encountered,
                -- rolls the entire transaction back
        DBMS_OUTPUT.PUT_LINE('Source Log Process Aborted. ' ||
            'No Records Inserted. ');
        DBMS_OUTPUT.PUT_LINE('Oracle Error Code: ' ||
            TO_CHAR(SQLCODE) || '   Oracle Error Message: ' ||
            SUBSTR(SQLERRM,1,150));
END log_source;
--------------------------------------------------------------------
/
CREATE PUBLIC SYNONYM log_source FOR log_source;

GRANT EXECUTE ON log_source TO PUBLIC;
```

Without providing SELECT privilege on the two DBA views directly to user PLSQL_USER, the procedure creation would fail, since a user creating a stored PL/SQL program unit cannot be granted access to objects referenced in the stored object through a role. Access to objects referenced must be directly to the schema (remember access is provided to the DBA_OBJECTS and DBA_SOURCE views by being part of the DBA role, but this will not suffice).

In regards to the preceding method, access to the source_log table can be limited to specific users by changing the GRANT statement at the end of the 3_5.sql script. Likewise, execution of the log_source procedure can be limited to specific users by changing the GRANT statement at the end of the 3_6.sql script. For a more in-depth discussion of privileges as they relate to PL/SQL stored objects, refer to Chapter 10.

The final step in automating this backup source code method is to submit the log_source procedure to the job scheduler through DBMS_JOB. The DBMS_JOB package provided by Oracle allows stored PL/SQL program units to be submitted to a job scheduler to execute at a specified interval. The interval can be set, and the internal will be dependent on your environment. For more information on how to use the DBMS_JOB package, refer to Chapter 12.

My original approach to accomplishing the automated backup was to place a BEFORE INSERT database trigger on the underlying table of the DBA_SOURCE view, namely, the source$ table. Every time source code was inserted in this table, the records would be inserted to the source_log table. Unfortunately, this approach failed, since database triggers are not allowed on Oracle system tables.

It is important to note that database trigger source code can also be versioned in the same method as previously outlined for packages, procedures, and functions with some minor changes. The reason database triggers cannot be logged in the preceding table is that the source code for database triggers reside in its own table (DBA_TRIGGERS and is not part of DBA_SOURCE), even though database trigger compilation was introduced in PL/SQL version 2.3.

Summary

PL/SQL coding standards are extremely important to your development environment. There are major benefits that result to ensure continued success, even after deployment. The readability and maintainability alone are two benefits that are well worth the initial investment of establishing standards and ongoing efforts to enforce standard adherence.

This chapter established PL/SQL Coding Standards, which is the first component of establishing a PL/SQL Development Foundation. The two other components to this development foundation are established in Chapter 4 and Chapter 5.

All standards established in this chapter are used throughout the book with the following exceptions:

- **Filenames**   Due to the format and the flow of the book, filenames do not follow the naming convention outlined in this chapter. Typically, all filenames in the book are named sequentially, with the chapter number starting the filename prefix and the extension of sql. The filenames in this chapter, therefore, are 3_1.sql, 3_2.sql, and so forth.

- **White space**   Due to space limitations, the number of blank lines have been reduced, so many code segments do not have the stated standard blank lines to break up the code.

Tips Review

- Use filenames with a prefix of eight characters or less and use an extension of three characters or less. Because filename lengths are not consistent across all platforms, choosing the lowest common denominator is best.

- Ensure SQL and PL/SQL reserved words are not used for any object creation in your database. In addition, do not use PL/SQL reserved words in your

PL/SQL source code to name any variables or other module components. This causes confusion when debugging PL/SQL source code and extra coding to work around this issue.

■ Ample use of blank lines increases code readability by creating logical blocks that are easily visible to the human eye.

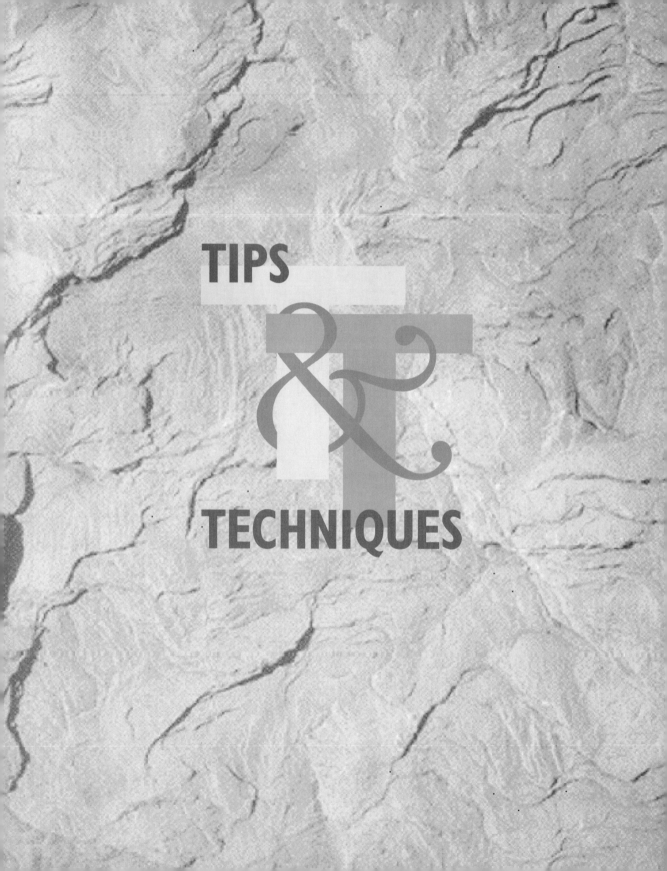

TIPS & TECHNIQUES

CHAPTER
4

Defining Standard
PL/SQL Coding
Techniques
(Developer and DBA)

The PL/SQL language has become the core procedural language of most Oracle-based applications. This forces a developer not only to learn the language, but also to develop a methodology and standard techniques for PL/SQL development and deployment. This chapter takes the next step in the process of standardizing PL/SQL coding by defining several PL/SQL techniques to follow when developing PL/SQL in an application development environment. This chapter combined with Chapter 3 and Chapter 5 comprise a PL/SQL Development Foundation. Applying these techniques improves PL/SQL development, maintainability, performance, and overall effectiveness of PL/SQL deployment.

A solid set of standards and coding techniques combine to create a development foundation necessary in any application development environment. The goal of this chapter is to define standard PL/SQL coding techniques to help a developer become more effective in PL/SQL development. The tips and techniques outlined in this chapter are as follows:

- Learn your application development schema

- Understand your application development and deployment environment

- Know the database and product versions you are working with

- Use variable type casting to shield PL/SQL code from schema changes (%TYPE and %ROWTYPE)

- Default PL/SQL variables to eliminate hidden problem conditions

- Take special care when dealing with NULL and DATE values

- Use Boolean to reduce coding errors and to simplify conditional tests

- Use DBMS_OUTPUT.PUT_LINE effectively

- Use explicit cursors versus implicit cursors

- Use cursor for loops to reduce coding and margin for error

- Use parameters in explicit cursors to improve readability

- Implement cursor variables for similar queries with different data sources

- Implement PL/SQL records to limit local variables and improve maintainability

- Implement PL/SQL tables to improve performance of reference tables and to provide temporary storage

- Use PL/SQL VARCHAR2 data type to search and manipulate LONG database columns

- Ensure variable names do not mimic column names

■ Specify table columns with INSERT statements

■ Use synonyms for portability of PL/SQL code

■ Use a database table to make program units dynamically adjustable

■ Use ROWID to improve transaction processing performance

■ Use FOR UPDATE to lock records for transaction processing

■ Choose large rollback segments when processing large transaction sets

■ Use a counter to limit the size of transactions per commit

■ Develop a monitoring facility for long-running processes

Learn Your Application Development Schema

Developers must become familiar with the application structure and environment when they are involved in any application development effort. If the developers are involved from the beginning of the project, it is much easier. Unfortunately, developers are often integrated into an application development project after it has already started. When this happens, developers must get to know the application structure to be an efficient and effective team member on the project. Application background can be transferred from team members; however, it is imperative to have the following details close whenever you develop source code:

■ **Table and view definitions**   A listing of column definitions of the tables and views in the development schema (an ER diagram would also be extremely helpful)

■ **Constraint definitions**   A listing of all the constraints in the development schema

■ **Index definitions**   A listing of all indexes on every table in the development schema

■ **Sequence definitions**   A listing of all sequence numbers in the development schema

■ **Synonym definitions**   A listing of all PUBLIC synonyms in the development environment

Many pieces of information are useful throughout the development life cycle, but the previous list of information is a must to ensure a complete understanding of the environment. The following scripts enable you to obtain this valuable information (except for the first script, the formatting commands for the output are not included due to space limitations, and all output is limited to a subset of the result).

The table and view definition script is illustrated, followed by the output. This script is extremely valuable as a reference for the name, the data type, and the NULL attribute of each column for each table. This becomes useful when the %TYPE and %ROWTYPE variable declarations are used.

File: 4_1.sql

```
--  ***********************************************************
--  4_1.SQL
--  ***********
--  Table Descriptions
--  All Tables for Current Schema
--  ***********************************************************
SET NUMWIDTH 3
SET WRAP ON
SET VERIFY OFF
SET RECSEP OFF
SET FEEDBACK ON
SET SPACE 1
SET NEWPAGE 0
SET PAGESIZE 56
SET LINESIZE 80
SET TAB OFF
--  ***********************************************************
BREAK ON today
COLUMN today NEW_VALUE _DATE
column user  NEW_VALUE _USER
SELECT TO_CHAR(SYSDATE, 'mm/dd/yyyy') today,
       USER
FROM   DUAL;
CLEAR BREAKS
--  ***********************************************************
TTITLE LEFT '4_1.sql' RIGHT 'Printed: ' _DATE  SKIP 1 -
       CENTER 'Table / View Descriptions' SKIP 1-
       CENTER 'All Tables and Views for Schema ' _USER SKIP 2;
BTITLE SKIP 2 CENTER 'Page  ' SQL.PNO
BREAK ON table_name SKIP 1
```

```
COLUMN table_name   FORMAT A20     HEADING 'Table'
COLUMN column_name  FORMAT A22     HEADING 'Column'
COLUMN data_type    FORMAT A10     HEADING 'Data|Type'
COLUMN data_length  FORMAT 999999  HEADING 'Length'
COLUMN data_scale   FORMAT 99999   HEADING 'Scale'
COLUMN nullable     FORMAT A5      HEADING 'Null'

SPOOL 4_1.lis
SELECT table_name, column_name, data_type,
       DECODE(data_length, 22, data_precision,
              data_length) data_length,
       data_scale, nullable
FROM   user_tab_columns
ORDER BY table_name, column_id;
SPOOL OFF
```

Output (4_1.sql)

```
4_1.sql                                           Printed: 03/09/1999
                        Table / View Descriptions
                All Tables and Views for Schema PLSQL_USER
                                          Data
Table                 Column               Type       Length  Scale Null
--------------------  --------------------- ---------- ------- ------ -----

S_DEPARTMENT          DEPARTMENT_ID         NUMBER          7     0 N
                      DEPARTMENT_NAME       VARCHAR2       50       N
                      REGION_ID             NUMBER          7     0 Y

S_EMPLOYEE            EMPLOYEE_ID           NUMBER          7     0 N
                      EMPLOYEE_LAST_NAME    VARCHAR2       25       N
                      EMPLOYEE_FIRST_NAME   VARCHAR2       25       Y
                      USERID                VARCHAR2        8       Y
                      START_DATE            DATE            7       Y
                      COMMENTS              VARCHAR2      255       Y
                      MANAGER_ID            NUMBER          7     0 Y
                      TITLE                 VARCHAR2       25       Y
                      DEPARTMENT_ID         NUMBER          7     0 Y
                      SALARY                NUMBER         11     2 Y
                      COMMISSION_PCT        NUMBER          4     2 Y
```

The constraint definition script is illustrated, followed by the output. This script contains two queries. The first query returns all constraints (.lis output file extension) and the second query returns only the disabled constraints (.alt output file extension). The first query is extremely valuable in determining the primary and foreign keys, as well as the constraints at the database level. The second query is helpful in identifying any constraints not enabled at the current time.

File: 4_2.sql

```
-- Query 1
SELECT  dc.table_name, dcc.column_name, dcc.position,
        dcc.constraint_name, dc.constraint_type, dc.search_condition
FROM    user_constraints dc, user_cons_columns dcc
WHERE   dcc.table_name     = dc.table_name
AND     dcc.owner          = dc.owner
AND     dcc.constraint_name = dc.constraint_name
ORDER BY dcc.table_name, dcc.owner, dcc.position, dcc.column_name;

-- Query 2
SELECT  dc.table_name, dc.constraint_type, dc.constraint_name,
        dcc.column_name, dc.status
FROM    user_constraints dc, user_cons_columns dcc
WHERE   dc.status          = 'DISABLED'
AND     dc.table_name      = dcc.table_name
AND     dc.constraint_name = dcc.constraint_name
ORDER BY dc.table_name;
```

Output (4_2.sql:4_2.lis)

```
4_2.sql                                                    Printed: 03/09/1999
                  Constraint Listing by Table for Schema PLSQL_USER
                  Constraint Type: P:Primary Key R:Foreign Key C:Condition


                                                            Cons
Table           Column          Seq Name                    Type Constraint
--------------- --------------- ---- --------------------------------- ---- -------------
S_INVENTORY     PRODUCT_ID          S_INVENTORY_PRODUCT_ID_NN          C    PRODUCT_ID IS
                                                                            NOT NULL
S_INVENTORY     WAREHOUSE_ID        S_INVENTORY_WAREHOUSE_ID_NN        C    WAREHOUSE_ID
                                                                            IS NOT NULL
S_ITEM          ORDER_ID        1   S_ITEM_ORDER_ID_FK                 R
S_ITEM          ORDER_ID        1   S_ITEM_ORDER_ID_ITEM_ID_PK         P
S_ITEM          ORDER_ID        1   S_ITEM_ORDER_ID_PRODUCT_ID_UK      U
S_ITEM          PRODUCT_ID      1   S_ITEM_PRODUCT_ID_FK               R
S_ITEM          ITEM_ID         2   S_ITEM_ORDER_ID_ITEM_ID_PK         P
S_ITEM          PRODUCT_ID      2   S_ITEM_ORDER_ID_PRODUCT_ID_UK      U
S_ITEM          ITEM_ID             S_ITEM_ID_NN                       C    ITEM_ID IS
                                                                            NOT NULL
S_ITEM          ORDER_ID            S_ITEM_ORDER_ID_NN                 C    ORDER_ID IS
                                                                            NOT NULL
S_ITEM          PRODUCT_ID          S_ITEM_PRODUCT_ID_NN               C    PRODUCT_ID IS
                                                                            NOT NULL
```

Output (4_2.sql:4_2.alt)

```
4_2.sql                                                    Printed: 03/09/1999
                    Disabled Constraints for Schema PLSQL_USER
              Constraint Type: P:Primary Key R:Foreign Key C:Condition

Table        Type Constraint                    Column            Status
----------- ---- -------------------------- ---------------- --------
S_ORDER      C    S_ORDER_PAYMENT_TYPE_CK     PAYMENT_TYPE      DISABLED
```

The index definition script is illustrated, followed by the output. This script is extremely instrumental in determining what columns are indexed and becomes a mandatory piece of information to have when optimizing SQL statements.

File: 4_3.sql

```
SELECT dic.table_name, dic.index_name,
       DECODE(di.uniqueness, 'UNIQUE', 'YES', 'NO')uniqueness,
       dic.column_position, dic.column_name
FROM   user_indexes di, user_ind_columns dic
WHERE  dic.table_name  = di.table_name
AND    dic.index_name  = di.index_name
ORDER BY dic.table_name, dic.index_name,
         di.uniqueness desc, dic.column_position;
```

Output (4_3.sql)

```
4_3.sql                                          Printed: 03/09/1999
            Index Listing by Table for Schema PLSQL_USER


Table          Index                           Unique Seq Column
-------------- ------------------------------- ------ --- --------------
S_CUSTOMER     S_CUSTOMER_ID_PK                YES      1 CUSTOMER_ID
S_DEPARTMENT   S_DEPARTMENT_ID_PK              YES      1 DEPARTMENT_ID
               S_DEPARTMENT_NAME_REGION_ID_UK YES      1 DEPARTMENT_NAME
               S_DEPARTMENT_NAME_REGION_ID_UK YES      2 REGION_ID
```

The sequence definition script is illustrated, followed by the output. This script is extremely valuable in determining what sequences must be used in the application.

File: 4_4.sql

```
SELECT sequence_name, increment_by,
       DECODE(cycle_flag,'y','  cycle','n', 'nocycle', 'nocycle')
            cycle_flag,
       DECODE(order_flag,'y','  order','n', 'noorder', 'noorder')
            order_flag,
       max_value, min_value, cache_size, last_number
FROM   user_sequences
ORDER BY sequence_name;
```

Output (4_4.sql)

```
4_4.sql                                          Printed: 03/09/1999
          Sequence Description for Schema PLSQL_USER
```

Sequence Name	Inc By	Cycle Flag	Order Flag	Maximum Value	Minimum Value	Cache Size	Last Number
S_CUSTOMER_ID	1	nocycle	noorder	1.0000E+07	1	0	216
S_DEPARTMENT_ID	1	nocycle	noorder	1.0000E+07	1	0	51
S_EMPLOYEE_ID	1	nocycle	noorder	1.0000E+07	1	0	26
S_IMAGE_ID	1	nocycle	noorder	1.0000E+07	1	0	1,981
S_LONGTEXT_ID	1	nocycle	noorder	1.0000E+07	1	0	1,369
S_ORDER_ID	1	nocycle	noorder	1.0000E+07	1	0	113
S_PRODUCT_ID	1	nocycle	noorder	1.0000E+07	1	0	50,537
S_REGION_ID	1	nocycle	noorder	1.0000E+07	1	0	6
S_WAREHOUSE_ID	1	nocycle	noorder	1.0000E+07	1	0	10,502

The synonym definition script is illustrated, followed by the output. This script is extremely valuable in determining the PUBLIC synonyms for the objects in the application.

File: 4_5.sql

```
SELECT  ds.owner owner, table_owner,
        SUBSTR(dc.table_type,1,6) table_type,
        ds.table_name table_name, synonym_name
FROM    dba_synonyms ds, user_catalog dc
WHERE   ds.table_name = dc.table_name
ORDER BY ds.owner, table_owner, table_type, ds.table_name;
```

Output (4_5.sql)

```
4_5.sql                                             Printed: 03/09/1999
                    Synonyms for Schema PLSQL_USER

Synonym
Owner           Object Owner   Type    Object Name       Synonym Name
-------------   ------------   ------  ---------------   ---------------
PUBLIC          PLSQL_USER     TABLE   SOURCE_LOG        SOURCE_LOG
PUBLIC          PLSQL_USER     TABLE   S_CUSTOMER        S_CUSTOMER
PUBLIC          PLSQL_USER     TABLE   S_DEPARTMENT      S_DEPARTMENT
PUBLIC          PLSQL_USER     TABLE   S_EMPLOYEE        S_EMPLOYEE
PUBLIC          PLSQL_USER     TABLE   S_IMAGE           S_IMAGE
PUBLIC          PLSQL_USER     TABLE   S_INVENTORY       S_INVENTORY
PUBLIC          PLSQL_USER     TABLE   S_ITEM            S_ITEM
PUBLIC          PLSQL_USER     TABLE   S_LONGTEXT        S_LONGTEXT
PUBLIC          PLSQL_USER     TABLE   S_ORDER           S_ORDER
PUBLIC          PLSQL_USER     TABLE   S_PRODUCT         S_PRODUCT
PUBLIC          PLSQL_USER     TABLE   S_REGION          S_REGION
PUBLIC          PLSQL_USER     TABLE   S_TITLE           S_TITLE
PUBLIC          PLSQL_USER     TABLE   S_WAREHOUSE       S_WAREHOUSE
```

TIP

Creating a PUBLIC synonym on all production objects (tables, views, sequences, stored PL/SQL objects, and so forth) is recommended to eliminate the need to precede object references with the username. This also improves application portability and flexibility.

TIP

Always name the synonyms the same as the underlying object. This eliminates confusion and ensures accuracy and efficiency. This should be a standard in any environment. I have worked in environments where this was not the case; it increases development time by adding an unnecessary level of complexity, especially when new developers are integrated into the project.

TIP

Execution of the preceding five scripts to learn the application schema saves valuable development time in the long run. Schema changes should be communicated to all team members when made. A new version of the previous output should immediately be created each time schema changes are made and distributed to each team member.

Some of the preceding scripts may seem common sensical, but time has told me many environments do not use the data dictionary on a regular basis; therefore, these scripts become even more valuable in those environments.

Understand Your Application Development and Deployment Environment

In addition to knowing the application development schema, becoming familiar with the application development and deployment environment is important. The method you design, develop, implement, and maintain applications impacts several considerations when you develop PL/SQL source code in your environment.

Is it a client-server or Web-based production environment? Is the production environment on an intranet or the Internet? How many concurrent users will be using the application? With what type of devices will they be connecting? What

Application Development and Deployment Environment

type of processing is more prevalent in the system: batch oriented or transaction oriented? What is the projected data volume of the database tables? Many people think these are only DBA-related questions that must be known. I believe this is also important knowledge for developers to know. This helps in determining the best method to follow when developing PL/SQL source code.

One of the standards at most Oracle sites is the existence of SQL*Plus for development, debugging, and testing. Many environments have additional PL/SQL tools available to help in the development and maintenance of PL/SQL source code, such as Procedure Builder, SQL*Navigator, TOAD, or SQL*Station (many others are on the market). I am still old-fashioned; therefore, I tend to use SQL*Plus for a large percentage of my PL/SQL development, testing, and debugging. No matter what the environment, get to know it and use it to your benefit to ensure you are efficient, productive, and accurate.

When debugging, testing, or optimizing source code, break down the code into smaller segments for testing to locate the real problem. If possible, test this smaller code segment in SQL*Plus or your tool of choice. The following are a few quick examples of breaking down code into smaller segments to determine the real problem:

- If you have a procedure in a package that does not seem to work properly, cut out that procedure, test it standalone, and set any global variables with SQL*Plus variable commands.

- If you have a SELECT statement in a program unit that is failing or not returning the proper information, pull the statement into SQL*Plus and get it to work properly in SQL*Plus first.

- If you have an UPDATE or DELETE statement in a procedure that is not manipulating the data properly, pull the statement into SQL*Plus and get it to work properly in SQL*Plus first. You can execute the statement and then SELECT the information to verify if the UPDATE or DELETE worked properly and then roll back the information. Remember, when you manipulate data in SQL*Plus, you can requery the data to verify if the data was changed as desired. This can be an iterative process, and the greatest part of this method is no users see the changes you are making until you perform a COMMIT.

- SQL*Plus is also a great product to use for optimizing SQL statements. This is discussed in further detail in Chapter 7 but, again, the standard method is to remove the statement to optimize from the procedure and work with it in SQL*Plus.

TIP
An UPDATE and DELETE statement first performs a SELECT to fetch the records being manipulated and then performs the UPDATE or DELETE operation. An UPDATE and DELETE, therefore, can be changed to a SELECT statement first to review the result set that is going to be manipulated to ensure these statements are manipulating the desired records.

Know the Database and Product Versions You Are Working with

With the Oracle database and development product versions changing on a regular basis, knowing what versions of the products you are working with has become essential. Times have changed since 1985 when I first started in Oracle. Back then, major version upgrades took several years, so you actually were afforded the opportunity to get to know the intricacies of the products. Today, several upgrades occur a year, and with each new upgrade come major enhancements to the capabilities of the products. Larger Oracle environments with multiple instances typically have different product versions on the different instances, different platforms, and different environments (development, testing, quality assurance, and production). With this disparity comes an incongruity in the features available on these environments. Knowing the product versions for the development environment is mandatory, but it's even more important for the production environment. Having the development and production environments on the same versions for all products is ideal. If this is the case in your environment, you can skip this section.

With different versions at the database and/or development product level, you have to add a layer of testing and understanding of the version differences. Developing your source code so it works on the lowest version in the application environment is the safest approach; products are generally upwardly compatible but not downwardly compatible. When a new feature in the latest release makes your coding much easier, but you cannot use this feature because you are coding to the least common version, your work becomes increasingly difficult.

A good example of this scenario is the Oracle supplied package UTL_FILE. This package was introduced in version 2.3 of PL/SQL. Prior to this version, the typical method of outputting information from a PL/SQL program was to INSERT the information into a temporary database table and then report off that table while spooling to a file. The introduction of the UTL_FILE package makes this process much easier and cleaner for developers and DBAs.

If the new feature improves functionality or performance, then I recommend supporting both versions and controlling the processing by a switch that is dependent on version notification to the executing program. The switching between source code can be handled by reading the database, setting a switch in a database table (discussed in more detail later in this chapter), or setting a package global variable (discussed in further detail in Chapter 5).

Use Variable Type Casting to Shield PL/SQL Code from Schema Changes (%TYPE and %ROWTYPE)

One of the most important concepts to keep in mind when coding PL/SQL or any other language is maintainability. At the time development occurs, either preproduction or postproduction, the database schema often seems stable. As we all know, things change. The change may be the addition of a new column to a database table or a column data type change. This may occur after the discovery that a column thought to store only numeric values actually needs to store alphanumeric values. The change could be as simple as increasing the length of an existing column. In any of these cases, all PL/SQL code involving these tables and columns must be analyzed and possibly modified. This includes variable and parameter declarations that no longer match column data types and cursors that no longer represent all the columns within a database table.

The use of the PL/SQL %TYPE and %ROWTYPE declaration attributes reduces and often eliminates the problems the previous changes would have caused and makes PL/SQL code easier to maintain. The following segment of code illustrates the use of the %TYPE attribute.

```
DECLARE
-- Examples of %TYPE Usage
lv_order_num          s_order.order_id%TYPE;       -- Instead of NUMBER(7)
lv_order_total_num  s_order.total%TYPE;        -- Instead of NUMBER(11,2)
lv_payment_type_txt s_order.payment_type%TYPE; -- Instead of VARCHR2(6)
lv_order_date         s_order.date_ordered%TYPE; -- Instead of DATE
lv_order_num          NUMBER(5);
lv_order_num2         lv_order_num%TYPE;           -- Instead of NUMBER(5)
```

In the preceding example, if the database column data type changes, the next time the code segment is executed, this PL/SQL declaration inherits the new data type. As shown with the lv_order_num2 variable declaration, the %TYPE attribute can also be used to link PL/SQL defined variable data types. This becomes extremely valuable when creating variables of the same type and using these throughout a procedure or entire package. Type casting allows the same maintainability for PL/SQL variables that exist for database columns.

Using %TYPE does not guarantee the PL/SQL code segment will still be valid upon the next execution. If a database column is changed from a NUMBER data type to a VARCHAR2 data type, the conversion causes execution problems in the PL/SQL code if type casting is used (for example, the variable is used in an arithmetic calculation). Typical database table modifications involve increasing a column length or adding additional columns. The operation of changing a column from a NUMBER data type to a VARCHAR2 data type is less the norm and involves the operation of dropping and recreating the table.

TIP
When a database table is modified in any manner, any stored PL/SQL objects such as packages (bodies), procedures, function, and triggers that reference that object become INVALID. After making a table change, make sure to check the INVALID objects (shown in Chapter 5, Chapter 9 and Chapter 13) and recompile these INVALID objects. Oracle automatically recompiles the stored object when the next call to this object occurs. The compilation can fail, and this failure will occur during production hours if you do not manually handle the recompilation to ensure all objects recompile without error.

TIP
Always make database changes (tables, stored objects, and so forth) during off-hours to ensure all system objects are recompiled and revalidated prior to production. This method avoids a lot of pain and agony.

Similar to the %TYPE attribute, the %ROWTYPE links PL/SQL definitions to database table definitions. However, the %ROWTYPE attribute links more than one column data type; it links all column data types for a table. The following segment of code displays the use of the %ROWTYPE attribute.

File: 4_6.sql

```
SET SERVEROUTPUT ON SIZE 1000000
DECLARE
    -- Examples of %ROWTYPE Usage
    -- PL/SQL Record mirroring S_ORDER table
```

```
   lv_ord_rec s_order%ROWTYPE;
   CURSOR cur_get_order IS
      SELECT order_id, customer_id, total
      FROM    s_order;
   -- Mirroring cur_get_order cursor
   lv_ord_cur_rec cur_get_order%ROWTYPE;
BEGIN
   -- Customer Processing...
   lv_ord_rec.total := 10;
   DBMS_OUTPUT.PUT_LINE('Total: '|| lv_ord_rec.total);
   lv_ord_cur_rec.total := 20;
   DBMS_OUTPUT.PUT_LINE('Total: '|| lv_ord_cur_rec.total);
END;
/
```

When %ROWTYPE is used, the variable declared is now actually a record comprised of all columns in the database table or cursor referred to in the declaration. In the previous example, the following PL/SQL variables are defined for the lv_ord_rec variable:

lv_ord_rec.order_id	NUMBER(7)
lv_ord_rec.customer_id	NUMBER(7)
lv_ord_rec.date_ordered	DATE
lv_ord_rec.date_shipped	DATE
lv_ord_rec.sales_rep_id	NUMBER(7)
lv_ord_rec.total	NUMBER(11, 2)
lv_ord_rec.payment_type	VARCHAR2(6)
lv_ord_rec.order_filled	VARCHAR2(1)

One variable is declared for every database column in the s_order table, whereas, the lv_ord_cur_rec variable has three PL/SQL variables declared, one for each column in the cursor cur_get_order. The same rules and tips highlighted for the %TYPE attribute apply to the %ROWTYPE attribute.

TIP

Attempt to use type casting with database columns whenever possible. This eases maintenance changes in the future by reducing the necessary code modifications. Remember, type casting is not a cure-all, and you still should perform impact analysis for any change.

TIP
The %TYPE and %ROWTYPE only assign the referenced data type to the PL/SQL variable and will not mirror the characteristics related to NOT NULL or default values.

Default PL/SQL Variables to Eliminate Hidden Problem Conditions

PL/SQL variables will be used extensively in your PL/SQL development. Each variable you create has a purpose that will be exploited somewhere within your source code. Developers often declare their PL/SQL variables in the declaration section and later assign default values or rely on some other process to set the variable.

Always default your PL/SQL variables in the declaration, if possible, especially Boolean and Number variables. A Boolean should always be defaulted to either TRUE or FALSE and a number should typically be defaulted to 0. Character variables can also be defaulted if a default value makes sense, but the character family variables are less likely to be defaulted. If a variable is not defaulted, then hidden problems can be introduced into your PL/SQL source code, especially in the form of NULL values.

The following code illustrates the problem of not assigning default values to PL/SQL variables:

File: 4_7.sql

```
SET SERVEROUTPUT ON SIZE 1000000
DECLARE
   lv_test_num     NUMBER(3);
   lv_test_txt     VARCHAR2(5);
   lv_complete_bln BOOLEAN;
BEGIN
   IF lv_test_num != 10 THEN                     -- lv_test_num is NULL
      DBMS_OUTPUT.PUT_LINE('Number Test: TRUE');
   ELSE
      DBMS_OUTPUT.PUT_LINE('Number Test: FALSE');
   END IF;
   IF lv_test_txt != 'TEMP' THEN                 -- lv_test_txt is NULL
      DBMS_OUTPUT.PUT_LINE('Character Test: TRUE');
   ELSE
      DBMS_OUTPUT.PUT_LINE('Character Test: FALSE');
   END IF;
```

```
    IF NOT lv_complete_bln THEN                     -- lv_complete is NULL
        DBMS_OUTPUT.PUT_LINE('Boolean Test: TRUE');
    ELSE
        DBMS_OUTPUT.PUT_LINE('Boolean Test: FALSE');
    END IF;
END;
/
```

Output (4_7.sql)

```
Number Test: FALSE
Character Test: FALSE
Boolean Test: FALSE

PL/SQL procedure successfully completed.
```

As shown in the preceding example, all three of these conditions (number, character, Boolean) result in a FALSE comparison. This is due to the result of comparing NULL values. The outcome of this example is much different if we change the declaration section and default each value as illustrated in the following.

```
DECLARE
    lv_test_num     NUMBER(3)   DEFAULT 0;
    lv_test_txt     VARCHAR2(5) DEFAULT 'N/A';
    lv_complete_bln BOOLEAN     DEFAULT FALSE;
```

```
Number Test: TRUE
Character Test: TRUE
Boolean Test: TRUE

PL/SQL procedure successfully completed.
```

As seen above, the result is more of what is expected. The problem with handling NULL values is covered more in the following section, but defaulting PL/SQL variables can avoid this hidden problem.

Knowing the default value assignment should be treated the same as an assignment in your code is important. Knowing a default value assignment can use all PL/SQL functions available for the data type family is also important. This is illustrated in the following example.

File: 4_8.sql

```
DECLARE
    lv_three_month_forecast_date DATE           := ADD_MONTHS(SYSDATE,3);
    lv_current_user_txt                VARCHAR2(40) := TO_CHAR(UID) ||
```

```
                                                  ':  '  ||  USER;
   lv_date_as_number_num          PLS_INTEGER   := TO_NUMBER(TO_CHAR(
                                                  SYSDATE,  'YYYYMMDD'));
BEGIN
   DBMS_OUTPUT.PUT_LINE(lv_three_month_forecast_date);
   DBMS_OUTPUT.PUT_LINE(lv_current_user_txt);
   DBMS_OUTPUT.PUT_LINE(lv_date_as_number_num);
END;
/
```

Output (4_8.sql)

```
11-SEP-98
19: PLSQL_USER
19980911


PL/SQL procedure successfully completed.
```

TIP
When possible, default PL/SQL variables to avoid hidden NULL value problems. The default assignment is very flexible because it allows the use of any function available in the PL/SQL, including any functions you created.

TIP
The DBMS_OUTPUT.PUT_LINE procedure is overloaded and can accept either a character, numeric, or date data type (this is illustrated in the preceding example). If you want to mix values to pass to this function, use the TO_DATE, TO_NUMBER, and TO_CHAR functions.

Take Special Care When Dealing with NULL and DATE Values

NULL values and DATE data types in PL/SQL introduce the same potential problems that exist when dealing with NULL values and DATE data types (including SYSDATE) in SQL. An extensive discussion covering the problems encountered in SQL with these values is provided in Chapter 2. PL/SQL developers must be aware the same problem is hidden in PL/SQL and can cause you undue problems if a proactive approach and understanding of these issues does not exist.

The Boolean variable is an additional variable that must be addressed in PL/SQL regarding NULL values. The Boolean data type does not exist in SQL. If you default Boolean variables to TRUE or FALSE, and remember a Boolean that is not set has a value of NULL, which is not equal to TRUE or FALSE, then you can address the Boolean NULL value problem.

The following PL/SQL code illustrates the NULL problem in PL/SQL.

File: 4_9.sql

```
SET SERVEROUTPUT ON SIZE 1000000
<<default_test>> -- Naming the PL/SQL block
DECLARE
   lv_first_num       NUMBER(10) DEFAULT 0;      -- Defaulted to 0
   lv_second_num      NUMBER(10) := 10;          -- Defaulted to 10
   lv_third_num       NUMBER(10);                -- Defaulted to NULL
   lv_processed_bln   BOOLEAN DEFAULT FALSE;     -- Defaulted to FALSE
   lv_complete_bln1   BOOLEAN;                   -- Defaulted to NULL
   lv_complete_bln2   BOOLEAN;                   -- Defaulted to NULL
BEGIN
   -- Note the second reference to the lv_second_num variable. The
   -- result in this example is to print the same variable.
   DBMS_OUTPUT.PUT_LINE('lv_first_num:        ' ||
           TO_CHAR(lv_first_num)  ||
           CHR(10) || 'lv_second_num:       ' ||
           TO_CHAR(lv_second_num) ||
           CHR(10) || 'lv_third_num:        ' ||
           TO_CHAR(lv_third_num)  ||
           CHR(10) || 'lv_processed_bln:  ' || 'FALSE' ||
           CHR(10) || 'lv_complete_bln1:  ' || ''       ||
           CHR(10) || 'lv_complete_bln2:  ' || ''       ||
           CHR(10) ||
           'default_test.lv_second_num: ' ||
           TO_CHAR(default_test.lv_second_num) || CHR(10));
   DBMS_OUTPUT.PUT_LINE('Is lv_second_num > lv_third_num?');
   IF lv_second_num > lv_third_num THEN
      DBMS_OUTPUT.PUT_LINE('lv_second_num > lv_third_num' || CHR(10));
   ELSE
      DBMS_OUTPUT.PUT_LINE('lv_second_num < lv_third_num' || CHR(10));
   END IF;
   DBMS_OUTPUT.PUT_LINE('Is lv_first_num = lv_third_num?');
   IF lv_first_num = lv_third_num THEN
      DBMS_OUTPUT.PUT_LINE('lv_first_num = lv_third_num');
   ELSE
      DBMS_OUTPUT.PUT_LINE('lv_first_num <> lv_third_num');
   END IF;
   DBMS_OUTPUT.PUT_LINE('Is lv_complete_bln1 = TRUE?');
```

```
   IF lv_complete_bln1 THEN
      DBMS_OUTPUT.PUT_LINE('lv_complete_bln1 = TRUE');
   ELSE
      DBMS_OUTPUT.PUT_LINE('lv_complete_bln1 <> TRUE');
   END IF;
   DBMS_OUTPUT.PUT_LINE('Is NOT lv_complete_bln1 = TRUE?');
   IF NOT lv_complete_bln1 THEN
      DBMS_OUTPUT.PUT_LINE('NOT lv_complete_bln1 = TRUE');
   ELSE
      DBMS_OUTPUT.PUT_LINE('NOT lv_complete_bln1 <> TRUE');
   END IF;
   DBMS_OUTPUT.PUT_LINE('Is lv_complete_bln1 = lv_complet_bln2?');
   IF lv_complete_bln1 = lv_complete_bln2 THEN
      DBMS_OUTPUT.PUT_LINE('lv_complete_bln1 = lv_complete_bln2');
   ELSE
      DBMS_OUTPUT.PUT_LINE('lv_complete_bln1 <> lv_complete_bln2');
   END IF;
END default_test;
/
```

Output (4_9.sql)

```
lv_first_num:        0
lv_second_num:       10
lv_third_num:
lv_processed_bln:   FALSE
lv_complete_bln1:
lv_complete_bln2:

default_test.lv_second_num: 10

Is lv_second_num > lv_third_num?
lv_second_num < lv_third_num

Is lv_first_num = lv_third_num?
lv_first_num <> lv_third_num

Is lv_complete_bln1 = TRUE?
lv_complete_bln1 <> TRUE

Is NOT lv_complete_bln1 = TRUE?
NOT lv_complete_bln1 <> TRUE

Is lv_complete_bln1 = lv_complet_bln2?
lv_complete_bln1 <> lv_complete_bln2

PL/SQL procedure successfully completed.
```

Dealing with NULL and DATE Values

TIP
*Any PL/SQL block can be labeled by adding a label
identifier prior to the DECLARE statement (illustrated in
the preceding example). This adds flexibility in
uniquely identifying a variable if the same variable is
used in an outer or nested block. It is not needed by
default because Oracle determines the variable you are
referring to by the name and scope, but it is available
for readability and referencing an outer variable.*

If all number variables had been defaulted to 0 and all Boolean variables
had been defaulted to FALSE, the result would be much different, as the
following illustrates.

```
lv_first_num:        0
lv_second_num:       10
lv_third_num:        0
lv_processed_bln:    FALSE
lv_complete_bln1:    FALSE
lv_complete_bln2:    FALSE
default_test.lv_second_num: 10

Is lv_second_num > lv_third_num?
lv_second_num > lv_third_num

Is lv_first_num = lv_third_num?
lv_first_num = lv_third_num

Is lv_complete_bln1 = TRUE?
lv_complete_bln1 <> TRUE

Is NOT lv_complete_bln1 = TRUE?
NOT lv_complete_bln1 = TRUE

Is lv_complete_bln1 = lv_complete_bln2?
lv_complete_bln1 = lv_complete_bln2

PL/SQL procedure successfully completed.
```

This outcome is more in line with what logically makes sense.

TIP

If you have any doubt of how NULL values and DATE data types work and should be handled, go directly to Chapter 2 and review the conditions. Both issues must be understood and addressed proactively. NULL is not equal to anything, not even another NULL value. Default all PL/SQL variables when possible and use the NVL function to assist in addressing this NULL problem. TRUNCate all dates when possible and remember the SYSDATE variable contains the date and time. Instead of having to remember to truncate the date, set a package variable and reference this variable. The following illustrates this technique.

File: 4_10.sql

```
CREATE OR REPLACE PACKAGE globals IS
   pvg_global_sysdate DATE DEFAULT TRUNC(SYSDATE);
END globals;
```

The pvg_global_sysdate variable can be referenced from any session that has EXECUTE privilege on the globals package as follows:

Output (4_10.sql)

```
SET SERVEROUTPUT ON SIZE 1000000
EXECUTE DBMS_OUTPUT.PUT_LINE(globals.pvg_global_sysdate)
```

```
13-SEP-98
```

```
PL/SQL procedure successfully completed.
```

To understand variable declaration and scope in more detail, refer to Chapter 5.

TIP

If a DATE variable has a time other than midnight (00:00:00), then the comparison condition that can be performed to verify the DATE value is within a specific date range is illustrated in the following example (note the use of setting the low-range date time value to 00:00:00 and the high-range date time value to 23:59:59).

File: 4_11.sql

```
CREATE OR REPLACE FUNCTION date_range
   (p_low_end_date  DATE,
    p_high_end_date DATE,
    p_to_check_date DATE)
    RETURN BOOLEAN IS
-- This function accepts a low range date, a high range date, and a
-- date to check. Then the function determines if the date to check
-- is between the low range and high range. This function handles
-- dates with time values other than 00:00:00.
-- If the date to check is in the range, then a TRUE is returned.
   lv_return_bln BOOLEAN := FALSE;
   lv_low_date   DATE := TRUNC(p_low_end_date); -- Time 00:00:00
   -- The next date value is defaulted to the current date and
   -- time of 23:59:59
   lv_high_date  DATE := TRUNC(p_high_end_date + 1) - .000011574;
BEGIN
   IF p_to_check_date >  lv_low_date  AND
      p_to_check_date <= lv_high_date THEN
      lv_return_bln := TRUE;
   END IF;
   -- The display statements are used to see the values used
   DBMS_OUTPUT.PUT_LINE('Low Date     : ' ||
      TO_CHAR(lv_low_date, 'MM/DD/YYYY:HH24:MI:SS'));
   DBMS_OUTPUT.PUT_LINE('Date To Check: ' ||
      TO_CHAR(p_to_check_date, 'MM/DD/YYYY:HH24:MI:SS'));
   DBMS_OUTPUT.PUT_LINE('High Date    : ' ||
      TO_CHAR(lv_high_date,    'MM/DD/YYYY:HH24:MI:SS'));
   RETURN lv_return_bln;
END date_range;
/
```

File: 4_12.sql

```
SET SERVEROUTPUT ON SIZE 1000000
-- This PL/SQL block passes the SYSDATE as all three variables
-- into the date_range function. The 3 dates that are compared are
-- displayed to show the functionality of the date_range function.
DECLARE
   lv_date_check_bln BOOLEAN;
BEGIN
   lv_date_check_bln := date_range(SYSDATE, SYSDATE, SYSDATE);
   IF lv_date_check_bln THEN
      DBMS_OUTPUT.PUT_LINE('Date in Range: TRUE');
   ELSE
```

```
        DBMS_OUTPUT.PUT_LINE('Date in Range: FALSE');
    END IF;
END;
/
```

Output (4_12.sql)

```
Low Date     : 03/13/1999:00:00:00
Date To Check: 03/13/1999:14:31:54
High Date    : 03/13/1999:23:59:59
Date in Range: TRUE

PL/SQL procedure successfully completed.
```

Use Booleans to Reduce Coding Errors and to Simplify Conditional Tests

Even though the Boolean data type is not supported by the Oracle RDBMS and SQL, it is a powerful component of PL/SQL and should be used accordingly. Do not attempt to mimic Boolean variables using either character or numeric variables. While this in itself is not a difficult task, it must be done carefully to prevent the introduction of errors into your code. Consider the following example that uses a character data type to simulate a Boolean variable.

File: 4_13.sql

```
-- Assumes execution in SQL*Plus
DECLARE
    lv_product_exists_txt  VARCHAR2(1) := 'N'; -- Boolean simulator
    lv_product_num         s_product.product_id%TYPE;
    CURSOR cur_product IS
        SELECT product_id
        FROM   s_product
        WHERE  product_id = &&p_product;  -- Prompts for product
BEGIN
    OPEN cur_product;
    FETCH cur_product INTO lv_product_num;
    IF cur_product%ROWCOUNT > 0 THEN
        lv_product_exists_txt := 'Y';
    END IF;
    CLOSE cur_product;
```

```
   IF lv_product_exists_txt = 'y' THEN
      -- Product Processing Logic...
      DBMS_OUTPUT.PUT_LINE('Product Id: ' ||TO_CHAR(&&p_product) ||
         ' Exists. ');
   ELSE
      DBMS_OUTPUT.PUT_LINE('Product Id: ' ||TO_CHAR(&&p_product) ||
         ' Does NOT Exists. ');
   END IF;
END;
/
```

While the preceding block is syntactically correct, a logic error exists, which will prevent it from running as intended. In this block, a TRUE value is represented with *Y* and a FALSE value with *N*. In the conditional statement that performs the product processing logic, I have accidentally written the test statement using *y* instead of *Y*, and the conditional statement will never execute. The code will fail to process the product logic. The main problem with this technique is, with the exception of number of characters, there are no constraints as to what values a character variable can be set. Neither the PL/SQL compiler nor the runtime interpreter will catch the error, unless the capacity of the variable is exceeded.

Don't think the problem can be corrected using numeric variables to simulate Booleans. They also are susceptible to being accidentally set to or compared with a value that represents neither TRUE nor FALSE.

By rewriting the preceding block using true Boolean variables, the PL/SQL compiler detects any statements attempting to assign an illegal value to a Boolean variable. The logic errors caused by invalid Boolean variable assignments are avoided.

File: 4_14.sql

```
-- Assuming execution in SQL*Plus
DECLARE
   lv_product_exists_bln  BOOLEAN := FALSE;
   lv_product_num         s_product.product_id%TYPE;
   CURSOR cur_product IS
      SELECT product_id
      FROM   s_product
      WHERE  product_id = &&p_product;  -- Prompts for product
BEGIN
   OPEN cur_product;
   FETCH cur_product INTO lv_product_num;
   IF cur_product%ROWCOUNT > 0 THEN
      lv_product_exists_bln := TRUE;
   END IF;
```

```
    CLOSE cur_product;
    IF lv_product_exists_bln THEN
        -- Product Processing Logic...
        DBMS_OUTPUT.PUT_LINE('Product Id: ' ||TO_CHAR(&&p_product) ||
            ' Exists. ');
    ELSE
        DBMS_OUTPUT.PUT_LINE('Product Id: ' ||TO_CHAR(&&p_product) ||
                            ' Does NOT Exists. ');
    END IF;
END;
/
```

As an added benefit, the use of true Booleans simplifies the conditional statements ("IF lv_product_exists_txt = 'y' THEN" becomes "IF lv_product_exists_bln THEN"), reducing the risk of coding errors.

Use **DBMS_OUTPUT.PUT_LINE** Effectively

Most PL/SQL developers make extensive use of the Oracle supplied procedure DBMS_OUTPUT.PUT_LINE for debugging, testing, or informational display purposes when working with PL/SQL code in SQL*Plus. This procedure needs to be thoroughly understood to ensure it is used properly in development and production. Otherwise, unexpected or hidden problems will result. Since this procedure primarily displays information to the screen when called from PL/SQL code, it appears to be a basic function on the surface. However, there is much more to the DBMS_OUTPUT.PUT_LINE procedure and DBMS_OUTPUT package, which should be understood to ensure they are being used effectively. The following outlines a list of the DBMS_OUTPUT package features and functionality to ensure this understanding:

- When in SQL*Plus, the DBMS_OUTPUT.PUT_LINE procedure only displays information to the screen when the PL/SQL program unit has completed execution (successfully or unsuccessfully). This procedure is not truly interactive; it will only store information to a message buffer until the PL/SQL program unit is completed. If you have a process that loops 1,000 times and uses the DBMS_OUTPUT.PUT_LINE command to display information, and the process completes in ten minutes, then your 1,000 messages start displaying to your screen in ten minutes. This procedure does not store information to the message buffer unless the message buffer has been enabled. To enable the message buffer, one of two commands can be executed in SQL*Plus:

```
-- Command 1: Buffer set to 2000 bytes max
SET SERVEROUTPUT ON
-- Command 1: Buffer set to 1000000 bytes max
SET SERVEROUTPUT ON SIZE 1000000

-- Command 2: Buffer set to 20000 bytes max
EXECUTE DBMS_OUTPUT.ENABLE
-- Command 2: Buffer set to 1000000 bytes max
EXECUTE DBMS_OUTPUT.ENABLE(1000000)
```

■ The preceding message buffer is defaulted to 2,000 bytes for the SET command and 20,000 bytes for the DBMS_OUTPUT.ENABLE command. The maximum size of the message buffer is 1,000,000 bytes (minimum is 2,000 bytes) and is modifiable as illustrated in the preceding examples.

■ SET SERVEROUTPUT ON is a SQL*Plus command and is only available in SQL*Plus, not callable from within PL/SQL code. This command operates differently from the DBMS_OUTPUT.ENABLE command because it not only enables the message buffer, it also automatically reads the message buffer and displays the buffer to your screen when a PL/SQL program unit completes. The DBMS_OUTPUT.ENABLE command only enables the message buffer. It *does not* automatically read the buffer and display information to the screen upon completion of a PL/SQL program unit. With the DBMS_OUTPUT.ENABLE procedure, if in SQL*Plus, the SET SERVEROUTPUT still needs to be set to ON to have information read from the buffer and displayed to the screen. If in any other product and embedded in the PL/SQL program unit, then the DBMS_OUTPUT.GET_LINE(S) procedures must be used to read the message buffer. The DBMS_OUTPUT.GET_LINE(S) can also be used when in SQL*Plus to read and display the buffer, but these procedures become much less useful since you can issue the SET SERVEROUTPUT ON command is a SQL*Plus session to have the buffer always read and displayed automatically.

■ If the buffer is not flushed and becomes filled, a PL/SQL error will result. When the program aborts, all uncommitted transactions are rolled back. To eliminate the buffer overflow error, the buffer can be increased or the information logged to the buffer reduced. If the buffer overflows or any other error is encountered, and you are in SQL*Plus with the SET SERVEROUTPUT ON previously executed, the message buffer will be read and displayed, followed by the error encountered. If the DBMS_OUTPUT.ENABLE is called in a PL/SQL program unit and the program unit is called from within a product other than SQL*Plus (for example, Forms), when the message buffer overflows, the program will result in an error. This can be a hard problem to track down because it is impossible to repeat regularly.

There are other methods of logging processing information during debugging or long-running PL/SQL processing. These are discussed later in this chapter.

One of the following three methods should be used for handling the DBMS_OUTPUT.PUT_LINE calls in your PL/SQL code when deploying the PL/SQL code into production.

- Method 1: Delete all occurrences of this procedure from your code (however, this method eliminates this useful debugging and testing information if modifications are needed at a later time).

- Method 2: Comment out all occurrences of this procedure in your code (however, this can become time consuming if many of these calls are in your code).

- Method 3: Leave these procedure calls unchanged in your production code (allows for enabling the message buffer when future modifications are needed, so all these procedure calls are turned on during the modification phase).

Method 3 can be accomplished by keeping the DBMS_OUTPUT.PUT_LINE calls in your production code. The commands will be executed, but the information will not be placed in a buffer because the message buffer will not be enabled (this is assuming you do not call the DBMS_OUTPUT.ENABLE procedure).

File: 4_15.sql

```
CREATE OR REPLACE PROCEDURE LOAD_DATA IS
-- Declarations
BEGIN
   DBMS_OUTPUT.PUT_LINE('Load Data Processing Starting...');
   -- Processing Logic...
   DBMS_OUTPUT.PUT_LINE('Load Data Processing Complete.');
END;
/
```

When the preceding procedure is called from any product other than SQL*Plus, the DBMS_OUTPUT.PUT_LINE calls have no effect. If the procedure is called within SQL*Plus and the message buffer is enabled with the SET command, however, these lines will display to the screen. This is illustrated in the following code:

Output (4_15.sql)

```
SET SERVEROUTPUT ON SIZE 1000000
EXECUTE load_data
```

Using DBMS_OUTPUT.PUT_LINE

```
Load Data Processing Starting...
Load Data Processing Complete.

PL/SQL procedure successfully completed.
```

TIP

Enable the serveroutput buffer to log DBMS_OUTPUT.PUT_LINE calls to assist in debugging and screen I/O when in SQL*Plus. Remember, the maximum buffer size is 1,000,000 bytes and the maximum line length that can be written to the buffer is 255 bytes.

TIP

In SQL*Plus, you can wrap the output of this procedure on a word by using the FORMAT WORD_WRAPPED attribute on the SET SERVEROUTPUT command as shown in the following code. The line wrapping is dependent on the setting of the LINESIZE parameter.

```
SET LINESIZE 20
SET SERVEROUTPUT ON SIZE 1000000 FORMAT WORD_WRAPPED
EXECUTE.DBMS_OUTPUT.PUT_LINE('12345678901234567890123456789' ||
    '12345678901234567890')
```

```
12345678901234567890
12345678901234567890
1234567890

PL/SQL procedure successfully completed.
```

TIP

I strongly recommend using DBMS_OUTPUT.PUT_LINE for message display or screen display with the intent that this display is used only in SQL*Plus for debugging and testing with the SET SERVEROUTPUT ON command executed. Never use the DBMS_OUTPUT.ENABLE in your PL/SQL coding because this introduces the potential for hidden errors. Turn the buffer on and off with the SET command in SQL*Plus. You can leave your DBMS_OUTPUT.PUT_LINE statements in your code and they will have no effect unless the message buffer is enabled.

TIP
If you want to buffer information while processing for later use, use the PL/SQL table structure available in PL/SQL, do not use the message buffer with DBMS_OUTPUT.PUT_LINE, GET_LINE, or ENABLE. You will have far greater control over the PL/SQL table and you will not have to worry about overflowing the message buffer.

For more information on the DBMS_OUTPUT package, refer to Chapter 12.

Use Explicit Cursors Versus Implicit Cursors

When you develop SQL statements in your PL/SQL source code, you are faced with the decision of whether to use explicit or implicit cursors. All INSERT, UPDATE, and DELETE statements are executed with implicit cursors because you do not have the option to set up a cursor for these statements. When creating a SELECT statement and you only need to return one record, you have the option of creating an explicit or implicit cursor.

I recommend using an explicit cursor for single record SELECT statements. The main reasons for using an explicit cursor are evident from a brief outline of the operation of explicit and implicit cursors.

An implicit cursor executes in a similar method as an explicit cursor: open, fetch, close. Oracle performs these three operations internally for implicit cursors, but the developer is required to perform these three operations for explicit cursors. If the fetch of an implicit cursor does not return a record, then the exception NO_DATA_FOUND is raised. This causes processing to branch to the EXCEPTION section of a block. With explicit cursors, you can open, fetch, and close the cursor. The %FOUND and %NOTFOUND attributes of the cursor can be checked to determine processing logic based on these two conditions. If the first fetch of an implicit cursor returns a record, then a second fetch is attempted to determine if the exception TOO_MANY_ROWS should be raised. Explicit cursors provide more control over the processing of the cursor logic once the fetch is executed.

The first two examples illustrate implicit cursors and the processing logic when too many records or no records are found. These examples are followed by two examples of the same processing with explicit cursors.

File: 4_16.sql

```
DECLARE  -- Implicit Cursor: Too many rows
   lv_emp_rec s_employee%ROWTYPE;
```

```
BEGIN
   SELECT * INTO lv_emp_rec
   FROM   s_employee;
EXCEPTION
   WHEN NO_DATA_FOUND THEN
      DBMS_OUTPUT.PUT_LINE('No Employee Record Found.');
   WHEN TOO_MANY_ROWS THEN
      DBMS_OUTPUT.PUT_LINE('More Than One Employee Record Found.');
   WHEN OTHERS THEN
      DBMS_OUTPUT.PUT_LINE('Unknown Error.');
END;
/
```

Output (4_16.sql)

```
More Than One Employee Record Found.

PL/SQL procedure successfully completed.
```

File: 4_17.sql

```
DECLARE   -- Implicit Cursor: No rows found
   lv_emp_rec s_employee%ROWTYPE;
BEGIN
   SELECT * INTO lv_emp_rec
   FROM   s_employee
   WHERE  employee_id = 999;    -- This line added
EXCEPTION
   WHEN NO_DATA_FOUND THEN
      DBMS_OUTPUT.PUT_LINE('No Employee Record Found.');
   WHEN TOO_MANY_ROWS THEN
      DBMS_OUTPUT.PUT_LINE('More Than One Employee Record Found.');
   WHEN OTHERS THEN
      DBMS_OUTPUT.PUT_LINE('Unknown Error.');
END;
/
```

Output (4_17.sql)

```
No Employee Record Found.

PL/SQL procedure successfully completed.
```

File: 4_18.sql

```
DECLARE  --Explicit Cursor: Too many rows
   CURSOR cur_employee IS
      SELECT *
      FROM   s_employee;
   lv_emp_rec s_employee%ROWTYPE;
BEGIN
   OPEN cur_employee;
   FETCH cur_employee INTO lv_emp_rec;
   IF cur_employee%NOTFOUND THEN
      DBMS_OUTPUT.PUT_LINE('No Employee Record Found.');
   END IF;
   CLOSE cur_employee;
EXCEPTION
   WHEN OTHERS THEN
      DBMS_OUTPUT.PUT_LINE('Unknown Error.');
      IF cur_employee%ISOPEN THEN
         CLOSE cur_employee;
      END IF;
END;
/
```

There is no output message, since the explicit logic only fetched once and a record was found.

File: 4_19.sql

```
DECLARE  -- Explicit Cursor: No rows found
   CURSOR cur_employee IS
      SELECT *
      FROM   s_employee
      WHERE employee_id = 999; -- This line added
   lv_emp_rec s_employee%ROWTYPE;
BEGIN
   OPEN cur_employee;
   FETCH cur_employee INTO lv_emp_rec;
   IF cur_employee%NOTFOUND THEN
      DBMS_OUTPUT.PUT_LINE('No Employee Record Found.');
   END IF;
   CLOSE cur_employee;
EXCEPTION
   WHEN OTHERS THEN
      DBMS_OUTPUT.PUT_LINE('Unknown Error.');
      IF cur_employee%ISOPEN THEN
         CLOSE cur_employee;
      END IF;
END;
/
```

Explicit Cursors Versus Implicit Cursors

Reducing Coding and Margin for Error

Output(4_19.sql)

```
No Employee Record Found.

PL/SQL procedure successfully completed.
```

TIP
*Always close the cursors that you open for performance
reasons. Every cursor requires memory. If the cursor is
no longer needed, close it. Remember to do this in your
error-handling routines, as shown in the preceding
example. Prior to executing the CLOSE statement, the
ISOPEN cursor attribute can be checked to make sure an
attempt is not made to close an already closed cursor. If
a close is attempted on a closed cursor, an error will be
raised: ORA-01001: invalid cursor.*

Use CURSOR FOR LOOPs to Reduce Coding and Margin for Error

You can deploy a variety of techniques when you work with explicit cursors. The
standard convention is to open the cursor, start a loop, fetch each record (followed
by processing logic), and then close the cursor. Some people forget to close cursors,
which increases the memory required. This could eventually lead to an error
indicating you exceeded the number of open cursors for your session. The number
of open cursors is set by the open_cursors parameter in the init.ora parameter file
and the default is 50, indicating 50 open cursors maximum in any session at any
one time. This is usually adjusted higher to accommodate larger systems, but it is
still a developer's responsibility to develop tight code, including closing cursors
when they are no longer needed.

I recommend the use of the CURSOR FOR LOOP for any explicit cursor created
to process multiple records. The CURSOR FOR LOOP automatically handles the
open, fetch, and close operations for the cursor. It also automatically declares a
PL/SQL record variable with the name of the variable specified in the CURSOR FOR
LOOP. When Oracle executes the CURSOR FOR LOOP statement, it internally
does the following:

- Declares a record variable for the PL/SQL variable specified in the CURSOR
  FOR LOOP (same as %ROWTYPE of the cursor)

- Opens the cursor (it does not perform an %ISOPEN check prior)

- Fetches the first record

- Each time it reaches the END LOOP statement, it loops to the beginning of the loop and fetches the next record

- If a fetch results in no more records, the cursor is closed and the processing passes to the PL/SQL statement after the END LOOP statement

- If an exception is raised (implicitly or explicitly) in a CURSOR FOR LOOP, the cursor is closed and the processing passes to the exception handler

Based on the preceding list of internal handling performed for CURSOR FOR LOOPs, the benefits that come by using this command—versus controlling the cursor explicitly—are obvious. The following examples illustrate identical logic. The first example demonstrates the use of a CURSOR FOR LOOP. The second example demonstrates the necessary code to mimic the same functionality without the CURSOR FOR LOOP.

File: 4_20.sql

```
DECLARE
   CURSOR cur_employee IS
      SELECT employee_id,
             employee_last_name || ', ' ||employee_first_name emp_name
      FROM   s_employee
      ORDER BY employee_id;
BEGIN
   FOR lv_cur_employee_rec IN cur_employee LOOP
      DBMS_OUTPUT.PUT_LINE('Employee: ' ||
         TO_CHAR(lv_cur_employee_rec.employee_id) ||
         ' ' || lv_cur_employee_rec.emp_name);
   END LOOP;
   EXCEPTION
      WHEN OTHERS THEN
         DBMS_OUTPUT.PUT_LINE('Error in Employee Procssing.');
END;
/
```

Output (4_20.sql)

```
Employee: 1 VELASQUEZ, CARMEN
Employee: 2 NGAO, LADORIS
Employee: 3 NAGAYAMA, MIDORI
Employee: 4 QUICK-TO-SEE, MARK

PL/SQL procedure successfully completed.
```

Reducing Coding and Margin for Error

The preceding output only displays a subset of the result. The following source code provides the identical results (the output is not shown). Each of the additional lines of code needed for this example is commented with '-- Not necessary'.

File: 4_21.sql

```
DECLARE
   CURSOR cur_employee IS
      SELECT employee_id,
             employee_last_name || ', ' ||employee_first_name emp_name
      FROM   s_employee
      ORDER BY employee_id;
   lv_cur_employee_rec cur_employee%ROWTYPE;            -- Not necessary
BEGIN
   OPEN cur_employee;                                   -- Not necessary
   LOOP
      FETCH cur_employee INTO lv_cur_employee_rec; -- Not necessary
      EXIT WHEN cur_employee%NOTFOUND;                  -- Not necessary
      DBMS_OUTPUT.PUT_LINE('Employee: ' ||
         TO_CHAR(lv_cur_employee_rec.employee_id) ||
         ' ' || lv_cur_employee_rec.emp_name);
   END LOOP;

   CLOSE cur_employee;                                  -- Not necessary
EXCEPTION
   WHEN OTHERS THEN
      DBMS_OUTPUT.PUT_LINE('Error in Employee Procssing.');
      IF cur_employee%ISOPEN THEN                       -- Not necessary
         CLOSE cur_employee;                            -- Not necessary
      END IF;                                           -- Not necessary
END;
/
```

As evident in the preceding example, a number of additional statements must be added to ensure the same type of processing is accomplished with the inherent use of the CURSOR FOR LOOPs for explicit cursors.

TIP
Use CURSOR FOR LOOPs to create less error-prone code and eliminate extra code inherently handled with the use of this command. Any time Oracle internally performs operations for you without adding overhead, without eliminating control, and without forcing you to add more code in the long run, let it. One of your goals of developing in PL/SQL should always be to reduce code volume, which reduces the possibility for runtime errors.

TIP
If a cursor is only being used to check for existence (one record exists), use the OPEN, FETCH, CLOSE statements. The CURSOR FOR LOOP always performs at least two fetches because it must know when there are no more records.

Implement PL/SQL Records to Limit Local Variables and Improve Maintainability

Whenever the number of local variables can be reduced, a program becomes easier to understand and maintain. If two local variables are in a procedure, the logic becomes easier to follow and understand than another procedure with 10 or 20 local variables. Many PL/SQL developers who have made the transition from other languages continue to find they are performing more work than necessary by keeping track of dozens of local PL/SQL variables. Most of these local variables can be grouped together in categories of functionality or purpose.

PL/SQL records provide the capability to create composite variables, containing related pieces of information. Each of the individual items of data within a PL/SQL record can be accessed or manipulated like other PL/SQL variables. Increasing the effectiveness of this concept is the capability to base records on cursors and tables.

When creating local variables for fetching data, it is recommended to use PL/SQL records based on cursors and using the %ROWTYPE attribute. The %ROWTYPE method, as described in an earlier section in this chapter, considerably reduces the amount of maintenance involved in schema changes. In addition, using the %ROWTYPE attribute based on a table is helpful. This practice could be used to create generic PL/SQL records for common processing on a table.

The following example implements cursor-based PL/SQL records for processing information for a customer. First, initial customer data is retrieved, followed by order information retrieval for the customer. In both cases, PL/SQL records are implemented. Note that the retrieval of the order information is performed by a CURSOR FOR LOOP and the PL/SQL record variable is self-declaring, identical to typical FOR loop variables.

File: 4_22.sql

```
CREATE OR REPLACE PROCEDURE total_customer
   (p_cust_num s_customer.customer_id%TYPE) IS
   CURSOR cur_customer IS
     SELECT *
```

```
      FROM    s_customer
      WHERE   customer_id = p_cust_num;
   CURSOR cur_orders IS
      SELECT order_id, date_ordered, total
      FROM    s_order
      WHERE   customer_id = p_cust_num
      ORDER BY date_ordered;
   lv_cust_rec s_customer%ROWTYPE;
BEGIN
   -- Fetch customer information, using the customer id parameter.
   OPEN cur_customer;
   FETCH cur_customer INTO lv_cust_rec;
   IF (cur_customer%FOUND) THEN
      -- Output customer name, followed by a blank line
      DBMS_OUTPUT.PUT_LINE('Customer: ' ||
         lv_cust_rec.customer_name || CHR(10));
      -- Loop through all orders, output order information
      FOR lv_ord_rec IN cur_orders LOOP
         DBMS_OUTPUT.PUT_LINE('Order: ' || lv_ord_rec.order_id ||
            ' Date: '  || TO_CHAR(lv_ord_rec.date_ordered,
            'MM/DD/YYYY') || '  Total: ' ||
            TO_CHAR(lv_ord_rec.total, '$99,999.00'));
      END LOOP;
   ELSE
      -- Output message if customer id passed to procedure was invalid
      DBMS_OUTPUT.PUT_LINE('Customer ID: ' || p_cust_num ||
         ' does not exist.');
   END IF;
   CLOSE cur_customer;
EXCEPTION
   WHEN OTHERS THEN
      Raise_Application_Error(-20100,
      'Error in procedure TOTAL_CUSTOMER.', FALSE);
END total_customer;
/
```

In addition to cursor- and table-based records, user-defined record types can be implemented. These types of records provide enhanced composite data types for more specific implementations. For user-defined PL/SQL records to be used, a TYPE must be declared.

The following example creates a user-defined PL/SQL record to group compensation information for an employee and shows the declaration of two variables declared with that type.

File: 4_23.sql

```
DECLARE
   TYPE type_emp_comp_rec IS RECORD
```

```
      (emp_last_name_txt         s_employee.employee_last_name%TYPE,
       emp_first_name_txt        s_employee.employee_first_name%TYPE,
       emp_salary_num            s_employee.salary%TYPE,
       emp_commission_pct_num s_employee.commission_pct%TYPE );
   lv_emp_comp_rec1 type_emp_comp_rec;
   lv_emp_comp_rec2 type_emp_comp_rec;
BEGIN
   lv_emp_comp_rec1.emp_last_name_txt  := 'TREZZO';
   lv_emp_comp_rec2.emp_first_name_txt := 'JOE';
END;
/
```

A PL/SQL record is the same as defining a table in the database, with the exception that the PL/SQL record is used for storage in a PL/SQL program unit to enable the manipulation of information.

TIP
If two PL/SQL records were created with exactly the same structure (for example, exact column names and data types), they are considered two distinct PL/SQL record types. An error would occur if an attempt was made to set two PL/SQL record types variable equal to each other, even if they had exactly the same definition. This is illustrated in the following example:

File: 4_24.sql

```
DECLARE
   TYPE type_emp_rec1 IS RECORD
      (emp_last_name_txt  s_employee.employee_last_name%TYPE,
       emp_first_name_txt s_employee.employee_first_name%TYPE);
   TYPE type_emp_rec2 IS RECORD
      (emp_last_name_txt  s_employee.employee_last_name%TYPE,
       emp_first_name_txt s_employee.employee_first_name%TYPE);
   lv_emp_type_rec1    type_emp_rec1;
   lv_emp_type_rec2    type_emp_rec2;
   lv_emp_type_rec3    type_emp_rec2;
BEGIN
   -- Fails with PL/SQL error (PLS-00382: expression is of wrong type)
   lv_emp_type_rec1 := lv_emp_type_rec2;
   -- Executes without error
   lv_emp_type_rec1.emp_last_name_txt :=
      lv_emp_type_rec2.emp_last_name_txt;
   -- Executes without error
   lv_emp_type_rec2 := lv_emp_type_rec3;
END;
/
```

This operation of setting the two PL/SQL records equal raises a PL/SQL error, namely, *PLS-00382: expression is of wrong type*, because the PL/SQL records are considered different type declarations. If the individual components of the records are set equal to each other, the assignment will succeed as long as the individual data types match. Likewise, as shown in the last example, if two PL/SQL record variables declared with the same type declaration, as lv_emp_type_rec2 and lv_emp_type_rec3, then the variables can be set equal.

PL/SQL records provide flexibility and functionality, which when used properly, can increase readability and maintainability.

Implement PL/SQL Tables of Records to Improve Performance and Provide a Temporary Storage Table

The majority of processing time of any program that has embedded SQL statements is spent on processing the SQL statements. PL/SQL programs have the same problems with the embedded SQL statements. Developers should, and normally do, concentrate the majority of their time attempting to improve performance by optimizing the SQL statements.

SQL statements optimized today may become slower over time because of growth, in terms of the number of records being stored and processed. Even though a SQL statement may execute quickly (less than one second), each time the statement is executed it may be a potential for performance improvements because the true time of execution is based on the number of times it is executed. Do the math on a statement that takes one second to execute. If the SQL statement is executed 9,000 times, how long does it take to process that one statement alone? The answer is 2.5 hours (150 minutes). Reducing that statement alone down to 0.1 second would reduce the execution time of the overall program by 2 hours and 15 minutes (135 minutes). Therefore, always consider the optimization of iterative executions, especially in the SQL area. Refer to Chapter 7 and Chapter 8 for further details on SQL and PL/SQL tuning, respectively. Iterative executions of SQL statements are often merely performing common lookups to get some supplementary information, such as the name or description for a code value. These types of SELECT statements can often be replaced with PL/SQL tables to reduce the overall processing time significantly.

TIP
*Use the speed of PL/SQL tables to limit the number of
lookups performed against the database. Accessing
information contained within a PL/SQL table (in
memory) is considerably faster than accessing
information from a database table. This is because the
data is being stored in memory for PL/SQL tables. The
ideal candidate database table is one that has limited
records with a numeric unique key. This unique key
can be loaded as the array index for index searches. If
the lookup is not on the array index, the process by
which the information in PL/SQL tables is searched is a
little more involved. Procedures and functions can be
set up to make this process easier, and the time spent
to develop these modules is worth the performance
improvements realized.*

In addition to defining and manipulating the contents of a PL/SQL table, PL/SQL
table functions, referred to as attributes, can be called to make common processing
easier. These attributes are DELETE, COUNT, EXISTS, NEXT, PRIOR, FIRST, and
LAST (the names clearly identify their use).

The basic steps for implementing a PL/SQL table are

1. Define the PL/SQL table(s).

2. Load the PL/SQL table(s) with data prior to PL/SQL processing.

3. Access the PL/SQL table(s) for common lookup information versus
   performing a query.

The following example illustrates the use of PL/SQL tables for common lookups,
the method of accessing PL/SQL tables by the array index, the method of accessing
PL/SQL tables without the array index to find information, and several of the PL/SQL
table attributes. The package example uses the package initialization section to
populate a PL/SQL table automatically with all the product information when the
package is first referenced. At this point, all the product information is stored in
memory for quick access throughout the database session.

Improving Performance

File: 4_25.sql

```
CREATE OR REPLACE PACKAGE process_products IS
   -- Creates the PL/SQL table structure based on the s_product table
   TYPE type_prod_table IS TABLE OF s_product%ROWTYPE
       INDEX BY BINARY_INTEGER;
   pvg_prod_table type_prod_table;
   -- This procedure populates the product PL/SQL table with the
   -- entire contents of the s_product table.
   PROCEDURE populate_prod_table;
-- This procedure scans the product PL/SQL table by the product id
   PROCEDURE check_product_id (p_prod_id_num s_product.
       product_id%TYPE);
-- This procedure scans the product PL/SQL table by the product name
   PROCEDURE check_product_name (p_prod_name_txt s_product.
       product_name%TYPE);
END process_products;
/
```

File: 4_25a.sql

```
CREATE OR REPLACE PACKAGE BODY process_products IS
-------------------------------------------------------------------
PROCEDURE populate_prod_table IS
   CURSOR cur_product IS
       SELECT *
       FROM   s_product;
BEGIN
   -- First, empty current PL/SQL table
   pvg_prod_table.DELETE;
   -- Loop through all products, placing into PL/SQL table
   FOR lv_prod_rec IN cur_product LOOP
       -- The product_id is used as the array index, but also loaded
       -- for the searches that are on product_name and need to
       -- return the product_id.
       pvg_prod_table(lv_prod_rec.product_id).product_id
           := lv_prod_rec.product_id;
       pvg_prod_table(lv_prod_rec.product_id).product_name
           := lv_prod_rec.product_name;
       pvg_prod_table(lv_prod_rec.product_id).short_desc
           := lv_prod_rec.short_desc;
       pvg_prod_table(lv_prod_rec.product_id).suggested_wholesale_price
           := lv_prod_rec.suggested_wholesale_price;
   END LOOP;
EXCEPTION
   WHEN OTHERS THEN
       RAISE_APPLICATION_ERROR(-20100,
```

```
                'Error in procedure POPULATE_PROD_TABLE.', FALSE);
END populate_prod_table;
-------------------------------------------------------------------
PROCEDURE check_product_id
   (p_prod_id_num s_product.product_id%TYPE) IS
BEGIN
   -- One statement to see if the product exists, since the
   -- array index is the product_id.
   IF pvg_prod_table.EXISTS(p_prod_id_num) THEN
      DBMS_OUTPUT.PUT_LINE('PL/SQL Table Index: ' ||
         pvg_prod_table(p_prod_id_num));
      DBMS_OUTPUT.PUT_LINE('Product ID: ' ||
         pvg_prod_table(p_prod_id_num).product_id );
      DBMS_OUTPUT.PUT_LINE('Product Name: ' ||
         pvg_prod_table(p_prod_id_num).product_name );
      DBMS_OUTPUT.PUT_LINE('Description: ' ||
         pvg_prod_table(p_prod_id_num).short_desc );
      DBMS_OUTPUT.PUT_LINE('Wholesale Price: ' ||
         TO_CHAR(pvg_prod_table(p_prod_id_num).
         suggested_wholesale_price, '$9999.00'));
      DBMS_OUTPUT.PUT_LINE(CHR(10));
   ELSE
      DBMS_OUTPUT.PUT_LINE('Product: ' || TO_CHAR(p_prod_id_num) ||
         ' is invalid.');
   END IF;
EXCEPTION
   WHEN OTHERS THEN
      RAISE_APPLICATION_ERROR(-20102,
         'Error in procedure CHECK_PRODUCT_ID.', FALSE);
END check_product_id;
-------------------------------------------------------------------
PROCEDURE check_product_name
   (p_prod_name_txt s_product.product_name%TYPE) IS
   lv_index_num      NUMBER;
   lv_match_bln      BOOLEAN := FALSE;
BEGIN
   -- First check if table has any records
   IF pvg_prod_table.COUNT <> 0 THEN
      -- Attain starting table index for loop
      lv_index_num := pvg_prod_table.FIRST;
      -- Loop through all products looking for a match on product_name
      LOOP
         -- Check existence of the product name (not exact match
         -- check, only a check to see if the input name is contained
         -- in a product name in the table).
         IF (INSTR(UPPER(pvg_prod_table(lv_index_num).product_name),
            UPPER(p_prod_name_txt)) > 0) THEN
            -- Assign TRUE to search boolean
```

```
                  lv_match_bln := TRUE;
                  -- Output record data from PL/SQL table
                  DBMS_OUTPUT.PUT_LINE('PL/SQL Table Index: ' ||
                     pvg_prod_table(lv_index_num));
                  DBMS_OUTPUT.PUT_LINE('Product ID: ' ||
                     pvg_prod_table(lv_index_num).product_id );
                  DBMS_OUTPUT.PUT_LINE('Product Name: ' ||
                     pvg_prod_table(lv_index_num).product_name );
                  DBMS_OUTPUT.PUT_LINE('Description: ' ||
                     pvg_prod_table(lv_index_num).short_desc );
                  DBMS_OUTPUT.PUT_LINE('Wholesale Price: ' ||
                     TO_CHAR(pvg_prod_table(lv_index_num).
                     suggested_wholesale_price, '$9999.00'));
                  DBMS_OUTPUT.PUT_LINE(CHR(10));
               END IF;
               EXIT WHEN (lv_index_num = pvg_prod_table.LAST) OR
                  lv_match_bln;
               lv_index_num := pvg_prod_table.NEXT(lv_index_num);
            END LOOP;
            IF NOT lv_match_bln THEN
               -- Output record data from PL/SQL table
               DBMS_OUTPUT.PUT_LINE('Product: ' || p_prod_name_txt ||
                  ' is invalid.');
            END IF;
         ELSE
            -- Output record data from PL/SQL table
            DBMS_OUTPUT.PUT_LINE('There are no products in the table.');
         END IF;
EXCEPTION
   WHEN OTHERS THEN
      RAISE_APPLICATION_ERROR(-20102,
         'Error in procedure CHECK_PRODUCT_NAME.', FALSE);
END check_product_name;
-------------------------------------------------------------------
-- Package Initialization Section
BEGIN
   -- Call procedure to populate product PL/SQL table
   populate_prod_table;
END process_products;
/
```

New in PL/SQL 2.3:

- PL/SQL tables extend beyond the limitation of scalar types to include records

- PL/SQL attributes are introduced

PL/SQL Table recommendations:

- Store elements in PL/SQL tables sequentially and set a standard of the first array index being 1 and increment by 1's (if you are storing a database table and the unique key is an integer, use the unique key as the array index).

- Use PL/SQL tables for small lookup tables that will be retrieved from iterative processes.

- Use PL/SQL tables for temporary storage of information that will be needed at a later time. This often eliminates the need for the creation of temporary database tables.

Important information to know about PL/SQL tables:

- PL/SQL tables are not constrained and records can be inserted in any order and are bound by the BINARY_INTEGER type.

- PL/SQL tables are manipulated like arrays, but they are more like database tables.

- PL/SQL table storage is created initially when a variable is defined as a PL/SQL table. Additional space is allocated to a PL/SQL table each time records are inserted into the PL/SQL table.

PL/SQL tables are extremely powerful, but like any other PL/SQL construct, they must be used properly and for the right purpose.

Use Parameters in Explicit Cursors to Improve Readability

When developing PL/SQL code, explicitly defined cursors are a necessity. In most instances, the PL/SQL developer does not implement all the available features of this basic PL/SQL concept. Developers do not always check for the value of the %FOUND or %NOTFOUND cursor attributes after attempting to fetch a record. Developers also do not always check or use the %ISOPEN cursor attribute to verify the cursor has already been opened. Moreover, developers do not always use the CLOSE command at the termination of cursor processing, freeing up resources, and avoiding the limit of open cursors for a session. One feature of explicitly defined cursors that should definitely be implemented is parameterization.

Cursor parameters provide PL/SQL developers with two opportunities: first, to stop setting local variables before opening a cursor and, second, to stop having multiple cursors with different conditions for the same columns. Implementing cursor parameters in the body of a PL/SQL block structure provides improved readability and a consistent flow of overriding logic. For example, when analyzing a large piece of PL/SQL code with several cursors involved, a cursor parameter provided in the OPEN statement makes it obvious that the piece of information is used to determine the result set of the cursor. If local variables were used, however, it is not obvious, unless the declaration section of the PL/SQL block is reviewed, more specifically, the declaration section where the variables are being used.

Identical to the declaration of PL/SQL variables and parameters for procedures and functions, the %TYPE feature can be implemented for the data type specification.

The following example implements cursor parameters, along with the use of the %TYPE feature for specifying the parameter data type:

File: 4_26.sql

```
CREATE OR REPLACE PROCEDURE order_process
    (p_ordering_num NUMBER) IS
    -- This procedure returns the total from an order number being
    -- passed in.
    CURSOR cur_get_order (p_ord_num s_order.order_id%TYPE) IS
        SELECT *
        FROM    s_order
        WHERE   order_id = p_ord_num;
    lv_order_rec cur_get_order%ROWTYPE;
BEGIN
    OPEN cur_get_order (p_ordering_num);
    FETCH cur_get_order INTO lv_order_rec;
    DBMS_OUTPUT.PUT_LINE('Order Total: ' ||
        TO_CHAR(lv_order_rec.total));
    CLOSE cur_get_order;
    EXCEPTION
        WHEN OTHERS THEN
            RAISE_APPLICATION_ERROR(-20100, 'Order Problem.', FALSE);
END;
/
```

TIP
Cursor parameters should be viewed in the same manner as procedures that pass parameters: define them when it is necessary to make the cursor dynamic and to eliminate hardcoding. Likewise, cursor parameters can also have default values assigned when declared and when opening the cursor, the same default rules apply as procedures.

Implement Cursor Variables for Similar Queries with Different Data Sources

A PL/SQL developer often develops several similar routines in an application but with slight variations, depending on the location of the application in which the code is implemented. Because of the slight variation, continuing to develop and maintain similar code is necessary . . . or is it?

We are taught to modularize code to make it more generic and reusable. Therefore, PL/SQL developers typically create common procedures and functions, and then group these objects into a database package. The %TYPE and %ROWTYPE attributes are also used to streamline maintenance of an application by allowing limited maintenance when modifying tables and columns. These techniques create more generic source code and other capabilities within PL/SQL provide additional assistance in this area.

PL/SQL developers constantly implement cursors. Cursors can have very similar structures with the same select column list, but varying predicate clauses. PL/SQL REF CURSORs, also known as cursor variables, allow the same cursor pointer to be opened with varying queries. This cursor variable is used when fetches are made, allowing the functionality surrounding the actual fetches to be generic.

TIP
Implement the generic functionality provided by cursor variables for similar queries or in cases where a cursor may be opened numerous ways, but always follows through the same processing. Cursor variables have several similar properties as normal variables, allowing them to be passed as parameters to procedures and functions. These properties are what make cursor variables good for generalizing PL/SQL code.

TIP
PL/SQL REF CURSORs were introduced with PL/SQL 2.2 and greatly enhanced with PL/SQL 2.3. PL/SQL REF CURSORs provide a great deal of flexibility and can be used when this type of flexibility is needed. Several rules surround their use and must be considered. I would not recommend using this feature until you are on PL/SQL 2.3.

The steps for implementing PL/SQL cursor variables are similar to those for implementing standard explicit cursors. In addition, the declaration needs a PL/SQL variable declared for the declared REF CURSOR type. The actual cursor is not defined until the OPEN cursor statement. Two examples of REF CURSORs are illustrated in the following declaration.

```
DECLARE
    TYPE type_emp_refcur      IS REF CURSOR RETURN s_employee%ROWTYPE;
    TYPE type_general_refcur IS REF CURSOR;

    lv_emp_rec       type_emp_refcur;
    lv_general_rec type_general_refcur;
```

The type_emp_refcur declaration is an example of a constrained REF CURSOR (commonly referred to as a *strong-type declaration*) because a RETURN is specified. The RETURN in the preceding example constrains the cursor referenced for this REF CURSOR to return all the columns in the s_employee table. When the cursor is opened and the actual SELECT is defined, it must return the same columns as s_employee (exact number of columns and exact data types). The lv_emp_rec is the variable that will be referenced in the OPEN cursor statement. This variable is a pointer to a memory location for the cursor.

The type_general_refcur declaration is an example of an unconstrained REF CURSOR (commonly referred to as a *weak-type declaration*) because no RETURN is specified. Any SQL statement, therefore, can be defined in the OPEN command for this cursor. The resulting columns can vary, as can the table and predicate (WHERE) clause.

Therefore, the RETURN is used when the same columns are being returned from a table with a different predicate, which often depends on where the cursor is called from or on the need to manipulate multiple tables with the same structure (partitioned tables is a good example of this use). The RETURN is not used when data will be pulled from a variety of tables and the result set will vary in data type or in the number of columns returned.

Most errors encountered when implementing constrained cursor variables occur at compilation time because the RETURN specified can be verified to ensure a match occurs with the OPEN cursor statement. Most errors encountered when implementing unconstrained cursor variables occur at execution time because the verification for matching data types is performed on the OPEN cursor statement and the FETCH cursor statement. Therefore, the main error resulting from this data type match verification is the ROWTYPE_MISMATCH, which results when the RETURN declaration does not match the return from the cursor actually used.

When cursor variables are opened, a SELECT statement is specified. Once the cursor is opened, the cursor variable can be sent elsewhere, fetched from, and processed. Cursor variables can and should be closed when the processing is complete, the same as explicit cursors. The %ISOPEN, %FOUND, %NOTFOUND, and %ROWCOUNT cursor attributes are also available for cursor variables.

The following package provides the functionality to retrieve a name for an ID value within several different tables. A call to the name_pkg.get_name function returns the name for the specified ID within the desired table.

File: 4_27.sql

```
CREATE OR REPLACE PACKAGE name_pkg IS
-- This package uses constrained cursor variables to
-- return the name for a given id of a specified table.
   -- Declare user-defined record type
   TYPE type_name_rec IS RECORD (name VARCHAR2(100));
   -- Declare constrained cursor variable
   TYPE type_name_refcur IS REF CURSOR
      RETURN type_name_rec;
   -- Opens the cursor based on the name, and uses the p_id_num in
   -- the predicate clause to only return one value.
   FUNCTION open_name (p_table_txt IN VARCHAR2, p_id_num IN NUMBER)
      RETURN type_name_refcur;
   -- Calls the open_name function to open the cursor and return the
   -- the name of the p_id_num passed. If no match is found, the
   -- NO_DATA_FOUND exception is raised.
   FUNCTION get_name (p_table_txt IN VARCHAR2, p_id_num IN NUMBER)
      RETURN VARCHAR2;
END name_pkg;
/
```

File: 4_27a.sql

```
CREATE OR REPLACE PACKAGE BODY name_pkg IS
-------------------------------------------------------------------
FUNCTION open_name (p_table_txt IN VARCHAR2, p_id_num IN NUMBER)
   RETURN type_name_refcur IS
   lv_table_txt  VARCHAR2(100) := UPPER(p_table_txt);
   lv_name_rec   type_name_refcur;
BEGIN
   IF lv_table_txt = 'EMPLOYEE' THEN
      OPEN lv_name_rec FOR
         SELECT employee_last_name || ', '|| employee_first_name
         FROM   s_employee
         WHERE  employee_id = p_id_num;
   ELSIF lv_table_txt = 'CUSTOMER' THEN
      OPEN lv_name_rec FOR
         SELECT customer_name
         FROM   s_customer
         WHERE  customer_id = p_id_num;
   ELSIF lv_table_txt = 'PRODUCT' THEN
```

```
      OPEN lv_name_rec FOR
         SELECT product_name
         FROM   s_product
         WHERE  product_id = p_id_num;
   ELSE
      RAISE_APPLICATION_ERROR (-20222,
         'Invalid table specified for name request.');
   END IF;
   RETURN lv_name_rec;
END open_name;
-----------------------------------------------------------------
FUNCTION get_name (p_table_txt IN VARCHAR2, p_id_num IN NUMBER)
   RETURN VARCHAR2 IS
   lv_name_rec    type_name_rec;
   lv_name_refcur type_name_refcur;
BEGIN
   -- Call function to return opened cursor variable
   lv_name_refcur := open_name(p_table_txt, p_id_num);
   -- Fetch data for given id from specified table
   FETCH lv_name_refcur INTO lv_name_rec;
   -- Check if data was found
   IF (lv_name_refcur%NOTFOUND) THEN
      CLOSE lv_name_refcur;
      RAISE NO_DATA_FOUND;
   ELSE
      CLOSE lv_name_refcur;
   END IF;
   RETURN lv_name_rec.name;
END get_name;
-----------------------------------------------------------------
END name_pkg;
/
```

The following segment demonstrates two calls to the name_pkg.get_name
function for two different tables with the output.

Output (4_27.sql)

```
SET SERVEROUTPUT ON SIZE 1000000
BEGIN
   DBMS_OUTPUT.PUT_LINE(name_pkg.get_name('CUSTOMER',201));
   DBMS_OUTPUT.PUT_LINE(name_pkg.get_name('EMPLOYEE',1));
END;
/

UNISPORTS
VELASQUEZ, CARMEN

PL/SQL procedure successfully completed.
```

TIP
Cursor variables (REF CURSORs) are an attractive feature and offer extreme flexibility, but I recommend using them with caution. Use cursor variables only when they are truly needed. Remember, the more flexible something is, the more prone it is to errors.

Use PL/SQL VARCHAR2 Data Type to Search and Manipulate LONG Database Columns

Ever since Oracle provided the capability to store LONG data types in a database table, there has been the problem of searching and/or manipulating the information in these types of columns. As a general rule, a column should only be defined as a LONG data type if it has to store extremely large amounts of text. The VARCHAR2 data type should be used, if possible.

TIP
In Oracle 8.0, the VARCHAR2 maximum length is increased from 2,000 characters to 4,000.

With Oracle 8.0 doubling the maximum storage size of VARCHAR2 columns, the VARCHAR2 column continues as the preferred data type for large character data, if possible. However, the LONG data type continues to be necessary in some cases, and starting with Oracle7 can store up to 2G of data.

LONG columns cannot be searched, used in any functions, indexed, nor used in a WHERE, GROUP BY, HAVING, or ORDER BY clause of a SQL statement. An Oracle database table is limited to having only one LONG column. The purpose of a LONG column is simply for storage.

The LONG and VARCHAR2 data types of database columns do not have the same properties as their PL/SQL counterparts. The PL/SQL VARCHAR2 data type has a maximum length of 32,767 bytes, which is much larger than its database counterpart. However, the PL/SQL LONG data type has a maximum length of 32,760 bytes, which is much smaller than its database counterpart. A search can be performed on PL/SQL LONG data types. The length differences between database data types and PL/SQL data types provides new possibilities for processing LONG data types from the database.

TIP
*Use 32K-length PL/SQL VARCHAR2 variables to search
LONG database columns that are less than 32K in
length. In many cases, text stored within a LONG
database column is less than 32K in length, enabling
you to implement this functionality. The logic can be
used to process application data, as well as data
dictionary information. In fact, several data dictionary
views contain columns defined as a LONG data type.
For example, the USER_VIEWS view has the text column
defined as a LONG and, in most cases, is less than 32K
in length. Likewise, the trigger_body column of the
USER_TRIGGERS view is also defined as a LONG.*

The "search" feature of a LONG column can be performed by selecting the
column value into a PL/SQL VARCHAR2 variable. Error handling must accompany
this process because the possibility exists that a LONG column contains more than
32K of data.

The following procedure provides the capability to search database trigger
text—stored in the data dictionary—for particular character strings if the trigger
text is less than 32K in length. The procedure allows the search string to be
provided, as well as a specific trigger name if desired. Otherwise, all user triggers
are searched by default.

File: 4_28.sql

```
CREATE OR REPLACE PROCEDURE search_trigs
   (p_search_txt VARCHAR2, p_trigger_txt VARCHAR2 := NULL) IS
   CURSOR cur_get_trigger_body IS
      SELECT trigger_name, table_name, trigger_body
      FROM   user_triggers
      WHERE  trigger_name = NVL(UPPER(p_trigger_txt), trigger_name);
   lv_body_txt          VARCHAR2(32767);
   lv_trigger_name_txt  VARCHAR2(30);
   lv_table_name_txt    VARCHAR2(30);
   lv_counter_num       NUMBER;
   lv_error_occurred_bln BOOLEAN := FALSE;
BEGIN
   OPEN cur_get_trigger_body;
   LOOP
      -- Initialize local variables on each loop pass
      lv_trigger_name_txt := NULL;
      lv_table_name_txt   := NULL;
      lv_body_txt         := NULL;
```

```
            -- Use nested PL/SQL block to trap exceptions
        BEGIN << fetch_body >>
            FETCH cur_get_trigger_body INTO lv_trigger_name_txt,
                lv_table_name_txt, lv_body_txt;
            IF cur_get_trigger_body%NOTFOUND THEN
                -- When no more triggers, exit loop
                EXIT;
            END IF;
        EXCEPTION
            WHEN VALUE_ERROR THEN
                IF p_trigger_txt IS NOT NULL THEN
                    lv_error_occurred_bln := TRUE;
                    DBMS_OUTPUT.PUT_LINE('Trigger body too long to ' ||
                        'search.');
                ELSE
                    DBMS_OUTPUT.PUT_LINE('Trigger body too long to ' ||
                        'search for  Trigger: ' ||
                        RPAD(lv_trigger_name_txt,30) ||
                        ' Table: ' || lv_table_name_txt);
                END IF;
        END fetch_body;
        -- Use INSTR function to check if search string is found
        IF INSTR(UPPER(lv_body_txt), UPPER(p_search_txt)) > 0 THEN
            lv_counter_num := NVL(lv_counter_num, 0) + 1;
            DBMS_OUTPUT.PUT_LINE('Match found in  Trigger: ' ||
                RPAD(lv_trigger_name_txt,30) || ' Table: ' ||
                lv_table_name_txt);
        END IF;
    END LOOP;
    CLOSE cur_get_trigger_body;
    -- If no previous messages were displayed, then create generic one
    IF NVL(lv_counter_num,0) = 0 AND NOT lv_error_occurred_bln THEN
        DBMS_OUTPUT.PUT_LINE('Search found no matches.');
    END IF;
END search_trigs;
/
```

The following illustrates the output from the previous procedure produced by basic calls from SQL*Plus:

Output (4_28.sql)

```
SET SERVEROUTPUT ON SIZE 1000000
EXECUTE search_trigs('REGION')
Match found in  Trigger: BU_REGION                Table: S_REGION

PL/SQL procedure successfully completed.
```

```
EXECUTE search_trigs('BEGIN')
Match found in  Trig: BI_CUSTOMER              Table: S_CUSTOMER
Match found in  Trig: BU_REGION               Table: S_REGION

PL/SQL procedure successfully completed.

EXECUTE search_trigs('ORDER')
Search found no matches.

PL/SQL procedure successfully completed.
```

Ensure PL/SQL Variable Names Do Not Mimic Column Names

Complex or large PL/SQL program units can often contain an unwieldy number of variables. Most seasoned developers have developed some type of naming convention that helps them to organize a program unit with numerous variables. The easiest technique is to use variable names similar to their database equivalents, which promotes easy memorization and fewer trips back to the program declaration section. Unfortunately, many less experienced developers make the mistake of duplicating column names as variable names. This may seem like a plausible approach because little variable memorization is required. However, a problem arises when these variables are used in a DML statement. Consider the following procedure:

File: 4_29.sql

```
CREATE OR REPLACE PROCEDURE reset_ship_dates
   (date_shipped IN DATE) IS
BEGIN
   UPDATE s_order
   SET    date_shipped = NULL
   WHERE  date_shipped = date_shipped;
   COMMIT;
END reset_ship_dates;
/
```

The purpose of this procedure is to reset all ship dates, which accidentally were updated to an incorrect date and were not yet shipped. The intent of this procedure seems straightforward: call the procedure reset_ship_dates with an incorrect shipping date and have all those ship dates reset. The problem is the variable date_shipped mimics the name of a table column. When Oracle parses SQL statements in a program unit, it checks for column references before checking for variable references, thus the variable called date_shipped was never used in the predicate clause of the DML statement. The names in that clause were all resolved to the date_shipped column, so every date_shipped in the table will be removed.

TIP
Set standards as outlined in Chapter 3 for variable names, and do not mimic database column names with PL/SQL variable names. Standard variable names or preceding PL/SQL variable names in SQL statements with the name of the procedure will eliminate the potentially disastrous result.

Specify Table Columns with INSERT Statements

When you develop PL/SQL code, there are several simple techniques to implement to make your code easier to read and maintain. To save time and energy, PL/SQL developers often take shortcuts. These shortcuts usually work short term, but often demonstrate a lack of foresight. One of those areas where PL/SQL developers often cut corners is leaving out the table columns with INSERT statements.

TIP
Always include listings of table columns with INSERT statements. Oracle does not force developers to specify each table column that a value is being inserted into if the number of values matches the number of columns defined for a table. Leaving out the table column names causes problems for readability and maintainability. When you attempt to view source code containing an INSERT statement without columns, it is difficult to know the columns into which the values are being inserted unless a table specification is available.

More important, if the table structure is modified, the INSERT statement often is no longer valid. An INSERT statement without column specifications must have the same number of data items with the same data types to be valid. If table columns are specified, the INSERT statement will remain valid and will not cause any PL/SQL code to encounter problems.

The following two examples illustrate the same INSERT statement. Example 1 does not contain the explicit column names. Example 2 contains the explicit column names.

```
--Example 1: Does not specify all columns included in insert statement
INSERT INTO s_customer
VALUES
(lv_cust_rec.customer_id, lv_cust_rec.customer_name,
 lv_cust_rec.phone, lv_cust_rec.address, lv_cust_rec.city,
 lv_cust_rec.state, lv_cust_rec.country, lv_cust_rec.zip_code,
 lv_cust_rec.credit_rating, lv_cust_rec.sales_rep_id,
 lv_cust_rec.region_id, lv_cust_rec.comments,
 lv_cust_rec.preferred_customer, lv_cust_rec.shipping_method);
```

```
--Example 2: Specifies all columns included in insert statement
INSERT INTO s_customer
(customer_id, customer_name,
 phone, address, city,
 state, country, zip_code,
 credit_rating, sales_rep_id,
 region_id, comments,
 preferred_customer, shipping_method)
VALUES
(lv_cust_rec.customer_id, lv_cust_rec.customer_name,
 lv_cust_rec.phone, lv_cust_rec.address, lv_cust_rec.city,
 lv_cust_rec.state, lv_cust_rec.country, lv_cust_rec.zip_code,
 lv_cust_rec.credit_rating, lv_cust_rec.sales_rep_id,
 lv_cust_rec.region_id, lv_cust_rec.comments,
 lv_cust_rec.preferred_customer, lv_cust_rec.shipping_method);
```

If you add a new column to the s_customer table, Example 1 will fail with the error *ERROR at line 1: ORA-00947: not enough values* because more columns are now in the table than referenced in the VALUES clause. In the same scenario, Example 2 will work without error, but the added column will contain a NULL value.

Use Synonyms for Portability of PL/SQL Code

For most applications, many stored PL/SQL program units are executable by all application users, both the user who owns the tables being accessed and other users who do not own the tables. Without synonyms, for a user to reference database objects owned by other users or on remote databases, the reference must include the schema name (and database link, if one exists on the database object). The use of schema names and database link names within PL/SQL source code can prove to be a maintenance nightmare. If a table is moved from one schema to another, that reference must be accounted for in all of the PL/SQL and other application code. On the other hand, if a database table were moved to another remote database, the database link reference must be modified throughout the application and PL/SQL code. The magnitude of maintenance in response to one of these changes is far too great. For these reasons, the use of synonyms is highly recommended.

A synonym creates an alternative name for a database object reference. Synonyms can reference tables, views, sequences, packages, procedures, functions, and most other database objects. They are used to make database object references less complicated and more portable. Some examples of creating PUBLIC synonyms are illustrated in the following code:

```
-- Public synonym on PLSQL_USER s_employee table on remote
-- database prod1
CREATE PUBLIC SYNONYM s_employee FOR plsql_user.s_employee@prod1;

-- Public synonym on PLSQL_USER s_customer table
CREATE PUBLIC SYNONYM s_customer FOR plsql_user.s_customer;

-- Public synonym on PLSQL_USER search_trigs procedure
CREATE PUBLIC SYNONYM search_trigs FOR plsql_user.search_trigs;

-- Public synonym on PLSQL_USER name_pkg package (now all contents
-- of the name_pkg package are accessible without preceding the calls
-- with the schema name)
CREATE PUBLIC SYNONYM name_pkg FOR plsql_user.name_pkg;
```

I strongly recommend using PUBLIC synonyms. Otherwise, the synonym is not available to all users (a non-PUBLIC synonym is only visible to the schema that created the synonym), and you must create the synonym for each user to receive the benefit of synonyms. I also strongly recommend standardization to make the name of the synonym mirror the name of the database object for which you are creating the synonym. This method eliminates unnecessary confusion and the extra layer of complexity introduced when this naming convention is not followed.

TIP
Always implement PUBLIC synonyms to reference database objects through any portion of application code, including stored PL/SQL program units. Using synonyms can be beneficial in several respects: reducing maintenance efforts, allowing for code to be portable to other databases, and developing against development schemas (only having to change the synonym object references for moving to production).

Remember, synonyms simply create alternative names for object references, and normal privileges must still be granted to those trying to access the underlying objects. If the object reference must be changed, the PL/SQL code and other application code does not need to be modified. Information pertaining to synonyms can be found in the DBA_SYNONYMS, ALL_SYNONYMS, and USER_SYNONYMS data dictionary views (see Chapter 13 and Appendix C for more on Oracle's data dictionary).

I have heard people say there is overhead in using synonyms because of an internal Oracle data dictionary step to determine the synonym reference. This overhead is negligible, and the previously outlined advantages of using synonyms far outweigh this small overhead. If performance is suffering, eliminating synonyms and using direct references is not your problem. Many other areas can be fixed before you ever change this area.

TIP

When Oracle parses statements and attempts to determine which database object is being referenced, it follows the path outlined:
- Searches current user for object existence
- Searches private synonyms for current user
- Searches PUBLIC synonyms

Use a Database Table to Make Program Units Dynamically Adjustable

PL/SQL programs invariably require revisions at some point. The revisions are to eliminate bugs, introduce new functionality, or tweak existing code. For example, when the specifications for the employee commission structure were originally written, the default commission percentage for an entry-level salesperson was three percent and should default when a new salesperson is entered in the system. If two months later, the decision is made to change this to five percent, a change must be made to the system. It was known up-front or anticipated that this percentage would change, therefore a change of this nature should *not* require a change to source code, but all too often, it does. The beauty of writing database applications is you have easy access to an object that is perfect for storing dynamic configuration information—a database table.

You can define a basic control table. Consider the following application_control table, which I have been using for years.

Column Name	Data Type	Description
app_code	VARCHAR2(20)	A unique application code used to segregate records by the application to which they belong. (This column in conjunction with the control_name column comprises the primary key.)
control_name	VARCHAR2(50)	A unique identifier within an application code. (This column, in conjunction with the app_code column, comprises the primary key.)
control_value	VARCHAR2(500)	The value associated with the unique identifier.
valid_control_values	VARCHAR2(1000)	A thorough description of the unique identifier, including any limitations on the associated values.

A GUI interface can be created to assist in manipulating the data in the application_control table. Within this table, a record should be stored for any functionality that should be adjustable at runtime. Returning to the example of the commission percentage, a record similar to the following would be added to the application_control table:

Column Name	Value
App_Code	PAYROLL SYSTEM
Control_Name	COMMISSION PERCENTAGE DEFAULT
Control_Value	3
Valid_Control_Values	The default commission percentage for entry-level salespeople.

Making Program Units Dynamically Adjustable

Making Program Units
Dynamically Adjustable

Now, the commission percentage default should be revised to retrieve the commission percentage from the application_control table each time it is referenced. The result is a program whose functionality can be adjusted dynamically without the need to revise source code.

Perhaps the most difficult part of incorporating dynamic adjustability is determining just what pieces of a program unit should be adjustable. Here are some suggestions:

- Program units driven by date windows (starting point, ending point, and range) should have the window parameters in the control table.

- Program units that drop and re-create indexes (perhaps to increase performance of a batch-load) could have the DDL statements to create the indexes in the control table. This makes implementing new storage definitions or moving the index to a different tablespace easier.

- Programs are often written to perform data analysis and report when a threshold has been exceeded. For example, a data warehouse might be analyzed with each update to identify monetary imbalances against the source system in excess of 50 cents. Any thresholds for analysis should be stored in the control table.

- Programs that rely on files outside the database system (such as files being sent via FTP to/from another system) could have the directory paths and file names stored in the control table. This creates easy implementation of directory and name changes.

- The availability of an application or one of its components could be stored in the control table. An entire application (or any module within it) should be able to be brought offline without having to contact a DBA to shut down the database listener. As users attempt to connect to modules within an application, those modules should query the control table to determine if they are online. If not, a friendly message could instruct the user to try again later. A practical implementation of this functionality is to keep users out of a query and reporting module until some type of batch update is completed.

TIP

A control table adds a tremendous amount of flexibility when an application is in production and is the easiest form of maintenance that can be performed to change the functionality of your system. I strongly recommend adding a control table for all applications. As you develop the application, think about what will most likely change over time. Rely on your experience of past applications to determine what typically changes. Most systems are similar in this area.

Use ROWID to Improve Transaction Processing Performance

Throughout your PL/SQL development, you will be asked many times to improve the performance of a PL/SQL module you developed. Improving performance of PL/SQL code you develop should be something that becomes part of your development process. Most of your PL/SQL program units contain a large percentage of PL/SQL commands and a small percentage of SQL statements, but the SQL statements are typically the portion of the PL/SQL module that consumes the majority of processing time. Therefore, SQL statements should be reviewed first to determine if improvements can be made to optimize these statements. The use of the ROWID is one potential optimization capability (refer to Chapter 7 and Chapter 8 for other SQL and PL/SQL performance tuning tips). Anytime a PL/SQL module repetitively fetches a record and then manipulates that record via SQL, the ROWID can be used. The ROWID is the fastest access method for Oracle, so ROWID should be used whenever possible.

A typical scenario where the ROWID can be used follows:

■ All employees are receiving a salary increase, but the raise is dependent on the department to which they belong and their current salary. Update the salaries based on the following criteria.

Department	10% Raise	5% Raise
10	<= $1,000	> $1,000
31	<= $1,400	> $1,400
41	<= $1,000	> $1,000
51	<= $2,000	> $2,000

The PL/SQL code to accomplish the previous logic is shown in the following:

File: 4_30.sql

```
DECLARE
   CURSOR cur_employee IS
      SELECT employee_id, department_id, NVL(salary,0) salary, ROWID
      FROM   s_employee;
   lv_record_num PLS_INTEGER DEFAULT 0;
BEGIN
   FOR lv_emp_rec IN cur_employee LOOP
      lv_record_num := lv_record_num + 1;
      -- Determining the raise amount based on raise criteria
    IF lv_emp_rec.department_id = 10 OR
       lv_emp_rec.department_id = 41 THEN
```

```
            IF lv_emp_rec.salary > 1000 THEN
                lv_emp_rec.salary := lv_emp_rec.salary * 1.05;
            ELSE
                lv_emp_rec.salary := lv_emp_rec.salary * 1.10;
            END IF;
        ELSIF lv_emp_rec.department_id = 31 THEN
            IF lv_emp_rec.salary > 1400 THEN
                lv_emp_rec.salary := lv_emp_rec.salary * 1.05;
            ELSE
                lv_emp_rec.salary := lv_emp_rec.salary * 1.10;
            END IF;
        ELSIF lv_emp_rec.department_id = 50 THEN
            IF lv_emp_rec.salary > 2000 THEN
                lv_emp_rec.salary := lv_emp_rec.salary * 1.05;
            ELSE
                lv_emp_rec.salary := lv_emp_rec.salary * 1.10;
            END IF;
        END IF;
        UPDATE s_employee
        SET    salary = lv_emp_rec.salary
        WHERE  rowid  = lv_emp_rec.ROWID;
    DBMS_OUTPUT.PUT_LINE(' Employee: '    || lv_emp_rec.employee_id  ||
        ' Department: ' || lv_emp_rec.department_id ||' New Salary: ' ||
        to_char(lv_emp_rec.salary, '$999,999.99'));
    END LOOP;
    COMMIT;
    DBMS_OUTPUT.PUT_LINE('Update Process Complete. ' ||
        lv_record_num || ' Records Processed.');
    EXCEPTION
        WHEN OTHERS THEN
            DBMS_OUTPUT.PUT_LINE('Error on Record ' || lv_record_num ||
            ': Update Process Aborted.');
            ROLLBACK;
END;
/
```

Each employee record is selected, the new salary is determined, and then the employee record is updated. The ROWID is selected and then used to update the employee record with the new salary. If the entire employee table is processed successfully, the process is committed. If any errors occur in the update process, the process is rolled back and an error logged to the screen of the record being processed. The IF logic in this PL/SQL module has a lot of redundancy, which can be enhanced by turning the IF logic into a function and calling it for each employee.

TIP
When looping through cursor records and then performing DML statements on the selected tables, select the ROWID as an additional column. The use of the ROWID pseudo-column in SQL statements provides the fastest possible performance. Refer to Chapter 2 for more details on the Oracle ROWID.

Use FOR UPDATE to LOCK Records for Transaction Processing

The FOR UPDATE clause, which is available for use with explicitly defined cursors, is a valuable option when you need to lock a small segment of records and ensure they do not change throughout transactional processing. Using the FOR UPDATE clause within a cursor forces an explicit lock to be placed on each of the records in the result set when the cursor is opened, not when the cursor is declared. The records are then locked until there is a transaction command (for example, COMMIT or ROLLBACK) performed. When using the FOR UPDATE clause, the open cursor statement first checks all the records in the result set to ensure no locks exist on any of these records. If no current row-level locks exist on all records in the result set, then a row-level lock will be placed on all the records in the result set. At this point, other users can query any of the records in the result set you currently have locked, but they will be unable to modify them until you issue a COMMIT or ROLLBACK. If other users query any of the records in your result set, they will see the record as it was when you queried the record, not any changes you may have pending.

If the open cursor statement finds a lock on any of the records, the process will be placed in a wait state until all the row-level locks are released by the locking session. Once the locks are released (by a transaction command), the process previously outlined takes place.

Once your cursor is opened and all the records are locked, if a COMMIT or ROLLBACK is performed prior to processing all records in the result set, then an attempt to fetch the next record will result in the Oracle error *ORA-01002: fetch out of sequence.* This error occurs because the COMMIT or ROLLBACK released the record locks and invalidated the FOR UPDATE cursor. No transaction command, not even the use of SAVEPOINTS, can be implemented when the FOR UPDATE cursor is active. For this reason, this clause is only good for small sets of records, where small is relative to the size of your rollback segment (refer to the next section on rollback segments for more information) storing the changed records for read consistency. The size of records that can be processed in this manner, therefore, is dependent on your system's configuration.

In the previous section, a PL/SQL progam unit was developed to update salaries for all employees. The ROWID was used to improve processing performance. The ROWID can be used with the FOR UPDATE statement, as well to obtain the performance gain as outlined.

If we look at the previous PL/SQL program unit, when we did not use the FOR UPDATE clause on the cur_employee cursor, what would happen if another user had a lock on employee record 25? The following order of events would have occurred

- The cursor FOR LOOP would have executed the open cursor, which would have selected all the records in the s_employee table into the result set.

- Each employee would have been fetched, one by one, and the IF logic that updates the salaries would have been performed. For each employee, the UPDATE statement would have been executed until employee record 25 was fetched.

- At this point, an attempt to UPDATE employee record 25 would have been made. When an UPDATE was attempted, Oracle internally performs the same function as a FOR UPDATE on a SELECT statement; therefore, Oracle would attempt to lock employee record 25. When Oracle determines that employee record 25 is locked, it waits until the lock is released.

- Once the lock is released, the employee record 25 is updated to the new salary.

Therein lies the problem! What if the salary were $1,100 when my process performed the open cursor? Then I would have updated the salary to $1,155 (1.05 * $1,100) based on the salary update logic. If the process holding the lock at the time I attempted the UPDATE updated the salary to $1,200 and committed, then I would effectively have overwritten the change. Unless this is your intent, this is a problem.

If my process used the FOR UPDATE in the cur_employee cursor, however, the end result of the previous scenario would have been that employee record 25 would have been updated to $1,280 (1.05 * $1,200). This would typically be what I wanted. The reason for the different outcome is my process would *not* have been able to retrieve the result set until the other session had released the record. Once my process locked all the records, then no other user could modify the records in my result set until I released them.

To accomplish the FOR UPDATE, the only segment of the PL/SQL code from the previous section I must change is the cursor; this is illustrated in the following declaration:

```
DECLARE
  CURSOR cur_employee IS
    SELECT employee_id, department_id, NVL(salary,0) salary, ROWID
    FROM   s_employee
    FOR UPDATE;              -- Only modification
  lv_record_num PLS_INTEGER DEFAULT 0;
BEGIN
```

TIP
When the FOR UPDATE clause is used, Oracle enables the use of a WHEN CURRENT OF clause to be used with an UPDATE or DELETE statement to reference the current record. Even though this works, I recommend the use of the ROWID over this use because the ROWID works whether the FOR UPDATE is used, and it is faster.

The FOR UPDATE is a valuable command extension to cursors in PL/SQL to ensure information does not change until processing is complete. The size of the result set that can be processed in your environment with the FOR UPDATE depends on your environment.

One problem of the FOR UPDATE is when you are put in a wait state. You are not notified of this condition; your process just sits there. If your PL/SQL process typically takes several hours to complete, you would never know your process was waiting. I have seen this happen many times in a production environment: a nightly PL/SQL process executes that uses the FOR UPDATE clause and a user on the system leaves at the end of the day in the middle of a Form where he or she made a change and did not COMMIT. In this case, if the nightly process was attempting to lock that record in the result set, the process would never execute. What makes this scenario even more painful is the process just sits there with no feedback to anyone that it is waiting on a record lock.

How do you ensure this is not happening in your nightly processes?

■ Do not use the FOR UPDATE unless you must. You only have to use a FOR UPDATE if you are selecting records and then performing an UPDATE or DELETE on them, one by one. This occurs more in batch-type processes.

LOCKing Records for Transaction Processing

■ If you are using the FOR UPDATE, use the NOWAIT argument on this clause (FOR UPDATE NOWAIT) to force your program to return an Oracle error *ORA-00054: resource busy and acquire with NOWAIT specified* if the open cursor is unable to lock the entire result set. This method at least signifies to the user that someone is holding a lock on the record set desired.

If you are in the following situation, an alternative technique must be implemented:

■ You are querying records and are either updating or deleting them

■ The process is taking several hours

■ You want to ensure that from the time the open cursor is executed (result set created) to the time you modify the records in the result set, the information has not changed

■ You either do not have the configuration to support the locking of a large result set or locking the records during the day would impede operations

You can deploy the following technique to ensure you are updating the most recent version of the record and you do not impede daily transactional processing. A good example of this situation is when a nightly process does not complete for some reason and must be executed during the day.

File: 4_31.sql

```
DECLARE
   -- Declared prior to the cursor reference
   lv_prev_rowid ROWID;
   -- Main query for all employee records
   CURSOR cur_employee IS
      SELECT employee_id, department_id, NVL(salary,0) salary, ROWID
      FROM   s_employee;
   -- Queries the current employee record to get the most up to date
   -- contents of the record and locks the record
   CURSOR cur_employee_lock IS
      SELECT employee_id, department_id, NVL(salary,0) salary
      FROM   s_employee
      WHERE  rowid = lv_prev_rowid
      FOR UPDATE NOWAIT;              -- Attempts to lock the record
   lv_record_num number DEFAULT 0;
   lv_failed_num number DEFAULT 0;
   lv_emp_rec    cur_employee_lock%ROWTYPE;
BEGIN
   FOR lv_emp_nolock_rec IN cur_employee LOOP
```

```
     lv_record_num := lv_record_num + 1;
     lv_prev_rowid := lv_emp_nolock_rec.rowid;
     BEGIN  -- Must create another block to trap NOWAIT error
        OPEN cur_employee_lock; -- Requery record-FOR UPDATE NOWAIT
        FETCH cur_employee_lock into lv_emp_rec;
        -- Determining the raise amount based on conditions
        IF lv_emp_rec.department_id = 10 OR
           lv_emp_rec.department_id = 41 THEN
           IF lv_emp_rec.salary > 1000 THEN
              lv_emp_rec.salary := lv_emp_rec.salary * 1.05;
           ELSE
              lv_emp_rec.salary := lv_emp_rec.salary * 1.10;
           END IF;
        ELSIF lv_emp_rec.department_id = 31 THEN
           IF lv_emp_rec.salary > 1400 THEN
              lv_emp_rec.salary := lv_emp_rec.salary * 1.05;
           ELSE
              lv_emp_rec.salary := lv_emp_rec.salary * 1.10;
           END IF;
        ELSIF lv_emp_rec.department_id = 50 THEN
           IF lv_emp_rec.salary > 2000 THEN
              lv_emp_rec.salary := lv_emp_rec.salary * 1.05;
           ELSE
              lv_emp_rec.salary := lv_emp_rec.salary * 1.10;
           END IF;
        END IF;
        UPDATE s_employee
        SET    salary = lv_emp_rec.salary
        WHERE  rowid  = lv_emp_nolock_rec.rowid;
        DBMS_OUTPUT.PUT_LINE(' Employee: '     ||
           lv_emp_rec.employee_id   || ' Department: '  ||
           lv_emp_rec.department_id || ' New Salary: '  ||
           to_char(lv_emp_rec.salary, '$999,999.99'));
        CLOSE cur_employee_lock;
        COMMIT;
     EXCEPTION
        WHEN OTHERS THEN
           DBMS_OUTPUT.PUT_LINE('***** Employee Id: ' ||
              lv_emp_nolock_rec.employee_id ||
              ' Not Processed Due to Lock *****');
           lv_failed_num := lv_failed_num + 1;
           ROLLBACK; -- Rollback any records with errors
           IF cur_employee_lock%ISOPEN THEN
              CLOSE cur_employee_lock;
           END IF;
     END;
END LOOP;
lv_record_num := lv_record_num - lv_failed_num;
```

LOCKing Records for Transaction Processing

```
    DBMS_OUTPUT.PUT_LINE('Update Process Complete. ' ||
        lv_record_num || ' Records Processed.');
    DBMS_OUTPUT.PUT_LINE(lv_failed_num || ' Records Not Processed.');
EXCEPTION
    WHEN OTHERS THEN
        DBMS_OUTPUT.PUT_LINE('Error on Record ' || lv_record_num ||
            ': Update Process Aborted.');
        ROLLBACK;
END;
/
```

The preceding PL/SQL program unit performs the following:

- Creates a result set without locking the records, which is necessary to ensure the entire set of records you want to change is processed.

- Does not lock any records until the time each record is processed.

- Queries the record to be processed a second time and locks the record with the FOR UPDATE clause (this ensures when a record is processed, it has the most recent information and the record will be locked).

- Skips records currently locked by another session. In this code, it does not handle these locked records. A more robust technique would be to log the ROWID of locked records that are not processed to a PL/SQL table and then, at the end of this process, loop back through the records in the PL/SQL table and process them. If a record is still locked, the record could be recorded to a log file or inserted into a database table for further handling.

- Commits for each record, but avoids the FOR UPDATE error because this cursor only fetches one record.

This PL/SQL program unit does have additional overhead associated with it because it queries each record twice, but it is a viable and extremely valuable solution when faced with this difficult scenario.

 TIP
The FOR UPDATE clause enables you to specify columns as attributes (FOR UPDATE OF col1,col2) to specify the columns you will be updating. I recommend leaving this attribute off because it adds little value. With or without the column specification, the records are locked and you can update any column in the database table.

TIP

The last PL/SQL program unit presented in this section provides a valuable solution to executing large PL/SQL batch processing routines during production hours without locking large segments of records, thus, without affecting other users.

Choose Large Rollback Segments When Processing Large Transaction Sets

When performing large amounts of DML statements (INSERT, UPDATE, and DELETE) a critical decision needs to be made. Should one COMMIT be performed at the end of the entire process or should a COMMIT be performed periodically? Committing once at the end of the process is typically much safer. If the process failed anywhere during execution, it can be rerun and started over. On the other hand, if commits were being performed throughout the execution, often just rerunning the process can cause undesired results. Logical methods exist to track the commits and to develop a mechanism for restarting the process at the point of failure. The complexity of developing this type of logic is entirely dependent on the specific process.

Devising a method to restart the process can be created and, if the process is a long running routine, this would be the preferred method to deploy. This way, if the process does abort, restarting it will not eliminate the time it was already processing. Remember, the method of restarting a process where it left off must be logically sound to ensure accuracy.

This section explores the option of committing once at the end of the process. If the process involves processing large amounts of data, then one COMMIT at the end of the execution may never work. Remember, the total size of all the transactions since the last COMMIT in a session must fit into a single rollback segment. For large transaction sets, normal-sized rollback segments most likely will not be large enough. In cases where the rollback segment is not large enough, the *ORA-01562: failed to extend rollback segment number 7* and *ORA-01628: max # extents (2) reached for rollback segment RB_1* errors will occur. These errors are not limited to DML operations and could appear when a query contains an extremely large result set.

Typical rollback segments are designed for transaction processing (large numbers of small transactions); therefore, they are often too small for special processing of large transaction sets. Therefore, a few larger sized rollback segments must be created to handle the larger processing and larger transaction sets. Once larger rollback segments are created, the PL/SQL programs must be modified to use these segments specifically. If the rollback segment is not specified in the program, then the session executing the program will function like all other sessions and be assigned to a rollback segment automatically by Oracle.

Oracle provides a SET command to allow the rollback segment to be specified. In SQL*Plus, the following illustrates the use of the SET command to choose a specific rollback segment for a transaction:

File: 4_32.sql

```
-- RB_BIG will be used for the update transaction
COMMIT;
SET TRANSACTION USE ROLLBACK SEGMENT rb_big;
UPDATE s_employee
SET    salary = NVL(salary, 0) * 1.10;
COMMIT;
```

In PL/SQL, however, the SET command is unavailable. In PL/SQL, the Oracle supplied packages DBMS_SQL or DBMS_TRANSACTION must be used. See Chapter 11 and Chapter 12 for more information regarding Oracle's supplied packages.

TIP

Implement the DBMS_TRANSACTION.USE_ROLLBACK_SEGMENT procedure to choose a rollback segment large enough to handle the size of the transaction set. Call this procedure before new transactions take place and after any intermediate commits or rollbacks occur. This will ensure the specified rollback segment will be used to store the pending transactions.

The following statement is an example implementation of using this procedure.

```
DBMS_TRANSACTION.USE_ROLLBACK_SEGMENT('rb_big');
```

Typically, large rollback segments used only for special processing are created in separate tablespaces and have very large initial extent sizes. The reason for the large initial extent size is to eliminate the overhead of allocating space as the segment grows and to eliminate the overhead of fragmentation.

The data dictionary view, DBA_ROLLBACK_SEGS, can be queried to check rollback segment sizes, as well as to determine whether the rollback segments are online. If an attempt is made to use a rollback segment that is not online, then the *ORA-01598: rollback segment 'RB_BIG' is not online* error occurs. If a rollback segment is only to be used by special processing, it can be dynamically put online, using the DBMS_SQL package. The DDL statement, *ALTER ROLLBACK SEGMENT segment_name ONLINE*, can be dynamically created and executed with the DBMS_SQL package. See Chapters 11 and 12 for further explanation of the DBMS_SQL package.

The following is a generic procedure, using DBMS_SQL, to perform basic DDL and DCL statements, as well as to exemplify putting a rollback segment online:

File: 4_33.sql

```
CREATE OR REPLACE PROCEDURE exec_ddl
   (p_statement_txt VARCHAR2) IS
-- This procedure provides a way to dynamically perform any
-- DDL statements from within your normal PL/SQL processing.
   lv_exec_cursor_num    PLS_INTEGER := DBMS_SQL.OPEN_CURSOR;
   lv_rows_processed_num NUMBER := 0;
   lv_statement_txt      VARCHAR2(30000);
BEGIN
   lv_statement_txt := p_statement_txt;
   DBMS_SQL.PARSE (lv_exec_cursor_num, lv_statement_txt,
      DBMS_SQL.NATIVE);
   lv_rows_processed_num := DBMS_SQL.EXECUTE (lv_exec_cursor_num);
   DBMS_SQL.CLOSE_CURSOR (lv_exec_cursor_num);
EXCEPTION
   WHEN OTHERS THEN
      IF DBMS_SQL.IS_OPEN (lv_exec_cursor_num) THEN
         DBMS_SQL.CLOSE_CURSOR (lv_exec_cursor_num);
      END IF;
   RAISE;
END exec_ddl;
/
```

```
-- Example implementation of the exec_ddl procedure
EXECUTE exec_ddl ('ALTER ROLLBACK SEGMENT rb_big ONLINE')
```

The necessary system privileges must be granted to users implementing these techniques, and these operations are usually controlled by the DBA.

A little-known fact is Oracle uses rollback segments during the processing of cursors, even if no DML statements are being issued from within the cursor loop. The rollback segments are being used as a type of work area as a cursor loop is being executed. Thus, having a cursor loop fail if a rollback segment of insufficient size is used to read the cursor is quite possible. The failure does not occur immediately; it happens only after numerous iterations of the cursor loop have been performed. Because the error message returned is the same as what would be returned when a single DML statement fails, many developers are fooled into thinking the error lies elsewhere in their code. Valiant efforts are made to manage transaction sizes properly within the cursor loops, but to no avail. To open a large cursor successfully, setting a large rollback segment just prior to the opening of the cursor is imperative.

TIP
If you are manipulating large sets of records between transactions, make sure to assign the transaction to a rollback segment. This will ensure completion without receiving an error for exceeding the rollback segment size. Any time a COMMIT or ROLLBACK is executed, the rollback segment used for the transaction is released. Therefore, if a process commits periodically during large transactions, the rollback segment assignment command must be included in the process after every COMMIT.

Use a Counter to Limit Size of Transactions per COMMIT

As mentioned in the previous section, a process that creates numerous transactions (DML operations) can overflow the size of the current rollback segment. In many cases, with transaction processing, no dependence exists upon previously processed transactions. In this case, it is possible and desirable to commit transactions at certain time intervals throughout the processing. More important, during longer processes containing DML statements (UPDATEs and DELETEs), a row-level lock is placed on each record modified and, therefore, these record modifications are invisible to other sessions until the locks are released. These locks are released when a COMMIT or ROLLBACK occurs, so performing commits throughout this type of processing can limit the number of locked rows within tables at any given time.

TIP
Implement the use of a counter to perform a COMMIT for a specified number of transactions. This technique is most commonly implemented within loops, particularly those based on cursors. Deciding on the interval size of committing transactions is dependent upon the size of the transactions and your Oracle and application configuration. Many PL/SQL developers choose to commit every time through a loop, which is unnecessary. When a COMMIT occurs and additional transactions occur, Oracle flushes the rollback segment information and chooses another rollback segment for the next transaction. Although this process of flushing rollback segments and switching to others is quick, it introduces overhead that can be avoided by only committing at periodic intervals.

Performing a COMMIT every 100 (the higher the better; I generally test this to determine what to use for different systems; I prefer using 1,000 as a standard) records processed should not cause rollback segment problems on most systems. Again, this is an arbitrary number chosen to reduce the number of rollback segment switches significantly, as well as to ensure all transactions within that set can be processed by one rollback segment.

Remember, commits cannot occur within a loop involving cursors selected with the FOR UPDATE clause.

The following example illustrates the technique of committing at regular intervals during lengthy transaction processing.

File: 4_34.sql

```
CREATE OR REPLACE PROCEDURE salary_update
   (p_dept_num              s_employee.department_id%TYPE,
    p_update_percentage_num NUMBER,
    p_commit_interval_num   NUMBER := 100) IS

  CURSOR cur_salary (p_department_num s_employee.department_id%TYPE)
    IS
    SELECT employee_id, NVL(salary,0) salary, rowid
```

```
     FROM    s_employee
     WHERE   department_id = p_department_num
     ORDER BY employee_id;
   lv_counter_num    PLS_INTEGER := 0;
   lv_error_code     NUMBER;
   lv_error_message VARCHAR2(150);
BEGIN
   FOR lv_salary_rec IN cur_salary (p_dept_num) LOOP
      -- Increment transaction counter
      lv_counter_num := lv_counter_num + 1;
      -- Update each employee salary with the p_update_percentage_num
      UPDATE s_employee
      SET salary = salary * NVL(1 + p_update_percentage_num/100, 1)
      WHERE rowid = lv_salary_rec.ROWID;
      -- Perform commit every commit_interval as passed to procedure
      IF MOD(lv_counter_num, p_commit interval_num) = 0 THEN
         DBMS_OUTPUT.PUT_LINE('Commit at Record: ' || lv_counter_num);
         COMMIT;
      END IF;
   END LOOP;
   -- Perform commit for any outstanding transactions
   DBMS_OUTPUT.PUT_LINE('Commit at Record: ' || lv_counter_num);
   COMMIT;
   DBMS_OUTPUT.PUT_LINE('Process Complete.');
   EXCEPTION
      WHEN OTHERS THEN
          DBMS_OUTPUT.PUT_LINE('Process Aborted at Record: ' ||
             lv_counter_num);
          ROLLBACK;
          lv_error_code := SQLCODE;
          lv_error_message := SUBSTR(SQLERRM, 1, 150);
          DBMS_OUTPUT.PUT_LINE('Error Code: ' || lv_error_code);
          DBMS_OUTPUT.PUT_LINE('Error Message: ' || lv_error_message);
END salary_update;
/
```

Output (4_34.sql)

```
-- 7% Raise for Dept 41, commit every 5 recs
EXECUTE salary_update(41,7,5)

Commit at Record: 5
Commit at Record: 10
Commit at Record: 15
Commit at Record: 16
Process Complete.

PL/SQL procedure successfully completed.
```

```
-- 7% Raise for Dept 41 commit every 100 recs
EXECUTE salary_update(41,7)

Commit at Record: 16
Process Complete.

PL/SQL procedure successfully completed.
```

```
-- Same as previous
EXECUTE salary_update(41,7,0)

Commit at Record: 16
Process Complete.

PL/SQL procedure successfully completed.
```

```
-- 100000000 Raise for Dept 41
EXECUTE salary_update(41,100000000)

Process Aborted at Record: 1
Error Code: -1438
Error Message: ORA-01438: value larger than specified precision
allows for this column

PL/SQL procedure successfully completed.
```

TIP
*Evaluate your processes and, if possible, COMMIT
periodically based on your system configuration. When
you COMMIT periodically, however, log the commit
point information to ensure that if the process aborts,
you are able to restart the process at the point of failure.*

TIP
*Regarding transaction processing, make sure you
control all commits and rollbacks. The commits are
usually easy, but make sure you are handling
unanticipated errors and providing the desired
transaction control when errors occur.*

Develop a Monitoring Facility for Long-running Processes

When a PL/SQL program unit is executing, which spans more than ten minutes, you
should establish a monitoring facility to determine the progress of the process. This

is extremely important if the program you are executing is performing any data manipulation, which means your process may have to wait for someone else or vice versa.

The DBMS_OUTPUT package is the most frequently used of Oracle's supplied PL/SQL packages. This package simply provides the capability to send text output to the screen through a message buffer. The DBMS_OUTPUT.PUT_LINE procedure is most commonly used to send a character string to the message buffer, as implemented in the following example:

File: 4_35.sql

```
SET SERVEROUTPUT ON SIZE 1000000
BEGIN
    DBMS_OUTPUT.PUT_LINE('Procedure Starting...');
    FOR lv_counter_num in 1..100000 LOOP
        NULL;
    END LOOP;
    DBMS_OUTPUT.PUT_LINE('Procedure Complete.');
END;
/
```

A problem arises when real-time feedback is desired. DBMS_OUTPUT package does not provide this type of functionality. The DBMS_OUTPUT package flushes the message buffer at completion or interruption of the program that is executing, not when the DBMS_OUTPUT.PUT_LINE statement is executed. In the previous example, the following processing occurred.

- ■ "Procedure Starting..." was placed in the message buffer

- ■ The FOR LOOP executed

- ■ "Procedure Complete." was placed in the message buffer

- ■ The PL/SQL block completed (END statement executed)

- ■ The two messages were flushed from the message buffer and displayed to the screen

If an error had occured in the FOR LOOP, then the process would have been aborted and the first message would have been flushed from the message buffer and displayed to the screen, followed by the error message. In summary, real-time information cannot be displayed to the screen using the DBMS_OUTPUT package during processing.

The simplicity and usefulness of the DBMS_OUTPUT package causes most PL/SQL developers to implement the package as their primary debugging process. For most scenarios where quick and dirty debugging is necessary, this package will suffice. In most complex production environments, however, the PL/SQL processing is usually much harder to follow and debug. This also applies to commonly executed PL/SQL program units that take long periods to execute.

When routines are executing over long periods of time, what is helpful and often necessary to know is how long the process has been executing and how far along the process is so you can determine the remaining time to completion. How embarrassing to tell someone a process will be complete in one hour and then five hours later, the process is still running!

To fulfill this need of providing information during a long-executing PL/SQL program, four methods can be implemented:

- Log information to a database table at specified intervals.

- Log information to an operating system file using the Oracle package UTL_FILE at specified intervals.

- Log information to a pipe and read from the pipe using the Oracle package DBMS_PIPE at specified intervals.

- Log information to the V$SESSION view describing the execution time and progress using the Oracle package DBMS_APPLICATION_INFO at specified intervals.

The method of logging information to a database table is demonstrated in this section. The other three methods are described in more detail in Chapter 8 and Chapter 12. There are caveats to all four methods; therefore, you must determine what will work best in your environment.

If you want to log information to a database table, you must perform a COMMIT periodically. The example in the previous section would be a common type of program in which this technique would be used. In this scenario, we are processing employee records and updating salaries for departments. Assuming the departments have thousands of employees (more than our example s_employee table), knowing where the process is once started would be ideal. Every time a COMMIT is performed, you can log the time and number of total records committed, the same as the DBMS_OUTPUT.PUT_LINE call. We would perform the following steps:

- Create an employee log table with four columns (user, date, time, and number of records committed)

- Modify the salary_update procedure to INSERT a record into the employee log table every time a COMMIT is performed

The code for both of these is illustrated next.

Developing a Monitoring Facility

File: 4_36.sql

```
-- Creates the employee log table
CREATE TABLE EMPLOYEE_PROCESS_LOG
(PROCESS_USER        VARCHAR2(30),
 PROCESS_DATE        DATE,
 PROCESS_TIME        VARCHAR2(6),
 RECORDS_PROCESSED NUMBER(10));
```

```
-- The INSERT replaces the DBMS_OUTPUT.PUT_LINE calls
CREATE OR REPLACE PROCEDURE salary_update
    (p_dept_num s_employee.department_id%TYPE,
     p_update_percentage_num NUMBER,
     p_commit_interval_num NUMBER := 100) IS
 .       .       .       .       .       .       .
 .       .       .       .       .       .       .
    IF MOD(lv_counter_num, p_commit_interval_num) = 0 THEN
       INSERT INTO EMPLOYEE_PROCESS_LOG
           (process_user, process_date, process_time,
           records_processed)
       VALUES
           (USER, TRUNC(SYSDATE), TO_CHAR(SYSDATE, 'HH24MISS'),
           lv_counter_num);
       COMMIT;
    END IF;
 .       .       .       .       .       .       .
 .       .       .       .       .       .       .
END salary_update;
/
```

When the salary_update procedure is executed, the employee_process_log table can be queried to verify how far along the procedure is at any time. One record will be logged to this table at the COMMIT interval. This technique is extremely valuable for monitoring long-running processes.

This technique can be used in any situation where you want to monitor a process and you can perform commits at periodic intervals. The commits should not interfere with any other processing logic and should be placed in your PL/SQL processing where it makes sense and after the functionality is coded. This technique can be enhanced in several ways, a few of which follow: to delete all records in the log table at the beginning of the program; to become a generic logging mechanism by adding a procedure name column to the process log database table; to log start and end statuses.

TIP
Always build a monitoring mechanism into your PL/SQL modules if they take more than ten minutes to complete processing. This is a powerful mechanism, which will always enable you to monitor processing and recognize when a problem exists that normally would not be detected as easily.

Summary

In this chapter, we highlighted important standard PL/SQL coding techniques. This chapter can be combined with Chapter 3 and Chapter 5 to form a PL/SQL Development Foundation. This PL/SQL Development Foundation provides a robust set of standards and techniques that can, and should, be deployed in most PL/SQL development environments.

Developing a PL/SQL Development Foundation in your environment is imperative. This is critical to ensure your application core, namely, PL/SQL developed code is functional, consistent, readable, maintainable, dynamic, flexible, and efficient. Once your PL/SQL Development Foundation is established, the next step is the education of your current development staff (and future staff, as they come aboard). Finally, the hardest task of all is to enforce the Development Foundation.

Tips Review

- Creating a PUBLIC synonym on all production objects (tables, views, sequences, stored PL/SQL objects, and so forth) is recommended to eliminate the need to precede object references with the username. This also improves application portability and flexibility.

- Always name the synonyms the same as the underlying object.

- Execution of standard application scripts to learn the application schema saves valuable development time in the long run. Schema changes should be communicated to all team members when made.

- An UPDATE and DELETE statement first performs a SELECT to fetch the records being manipulated and then performs the UPDATE or DELETE operation. An UPDATE and DELETE, therefore, can be changed to a SELECT statement first to review the result set that is going to be manipulated to ensure these statements are manipulating the desired records.

Tips Review

■ When a database table is modified in any manner, any stored PL/SQL objects such as packages, procedures, function, and triggers that reference that object become INVALID. After making a table change, therefore, make sure to check the INVALID objects (shown in Chapters 5, 9, and 13) and recompile these INVALID objects. Oracle automatically recompiles the stored object when the next call to this object occurs. The compilation can fail, however, and this failure will occur during production hours if you do not manually handle the recompilation to ensure all objects recompile without error.

■ Always make database changes (tables, stored objects, and so forth) during off-hours to ensure all system objects are recompiled and revalidated prior to production.

■ Attempt to use type casting with database columns whenever possible.

■ The %TYPE and %ROWTYPE only assign the referenced data type to the PL/SQL variable and do not mirror the characteristics related to NOT NULL or default values.

■ When possible, default PL/SQL variables to avoid hidden NULL value problems. Remember, the default assignment is very flexible because it allows use of any function available in the PL/SQL, including any functions you created.

■ The DBMS_OUTPUT.PUT_LINE procedure is overloaded and can accept either a character, numeric, or date data type. If you want to mix values to pass to this function, use the TO_DATE, TO_NUMBER, and TO_CHAR functions.

■ Any PL/SQL block can be labeled by adding a label identifier prior to the DECLARE statement. This adds flexibility in uniquely identifying a variable if the same variable is used in an outer or nested block. It is not needed by default because Oracle determines the variable you are referring to by the name and scope, but it is available for readability and referencing an outer variable.

■ If you have any doubt of how NULL values and DATE data types work and should be handled, go directly to Chapter 2 and review the conditions. Both issues must be understood and addressed proactively. NULL is not equal to anything, not even another NULL value. Default all PL/SQL variables when possible and use the NVL function to assist in addressing this NULL problem. TRUNCate all dates when possible and remember the SYSDATE variable contains the date and time. Instead of having to remember to truncate this date, set a package variable and reference this variable.

- If a DATE variable has a time other than midnight (00:00:00), then the comparison condition performed to verify if the DATE value is within a specific date range should set the low-range date time value to 00:00:00 and the high-range date time value to 23:59:59.

- Enable the server output buffer to log DBMS_OUTPUT.PUT_LINE calls to assist in debugging and screen I/O when in SQL*Plus. Remember, the maximum buffer size is 1,000,000 bytes and the maximum line length that can be written to the buffer is 255 bytes.

- In SQL*Plus, you can wrap the output of the DBMS_OUTPUT.PUTLINE procedure on a word by using the FORMAT WORD_WRAPPED attribute on the SET SERVEROUTPUT command. The line wrapping is dependent on the setting of the LINESIZE parameter.

- I strongly recommend using DBMS_OUTPUT.PUT_LINE for message display or screen display with the intent that this display is used only in SQL*Plus for debugging and testing with the SET SERVEROUTPUT ON command executed. NEVER use the DBMS_OUTPUT.ENABLE in your PL/SQL coding because this introduces the potential for hidden errors. Turn the buffer on and off with the SET command in SQL*Plus. You can leave your DBMS_OUTPUT.PUT_LINE statements in your code and they will have no effect unless the message buffer is enabled.

- If you want to buffer information while processing for later use, use the PL/SQL table structure available in PL/SQL, do not use the message buffer with DBMS_OUTPUT.PUT_LINE, GET_LINE, and ENABLE. You will have far greater control over the PL/SQL table, and you will not have to worry about overflowing the message buffer.

- Always close the cursors that you open for performance reasons. Every cursor requires memory. If the cursor is no longer needed, close it. Remember to do this in your error-handling routines. Prior to executing the CLOSE statement, the ISOPEN cursor attribute can be checked to make sure an attempt is not made to close an already closed cursor. If a close is attempted on a closed cursor, an error will be raised: *ORA-01001: invalid cursor.*

- Use cursor FOR LOOPs to create less error-prone code and eliminate extra code inherently handled with the use of this command. Any time Oracle internally performs operations for you without adding overhead, without eliminating control, and without forcing you to add more code in the long run, let it. One of your goals of developing in PL/SQL should always be reduce code volume, which reduces the possibility for runtime errors.

■ If a cursor is only being used to check for existence (one record exists), use the OPEN, FETCH, CLOSE statements. The cursor FOR LOOP always performs at least two fetches because it must know when there are no more records.

■ If two PL/SQL records were created with exactly the same structure (for example, exact column names and data types), they are considered two distinct PL/SQL record types. Therefore, an error would occur if an attempt was made to set two PL/SQL record types variable equal to each other, even if they had exactly the same definition.

■ Use the speed of PL/SQL tables to limit the number of lookups performed against the database. Accessing information contained within a PL/SQL table (in memory) is considerably faster than accessing information from a database table. This is because the data being stored in memory for PL/SQL tables. The ideal candidate database table is one that has limited records with a numeric unique key. This unique key can be loaded as the array index for index searches. If the lookup is not on the array index, the process by which the information in PL/SQL tables is searched is a little more involved. Procedures and functions can be set up to make this process easier, and the time spent to develop these modules is worth the performance improvements realized.

■ Cursor parameters should be viewed in the same manner as procedures that pass parameters: define them when it is necessary to make the cursor dynamic and to eliminate hardcoding. Likewise, cursor parameters can also have default values assigned when declared and when opening the cursor, the same default rules apply as procedures.

■ Implement the generic functionality provided by cursor variables for similar queries or in cases where a cursor may be opened numerous ways, but always follows through the same processing. Cursor variables have several similar properties as normal variables, allowing them to be passed as parameters to procedures and functions. These properties are what make cursor variables good for generalizing PL/SQL code.

■ PL/SQL REF CURSORs were introduced with PL/SQL 2.2 and greatly enhanced with PL/SQL 2.3. PL/SQL REF CURSORs provide a great deal of flexibility and can be used when this type of flexibility is needed. Several rules surround their use and must be considered. I would not recommend using this feature until you are on PL/SQL 2.3.

■ Cursor variables (REF CURSORs) are an attractive feature and offer extreme flexibility, but I recommend using them with caution. Use cursor variables only when they are truly needed. Remember, the more flexible something is, the more prone it is to error, unless used and tested properly.

■ In Oracle 8.0, the VARCHAR2 maximum length is increased from 2,000 characters to 4,000.

■ Use 32K-length PL/SQL VARCHAR2 variables to search LONG database columns that are less than 32K in length. In many cases, text stored within a LONG database column is less than 32K in length, enabling you to implement this functionality.

■ Set standards as outlined in Chapter 3 for variable names, and do not mimic database column names with PL/SQL variable names. Standard variable names or preceding PL/SQL variable names in SQL statements with the name of the procedure will eliminate the potentially disastrous result.

■ Always include listings of table columns with INSERT statements.

■ Always implement PUBLIC synonyms to reference database objects through any portion of application code, including stored PL/SQL program units. Using synonyms can be beneficial in several respects: reducing maintenance efforts, allowing for code to be portable to other databases, and developing against development schemas (only having to change the synonym object references for moving to production).

■ When Oracle parses statements and attempts to determine which database object is being referenced, it follows the path outlined:

  - Searches current user for object existence
  - Searches private synonyms for current user
  - Searches PUBLIC synonyms

■ A control table adds a tremendous amount of flexibility when an application is in production and is the easiest form of maintenance that can be performed to change the functionality of your system. I strongly recommend adding a control table for all applications.

■ When looping through cursor records and then performing DML statements on the selected tables, select the ROWID as an additional column. The use of the ROWID pseudo-column in SQL statements provides the fastest possible performance. Refer to Chapter 2 for more details on the Oracle ROWID.

Tips Review

■ When the FOR UPDATE clause is used, Oracle enables the use of a WHEN CURRENT OF clause to be used with an UPDATE or DELETE statement to reference the current record. Even though this works, I recommend the use of the ROWID over this use because the ROWID works whether or not the FOR UPDATE is used, and it is faster.

■ The FOR UPDATE clause enables you to specify columns as attributes (FOR UPDATE OF col1,col2) to specify the columns you will be updating. I recommend leaving this attribute off because it adds little value. With or without the column specification, the records are locked and you can update any column in the database table.

■ Implement the DBMS_TRANSACTION.USE_ROLLBACK_SEGMENT procedure to choose a rollback segment large enough to handle the size of the transaction set. Call this procedure before new transactions take place and after any intermediate commits or rollbacks occur. This will ensure the specified rollback segment will be used to store the pending transactions.

■ If you are manipulating large sets of records between transactions, make sure to assign the transaction to a rollback segment. This will ensure completion without receiving an error for exceeding the rollback segment size. Any time a COMMIT or ROLLBACK is executed, the rollback segment used for the transaction is released. Therefore, if a process commits periodically during large transactions, the rollback segment assignment command must be included in the process after every COMMIT.

■ Implement the use of a counter to perform a COMMIT for a specified number of transactions.

■ Evaluate your processes and, if possible, COMMIT periodically based on your system configuration. When you COMMIT periodically, however, log the commit point information to ensure that if the process aborts, you are able to restart the process at the point of failure.

■ Regarding transaction processing, make sure you control all commits and rollbacks. The commits are usually easy, but make sure you are handling unanticipated errors and providing the desired transaction control when errors occur.

■ Always build a monitoring mechanism into your PL/SQL modules if they take more than ten minutes to complete processing. This is a powerful mechanism, which will always enable you to monitor processing and recognize when a problem exists that normally would not be detected as easily.

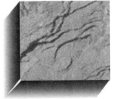

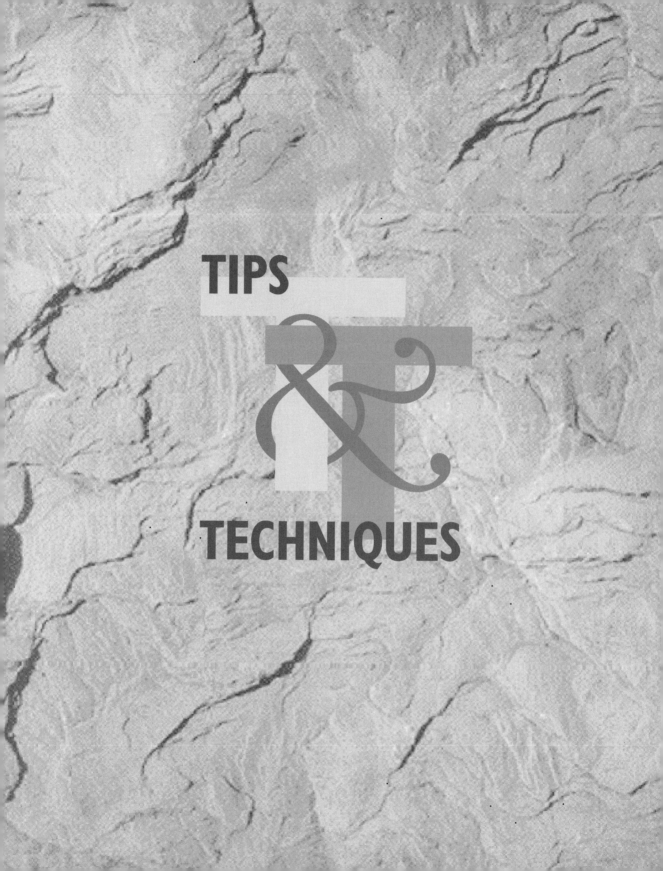

TIPS & TECHNIQUES

CHAPTER
5

Defining Standard
PL/SQL Program
Unit Techniques
(Developer and DBA)

Oracle development began to evolve when Oracle introduced the capability of storing PL/SQL source code in the database. Prior to this major enhancement (version 2.0 of PL/SQL), all PL/SQL source code was created and stored at the operating system level embedded in the product source code, whether it was forms, reports, or a third-party product. With the capability of storing PL/SQL program units in the database came major enhancements in performance and major changes in development methodologies.

When Oracle introduced the option of storing PL/SQL program units in the database, they also introduced the new PL/SQL program unit types: packages (groups of procedures and functions) and database triggers (triggers at the database table level executing PL/SQL code based on DML statements). Stored PL/SQL program units, namely packages, procedures, functions, and database triggers, became a major component of development, and the evolution of modularizing PL/SQL code and storing this code in the database started taking shape. This evolution helps with maintainability and provides improved performance.

Storing PL/SQL program units in the database should be a standard method of any development environment. This technique forces a developer to create a methodology and standard techniques using PL/SQL program units. A solid set of standards and coding techniques combines to create a development foundation that is necessary in any application development environment. This chapter takes the final step in the process of standardizing PL/SQL coding by defining several PL/SQL program unit techniques to follow when developing PL/SQL program units in an application development environment. Applying these techniques will improve PL/SQL development and maintainability, as well as improve performance and overall effectiveness of PL/SQL deployment.

The goal of this chapter is to define standard PL/SQL program unit coding techniques to help a developer be more effective in PL/SQL development. The following tips and techniques provide useful background for developing, implementing, and maintaining stored PL/SQL code in packages, procedures, functions, and database triggers.

- Understand the advantages of stored PL/SQL program units
- Locate stored PL/SQL program units components correctly
  - Package specification
  - Package body
  - Procedures
  - Functions
  - Database triggers

- Declare a program unit within a program unit
- Understand variable location declaration scope
- Encapsulate PL/SQL logic for error handling
- Store source code for stored program units in flat files
- Implement stored PL/SQL packages
  - Understand features of PL/SQL packages
    - Increase modularization
    - Improve performance
    - Separation of specification and body
  - Modularize code with PL/SQL packages
  - Create session-wide global variables and elements with package specifications
  - Implement version reporting in PL/SQL packages
  - Separate package specification and body
- Make stored PL/SQL program unit compilation easy
- Limit PL/SQL functions to a single RETURN statement
- Use functions to simplify complex or common SQL statement logic
- Implement packaged inline functions
- Use database triggers to enforce data integrity
- Use database triggers to create audit logs for data manipulation
- Avoid mutating tables (ORA-04091) in database triggers
- Overload procedures and functions to make calls more flexible
- Provide default parameter values when possible
- Use named-notation for parameters
- Use PL/SQL tables as parameters to pass data to program units
- Provide labels for all END statements
- Encrypt stored PL/SQL program unit source code
- Use PL/SQL tables to build a custom error stack

■ Use RAISE_APPLICATION_ERROR and user-defined exceptions to supplement error handling

■ Create a standard user-defined exception to communicate program unit failure

■ Create generic error handler to log errors

Understand the Advantages of Stored PL/SQL Program Units

Major advantages are evident when you store PL/SQL program units in the database. I highly recommend a standard of storing PL/SQL program units in the database when a segment of PL/SQL source code is modularized into a PL/SQL program unit.

Remember, product specific references to non-server stored product PL/SQL packages result in an error, if an attempt is made to store the program unit in the database. Therefore, any PL/SQL program unit created in a client-side product that references product specific PL/SQL program units should remain on the client-side and be stored either in the product source code or with a mechanism of the product, such as a PL/SQL library, if using Oracle Developer.

Whenever I typically create a PL/SQL code segment that I plan to use elsewhere in my application, I create the PL/SQL code segment as a stored PL/SQL program unit. If the PL/SQL program unit is one of many modules performing a certain set of business logic, or if it is logic that needs to share variables, then I create the PL/SQL program unit as a part of a package.

Typically, I create most of my PL/SQL program units in the database. Many advantages to storing PL/SQL program units in the database are outlined in the following list.

■ Provides a central location of application logic for ease of maintenance

■ Reduces redundancy of business logic and ensures consistency

■ Provides security benefits of stored PL/SQL program units

■ Enables PL/SQL source code and attributes to be viewed through the Oracle data dictionary

■ Performance of PL/SQL is better because the code is compiled

■ Performance of PL/SQL is better because the code is consistent and typically uses the Shared Pool more efficiently

■ Reduces network traffic

- Increases performance because Oracle stores a compiled version of a stored PL/SQL module in memory after being called for the first time, enabling subsequent calls to be made against memory

- Introduces an additional layer of grouping PL/SQL program units with PL/SQL packages

- Adds another validation level with database triggers performed as database transactions occur

The preceding list of advantages for storing PL/SQL source code, which is not all-encompassing, typically outweighs any disadvantages. Even though stored PL/SQL source code is generally the best choice for application partitioning of logic source code, the complete development environment, including all development tools, should be evaluated prior to development to determine the correct location of PL/SQL source code.

TIP
*PL/SQL program units should be stored in the database
to improve development consistency, maintenance,
and performance.*

Locate Stored PL/SQL Program Units Components Correctly

The business and functional logic developed dictates the type of programming logic necessary. The PL/SQL language and structure offers a variety of options when it comes to the location of a variable, segment of code, program unit, and so forth. Understanding these options, their implications, and the scope associated with each option is important. The following sections provide an outline of location implications and scope associated with PL/SQL program units.

Package Specification

A *package specification* typically is created with an associated package body. The package specification defines all PUBLIC PL/SQL elements. Any variable declared in the package specification exists throughout the life of a session and maintains its package state. This applies to any declarations, including PL/SQL tables, cursors, and so forth. Therefore, the scope of the package specification is global (viewable to all users for the duration of the session). Any procedures and functions defined in the package body that are to be PUBLIC (callable outside the package) are defined

in the package specification. Reference to any package specification element loads
the entire package specification and package body into memory.

Referenced package specification elements need to be preceded by the package
name. The package specification is treated as a separate object in the database and
is compiled separately from the package body. A package specification can be
created without a corresponding package body, if only variable or cursor
declarations are created for access session-wide. Packages possess many positive
attributes outlined later in this chapter. Create packages to group collections of
PL/SQL elements and PL/SQL program units, having a common function or purpose.
When stored PL/SQL program units are compiled that reference package elements
or program units, the package specification is the only object referenced in the
compilation.

The following example illustrates the scope of a variable defined in the
package specification.

File: 5_1.sql

```
CREATE OR REPLACE PACKAGE global_def IS
    pvg_execution_num PLS_INTEGER := 0;
    PROCEDURE increment_value (p_increment_num PLS_INTEGER);
END global_def;
/
```

Once the package specification is created, the pvg_execution_num variable and
increment_value procedure can be called. Calls to the pvg_execution_num variable
are illustrated in the following code.

File: 5_2.sql

```
BEGIN
    DBMS_OUTPUT.PUT_LINE('Variable Value: ' ||
        global_def.pvg_execution_num);
    global_def.pvg_execution_num := global_def.pvg_execution_num + 1;
    DBMS_OUTPUT.PUT_LINE('Variable Value: ' ||
        global_def.pvg_execution_num);
    global_def.pvg_execution_num := global_def.pvg_execution_num + 1;
    DBMS_OUTPUT.PUT_LINE('Variable Value: ' ||
        global_def.pvg_execution_num);
    global_def.pvg_execution_num := global_def.pvg_execution_num + 1;
    DBMS_OUTPUT.PUT_LINE('Variable Value: ' ||
        global_def.pvg_execution_num);
END;
/
```

Output (5_2.sql)

```
Variable Value: 0
Variable Value: 1
Variable Value: 2
Variable Value: 3

PL/SQL procedure successfully completed.
```

The preceding example illustrates the method of referencing package variables and the variable existence for the duration of the session.

Package Body

A *package body* contains the procedure and function logic identified in the package specification. Any procedure or function identified in the package specification must be created in the package body and must be identical to the package specification definition (name, parameter name, type, and order). Declarations can be defined in the package body at the beginning of the code segment identical to other program unit declaration sections. Any declaration in a package body can only be viewed and referenced by the package body program units, and maintains state for the session identical to package specification defined variables. Likewise, any procedure or function defined in the package body that is not defined in the package specification can only be viewed and referenced by the package body program units. At the end of the package body program unit, an initialization section can be created to initialize package components, such as loading a PL/SQL table.

The elements and program units defined in the package body—not in the package specification—are considered PRIVATE and are only known to the package body components. PRIVATE components cannot be called directly from PL/SQL program units outside the package because they are unknown to program units outside the package in which they are defined. PRIVATE components are created to hide logic used by program units and logic that should not be viewable or accessible outside the package contained logic.

The package body is treated as a separate object in the database and is compiled separately from the package specification. The package body compilation relies on the package specification for successful compilation. A package body cannot be created without a corresponding package specification.

If packages contain proprietary or confidential business algorithms or contain logic that should not be viewed or modified, the package body can be encrypted. A common method of deployment is to create the package specification without encryption and create the package body encrypted with the WRAP facility. The WRAP facility is detailed later in this chapter.

The following example illustrates the use of PRIVATE and PUBLIC PL/SQL elements. The global_def package body defines the increment_value procedure,

Locating Stored PL/SQL Program Units Components

defined in the global_def package specification, created in the preceding section. It also defines the lv_execution_num variable and the increment_display procedure that are PRIVATE to the package body.

File: 5_3.sql

```
CREATE OR REPLACE PACKAGE BODY global_def IS
   lv_execution_num PLS_INTEGER := 0;
   PROCEDURE increment_display (p_value_num PLS_INTEGER) IS
   BEGIN
      DBMS_OUTPUT.PUT_LINE('--------------------------------');
      DBMS_OUTPUT.PUT_LINE('Variable Value: ' || p_value_num);
      DBMS_OUTPUT.PUT_LINE('--------------------------------');
   END increment_display;
   PROCEDURE increment_value (p_increment_num PLS_INTEGER) IS
   BEGIN
      lv_execution_num := lv_execution_num + p_increment_num;
      increment_display (lv_execution_num);
   END increment_value;
END global_def;
/
```

The following PL/SQL code segment illustrates the execution of the package procedure.

File: 5_4.sql

```
BEGIN
   global_def.increment_value(5);
   global_def.increment_value(3);
   global_def.increment_value(1);
END;
/
```

Output (5_4.sql)

```
--------------------------------
Variable Value: 5
--------------------------------
--------------------------------
Variable Value: 8
--------------------------------
--------------------------------
Variable Value: 9
--------------------------------
PL/SQL procedure successfully completed.
```

Procedures

Procedures can be created standalone and stored in the database. A procedure should be created when business logic or functional logic requires processing that needs input and/or output variables. If a procedure does not have an association with other program units or need to share variables, the procedure can be created as a standalone stored PL/SQL procedure. A procedure can later be re-created as part of a package, by defining the procedure in the package specification, by moving the procedure logic into the package body, and by modifying existing calls of the procedure to include the package name.

Functions

Functions can be created standalone and stored in the database. A function should be created when business logic or functional logic requires processing that returns one value. If a function does not have an association with other program units or need to share variables, the function can be created as a standalone stored PL/SQL function. A function can later be re-created as part of a package, by defining the function in the package specification, by moving the function logic in the package body, and by modifying existing calls of the function to include the package name. A stored PL/SQL function can be called from a SQL statement, which is known as an inline function. The process of creating and using inline functions is detailed later in this chapter.

The question often arises as to whether a procedure or a function should be created. A function or a procedure can actually be used to accomplish the same task. Functions can also return more than one value by using output parameters. I recommend using a procedure if more than one output parameter will be returned. The program unit choice of procedure or function when no or one output value is returned comes down to personal preference. I know of developers who create all their program units as functions, returning the one return output value for a single return and return a BOOLEAN for success or failure when no output values need to be returned. I generally use procedures for most of my program unit logic when output values are not required, unless I am only concerned about the success or failure of the program unit. I generally use functions when one-output-value return is required because it is a cleaner approach for one output value returns.

Functions give you the added benefit of being able to use them as inline functions in SQL statements. Functions are not callable directly from the Web server interface; therefore, functions in a Web-based environment need to be created in a package to allow for an indirect call to the functions.

TIP
Oracle 8.1 introduces functional-based indexes, which provide the capability to index a PL/SQL function used as an inline function in SQL. Refer to Chapter 16 for further details.

Locating Stored PL/SQL Program Units Components

Locating Stored PL/SQL Program Units Components

Database Triggers

Database triggers provide an excellent vehicle for performing application logic at the database level, independent of the application interface. Database triggers execute implicitly based on the definition and are defined on a database table. Database triggers can include PL/SQL source code directly in the definition of the trigger, as well as calls to PL/SQL program units.

Database triggers provide an additional level of application partitioning logic. Remember, database triggers are executed for every record operation and add overhead to the processing. Database triggers can also be used to supplement security methods. Several database trigger uses are outlined later in this chapter.

TIP
Oracle 8.1 introduces eight new trigger types expanding the database trigger concept beyond database table triggers. Refer to Chapter 16 for further details.

Declare a Program Unit within a Program Unit

How many times have you created a PL/SQL program unit containing several lines of repetitious source code? When you make a change to one of the repetitious lines of source code, you must make the change multiple times throughout the program unit. This becomes extremely cumbersome and tedious. The several lines of code are specific to the program unit and are never used in any location outside this program unit; therefore, creating a stored PL/SQL program unit is undesirable.

This type of source code is a perfect candidate for a program unit to be created within the current program unit. This is similar to creating a stored procedure or function, only it is defined and callable only within the current program unit. Therefore, the scope is the current program unit. The following example illustrates the creation of a procedure within a program unit to display a value to the screen preceded and followed by a line of dashes.

File: 5_5.sql

```
DECLARE
    lv_count_num PLS_INTEGER := 0;
    -- PL/SQL program unit defined within the PL/SQL program unit
    PROCEDURE DISPLAY_VALUE (p_value_num PLS_INTEGER) IS
    BEGIN
        DBMS_OUTPUT.PUT_LINE('-------------------------------');
        DBMS_OUTPUT.PUT_LINE('Variable Value: ' || p_value_num);
```

```
        DBMS_OUTPUT.PUT_LINE('--------------------------------');
   END;
BEGIN
   display_value(lv_count_num);
   lv_count_num := lv_count_num + 2;
   display_value(lv_count_num);
   lv_count_num := lv_count_num + 4;
   display_value(lv_count_num);
   lv_count_num := lv_count_num + 8;
   display_value(lv_count_num);
END;
/
```

Output (5_5.sql)

```
--------------------------------
Variable Value: 0
--------------------------------
--------------------------------
Variable Value: 2
--------------------------------
--------------------------------
Variable Value: 6
--------------------------------
--------------------------------
Variable Value: 14
--------------------------------

PL/SQL procedure successfully completed.
```

TIP
Create a procedure or function within a PL/SQL program unit when the code segment is executed multiple times in the program and is specific only to the current program unit.

Understand Variable Location Declaration Scope

PL/SQL blocks can be nested in program units. Variable scope is extremely important to understand to ensure program units are designed and developed properly. The easiest way to remember variable scope is to remember the following rules:

- A variable is known to the program unit, in which it is declared, and any nested program units within the current program unit. Outside the current program unit, the variable is unknown.

- If the same variable is declared in a nested program unit, then the nested program unit variable becomes the overriding variable. The variable declared in the outer program unit can be referenced by preceding the variable with a label identifying the outer PL/SQL block.

- If a procedure or function is called from a program unit, the only variables known to the called procedure or function are the variables passed into the procedure or function (as well as package specification variables).

- Variables declared in a package specification are in scope for the entire session and are referenced by preceding the variable with the package name.

The following example illustrates variable scope.

File: 5_6.sql

```
<<main_loop>>
DECLARE
   lv_var_num_1 PLS_INTEGER := 5;
BEGIN
   -- Refers to the main_loop variable
   DBMS_OUTPUT.PUT_LINE('Step 1: ' || lv_var_num_1);
   <<inner_loop>>
   DECLARE
      -- Overrides the main_loop variable
      lv_var_num_1 PLS_INTEGER := 3;
      lv_var_num_2 PLS_INTEGER := 9;
   BEGIN
      -- Refers to the inner_loop variable
      DBMS_OUTPUT.PUT_LINE('Step 2: ' || lv_var_num_1);
      -- Refers to the main_loop variable
      DBMS_OUTPUT.PUT_LINE('Step 3: ' || main_loop.lv_var_num_1);
      DBMS_OUTPUT.PUT_LINE('Step 4: ' || lv_var_num_2);
      -- Changes the value of the inner_loop variable
      lv_var_num_1 := 6;
      DBMS_OUTPUT.PUT_LINE('Step 5: ' || lv_var_num_1);
   END;
   -- Refers to the main_loop variable that does not know about the
   -- value change that took place in the inner_loop
   DBMS_OUTPUT.PUT_LINE('Step 7: ' || lv_var_num_1);
END;
/
```

Output (5_6.sql)

```
Step 1: 5
Step 2: 3
Step 3: 5
Step 4: 9
Step 5: 6
Step 7: 5

PL/SQL procedure successfully completed.
```

Encapsulate PL/SQL Logic for Error Handling

Always have an error-handling routine included in any PL/SQL program unit (note: this recommendation is not followed in this book because of space limitations). A standard error handler is outlined later in this chapter. Even though an EXCEPTION section is included in a program unit with a WHEN OTHERS condition, this often does not provide a means for controlling error handling as desired.

Identifying an error and handling the error exactly where the error occurred is extremely important. A common method of solving this problem is to encapsulate PL/SQL logic in a nested PL/SQL block to handle the error at the point of failure. This often entails adding a BEGIN statement prior to a statement or group of statements, adding an EXCEPTION section, and adding an END statement. Despite the extra steps, it will provide a more granular error-handling process.

The following example illustrates the difference between creating one error handler to process all errors and creating multiple, more granular error handling.

File: 5_7.sql

```
DECLARE
    lv_region_name_txt          s_region.region_name%TYPE;
    lv_employee_last_name_txt s_employee.employee_last_name%TYPE;
BEGIN
    SELECT region_name INTO lv_region_name_txt
    FROM    s_region
    WHERE   region_id = &&region_id;
    SELECT employee_last_name INTO lv_employee_last_name_txt
    FROM    s_employee
    WHERE   employee_id = &&employee_id;
    DBMS_OUTPUT.PUT_LINE('Region Name: ' || lv_region_name_txt);
    DBMS_OUTPUT.PUT_LINE('Emp Last Name: ' ||
        lv_employee_last_name_txt);
EXCEPTION
  WHEN NO_DATA_FOUND THEN
      DBMS_OUTPUT.PUT_LINE('Error: One of the Selects Failed.');
```

```
    WHEN OTHERS THEN
        DBMS_OUTPUT.PUT_LINE(SUBSTR(SQLERRM, 1, 80));
END;
/
```

The preceding example prompts for two values—namely, a region_id and an employee_id. For both, a value of 25 was entered, which results in the s_region table SELECT raising the NO_DATA_FOUND exception. As shown in the following output, no mechanism exists to reveal the SELECT causing this exception. Therefore, the error message is generic.

Output (5_7.sql)

```
Error: One of the Selects Failed.

PL/SQL procedure successfully completed.
```

The preceding PL/SQL code segment can be modified, as illustrated in the following code, providing a more robust and accurate error handler.

File: 5_8.sql

```
DECLARE
    lv_region_name_txt          s_region.region_name%TYPE;
    lv_employee_last_name_txt s_employee.employee_last_name%TYPE;
BEGIN
  BEGIN
    SELECT region_name INTO lv_region_name_txt
    FROM    s_region
    WHERE   region_id = &&region_id;
    DBMS_OUTPUT.PUT_LINE('Region Name: ' || lv_region_name_txt);
  EXCEPTION
    WHEN NO_DATA_FOUND THEN
        DBMS_OUTPUT.PUT_LINE('Error: Region Select Failed.');
  END;
  BEGIN
    SELECT employee_last_name INTO lv_employee_last_name_txt
    FROM    s_employee
    WHERE   employee_id = &&employee_id;
    DBMS_OUTPUT.PUT_LINE('Emp Last Name: ' ||
        lv_employee_last_name_txt);
  EXCEPTION
    WHEN NO_DATA_FOUND THEN
        DBMS_OUTPUT.PUT_LINE('Error: Employee Select Failed.');
  END;
```

```
EXCEPTION
   WHEN OTHERS THEN
      DBMS_OUTPUT.PUT_LINE(SUBSTR(SQLERRM, 1, 80));
END;
/
```

Output (5_8.sql)

```
Error: Region Select Failed.
Emp Last Name: SCHWARTZ

PL/SQL procedure successfully completed.
```

As illustrated in the preceding output, the error handling provides more accurate handling of the process.

TIP
To isolate an error, encapsulate the PL/SQL source code in a nested PL/SQL block with an EXCEPTION handler.

Store Source Code for Stored Program Units in Flat Files

Many of the developer tools, such as Oracle Procedure Builder, attempt to simplify the development cycle by enabling developers to work directly with PL/SQL code stored in the database (packages, procedures, functions, and database triggers). This technique sounds ideal in theory; however, many advantages exist when storing source code in flat files. Among the more obvious advantages are

- Flat files are readily transferable to any operating system platform

- The majority of programs can read flat files

- Text editors have leaner system requirements (disk space, memory, and processor speed)

- Flat files lend themselves to visual differences

- Flat files can be processed by third-party software versioning tools

Furthermore, several less obvious advantages give a decisive edge to flat files for permanent source-code storage:

■ **Code Organization** Using standardized filename suffixes, the source code can be easily categorized. For example, the naming convention for SQL*Plus scripts might be xxxx.sql, while stored procedures might be xxxx.prc. (Refer to Chapter 3 for further details related to file naming standards.)

■ **Code Regression** Embedding the revision date (or revision number) of a program unit in the filename creates a simple method of reverting a program to any prior state. For example, revision 3 of a stored procedure might be xxxx003.prc. This technique is most important when versioning software is not being used.

■ **Segregating package specifications from package bodies** By keeping the two components of a package separated, installing the pieces independently becomes possible. Only installing a package body does not cause program units referencing the package specification to become INVALID. All references to a package are through the specification, and as long as the specification is not altered the objects that reference the package will remain VALID.

Implement Stored PL/SQL Packages

Stored PL/SQL packages provide a tremendous number of advantages for application development, including increased flexibility, easier maintainability, and increased performance. The many advantages are highlighted in the following sections.

Understand Features of PL/SQL Packages

PL/SQL packages are the recommended method of modularizing and coding in PL/SQL. The following subsections list the advantages to using this powerful PL/SQL structure.

Increase Modularization

Modularized code is recommended. With PL/SQL packages, related processes can be grouped together. Even though PL/SQL is not truly object-oriented, packages provide the object-oriented concept of encapsulation.

Improve Performance

When a stored PL/SQL program unit is referenced for the first time, the compiled version of the program unit is placed into memory (Shared Pool of the SGA). The first reference to a component of a PL/SQL package forces the entire compiled package source to be loaded into memory. Subsequent calls to modules within the package have been loaded into memory and are accessed much faster.

Separation of Specification and Body

A PL/SQL package consists of two parts: specification and body. The *package specification* contains a list of all PUBLIC (global) package objects. The *package body* contains all the source code to the modules corresponding to those within the specification and others that can be considered PRIVATE to the package body. This separation of the specification and body provides significant functionality.

References to package objects or modules are directed to the package specification. This allows the package body to be re-compiled without invalidating any stored objects that reference the package. A segment of PL/SQL code referencing a procedure within a package compiles successfully if the procedure is defined within the package specification. It will not look at the package body until it is executed. Even though the specification and body are dependent on each other, they are treated as two separate objects from a creation, compilation, and storage standpoint.

Second, modules within the same package that need to share logic or information can be made PRIVATE. The modules can be made PRIVATE by not placing the module definition into the package specification. Without a definition within the package specification, the module cannot be called from outside the package.

Modularize Code with PL/SQL Packages

The PL/SQL language supports modular code by requiring it to be placed into a block structure. The PL/SQL language enables a PL/SQL block to be converted into either a procedure or function, and then stored in the database. These procedures and functions can be called as assignments or executable statements from elsewhere. Each of these procedures and functions performs a task, either processing a business rule or performing a function to return a specific value. When developing numerous PL/SQL modules (program units) for a particular application or over a period of time, many of the modules are often used together to perform a process or are related in their processing. Packaging these modules together as components to perform a specific process or group of processes is ideal.

TIP
Use database packages to further modularize your PL/SQL code, grouping related procedures and functions to take advantage of the many inherent features and benefits of PL/SQL packages.

Implementing Stored PL/SQL
Packages

Create Session-Wide Global Variables and Elements with Package Specifications

One of the best features of database packages is the capability to create variables that scope more than the procedure or function in which they are defined. By defining a variable in the declaration section of a package body, that variable can be used by all procedures and functions in the package. If that same variable is moved into the package specification, a session-wide global variable is created. Any package, procedure, function, or PL/SQL block can access these global variables. The values placed in the global variables will be maintained until the database session is terminated. The variables must reside in the package specification, and only there are they accessible by all program units. In fact, creating a package body to mate with the specification is unnecessary—package specifications can exist independently without the support of a package body.

So just what does a package created only with a package specification give the developer? First, the developer is given a means of sharing control data that might otherwise have to be queried from a database table by every program unit that needed it. And, second, the developer is given a method of creating a common work area for processing logic that is spread out among numerous program units.

TIP

As with globals in any language, use package globals with care. Misuse can result in code that is difficult to debug and maintain.

Only data that must last for session duration should be kept in package globals. Do not create package globals to avoid passing parameters. If large parameters must be passed, use the NOCOPY modifier (available with Oracle 8.1 and covered in Chapter 16).

TIP

Package globals are not directly accessible from the client-side. Refer to Chapter 14 for a technique to provide access to package globals from client-side products.

PL/SQL package specifications also provide the capability to create global, user-defined object types, exceptions, and cursors. You might ask: "How does this change my current PL/SQL coding techniques?" Using the package specification to define global session objects should not change your PL/SQL coding techniques; instead, it should add to your arsenal of techniques to be used as required.

TIP

Implement PL/SQL package specifications as repositories for reusable PL/SQL objects, such as user-defined data types, cursors, and exceptions.

The following package specification contains several objects whose structures can be referred to globally. For instance, the user-defined types can be used elsewhere as data types for variables.

File: 5_9.sql

```
CREATE OR REPLACE PACKAGE global_pkg IS
   -- Declare user-defined data types to be referenced globally
   TYPE pv_stats_rec IS RECORD
      (pvg_rep_last_name_txt    s_employee.employee_last_name%TYPE,
       pvg_rep_first_name_txt   s_employee.employee_first_name%TYPE,
       pvg_salary_num           s_employee.salary%TYPE,
       pvg_commission_pct_num   s_employee.commission_pct%TYPE,
       pvg_cust_count_num       NUMBER,
       pvg_order_count_num      NUMBER,
       pvg_orders_total_num     NUMBER,
       pvg_last_order_date      DATE,
       pvg_avg_order_tot_num    NUMBER );
   TYPE pv_prod_table_rec IS TABLE OF s_product%ROWTYPE
      INDEX BY BINARY_INTEGER;
   -- Declare global variable based on user-defined types
   pvg_prod_tab pvg_prod_table_rec;
   -- Declare global PL/SQL cursors
   CURSOR cur_employee (p_emp_id_num s_employee.employee_id%TYPE) IS
      SELECT *
      FROM    s_employee
      WHERE   employee_id = p_emp_id_num;
   CURSOR cur_customer (p_cust_id_num s_customer.customer_id%TYPE) IS
      SELECT *
      FROM    s_customer
      WHERE   customer_id = p_cust_id_num;
   CURSOR cur_warehouse (p_ware_id_num s_warehouse.warehouse_id%TYPE)
      IS
      SELECT *
      FROM    s_warehouse
      WHERE   warehouse_id = p_ware_id_num;
   CURSOR cur_order (p_ord_id_num s_order.order_id%TYPE) IS
      SELECT *
      FROM    s_order
      WHERE   order_id = p_ord_id_num;
   CURSOR cur_product (p_prod_id_num s_product.product_id%TYPE) IS
```

```
      SELECT *
      FROM    s_product
      WHERE   product_id = p_prod_id_num;
   -- Declare global, cursor-based record variables
   pvg_cust_rec cur_customer%ROWTYPE;
   pvg_emp_rec   cur_employee%ROWTYPE;
   pvg_whs_rec   cur_warehouse%ROWTYPE;
   pvg_ord_rec   cur_order%ROWTYPE;
   pvg_prod_rec cur_product%ROWTYPE;
END global_pkg;
/
```

The following example illustrates a package that populates a PL/SQL table with all employees, which then becomes available for searching and analyzing. The populate_emp_table procedure is called from the package initialization and the check_emp procedure is called to check for a certain employee, providing output to the screen.

File: 5_10.sql

```
CREATE OR REPLACE PACKAGE process_emps IS
   TYPE emp_table_type IS TABLE OF s_employee.employee_last_name%TYPE
      INDEX BY BINARY_INTEGER;
   pvg_emp_tab emp_table_type;
   PROCEDURE populate_emp_table;
   PROCEDURE check_emp(p_emp_id_num s_employee.employee_id%TYPE);
END process_emps;
/
```

File: 5_10a.sql

```
CREATE OR REPLACE PACKAGE BODY process_emps IS
-----------------------------------------------------------------
PROCEDURE populate_emp_table IS
   CURSOR cur_employee IS
      SELECT *
      FROM    s_employee;
BEGIN
   -- First, empty current PL/SQL table
   pvg_emp_tab.DELETE;
   FOR cur_employee_rec IN cur_employee LOOP
      pvg_emp_tab(cur_employee_rec.employee_id) :=
         cur_employee_rec.employee_last_name;
   END LOOP;
```

```
EXCEPTION
   WHEN OTHERS THEN
      RAISE_APPLICATION_ERROR(-20101,
         'Error in procedure POPULATE_EMP_TABLE.', FALSE);
END populate_emp_table;
------------------------------------------------------------------
PROCEDURE check_emp(p_emp_id_num s_employee.employee_id%TYPE) IS
BEGIN
   -- Check existence of an employee, given the employee id
   IF pvg_emp_tab.EXISTS(p_emp_id_num) THEN
      DBMS_OUTPUT.PUT_LINE('Employee ID:' || p_emp_id_num ||
         ' is valid for '|| pvg_emp_tab(p_emp_id_num) || '.');
   ELSE
      DBMS_OUTPUT.PUT_LINE('Employee ID:' || p_emp_id_num ||
         ' is not found.');
   END IF;
EXCEPTION
   WHEN OTHERS THEN
      RAISE_APPLICATION_ERROR(-20100,
         'Error in procedure CHECK_EMPLOYEE.', FALSE);
END check_emp;
------------------------------------------------------------------
-- Package Initialization Section
BEGIN
   -- Call procedure to populate employee PL/SQL table
   populate_emp_table;
END process_emps;
/
```

In the first reference to the process_emps package, the package initialization section will be executed, populating the PL/SQL table. The following is an example call to the check_emp procedure of the package.

```
EXECUTE process_emps.check_emp(4)
```

Output (5_10.sql)

```
Employee ID:4 is valid for QUICK-TO-SEE.

PL/SQL procedure successfully completed.
```

The preceding example shows an implementation of PL/SQL tables for a scalar type; however, PL/SQL tables are capable of storing records by defining the content of the table to be a record type. Refer to Chapter 4 for tips and techniques for implementing PL/SQL tables of records.

Implement Version Reporting in PL/SQL Packages

Quite often it becomes difficult to determine if the changes made to a package's source code was installed into the database. Stored PL/SQL program units undergo minor formatting changes as source code is moved into the database, making it difficult to check the installed code by extracting it and comparing it to the source script. A simple solution to this problem is to add a versioning variable to the package body and to update it to the current date when the source code has changed.

A decimal addition to the date stamp value enables multiple changes within the same day to be traced. The variable should be highlighted with text and kept near the top of the package body or the developers may forget to update it. A simple query against the USER_SOURCE view (filtering the name column by the package name and the text column by the string '%version%') will yield the version of a package installed into the database.

Taking this approach one step further, a simple function can be added to the package to return the contents of the pv_version_txt variable. The version function is illustrated in the following PL/SQL code segment.

File: 5_11.sql

```
CREATE OR REPLACE PACKAGE globals IS
    FUNCTION what_version RETURN VARCHAR2;
    PRAGMA RESTRICT_REFERENCES(what_version, WNDS, WNPS, RNDS);
END globals;
/
```

File: 5_11a.sql

```
CREATE OR REPLACE PACKAGE BODY globals IS
    -- Declare package variables.
    -- You must change the version variable with every package change.
    pvg_version_txt VARCHAR2(30) := '19980519.1';
    -- Declare local program units.
    -- Declare global program units.
    FUNCTION what_version RETURN VARCHAR2 IS
    BEGIN
        RETURN pvg_version_txt;
    END; -- what_version
END globals;
/
```

Now the packages can be probed individually to return the version string, or a simple PL/SQL block, such as the following, can be used to probe all packages at once.

File: 5_12.sql

```
SET SERVEROUTPUT ON SIZE 1000000
DECLARE
   lv_dml_statement_txt    VARCHAR2(100);
   lv_package_version_txt VARCHAR2(100);
   lv_record_count_num     PLS_INTEGER;
   lv_version_cursor_num   PLS_INTEGER;
   CURSOR cur_source IS
      SELECT DISTINCT name
      FROM   user_source
      WHERE  type = 'PACKAGE BODY';
BEGIN
   FOR cur_source_rec IN cur_source LOOP
      lv_version_cursor_num := DBMS_SQL.OPEN_CURSOR;
      lv_dml_statement_txt := 'SELECT ' || cur_source_rec.name ||
         '.what_version FROM DUAL';
      BEGIN
         DBMS_SQL.PARSE(lv_version_cursor_num, lv_dml_statement_txt,
            DBMS_SQL.NATIVE);
         DBMS_SQL.DEFINE_COLUMN(lv_version_cursor_num, 1,
            lv_package_version_txt, 100);
         lv_record_count_num :=
            DBMS_SQL.EXECUTE(lv_version_cursor_num);
         IF DBMS_SQL.FETCH_ROWS(lv_version_cursor_num) > 0 THEN
            DBMS_SQL.COLUMN_VALUE(lv_version_cursor_num, 1,
               lv_package_version_txt);
         ELSE
            lv_package_version_txt := 'Version Reporting Failed';
         END IF;
      EXCEPTION
         WHEN OTHERS THEN
            lv_package_version_txt := 'Version Reporting Not ' ||
               'Supported';
      END;
      DBMS_OUTPUT.PUT_LINE(LOWER(cur_source_rec.name) || ': ' ||
         lv_package_version_txt);
      DBMS_SQL.CLOSE_CURSOR(lv_version_cursor_num);
   END LOOP;
END;
/
```

Implementing Stored PL/SQL Packages

A sample output from executing the preceding PL/SQL block is included in the following output.

Output (5_12.sql)

```
order_shipped: 19980609.1
customer_created: 19980610.1
new_employee: 19980611.1
generic: 19980613.1
globals: 19980519.1
process_terminations: 19980610.1
standard_program_units: 19980505.1
trend_analysis: Version Reporting Not Supported
web_security: 19980611.1

PL/SQL procedure successfully completed.
```

The preceding approach can also be a method of handling version-dependent packages and procedures. A client-side or server-side application module can verify the version of a procedure to ensure the proper processing will result. It can also be used at the startup of an application that requires distribution of packages across an environment to ensure all package versions are at the proper level. A master table can store the correct version required and the login can check the local version against the master table to ensure proper versioning. This logic can prohibit users from logging in, if their system has not been upgraded to the proper version.

This versioning method can be implemented at the package specification or package body level. The main advantage of supplying this logic in the package body pertains to compilation efficiency, covered later in this chapter.

Separate Package Specification and Body

This section is critical to understand and follow. It will save you a tremendous amount of time and headaches.

The package specification and package body should always be separated into two operating system files to eliminate unnecessary compilation steps. Placing the two object creations in the same file is natural because they are each a component of the same package. Instead, separate these objects into two distinct files and use the naming convention outlined in Chapter 3 to name the files uniquely in a manner that signifies the two files comprise the specification and the body.

An object referencing a package only references the package specification, which applies during compilation and execution. Therefore, when a procedure is compiled that refers to a package component, the compilation checks the package specification for compilation information—including the content of the package specification—and verifies the status of the package specification to ensure it is VALID (compiled successfully). If the package specification is recompiled, any object that references the package specification becomes INVALID and needs to be recompiled.

If the package body is recompiled, there is no effect on any of the objects that reference the package. Typically, once the package is created, future enhancements are made to the package body content, thus eliminating any need to recompile the package specification.

Consider the following scenario to illustrate this point: A package (test_pack) is created containing two procedures, namely, test_proc1 and test_proc2. A standalone procedure (call_test_proc) is created that references the test_proc1 procedure. Both of these creations are illustrated in the following examples.

File: 5_13.sql

```
CREATE OR REPLACE PACKAGE test_pack IS
PROCEDURE test_proc1;
PROCEDURE test_proc2;
END test_pack;
/
```

File: 5_13a.sql

```
CREATE OR REPLACE PACKAGE BODY test_pack IS
PROCEDURE test_proc1 IS
   BEGIN
      DBMS_OUTPUT.PUT_LINE('Executing test_proc1.');
   END test_proc1;
PROCEDURE test_proc2 IS
   BEGIN
      DBMS_OUTPUT.PUT_LINE('Executing test_proc2.');
   END test_proc2;
END test_pack;
/
```

File: 5_14.sql

```
CREATE OR REPLACE PROCEDURE call_test_proc IS
BEGIN
   test_pack.test_proc1;
END;
/
```

Once the test_pack package specification and body, and the call_test_proc are created, all three objects are compiled and reflect a VALID status in the USER_OBJECTS view, as shown in the following query.

File: 5_15.sql

```
SELECT object_name, object_type, status
FROM   user_objects
WHERE  OBJECT_NAME IN ('TEST_PACK', 'CALL_TEST_PROC')
ORDER BY object_name, object_type;
```

Output (5_15.sql)

```
OBJECT_NAME              OBJECT_TYPE     STATUS
------------------------ --------------- -------
CALL_TEST_PROC           PROCEDURE       VALID
TEST_PACK                PACKAGE         VALID
TEST_PACK                PACKAGE BODY    VALID
```

When the test_pack body is recompiled, the following results.

Output (5_15.sql)

```
OBJECT_NAME              OBJECT_TYPE     STATUS
------------------------ --------------- -------
CALL_TEST_PROC           PROCEDURE       VALID
TEST_PACK                PACKAGE         VALID
TEST_PACK                PACKAGE BODY    VALID
```

In the preceding example, all objects are still VALID because the test_pack body recompilation has no effect on the compilation of procedure call_test_proc.

When the test_pack specification and body are recompiled, the following results.

Output (5_15.sql)

```
OBJECT_NAME              OBJECT_TYPE     STATUS
------------------------ --------------- -------
CALL_TEST_PROC           PROCEDURE       INVALID
TEST_PACK                PACKAGE         VALID
TEST_PACK                PACKAGE BODY    VALID
```

The preceding example illustrates the dependency of package references on the package specification, not on the package body. This dependency can also be viewed in the USER_DEPENDENCIES view, as shown in the following query.

File: 5_16.sql

```
SELECT name, type, referenced_owner r_owner, referenced_name r_name,
       referenced_type r_type
FROM   user_dependencies
WHERE  name IN ('CALL_TEST_PROC', 'TEST_PACK')
OR     referenced_name IN ('CALL_TEST_PROC', 'TEST_PACK');
```

Output (5_16.sql)

NAME	TYPE	R_OWNER	R_NAME	R_TYPE
TEST_PACK	PACKAGE BODY	PLSQL_USER	TEST_PACK	PACKAGE
CALL_TEST_PROC	PROCEDURE	PLSQL_USER	TEST_PACK	PACKAGE

The preceding example illustrates the dependency of the test_pack package body and call_test_proc procedure on the test_pack package specification.

TIP
Separate the package specification and package body into two files and only compile each object if the content of the object has changed. Recompiling the package specification every time the package body is compiled causes extra compilation steps that can cause extra unnecessary work.

Make Stored PL/SQL Program Unit Compilation Easy

This section is critical to understand and follow. It will save you a tremendous amount of time and headaches.

Several locations in this book discuss the subject of stored PL/SQL program unit compilation, namely in Chapter 9, Chapter 12, and Chapter 13. When a stored PL/SQL program unit is recompiled, any object that references or is dependent on the program unit that is recompiled will become INVALID. This side effect of recompiling can cause a domino effect because each program unit that becomes INVALID causes all dependent program units to become INVALID and the dominoes continue to fall. Therefore, if one of the main program units is recompiled, it could cause a ripple effect leaving all or many program units INVALID.

The standard method of recompiling all these INVALID program units is to create a dynamic SQL script against the USER_OBJECTS view to build an

ALTER...COMPILE script, followed by the execution of this recompilation script. This process is confusing, because when completed, INVALID program units still exist.

The following is an explanation of how this process really works, followed by a solution to this recompilation problem to make this process easier.

Let's set up a dependency scenario to illustrate the problem with recompilation of all INVALID objects. The following five procedures are dependent on each other. The procedures are created and the statuses of the objects are verified.

File: 5_17.sql

```
CREATE OR REPLACE PROCEDURE EE AS
BEGIN
    NULL;
END;
/
CREATE OR REPLACE PROCEDURE DD AS
BEGIN
    EE;
END;
/
CREATE OR REPLACE PROCEDURE CC AS
BEGIN
    DD;
END;
/
CREATE OR REPLACE PROCEDURE BB AS
BEGIN
    CC;
END;
/
CREATE OR REPLACE PROCEDURE AA AS
BEGIN
    BB;
END;
/
```

File: 5_18.sql

```
SELECT object_name, object_type, status
FROM   user_objects
WHERE  object_name IN ('AA', 'BB', 'CC', 'DD', 'EE')
ORDER BY object_name, object_type;
```

Output (5_18.sql)

```
OBJECT_NAME      OBJECT_TYPE    STATUS
---------------  -------------  -------
AA               PROCEDURE      VALID
BB               PROCEDURE      VALID
CC               PROCEDURE      VALID
DD               PROCEDURE      VALID
EE               PROCEDURE      VALID
```

All five procedures are compiled and VALID at this point. When the following COMPILE command is executed, the ee procedure is recompiled, which INVALIDates the remaining four procedures because dd becomes INVALID, cc follows, then bb, and, lastly, aa.

```
ALTER PROCEDURE EE COMPILE;
```

Output (5_18.sql)

```
OBJECT_NAME      OBJECT_TYPE    STATUS
---------------  -------------  -------
AA               PROCEDURE      INVALID
BB               PROCEDURE      INVALID
CC               PROCEDURE      INVALID
DD               PROCEDURE      INVALID
EE               PROCEDURE      VALID
```

The preceding output shows the domino effect takes place because of object dependencies. The following script illustrates the standard method of recompiling PL/SQL program units. The dynamic SQL script executes to create a DDL script to recompile all INVALID program units.

File: 5_19.sql

```
SELECT 'ALTER ' || object_type || ' ' ||
       object_name || ' COMPILE;'
FROM   user_objects
WHERE  object_name IN ('AA', 'BB', 'CC', 'DD', 'EE')
AND    status='INVALID'
ORDER BY object_type, object_name;
```

Making Compilation Easy

Output (5_19.sql)

```
ALTER PROCEDURE AA COMPILE;
ALTER PROCEDURE BB COMPILE;
ALTER PROCEDURE CC COMPILE;
ALTER PROCEDURE DD COMPILE;
```

Once the preceding DDL COMPILE statements are executed, the following USER_OBJECTS output reveals the state of the program units. As evident in the following output, three program units are still INVALID.

Output (5_18.sql)

OBJECT_NAME	OBJECT_TYPE	STATUS
AA	PROCEDURE	INVALID
BB	PROCEDURE	INVALID
CC	PROCEDURE	INVALID
DD	PROCEDURE	VALID
EE	PROCEDURE	VALID

When procedure aa is compiled, it checks all dependent (referenced) objects of procedure aa (in this case, procedure bb) to verify the dependent objects are VALID; if the dependent object(s) are not VALID, then the dependent objects are compiled, and so forth. When the compile for procedure aa begins, it sees procedure bb is INVALID, and it attempts to compile procedure bb. Procedure bb sees procedure cc is INVALID and it then attempts to compile cc. Procedure cc sees procedure dd is INVALID, and it then attempts to compile procedure dd. Procedure dd compiles successfully, then procedure cc compiles successfully, followed by procedure bb, and then procedure aa.

If we stop at this point—the point of only issuing the COMPILE for procedure aa—all program units would be VALID. However, our dynamic script does not enable the checking of the INVALID statuses intermittently. When the compile for procedure bb is attempted, procedure aa becomes INVALID because it is dependent on bb and bb follows the compilation dependency tree. The last compile statement compiles procedure dd and the end result is procedure aa, bb, and cc remain (5_19.sql) INVALID. The next natural step is to re-run the preceding dynamic SQL script and re-run the compiles. This is then performed two more times after this execution. At that point, all is VALID. This seems cumbersome because it is.

A better way exists. What if the only compilation was on procedure aa? If this were performed, the compilation process would compile all procedures and only one compilation statement would have been necessary. Therefore, the following PL/SQL program unit will accomplish the task of recompilation by running this recompilation module one time. The compilation logic compiles one object at a time, re-querying the USER_OBJECTS view for INVALID objects fetching only one object at a time.

The compilation procedure is shown in the following example. The procedure contains logic to attempt a COMPILE for all program units that remain INVALID once. If a program unit contains an error that will not allow a successful compilation, the program unit is skipped after the first unsuccessful compilation attempt.

File: 5_20.sql

```
CREATE OR REPLACE PROCEDURE recompile_all_objects IS
-- Compiles all objects under the current schema by executing this
-- procedure once.
-- The schema creating this procedure must be granted SELECT privilege
-- directly to the USER_OBJECTS view (not through a role).
   -- Fetches INVALID stored PL/SQL program units
   CURSOR cur_objects_invalid IS
      SELECT object_id, object_name, object_type
      FROM   user_objects
      WHERE  status      = 'INVALID'
      AND    object_type IN ('PACKAGE', 'PACKAGE BODY',
                              'FUNCTION', 'PROCEDURE', 'TRIGGER')
      ORDER BY object_type, object_name;
   -- Queries PL/SQL program unit compiled to ensure it was successful
   CURSOR cur_objects_valid (p_object_id_num NUMBER) IS
      SELECT 'FOUND'
      FROM   user_objects
      WHERE  STATUS      = 'VALID'
      AND    object_id   = p_object_id_num;
   -- Stores PL/SQL program units that failed compile
   TYPE lv_invalid_tab IS TABLE OF cur_objects_invalid%ROWTYPE
      INDEX BY BINARY_INTEGER;
   lv_invalid_tab_rec     lv_invalid_tab;
   lv_count_compiled_num  PLS_INTEGER; -- compiled counter
   lv_column_valid_txt    VARCHAR2(5);
   lv_exec_cursor_num     PLS_INTEGER := DBMS_SQL.OPEN_CURSOR;
   lv_sql_statement_txt   VARCHAR2(200);
   lv_object_count_num    PLS_INTEGER := 0; -- VALID counter
BEGIN
   DBMS_OUTPUT.PUT_LINE('Starting Re-Compilation of Objects');
   DBMS_OUTPUT.PUT_LINE('-----------------------------------------');
   LOOP
      -- set to 0 to determine if any program units compiled this loop
      lv_count_compiled_num := 0;
      FOR cur_objects_invalid_rec IN cur_objects_invalid LOOP
         -- Make sure PL/SQL program unit was not already
```

```
           -- unsuccessfully compiled. If it is in the PL/SQL table,
           -- the program unit previously failed and is skipped.
       IF NOT lv_invalid_tab_rec.
           EXISTS(cur_objects_invalid_rec.object_id) THEN
           -- Builds COMPILE DDL statements
           IF cur_objects_invalid_rec.object_type =
              'PACKAGE BODY' THEN
               lv_sql_statement_txt := 'ALTER PACKAGE ' ||
                  cur_objects_invalid_rec.object_name ||
                  ' COMPILE BODY';
           ELSE
               lv_sql_statement_txt := 'ALTER ' ||
                  cur_objects_invalid_rec.object_type ||
                  ' ' || cur_objects_invalid_rec.object_name ||
                  ' COMPILE';
           END IF;
           -- The DBMS_SQL.PARSE executes a DDL statement, therefore
           -- DBMS_SQL.EXECUTE is not required. Prior to Oracle8, if
           -- the DBMS_SQL.PARSE command resulted in an Oracle error,
           -- no error was returned to the PL/SQL calling code. After
           -- Oracle8, an error is passed back, therefore, this call
           -- is in a nested PL/SQL block to bypass the error, the
           -- query to USER_OBJECTS for the object being VALID tells
           -- this program if the compile succeeded or failed.
           BEGIN
               lv_object_count_num := lv_object_count_num + 1;
               DBMS_SQL.PARSE(lv_exec_cursor_num,
                  lv_sql_statement_txt, DBMS_SQL.NATIVE);
           EXCEPTION
               WHEN OTHERS THEN
                  NULL;
           END;
           -- If object VALID, compile successful, otherwise failed.
           OPEN cur_objects_valid(cur_objects_invalid_rec.object_id);
           FETCH cur_objects_valid INTO lv_column_valid_txt;
           IF CUR_OBJECTS_VALID%ROWCOUNT > 0 THEN
               -- Display Success and exit loop
               DBMS_OUTPUT.PUT_LINE('Object Compilation: ' ||
                  cur_objects_invalid_rec.object_type ||
                  ' - ' || cur_objects_invalid_rec.object_name ||
                  ' SUCCEEDED');
               lv_count_compiled_num := lv_count_compiled_num + 1;
               CLOSE cur_objects_valid;
               EXIT;
           ELSE
               -- Display failure and add to PL/SQL table
               DBMS_OUTPUT.PUT_LINE('Object Compilation: ' ||
                  cur_objects_invalid_rec.object_type ||
                  ' - ' || cur_objects_invalid_rec.object_name ||
```

```
                        ' FAILED');
                lv_invalid_tab_rec(cur_objects_invalid_rec.object_id).
                    object_name := cur_objects_invalid_rec.object_name;
                lv_invalid_tab_rec(cur_objects_invalid_rec.object_id).
                    object_type := cur_objects_invalid_rec.object_type;
                CLOSE cur_objects_valid;
            END IF;
        END IF;
    END LOOP;
    -- When no more INVALID PL/SQL program units exist that have not
    -- been attempted to be compiled in this program unit, exit.
    IF lv_count_compiled_num = 0 THEN
        EXIT;
    END IF;
    END LOOP;
    -- Displays the fact that no INVALID PL/SQL program units found
    IF lv_object_count_num = 0 THEN
        DBMS_OUTPUT.PUT_LINE('No Objects to Re-Compile - All VALID.');
    END IF;
    DBMS_OUTPUT.PUT_LINE('-------------------------------------------');
    DBMS_OUTPUT.PUT_LINE('Re-Compilation of Objects Complete');
    DBMS_SQL.CLOSE_CURSOR(lv_exec_cursor_num);
EXCEPTION
    WHEN OTHERS THEN
        DBMS_OUTPUT.PUT_LINE('-------------------------------------------');
        DBMS_OUTPUT.PUT_LINE('Re-Compilation Aborted.');
        DBMS_OUTPUT.PUT_LINE(SUBSTR(SQLERRM, 1, 100));
        -- Closes any cursor left open upon an error
        IF DBMS_SQL.IS_OPEN(lv_exec_cursor_num) THEN
            DBMS_SQL.CLOSE_CURSOR(lv_exec_cursor_num);
        END IF;
        IF cur_objects_valid%ISOPEN THEN
            CLOSE cur_objects_valid;
        END IF;
END recompile_all_objects;
/
```

TIP

Prior to release Oracle 8.0, when DBMS_SQL.PARSE for DDL commands was executed in a PL/SQL program unit, no error was returned if the command failed. Therefore, an exception was not raised. After the release of Oracle 8.0, this processing changed; therefore, if you want to trap the error, the DBMS_SQL.PARSE can be encapsulated in a nested block to handle the error as desired. This is illustrated in the preceding PL/SQL code segment.

Making Compilation Easy

The preceding PL/SQL program unit can be executed under a schema to recompile all PL/SQL program units. The logic is such that if Oracle internally VALIDates a program unit when another program unit is compiled, it is not recompiled again. The preceding example that created the five dependent procedures is used in the following example to illustrate the recompile_all_objects procedure execution. All objects are currently INVALID with the exception of the ee procedure, as illustrated in the following output.

Output (5_18.sql)

```
OBJECT_NAME        OBJECT_TYPE       STATUS
---------------    --------------    -------
AA                 PROCEDURE         INVALID
BB                 PROCEDURE         INVALID
CC                 PROCEDURE         INVALID
DD                 PROCEDURE         INVALID
EE                 PROCEDURE         VALID
```

```
EXECUTE recompile_all_objects
```

Output (5_20.sql)

```
Starting Re-Compilation of Objects
------------------------------------------
Object Compilation: PROCEDURE - AA SUCCEEDED
------------------------------------------
Re-Compilation of Objects Complete

PL/SQL procedure successfully completed.
```

The preceding output from the recompile_all_objects execution reveals the only procedure explicitly compiled was the aa procedure. When the USER_OBJECTS view is reviewed, all PL/SQL objects are now VALID.

Output (5_18.sql)

```
OBJECT_NAME        OBJECT_TYPE       STATUS
---------------    --------------    -------
AA                 PROCEDURE         VALID
BB                 PROCEDURE         VALID
CC                 PROCEDURE         VALID
DD                 PROCEDURE         VALID
EE                 PROCEDURE         VALID
```

Therefore, any time an object is recompiled, the USER_OBJECTS view should be reviewed to reveal if objects are INVALID. If any objects are INVALID, the recompile_all_objects procedure should be executed, followed by a review of the USER_OBJECTS view. Prior to production hours, all PL/SQL objects should be VALID. Additional information related to compilation can be found in Chapter 9, Chapter 12, and Chapter 13.

TIP
The DBMS_SQL calls in the recompile_all_objects procedure can be superseded with the new EXECUTE IMMEDIATE PL/SQL command introduced in the release of Oracle 8.1. Refer to Chapter 16 for further details.

Limit PL/SQL Functions to a Single RETURN Statement

A PL/SQL function serves the purpose of returning a value or, in some cases, a composite data type value. Within the logic of the function, the RETURN value of the function is determined by conditional logic. Since the RETURN statement is allowed anywhere within the function logic, many PL/SQL developers place separate RETURN statements throughout the code. This is usually not recommended for readability, allowing for top-down design, and promoting maintainability.

More important, all the normal PL/SQL logic will have been processed or bypassed, depending on conditional logic. The local variable that is used can be referenced in error handling by adding the value to an error message, using RAISE_APPLICATION_ERROR, saving the value to an error table, or displaying the value to the screen using the DBMS_OUTPUT.PUT_LINE procedure. The following example illustrates a function providing a consistent formatting for all money values. A call to the format_money function would be used in all locations where this formatted output is required. The function also shows a local variable can be used to store the value that is going to be returned. The last statement of the function returns the local variable value.

File: 5_21.sql

```
CREATE OR REPLACE FUNCTION format_money (p_value_num NUMBER)
   RETURN VARCHAR2 IS
   lv_value_txt VARCHAR2(100);
BEGIN
   -- This function assumes the value is not > $999,999,999.99
   IF (p_value_num >= 1000000) THEN
```

```
     lv_value_txt := LTRIM(TO_CHAR(p_value_num, '$999,999,999.00'));
   ELSIF (p_value_num < 1000000) AND (p_value_num >= 1000) THEN
     lv_value_txt := LTRIM( TO_CHAR(p_value_num, '$999,999.00'));
   ELSE
     lv_value_txt := LTRIM(TO_CHAR(p_value_num, '$999.00'));
   END IF;
   RETURN lv_value_txt;
EXCEPTION
   WHEN OTHERS THEN
     RAISE_APPLICATION_ERROR( -20123, 'Error occurred in MONEY ' ||
        'function for incoming value:' || TO_CHAR(p_value_num) ||
        ' and outgoing value:' || lv_value_txt);
END format_money;
/
```

The preceding function's EXCEPTION section was capable of referencing the local variable value, which would be impossible had multiple RETURN statements been used.

TIP

When creating a PL/SQL function, provide a common exit to the module by having only one RETURN statement. The returned value can be assigned to a local variable. This local variable can then be referenced in the RETURN statement and is recommended to be the last statement of the function.

Use Functions to Simplify Complex or Common SQL Statement Logic

Embedding SQL statements within PL/SQL code proves to be powerful and useful. What separates PL/SQL from many other languages is the ease by which any DML statement can be performed. Nearly all the PL/SQL program units created for an application contain SQL.

Commonly, a PL/SQL cursor is implemented to query data from the database, and then normal PL/SQL constructs like LOOPs and IF THEN control structures are implemented to perform special processing. The results of the query can be manipulated and used in calculations to attain valuable information. A PL/SQL developer incorporates complex logic into SQL statements using several calls to many of the built-in Oracle functions or by executing PL/SQL logic against the results. The PL/SQL logic can be turned into stored PL/SQL functions that can then be called within SQL statements. This method allows developers to extend the standard SQL functions that come with the SQL language by using the PL/SQL language to create new functions, known as inline functions.

The capability to create inline functions reverses the normal roles of SQL and PL/SQL. Many Oracle developers continue to copy a complex SQL statement from one module to another. Moving this complex logic to a function that can be called inline would significantly reduce redundancy and margin of error. The functionality of inline functions is tremendously underused.

TIP
Implement inline functions to simplify complex SQL logic and reduce redundancy. Creating a standalone function that can be used inline is no different than any Oracle-supplied SQL or PL/SQL function.

Certain restrictions and rules are enforced by Oracle to govern whether a function is pure enough to be called from within a SQL statement. First, a few basic restrictions must be followed:

- Parameters to the function can only be IN parameters and must only consist of database data types (DATE, CHAR, VARCHAR2, NUMBER, ROWID, LONG, and LONG RAW)

- Return data types also must only consist of database data types

- Functions must be stored in the database as a PL/SQL function

Second, the standalone function must be determined to be "pure" enough to be called inline. The following table lists four purity levels to which functions can adhere to determine in which places, or if, they can be called from within SQL.

Purity Level (Abbreviation)	Description
Writes No Database State (WNDS)	Function does not INSERT into, UPDATE, or DELETE from any database tables.
Reads No Database State (RNDS)	Function does not SELECT from the database.
Writes No Package State (WNPS)	Function does not change values of any package variables.
Reads No Package State (RNPS)	Function does not read the values of any package variables.

For standalone stored PL/SQL functions, Oracle implicitly determines the purity level during compilation of the stored objects or at execution of an anonymous PL/SQL block.

The purity levels provide the following limitations on the use of the function inline.

- All functions called inline must meet the WNDS purity level

- All functions called inline remotely—across a database link—must also meet the RNPS and WNPS purity levels

- All functions called inline from clauses—other than SELECT, SET, or VALUES—must meet the WNPS purity level

- Calls to subprograms, like other procedures or functions, affect the purity levels of functions

Several rules and restrictions exist for calling PL/SQL functions inline, but they still provide several advantages to modularized and reusable development. The following example provides a consistent formatting for the city, state, zip, and country for a customer. This should be used in all locations where this formatted output is required.

File: 5_22.sql

```
CREATE OR REPLACE FUNCTION customer_csz
   (p_cust_id_num s_customer.customer_id%TYPE)
   RETURN VARCHAR2 IS
   CURSOR cur_customer IS
      SELECT RTRIM(city || ', '|| state) ||
             RTRIM(' ' || zip_code) ||
             RTRIM(' ' || country)
      FROM   s_customer
      WHERE  customer_id = p_cust_id_num;
   lv_citystatezip_txt VARCHAR2(75);
BEGIN
   -- Fetch the already formatted string for the customer
   OPEN cur_customer;
   FETCH cur_customer INTO lv_citystatezip_txt;
   CLOSE cur_customer;
   RETURN lv_citystatezip_txt;
END;
/
```

Once created, the PL/SQL function can be referenced in a SQL statement, as illustrated in the following example.

File: 5_23.sql

```
SELECT customer_name || CHR(10) ||
       address || CHR(10) ||
       customer_csz(customer_id) full_address
FROM   s_customer;
```

Output (5_23.sql)

```
FULL_ADDRESS
-------------------------------------------------------
UNISPORTS
72 VIA BAHIA
SAO PAOLO, BRAZIL

SIMMS ATHELETICS
6741 TAKASHI BLVD.
OSAKA, JAPAN

DELHI SPORTS
11368 CHANAKYA
NEW DELHI, INDIA
```

The preceding output has been limited to the first three records.

Implement Packaged Inline Functions

In the previous section, inline PL/SQL functions and background necessary to implement these functions standalone was detailed. However, as PL/SQL developers continue to modularize complimentary subprograms by placing them into packages, a few more steps become necessary for implementing inline PL/SQL functions.

Unlike standalone stored PL/SQL functions, the PL/SQL Engine does not determine the purity level of packaged functions. Therefore, the PL/SQL developer must explicitly assign the correct purity levels for the function to be called inline.

The RESTRICT_REFERENCES PRAGMA is placed in the package specification and refers to the defined function by the name. If a function is overloaded, a separate PRAGMA must follow each function definition in the package specification. Assigned purity levels can be listed in any order. At the time of compilation, errors will occur if the PL/SQL Engine determines the function does not meet the specified purity levels.

The following example implements overloaded functions allowing either the customer ID or the customer name to be passed as a parameter; each function is defined with PRAGMAS enabling both to be called inline.

File: 5_24.sql

```
CREATE OR REPLACE PACKAGE inline_pkg IS
-- First overloaded function version accepts customer_id
FUNCTION customer_csz (p_cust_id_num s_customer.customer_id%TYPE)
   RETURN VARCHAR2;
   PRAGMA RESTRICT_REFERENCES(customer_csz, WNDS, WNPS, RNPS);
-- Second overloaded function version accepts customer_name
FUNCTION customer_csz (p_cust_name_txt s_customer.customer_name%TYPE)
   RETURN VARCHAR2;
   PRAGMA RESTRICT_REFERENCES(customer_csz, WNDS, WNPS, RNPS);
END inline_pkg;
/
```

File: 5_24a.sql

```
CREATE OR REPLACE PACKAGE BODY inline_pkg IS
----------------------------------------------------------------
FUNCTION customer_csz (p_cust_id_num s_customer.customer_id%TYPE)
   RETURN VARCHAR2 IS
   CURSOR cur_customer IS
      SELECT RTRIM(city || ', '|| state) ||
             RTRIM(' ' || zip_code) ||
             RTRIM(' ' || country)
      FROM   s_customer
      WHERE  customer_id = p_cust_id_num;
   lv_citystatezip_txt VARCHAR2(75);
BEGIN
   -- Fetch the already formatted string for the customer
   OPEN cur_customer;
   FETCH cur_customer INTO lv_citystatezip_txt;
   CLOSE cur_customer;
   RETURN lv_citystatezip_txt;
END customer_csz;
----------------------------------------------------------------
FUNCTION customer_csz (p_cust_name_txt s_customer.customer_name%TYPE)
   RETURN VARCHAR2 IS
   CURSOR cur_customer IS
      SELECT RTRIM(city || ', '|| state) ||
             RTRIM(' ' || zip_code) ||
             RTRIM(' ' || country)
      FROM   s_customer
      WHERE  customer_name = p_cust_name_txt;
   lv_citystatezip_txt VARCHAR2(75);
BEGIN
   -- Fetch the already formatted string for the customer
```

```
    OPEN cur_customer;
    FETCH cur_customer INTO lv_citystatezip_txt;
    CLOSE cur_customer;
    RETURN lv_citystatezip_txt;
END customer_csz;
-------------------------------------------------------------------
END inline_pkg;
/
```

TIP
PL/SQL functions can be called from SQL statements.
When the PL/SQL function is created as a standalone
stored PL/SQL program unit, the purity level does not
have to be specified and is determined internally by
Oracle. If the PL/SQL function is defined within a
package, then the purity level must be defined through
the RESTRICTED_REFERENCES pragma definition in
the package specification.

Use Database Triggers to Enforce Data Integrity

Many avenues exist for developers to ensure data integrity. The best possible
method is to deploy database constraints on tables to ensure the data manipulation
follows these constraints. Database constraints cannot enforce all business rules and
validation; therefore, many of these constraints or rules are enforced at the time of
entry—in the front-end application interface. This front-end enforcement is required
to provide interactive validation and customized messaging at the point where a
constraint is violated versus waiting for the database to detect all the errors upon
commit. This involves stored PL/SQL program units to modularize routines and
business functions, but even these must be called within the front-end products.
Occasionally, developers forget about the "backdoor" access (SQL*Plus, Microsoft
Access through ODBC, and so forth), or front-end interfaces that missed some of the
validation rules.

Oracle's database trigger capability allows developers to build a layer of logic at
the database level, executing implicitly every time an INSERT, UPDATE, and/or
DELETE is executed on a table. Database triggers are extremely versatile because
they are composed of PL/SQL blocks, making the scope limitless as far as what can
be done at this level. Database triggers can be created as a transactional trigger (fires
once for each DML statement) or as row-level trigger (fires once for every row
affected by a DML statement). Database triggers can be defined to execute either
BEFORE or AFTER the database transaction occurs. Other optional clauses are

Enforcing Data Integrity

available to further enhance and specify the triggering process. The triggering DML events—of inserting, updating, and deleting—can be combined into one database-level trigger.

TIP

Combine different triggers on the same table, where redundant code is evident. No matter what triggering event has occurred, the logic is often the same. To create a combined trigger and also to separate different logic within it, the INSERTING, UPDATING, and DELETING keywords can be used. These Booleans evaluate to TRUE if the corresponding transaction type is occurring, enabling you to separate the logic within a combined trigger. In conjunction with the UPDATING Boolean option, you are able to specify a column name.

The database trigger level is independent of the front-end interface (be it Forms, SQL*Plus, SQL*Loader, Microsoft Access, or any other product interfacing to the database). The database trigger level does not rely on explicit source code executing and it is the last line of defense prior to data being manipulated in a database table.

What happens if we do not have all the necessary validation for applications? Incorrect data is inserted or manipulated, and developers are running cleanup routines to eliminate or undo corrupted data. In addition to creating our business rules and validation at the front-end level, providing the same validation at the database level could ensure the database tables remain accurate, no matter where the data is being inserted or from where it is being manipulated.

TIP

Implement database-level triggers to enforce validation to ensure data accuracy. Many Oracle developers have the false notion a trigger that fires on every INSERT, UPDATE, or DELETE will be slow. If a trigger contains just PL/SQL logic, the trigger will be almost unnoticeable. Likewise, if the trigger performs DML, the speed of the trigger relies tremendously on the speed of the DML. A poorly tuned query within a PL/SQL cursor causes the transaction by which the trigger is executing to be slow. For further information on tuning DML statements, refer to Chapter 7.

The following example shows the trigger creation script for a BEFORE INSERT trigger disallowing a customer with a poor credit rating to pay for an order with a credit card. This trigger enforces a business rule at the database level, with no reliance to any front-end application.

File: 5_25.sql

```
CREATE OR REPLACE TRIGGER bi_order
BEFORE INSERT
ON s_order
REFERENCING OLD AS OLD NEW AS NEW
FOR EACH ROW
WHEN (NEW.payment_type = 'CREDIT')
DECLARE
   CURSOR cur_check_customer IS
      SELECT 'x'
      FROM    s_customer
      WHERE   customer_id = :NEW.customer_id
      AND     credit_rating = 'POOR';
   lv_temp_txt VARCHAR2(1);
BEGIN
   OPEN cur_check_customer;
   FETCH cur_check_customer INTO lv_temp_txt;
   IF (cur_check_customer%FOUND) THEN
      CLOSE cur_check_customer;
      RAISE_APPLICATION_ERROR(-20111, 'Cannot process CREDIT ' ||
         'order for a customer with a POOR credit rating.');
   ELSE
      CLOSE cur_check_customer;
   END IF;
END bi_order;
/
```

With the preceding database-level trigger present, the desired validation is enforced independent of the entry point. If the validation logic fails, a descriptive error message is given, not allowing corrupted data to be sent into the database, as shown in the following example.

Output (5_25.sql)

```
ERROR at line 1:
ORA-20111: Cannot process CREDIT order for a customer with a POOR
   credit rating.
ORA-06512: at "PLSQL_USER.BI_ORDER", line 14
ORA-04088: error during execution of trigger 'PLSQL_USER.BI_ORDER'
```

Enforcing Data Integrity

The use of user-defined exceptions is often useful for improving readability of the logic. If a validation should fail, a user-defined exception can be raised. In the exception section of the trigger block, the exception can be handled by providing a more descriptive error message. This is extremely helpful when multiple conditions can possibly raise the same exception. A call to the RAISE_APPLICATION_ERROR procedure can be limited from within the exception section, reducing redundancy.

The following example shows the previous trigger, implementing a user-defined exception. The exception section of the trigger block performs the handling of the validation exception.

File: 5_26.sql

```
CREATE OR REPLACE TRIGGER bi_order
BEFORE INSERT
ON s_order
REFERENCING OLD AS OLD NEW AS NEW
FOR EACH ROW
WHEN (NEW.payment_type = 'CREDIT')
DECLARE
   CURSOR cur_check_customer IS
      SELECT 'x'
      FROM    s_customer
      WHERE   customer_id = :NEW.customer_id
      AND     credit_rating = 'POOR';
   lv_temp_txt           VARCHAR2(1);
   lv_poor_credit_excep EXCEPTION;
BEGIN
   OPEN cur_check_customer;
   FETCH cur_check_customer INTO lv_temp_txt;
   IF (cur_check_customer%FOUND) THEN
      CLOSE cur_check_customer;
      RAISE lv_poor_credit_excep;
   ELSE
      CLOSE cur_check_customer;
   END IF;
EXCEPTION
   WHEN lv_poor_credit_excep THEN
      RAISE_APPLICATION_ERROR(-20111, 'Cannot process CREDIT ' ||
         'order for a customer with a POOR credit rating.');
   WHEN OTHERS THEN
      RAISE_APPLICATION_ERROR(-20122, 'Unhandled error occurred in' ||
         ' BI_ORDER trigger for order#:' || TO_CHAR(:NEW.ORDER_ID));
END bi_order;
/
```

Enforcing Data Integrity

I am not recommending all logic be turned into database triggers. However, I do recommend further analyzing the logic and validation (as well as your development and production environments) and determining what the critical pieces of this logic are to decide if adding logic at the database level would be beneficial.

For further detailed information regarding the syntax and options for creating PLSQL database triggers, refer to *Oracle8: PL/SQL Programming Guide,* by Scott Urman (Oracle Press).

Use Database Triggers to Create Audit Logs for Data Manipulation

In many applications, the manipulation of data must be tracked. Providing an audit log to monitor each transaction for security reasons or to revert to a previous set of data can be helpful. The logical place for such functionality is within database-level triggers, where the transactions are taking place. Since the auditing usually logs to an unindexed table, the process is fast.

TIP

Implement "audit log" functionality by creating database-level triggers on tables that need to be audited. An audit log table can be created for each table being audited, storing only the changes to the information within the tables. The INSERT into the audit log table is within a transactional database trigger; therefore, the audit logging only occurs if the transaction is committed successfully. Creating audit logs from within front-end applications may cause transactions to be logged that were not completed successfully. Therefore, a database level trigger is the best place to put such logic.

Audit log tables typically are identical in structure to the table audited, with additional columns for storage of the application user and modification date. An operation flag column can be added to signify which type of DML operation occurred. An example of this type of database trigger is illustrated in the following example. Prior to executing the following database trigger, a new table called s_item_log needs to be created to enable the item logging to take place. The following shows the s_item_log table creation.

File: 5_27.sql

```
CREATE TABLE s_item_log
 (order_id           NUMBER(7),
  item_id            NUMBER(7),
  product_id         NUMBER(7),
  price              NUMBER(11, 2),
  quantity           NUMBER(9),
  quantity_shipped   NUMBER(9),
  log_type           VARCHAR2(1),
  log_user           VARCHAR2(30),
  log_date           DATE);
```

The following database trigger provides an audit of all records updated or deleted from the s_item table. If an UPDATE is performed, the values of the record prior to the update are logged to the s_item_log table along with the designation of a 'U' to signify an update and the username and date/time. If a DELETE is performed, the values of the record are logged to the s_item_log table along with the designation of a 'D' to signify a delete and the username and date/time.

File: 5_28.sql

```
CREATE OR REPLACE TRIGGER bud_item
BEFORE UPDATE OR DELETE
ON s_item
REFERENCING OLD AS OLD NEW AS NEW
FOR EACH ROW
BEGIN
   -- If updating, log "OLD" values and mark log_type as 'U'
   IF (UPDATING) THEN
      INSERT INTO s_item_log (ORDER_ID, ITEM_ID, PRODUCT_ID,
         PRICE, QUANTITY, QUANTITY_SHIPPED,
         LOG_TYPE, LOG_USER, LOG_DATE )
      VALUES ( :OLD.ORDER_ID, :OLD.ITEM_ID, :OLD.PRODUCT_ID,
         :OLD.PRICE, :OLD.QUANTITY, :OLD.QUANTITY_SHIPPED,
         'U', USER, SYSDATE );
   -- If deleting, log "OLD" values and mark log_type as 'D'
   ELSIF (DELETING) THEN
      INSERT INTO s_item_log ( ORDER_ID, ITEM_ID, PRODUCT_ID,
         PRICE, QUANTITY, QUANTITY_SHIPPED,
         LOG_TYPE, LOG_USER, LOG_DATE )
      VALUES ( :OLD.ORDER_ID, :OLD.ITEM_ID, :OLD.PRODUCT_ID,
         :OLD.PRICE, :OLD.QUANTITY, :OLD.QUANTITY_SHIPPED,
         'D', USER, SYSDATE );
   END IF;
END;
/
```

Database-level validation triggers are also used to prohibit invalid or inaccurate data from entering database tables. Front-end application interfaces are a great means of controlling data manipulation of the underlying database tables; however, no matter how bulletproof the application interface, there still exist other avenues of accessing the underlying database tables. As a result, database-level triggers are recommended

Typically, it is best to educate the users that their modifications are being tracked, so they feel a sense of ownership when making modifications. Making sure everyone is granted a unique Oracle username is imperative. Also important is to provide only INSERT privilege on the audit table to general users. If DELETE privileges were given, then the audit table would have a backdoor.

Avoid Mutating Tables (ORA-04091) in Database Triggers

As a PL/SQL developer trying to implement the most efficient and robust features of the language regarding the Oracle database, you occasionally encounter roadblocks. As previously mentioned, the use of database triggers is recommended, especially in Oracle 7.3 and subsequent releases (PL/SQL 2.3), where database-level triggers are compiled like other PL/SQL objects and stored in compiled format for faster execution.

Periodically, you may encounter the following error:

```
ERROR at line 1:
ORA-04091: table PLSQL_USER.S_ORDER is mutating, trigger/function
may not see it
ORA-06512: at "PLSQL_USER.AI_ORDER", line 2
ORA-04088: error during execution of trigger 'PLSQL_USER.AI_ORDER'
```

This can be a painstaking error because you may have developed the trigger that replaces many layers of front-end level validation and calculations. In addition, this error is not encountered until testing time.

The preceding error occurred when an INSERT to the s_order table was attempted, causing the ai_order trigger to fire (5_29.sql following), which inserts into the s_item table. When the INSERT is attempted in the s_item table, a foreign key constraint check is internally executed against the s_order table. This violates Oracle's rules for database level triggers and, thus, a mutating table error results.

The following are scenarios where the mutating table error occurs:

■ When a row-level trigger selects or modifies the contents of the same table where the trigger resides (except when a single record INSERT occurs; in this case, the mutating error does not occur)

■ When a row-level trigger selects or modifies key columns (primary, unique, or foreign) of tables related or constrained, through foreign key constraints

The following trigger example causes the mutating error to occur, because the s_order table is a parent to the s_item table. As a result, the INSERT into the s_item table while inserting into the s_order table causes the foreign key to be checked against the parent record. The foreign key constraint is performing a lookup against the s_order table while within the trigger.

File: 5_29.sql

```
CREATE OR REPLACE TRIGGER ai_order
AFTER INSERT
ON s_order
REFERENCING OLD AS OLD NEW AS NEW
FOR EACH ROW
BEGIN
    INSERT INTO s_item
        (order_id, item_id, product_id)
    VALUES
        (:NEW.order_id, 1, 232);
END ai_order;
/
```

The product_id in the preceding trigger is hardcoded to 232. I added a product in the s_product table with a product_id of 232 and a product_name of NEW PRODUCT to enable this trigger example to work properly.

The following trigger avoids the mutating table error because none of the key columns between the triggering and updating tables have been read or modified. Therefore, you are able to UPDATE or read parent record information from database-level triggers on child table records if none of the key columns are represented. This type of functionality is helpful in making sure summary information on parent records always matches the collection of child record values.

File: 5_30.sql

```
CREATE OR REPLACE TRIGGER bud_item
AFTER INSERT OR UPDATE OF price, quantity OR DELETE
ON s_item
FOR EACH ROW
BEGIN
    -- Update the total for the order by deducting the current line
```

```
    -- item total and adding the new line item total.
  UPDATE s_order
  SET total = NVL(total,0) +
              (NVL(:NEW.price,0) * NVL(:NEW.quantity,0)) -
              (NVL(:OLD.price,0) * NVL(:OLD.quantity,0))
  WHERE order_id = NVL(:OLD.order_id, :NEW.order_id);
END bud_item;
/
```

Finally, the following example is the exception to the rule in some cases. A row-level database trigger based on the INSERT event will enable the same table to be selected against if the INSERT statement that caused the trigger to fire inserted a single row. In other words, the INSERT was not performed as an INSERT INTO…SELECT. As a result, this trigger can cause errors in group INSERTs and not cause errors on singular INSERTs. If a similar trigger was also used for surrounding the UPDATE and DELETE events, any DML statements of those types would result in a mutating table error, regardless of whether the statements affected only one row.

File: 5_31.sql

```
CREATE OR REPLACE TRIGGER bi_item
BEFORE INSERT
ON s_item
REFERENCING OLD AS OLD NEW AS NEW
FOR EACH ROW
DECLARE
   CURSOR cur_check_item IS
      SELECT MAX(item_id)
      FROM    s_item
      WHERE   order_id = :NEW.order_id;
   lv_max_item_num NUMBER;
BEGIN
   IF (:NEW.item_id IS NULL) THEN
      OPEN cur_check_item;
      FETCH cur_check_item INTO lv_max_item_num;
      CLOSE cur_check_item;
      :NEW.item_id := NVL(lv_max_item_num, 0) + 1;
   END IF;
END bi_item;
/
```

Even though not all DML statements within row-level database triggers cause the mutating table error, the scenarios causing the error can be overcome with a little ingenuity.

Avoiding Mutating Tables in
Database Triggers

TIP
Create row- and statement-level database triggers to store and process information within a PL/SQL table to overcome instances where the mutating table error occurs. With this technique, few situations exist where the mutating error cannot be avoided.

The technique is based on the fact that detailed information is available within row-level database triggers. Within statement-level database triggers, even though detailed information is not present, nearly all DML statements are legal. A place to store the detailed information is all that is needed for the statement-level database trigger to perform the desired processing. A PL/SQL table will be used to accommodate the temporary storage requirement.

The following are steps for implementing this mutating error-avoidance technique:

1. Create a PL/SQL package specification, declaring a PL/SQL table variable to be used to store transaction information

2. Create a row-level database trigger placing record information into the PL/SQL table

3. Create a statement-level database trigger to read the previously populated PL/SQL table and perform processing for each record

A statement-level database trigger cannot be used to implement such functionality if a DELETE CASCADE operation is used.

The following example accomplishes the same functionality desired by the preceding ai_order database trigger (5_29.sql) using the error avoidance technique to avoid the mutating table error. A stored PL/SQL package specification was created to define and declare a PL/SQL table, along with an index variable. This PL/SQL table, declared in the package specification, offers "global" referencing and access, which will be implemented from multiple database-level triggers. Refer to the earlier section within this chapter for further information on implementing PL/SQL package specifications to provide global objects and information.

File: 5_32.sql

```
CREATE OR REPLACE PACKAGE order_insert IS
    -- Define a PL/SQL table type to store the order_id info
    TYPE pvg_order_tab IS TABLE OF s_order.order_id%TYPE
        INDEX BY BINARY_INTEGER;
    -- Declare variables for the PL/SQL table and counter
    pvg_order_tab_rec pvg_order_tab;
    pvg_tab_index_num PLS_INTEGER := 0;
END order_insert;
/
```

A row-level trigger was created in the following code segment to store information from each row inserted into the new PL/SQL table within the database package specification. In addition, the table index variable is incremented before adding more information into the PL/SQL table.

File: 5_33.sql

```
CREATE OR REPLACE TRIGGER bi_order_row
BEFORE INSERT
ON s_order
FOR EACH ROW
BEGIN
   -- Increment PL/SQL table index before inserting
   order_insert.pvg_tab_index_num := order_insert.pvg_tab_index_num +
1;
   -- Add the ORDER_ID to the PL/SQL table
   order_insert.pvg_order_tab_rec(order_insert.pvg_tab_index_num) :=
      NVL(:OLD.order_id, :NEW.order_id);
END bi_order_row;
/
```

Finally, in a statement-level trigger as illustrated in the following code segment, the PL/SQL table can be read and the desired processing can occur. In this case, whenever an order is created, a default item record will be created. Often, the statement-level trigger will be set to be processed *after* the transaction if the table information is queried during processing.

File: 5_34.sql

```
CREATE OR REPLACE TRIGGER bi_order_stmt
BEFORE INSERT
ON s_order
BEGIN
   -- Loop through the PL/SQL, performing processing for each order
   FOR lv_tab_index_num IN 1..order_insert.pvg_tab_index_num LOOP
      -- Insert initial item record for every item
      INSERT INTO s_item
      (order_id, item_id, product_id)
      VALUES
      (order_insert.pvg_order_tab_rec(lv_tab_index_num), 1, 232);
   END LOOP;
   -- Initialize package variable counter for subsequent inserts
   order_insert.pvg_tab_index_num := 0;
END bi_order_stmt;
/
```

The functionality that previously caused the mutating table error can be performed at the database level, without disabling or removing foreign key constraints or even creating a temporary table.

With a simple workaround, as outlined in this section, almost any occurrence of the *ORA: 04091* mutating table error can be overcome. Actually, this workaround can become very complex, depending upon the amount of information stored in the package PL/SQL table and the logic involved in processing the information. Even though the preceding example implemented a PL/SQL table of scalar values, PL/SQL tables of records can be created, in which several pieces of information can be held for processing purposes.

This technique of solving the mutating table problem can also be reviewed in the *Oracle8: PL/SQL Programming,* by Scott Urman (Oracle Press).

Overload Procedures and Functions to Make Calls More Flexible

When modular code is developed, often a specification for what is required to run the module is available. For example, a procedure providing salary increases may initially be required to accept an employee ID. An enhancement request may later be submitted to request the same process to be called using a name or social security number of the employee. Other requests may ask for additional flexibility by providing the capability to call the modules dynamically with more parameters. As a PL/SQL developer, you can create separate modules with slightly different names, performing the same process with the given parameters. You can also implement PL/SQL packages enabling multiple declarations of the same module with different types of parameters.

TIP

Implement overloaded procedures and functions to provide more generalized module calls. For several of the Oracle built-in functions and procedures, overloaded versions are available.

Oracle supplied packages that contain overloaded procedures and functions enable these modules to be called with different parameter data types, as well as with different numbers of parameters. By providing overloading, Oracle has provided generalized logic in their modules, enabling the most flexibility possible. This concept should also be considered in your PL/SQL development to provide added flexibility.

Overloading modules is performed by creating separate versions of each module within the PL/SQL package with parameters of different names, different data types, different ordering of parameters of differing data types, and a different number of parameters. Therefore, two declarations of the same module—each having a single VARCHAR2 parameter of different names—could be compiled. However, a module call sending a VARCHAR2 value into the parameter without using named notation would fail, because the PL/SQL Engine cannot determine which version of the module to execute.

For an example of overloading, refer to the inline_pkg package (5_24.sql).

Provide Default Parameter Values When Possible

Parameterizing procedures and functions is used to provide a reusable and more general component to an application. For example, a procedure needed to terminate an employee should not have a particular employee hardcoded, even though it was created for that purpose. A PL/SQL developer must look ahead and believe the same process will be requested of them at a later point in time. As a result, most PL/SQL developers appropriately parameterize their procedures and functions for these purposes.

Sometimes, while you are creating parameters for a specific procedure or function, you know the majority of time-specific parameter values will be used. As a result, nearly all calls to the procedure will consist of the same parameter values being passed, which becomes annoying.

TIP

When a parameter value is used in the majority of the cases, providing a default parameter value enables subsequent calls to be made easier. Rather than hardcoding a parameter value in the majority of the module calls, default the parameter value within the module. This enables a PL/SQL developer to simplify the module calls, removing the redundant parameter values. By defaulting the parameter values, it transforms more complex module calls into simpler ones, by removing many parameter value settings. In fact, with many module calls, it is unnecessary to have any parameters sent, thus assuming the defaulted values.

The following example provides default parameter values for the directory and filename. The string_line procedure provides the capability to search an operating system file line by line to determine if a literal text string is located in the file.

File: 5_35.sql

```
CREATE OR REPLACE PROCEDURE string_line (p_string_txt VARCHAR2,
   p_directory_txt VARCHAR2 := 'c:\temp',
   p_filename_txt VARCHAR2 := 'prodlist.dat') IS
-- This procedure searches the specified file line by line to
-- determine if the string is located in the file.
   lv_line_cnt_num PLS_INTEGER := 0;
   lv_buffer_txt    VARCHAR2(2000);
   lv_found_bln     BOOLEAN := FALSE;
   lv_file_id_num   UTL_FILE.FILE_TYPE;
BEGIN
   -- Open the data load file on the server so it can be read.
   lv_file_id_num := UTL_FILE.FOPEN(p_directory_txt,
      p_filename_txt, 'R');
   LOOP
      lv_buffer_txt    := NULL;
      lv_line_cnt_num := lv_line_cnt_num + 1;
      BEGIN << get_next_line >>
         UTL_FILE.GET_LINE(lv_file_id_num, lv_buffer_txt);
      EXCEPTION
         WHEN NO_DATA_FOUND THEN
            EXIT;
      END get_next_line;
      IF (INSTR(UPPER(lv_buffer_txt), UPPER(p_string_txt)) > 0) THEN
         DBMS_OUTPUT.PUT_LINE('Line ' || lv_line_cnt_num ||
            ': ' || lv_buffer_txt);
         lv_found_bln := TRUE;
      END IF;
   END LOOP;
   IF NOT lv_found_bln THEN
      DBMS_OUTPUT.PUT_LINE('The string was not found in the file.');
   END IF;
   UTL_FILE.FCLOSE_ALL;
EXCEPTION
   WHEN OTHERS THEN
      UTL_FILE.FCLOSE_ALL;
      RAISE_APPLICATION_ERROR(-20103,
         'Unhandled exception occurred while reading data file ' ||
         '(string_line).');
END string_line;
/
```

A call to this procedure can be made in the following ways:

Output (5_35.sql)

```
BEGIN
   -- Only send the search string and accept the defaulted values
   string_line('hello');
   -- Provide values for all parameters, overriding defaults
   string_line('hello', 'c:\utl_dir', 'new_file.dat');
END;
/
```

The defaulted parameter values makes the first call to the string_line procedure easy, providing the capability for overriding the defaulted values by sending values to the module call.

TIP

When providing a default value for a parameter, place the parameters with a default value last in the parameter declaration list. This provides an easier calling mechanism.

TIP

When passing parameters to a PL/SQL program unit, no length is specified for each parameter when the PL/SQL program unit is created. Therefore, care should be taken when processing input values to ensure the value passed into the PL/SQL program unit can be accommodated. If the length cannot be handled, the following error results: ORA-06502: PL/SQL: numeric or value error.

Use Named-Notation for Parameters

Modularized PL/SQL code provides reusability and consistent business processes through the implementation of procedures and functions. Procedures and functions may end up with numerous parameters, and calls to these modules become long lists of parameter values separated by commas. Trying to read such a module call makes it difficult to understand how each parameter value is being received, without looking up the module definition for the positions of each of the parameters.

TIP
Implement named notation to clarify program unit calls when a long parameter list exists or many of the parameters are defaulted. Named notation enables parameters within a module call to be specified by name when sending a value. Rather than assigning the parameter value by position, the actual parameter name from the module definition is specified, followed by "=>", and then the parameter value.

For example, with a procedure call having eight parameters, the last seven of which are defaulted, the first parameter value can be sent by positional notation and any of the last seven can be sent by name. The procedure call with eight parameters is illustrated in the following example.

File: 5_36.sql

```
BEGIN
-- Procedure do_all( p_1_num NUMBER,
--                   p_2_txt VARCHAR2 := NULL,
--                   p_3_txt VARCHAR2 := NULL,
--                   p_4_txt VARCHAR2 := NULL,
--                   p_5_txt VARCHAR2 := NULL,
--                   p_6_txt VARCHAR2 := NULL,
--                   p_7_txt VARCHAR2 := NULL,
--                   p_8_txt VARCHAR2 := NULL );
   do_all(1, p_4_txt => 'OLD', p_6_txt => 'NEW');
END;
/
```

The implementation of named notation simplifies the procedure call by eliminating NULL values in between real parameter values. Along with providing simplicity, using named notation clearly identifies each parameter's value.

When using a combination of positional and named notation, once named notation is used within a call, positional notation can no longer be used within the same call. Therefore, in the previous example, values for the P_7 and P_8 could not be sent following the reference to the P_6 parameter, without specifying the relevant parameter name.

Use PL/SQL Tables as Parameters to Pass Data to Program Units

Occasionally, a situation arises where a program unit needs to accept a variable number of records. The obvious approach might be to create an overloaded package, but this method could become tedious to code if it is possible for more than a handful of records to be passed. A better approach is to use a PL/SQL table to pass the records to the stored program unit. The program can then loop through all the records in the PL/SQL table, processing each one.

Consider a program processing vacation requests from an HTML front end. This vacation scheduler enables the user to enter up to ten vacations and/or days off. With each scheduled vacation, the user must indicate the individual who will perform his/her work for the vacation period. The processing program must also check for overlapping vacations and, if any are found, it must prohibit the entire schedule.

The business rules governing this vacation scheduler make it imperative that the entire schedule entered by the user be sent to the processing program as a single unit. An overloaded package to handle up to ten vacation records would be tedious to code. A program with a large argument list to accept the maximum number of vacation records would be possible, but developing the source code for this type of program would be very tedious and be inflexible to an increase in the number of vacations that could be scheduled at once. The best solution is a program that accepts the entire schedule loaded into a PL/SQL table. The creation segment of this PL/SQL program unit is shown in the following example.

File: 5_37.sql

```
CREATE OR REPLACE PACKAGE process_vacations IS
   TYPE pvg_vacation_rec IS RECORD
      (pvg_vacationing_user_txt     VARCHAR2(30),
       pvg_start_date               VARCHAR2(10),
       pvg_end_date                 VARCHAR2(10),
       pvg_redirect_interviews_txt VARCHAR2(30),
       pvg_redirect_reviews_txt     VARCHAR2(30));
   TYPE pvg_type_vacation_tab IS TABLE OF pvg_vacation_rec
      INDEX BY BINARY_INTEGER;
   PROCEDURE process_schedules (p_vac_tab IN pvg_type_vacation_tab);
END process_vacations;
/
```

File: 5_37a.sql

```
CREATE OR REPLACE PACKAGE BODY process_vacations IS

PROCEDURE process_schedules (p_vac_tab IN pvg_type_vacation_tab) IS
BEGIN
   FOR lv_loop_counter_num IN 1..p_vac_tab.COUNT LOOP
      NULL; -- Processing logic
   END LOOP;
END process_schedules;
END process_vacations;
/
```

The preceding example will only work in PL/SQL version 2.3 and subsequent releases; the earlier versions did not support PL/SQL tables of records. With earlier versions of PL/SQL, the single PL/SQL table must be broken into five individual tables (one for pvg_vacationing_user_txt, one for pvg_start_date, and so forth). The logical records in the five individual tables could be identified through the index value in each table.

Provide Labels for All END Statements

Within modularized PL/SQL program units, such as procedures and functions within packages or nested blocks, understanding where every module begins and ends can be difficult. Readability and maintainability are goals all PL/SQL developers should strive for within their code; therefore, anything that provides more clarity to nested or modularized blocks should be implemented.

TIP

Implement block labels at both the beginning and ending of nested blocks (including PL/SQL blocks and looping blocks), as well as within packaged code. This process of providing a name to a segment of logic and marking the end of the logic inevitably improves readability and, as a result, maintainability.

The use of labels at the end of PL/SQL program units is illustrated throughout this book. The use of END labels on nested block structures, such as anonymous blocks and loops, is illustrated in Chapter 6.

As the complexity of PL/SQL logic increases, the need increases for nested blocks, and the use of block labels in the END statements greatly improves readability.

Encrypt Stored PL/SQL Program Unit Source Code

Oracle provides a helpful feature of storing the source code for PL/SQL stored objects in the database. The source code is accessible in the USER_SOURCE (ALL_SOURCE and DBA_SOURCE) data dictionary view. Being able to view and query this information online is a powerful mechanism that can be extended to re-creating the SQL creation scripts for stored PL/SQL program units. However, the following are three reasons for potential danger to consider.

- Confidential or proprietary business rules or functionality can be embedded in the PL/SQL source code, accessible to Oracle users by querying the data dictionary.

- PL/SQL stored packages, procedures, and functions typically contain the major complexity of the applications. Modification of this logic by someone could damage the core of the application and, thus, cause major problems. The logic is in the data dictionary; therefore, it provides the capability to rebuild the PL/SQL stored program units in a SQL script, modify the logic, and then re-create the object. This re-creation of the object would require certain privileges, but it is still a potential danger.

- Many Oracle development environments follow standard development methodologies, one being a version control mechanism. This mechanism controls the access to the source code; however, if the version control mechanism is not used or bypassed, major problems can arise. If someone modifies a stored PL/SQL program unit, as outlined in the previous point, and implements the changes in production, the next time the proper steps are followed to make changes to the module, it will nullify the previous, non-standard change.

When reviewing your PL/SQL development environment, take the necessary steps to reduce the risk of the previously noted potential danger. Two methods can be deployed to minimize this risk, outside the normal Oracle standard security capabilities. First, access to the data dictionary views, USER_SOURCE, ALL_SOURCE, and DBA_SOURCE, can be limited to only certain Oracle schema. Second, the PL/SQL stored objects can be encrypted through the Oracle provided WRAP facility.

TIP
Use the WRAP facility to convert a stored PL/SQL program unit creation script into a wrapped version, disallowing curious minds from attaining source code access. This type of security is generally not needed because of the basic Oracle security where users must be granted rights to another schema's objects. If confidential business logic or critical core functionality is involved, wrapping the source code is the only way to be sure the logic is unreadable.

The following is an example of the command (under Windows 95, Oracle 7.3) for creating the wrapped source file. With your installation of Oracle, there should be an executable beginning with WRAP. In the following example, the version of the executable was WRAP23.EXE.

```
wrap23 INAME=5_38.sql ONAME=5_38.plb
```

The INAME parameter is required, and assumes a .SQL file extension if the extension is not provided. The ONAME parameter is not required and assumes the INAME parameter's filename with a .PLB extension if not provided.

 TIP
The WRAP facility will accept files that do not contain CREATE DDL statements for packages, procedures, and functions, and creates an output file. The output file created in this case is similar to the input files (minus the comments and extra spaces) because the WRAP facility only converts the statements for creation of packages, procedures, and functions.

The following is an example of a PL/SQL procedure creation script that was wrapped with the previous WRAP command.

File: 5_38.sql

```
CREATE OR REPLACE PROCEDURE exec_ddl (p_statement_txt VARCHAR2) IS
   lv_exec_cursor_num    PLS_INTEGER := DBMS_SQL.OPEN_CURSOR;
   lv_rows_processed_num PLS_INTEGER := 0;
BEGIN
   DBMS_SQL.PARSE (lv_exec_cursor_num, p_statement_txt,
      DBMS_SQL.NATIVE);
```

```
      lv_rows_processed_num := DBMS_SQL.EXECUTE (lv_exec_cursor_num);
      DBMS_SQL.CLOSE_CURSOR (lv_exec_cursor_num);
EXCEPTION
   WHEN OTHERS THEN
      IF DBMS_SQL.IS_OPEN (lv_exec_cursor_num) THEN
         DBMS_SQL.CLOSE_CURSOR (lv_exec_cursor_num);
      END IF;
   RAISE;
END exec_ddl;
/
```

The resulting file, 5_38.plb, contains a wrapped version of the PL/SQL procedure creation script. This script can be executed in SQL*Plus to create the stored PL/SQL procedure in its wrapped structure. When the script is executed, the PL/SQL syntax is checked, but the semantics, such as table and column names, are not. The errors from problems with semantics will arise at runtime; therefore, wrapped code needs to be executed for the semantics to be checked. The following code segment displays the first ten lines of the 5_38.plb file.

File: 5_39.sql (5_38.plb)

```
CREATE OR REPLACE PROCEDURE exec_ddl wrapped
0
abcd
abcd
abcd
abcd
abcd
abcd
abcd
abcd...
```

The wrapped file is in hexadecimal format and is executed in SQL*Plus the same as a nonwrapped PL/SQL creation object. Oracle can read the ASCII or hexadecimal version to create the stored object. The data dictionary will store the hexadecimal version of the object, if the PL/SQL object was created from the wrapped version.

Oracle uses the WRAP facility for a variety of their supplied packages. The standard deployment method of the Oracle PL/SQL packages is to create package specifications as unwrapped PL/SQL source code in operating system files with a .sql extension and package bodies as wrapped files with a .plb extension. Oracle separates the two portions of the package (specification and body) into two separate operating system files. This standard technique deployed by Oracle can be viewed by looking in the ORACLE_HOME/rdbms73/admin directory (Oracle 7.3; however, this location will vary depending on operating system and Oracle version), where all Oracle supplied package's creation scripts are located.

TIP

If you ever decide to wrap any PL/SQL source code, you should know the location of the original unwrapped source code file. This is necessary for any modifications in the future. Therefore, never lose the ASCII file of a wrapped file. The WRAP facility was introduced in PL/SQL 2.2.

Use PL/SQL Tables to Build a Custom Error Stack

The classic method of validating data coming from a front-end is to warn the user of validation errors in a piecemeal manner. Only after the user has corrected the indicated error will the next error be identified. A need may arise to create a data processing package to analyze incoming data and to return all data validation errors in a single pass. Such a scenario might be an HTML order form on the Internet. Long processing times may be encountered using a dial-up connection and would require the back-end processing packages to identify all validation errors at once, eliminating the user's frustration of having to submit data multiple times. The key to providing this type of functionality is to use a PL/SQL table to communicate validation errors between the processing package and the front end. The following example illustrates a server-side processing package returning all validation errors at once.

File: 5_40.sql

```
CREATE OR REPLACE PACKAGE order_entry IS
   TYPE pvg_type_error_tab IS TABLE OF VARCHAR2(500)
      INDEX BY BINARY_INTEGER;
   PROCEDURE process_errors
      (p_txt_1 IN VARCHAR2, p_txt_2 IN VARCHAR2, p_txt_3 IN VARCHAR2,
       p_txt_4 IN VARCHAR2, p_txt_5 IN VARCHAR2,
       p_error_tab OUT order_entry.pvg_type_error_tab);
END order_entry;
/
```

File: 5_40a.sql

```
CREATE OR REPLACE PACKAGE BODY order_entry IS
PROCEDURE process_errors
   (p_txt_1 IN VARCHAR2, p_txt_2 IN VARCHAR2, p_txt_3 IN VARCHAR2,
```

```
      p_txt_4 IN VARCHAR2, p_txt_5 IN VARCHAR2,
      p_error_tab OUT order_entry.pvg_type_error_tab) IS
BEGIN
   IF p_txt_1 IS NULL THEN
      p_error_tab(p_error_tab.COUNT + 1) :=
         'You must enter your first name.';
   END IF;
   IF p_txt_2 IS NULL THEN
      p_error_tab(p_error_tab.COUNT + 1) :=
         'You must enter your last name.';
   END IF;
   IF p_txt_3 IS NULL THEN
      p_error_tab(p_error_tab.COUNT + 1) :=
         'You must enter your credit card number.';
   END IF;
   IF p_txt_4 IS NULL THEN
      p_error_tab(p_error_tab.COUNT + 1) :=
         'You must enter the expiration date of your credit card.';
   END IF;
   IF p_txt_5 IS NULL THEN
      p_error_tab(p_error_tab.COUNT + 1) :=
         'You must indicate VISA or Mastercard.';
   END IF;
   -- Additional processing logic goes here.
EXCEPTION
   WHEN OTHERS THEN
      p_error_tab(p_error_tab.COUNT + 1) :=
         'Unable to process your order.';
      p_error_tab(p_error_tab.COUNT + 1) :=
         'Please call our 800 number for assistance';
END process_errors;
END order_entry;
/
```

The processing package never terminates with an exception. This is necessary to enable the values assigned to the OUT arguments to be returned to the calling program. If the processing package were to terminate with an active EXCEPTION, the values assigned to the OUT arguments would be lost.

When the front end performs a call to the processing package, it must interrogate the PL/SQL table for the presence of any records. The lack of records in the PL/SQL table would indicate a successful submission and the user could be notified. Otherwise, all records in the PL/SQL table would have to be presented to the user. If the front-end is an Oracle form, then the records might be parsed into a non-database block. In the case of the example HTML form, the records might be parsed into a separate browser frame.

Use **RAISE_APPLICATION_ERROR** and **User-Defined Exceptions to Supplement Error Handling**

Along with developing PL/SQL comes the process of debugging and providing information for error messages. Often the exact process flow would be nice to know, to determine the process is following the steps that are assumed. Questions like "Did it get into the loop?" and "Was the condition met?" are not easily answered unless certain flags are used as output.

Complete error-handling routines should be implemented in your development and production environments. The type of error handling can vary greatly depending on the type of processing, whether small transaction (verification) logic or large transaction (data loading) logic. In either case, the EXCEPTION section should be included in every one of your PL/SQL blocks. In the EXCEPTION sections, the RAISE_APPLICATION_ERROR procedure can be used to display a programmer-defined error number and message.

The following example shows the use of the RAISE_APPLICATION_ERROR procedure within the EXCEPTION section and how the raised exception appears as output in SQL*Plus:

File: 5_41.sql

```
DECLARE
   -- Define an exception
   lv_excep EXCEPTION;
BEGIN
   -- Block Processing Logic
   -- Call the exception logic
   RAISE lv_excep;
EXCEPTION
   WHEN lv_excep THEN
      RAISE_APPLICATION_ERROR(-20101, 'Defined exception occurred.');
   WHEN OTHERS THEN
      -- Executed when any error occurs
      RAISE_APPLICATION_ERROR(-20100, 'Unknown exception occurred.');
END;
/
```

Output (5_41.sql)

```
DECLARE
*
ERROR at line 1:
ORA-20101: Defined exception occurred.
ORA-06512: at line 7
```

The resulting error appears to be an Oracle error, but as evidenced in the source code, the PL/SQL block created the error. This technique of creating your own errors and raising them if certain conditions are met is extremely powerful, and provides for an extremely robust error trapping and logging schema.

The error number argument that can be used in the RAISE_APPLICATION_ERROR command range is –20000 to –20999.

Create a Standard User-Defined Exception to Communicate Program Unit Failure

To create a robust data processing program, it is imperative to maintain an open channel of communication between interactive program units. When a subordinate program has encountered an error that must be handled at a higher level, use the EXCEPTION handler infrastructure Oracle has provided. Raising an exception from within an active exception handler will cause that raised exception to propagate outward to the encompassing (calling) program. What remains is a method of differentiating between runtime errors in the current program unit and those in subordinate program units. Consider the following example of an order-processing package.

File: 5_42.sql

```
CREATE OR REPLACE PACKAGE process_orders IS
PROCEDURE fill_and_send;
PROCEDURE fill_orders;
END process_orders;
/
```

File: 5_42a.sql

```
CREATE OR REPLACE PACKAGE BODY process_orders IS
   lv_package_txt VARCHAR2(30) := 'PROCESS_ORDERS';
   lv_order_processed_num PLS_INTEGER;
PROCEDURE fill_and_send IS
   lv_procedure_txt VARCHAR2(30) := 'FILL_AND_SEND';
BEGIN
   -- Processing logic...
   NULL;
EXCEPTION
   WHEN NO_DATA_FOUND THEN
      -- Order data for this order could not be found.
      log_error(lv_package_txt, lv_procedure_txt);
      RAISE NO_DATA_FOUND;
   WHEN OTHERS THEN
      -- An unanticipated error has occurred.
      log_error(lv_package_txt, lv_procedure_txt);
      RAISE NO_DATA_FOUND;
END fill_and_send;
PROCEDURE fill_orders IS
   CURSOR cur_orders IS
      SELECT *
      FROM   s_order
      WHERE order_filled = 'N';
   lv_procedure_txt VARCHAR2(30) := 'FILL_ORDERS';
BEGIN
   FOR cur_orders_rec IN cur_orders LOOP
      BEGIN
         lv_order_processed_num := cur_orders_rec.order_id;
         -- Retrieve inventory for product type...
         -- Retrieve dependency data for current order...
         -- Processing logic...
         COMMIT;
      EXCEPTION
         WHEN NO_DATA_FOUND THEN
            log_error(lv_package_txt, lv_procedure_txt);
         WHEN OTHERS THEN
            -- An unanticipated error has occurred.
            -- Log the error then abort run...
            log_error(lv_package_txt, lv_procedure_txt);
            RAISE NO_DATA_FOUND;
      END;
   END LOOP;
EXCEPTION
   WHEN OTHERS THEN
      -- Handle condition...
```

```
     log_error(lv_package_txt, lv_procedure_txt);
END fill_orders;
END process_orders;
/
```

Note the calls in the exception handlers to the procedure log_error. The log_error procedure is detailed in a later section in this chapter and provides a general error logging mechanism. The mere presence of exception handlers in a program unit does not guarantee robust, proper behavior. The preceding package has two major shortcomings that would prevent the package from responding properly to runtime errors.

1. The use of the standard exception NO_DATA_FOUND to communicate a data error from the fill_and_send procedure when it fails for an order. Standard exceptions should never be used to communicate failure conditions from a subordinate program unit. The main program unit cannot differentiate between a NO_DATA_FOUND condition, originating from a subordinate program unit from one being generated by its own native code. Multiple conditions (a lookup failure in the main procedure or any error in the subordinate procedure) can raise an exception, and the error will be recorded twice by the error handlers—once in the NO_DATA_FOUND exception of the subordinate procedure, and once in the NO_DATA_FOUND exception of the main procedure. Removing the call to the error-logging procedure in the subordinate procedure is not recommended because this would destroy the capability to record runtime values of variables in the procedure in the error log at the point of failure.

2. No provision exists for the fill_and_send procedure to signal a fatal error to the main procedure. In fact, the same NO_DATA_FOUND standard exception is used to signal an unanticipated error to the main procedure. It is highly unlikely that a fatal system error (such as the failure to extend a tablespace) encountered in a subordinate program unit should be signaled to the calling procedure in the same way as a simple data error (failing to find inventory information for an order).

Both these limitations can be eliminated through the deployment of user-defined exceptions. This provides a precise control over the behavior of the application in the event of runtime errors. Correcting the example program is simply a matter of adding two user-defined exceptions:

■ **pu_failure_excep** - Used to indicate a Program Unit Failure. Used to indicate when a severe error was encountered and further processing should not be attempted.

- **data_error_excep** - Used to indicate a data lookup/validation error has occurred and further processing for the current record only should be aborted.

The revised package body would be changed to the following:

File: 5_42b.sql

```
CREATE OR REPLACE PACKAGE BODY process_orders IS
   lv_package_txt VARCHAR2(30) := 'PROCESS_ORDERS';
   lv_order_processed_num PLS_INTEGER;
   data_error_excep EXCEPTION;
   pu_failure_excep EXCEPTION;
PROCEDURE fill_and_send IS
   lv_procedure_txt VARCHAR2(30) := 'FILL_AND_SEND';
BEGIN
   -- Processing logic...
   NULL;
EXCEPTION
   WHEN NO_DATA_FOUND THEN
      -- Order data for this order could not be found.
      log_error(lv_package_txt, lv_procedure_txt);
      RAISE data_error_excep;
   WHEN OTHERS THEN
      -- An unanticipated error has occurred.
      log_error(lv_package_txt, lv_procedure_txt);
      RAISE pu_failure_excep;
END fill_and_send;
PROCEDURE fill_orders IS
   CURSOR cur_orders IS
      SELECT *
      FROM   s_order
      WHERE order_filled = 'N';
   lv_procedure_txt VARCHAR2(30) := 'FILL_ORDERS';
BEGIN
   FOR cur_orders_rec IN cur_orders LOOP
      BEGIN
         lv_order_processed_num := cur_orders_rec.order_id;
         -- Retrieve inventory for product type...
         -- Retrieve dependency data for current order...
         -- Processing logic...
         COMMIT;
      EXCEPTION
         WHEN NO_DATA_FOUND THEN
            log_error(lv_package_txt, lv_procedure_txt);
         WHEN pu_failure_excep THEN
            -- A subordinate package has encountered a severe error.
```

```
            -- Abort run.
            log_error(lv_package_txt, lv_procedure_txt);
            RAISE pu_failure_excep;
         WHEN OTHERS THEN
            -- A unanticipated error has occurred.
            -- Log the error then abort run...
            log_error(lv_package_txt, lv_procedure_txt);
            RAISE pu_failure_excep;
      END;
   END LOOP;
EXCEPTION
   WHEN pu_failure_excep THEN
      -- A subordinate package has encountered a severe error.
      -- Abort run.
      RAISE pu_failure_excep;
   WHEN OTHERS THEN
      -- Handle condition...
      log_error(lv_package_txt, lv_procedure_txt);
      RAISE pu_failure_excep;
END fill_orders;
END process_orders;
/
```

The revised version of the package is superior; the user-defined exceptions yield more granular control over the types of runtime errors being encountered. With this understood, one more point requires discussion: the propagation of user-defined exceptions between program units.

User-defined exceptions are meaningless outside the scope at which they are defined. Therefore, binding user-defined exceptions to Oracle error numbers is necessary to enable them to propagate between program units. This can be accomplished with the EXCEPTION_INIT pragma. Oracle errors numbers below -20000 are reserved for developers. The process_orders package body exception declarations are revised in the example program to read:

```
pu_failure_excep EXCEPTION;
PRAGMA EXCEPTION_INIT (pu_failure_excep, -20000);
data_error_excep EXCEPTION;
PRAGMA EXCEPTION_INIT (data_error_excep, -20001);
```

Now it is possible to propagate the new exceptions between program units. The propagation is possible when the identical user-defined exceptions are used in each program unit, and they are defined by the same error number via the EXCEPTION_INIT pragma.

It is also possible to declare exceptions and put in the EXCEPTION_INIT pragma in a package specification, so grouping all exceptions for an application or component in a package specification is possible. This ensures all units refer to the same exception number by the same name.

Create a Generic Error Handler to Log Errors

When developing large applications, the number of PL/SQL program units can be burdensome when attempting to identify errors in a program unit. This is only complicated more when dealing with various application interfaces. Therefore, it is extremely important to establish a consistent error-handling process to ensure error processing is consistent throughout the application. One solid method of providing a generic handler is to create an error table and log errors to this table.

The following example creates an error-logging table called system_errors and a sequence number to identify each record uniquely in this table. This is created on the database server and used to log all errors throughout the application. The usefulness is dependent on the amount of information logged in the system_errors table.

File: 5_43.sql

```
CREATE SEQUENCE system_error_id NOCACHE;

CREATE TABLE system_errors
    (system_error_id  NUMBER(10,0), package_name  VARCHAR2(50),
     procedure_name  VARCHAR2(50), execution_location  varchar2(20),
     oracle_error_text  VARCHAR2(200),
     additional_information  VARCHAR2(2000),
     call_stack  VARCHAR2(2000), error_stack  VARCHAR2(2000),
     insert_time  DATE, insert_user  VARCHAR2(30));

COMMENT ON TABLE system_errors IS
    'Errors generated by stored program units.';
COMMENT ON COLUMN system_errors.system_error_id IS
    'The system-wide ID to identify a system error. Useful for
     determining the order in which errors were encountered and
     logged.';
COMMENT ON COLUMN system_errors.package_name IS 'The package name.';
COMMENT ON COLUMN system_errors.procedure_name IS
    'The procedure/function name.';
COMMENT ON COLUMN system_errors.execution_location IS
    'A reference to a location in the executing code.';
```

```
COMMENT ON COLUMN system_errors.oracle_error_text IS
  'The text of the Oracle error message.';
COMMENT ON COLUMN system_errors.additional_information IS
  'Any pertinent information the developer may be trapping by the
  error handler.';
COMMENT ON COLUMN system_errors.call_stack IS
  'The call stack at the time of the error.';
COMMENT ON COLUMN system_errors.error_stack IS
  'The error stack at the time of the error.';
COMMENT ON COLUMN system_errors.insert_time IS
  'The date and time of record insertion.';
COMMENT ON COLUMN system_errors.insert_user IS
  'The user inserting the record.';
```

The preceding table creation also provides comments for the table and each of the columns to provide detail of the intent of each column value. The last component necessary to make this general error-handling mechanism a reality is to create a procedure to call that logs information into this table. The following code creates a procedure called log_error, which provides a means for logging information into the system_errors table.

File: 5_44.sql

```
-- log_error (procedure) - Records an error in the error logging table.
CREATE OR REPLACE PROCEDURE log_error
   p_package_txt    VARCHAR2 DEFAULT 'UNKNOWN',
   p_procedure_txt  VARCHAR2 DEFAULT 'UNKNOWN',
   p_location_txt   VARCHAR2 DEFAULT 'UNKNOWN',
   p_error_txt      VARCHAR2 DEFAULT 'UNKNOWN',
   p_text_txt       VARCHAR2 DEFAULT 'NONE',
   p_commit_bln     BOOLEAN  DEFAULT TRUE,
   p_user_txt       VARCHAR2 DEFAULT USER,
   p_time_date      DATE     DEFAULT SYSDATE) IS
   -- p_package_txt - The name of the package in which the error
   --     occurred.
   -- p_procedure_txt - The name of the procedure/function in which
   --     the error occurred.
   -- p_location_txt - The reference to a physical location within the
   --     procedure/function in which the error occurred.
   -- p_error_txt - The Oracle error message.
   -- p_text_txt - Any additional information provided by the
   --     developer to aid in identifying the problem. For example,
   --     this might be a rowid or account number.
   -- p_commit_bln - Boolean flag to determine if this procedure
   --     should perform a commit after writing to the error table.
```

```
    -- p_user_txt - The oracle user account that generated the
    --     error. If left NULL, the current user will be assumed.
    -- p_time_date - The date and time when the error occurred.
    --     If left NULL, the current date and time will be used.
    lv_call_stack_txt  VARCHAR2(2000);
    lv_error_stack_txt VARCHAR2(2000);
    pu_failure_excep     EXCEPTION;
    PRAGMA EXCEPTION_INIT (pu_failure_excep, -20000);
BEGIN
    lv_call_stack_txt := SUBSTR(DBMS_UTILITY.FORMAT_CALL_STACK,
        1, 2000);
    lv_error_stack_txt := SUBSTR(DBMS_UTILITY.FORMAT_ERROR_STACK,
        1, 2000);
    INSERT INTO system_errors
        (system_error_id, package_name, procedure_name,
         execution_location, oracle_error_text, additional_information,
         call_stack, error_stack, insert_time, insert_user)
    VALUES
        (system_error_id.NEXTVAL, SUBSTR(p_package_txt, 1, 50),
         SUBSTR(p_procedure_txt, 1, 50),
         SUBSTR(p_location_txt, 1, 20), SUBSTR(p_error_txt, 1, 200),
         SUBSTR(p_text_txt, 1, 2000), lv_call_stack_txt,
         lv_error_stack_txt, p_time_date, p_user_txt);
    IF p_commit_bln THEN
        COMMIT;
    END IF;
EXCEPTION
    WHEN OTHERS THEN
        RAISE pu_failure_excep;
END log_error;
/
```

The log_error procedure provides several comments to explain the usefulness of each parameter passed to this procedure. EXECUTE privilege can be provided to the schema that will call the log_error procedure. This procedure should then be added to each error handler where it is important to log error information. As for the values for each parameter passed to the log_error procedure, it is important to standardize in your environment with all developers to ensure the necessary level of detail is being logged in the system_errors table.

TIP

A front-end interface can be created to provide a convenient mechanism to interface to the system_errors table. This error table should be reviewed regularly to determine if the errors encountered are a cause for concern.

Summary

In this chapter, several tips and techniques were discussed surrounding modular PL/SQL development within packages, procedures, functions, and database triggers. Storing PL/SQL program units is an excellent option when faced with application partitioning. PL/SQL procedures and functions enable common functionality to become more modular and reusable. PL/SQL packages further the level of modularization and provide encapsulation of multiple, related modules. Many benefits exist in developing PL/SQL logic into packages. Database triggers enable PL/SQL logic to be executed for a DML operation. Validation is a major use for database-level triggers. With the extensive functionality, along with the performance benefits of having PL/SQL source code within the database, stored PL/SQL should be a standard. This chapter can be combined with Chapter 3 and Chapter 4 to form a PL/SQL Development Foundation. This PL/SQL Development Foundation provides a robust set of standards and techniques that can, and should, be deployed in most PL/SQL development environments.

Developing a PL/SQL Development Foundation in your environment is imperative. This is critical to ensure your application core, namely PL/SQL developed code, is functional, consistent, readable, maintainable, dynamic, flexible, and efficient. Once your PL/SQL Development Foundation is established, the next step is the education of your current development staff (and future staff, as they come aboard). Finally, the hardest task of all is to enforce the Development Foundation.

Tips Review

■ PL/SQL program units should be stored in the database to improve development consistency, maintenance, and performance.

■ Oracle 8.1 introduces functional based indexes, providing the capability to index a PL/SQL function used as an inline function in SQL. Refer to Chapter 16 for further details.

■ Oracle 8.1 introduces eight new trigger types that expand the database trigger concept beyond database table triggers. Refer to Chapter 16 for further details.

■ Create a procedure or function within a PL/SQL program unit when a code segment is executed multiple times in a program and is specific only to the current program unit.

■ To isolate an error, encapsulate the PL/SQL source code in a nested PL/SQL block with an EXCEPTION handler.

- Use database packages to further modularize your PL/SQL code, grouping related procedures and functions, to take advantage of the many inherent features and benefits of PL/SQL packages.

- As with globals in any language, use package globals with care. Misuse can result in code that is both difficult to debug and maintain.

- Package globals are not directly accessible from the client-side. Refer to Chapter 14 for a technique to provide access to package globals from client-side products.

- Implement PL/SQL package specifications as repositories for reusable PL/SQL objects, such as user-defined data types, cursors, and exceptions.

- Separate the package specification and package body into two files and only compile each object if the content of the object has changed. Recompiling the package specification every time the package body is compiled causes extra compilation steps, which can cause extra unnecessary work.

- Prior to release Oracle 8.0, when DBMS_SQL.PARSE for DDL commands was executed in a PL/SQL program unit, no error was returned if the command failed. Therefore, an exception was not raised. After the release of Oracle 8.0, this processing changed and, if you want to trap the error, the DBMS_SQL.PARSE can be encapsulated in a nested block to handle the error as desired.

- When creating a PL/SQL function, provide a common exit to the module by having only one RETURN statement. The returned value can be assigned to a local variable. This local variable can then be referenced in the RETURN statement and is recommended to be the last statement of the function.

- Implement inline functions to simplify complex SQL logic and reduce redundancy. Creating a standalone function that can be used inline is no different than any Oracle-supplied SQL or PL/SQL function.

- PL/SQL functions can be called from SQL statements. When the PL/SQL function is created as a standalone stored PL/SQL program unit, the purity level does not have to be specified and is determined internally by Oracle. If the PL/SQL function is defined within a package, then the purity level must be defined through the RESTRICTED_REFERENCES pragma definition in the package specification.

- Combine different triggers on the same table, where redundant code is evident. No matter what triggering event has occurred, the logic is often the same. To create a combined trigger and also separate different logic within it, the INSERTING, UPDATING, and DELETING keywords can be used. These Booleans evaluate to TRUE if the corresponding transaction type is occurring, enabling you to separate the logic within a combined trigger. In conjunction with the UPDATING Boolean option, you are able to specify a column name.

■ Implement database-level triggers to enforce validation to ensure data accuracy. Many Oracle developers have the false notion that a trigger that fires on every INSERT, UPDATE, or DELETE will be slow. If a trigger contains just PL/SQL logic, the trigger will be almost unnoticeable. Likewise, if the trigger performs DML, the speed of the trigger relies heavily on the speed of the DML. A poorly tuned query within a PL/SQL cursor will cause the transaction by which the trigger is executing to be slow. For more helpful information on tuning DML statements, refer to Chapter 7.

■ Implement "audit log" functionality by creating database-level triggers on tables that need to be audited. An audit log table can be created for each table audited, storing only the changes to the information within the tables. The INSERT into the audit log table is within a transactional database trigger; therefore, the audit logging only occurs if the transaction is committed successfully. Creating audit logs from within front-end applications may cause transactions that were not completed successfully to be logged. Therefore, a database-level trigger is the best place to put such logic.

■ Create row- and statement-level database triggers to store and process information within a PL/SQL table to overcome instances where the mutating table error occurs. With this technique, few situations exist where the mutating error cannot be avoided.

■ Implement overloaded procedures and functions to provide more generalized module calls. For several of the Oracle built-in functions and procedures, overloaded versions are available.

■ When a parameter value is used in the majority of the cases, providing a default parameter value enables subsequent calls to be made easier. Rather than hardcoding a parameter value in the majority of the module calls, default the parameter value within the module. This enables a PL/SQL developer to simplify the module calls, removing the redundant parameter values. By setting the default of the parameter values, it transforms more complex module calls into simpler ones, by removing many parameter value settings. In fact, with many module calls, it becomes unnecessary to have any parameters sent, thus assuming the defaulted values.

■ When providing a default value for a parameter, place the parameters with a default value last in the parameter declaration list. This provides an easier calling mechanism.

■ When passing parameters to a PL/SQL program unit, no length is specified for each parameter when the PL/SQL program unit is created. Therefore, care should be taken when processing input values to ensure the value passed into the PL/SQL program unit can be accommodated. If the length cannot be handled, the following error will result: *ORA-06502: PL/SQL: numeric or value error.*

■ Implement named notation to clarify program unit calls when there is a long parameter list or many of the parameters are defaulted. Named-notation enables parameters within a module call to be specified by name when sending a value. Rather than assigning the parameter value by position, the actual parameter name from the module definition is specified, followed by "=>", and the parameter value.

■ Implement block labels at both the beginning and ending of nested blocks (including PL/SQL blocks and looping blocks), as well as within packaged code. This process of providing a name to a segment of logic and marking the end of the logic inevitably improves readability and, as a result, maintainability.

■ Use the WRAP facility to convert a normal stored program creation script into a wrapped version, disallowing curious minds from attaining source code access.

■ The WRAP facility will accept files that do not contain CREATE DDL statements for packages, procedures, and functions and creates an output file. The output file created in this case is similar to the input files (minus the comments and extra spaces) because the WRAP facility only converts the statements for creation of packages, procedures, and functions.

■ If you ever decide to wrap any PL/SQL source code, you should know the location of the original unwrapped source code file. This is necessary for any modifications in the future. Therefore, never lose the ASCII file of a wrapped file. The WRAP facility was introduced in PL/SQL 2.2.

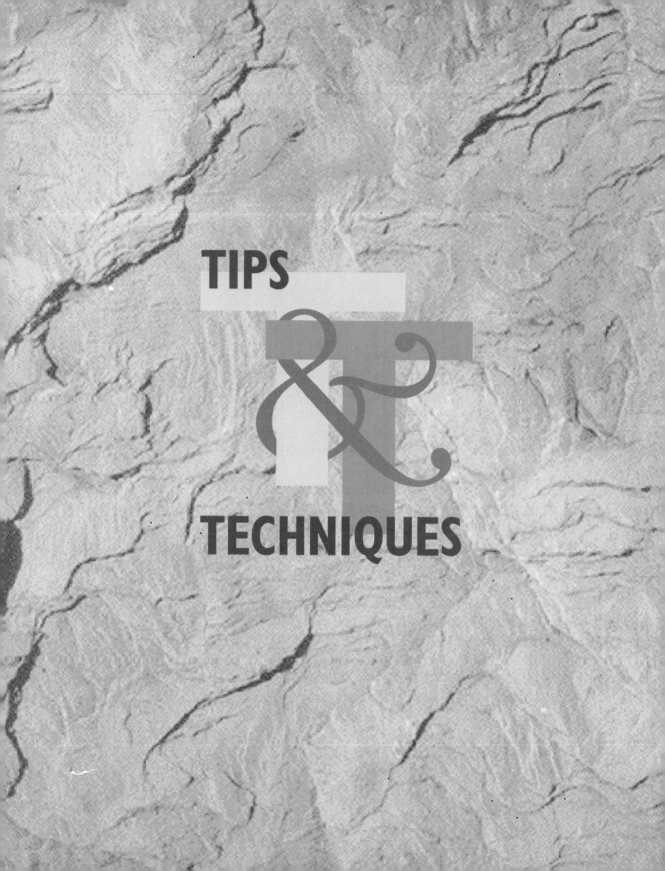

TIPS & TECHNIQUES

CHAPTER
6

Exploring the Expansive PL/SQL Language Commands

The PL/SQL language is similar to many other programming languages, so if you are familiar with other programming languages, the transition to PL/SQL will be natural. The commands and functional capabilities make PL/SQL a robust language. Once the basics of the commands and functionality have been learned, the next step is combining the commands and functionality to develop complex programs, followed by understanding the intricacies of these powerful commands.

This chapter focuses on the PL/SQL language commands and highlights the robustness of the language commands by providing a series of examples. These examples provide insight into many tips and techniques that can be deployed to take advantage of the many components of the PL/SQL language.

Many of the functions operate the same as their SQL counterpart. These functions are presented in this chapter in the PL/SQL context to highlight the flexibility of calling these functions directly in PL/SQL. The goal of this chapter is to highlight the language commands and the power built into the language to ensure developers are using the language to the fullest. This chapter provides tips and techniques on the following PL/SQL language areas:

- Build flexibility into the declaration section

  - Use constants for flexibility

  - Expand default values by using functions

  - Ease maintenance by using %ROWTYPE and %TYPE

  - Understand the NOT NULL attribute

- Name anonymous blocks to enable unique variable naming

- Expand LABEL use for LOOPs to allow more control

- Use PL/SQL cursor flexibility

  - Use column aliases in cursors

  - Check the %ROWCOUNT cursor attribute

  - Understand the %FOUND cursor attribute

- Use IF statements to the fullest

  - Use the ELSIF component of the IF statement

- Use the NULL command

- Control all transaction logic before a PL/SQL program unit completes

- Enable the use of literal single quotes in literal strings

- Beware of multiple line comments
- Examine the differences between SQL and PL/SQL
- Expand the standard operand capabilities

  - Extend the BETWEEN operand use
  - Expand the LIKE operand use
  - Expand the IN operand use

- Build a numeric function arsenal
  - Use MOD for controlling feedback
  - Use CEIL and FLOOR for forced rounding
  - Manipulate numbers with ROUND/TRUNC/SIGN/ABS

- Build a character function arsenal
  - Modify character strings with INITCAP/LOWER/UPPER
  - Format and convert character strings with RPAD/LPAD/CHR/TO_CHAR
  - Process character strings with INSTR/LENGTH/LTRIM/RTRIM
  - Transform character strings with REPLACE/TRANSLATE

- Build a date function arsenal
- Make data type conversion easy by using the conversion functions

  - Convert dates and numbers with TO_CHAR
  - Convert character strings to dates with TO_DATE
  - Convert character strings to numbers with TO_NUMBER
  - Ensure NULL values are handled as expected with NVL

Build Flexibility into the Declaration Section

The declaration section of a PL/SQL program unit offers a tremendous amount of flexibility and functionality, which is often unused. This functionality includes setting constants for use as format masks in the PL/SQL program units, setting default values that use PL/SQL functions, using %ROWTYPE and %TYPE to declare variables, and understanding the NOT NULL attribute.

Each of these declaration areas is explored and highlighted in the following sections.

Use Constants for Flexibility

Constants are a good method for setting certain necessary values throughout your application. Any value that has changed in the past, or may change in the future, can be set in a global package to ease maintenance and ensure the value can be changed in one location and replicated throughout your application.

Generally, I recommend limiting the use of PL/SQL constants to self-contained PL/SQL program units. I typically store all my constant variables, which may change later, in a global application-wide database table. The database storage approach eliminates the need for modifications to source code and recompilation of stored PL/SQL program units.

Constant values provide a wealth of flexibility, which is not limited only to setting constant values for calculations or thresholds. The following is an example of setting a format mask for a PL/SQL program unit used to display a value. The format mask is controlled by a constant value. One change to the format mask in the constant and all references to this constant variable format mask are changed.

The following example illustrates a format mask of 99999.99.

File: 6_1.sql

```
DECLARE
    lv_format_txt   CONSTANT VARCHAR2(11)  := '99999.99';
    lv_test_txt              VARCHAR2(11);
    lv_test_num              NUMBER := 54321;
BEGIN
    lv_test_txt := TO_CHAR(lv_test_num, lv_format_txt);
    DBMS_OUTPUT.PUT_LINE('Test Value: ' || lv_test_txt);
END;
/
```

Output (6_1.sql)

```
Test Value:  54321.00

PL/SQL procedure successfully completed.
```

The following example illustrates how easy it is to change the format mask to $99,999.99.

File: 6_2.sql

```
DECLARE
   lv_format_txt  CONSTANT VARCHAR2(11)  := '$99,999.99';
   lv_test_txt              VARCHAR2(11);
   lv_test_num              NUMBER := 54321;
BEGIN
   lv_test_txt := TO_CHAR(lv_test_num, lv_format_txt);
   DBMS_OUTPUT.PUT_LINE('Test Value: ' || lv_test_txt);
END;
/
```

Output (6_2.sql)

```
Test Value:  $54,321.00

PL/SQL procedure successfully completed.
```

The database table storage approach saves maintenance in an application when values that are constant throughout an application change. This approach can be expanded beyond the standard approach of threshold variables, as outlined in the preceding example.

Expand Default Values by Using Functions

When declaring variables, setting a default value to be used when the value is first referenced is often advantageous. If the value may not change, a default value should be specified. Number values used for counters typically should be set to 0 in the variable declaration. However, the capability of setting these default values extends well beyond constant values and enables PL/SQL functions to be used to assign a default value.

This capability is illustrated in the following example, where one variable is defaulted to SYSDATE and one variable is defaulted to the current month.

File: 6_3.sql

```
DECLARE
   lv_current_date      DATE := SYSDATE;
   lv_current_month_txt VARCHAR(3) := TO_CHAR(SYSDATE, 'MON');
BEGIN
   DBMS_OUTPUT.PUT_LINE('Current Date:  ' ||lv_current_date);
   DBMS_OUTPUT.PUT_LINE('Current Month: ' ||lv_current_month_txt);
END;
/
```

Building Flexibility into the Declaration Section

Output (6_3.sql)

```
Current Date:  26-APR-99
Current Month: APR

PL/SQL procedure successfully completed.
```

The preceding technique becomes extremely powerful when dynamic default values are needed.

Ease Maintenance by Using %ROWTYPE and %TYPE

The use of %ROWTYPE and %TYPE are helpful when developing applications to ensure references to the same columns in different locations have the same declaration. The use of these two declaration attributes becomes more advantageous when maintaining applications and a database column or application variable must change in terms of length. The expansion of the length of a character column is a common modification in many applications. The more %ROWTYPE and %TYPE are used in PL/SQL to tie variable declarations to the database and/or other PL/SQL variables used in many locations, the easier development and maintenance will be.

The declaration can be tied to a database record, database column, or PL/SQL variable previously defined in the declaration scope. This is illustrated in the following example with the use of %ROWTYPE and %TYPE.

File: 6_4.sql

```
DECLARE
   CURSOR cur_employee IS
      SELECT employee_last_name, employee_first_name, employee_id
      FROM   s_employee
      ORDER BY employee_last_name;
   CURSOR cur_customer IS
      SELECT *
      FROM   s_customer;
   -- Multiple variables declared based on cursor with
   -- columns listed (selected columns)
   lv_cur_emp_rec          cur_employee%ROWTYPE;
   -- Multiple variables declared based on cursor without
   -- columns listed (all columns)
   lv_cur_cust_rec         cur_customer%ROWTYPE;
   -- Multiple variables declared based on database
   -- table (all columns)
```

```
    lv_emp_rec                s_employee%ROWTYPE;
    -- One variable declared based on previously declared %ROWTYPE
    -- variable
    lv_emp_last_name_txt  lv_cur_emp_rec.employee_last_name%TYPE;
    -- One variable declared based on previous variable declaration
    lv_emp_last_name_txt2 lv_emp_last_name_txt%TYPE;
    -- Two variables declared based on database table column
    -- definitions
    lv_cust_name_txt          s_customer.customer_name%TYPE;
    lv_emp_first_name_txt s_employee.employee_first_name%TYPE;
BEGIN
    lv_cur_emp_rec.employee_last_name := 'TREZZO';
    lv_cur_cust_rec.customer_name     := 'TUSC';
    lv_emp_rec.employee_first_name    := 'JOE';
    lv_emp_last_name_txt              := 'TREZZO';
    lv_emp_last_name_txt2             := 'TREZZO';
    lv_cust_name_txt                  := 'TUSC';
    lv_emp_first_name_txt             := 'JOE';
END;
/
```

All of the preceding examples demonstrate the flexibility in using the %ROWTYPE and %TYPE declarations. The %TYPE cannot reference a cursor column directly. The following is line 20 from the preceding example:

```
    lv_emp_last_name_txt  lv_cur_emp_rec.employee_last_name%TYPE;
```

A natural change would be to reference the cur_employee cursor instead of the lv_cur_employee_rec variable, as shown in the following example.

```
    lv_emp_last_name_txt  cur_employee.employee_last_name%TYPE;
```

However, this results in the following error.

```
ORA-06550: line 18, column 26:
PLS-00201: identifier 'CUR_EMPLOYEE.EMPLOYEE_LAST_NAME' must be
declared
ORA-06550: line 18, column 26:
PL/SQL: Item ignored
ORA-06550: line 20, column 26:
PLS-00320: the declaration of the type of this expression is
incomplete or malformed
```

A %TYPE attribute cannot be used to reference a cursor variable directly. The reference must be to a variable declared with the %ROWTYPE.

Understand the **NOT NULL** Attribute

The NOT NULL attribute in a variable declaration is often misunderstood. PL/SQL does not transfer this attribute of a variable declaration when a database column or other PL/SQL variable defined as NOT NULL is referenced in the declaration of another variable. This is important to ensure that if a variable is to be defined as NOT NULL, then this attribute must be stated specifically. The NOT NULL attribute does not transfer with the use of %TYPE or %ROWTYPE.

When a variable is declared as NOT NULL, then a default value must be assigned in the declaration, or an error will result upon compilation. The following example demonstrates this assignment.

File: 6_5.sql

```
DECLARE
    lv_test_txt VARCHAR2(5) NOT NULL DEFAULT 'HELLO';
BEGIN
    DBMS_OUTPUT.PUT_LINE('Test Value: ' || lv_test_txt);
END;
/
```

Output (6_5.sql)

```
Test Value: HELLO

PL/SQL procedure successfully completed.
```

The NOT NULL attribute does not pass to the PL/SQL declaration when a %ROWTYPE or %TYPE is used. This characteristic is consistent whether the reference is to a database column or other PL/SQL variable. This is illustrated in the following example.

Notice the customer_name database column in the s_customer table is declared as NOT NULL, as the following listing shows.

```
DESCR s_customer
 Name                                      Null?     Type
 ---------------------------------------   --------  ----
 CUSTOMER_ID                               NOT NULL  NUMBER(7)
 CUSTOMER_NAME                             NOT NULL  VARCHAR2(50)
 PHONE                                               VARCHAR2(15)
 ADDRESS                                             VARCHAR2(400)
 CITY                                                VARCHAR2(35)
 STATE                                               VARCHAR2(30)
 COUNTRY                                             VARCHAR2(30)
```

ZIP_CODE	VARCHAR2(10)
CREDIT_RATING	VARCHAR2(9)
SALES_REP_ID	NUMBER(7)
REGION_ID	NUMBER(7)
COMMENTS	VARCHAR2(255)
PREFERRED_CUSTOMER	NOT NULL VARCHAR2(1)
SHIPPING_METHOD	NOT NULL VARCHAR2(1)

The following example illustrates a PL/SQL variable declaration referencing the database column customer_name. The data type is inherited, but the NOT NULL attribute is not inherited. Likewise, the lv_temp_txt variable is defined as NOT NULL and the lv_temp_txt2 variable references this variable in the declaration. Both are cases of the NOT NULL attribute not being inherited with the %TYPE attribute.

File: 6_6.sql

```
DECLARE
   lv_customer_name_txt s_customer.customer_name%TYPE;
   lv_temp_txt          VARCHAR2(10) NOT NULL DEFAULT 'Testing';
   lv_temp_txt2         lv_temp_txt%TYPE;
BEGIN
   DBMS_OUTPUT.PUT_LINE('Customer Name: ' ||
      NVL(lv_customer_name_txt, 'N/A'));
   DBMS_OUTPUT.PUT_LINE('Temp Var: ' ||
      NVL(lv_temp_txt, 'N/A'));
   DBMS_OUTPUT.PUT_LINE('Temp Var2: ' ||
      NVL(lv_temp_txt2, 'N/A'));
END;
/
```

Output (6_6.sql)

```
Customer Name: N/A
Temp Var: Testing
Temp Var2: N/A

PL/SQL procedure successfully completed.
```

TIP
If you use the %ROWTYPE or %TYPE attribute and the NOT NULL attribute is desired, it must be explicitly defined for each variable. Only the data type and length are transferred to the declared variable through these two attributes.

Building Flexibility into the Declaration Section

Name Anonymous Blocks to Enable Unique Variable Naming

PL/SQL program units often contain nested PL/SQL blocks to provide more refined error trapping or nested functionality. When PL/SQL program units become lengthy, keeping track of the start and end of PL/SQL blocks or the location of the variable declarations becomes increasingly difficult. Additionally, if the same variable is used in a nested block, there is no way to reference the same variable declared at a more global level, even though it is still in scope.

PL/SQL provides the capability to provide a name or a label to a block, as well as other objects, such as loops, to distinguish between blocks and to provide a means for referencing the variable. This technique is shown in the following and uses the label command.

File: 6_7.sql

```
<<BLOCK1>>
DECLARE
   lv_var_num1 NUMBER := 10;
BEGIN
   <<BLOCK2>>
   DECLARE
      lv_var_num1 NUMBER := 20;
   BEGIN
      DBMS_OUTPUT.PUT_LINE('Value for lv_var_num1:          ' ||
         lv_var_num1);
      DBMS_OUTPUT.PUT_LINE('Value for BLOCK1.lv_var_num1: ' ||
         block1.lv_var_num1);
      DBMS_OUTPUT.PUT_LINE('Value for BLOCK2.lv_var_num1: ' ||
         block2.lv_var_num1);
   END BLOCK2;
END BLOCK1;
/
```

Output (6_7.sql)

```
Value for lv_var_num1:          20
Value for BLOCK1.lv_var_num1: 10
Value for BLOCK2.lv_var_num1: 20

PL/SQL procedure successfully completed.
```

In the preceding example, the labels occur prior to the PL/SQL declaration section and can also be used in the END command for the blocks. In the preceding example, lv_var_num1 was declared in both blocks, but the inner block declaration takes precedence when referenced. If desired, the local block name can still be used as previously illustrated, but this is neither necessary nor recommended. The outer variable needs to contain the outer block name to reference the variable.

Expand LABEL Usage for LOOPs to Allow More Control

Creating a label for loops in addition to PL/SQL blocks is helpful, as outlined in the previous section. Providing a label for a loop provides the same advantages of being able to identify the start and end of large sections of PL/SQL code, as well as being able to break out of a certain loop by name when loops are nested.

Loop labeling is illustrated in the following example, with the EXIT signifying to break out of the outer loop.

File: 6_8.sql

```
DECLARE
    lv_counter_num PLS_INTEGER := 0;
BEGIN
  <<LOOP1>>
  LOOP
     <<LOOP2>>
     LOOP
        lv_counter_num := lv_counter_num + 1;
        DBMS_OUTPUT.PUT_LINE('Counter: ' ||
           lv_counter_num);
        EXIT LOOP1 WHEN lv_counter_num = 3;
     END LOOP LOOP2;
        DBMS_OUTPUT.PUT_LINE('Exited LOOP2');
  END LOOP LOOP1;
        DBMS_OUTPUT.PUT_LINE('Exited LOOP1');
END;
/
```

Output (6_8.sql)

```
Counter: 1
Counter: 2
Counter: 3
Exited LOOP1

PL/SQL procedure successfully completed.
```

TIP

Always make sure to default counters to 0 in the declaration, to ensure the increment is being made properly. If the default assignment of 0 to the lv_counter_num variable is removed in the preceding example, this PL/SQL program unit will be placed in an infinite loop until the DBMS_OUTPUT message buffer limit is exceeded. Remember, NULL plus 1 is NULL.

Use PL/SQL Cursor Flexibility

The majority of database interaction is in the form of SELECTing information from the database. An abundance of flexibility is built into PL/SQL cursors by default, which is either not used or misunderstood.

This flexibility includes using column aliases, cursor attributes associated with each cursor, SQL attributes associated with each DML statement, and the use of GROUP BY functions in SELECTs. Each of these areas is explored in the following sections. Refer to Chapter 4 for further information on SELECT cursors.

Use Column Aliases in Cursors

Any time a value is retrieved from the database, if the value is not the result of the column name in the database, then an alias needs to be created to reference this value in PL/SQL. Any function or modification to a result column must have an alias defined for that column. This is illustrated in the following example with the concatenation of two columns and the use of the DECODE function.

File: 6_9.sql

```
DECLARE
   CURSOR cur_employee IS
      SELECT employee_last_name || ', ' ||
             employee_first_name name,
             DECODE(commission_pct, NULL, 'NO',
                    0, 'NO', 'YES') comm_flag
      FROM   s_employee
      ORDER BY DECODE(COMMISSION_PCT, NULL, 'NO',
                      0, 'NO', 'YES') DESC;
BEGIN
   FOR lv_cur_employee_rec IN cur_employee LOOP
      DBMS_OUTPUT.PUT_LINE('Employee: ' ||
         lv_cur_employee_rec.name || CHR(9) ||
         'Commission?: ' || lv_cur_employee_rec.comm_flag);
```

```
   END LOOP;
END;
/
```

Output (6_9.sql)

```
Employee: MAGEE, COLIN  Commission?: YES
Employee: GILJUM, HENRY Commission?: YES
Employee: NGUYEN, MAI   Commission?: YES
Employee: VELASQUEZ, CARMEN     Commission?: NO
Employee: NGAO, LADORIS Commission?: NO
Employee: NAGAYAMA, MIDORI      Commission?: NO
Employee: MADURO, ELENA Commission?: NO

PL/SQL procedure successfully completed.
```

Only a subset of records is displayed in the preceding output.

Check the %ROWCOUNT Cursor Attribute

The %ROWCOUNT attribute for SELECT statements is either a 1 or a 0, depending on whether the FETCH found a record. The %ROWCOUNT becomes more valuable when used with DML statements. If the statement is an INSERT, the question is: "Did one or more records insert as expected?" If the statement is an UPDATE, the question is: "Did the UPDATE succeed, and how many records were updated?" If the statement is a DELETE, the question is: "Did the DELETE succeed, and how many records were deleted?"

The %ROWCOUNT attribute can also be used as part of the PL/SQL logic flow. I have used this technique in the past when performing data loading. To summarize: a nightly program would read a record from an operating system datafile, then attempt an update of the database by the unique record ID of the record. If the record did not exist, 0 records (SQL%ROWCOUNT = 0) would be updated and the record would be considered new and inserted into the database table. If the record updated an existing record (SQL%ROWCOUNT=1), then the next record would be read and processed.

The %ROWCOUNT attribute is illustrated in the following example.

File: 6_10.sql

```
BEGIN
   UPDATE s_employee
   SET    salary = nvl(salary, 0) * 1.10
   WHERE  department_id = 32;
   DBMS_OUTPUT.PUT_LINE('Number of Rows Updated: ' ||
```

```
        SQL%ROWCOUNT);
END;
/
```

Output (6_10.sql)

```
Number of Rows Updated: 0

PL/SQL procedure successfully completed.
```

Even though the UPDATE did not update any records, it still completed without error and would continue processing. The following example shows records being updated.

File: 6_11.sql

```
BEGIN
   UPDATE s_employee
   SET    salary = nvl(salary, 0) * 1.10
   WHERE  department_id = 31;
   DBMS_OUTPUT.PUT_LINE('Number of Rows Updated: ' ||
      SQL%ROWCOUNT);
END;
/
```

Output (6_11.sql)

```
Number of Rows Updated: 6

PL/SQL procedure successfully completed.
```

TIP
The %ROWCOUNT attribute only reflects the result from the most recent SQL statement. If you perform five updates, then refer to this attribute; only the updated count for the last update will be returned. It is a single variable that contains the value at a point in time that is overwritten every SQL statement execution.

Understand the %FOUND Cursor Attribute

The %FOUND and %NOTFOUND attributes of a cursor are useful to determine if processing should continue, if the cursor should be closed, or if some special functioning should be invoked. The following is a basic example.

File: 6_12.sql

```
DECLARE
   CURSOR cur_employee_salary IS
      SELECT salary
      FROM   s_employee
      WHERE  department_id = 44;
   lv_cur_employee_salary cur_employee_salary%ROWTYPE;
BEGIN
   OPEN cur_employee_salary;
   FETCH cur_employee_salary INTO lv_cur_employee_salary;
   IF cur_employee_salary%FOUND THEN
      DBMS_OUTPUT.PUT_LINE('Record Found.');
   ELSE
      DBMS_OUTPUT.PUT_LINE('Record NOT Found.');
   END IF;
   CLOSE cur_employee_salary;
END;
/
```

Output (6_12.sql)

```
Record NOT Found.

PL/SQL procedure successfully completed.
```

No records exist with the department_id of 44, so the %FOUND is set to FALSE. Be careful when using this attribute when the cursor involves a GROUP function. A GROUP function always returns a record. When no records meet the predicate and a GROUP function is present, a NULL record is returned, as the following example illustrates. Therefore, when working with GROUP functions, the %FOUND attribute should be treated differently, since it is always set to TRUE.

File: 6_13.sql

```
DECLARE
   CURSOR cur_employee_salary IS
      SELECT SUM(salary)
      FROM   s_employee
      WHERE  department_id = 44;
   lv_cur_employee_salary cur_employee_salary%ROWTYPE;
BEGIN
   OPEN cur_employee_salary;
   FETCH cur_employee_salary INTO lv_cur_employee_salary;
   IF cur_employee_salary%FOUND THEN
      DBMS_OUTPUT.PUT_LINE('Record Found.');
```

```
    ELSE
        DBMS_OUTPUT.PUT_LINE('Record NOT Found.');
    END IF;
    CLOSE cur_employee_salary;
END;
/
```

Output (6_13.sql)

```
Record Found.

PL/SQL procedure successfully completed.
```

TIP
If GROUP functions are being used in a cursor and the %FOUND or %NOTFOUND are being used, beware of the result even if no records meet the predicate criteria.

TIP
When referring to the %FOUND, %NOTFOUND, and %ROWCOUNT cursor attributes, the name of the cursor must precede the attribute when referencing an explicit cursor and the literal "SQL" must precede the attribute when referencing a DML or query statement (SELECT INTO, INSERT, UPDATE, or DELETE).

Use IF Statement to the Fullest

The IF statement is a basic structure in PL/SQL that can be greatly enhanced by using nested PL/SQL functions to process complex conditions. The determination of the logic of an IF statement is dependent on the result: TRUE or FALSE (or NULL— processes the same as if the result is FALSE). Therefore, Boolean logic is one method of extending the basics of the IF statement. Additionally, other methods of extending the IF statement are shown in the following example.

The following function is created to enable a date to be passed as an argument to verify the date follows the standard input format of 'MM/DD/YYYY'. If the input date is a valid date with a 4-digit year entered, then the function returns TRUE; otherwise, it returns FALSE. The IF statement in the function illustrates the flexibility of nested functions in PL/SQL.

Using the IF Statement to the Fullest

File: 6_14.sql

```
CREATE OR REPLACE FUNCTION validate_date_format
   (p_input_date VARCHAR2) RETURN BOOLEAN IS
   lv_result_date DATE;
BEGIN
   lv_result_date := TO_DATE(p_input_date, 'MM/DD/YYYY');
   IF LENGTH(SUBSTR(input_date,
      INSTR(input_date, '/', 1, 2) + 1)) = 4 THEN
      RETURN TRUE;
   ELSE
      RETURN FALSE;
   END IF;
EXCEPTION
   WHEN OTHERS THEN
      RETURN FALSE;
END validate_date_format;
/
```

The following PL/SQL program unit illustrates the use of a function in an IF statement returning either TRUE or FALSE. This program unit must be executed in SQL*Plus and prompts for a date. If the date input is valid as defined in the function validate_date_format, then the message displays the date is VALID; otherwise, the message displays INVALID.

File: 6_15.sql

```
BEGIN
   IF validate_date_format('&&valid_date') THEN
      DBMS_OUTPUT.PUT_LINE('Date: ' || '&&valid_date' ||
         CHR(9) || ' is a VALID Date.');
   ELSE
      DBMS_OUTPUT.PUT_LINE('Date: ' || '&&valid_date' ||
         CHR(9) || ' is an INVALID Date.');
   END IF;
END;
/
```

Output (6_15.sql)

```
Enter value for valid_date: 01/01/1999

Date: 01/01/1999          is a VALID Date.

PL/SQL procedure successfully completed.
```

Output (6_15.sql)

```
Enter value for valid_date: 01-JAN-99

Date: 01-JAN-99  is an INVALID Date.

PL/SQL procedure successfully completed.
```

Output (6_15.sql)

```
Enter value for valid_date: 01/01/99

Date: 01/01/99   is an INVALID Date.

PL/SQL procedure successfully completed.
```

In the preceding examples, three dates were entered (01/01/1999, 01-JAN-99, and 01/01/99) and only the date in the proper format and with a four-digit year is considered valid.

When using Boolean variables in conditional commands, such as an IF statement or a LOOP statement, the condition will evaluate to FALSE if the Boolean value is NULL. This is illustrated in the following example.

File: 6_16.sql

```
DECLARE
    lv_temp_bln BOOLEAN;
BEGIN
    IF lv_temp_bln THEN
        DBMS_OUTPUT.PUT_LINE('TRUE');
    ELSE
        DBMS_OUTPUT.PUT_LINE('FALSE');
    END IF;
END;
/
```

Output (6_16.sql)

```
FALSE

PL/SQL procedure successfully completed.
```

Use the ELSIF Component of the IF Statement

The PL/SQL language provides an added conditional shortcut in the IF statement not found in all other programming languages and makes for smaller, more readable code. The following two code segments illustrate the difference between using the IF-ELSIF-ELSE construct versus using only the IF-ELSE construct. The PL/SQL code segments produce the same result.

The first PL/SQL code segment illustrates the IF-ELSE construct.

File: 6_17.sql

```
DECLARE
   lv_test_num1 PLS_INTEGER := 5;
   lv_test_num2 PLS_INTEGER := 10;
   lv_test_num3 PLS_INTEGER := 15;
   lv_test_num4 PLS_INTEGER := 5;
BEGIN
   IF lv_test_num1 = lv_test_num2 THEN
      DBMS_OUTPUT.PUT_LINE('Test 1 and Test 2 Equal');
   ELSE
      IF lv_test_num1 = lv_test_num3 THEN
         DBMS_OUTPUT.PUT_LINE('Test 1 and Test 3 Equal');
      ELSE
         IF lv_test_num1 = lv_test_num4 THEN
            DBMS_OUTPUT.PUT_LINE('Test 1 and Test 4 Equal');
         ELSE
            DBMS_OUTPUT.PUT_LINE
               ('Test 1 Not Equal to Test 2,3 or 4');
         END IF;
      END IF;
   END IF;
END;
/
```

Output (6_17.sql)

```
Test 1 and Test 4 Equal

PL/SQL procedure successfully completed.
```

The following illustrates the same PL/SQL logic with the IF-ELSIF-ELSE construct.

File: 6_18.sql

```
DECLARE
   lv_test_num1 PLS_INTEGER := 5;
   lv_test_num2 PLS_INTEGER := 10;
   lv_test_num3 PLS_INTEGER := 15;
   lv_test_num4 PLS_INTEGER := 5;
BEGIN
   IF lv_test_num1 = lv_test_num2 THEN
      DBMS_OUTPUT.PUT_LINE('Test 1 and Test 2 Equal');
   ELSIF lv_test_num1 = lv_test_num3 THEN
      DBMS_OUTPUT.PUT_LINE('Test 1 and Test 3 Equal');
   ELSIF lv_test_num1 = lv_test_num4 THEN
      DBMS_OUTPUT.PUT_LINE('Test 1 and Test 4 Equal');
   ELSE
      DBMS_OUTPUT.PUT_LINE('Test 1 Not Equal to Test 2,3 or 4');
   END IF;
END;
/
```

Output (6_18.sql)

```
Test 1 and Test 4 Equal

PL/SQL procedure successfully completed.
```

The preceding example is only a simple illustration of the benefits of the ELSIF clause. As the processing complexity increases, the benefit of this clause escalates.

TIP
Use the ELSIF clause whenever possible to improve readability, improve maintenance, and reduce the amount of code.

Use of the NULL Command

A command structure must contain a valid PL/SQL command, and a comment line does not satisfy the requirement, because the compiler ignores comment lines. The NULL command is helpful when development must begin and the general logic is known, but some of the detailed logic is still undefined. In this case, the NULL command can be placed where your final logic will be placed and it can provide an easy method of searching your code for sections where later coding is needed.

The following provides an example of this use of the NULL command. The IF statement contains an ELSE clause and an EXCEPTION is defined and raised, but the logic for both is currently undefined. The NULL command is used as a stub and is placed there, as a reminder of future development needs.

File: 6_19.sql

```
DECLARE
   lv_general_excep EXCEPTION;
BEGIN
   IF '&&input_value' IS NULL THEN
      RAISE lv_general_excep;
   ELSE
      -- Process Logic
      NULL;
   END IF;
EXCEPTION
   WHEN lv_general_excep THEN
      NULL;
END;
/
```

Output (6_19.sql)

```
Enter value for input_value: XXX

PL/SQL procedure successfully completed.
```

Control All Transaction Logic Before a PL/SQL Program Unit Completes

A good programming practice always ends transaction processing with either a COMMIT or ROLLBACK. SQL*Plus performs an implicit COMMIT by default upon exiting, but if a ROLLBACK is executed prior to the SQL*Plus exit, all the changes performed in your PL/SQL program unit will be lost. Without one of these commands, it becomes the process that called the PL/SQL program unit to handle this transaction closure.

I recommend you close transactions, if possible, prior to the completion of a PL/SQL program unit. The processing flow often dictates a COMMIT to be performed if successful, and a ROLLBACK to be performed if problems or exceptions are encountered.

The following is a short illustration demonstrating transaction closure in a PL/SQL program unit.

File: 6_20.sql

```
BEGIN
   -- Complex Logic
   UPDATE s_employee
   SET    salary = nvl(salary, 0) * 1.10;
   COMMIT;
   DBMS_OUTPUT.PUT_LINE('Update Process Succeeded.');
EXCEPTION
   WHEN OTHERS THEN
      -- Additional Error Processing and Logging
      DBMS_OUTPUT.PUT_LINE('Update Process Failed.');
      ROLLBACK;
END;
/
```

Output (6_20.sql)

```
Update Process Succeeded.

PL/SQL procedure successfully completed.
```

Enable the Use of Literal Single Quotes in Literal Strings

Literal single quotes are often needed in a literal string. The location of the single quote in the code determines the number of single quotes necessary to signify one literal single quote to return in the literal string.

The following example illustrates when two, three, and four single quotes are necessary to return one single quote.

File: 6_21.sql

```
DECLARE
   lv_test_txt VARCHAR2(10) := 'JOE';
BEGIN
   DBMS_OUTPUT.PUT_LINE
      ('Joe''s example of literal quotes around text ''' ||
      lv_test_txt || '''');
END;
/
```

Output (6_21.sql)

```
Joe's example of literal quotes around text 'JOE'

PL/SQL procedure successfully completed.
```

TIP
To return one literal quote in a literal string equates to the need for two single quotes. If the occurrence does not have a single quote starting or ending the string, then only two single quotes are necessary. If the occurrence has a single quote starting or ending the string, then three single quotes are necessary. If the occurrence has a single quote starting and ending the string, then four single quotes are necessary.

Beware of Multiple Line Comments

Two commands can be used to comment your PL/SQL code, namely, the single line comment command and the multiple line comment command. The single line comment command uses a '--' prior to the beginning of each command. When extending beyond one line, the single comment command must be placed on each line. No need exists to end the comment line; from the first occurrence of the comment; the remainder of the line is treated as a comment.

With the multiline comment command, you must specify the beginning and ending of the comment with '/*' and '*/', respectively. From the first occurrence of the beginning of the comment command, all is considered a comment until the ending comment command is found.

This is convenient for commenting out large segments of source code when debugging, but it opens the door for a hidden problem when extending comments with the multiline comment over several lines. I have seen segments of code commented out in this manner and then additional source code inserted into the section that was commented out. Also, I have seen where developers have scanned segments of PL/SQL source code and have not realized entire sections of code were commented out with the multiline comment and, therefore, debugging became more difficult.

Therefore, I recommend always commenting your PL/SQL code with the single line comment command. This is a little more tedious on the front end, but it saves you time and pain as the complexity of your source code increases.

The following is an example of both comment commands, illustrating that the PL/SQL parser does not require any special coding to include the comment command in a literal text string.

File: 6_22.sql

```
BEGIN
    -- The single line comment can be used in a literal text string
    -- without any special coding to identify the usage as literal
    -- text versus the start of a comment.
    DBMS_OUTPUT.PUT_LINE
        ('This illustrates the use of a literal --');
    /* The multiple line comment can also be used in a literal text
       string without any special coding to identify the usage as
       literal text versus the start or end of a comment. */
    DBMS_OUTPUT.PUT_LINE
        ('This illustrates the use of a literal /* */');
END;
/
```

Output (6_22.sql)

```
This illustrates the use of a literal --
This illustrates the use of a literal /* */

PL/SQL procedure successfully completed.
```

Examine the Differences Between SQL and PL/SQL

As explained in Chapter 2, a variety of functions is available in both SQL and PL/SQL. The functionality and the result are the same using either language. The difference mainly lies in the location of the logic processing. The SQL Engine processes a function if used in a SQL statement and by the PL/SQL Engine if used in a PL/SQL command.

Other commands are unavailable in the PL/SQL language, but available in the SQL language, like the DECODE function. However, this function is easily accomplished with the PL/SQL language by using an IF statement.

Therefore, the PL/SQL developer has the flexibility to dictate where much of the logic is to be developed and processed. The resource load is placed on the server SQL Engine or the load will be more on the PL/SQL Engine, which could be local on the client machine or on the server if a local PL/SQL Engine does not exist or if a stored object is called.

I have never performed any extensive testing on the timing of each location. In terms of speed, I cannot make a recommendation either way. When I have a choice of either location, I usually integrate the logic into the SQL statement, if it is not too complex. This reduces the PL/SQL complexity and enables me to test the result set in SQL*Plus standalone for each SQL statement. When the logic becomes more complex, I often perform more of the logic in PL/SQL to provide more granular control and more debugging capabilities.

The choice is yours and is usually dependent on the type of functionality you are developing. It's more important to know extreme flexibility exists in this area to ensure the full scope of options are known.

A list of PL/SQL functions is provided in Appendix B.

Expand the Standard Operand Capabilities

The set of operands extends well beyond the standard set of equality and arithmetic operands in the PL/SQL language. The operands of BETWEEN, LIKE, and IN provide another level of flexibility in the PL/SQL language and function identical to the SQL language counterpart. Additionally, the use of operands to compare values and determine if a condition evaluates to TRUE or FALSE is often used in PL/SQL IF statements and LOOPing (LOOP, WHILE, FOR, and so forth) structures to determine if a segment of code should be executed or the direction of logic flow. However, the use of these operands can be extended to any location where a TRUE or FALSE value result is possible. This means these operands can also be used in assignment statements and default value declarations.

This greatly enhances the flexibility of these operands and enables the capability to develop more dynamic PL/SQL code. The following sections highlight this expansion with examples of each operand.

Expand the BETWEEN Operand Usage

The BETWEEN operator can be used to set a Boolean variable, as illustrated in the following example executed in SQL*Plus. This example compares numeric values.

File: 6_23.sql

```
DECLARE
  lv_test_bln BOOLEAN;
BEGIN
  lv_test_bln := &test_var BETWEEN 1 and 10;
  IF lv_test_bln THEN
    DBMS_OUTPUT.PUT_LINE('Result: TRUE');
  ELSE
    DBMS_OUTPUT.PUT_LINE('Result: FALSE');
```

```
    END IF;
END;
/
```

Output (6_23.sql)

```
Enter value for test_var: 11
Result: FALSE

PL/SQL procedure successfully completed.
```

Output (6_23.sql)

```
Enter value for test_var: 3
Result: TRUE

PL/SQL procedure successfully completed.
```

TIP

The BETWEEN operand can be used to compare numeric, character, and DATE values. The BETWEEN operator includes the lower and upper bounds for comparison inclusion. Character comparisons are performed character by character, based on the ASCII value equivalent of each character. For DATE comparisons remember a time portion is associated with a DATE data type. This is detailed in Chapter 2.

The following example illustrates the BETWEEN operator for comparing character values.

File: 6_24.sql

```
BEGIN
  IF '&input_txt' BETWEEN 'A' AND 'D' THEN
     DBMS_OUTPUT.PUT_LINE('TRUE');
  ELSE
     DBMS_OUTPUT.PUT_LINE('FALSE');
  END IF;
END;
/
```

Output (6_24.sql)

```
Enter value for input_txt: A
TRUE

PL/SQL procedure successfully completed.
```

Output (6_24.sql)

```
Enter value for input_txt: B
TRUE

PL/SQL procedure successfully completed.
```

Output (6_24.sql)

```
Enter value for input_txt: E
FALSE

PL/SQL procedure successfully completed.
```

When comparing DATE values with the BETWEEN operator, the comparison is performed based on the data type of the value being checked. In the following example, the lv_test_date is declared as a DATE and, therefore, the result of the PL/SQL program unit is TRUE as seen.

File: 6_25.sql

```
DECLARE
   lv_test_date DATE := '01-FEB-99';
BEGIN
   IF  lv_test_date BETWEEN '31-JAN-99' AND '10-FEB-99' THEN
      DBMS_OUTPUT.PUT_LINE('TRUE');
   ELSE
      DBMS_OUTPUT.PUT_LINE('FALSE');
   END IF;
END;
/
```

Output (6_25.sql)

```
TRUE

PL/SQL procedure successfully completed.
```

Expanding the Standard
Operand Capabilities

The two comparison values were converted to dates internally by the PL/SQL engine with the TO_DATE function unlike the following comparison, which appears to be the same but has a quite different result.

File: 6_26.sql

```
DECLARE
    lv_test_date VARCHAR2(10) := '01-FEB-99';
BEGIN
    IF  lv_test_date BETWEEN '31-JAN-99' AND '10-FEB-99' THEN
        DBMS_OUTPUT.PUT_LINE('TRUE');
    ELSE
        DBMS_OUTPUT.PUT_LINE('FALSE');
    END IF;
END;
/
```

Output (6_26.sql)

```
FALSE

PL/SQL procedure successfully completed.
```

The reason for the different result is the lv_test_date variable declaration was changed from a DATE to a VARCHAR2. When this is done, the BETWEEN comparison becomes a character comparison, not a DATE comparison. Because the first character of the text string is '0' and the lower bound first character is '3', the condition fails and 'FALSE' is returned.

TIP
When comparing DATE values, ensure the values are being compared as DATE values and not as character values. The results can be quite different and are often deceiving and hard to debug.

Expand the LIKE Operand Usage

The LIKE operator can be used to set a Boolean variable, illustrated in the following example, executed in SQL*Plus.

File: 6_27.sql

```
DECLARE
   lv_test_bln BOOLEAN;
BEGIN
   lv_test_bln := UPPER('&test_var') LIKE 'TRE%';
   IF lv_test_bln THEN
      DBMS_OUTPUT.PUT_LINE('Result: TRUE');
   ELSE
      DBMS_OUTPUT.PUT_LINE('Result: FALSE');
   END IF;
END;
/
```

Output (6_27.sql)

```
Enter value for test_var: trezzo
Result: TRUE

PL/SQL procedure successfully completed.
```

Output (6_27.sql)

```
Enter value for test_var: joe
Result: FALSE

PL/SQL procedure successfully completed.
```

The LIKE operand compares only character strings and does a character-by-character comparison from left to right.

TIP
The' %' represents a wildcard of one or multiple characters to be used in the LIKE function. The '_' represents a wildcard for one character. Remember this when you compare data that contains an '_' in the values to signify a condition. You must take this into account when you search a string specifically for the values containing the '_' character.

The following example illustrates the problem with the '_' character used in data for special significance when a search is necessary that entails the '_' character.

File: 6_28.sql

```
DECLARE
    lv_training_code_txt VARCHAR2(10) := 'T_CLASS1';
    lv_non_training_code_txt VARCHAR2(10) := 'TUSC';
    PROCEDURE training_class_check (p_class_check_txt VARCHAR2) IS
    BEGIN
        IF p_class_check_txt LIKE 'T_%' THEN
            DBMS_OUTPUT.PUT_LINE(p_class_check_txt ||
                ' is a Training Class');
        ELSE
            DBMS_OUTPUT.PUT_LINE(p_class_check_txt ||
                ' is a Non-Training Class');
        END IF;
    END training_class_check;
BEGIN
    training_class_check(lv_training_code_txt);
    training_class_check(lv_non_training_code_txt);
END;
/
```

Output (6_28.sql)

```
T_CLASS1 is a Training Class
TUSC is a Training Class

PL/SQL procedure successfully completed
```

In the preceding example, both codes return as training classes, when, in fact, only the codes that begin with 'T_' signify training classes. To get around this condition, one of the following can be deployed:

■ Do not use the '_' character in your data if possible

■ Convert the '_' character to another character when searching based on the '_' character (shown in the following example)

The preceding example is changed to convert all 'T_' occurrences to 'T-'. The lines that changed in the preceding example are commented at the end of each line (NL for New Line and CL for Changed Line). The result is now correct, based on our specific guidelines.

File: 6_29.sql

```
DECLARE
    lv_training_code_txt VARCHAR2(10) := 'T_CLASS1';
    lv_non_training_code_txt VARCHAR2(10) := 'TUSC';
    PROCEDURE training_class_check (p_class_check_txt VARCHAR2) IS
        lv_check_txt VARCHAR2(10) := p_class_check_txt;     -- NL
    BEGIN
        IF SUBSTR(lv_check_txt,1,2) = 'T_' THEN          -- NL
            lv_check_txt := 'T-' || SUBSTR(lv_check_txt, 3); -- NL
        END IF;                                          -- NL
        IF lv_check_txt LIKE 'T-%' THEN          -- CL
            DBMS_OUTPUT.PUT_LINE(p_class_check_txt ||
                ' is a Training Class');
        ELSE
            DBMS_OUTPUT.PUT_LINE(p_class_check_txt ||
                ' is a Non-Training Class');
        END IF;
    END training_class_check;
BEGIN
    training_class_check(lv_training_code_txt);
    training_class_check(lv_non_training_code_txt);
END;
/
```

Output (6_29.sql)

```
T_CLASS1 is a Training Class
TUSC is a Non-Training Class

PL/SQL procedure successfully completed.
```

TIP
Anytime a PL/SQL program unit is created and any repetitive logic occurs that is only needed for the current PL/SQL program unit, create a procedure or function within the current PL/SQL program unit. This eliminates the redundant code, enhances readability, and eases maintenance. This is illustrated in the preceding two examples.

Expand the IN Operand Usage

The IN operator can be used to set a Boolean variable. This is illustrated in the following example, executed in SQL*Plus.

File: 6_30.sql

```
DECLARE
   lv_test_bln BOOLEAN;
BEGIN
   lv_test_bln := UPPER('&test_var') IN ('TREZZO','BROWN','NIEMIEC');
   IF lv_test_bln THEN
      DBMS_OUTPUT.PUT_LINE('Result: TRUE');
   ELSE
      DBMS_OUTPUT.PUT_LINE('Result: FALSE');
   END IF;
END;
/
```

Output (6_30.sql)

```
Enter value for test_var: tre
Result: FALSE

PL/SQL procedure successfully completed.
```

Output (6_30.sql)

```
Enter value for test_var: brown
Result: TRUE

PL/SQL procedure successfully completed.
```

The IN operand works with both character and numeric values.

Build a Numeric Function Arsenal

The set of numeric functions provided with PL/SQL is similar to the SQL language. These functions provide extensive functionality and flexibility. The first half of the battle is knowing each of these functions exists. The second half is remembering to use them when they are needed and to combine these functions by nesting them to extend their usefulness. This section highlights several of these functions that can assist in PL/SQL development. A complete list of these functions is provided in Appendix B.

Use MOD for Controlling Feedback

When processing large volumes of records, it is important to log or communicate processing information periodically to ensure real-time processing characteristics are known. This can be used both to inform others and to inform yourself, which allows a mechanism to ensure the code is executing efficiently. It can also be used for further investigation for optimization.

The MOD function provides a useful means to determine an interval by dividing two numbers and returning the remainder. The remainder can be used to determine if the desired interval is reached. The MOD function is illustrated in the following example. The interval is set to 1000 (remainder is 0 every 1000 iterations through the loop), at which time the elapsed execution time and number of records processed is written to the output buffer through the DBMS_OUTPUT.PUT_LINE procedure.

File: 6_31.sql

```
DECLARE
    lv_counter_num         PLS_INTEGER := 0;
    lv_timer_start_num     NUMBER;
    lv_timer_previous_num  NUMBER;
    lv_timer_current_num   NUMBER;
BEGIN
    lv_timer_start_num     := DBMS_UTILITY.GET_TIME;
    lv_timer_previous_num  := lv_timer_start_num;
    DBMS_OUTPUT.PUT_LINE
        ('Timing Per Thousand Records Processed (in secs)');
    LOOP
        lv_counter_num := lv_counter_num + 1;
        IF MOD(lv_counter_num, 1000) = 0 THEN
            lv_timer_current_num := DBMS_UTILITY.GET_TIME;
            DBMS_OUTPUT.PUT_LINE('Time Elapsed-Total: ' ||
                (lv_timer_current_num - lv_timer_start_num)/100 ||
                CHR(9) || ' This Set: ' ||
                (lv_timer_current_num - lv_timer_previous_num)/100 ||
                CHR(9) || ' Records Processed: ' ||
                lv_counter_num);
            lv_timer_previous_num := lv_timer_current_num;
        END IF;
        EXIT WHEN lv_counter_num = 5540;
    END LOOP;
    lv_timer_current_num := DBMS_UTILITY.GET_TIME;
    DBMS_OUTPUT.PUT_LINE('Time Elapsed-Total: ' ||
        (lv_timer_current_num - lv_timer_start_num)/100 ||
        CHR(9) || ' This Set: ' ||
        (lv_timer_current_num - lv_timer_previous_num)/100 ||
        CHR(9) || ' Records Processed: ' ||
        lv_counter_num);
END;
/
```

Output (6_31.sql)

```
Timing Per Thousand Records Processed (in secs)
Time Elapsed-Total: .15   This Set: .15    Records Processed: 1000
Time Elapsed-Total: .24   This Set: .09    Records Processed: 2000
Time Elapsed-Total: .34   This Set: .1     Records Processed: 3000
Time Elapsed-Total: .39   This Set: .05    Records Processed: 4000
Time Elapsed-Total: .52   This Set: .13    Records Processed: 5000
Time Elapsed-Total: .59   This Set: .07    Records Processed: 5540

PL/SQL procedure successfully completed.
```

This code segment can be used in long-running processes to return timing statistics.

TIP
The use of the DBMS_OUTPUT.PUT_LINE procedure would suffice if you can wait until the entire PL/SQL program unit completes to get feedback. However, this feedback is desired more real-time and, therefore, the DBMS_OUTPUT.PUT_LINE procedure calls would be replaced by DBMS_PIPE, UTL_FILE, or DBMS_APPLICATION_INFO calls. This technique is detailed in Chapter 12.

Use CEIL and FLOOR for Forced Rounding

Based on the application logic, numbers often need to be rounded either to the next highest or the next lowest whole number. The CEIL and FLOOR functions provide this functionality, although they do not perform any rounding. These functions simply return the next highest or lowest whole number. If the number input is a whole number, the number returned is the same as the number input.

The CEIL and FLOOR functions are illustrated in the following example.

File: 6_32.sql

```
BEGIN
    DBMS_OUTPUT.PUT_LINE('Orignal Number: ' ||
        &&test_var || CHR(9) || ' Ceil Number: ' ||
        CEIL(&&test_var) || CHR(9) || ' Floor Number: '||
```

```
      FLOOR(&&test_var));
END;
/
```

Output (6_32.sql)

```
Enter value for test_var: 23.5

Orignal Number: 23.5      Ceil Number: 24          Floor Number: 23

PL/SQL procedure successfully completed.
```

Output (6_32.sql)

```
Enter value for test_var: -22.3

Orignal Number: -22.3    Ceil Number: -22          Floor Number: -23

PL/SQL procedure successfully completed.
```

Output (6_32.sql)

```
Enter value for test_var: 56

Orignal Number: 56       Ceil Number: 56          Floor Number: 56

PL/SQL procedure successfully completed.
```

Manipulate Numbers with ROUND/TRUNC/SIGN/ABS

Numbers can be manipulated with PL/SQL functions dependent on the desired result. Decimals are often removed with the ROUND or TRUNCATE commands to ease calculations. The absolute value is used when only positive numbers should be used in calculations. The sign of a number is often desired to determine positive or negative results.

The following examples demonstrate how each of these numeric functions works in PL/SQL.

The ROUND function defaults to 0 decimal places if a precision is not specified. If a negative value is used for the precision value, it rounds on the left side of the decimal, as illustrated in the following example.

File: 6_33.sql

```
BEGIN
    DBMS_OUTPUT.PUT_LINE(ROUND(3.5));
    DBMS_OUTPUT.PUT_LINE(ROUND(105.09,1));
    DBMS_OUTPUT.PUT_LINE(ROUND(-3.5));
    DBMS_OUTPUT.PUT_LINE(ROUND(105.15,-2));
    DBMS_OUTPUT.PUT_LINE(ROUND(150.15,-2));
END;
/
```

Output (6_33.sql)

```
4
105.1
-4
100
200

PL/SQL procedure successfully completed.
```

The TRUNC function defaults to 0 decimal places if a precision is not specified. If a negative value is used for the precision value, it truncates on the left side of the decimal, as illustrated in the following example.

File: 6_34.sql

```
BEGIN
    DBMS_OUTPUT.PUT_LINE(TRUNC(3.5));
    DBMS_OUTPUT.PUT_LINE(TRUNC(105.09,1));
    DBMS_OUTPUT.PUT_LINE(TRUNC(-3.5));
    DBMS_OUTPUT.PUT_LINE(TRUNC(105.15,-2));
    DBMS_OUTPUT.PUT_LINE(TRUNC(150.15,-2));
END;
/
```

Output (6_34.sql)

```
3
105
-3
100
100

PL/SQL procedure successfully completed.
```

The SIGN function determines if the number is 0, greater than 0, or less than 0, and, as a result, returns a 0, 1, or –1, respectively. This is illustrated in the following example.

File: 6_35.sql

```
BEGIN
   DBMS_OUTPUT.PUT_LINE(SIGN(3.5));
   DBMS_OUTPUT.PUT_LINE(SIGN(-3.5));
   DBMS_OUTPUT.PUT_LINE(SIGN(0));
END;
/
```

Output (6_35.sql)

```
1
-1
0

PL/SQL procedure successfully completed.
```

The SIGN function would be helpful in an accounting system if you want to keep track of both positive and negative totals to determine the amount of credits and the amount of debits you had processed. By checking the SIGN, you can determine to what variable to add the amount.

The ABS function returns the absolute value of a number. If the number is 0, then a 0 is returned. This is illustrated in the following example.

File: 6_36.sql

```
BEGIN
   DBMS_OUTPUT.PUT_LINE(ABS(3.5));
   DBMS_OUTPUT.PUT_LINE(ABS(-3.5));
   DBMS_OUTPUT.PUT_LINE(ABS(0));
END;
/
```

Output (6_36.sql)

```
3.5
3.5
0

PL/SQL procedure successfully completed.
```

The ABS function could be used in the preceding accounting example to keep track of the total amount of credits and debits. Each value can be converted using the ABS function to get the total amount of transaction volume, regardless of the type of transaction (credit or debit).

Build a Character Function Arsenal

The set of character functions provided with PL/SQL is similar to the SQL language. These functions provide extensive functionality and flexibility. The first half of the battle is knowing each of these functions exists. The second half is remembering to use them when they are needed and to combine these functions by nesting them to extend their usefulness. This section highlights several of these functions that can assist in PL/SQL development. A complete list of these functions is provided in Appendix B.

Modify Character Strings with INITCAP/LOWER/UPPER

Once information is retrieved from the database or manipulated, the information is to be logged to a file or displayed on the screen. The INITCAP, LOWER, and UPPER functions enables the manipulation of information prior to the display.

The use of each of these functions is shown in the following example.

File: 6_37.sql

```
DECLARE
   CURSOR cur_employee IS
      SELECT employee_first_name, employee_last_name
      FROM   s_employee
      ORDER by employee_last_name;
BEGIN
   FOR lv_cur_employee_rec IN cur_employee LOOP
      DBMS_OUTPUT.PUT_LINE('Name: ' ||
         INITCAP(lv_cur_employee_rec.employee_first_name) || ' ' ||
         INITCAP(lv_cur_employee_rec.employee_last_name));
      DBMS_OUTPUT.PUT_LINE('Name: ' ||
         UPPER(lv_cur_employee_rec.employee_first_name) || ' ' ||
         UPPER(lv_cur_employee_rec.employee_last_name));
      DBMS_OUTPUT.PUT_LINE('Name: ' ||
         LOWER(lv_cur_employee_rec.employee_first_name) || ' ' ||
         LOWER(lv_cur_employee_rec.employee_last_name));
   END LOOP;
END;
/
```

Output (6_37.sql)

```
Name: Ben Biri
Name: BEN BIRI
Name: ben biri
Name: Antoinette Catchpole
Name: ANTOINETTE CATCHPOLE
Name: antoinette catchpole

PL/SQL procedure successfully completed.
```

Only the subset of records is displayed in the preceding output. Information stored in the database can be stored as all uppercase, all lowercase, or mixed case. I strongly recommend forcing all database columns to uppercase, especially if they are going to be columns used for searching. This guideline enables all conditional statements to search for UPPER values and to eliminate any confusion with mixed case. Additionally, if you are forced to convert the column value to UPPERcase when searching, it suppresses the use of an index, if an index existed on the column being searched.

If this UPPERcase guideline is followed, then when prompting for input, the value received can always be converted to uppercase prior to the search.

TIP

If you are uncertain as to the contents of a string and you want to search the string for a value, use the UPPER function to convert the value to all uppercase and search on the uppercase value.

TIP

Oracle 8.1 introduces functional based indexes as described in Chapter 16. Functional based indexes would help when comparing database column data that is mixed case.

Format and Convert Character Strings with RPAD/LPAD/CHR/TO_CHAR

When information is written out to an operating system file for data loading into another system, an operating system file is being read for input into your system, or information needs to be formatted, the RPAD, LPAD, CHR, and TO_CHAR functions can be very useful.

The following PL/SQL program unit retrieves information from the s_employee table and then displays the information to the screen in a nice formatted display using these four functions.

File: 6_38.sql

```
DECLARE
   CURSOR cur_employee IS
      SELECT employee_last_name || ', ' ||
             employee_first_name name,
             DECODE(commission_pct, NULL, 'NO',
                    0, 'NO', 'YES') comm_flag,
             salary
      FROM   s_employee
      ORDER BY DECODE(COMMISSION_PCT, NULL, 'NO',
                      0, 'NO', 'YES') DESC;
BEGIN
   FOR lv_cur_employee_rec IN cur_employee LOOP
      DBMS_OUTPUT.PUT_LINE('Employee: ' ||
         RPAD(lv_cur_employee_rec.name, 18, ' ')   ||
         'Commission?: ' ||
         LPAD(lv_cur_employee_rec.comm_flag, 3) ||
         CHR(9) || ' Salary: ' ||
         TO_CHAR(lv_cur_employee_rec.salary, '$999,999.99'));
   END LOOP;
END;
/
```

Output (6_38.sql)

```
Employee: MAGEE, COLIN      Commission?: YES   Salary:   $1,540.00
Employee: GILJUM, HENRY     Commission?: YES   Salary:   $1,639.00
Employee: VELASQUEZ, CARMEN Commission?:  NO   Salary:   $2,500.00
Employee: NGAO, LADORIS     Commission?:  NO   Salary:   $1,658.80
Employee: DANCS, BELA       Commission?:  NO   Salary:     $983.84
Employee: PATEL, RADHA      Commission?:  NO   Salary:     $909.48
Employee: HAVEL, MARTA      Commission?:  NO   Salary:   $1,495.21

PL/SQL procedure successfully completed.
```

Only the subset of records is displayed in the preceding output.

TIP
LPAD can also be used to center text within a column or section on the display.

In the following example, the input_value is centered within the length of the
column. Therefore, the PL/SQL code segment example advances beyond the basic
left padding to the length_of_column. The starting point of the string is determined
and then added to the length of the input_value. Then the string is padded to this
calculated length, which provides for a value to be centered within a column. The
character used to left pad the string is determined by the value_to_pad value input.
The following example prompts for the string to center, the length of the column to
center the string within, and the value to use to left pad the string. The string is then
displayed, as well as the length of the string.

File: 6_39.sql

```
DECLARE
    lv_test_txt VARCHAR2(80);
    lv_test_num PLS_INTEGER;
BEGIN
    lv_test_txt := LPAD('&&input_value',
        (&&length_of_column - LENGTH('&&input_value'))/2 +
        LENGTH('&&input_value'), '&&value_to_pad');
    lv_test_num := LENGTH(lv_test_txt);
    DBMS_OUTPUT.PUT_LINE(lv_test_txt);
    DBMS_OUTPUT.PUT_LINE(lv_test_num);
END;
/
```

Output (6_39.sql)

```
Enter value for input_value: TUSC REPORT
Enter value for length_of_column: 80
Enter value for value_to_pad:
TUSC REPORT
46

PL/SQL procedure successfully completed.
```

The value_to_pad input was a space. This should have resulted in centering the text
'TUSC REPORT' within the 80-character column space. This did not happen because
the DBMS_OUTPUT.PUT_LINE performs an LTRIM of spaces on the first value printed.
This is proven with the following example execution with different input.

Output (6_39.sql)

```
Enter value for input_value: TUSC REPORT
Enter value for length_of_column: 80
Enter value for value_to_pad: 1234567890
```

Building a Character
Function Arsenal

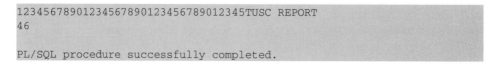

```
1234567890123456789012345678901234TUSC REPORT
46

PL/SQL procedure successfully completed.
```

As seen in the preceding output, the string is centered in the 80-character space. The input for the value_to_pad was used to enable for easy identification of the starting column of the centered text. As seen, the string starts at character location 36, which centers the text.

This logic can be used to center text dynamically that is returned to other programs.

Process Character Strings with INSTR/LENGTH/LTRIM/RTRIM

When information is written out to an operating system file for data loading into another system, an operating system file is read for input into your system, or information needs to be formatted, the INSTR, LENGTH, LTRIM, and RTRIM functions can be very useful.

The following PL/SQL program unit parses a filename and creates a log filename with the same name, but with an extension of '.log'. A value is parsed and all leading and trailing blanks are stripped from the value, and, lastly, the value lengths are displayed. This processing is accomplished using these four functions.

File: 6_40.sql

```
DECLARE
   lv_input_filename_txt VARCHAR2(40):= '\nightly\batch\main.dat';
   lv_log_filename_txt   VARCHAR2(40):=
      SUBSTR(lv_input_filename_txt,1, INSTR(lv_input_filename_txt,
      '.') - 1) || '.log';
   lv_input_column_txt   VARCHAR2(20):= '   RECORD1   ';
   lv_final_column_txt   VARCHAR2(20):=
      LTRIM(RTRIM(lv_input_column_txt, ' '));
   lv_input_length_num   PLS_INTEGER;
   lv_final_length_num   PLS_INTEGER;
BEGIN
   DBMS_OUTPUT.PUT_LINE('Input Filename:     ' ||
      lv_input_filename_txt);
   DBMS_OUTPUT.PUT_LINE('Log Filename:       ' ||
      lv_log_filename_txt);
   DBMS_OUTPUT.PUT_LINE('Input Column Value: ' ||
      lv_input_column_txt);
   DBMS_OUTPUT.PUT_LINE('Final Column Value: ' ||
      lv_final_column_txt);
   lv_input_length_num := LENGTH(lv_input_column_txt);
   lv_final_length_num := LENGTH(lv_final_column_txt);
```

Building a Character Function Arsenal

```
    DBMS_OUTPUT.PUT_LINE('Input Column Length: ' ||
        lv_input_length_num);
    DBMS_OUTPUT.PUT_LINE('Final Column Length: ' ||
        lv_final_length_num);
END;
/
```

Output (6_40.sql)

```
Input Filename:        \nightly\batch\main.dat
Log Filename:          \nightly\batch\main.log
Input Column Value:       RECORD1
Final Column Value:    RECORD1
Input Column Length: 13
Final Column Length: 7

PL/SQL procedure successfully completed.
```

Transform Character Strings with REPLACE/TRANSLATE

The REPLACE and TRANSLATE functions are useful character functions for transforming and masking character strings. Both functions are explored in further detail in Chapter 2. The following example is provided for reference.

The REPLACE function performs a replacement of a character string found in a value with a second character string. If the character string to be replaced is not found in the value, the value remains unchanged. If the character string to be replaced is found multiple times in the value, then each occurrence of the character string is replaced with the second character string. The following examples illustrate the REPLACE functionality.

File: 6_41.sql

```
DECLARE
    lv_temp_txt VARCHAR2(20);
BEGIN
    lv_temp_txt := UPPER('&input_value');
    DBMS_OUTPUT.PUT_LINE('Original Value: ' ||
        lv_temp_txt);
    lv_temp_txt := REPLACE(lv_temp_txt, UPPER('&value_to_replace'),
        UPPER('&replacement_value'));
    DBMS_OUTPUT.PUT_LINE('Replaced Value: ' ||
        lv_temp_txt);
END;
/
```

Output (6_41.sql)

```
Enter value for input_value: OPS$TREZZOJ
Enter value for value_to_replace: OPS$
Enter value for replacement_value:
Original Value: OPS$TREZZOJ
Replaced Value: TREZZOJ

PL/SQL procedure successfully completed.
```

The preceding example replaced the value of 'OPS$' with nothing, which is equivalent to striping out any occurrences of the value 'OPS$' from the string.

Output (6_41.sql)

```
Enter value for input_value: OPS$TREZZOJ
Enter value for value_to_replace: TREZO
Enter value for replacement_value: JOHNSON
Original Value: OPS$TREZZOJ
Replaced Value: OPS$TREZZOJ

PL/SQL procedure successfully completed.
```

In the preceding example, because no occurrence of value 'TREZO' was found in the string, no change occurred to the input_value.

The TRANSLATE function performs a replacement of a single character found in the value with a second character. The TRANSLATE function is a character-by-character replacement function, whereas the REPLACE function is a character string replacement function. The TRANSLATE function allows multiple single character replacements in one execution, whereas the REPLACE function allows one character string replacement per execution. The following examples illustrate the TRANSLATE functionality.

File: 6_42.sql

```
DECLARE
   lv_temp_txt VARCHAR2(20);
BEGIN
   lv_temp_txt := '&input_value';
   DBMS_OUTPUT.PUT_LINE('Original Value: ' ||
      lv_temp_txt);
   -- Every 0 is replaced by a 9, every 1 is replaced by a 9,
```

```
  -- every 2 is replaced by a 9 and so forth
  lv_temp_txt := TRANSLATE(lv_temp_txt,'012345678','999999999');
  DBMS_OUTPUT.PUT_LINE('Replaced Value: ' ||
    lv_temp_txt);
END;
/
```

Output (6_42.sql)

```
Enter value for input_value: 888-555-3254
Original Value: 888-555-3254
Replaced Value: 999-999-9999

PL/SQL procedure successfully completed.
```

Output (6_42.sql)

```
Enter value for input_value: (888) 555-0989
Original Value: (888) 555-0989
Replaced Value: (999) 999-9999

PL/SQL procedure successfully completed.
```

In these examples, the REPLACE function is a string replacement function, whereas the TRANSLATE function is a character-by-character replacement function. For the TRANSLATE function, any occurrence of a character in the first character set found in the string is replaced by the corresponding character in the second character set.

Build a Date Function Arsenal

The set of DATE functions provided with PL/SQL is similar to the SQL language. These functions provide extensive functionality and flexibility. The first half of the battle is knowing each of these functions exists. The second half is remembering to use them when they are needed and to combine these functions by nesting them to extend their usefulness. This section highlights several of these functions that can assist in PL/SQL development. A complete list of these functions is provided in Appendix B in the following examples.

Several DATE functions are illustrated below to provide insight into these powerful functions that are often necessary when date processing is performed. Comments are embedded in the PL/SQL code segment to explain each section.

File: 6_43.sql

```
DECLARE
   lv_test_date DATE := SYSDATE;
   -- The separator_line procedure is called on each break of each
   -- date function.
   PROCEDURE separator_line IS
   BEGIN
      DBMS_OUTPUT.PUT_LINE('-------------------------------------');
   END separator_line;
BEGIN
   separator_line;
   DBMS_OUTPUT.PUT_LINE(lv_test_date);
   separator_line;
   -- Shows the date and time, the date without the time, and the
   -- time on the West coast
   DBMS_OUTPUT.PUT_LINE(TO_CHAR(lv_test_date,
      'DD-MON-YYYY HH24:MI:SS'));
   DBMS_OUTPUT.PUT_LINE(TO_CHAR(TRUNC(lv_test_date),
      'DD-MON-YYYY HH24:MI:SS'));
   DBMS_OUTPUT.PUT_LINE(TO_CHAR(NEW_TIME(lv_test_date,
      'CST', 'PST'), 'DD-MON-YYYY HH24:MI:SS'));
   separator_line;
   -- Dates can be modified to go forward or backward by integers,
   -- the last example returns the same date
   DBMS_OUTPUT.PUT_LINE(TO_CHAR(ADD_MONTHS(lv_test_date, 9),
      'MM/DD/YYYY'));
   DBMS_OUTPUT.PUT_LINE(TO_CHAR(ADD_MONTHS(lv_test_date, -5),
      'MM/DD/YYYY'));
   DBMS_OUTPUT.PUT_LINE(TO_CHAR(ADD_MONTHS(lv_test_date, .5),
      'MM/DD/YYYY'));
   separator_line;
   -- Provides the last day of the month
   DBMS_OUTPUT.PUT_LINE(TO_CHAR(LAST_DAY(lv_test_date),
      'MM/DD/YYYY'));
   separator_line;
   -- Returns the number of months between 2 dates entered, it
   -- returns a number (+ or -), and fraction if the dates are not
   -- the same day of the months being compared or if the dates
   -- are not the last day of each month
   DBMS_OUTPUT.PUT_LINE(MONTHS_BETWEEN(lv_test_date,
      lv_test_date + 32));
   DBMS_OUTPUT.PUT_LINE(MONTHS_BETWEEN(LAST_DAY(lv_test_date+32),
      LAST_DAY(lv_test_date)));
   separator_line;
   -- Provides the date of the next occurrence of the day
   DBMS_OUTPUT.PUT_LINE(TO_CHAR(NEXT_DAY(lv_test_date, 'MON'),
```

```
    'MM/DD/YYYY'));
  separator_line;
  -- Rounds the date to the specified precision, the first is by
  -- date, the second is the nearest year
  DBMS_OUTPUT.PUT_LINE(TO_CHAR(ROUND(lv_test_date),
    'MM/DD/YYYY'));
  DBMS_OUTPUT.PUT_LINE(TO_CHAR(ROUND(lv_test_date, 'YYYY'),
    'MM/DD/YYYY'));
  separator_line;
END;
/
```

Output (6_43.sql)

```
------------------------------------
29-APR-99
------------------------------------
29-APR-1999 05:49:06
29-APR-1999 00:00:00
29-APR-1999 03:49:06
------------------------------------
01/29/2000
11/29/1998
04/29/1999
------------------------------------
04/30/1999
------------------------------------
-1.0645161290322580645161290322580645161613
1
------------------------------------
05/03/1999
------------------------------------
04/29/1999
01/01/1999
------------------------------------

PL/SQL procedure successfully completed.
```

Make Data Type Conversion Easy by Using the Conversion Functions

The last set of useful functions is classified as conversion functions, which are provided with PL/SQL and are similar to the SQL language. These functions provide an extensive set of functionality and flexibility when working with different data types. The first half of the battle is knowing each of these functions exists. The second half is remembering to use them when they are needed and to combine these functions by nesting them to extend their usefulness. This section highlights several of these functions that can assist in PL/SQL development. A complete list of these functions is provided in Appendix B.

The conversion functions are explored in the following sections.

Convert Dates and Numbers with TO_CHAR

The TO_CHAR function is used for converting number data types to character strings for use in character functional processing, as well as formatting numeric strings for output. The TO_CHAR function is helpful for converting date values to a character string of a different format. The complete set of format masks is quite extensive and well worth reviewing to understand the robustness of this capability.

The following example illustrates the conversion of a numeric value when displayed.

File: 6_44.sql

```
DECLARE
   lv_test_num NUMBER := 9324.66;
BEGIN
   DBMS_OUTPUT.PUT_LINE(TO_CHAR(lv_test_num, '$999,999.99'));
END;
/
```

Output (6_44.sql)

```
$9,324.66

PL/SQL procedure successfully completed.
```

The following example illustrates the conversion of a DATE value when displayed. A variety of formats are shown and comments are provided to explain some of the formatting.

File: 6_45.sql

```
DECLARE
   lv_test_date DATE := SYSDATE;
BEGIN
```

```
   DBMS_OUTPUT.PUT_LINE(lv_test_date);
   DBMS_OUTPUT.PUT_LINE(TO_CHAR(lv_test_date,
      'MM/DD/YYYY: HH24:MI:SS'));
   DBMS_OUTPUT.PUT_LINE(TO_CHAR(lv_test_date, 'MM/DD/YYYY'));
   -- The Q preceding the YYYY will equate to the quarter the
   -- date falls in
   DBMS_OUTPUT.PUT_LINE(TO_CHAR(lv_test_date, 'Q, YYYY'));
   DBMS_OUTPUT.PUT_LINE(TO_CHAR(lv_test_date, 'YEAR'));
   -- The FM preceding the MONTH returns the actual length of the
   -- month, without the FM, the month is padded out to 9 spaces.
   DBMS_OUTPUT.PUT_LINE(TO_CHAR(lv_test_date,
      'FMMONTH DDTH, YYYY'));
   -- The SP on the end of the DD, specifies to spell out the
   -- number.
   DBMS_OUTPUT.PUT_LINE(TO_CHAR(lv_test_date,
      'FMMONTH DDSPTH, YEAR'));
END;
/
```

Output (6_45.sql)

```
29-APR-99
04/29/1999: 04:25:40
04/29/1999
2, 1999
NINETEEN NINETY-NINE
APRIL 29TH, 1999
APRIL TWENTY-NINTH, NINETEEN NINETY-NINE

PL/SQL procedure successfully completed.
```

The preceding example only demonstrates a small subset of format masks for the conversion of DATE values. The list is extensive and often provides the necessary conversion, rather than attempting to create your own routine to convert dates.

TIP
In most cases, the format masks for dates are case-sensitive and therefore result in formatting the date according to the case used in the source code (for example, MONTH will display the month in all uppercase, and Month will display the month in all lowercase with only the first character in uppercase).

Making Data Type Conversion Easy

TIP
*The DATE format masks provide means of specifying
whether to return numbers to represent the date
components or to spell out the numbers into words.
A package exists, called DH_UTIL, allowing a numeric
dollar amount to be passed into one of the procedures to
return the spelled-out string of the value passed. This
package is ideal for printing checks. Dave Hunt of
Oracle Education Services created the package. Dave
can be reached at dhunt@oracle.com for the rights to
use this package. This is not supported by Oracle, but is
provided for use and to exemplify the power of PL/SQL.
This package can also be viewed in its entirety in the
Oracle Press book by Scott Urman,* Oracle PL/SQL
Programming.

Convert Character Strings to Dates with **TO_DATE**

The TO_DATE function is helpful for converting character strings into DATE values.
This is helpful prior to comparing dates or when inserting into a DATE column in
the database. The TO_DATE conversion allows the format mask to be specified to
ensure a successful conversion. When the TO_DATE function is called without
a specified format, the default format used is 'DD-MON-YY' (or the current date
format defined by the nls_date_format variable for the current session).

The format masks allowed are the same as for the TO_CHAR function when
converting dates.

Convert Character Strings to Numbers with **TO_NUMBER**

Sometimes, it is necessary to determine if a value is numeric. This is often the
case when data is being loaded from a data file. The columns are often read
into character variables and then inserted into the database. Numeric columns
are internally converted by the SQL Engine upon the insertion attempt. The
TO_NUMBER function enables the conversion to be addressed prior to the attempt

of loading a record into the database. The TO_NUMBER provides a method of determining if the value only contains numeric content; therefore, an attempt to load corrupted data is determined before the attempted load.

Also, a good programming practice is to ensure the conversion of a variable is performed explicitly versus implicitly by the SQL or PL/SQL Engine. This provides another means of error trapping prior to sending the PL/SQL program unit to the PL/SQL engine for compilation and execution.

The following example illustrates a method of determining invalid numbers and handling these numbers by striping out the invalid characters or nonnumeric digits.

File: 6_46.sql

```
DECLARE
    lv_test_num NUMBER;
    lv_test_txt VARCHAR2(10);
    FUNCTION validate_number (p_test_txt VARCHAR2)
        RETURN NUMBER IS
            lv_return_num NUMBER;
        BEGIN
            lv_return_num := TO_NUMBER(p_test_txt);
            RETURN lv_return_num;
        EXCEPTION
            WHEN OTHERS THEN
                lv_return_num := REPLACE(TRANSLATE(p_test_txt,
                    'ABCDEFGHIJKLMNOPQRSTUVWXYZ',
                                              '),' ');
            RETURN lv_return_num;
    END validate_number;
BEGIN
    lv_test_txt := '43546.66';
    lv_test_num := validate_number(lv_test_txt);
    DBMS_OUTPUT.PUT_LINE('Original Value: ' || lv_test_txt);
    DBMS_OUTPUT.PUT_LINE('New Value:      ' || lv_test_num);
    lv_test_txt := 'A5A46.896';
    lv_test_num := validate_number(lv_test_txt);
    DBMS_OUTPUT.PUT_LINE('Original Value: ' || lv_test_txt);
    DBMS_OUTPUT.PUT_LINE('New Value:      ' || lv_test_num);
END;
/
```

Making Data Type Conversion Easy

Output (6_46.sql)

```
Original Value: 43546.66
New Value:      43546.66
Original Value: A5A46.896
New Value:      546.896

PL/SQL procedure successfully completed.
```

In the preceding example, the PL/SQL program unit only removes a character if it is one of the letters in the alphabet. With some enhancements, this program unit can handle all characters, including nondisplayed characters like TABS and so forth. The logic shown here is one method of dealing with invalid characters found within a supposed numeric string. Many other methods exist to handle this circumstance and the method chosen will depend on your environment.

Ensure NULL Values Are Handled as Expected with NVL

The NVL function must be used extensively when developing programs that manipulate numeric or character values that can contain NULL values. It provides the means to pre-determine a NULL value as a specified value for comparisons, as well as when performing numeric operations. This function is described in extensive detail in Chapter 2.

Summary

In this chapter, we have examined many of the PL/SQL language commands and highlighted many of the robust capabilities of these commands. The true power of the language becomes more evident as these commands are used in combination to create more complex functionality in real-world applications. This chapter focused on many of the PL/SQL language commands, but not all commands. The tips and techniques presented in this chapter highlight several of the PL/SQL language commands' more robust features and capabilities.

To view the entire list of PL/SQL language commands, refer to Appendix B. The more these commands are used and combined, the more intricacies will be discovered and the more complex and powerful PL/SQL programs you will be able to develop.

Tips Review

- If you use the %ROWTYPE or %TYPE attribute and the NOT NULL attribute is desired, it must be explicitly defined for each variable. Only the data type and length are transferred to the declared variable through these two attributes.

- Always make sure to default counters to 0 in the declaration, to ensure the increment is being made properly. Also, remember NULL plus 1 is NULL.

- The %ROWCOUNT attribute only reflects the result from the most recent SQL statement. If you perform five updates, then refer to this attribute, only the count for the last update will be returned. It is a single variable that contains the value at a point in time that is overwritten every SQL statement execution.

- If GROUP functions are being used in a cursor and the %FOUND or %NOTFOUND are being used, beware of the result even if no records meet the predicate criteria.

- When referring to the %FOUND, %NOTFOUND, and %ROWCOUNT cursor attributes, the name of the cursor must precede the attribute when referencing an explicit cursor, and the literal "SQL" must precede the attribute when referencing a DML or query statement (SELECT INTO, INSERT, UPDATE, and DELETE).

- To return one literal quote in a literal string equates to the need for two single quotes. If the occurrence does not have a single quote starting or ending the string, then only two single quotes are necessary. If the occurrence has a single quote starting or ending the string, then three single quotes are necessary. If the occurrence has a single quote starting and ending the string, then four single quotes are necessary.

- The BETWEEN operand can be used to compare numeric, character, and DATE values. The BETWEEN operator includes the lower and upper bounds for comparison inclusion. Character comparisons are on a character-by-character basis, based on the ASCII value equivalent. For DATE comparisons, remember a time portion is associated with a DATE data type.

Tips Review

- When comparing DATE values, ensure the values are being compared as DATE values and not as character values. The results can be different and are often deceiving and hard to debug.

- The' %' represents a wildcard of one or multiple characters to be used in the LIKE function. The '_' represents a wildcard for one character. Remember this when comparing data that contains an '_' in the values to signify a condition. You must take this into account when searching a string specifically for the values containing the '_' character.

- Anytime a PL/SQL program unit is created and any repetitive logic exists that is only needed for the current PL/SQL program unit, create a procedure or function within the current PL/SQL program unit. This will eliminate the redundant code, enhance readability, and ease maintenance.

- The use of the DBMS_OUTPUT.PUT_LINE procedure would suffice if you can wait until the entire PL/SQL program unit completes to get feedback. Most often, however, this feedback is desired more real-time and, therefore, the DBMS_OUTPUT.PUT_LINE procedure calls could be replaced by DBMS_PIPE, UTL_FILE, or DBMS_APPLICATION_INFO calls.

- If you are uncertain about the contents of a string and you want to search the string for a value, use the UPPER function to convert the value to all uppercase and search on the uppercase value.

- Oracle 8.1 introduces functional based indexes as described in Chapter 16. Functional based indexes would help when comparing database column data that is mixed case.

- LPAD can also be used to center text within a column or section on the display.

- In most cases, the format masks for dates are case-sensitive and, therefore, result in formatting the date according to the case used in the source code (for example, MONTH will display the month in all uppercase letters, and Month will display the month in all lowercase letters, with only the first character in uppercase).

- The DATE format masks provide means of specifying whether to return numbers to represent the date components or to spell out the numbers into words. A package exists, called DH_UTIL, allowing a numeric dollar amount to be passed into one of the procedures to return the spelled-out

string of the value passed. This package is ideal for printing checks. Dave
Hunt of Oracle Education Services created the package. Dave can be
reached at dhunt@oracle.com for the rights to use this package. The
package is not supported by Oracle, but is provided for use and to
exemplify the power of PL/SQL. This package can also be viewed
in its entirety in the Oracle Press book by Scott Urman, *Oracle PL/SQL
Programming.*

Tips Review

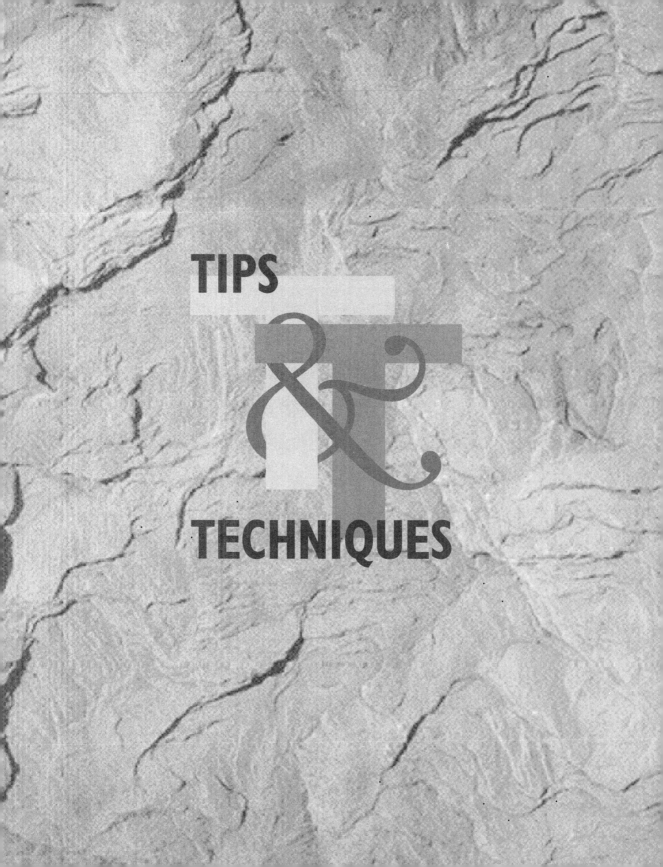

TIPS & TECHNIQUES

CHAPTER
7

Maximizing PL/SQL By
Optimizing SQL
(Developer and DBA)

S QL optimization is a critical aspect of any successful system. The number of SQL statements comprise a small portion of the overall source code; however, it is the most critical section of any source code written. The code must produce accurate results, as well as process the results efficiently. PL/SQL program units comprise a large portion of the source code developed in Oracle-based applications and, therefore, the SQL statements in these program units need to be optimized.

A production application that is deployed and functionally accurate is important, but if the application does not perform optimally, it is considered a failure. With the new paradigm of Web-based interactive applications, the bar has been raised in terms of what is acceptable performance because of the larger deployment base and hardware/software communication inefficiencies inherent with the Internet model today. Therefore, the need for speed has become even more critical in application development.

SQL tuning should be considered an integral part of any application development effort. SQL statements should be optimized during development and on an ongoing basis to ensure a system is deployed optimally and that it remains optimal as the system grows in terms of data, users, and source code.

Many developers view SQL tuning as a DBA responsibility. In my opinion, this is inaccurate. SQL tuning is every developer's responsibility; the more developers embrace this responsibility and optimize their source code, the more likely the system will be deployed successfully. Many components must be embraced to master SQL tuning; however, this expansive realm becomes easier and a more natural part of development the more it is performed. Therefore, if you are a developer and you do not consider SQL tuning your responsibility, or you do not feel you possess the ability to take on this challenge, stop right here! Learn this extremely important aspect of development today.

Believe me, the first time you take a program or segment of code from hours to seconds by optimizing SQL statements, you will feel the same accomplishment as when you see the users of your organization all using the form or report you developed. The goal of this chapter is to provide basic to intermediate aspects of SQL tuning. This chapter is not intended for experienced performance tuning application developers. If you think you are good at SQL performance tuning, read this chapter to ensure you truly understand all areas of the information provided. The chapter covers a wide variety of areas specific to SQL tuning for developers, with some interspersed topics that will also assist DBAs. This chapter includes the following tips and techniques.

- Understand the value of SQL performance tuning

- Understand Oracle index use

  - Create an application index listing

- Examine rule-based versus cost-based optimization
- Pinpoint problem SQL statements
    - User information/feedback
    - V$SQLAREA view
    - Session TRACE statistics
- Establish a developer tuning methodology
    - Optimize in SQL*Plus
        - Use AUTOTRACE
        - Set TIMING ON
        - Remove the ORDER BY clause
    - Use TRACE/TKPROF
    - Use Explain Plan
- Establish the developer-tuning checklist
    - Execute statements twice to get true timings
    - Beware of index suppression
    - Ensure the leading column of a concatenated index is used
    - Watch adding indexes
    - Improve subquery execution
    - Beware of the optimizer and distribution of data
    - Understand UPDATE/DELETE (SELECT first)
    - Force the driving table
    - Use hints to alter the plan
    - Watch out for database links
    - Limit dynamic SQL statements
    - Fine tune Web-based application SQL statements
    - Modify NOT EQUAL operators to use an index
    - Determine selectivity of a SQL statement
    - Cache small tables in memory

■ Use the most selective index when multiple indexes can be used

■ Understand the overhead associated with large transactions

This chapter, combined with Chapter 8 on PL/SQL tuning, will greatly enhance your capability to turn good PL/SQL source code into great PL/SQL source code. This could mean the difference between success and failure. For further detailed performance tuning information, refer to *Oracle Performance Tuning Tips and Techniques,* by Richard J. Niemiec (Oracle Press).

All the tuning examples in this chapter have been created around the example database included in Chapter 1 and Appendix A. These examples create a small testing environment for you to test the techniques in this chapter on your own, as well as to test other scenarios. Many of the techniques covered in this chapter will result in even larger performance improvements in your application environment.

Understand the Value of SQL Performance Tuning

Many people can develop SQL statements and return the desired results or manipulate the data to obtain the desired results. However, in Oracle application environments, the retrieval and manipulation behind the scenes must execute efficiently. Users will not tolerate downtime or lag time, and corporate America has become obsessed with efficiency. Simply stated, time and time again, "Time is money," is a true statement.

Being able to identify performance problem areas and optimizing these areas within an application is extremely important. Optimization can be accomplished at three levels—namely, the hardware and operating system level (larger or more efficient hardware and/or operating system performance tuning), the database level (tuning the init.ora parameters to optimize the SGA or configuration optimization to reduce contention), and the application level (optimizing source code, primarily SQL statements). Each area typically has an effect on the performance of a system, but the application level is one area that affects a system no matter what is done at the other two levels. The application level performance problems in the majority of applications are attributable to slow or not optimized SQL statements.

Who is responsible for optimizing a system? Depending on the person you ask and the company you talk to, the answer varies. My general recommendation is that the hardware and operating system level is the system administrator's/DBA's responsibility, the database level is the DBA's responsibility, and the application level (SQL statements) is 80 percent the developer's responsibility and 20 percent the DBA's responsibility.

SQL Performance Tuning

The goal of the following sections is to highlight techniques to assist developers in conquering their 80 percent responsibility in the optimization effort. SQL tuning is not an exact science, but the more you work with it, the better you will become. This is like most things in life: If you take the initiative and understand your responsibility, you are destined to be successful and the methods of acting upon this responsibility will become intuitive over time.

SQL performance tuning typically comes into play or is addressed when an application is nearing implementation. The first and foremost priority is to ensure the application meets the business requirements. Once accomplished, and at implementation, the question of performance is always raised. By reading the following sections and developing source code with SQL statement optimization in mind, most of the SQL tuning will be accomplished during the development of the application and the initial creation of the SQL statements, because you will inherently develop efficient code.

SQL tuning relies heavily on understanding how to use indexes effectively and knowing the data distribution of the application tables. Tuning prior to production implementation is critical to the success of an application and can make the difference between success and failure.

Remember, users are typically reluctant to change and when introducing a new system, it must perform functionally and optimally. You only get one chance at a first impression; make sure it is a good impression. Once an application is deployed, it is important to continue post-production monitoring and on-going performance tuning to ensure the application continues to function optimally.

The following sections define how Oracle uses indexes, illustrate how to identify problem SQL statements, establish a tuning methodology, and provide a developer's tuning checklist.

Understand Oracle Index Use

The first step in SQL statement performance tuning is to understand how Oracle indexes work. Understanding the method in which an index works aids in realizing the importance of indexing properly and understanding Oracle's internal optimization process. This is the short answer, but it is enough to point you in the right direction.

Oracle bases the execution of every SQL statement on an execution plan. An execution plan is created internally by Oracle during the SQL statement parsing process. The execution plan tells Oracle what path to follow to process a SQL statement. The plan dictates the order to process each statement to return the requested result set. Oracle's optimizer determines the execution plan based on the manner in which the SQL statement is written and varies based on the optimizer mode used.

Oracle uses one of two optimization methods depending on the init.ora setting, either rule-based or cost-based. Rule-based optimization is the older method that Oracle used by default prior to Oracle7. *Rule-based optimization* creates an execution plan based on a set of precedence rules when parsing a SQL statement. *Cost-based optimization* was introduced in Oracle7, and it creates an execution plan based on statistics (logged into the data dictionary when tables and indexes are analyzed) when parsing a SQL statement.

Depending on how your system is configured, it can drastically change the method in which SQL statements are processed. The system configuration is controlled by the DBA. Understanding the differences between the optimizers is important, but it is equally important to understand and build an arsenal of tuning techniques that can be applied during the laborious trial and error tuning process. The goal of SQL performance tuning is to make each SQL statement faster. The execution plan provides the window into the current path. Many techniques can be applied to change the execution plan that will ideally result in improved performance.

Once Oracle determines the execution plan, the SQL Engine executes the statement in the execution plan order to obtain the result set. The goal of most SQL statements is to use indexes as a common practice to improve SQL performance. The question is how does Oracle use an index?

When a request is made to create an index on a column, the column(s) indexed and the ROWID are stored in the index object. When a SQL statement is written that uses an index, Oracle searches the index for the record(s) that match the column criteria. Once found, the ROWID(s) for the matched record(s) are used to search the base table. The fastest search on a table is by ROWID because it is the address of the location on disk. For further information on ROWID, refer to Chapter 2 and Chapter 4.

If an index contains the entire contents of the information selected, then the SQL statement is satisfied entirely by the index contents and no need exists to go to the table and search by ROWID. This is illustrated in the following two scripts that both SELECT from the s_order table: the first cannot be satisfied by the index alone and the second can be satisfied by the index alone. A unique index is on the order_id column of the s_order table. The following example displays the SQL statement, the result set, and an Explain Plan obtained in SQL*Plus with AUTOTRACE set ON. AUTOTRACE is described in detail later in this chapter.

The following example illustrates the use of an index.

File: 7_1.sql

```
SELECT order_id, customer_id
FROM   s_order
WHERE  order_id = 100;
```

Output (7_1.sql)

```
ORDER_ID CUSTOMER_ID
--------- -----------
      100         204


Execution Plan
----------------------------------------------------------
   0      SELECT STATEMENT Optimizer=CHOOSE
   1    0   TABLE ACCESS (BY ROWID) OF 'S_ORDER'
   2    1     INDEX (UNIQUE SCAN) OF 'S_ORDER_ID_PK' (UNIQUE)
```

Notice the 3rd line of the Explain Plan shows how the unique index was used. The 2nd line shows the s_order table was accessed once the ROWID was retrieved from the index. The 1st line reveals the init.ora optimizer parameter is set to CHOOSE. CHOOSE means the method of optimization used could have been rule-based or cost-based, depending on whether the s_order table was ever analyzed (if previously analyzed, cost-based optimization is used; otherwise, rule-based optimization is used).

The following example shows the index use to satisfy the search and result set without accessing the database table.

File: 7_2.sql

```
SELECT order_id
FROM   s_order
WHERE  order_id = 100;
```

Output (7_2.sql)

```
ORDER_ID
---------
      100


Execution Plan
----------------------------------------------------------
   0      SELECT STATEMENT Optimizer=CHOOSE
   1    0   INDEX (UNIQUE SCAN) OF 'S_ORDER_ID_PK' (UNIQUE)
```

The execution plan shows the index was used and satisfied the SQL statement because the selection criteria and predicate were both included in the index. Any time the index can satisfy the predicate and result set, Oracle will internally identify that no need exists to go back to the table, as shown in the preceding example.

If Oracle can use multiple indexes on a table, it often will, as illustrated in the following example (typically only in the rule-based optimization). The s_order table has one index on the title column and a separate index on the start_date column.

File: 7_3.sql

```
SELECT employee_last_name, employee_first_name, start_date, title
FROM   s_employee
WHERE  title = 'STOCK CLERK'
AND    start_date = '08-MAR-90';
```

Output (7_3.sql)

```
EMPLOYEE_LAST_NAME EMPLOYEE_FIRST_NAME  START_DAT TITLE
------------------ -------------------- --------- ----------------

SMITH              GEORGE               08-MAR-90 STOCK CLERK

Execution Plan
----------------------------------------------------------
   0       SELECT STATEMENT Optimizer=CHOOSE
   1    0    TABLE ACCESS (BY ROWID) OF 'S_EMPLOYEE'
   2    1      AND-EQUAL
   3    2        INDEX (RANGE SCAN) OF 'EMP_IDX2' (NON-UNIQUE)
   4    2        INDEX (RANGE SCAN) OF 'EMP_IDX3' (NON-UNIQUE)
```

As illustrated in the preceding example, in the 4th and 5th lines of the Explain Plan, Oracle will use multiple indexes, if available.

Oracle can use a concatenated index, but only if the first portion of the index is in the predicate. Assume the s_order table is changed to combine the title and start_date columns, in that order, into one index. The following two scripts illustrate how Oracle processes and uses concatenated indexes.

The following illustrates the use of the index.

File: 7_4.sql

```
SELECT employee_last_name, employee_first_name, start_date, title
FROM   s_employee
WHERE  title = 'STOCK CLERK'
AND    start_date = '08-MAR-90';
```

Output (7_4.sql)

```
EMPLOYEE_LAST_NAME EMPLOYEE_FIRST_NAME  START_DAT TITLE
------------------ -------------------- --------- ----------------
SMITH              GEORGE               08-MAR-90 STOCK CLERK
```

```
Execution Plan
-----------------------------------------------------------------
   0        SELECT STATEMENT Optimizer=CHOOSE
   1    0     TABLE ACCESS (BY ROWID) OF 'S_EMPLOYEE'
   2    1       INDEX (RANGE SCAN) OF 'EMP_IDX4' (NON-UNIQUE)
```

The index was used to find the ROWID and then the table was accessed to retrieve the column values.

The following illustrates the inability to use the index because only the second part of a two-part index is referenced in the predicate clause.

File: 7_5.sql

```
SELECT employee_last_name, employee_first_name, start_date, title
FROM   s_employee
WHERE  start_date = '08-MAR-90';
```

Output (7_5.sql)

```
EMPLOYEE_LAST_NAME EMPLOYEE_FIRST_NAME   START_DAT TITLE
------------------ -------------------   --------- ---------------
GAO                LADORIS               08-MAR-90 VP, OPERATIONS
SMITH              GEORGE                08-MAR-90 STOCK CLERK


Execution Plan
-----------------------------------------------------------------
   0        SELECT STATEMENT Optimizer=CHOOSE
   1    0     TABLE ACCESS (FULL) OF 'S_EMPLOYEE'
```

Notice the 2nd line indicates a full table scan is performed on the s_employee table and no index was used. If the index was re-created with the first column being the start_date, then the index would have been used (the first portion of the index).

Prior to production the hardest part is guesstimating indexes to optimize your SQL statements. The following is a set of guidelines to assist in determining appropriate indexes prior to production:

- Index all primary keys.

- Index all foreign keys.

- In highly transaction-oriented environments, keep indexes to a minimum because every data INSERT, UPDATE, or DELETE will require the overhead of indexes to be updated (an UPDATE only affects an index if the changed column is in the index). Index the main columns that are retrieved (I recommend limiting indexes to three per table with a maximum of five per table).

Understanding Oracle Index Use

- In highly batch-oriented environments, index more because index maintenance is reduced and the need for retrieval speed becomes more important with larger processing.

- Scan all source code for SQL statements and build indexes that encompass the predicate columns (concatenated indexes will generally result and the number of indexes deemed necessary will usually be limited).

- Test programs and monitor speed: on a program-by-program basis and with user activity (additional indexes may be required).

By following the preceding guidelines, you can improve your efforts in selecting appropriate indexes.

When accessing data from tables Oracle has two options: to read every row in the table also referred to as a full table scan or to access a single row at a time by ROWID. When accessing less than 5 percent of the rows of a table, you generally want to use an index. If an index doesn't exist, then you may want to create one. Indexes increase performance for SELECT, UPDATE, and DELETE statements (when few rows are accessed) and decrease performance for INSERT statements (because inserts must be performed to both the table and index). However, a DELETE statement deleting half a table will also need to delete half the rows for the index (very costly for this specific situation).

Create an Application Index Listing

When it comes to SQL performance tuning, despite your role in the organization, you must know the indexes that exist in your system. This will enable you to review SQL statements to determine if an index can be used or if an index should be added to the system. The more familiar you are with the application indexes, the more natural the SQL statement can be written to use the indexes.

Therefore, it is important to execute the following script periodically under the development schema to obtain a listing of the indexes in your application.

File: 7_6.sql

```
SELECT a.table_name, a.index_name, uniqueness,
       column_position, column_name
FROM   user_indexes a, user_ind_columns b
WHERE  a.index_name = b.index_name
ORDER BY table_name, index_name, column_position;
```

Output (7_6.sql)

```
TABLE_NAME    INDEX_NAME                          UNIQUE POS COLUMN_NAME
------------- ----------------------------------- ------ --- ---------------
S_CUSTOMER    S_CUSTOMER_ID_PK                    UNIQUE   1 CUSTOMER_ID
S_DEPARTMENT  S_DEPARTMENT_ID_PK                  UNIQUE   1 DEPARTMENT_ID
S_DEPARTMENT  S_DEPARTMENT_NAME_REGION_ID_UK      UNIQUE   1 DEPARTMENT_NAME
S_DEPARTMENT  S_DEPARTMENT_NAME_REGION_ID_UK      UNIQUE   2 REGION_ID
S_EMPLOYEE    S_EMPLOYEE_ID_PK                    UNIQUE   1 EMPLOYEE_ID
S_EMPLOYEE    S_EMPLOYEE_USERID_UK               UNIQUE   1 USERID
S_IMAGE       S_IMAGE_ID_PK                       UNIQUE   1 IMAGE_ID
S_INVENTORY   S_INVENTORY_PROD_ID_WHSE_ID_PK     UNIQUE   1 PRODUCT_ID
S_INVENTORY   S_INVENTORY_PROD_ID_WHSE_ID_PK     UNIQUE   2 WAREHOUSE_ID
S_ITEM        S_ITEM_ORDER_ID_ITEM_ID_PK         UNIQUE   1 ORDER_ID
S_ITEM        S_ITEM_ORDER_ID_ITEM_ID_PK         UNIQUE   2 ITEM_ID
S_ITEM        S_ITEM_ORDER_ID_PRODUCT_ID_UK      UNIQUE   1 ORDER_ID
S_ITEM        S_ITEM_ORDER_ID_PRODUCT_ID_UK      UNIQUE   2 PRODUCT_ID
S_LONGTEXT    S_LONGTEXT_ID_PK                    UNIQUE   1 LONGTEXT_ID
S_ORDER       S_ORDER_ID_PK                       UNIQUE   1 ORDER_ID
S_PRODUCT     S_PRODUCT_ID_PK                     UNIQUE   1 PRODUCT_ID
S_PRODUCT     S_PRODUCT_NAME_UK                   UNIQUE   1 PRODUCT_NAME
S_REGION      S_REGION_ID_PK                      UNIQUE   1 REGION_ID
S_REGION      S_REGION_NAME_UK                    UNIQUE   1 REGION_NAME
S_TITLE       S_TITLE_PK                          UNIQUE   1 TITLE
S_WAREHOUSE   S_WAREHOUSE_ID_PK                   UNIQUE   1 WAREHOUSE_ID
```

Note the uniqueness column specifies whether the index contains unique or nonunique values. In this listing, all the indexes are unique and there are four concatenated indexes. This is apparent by looking at the position column and noting the 2 for a column position.

Examine RULE-Based versus COST-Based Optimization

Many Oracle systems are now using cost-based optimization. Many areas exist to look at to determine the optimization method in your environment, such as the Explain Plan output, TKPROF output, and viewing the system parameter setting in the init.ora (SELECT privilege must be granted on the V_$PARAMETER view).

The following illustrates the query from the V$PARAMETER view.

File: 7_7.sql

```
SELECT name, value
FROM   v$parameter
WHERE  name = 'optimizer_mode';
```

Output (7_7.sql)

```
NAME                    VALUE
--------------------    --------------------
optimizer_mode          CHOOSE
```

The value of CHOOSE indicates the optimizer mode will be cost-based as long as one of the objects referenced in the SQL statement has been analyzed. The optimizer will use rule-based if the value is CHOOSE and the object(s) have not been analyzed or if the value of this parameter is RULE.

The following table is an example of the difference in the optimizer mode execution plan. The example uses the s_employee table, and an index exists on the department_id column. The breakdown of department_id values for the records currently is shown in the following table:

Department	Number of Records
10	1
31	6
41	16
50	2

The first example uses the rule-based optimizer (optimizer is set to CHOOSE, but the s_employee table is not analyzed) and shows the use of an index.

File: 7_8.sql

```
SELECT employee_last_name, employee_first_name
FROM   s_employee
WHERE  department_id = 31;
```

Output (7_8.sql)

```
Execution Plan
-------------------------------------------------------------
   0      SELECT STATEMENT Optimizer=CHOOSE
   1    0    TABLE ACCESS (BY ROWID) OF 'S_EMPLOYEE'
   2    1       INDEX (RANGE SCAN) OF 'S_EMPLOYEE_DEPT' (NON-UNIQUE)
```

In the preceding example, the 1st line reveals the optimizer mode is set to CHOOSE in the init.ora. Because no cost-based information is at the end of the 1st line, the optimizer mode is RULE.

The following example uses the cost-based optimizer (the table has been analyzed: ANALYZE TABLE s_employee COMPUTE STATISTICS) and shows a full table scan and no use of an index.

Output (7_8.sql)

```
Execution Plan
----------------------------------------------------------
   0      SELECT STATEMENT Optimizer=CHOOSE (Cost=1 Card=7 Bytes=287)
   1    0     TABLE ACCESS (FULL) OF 'S_EMPLOYEE' (Cost=1 Card=7 Bytes=2
          87)
```

Cost-based information is at the end of the 1st line; therefore, the optimizer mode is COST.

The preceding example shows the different manner in which the optimizer works. The rule-based method follows the rule order independent of the data distribution, whereas the cost-based method adds the benefit of the important statistical information logged in the data dictionary views when the objects are analyzed. In the preceding example, the cost-based optimizer decided to pass on using the index and perform a full table scan because the department_id of 31 comprised 24 percent (6/25) of the data.

It is helpful to know what method of optimization is being used to help in the SQL tuning process and to understand the reason Oracle is choosing a certain path. The method of SQL tuning is similar independent of optimizer setting, so the remainder of this chapter concentrates on techniques of optimizing SQL statements, regardless of the optimizer mode.

Pinpoint Problem SQL Statements

During system testing before, as well as after, an application is deployed, monitoring the performance and determining if the application is performing efficiently is important. A variety of areas can be modified to enhance performance but, in terms of SQL tuning, three useful areas exist to check once an application has been deployed in production. A developer should be able to review these three areas outlined:

- User information/feedback
- V$SQLAREA view
- Session TRACE statistics

User Information/Feedback

Probably the best source to find out where performance problems reside has nothing to do with monitoring the system with scripts or tools; instead, it deals with user reaction and feedback. People generally complain more about negative things in their lives than compliment the positive things. Users of new applications are no different. Users typically have a negative attitude when a new system is deployed; therefore, if any problems occur with the new system, users bring them to your attention. All you must do is ask the users about the system and they are usually more than happy to give you a realistic critique of the system.

SQL performance can be determined by talking to the users. If SQL statements are not optimized correctly or can be optimized further, the statements are consistently slow. And, over time, the slowness gradually becomes slower. New applications with minimal data are always fast initially but, once volumes of data are loaded into the system, the system should be evaluated for acceptable performance.

TIP
Application users are a good source of identifying areas where performance problems exist in an application.

V$SQLAREA View

All SQL statements are processed by Oracle, and they are cached in the SGA for processing, more specifically in the Shared Pool SQL Area, which caches a variety of detailed information for each SQL statement—in particular the disk and memory reads. The real-time view V$SQLAREA can be monitored to display all SQL statements executed and more important, the disk-intensive and memory-intensive SQL statements can be highlighted and reviewed for further SQL optimization.

The V$SQLAREA view must be accessible to the developer. It is not by default accessible to most users. A DBA can grant access on the V$SQLAREA view by issuing the following statement:

```
GRANT SELECT ON v_$sqlarea TO plsql_user;
```

The reason the privilege must be granted on V_$SQLAREA is that is the name of the view and a public synonym on this view are named V$SQLAREA. Once this access is provided, the following scripts can be executed to highlight the top resource-intensive SQL statements. These can then be further analyzed to determine if the SQL statement(s) can be optimized.

File: 7_9.sql

```
SELECT disk_reads reads, executions exe,
       ROUND(disk_reads/DECODE(executions, 0, 1, executions)) ratio,
       command_type type, sql_text text
FROM   v$sqlarea
WHERE  disk_reads > &disk_read_threshold
ORDER BY disk_reads/DECODE(executions, 0, 1, executions) DESC;
```

The results of executing the preceding script and entering 100 for the threshold are illustrated in the following output.

Output (7_9.sql)

```
READS         EXE  RATIO TYPE TEXT
----------  ------ ------ ---- ----------------------------------------
435            2    218    3 SELECT disk_reads reads, executions exe,
                             ROUND(disk_reads/DECODE(executio
                             ns, 0, 1, executions)) ratio,       com
                             mand_type type, sql_text text FROM    v$s
                             qlarea WHERE  disk_reads > 100 ORDER BY
                             disk_reads/DECODE(executions, 0, 1, exec
                             utions) DESC
2352          20    118   47 DECLARE job BINARY_INTEGER := :job; next
                             _date DATE := :mydate;   broken BOOLEAN :
                             = FALSE; BEGIN declare rc binary_integer
                             ; begin rc := sys.dbms_defer_sys.purge(
                             purge_method=>2); end; :mydate := next_d
                             ate; IF broken THEN :b := 1; ELSE :b :=
                             0; END IF; END;
340           77     4     7 delete from source$ where obj#=:1
107           29     4     2 insert into source$(obj#,line,source) va
                             lues (:1,:2,:3)
254          168     2     3 select /*+ index(idl_ub1$ i_idl_ub11) +*
                             / piece#,length,piece from idl_ub1$ wher
                             e obj#=:1 and part=:2 and version=:3 ord
                             er by piece#
```

Displayed in the preceding example is a subset of the result set. The disk_reads column reveals the amount of disk reads performed for the execution of each statement. The execution column reveals how many times each statement is executed. The ratio provides the reads per execution. The type signifies the command type of each statement. The text returned is the actual SQL statement executed in the system, once the statement was passed to the SQL Engine for execution.

The first statement is the SELECT statement executed in the preceding example. The second statement is the execution of a PL/SQL block. The third statement is an internal Oracle statement that is deleting from the underlying user_source view table source$, indicating a stored PL/SQL program unit was deleted. The fourth statement is an internal Oracle statement that inserted into the underlying user_source view table source$, indicating a stored PL/SQL program unit was created. The third and fourth statements are the result of a CREATE OR REPLACE statement. The fifth statement is an internal Oracle statement that is retrieving a stored PL/SQL program unit's p-code from an internal Oracle table and loading the program unit into memory. As evidenced by the third through fifth statements shown in the previous example, a great deal can be learned about the internal execution of Oracle by viewing the contents of the SQL Area (V$SQLAREA view).

If a SQL statement was returned with 100,000 disk_reads and the statement was executed 100,000 times, the statement should not require further optimization because the statement is performing one disk_read per execution. The statement can be investigated to ensure it needs to be executed that many times. If a SQL statement was returned with 100,000 disk_reads and the statement was executed two times, the statement should be investigated for optimization because it is performing 50,000 disk_reads per execution (very costly).

The command type for the most common statements is found in the following table:

Command Type	Description of Command
3	SELECT statement
2	INSERT statement
6	UPDATE statement
7	DELETE statement
47	PL/SQL program unit

The sql_text column only returns the first 1,000 characters of the SQL statement, which, in most cases, contains the entire statement. If the entire statement is needed (for SQL statements of more than 1,000 characters), the preceding script can be joined to the V$SQLTEXT view (joined by the address and hash_value columns of both views). Access needs to be granted on V_$SQLTEXT and the result set needs to be ordered by the piece column of the V$SQLTEXT view because the SQL statement is stored in this view in 64-character segments.

Depending on the environment configuration and complexity of the application you are operating, the threshold should be increased to limit the result set to the top

SQL statements; therefore, the threshold entered can be 10,000 or higher in many cases. The goal of the preceding script is to return the resource-intensive SQL statements in your system.

The V$SQLAREA view stores all SQL statements that have been executed in your system since startup. There is a possibility SQL statements will be flushed from the V$SQLAREA view (SQL Area), as this cache follows a Least Recently Used (LRU) algorithm to age out statements when no more free space exists in the cache. The V$SQLAREA view returns Oracle internal statements that are executed, shown in the preceding example.

The preceding script can be changed to order by the disk_reads in descending order (change the ORDER BY clause), to only display a certain command type (change the predicate clause to contain a condition for the command_type column), to eliminate Oracle internal statements (change the predicate clause to contain a condition for the parsing_user_id column not equal to 0), or to return certain SQL statements (change the predicate clause to contain an INSTRing on the sql_text column).

One important alternate to the preceding example is to return the SQL statements by the buffer_gets or number of memory reads. This alternate script is illustrated in the following example.

File: 7_10.sql

```
SELECT  buffer_gets gets, executions exe,
        ROUND(buffer_gets/DECODE(executions, 0, 1, executions)) ratio,
        command_type type, sql_text text
FROM    v$sqlarea
WHERE   buffer_gets > &buffer_gets_threshold
ORDER BY buffer_gets/DECODE(executions, 0, 1, executions) DESC;
```

The buffer_gets are the number of memory reads performed for each SQL statement execution. If tuning is required, the same analysis should be applied to buffer_gets as outlined for disk_reads. A large amount of buffer_gets could indicate that an existing index is a bad index to use for the statement or a SELECT statement involving multiple tables is using the wrong driving table. Both these conditions can result in a larger number of buffer_gets than necessary.

TIP
The V$SQLAREA view is a valuable area to monitor to pinpoint the top SQL statements that need to be optimized.

Session TRACE Statistics

The TRACE facility is a powerful mechanism allowing the logging of statistical information of all SQL statements for a session, or for all sessions, and can be turned on when the database is started or for a particular session. When a session terminates, the TRACE is automatically turned off for the session. The TRACE can also be turned off by explicitly issuing a command to turn TRACE off. When TRACE is active, every SQL statement executed for the session that is being traced is logged to an operating system file, along with statistics for each SQL statement executed.

Once the TRACE is complete, and prior to viewing the output, the operating system file logged must be converted to a readable format. This is accomplished with the TKPROF operating system command. TKPROF converts the statistics output file to a readable formatted file. Several arguments can also be applied to the TKPROF command to tailor the formatted report to your needs. The converted file can then be reviewed to enable SQL statements to be identified for performance improvements.

The following init.ora parameters must be set prior to using the TRACE facility.

```
time_statistics = TRUE              --turns on timing statistics
max_dump_file_size = 1000000        --sets the maximum TRACE file size
user_dump_dest = /oracle8/jct_trace --specifies the TRACE directory
```

To turn on TRACE system wide, the init.ora parameter below can be set.

```
sql_trace = TRUE --all SQL will be logged once the database is started
```

TIP
It is generally not recommended to turn TRACE on at the database level, since the logging of statistics for every SQL statement executed in the system introduces overhead per statement that can result in noticeable overall performance degradation.

The following SQL statement can be executed to turn TRACE on/off for a session.

```
ALTER SESSION SET SQL_TRACE TRUE;
ALTER SESSION SET SQL_TRACE FALSE;
```

The following PL/SQL methods supplied by Oracle in the DBMS_SESSION and DBMS_SYSTEM supplied packages turn TRACE on/off for a session.

```
-- Turns on TRACE for the current session
EXECUTE DBMS_SESSION.SET_SQL_TRACE(TRUE)
-- Turns off TRACE for the current session
EXECUTE DBMS_SESSION.SET_SQL_TRACE(FALSE)
-- Turns on TRACE for a session with sid=8 and serial#=255; the
-- sid & serial# can be found in the V$SESSION view and other V$ views
EXECUTE DBMS_SYSTEM.SET_SQL_TRACE_IN_SESSION(8, 255, TRUE)
-- Turns off TRACE for a session with sid=8 and serial#=255
EXECUTE DBMS_SYSTEM.SET_SQL_TRACE_IN_SESSION(8, 255, FALSE)
```

For further information related to the preceding DBMS_SESSION and DBMS_SYSTEM packages, refer to Chapters 11 and 12.

The TKPROF facility is an operating system (OS) facility and is executed with the following command.

```
tkprof input_trace_file output_formatted_file [options]
```

The input_trace_file is the file logged when TRACE is turned on and the output_formatted_file is the formatted file that is created. The following list outlines various options:

- **sort=parameters** is the order of statements in output_formatted_file [more than one of these parameters can be specified and include FCHCPU (CPU time of fetch), FCHDSK (disk reads of fetch), FCHCU and FCHQRY (memory reads for fetch), FCHROW (number of rows fetched), EXECPU (CPU execution time), EXEDSK (disk reads during execution), EXECU and EXEQRY (memory reads during execution), and EXEROW (row processed during execution)]. This is entirely dependent on what is most important to the developer/DBA reviewing the output.

- **print=number** is the number of statements to include in the output_formatted_file; the default is all statements (typically all statements would be desired).

- **explain=username/password** provides an Explain Plan for all statements in the output (helpful for viewing the execution plan; set the username and password to the session the trace file was created from).

- **insert=filename** creates a file containing SQL statements to create a table and insert all TRACE file statistics per SQL statement (helpful for logging history for review of tuning progress).

- **record=filename** creates a file containing all the SQL statements that were TRACEd.

■ **sys=yes/no** enables the recursive statements to be eliminated from the output_formatted_file (defaults to yes).

Following is a quick example of a TRACE in a SQL*Plus session under schema PLSQL_USER.

Step 1: TRACE is turned on for a session

```
ALTER SESSION SET SQL_TRACE TRUE;
```

Step 2: One SQL statement is executed

```
SELECT employee_last_name, employee_first_name
FROM    s_employee a
WHERE   EXISTS
(SELECT 'X'
FROM    s_employee_test
WHERE   employee_last_name = a.employee_last_name);
```

Step 3: TRACE is turned off for the session

```
ALTER SESSION SET SQL_TRACE FALSE;
```

Step 4: TKPROF is executed for the statistics file (at the OS)

```
tkprof ora02483.trc ora02483.prf explain=plsql_user/plsql_user
```

Step 5: The output file from TKPROF is viewed

```
SELECT employee_last_name, employee_first_name
FROM    s_employee a
WHERE   EXISTS
(SELECT 'X'
FROM    s_employee_test
WHERE   employee_last_name = a.employee_last_name)
```

call	count	cpu	elapsed	disk	query	current	rows
Parse	1	0.00	0.18	0	0	0	0
Execute	1	0.00	0.00	0	0	0	0
Fetch	2	0.00	0.00	0	51	52	25
total	4	0.00	0.18	0	51	52	25

```
Misses in library cache during parse: 0
Optimizer goal: CHOOSE
Parsing user id: 19  (PLSQL_USER)


Rows     Execution Plan
-------  --------------------------------------------------------
      0  SELECT STATEMENT    GOAL: CHOOSE
     25   FILTER
     25    TABLE ACCESS   GOAL: ANALYZED (FULL) OF 'S_EMPLOYEE'
    321    TABLE ACCESS   GOAL: ANALYZED (FULL) OF 'S_EMPLOYEE_TEST'
```

The following are important areas of interest in a TKPROF output file:

- **Parse Count**   If high, the Shared Pool (SHARED_POOL_SIZE parameter) may need to be increased to reduce the amount of re-parsing taking place.

- **Disk Fetches**   If high, indexes may need to be added or reviewed for proper index use.

- **Query and/or Current Fetches**   If high, this may be an indicator that indexes may be unnecessary; it may be more efficient to drop indexes or suppress the use of certain indexes.

- **Elapsed Parse Time**   If high, this may be an indicator of too many cursors opened.

- **Misses in Library Cache**   If greater than 1, the Shared Pool (SHARED_POOL_SIZE parameter) may need to be increased to eliminate aging of the object.

- **Rows in Explain Plan (refers to the Rows column)**   If high, may be an indicator of poor index use or a statement that needs to be reworked.

The TRACE facility is extremely valuable and enables developers and DBAs to identify potential problem SQL statements. The TRACE facility can be turned on for certain programs, when testing performance, or if a program has been identified as a potential performance bottleneck.

Establish a Developer Tuning Methodology

Once SQL statements are identified for potential performance optimization, the tuning process becomes a repetition of trial and error. The SQL statement tuning iterative process should begin with an execution of the original statement in SQL*Plus with AUTOTRACE on and timing on (each described in this section). The SQL statement can be modified and re-executed to review the timing. Use the

Explain Plan to ensure the proper indexes are being used and the execution plan is what is expected, and review the statistics to ensure that the resource requirements are decreasing. The ultimate goal is to decrease the overall time of execution for a SQL statement.

The remainder of this chapter relies on the creation of a test scenario to illustrate various techniques. To create the test scenario, the following script was executed. The s_employee_test table is created to mirror the s_employee table structure. The PL/SQL program unit creates sample test data resulting in 25,000 records. The 25 employee records from the s_employee table are used to duplicate the records 1,000 times with a unique employee_id and a different salary (salary + iteration) for each employee record.

File: 7_11.sql

```
SET SERVEROUTPUT ON SIZE 1000000
-- Create the s_employee_test table without records
CREATE TABLE s_employee_test AS
SELECT * FROM s_employee
WHERE  1 = 2;
--Duplicates Employees with unique id and salary modification
DECLARE
    CURSOR cur_employee IS
        SELECT *
        FROM    s_employee
        ORDER BY employee_id;
    lv_total_emps_num PLS_INTEGER:= 0;
BEGIN
    FOR lv_loop_num IN 1..1000 LOOP
        FOR lv_emp_rec IN cur_employee LOOP
            INSERT INTO s_employee_test
                (employee_id, employee_last_name,
                employee_first_name, userid,
                start_date, comments,
                manager_id, .title,
                department_id, salary,
                commission_pct)
            VALUES
                (s_employee_id.nextval, lv_emp_rec.employee_last_name,
                lv_emp_rec.employee_first_name, lv_emp_rec.userid,
                lv_emp_rec.start_date, lv_emp_rec.comments,
                lv_emp_rec.manager_id, lv_emp_rec.title,
                lv_emp_rec.department_id, lv_emp_rec.salary + lv_loop_num,
                lv_emp_rec.commission_pct);
            lv_total_emps_num := lv_total_emps_num + 1;
        END LOOP;
        COMMIT;   -- Commits every 25 records
    END LOOP;
```

```
    DBMS_OUTPUT.PUT_LINE('Total Employees Inserted: ' ||
        lv_total_emps_num);
END;
/
```

Optimize in SQL*Plus

Once a SQL statement is identified for potential optimization, cut out the SQL statement from the program that contains it. Attempt to optimize one SQL statement at a time, ensuring the statement is isolated and tested in a controlled test environment. Otherwise, the tuning process becomes more tedious and it is more difficult to eliminate other aspects that may be causing the performance problem.

As a general guideline, therefore, once a SQL statement is identified for necessary tuning, test the statement directly in SQL*Plus. Experiment with the statement in SQL*Plus by itself.

The only problem that arises in SQL*Plus is when you perform a SELECT statement, the data retrieved is returned to the screen and what you are truly concerned with is the time to return the first record. This time tells you how long the statement takes to execute, independent of the values being displayed on your screen. Therefore, I have created a small PL/SQL code segment that prompts for the SELECT statement and then opens the cursor, fetches the first record, and closes the cursor. The timing is set on in SQL*Plus; therefore, I retrieve the timing of the SELECT statement execution, without the data being returned. This PL/SQL code segment is shown with the following two example executions.

File: 7_12.sql

```
SET TIMING ON
SET SERVEROUTPUT ON SIZE 1000000
DECLARE
   CURSOR cur_test_sql IS
      &select_statement;
   lv_test_sql_rec cur_test_sql%ROWTYPE;
BEGIN
   DBMS_OUTPUT.PUT_LINE('********************');
   OPEN cur_test_sql;
   FETCH cur_test_sql INTO lv_test_sql_rec;
   DBMS_OUTPUT.PUT_LINE('SELECT Succeeded.');
   IF cur_test_sql%FOUND THEN
      DBMS_OUTPUT.PUT_LINE('Records Found.');
   ELSE
      DBMS_OUTPUT.PUT_LINE('NO Records Found.');
   END IF;
   CLOSE cur_test_sql;
END;
/
```

Output (7_12.sql)

```
Enter value for select_statement: select employee_last_name from
s_employee_test order by salary
old    3:        &select_statement;
new    3:        select employee_last_name from s_employee_test order
                 by salary;
********************
SELECT Succeeded.
Records Found.

PL/SQL procedure successfully completed.

 real: 3240
```

Output (7_12.sql)

```
Enter value for select_statement: select employee_last_name from
s_employee_test
old    3:        &select_statement;
new    3:        select employee_last_name from s_employee_test;
********************
SELECT Succeeded.
Records Found.

PL/SQL procedure successfully completed.

 real: 110
```

Use AUTOTRACE

In SQL*Plus 3.3 and subsequent releases, Oracle provides a valuable tool called *AUTOTRACE*, which provides the capability to turn on Explain Plan and TRACE statistics for every SQL statement executed in SQL*Plus. This provides a similar capability as the Explain Plan utility, but automatically executes for each statement executed and automatically displays the Explain Plan output after the result set is retrieved. All examples in this chapter that display an Explain Plan used the AUTOTRACE tool.

To turn on AUTOTRACE, the following command can be executed in SQL*Plus:

```
SET AUTOTRACE ON
```

SET AUTOTRACE ON is a SQL*Plus command and it remains in effect until SQL*Plus is exited or the command is executed with the OFF attribute. The one main difference between AUTOTRACE and Explain Plan is Explain Plan provides information without actually executing the SQL statement, whereas AUTOTRACE executes the Explain Plan and statistics after the SQL statement has completed execution.

An example of the information returned is shown in the following script:

File: 7_13.sql

```
SELECT *
FROM   DUAL;
```

Output (7_13.sql)

```
D
-
X

Execution Plan
-------------------------------------------------------------
   0        SELECT STATEMENT Optimizer=CHOOSE
   1    0   TABLE ACCESS (FULL) OF 'DUAL'

Statistics
-------------------------------------------------------------
         0   recursive calls
         2   db block gets
         1   consistent gets
         0   physical reads
         0   redo size
       181   bytes sent via SQL*Net to client
       256   bytes received via SQL*Net from client
         3   SQL*Net roundtrips to/from client
         0   sorts (memory)
         0   sorts (disk)
         1   rows processed
```

The Explain Plan and statistics returned are critical pieces of information for SQL optimization. The Explain Plan reveals the execution plan Oracle has chosen and the statistics reveal the resources required to complete execution of the SQL statement.

Prior to the first execution, spool the output of the SQL*Plus session (SPOOL filename), so it can be reviewed later. For the statistics returned, the main statistics to review are the physical reads (disk reads), db block gets and consistent gets (memory reads), and the recursive calls (internal Oracle recursive calls that are costly). To ensure the modification attributable to the performance gain is truly recognized, only one modification should be made to a statement at a time between timing executions. Once the statement is optimized to an acceptable level, the modified statement can be inserted back into the main program and tested for performance improvements within the complete environment.

The Explain Plan can get complex quickly. Differing views exist on how to read the plan correctly to determine the actual path Oracle is taking when executing a statement. The differing views center around the correct order of the plan: is it top-down or bottom-up? The correct answer is dependent on the manner in which the SQL statement to retrieve the execution plan is written. A later section in this chapter describes the Explain Plan facility and illustrates one SQL statement used to retrieve the execution plan. With AUTOTRACE, the Explain Plan is displayed in a top-down order, as illustrated in the following example.

File: 7_14.sql

```
SELECT employee_last_name, employee_first_name
FROM    s_employee
WHERE   employee_last_name IN
(SELECT employee_last_name
FROM    s_employee_test);
```

Output (7_14.sql)

```
Execution Plan
-----------------------------------------------------------
   0         SELECT STATEMENT Optimizer=CHOOSE
   1     0     MERGE JOIN
   2     1       SORT (JOIN)
   3     2         TABLE ACCESS (FULL) OF 'S_EMPLOYEE'
   4     1       SORT (JOIN)
   5     4         VIEW
   6     5           SORT (UNIQUE)
   7     6             TABLE ACCESS (FULL) OF 'S_EMPLOYEE_TEST'
```

Based on the 1st line (the line with the first column set to 0), the optimizer mode is RULE (the init.ora optimizer mode is set to CHOOSE and no COST information is present). The first column numbers signify the parent of the dependent execution steps, whereas the second column numbers signify the dependent execution steps. To read the order of execution for the AUTOTRACE Explain Plan, disregard the parent and dependent numbers. The plan is read from top to bottom, from innermost indentation to outermost indentation. Therefore, the order of execution in the preceding example is illustrated in the following steps (columns 1 and 2 are shown in parenthesis after the step designation).

- Step 1 (7,6): A full table scan is performed on the s_employee_test table.

- Step 2 (6,5): A unique sort is performed on the s_employee_test records returned.

- Step 3 (3,2): A full table scan is performed on the s_employee table.

- Step 4 (5,4): A view is internally created for the s_employee_test records.

- Step 5 (2,1): A sort join is performed.

- Step 6 (4,1): A sort join is performed.

- Step 7 (1,0): The two sets of records are merged.

The first line performs no execution, but provides the detail of the type of SQL statement and the optimizer mode. For a developer, the important part of reading an Explain Plan is not necessarily knowing what each step of the plan means because it becomes extremely confusing fast. Being able to recognize the general order of the execution steps to identify the execution plan modification when a change is made to the SQL statement (either the order of the SQL statement tables in the FROM clause, the modification of the predicate clause, or the introduction of a HINT) is important. The following is one more example to ensure the execution plan is read correctly.

File: 7_15.sql

```
SELECT employee_last_name, employee_first_name, department_name
FROM   s_department dept, s_employee emp
WHERE  emp.department_id = dept.department_id;
```

Output (7_15.sql)

```
Execution Plan
-----------------------------------------------------------
   0        SELECT STATEMENT Optimizer=CHOOSE
   1    0     NESTED LOOPS
   2    1       TABLE ACCESS (FULL) OF 'S_EMPLOYEE'
   3    1       TABLE ACCESS (BY ROWID) OF 'S_DEPARTMENT'
   4    3         INDEX (UNIQUE SCAN) OF 'S_DEPARTMENT_ID_PK' (UNIQUE)
```

Based on the 1st line, the optimizer mode is RULE. This example identifies one additional important concept to understand when reading the Explain Plan output. When TABLE ACCESS steps are in the plan and steps are indented below this type of step, the first TABLE ACCESS, with respect to the top of the plan, takes precedence. The indented steps below this particular step are executed first from most indented to least indented, followed by the TABLE ACCESS step execution. Then the next TABLE ACCESS, with respect to the top of the plan at the same indentation, is processed by following the same steps. This is illustrated in the following steps.

- Step 1 (2,1): A full table scan is performed on the s_employee table.

- Step 2 (4,3): An index (department_id) search is performed on the s_department table.

- Step 3 (3,1): A ROWID search is performed on the s_department table based on Step 2.

- Step 4 (1,0): Nested loops are then performed.

Variations to the AUTOTRACE option exist to change the information displayed. The following are the options for AUTOTRACE:

Command	Display Explain Plan	Display Statistics	Display Result Set to Screen
SET AUTOTRACE ON	Yes	Yes	Yes
SET AUTOTRACE ON EXPLAIN	Yes	No	Yes
SET AUTOTRACE ON STATISTICS	No	Yes	Yes
SET AUTOTRACE TRACEONLY	Yes	Yes	No

TIP
The TRACEONLY option of AUTOTRACE is ideal for tuning because it does not display the result set to the screen, but includes the number of records retrieved.

Finally, some initial configurations are required by the DBA for the AUTOTRACE option to work for each user. Once AUTOTRACE is configured for a user, it is available every time the user logs into SQL*Plus.
Requirements to use all options of AUTOTRACE:

- **Explain Plan** The user must have access to a PLAN_TABLE, which is created by executing the utlxplan.sql script under the user (this script is supplied by Oracle and typically is in the admin directory under the ORACLE_HOME/rdbms directory). If this is not set up properly, the following message displays when attempting to turn AUTOTRACE ON:

```
SET AUTOTRACE ON

Unable to verify PLAN_TABLE format or existence
Error enabling EXPLAIN report
```

■ **Statistics**   The user must be granted the PLUSTRACE role by a DBA. The
PLUSTRACE role and necessary privileges granted to the PLUSTRACE role
are created by executing the plustrce.sql script under the SYS user (this
script is supplied by Oracle and typically is in the plus33 directory under
the oracle_home directory, where 33 changes, dependent on the version of
SQL*Plus). If this is not configured properly, the following message displays
when attempting to turn AUTOTRACE ON:

```
SET AUTOTRACE ON

Cannot find the Session Identifier.  Check PLUSTRACE role is
enabled
Error enabling STATISTICS report
```

Set TIMING ON

When optimizing SQL statements in SQL*Plus, the timing function can be enabled
by using the SQL*Plus timing function. This timing function displays the real time to
execute each statement executed in SQL*Plus as illustrated in the following
example:

File: 7_16.sql

```
SET TIMING ON
SELECT COUNT(*)
FROM   s_employee;
```

Output (7_16.sql)

```
COUNT(*)
----------
        25

real: 770
```

The real-time is displayed in thousandths of seconds; therefore, the actual time
elapsed is .77 seconds. This timing function can be turned off by replacing the ON
attribute with OFF.

Remove the ORDER BY Clause

Many times, the driving query of a program retrieves a large set of records and
contains an ORDER BY clause. This query potentially takes a considerable amount
of time, depending on the amount of data it is returning. This SQL statement

typically is highlighted as a candidate for SQL optimization. When this statement is pulled into SQL*Plus for optimization, remove the ORDER BY clause and review the performance of the statement without this clause. If the result is retrieved immediately, which is often the case, the statement is optimized, as much as it will be from a developer standpoint.

TIP
When optimizing SQL statements, remove the ORDER BY clause because the ORDER BY is performed once the result set is retrieved and no SQL tuning can be performed to enhance the performance of an ORDER BY.

Use TRACE/TKPROF

The TRACE/TKPROF facility should be a standard component in your tuning arsenal and tuning methodology, especially when attempting to optimize large programs with many SQL statements. This facility provides a robust mechanism to track key information during execution to enable potential problem SQL statements to be identified.

Refer to the section earlier in this chapter for further information on the TRACE/TKPROF facility.

Use Explain Plan

Explain Plan provides a powerful mechanism for viewing the execution plan of a SQL statement. When tuning, SQL statements can be modified by rewriting the SQL code or by introducing HINTs to force the optimizer down a different path to improve the overall performance of a SQL statement. In the process, the Explain Plan can be viewed to determine how the execution plan chosen by Oracle is changing with the SQL statement modifications.

The Explain Plan can be viewed in the TRACE/TKPROF facility, through AUTOTRACE in SQL*Plus, or by using Explain Plan alone in SQL*Plus. Refer to the sections earlier in this chapter for further information on Explain Plan in the TRACE/TKPROF and AUTOTRACE facilities.

The main advantage of using Explain Plan alone is the SQL statement is not executed in order to view the execution plan. It is much faster and more efficient to use Explain Plan over TRACE/TKPROF or AUTOTRACE when a SQL statement takes two hours to complete execution. The statement is parsed and the execution plan is determined by Oracle and logged into a database table. Once the execution plan is logged in the database table, the plan can be retrieved and displayed to enable review of the plan.

Prior to using Explain Plan, the utlxplan.sql (this script is supplied by Oracle and typically is in the admin directory under the ORACLE_HOME/rdbms directory) must be executed under the account that will be using Explain Plan. Executing this script creates a table named plan_table.

An Explain Plan is performed on a SQL statement by using one of the following methods:

- **Method 1**   The following statement inserts plan information into the plan_table with no identifier (use if the plan_table records will be deleted prior to every execution).

    File: 7_17.sql

    ```
    EXPLAIN PLAN FOR
    SELECT employee_last_name, employee_first_name
    FROM    s_employee a
    WHERE   EXISTS
    (SELECT 'X'
    FROM     s_employee_test
    WHERE    employee_last_name = a.employee_last_name);
    ```

- **Method 2**   The following statement inserts plan information into the plan_table with an identifier (use if the plan_table records will not be deleted each execution or if multiple users are sharing the same plan_table).

    File: 7_18.sql

    ```
    EXPLAIN PLAN
    SET STATEMENT_ID = 'emp_exist' FOR
    SELECT employee_last_name, employee_first_name
    FROM    s_employee a
    WHERE   EXISTS
    (SELECT 'X'
    FROM     s_employee_test
    WHERE    employee_last_name = a.employee_last_name);
    ```

Once these statements have been executed, the execution plan can be retrieved for the SQL statements. The following query is one of many in regular circulation in the Oracle community to retrieve the execution plan from the plan_table.

Establishing a Developer Tuning Methodology

File: 7_19.sql

```
SELECT LPAD(' ', 2*(level - 1)) || level || '.' ||
       NVL(position, 0) || ' ' || operation || ' ' ||
       options || ' ' || object_name || ' ' || object_type ||
       ' ' || DECODE(id, 0, statement_id || ' Cost = ' ||
       position) || ' ' || object_node "Query Plan"
FROM   plan_table
START WITH id = 0
AND     statement_id = '&&statement_id'
CONNECT BY PRIOR id = parent_id
AND     statement_id = '&&statement_id';
UNDEFINE statement_id
```

Output (7_19.sql)

```
Query Plan
---------------------------------------------------------------
1.1 SELECT STATEMENT      emp_exist Cost = 1
  2.1 FILTER
    3.1 TABLE ACCESS FULL S_EMPLOYEE
    3.2 INDEX RANGE SCAN S_EMPLOYEE_TEST_IDX3 NON-UNIQUE
```

TIP

Use Explain Plan natively when a statement takes a long time to execute and only the execution plan is desired. The TRACE/TKPROF and AUTOTRACE does not provide an Explain Plan until the statements complete execution.

Establish the Developer Tuning Checklist

Optimizing SQL statements is not an exact science. Therefore, it is important to understand how optimization works, including pinpointing SQL statement candidates for possible improvements, understanding indexing, understanding data distribution, understanding how to test for performance improvements, and what can be done to change the execution plan to make a SQL statement more efficient. All the components to SQL statement tuning have been covered in this chapter, except for the knowledge base of the actual SQL statement modifications to make statements more efficient.

This section focuses on techniques that can be applied to improve SQL statements by providing detailed insight into several methods of attacking different types of statements. These techniques should be added to your knowledge base of SQL statement tuning, enabling you to tackle SQL statements. As stated earlier in this chapter, SQL statement tuning is not an exact science; therefore, the more techniques you have in your arsenal, the more likely you will succeed in your optimization efforts.

The techniques covered in the following sections do not show the result set of each query but, instead, focus specifically on the timing and the execution plan (Explain Plan). Each statement was executed in SQL*Plus with the following commands already executed.

```
SET TIMING ON
SET AUTOTRACE ON
SET SERVEROUTPUT ON SIZE 1000000
```

The goal of the following sections is to improve on the overall execution speed of the SQL statements. Most of the results were tested on multiple versions of Oracle. Slight variations exist between Oracle versions and, therefore, the outcome of each of these executions may vary slightly, depending on the configuration of your Oracle environment. Some of the examples show the differences between rule-based and cost-based optimizers, but because of space limitations, this was only performed in a select number of sections.

Execute Statements Twice to Get True Timings

Have you ever executed the same SQL statement twice in SQL*Plus, and the second time seems to execute considerably faster? The second execution is generally faster because the first execution involves overhead that is not present in the second execution. When Oracle processes a SQL statement, it performs several steps internally, which are transparent to the user executing the statement.

The first time a SQL statement is executed it is parsed, an execution plan is created, the statement is loaded into the SQL Area (viewable through V$SQLAREA view), the result set is loaded into memory (database block buffers), and the result set is returned to the user. When the same statement is executed, Oracle is able to bypass several of these steps because they are already cached in memory. Oracle is often able to bypass the parsing, the execution plan, the SQL Area load, and the loading of the result set into memory.

The following example illustrates the second execution performance gain.

File: 7_20.sql

```
SELECT COUNT(*)
FROM    s_employee_test
WHERE   employee_last_name = 'PATEL';
```

Output (7_20.sql)

```
  COUNT(*)
----------
      2000

real: 330
```

Output (7_20.sql)

```
COUNT(*)
----------
     2000

real: 60
```

When optimizing SQL statements, always execute the statement more than once to determine the true timing involved.

TIP
When a query is run multiple times in succession, it becomes faster because you have cached the data in memory (full table scans are aged out of memory quicker than indexed scans). At times, people are tricked into believing they have made a query faster when, in actuality, they are accessing data stored in memory.

Beware of Index Suppression

Oracle determines if an index can be used to perform a more efficient retrieval of information. In rule-based, the optimizer attempts to use an index if one exists, with no regard to data distribution. In cost-based, the optimizer determines if an index exists, then views the statistics on the table and index(es) to determine if an index should be used. However, neither optimizer can use an index if the column that is used in the predicate clause is modified in any manner. This is illustrated in the following example.

A unique index is created on the employee_id column of the s_employee_test table in the following script:

```
CREATE UNIQUE INDEX s_employee_test_idx1
   ON s_employee_test(employee_id);
```

The following illustrates a query executed against the s_employee_test table for a specific employee.

File: 7_21.sql

```
SELECT employee_last_name, employee_first_name
FROM   s_employee_test
WHERE  employee_id = 76031;
```

Output (7_21.sql)

```
real: 440

Execution Plan
----------------------------------------------------------
   0      SELECT STATEMENT Optimizer=CHOOSE
   1    0    TABLE ACCESS (BY ROWID) OF 'S_EMPLOYEE_TEST'
   2    1       INDEX (UNIQUE SCAN) OF 'S_EMPLOYEE_TEST_IDX1' (UNIQUE)
```

The result in the preceding example indicates the rule-based optimizer was used and the unique index created on the employee_id column was used. However, if a SUBSTRing function was performed on the employee_id column, Oracle can no longer use the index because the database column was modified, as illustrated in the following script.

File: 7_22.sql

```
SELECT employee_last_name, employee_first_name
FROM   s_employee_test
WHERE  substr(employee_id,1,5) = 76031;
```

Output (7_22.sql)

```
real: 1710

Execution Plan
---------------------------------------------------------------
   0       SELECT STATEMENT Optimizer=CHOOSE
   1    0    TABLE ACCESS (FULL) OF 'S_EMPLOYEE_TEST'
```

Notice a full table scan was performed. This suppression of the index will happen whether you are using the rule- or cost-based optimizer. It will occur if any function or modification is performed on the indexed column in the predicate clause, including any character (UPPER, INSTR, TO_CHAR, etc.), numeric (TO_NUMBER, ROUND, TRUNC, etc.), or date (TO_DATE, TRUNC, ADD_MONTHS, etc.) function. Index suppression typically is not desired because an index is created with the intent to use the index.

SQL statements are often written with unintentional index suppression. The following example illustrates a SQL statement suppressing the use of an index on the start_date column, followed by a re-write of the SQL statement to allow for the use of the index.

The index on the start_date column cannot be used in the following query.

File: 7_23.sql

```
SELECT employee_id, employee_last_name, employee_first_name,
       start_date
FROM   s_employee
WHERE  TRUNC(start_date) = '08-MAR-90';
```

To modify the preceding query to enable the use of the start_date column index, the statement can be rewritten as follows.

File: 7_24.sql

```
SELECT employee_id, employee_last_name, employee_first_name,
       start_date
FROM   s_employee
WHERE  start_date BETWEEN '08-MAR-90' AND
       TO_DATE('08-MAR-90') + 1 - .000011574;
```

Columns defined with a DATE data type contain a time portion; therefore, the BETWEEN operator captures all records with a DATE of 08-MAR-90, independent of the time portion.

Index suppression may be desired if you need to force the optimizer to disregard an index in certain cases. To suppress an index, the SQL statement must be changed in a manner to ensure the same result set. To suppress predicate conditions for numeric values, add a 0 to the column. To suppress predicate conditions for character values, add a NULL string to the column.

The following illustrates the suppression of a numeric column.

File: 7_25.sql

```
SELECT  employee_last_name, employee_first_name
FROM    s_employee_test
WHERE   employee_id + 0 = 76031;
```

The following illustrates the suppression of a character column.

File: 7_26.sql

```
SELECT  employee_id, employee_last_name, employee_first_name
FROM    s_employee_test
WHERE   employee_last_name || '' = 'PATEL';
```

Beware of Oracle internal suppression. If you are comparing mismatched data types in the predicate clause, Oracle is forced to convert one of the values to perform the comparison. The employee_id column is defined as a number. The following illustrates a query containing an equality that compares the employee_id column to a character column.

File: 7_27.sql

```
SELECT  employee_last_name, employee_first_name
FROM    s_employee_test
WHERE   employee_id = '76031';
```

Output (7_27.sql)

```
real: 440

Execution Plan
---------------------------------------------------------------
   0      SELECT STATEMENT Optimizer=CHOOSE
   1    0   TABLE ACCESS (BY ROWID) OF 'S_EMPLOYEE_TEST'
   2    1     INDEX (UNIQUE SCAN) OF 'S_EMPLOYEE_TEST_IDX1' (UNIQUE)
```

The resulting Explain Plan indicates the index was still used. When Oracle compares a numeric value to a character value, it converts the character value to a number internally. In the preceding scenario, the conversion did not cause the suppression of an index.

This is not the case in the following example, however. The next scenario illustrates the internal conversion by Oracle causing the suppression of an index. When Oracle performs an internal modification to the statement, it is hard to track down, unless the Explain Plan is reviewed.

To create the following scenario, the employee_id column is duplicated in the s_employee_test table as employee_dup_id and is defined as a VARCHAR2(7). The statements follow to add the column, fill the column, and create an index on the column.

File: 7_28.sql

```
-- Adds the new column
ALTER TABLE s_employee_test
   ADD employee_dup_id VARCHAR2(7);
-- Updates the new column with the value of the employee_id column
UPDATE s_employee_test
SET     employee_dup_id = employee_id;
-- Creates an index on the new column
CREATE UNIQUE INDEX s_employee_test_idx2
   ON s_employee_test(employee_dup_id);
```

When the employee_dup_id column is searched, the Explain Plan reveals the use of an index.

File: 7_29.sql

```
SELECT employee_last_name, employee_first_name
FROM    s_employee_test
WHERE   employee_dup_id = '76031';
```

Output (7_29.sql)

```
real: 490

Execution Plan
----------------------------------------------------------
    0      SELECT STATEMENT Optimizer=CHOOSE
    1    0   TABLE ACCESS (BY ROWID) OF 'S_EMPLOYEE_TEST'
    2    1     INDEX (UNIQUE SCAN) OF 'S_EMPLOYEE_TEST_IDX2' (UNIQUE)
```

If we modify the statement slightly, changing the value from a character to a numeric value by removing the single quotes, the execution plan changes and does not use the index, as illustrated in the following example.

File: 7_30.sql

```
SELECT employee_last_name, employee_first_name
FROM   s_employee_test
WHERE  employee_dup_id = 76031;
```

Output (7_30.sql)

```
real: 1590

Execution Plan
------------------------------------------------------------
    0       SELECT STATEMENT Optimizer=CHOOSE
    1    0    TABLE ACCESS (FULL) OF 'S_EMPLOYEE_TEST'
```

The employee_dup_id column was modified internally by Oracle with a TO_NUMBER function, thus suppressing the use of the index.

TIP

Any modification to a column in a predicate clause eliminates the use of an index on that column. The predicate clause can often be rewritten to allow for the optimizer to use the index, if desired. If index suppression is desired, add 0 to a numeric column and concatenate a NULL string to a character column.

TIP

Be careful of Oracle internally adding a function to a column to convert a column to compare the same data types. Always compare the same data types in predicate clauses to eliminate the hidden Oracle internal conversion.

Ensure the Leading Column of a Concatenated Index is Used

When a concatenated (composite or multipart) index is used, the leading part of the index must be used. Consider the following example to build a two-part index on the s_employee table.

```
CREATE INDEX s_employee_test_idx3 ON s_employee_test
   (employee_last_name, salary);
```

The following example illustrates the use of the index.

File: 7_31.sql

```
SELECT  employee_last_name, employee_first_name, salary
FROM    s_employee_test
WHERE   employee_last_name  = 'PATEL'
AND     salary              = 11876.47;
```

Output (7_31.sql)

```
1 rows selected.

real: 500

Execution Plan
-------------------------------------------------------------
   0        SELECT STATEMENT Optimizer=CHOOSE (Cost=2 Card=1 Bytes=68)
   1    0    TABLE ACCESS (BY ROWID) OF 'S_EMPLOYEE_TEST' (Cost=2 Card=
             1 Bytes=68)
   2    1     INDEX (RANGE SCAN) OF 'S_EMPLOYEE_TEST_IDX3' (NON-UNIQUE
             )
```

The following example illustrates that a predicate clause referencing only the second part of an index will not use the index.

File: 7_32.sql

```
SELECT  employee_last_name, employee_first_name, salary
FROM    s_employee_test
WHERE   salary = 11876.47;
```

Output (7_32.sql)

```
1 rows selected.

real: 1160

Execution Plan
-------------------------------------------------------------
   0        SELECT STATEMENT Optimizer=CHOOSE (Cost=153 Card=2 Bytes=108
             )
   1    0    TABLE ACCESS (FULL) OF 'S_EMPLOYEE_TEST' (Cost=153 Card=2
             Bytes=108)
```

TIP

For a concatenated index to be used in full or in part, the leading edge of the index must be present. If any column contained in the index is not present in the predicate clause, then all columns of the index following that column cannot use the index.

Watch Adding Indexes

Indexes are generally helpful for increasing performance of SQL statements. Beware when adding indexes in your application. The addition of an index can change the execution plan of existing statements because each time a statement is executed, an execution plan is created. The execution plan takes into consideration all existing indexes.

TIP

When you want to use the cost-based optimizer, tables must be analyzed in your application. By analyzing the tables, the indexes are also analyzed. If you add an index of an already analyzed table, therefore, make sure to analyze the index. It is unnecessary to re-analyze the table when an index is added; the index can be analyzed separately.

The following example illustrates the potential problem when adding an index. An index is created on the employee_last_name column of the s_employee_test table.

```
CREATE INDEX s_employee_test_idx3
  s_employee_test (employee_last_name);
```

The following query illustrates the execution plan that Oracle will use when executing a query that references the employee_last_name and employee_first_name column.

File: 7_33.sql

```
SELECT employee_last_name, employee_first_name
FROM   s_employee_test
WHERE  employee_last_name  = 'PATEL'
AND    employee_first_name = 'RADHA';
```

Output (7_33.sql)

```
real: 170

Execution Plan
-------------------------------------------------------------
   0      SELECT STATEMENT Optimizer=CHOOSE
   1    0   TABLE ACCESS (BY ROWID) OF 'S_EMPLOYEE_TEST'
   2    1     INDEX (RANGE SCAN) OF 'S_EMPLOYEE_TEST_IDX3'(NON-UNIQUE)
```

An additional index is created on the employee_first_name column of the s_employee_test table, as illustrated in the following script.

```
CREATE INDEX s_employee_test_idx4
    ON s_employee_test (employee_first_name);
```

When the preceding query is executed with the new index created, the execution plan changes, as illustrated in the following output.

Output (7_33.sql)

```
real: 440

Execution Plan
-------------------------------------------------------------
   0      SELECT STATEMENT Optimizer=CHOOSE
   1    0   AND-EQUAL
   2    1     INDEX (RANGE SCAN) OF 'S_EMPLOYEE_TEST_IDX3'(NON-UNIQUE)
   3    1     INDEX (RANGE SCAN) OF 'S_EMPLOYEE_TEST_IDX4'(NON-UNIQUE)
```

In the preceding output, both indexes will be used. As displayed, the preceding example is using the rule-based optimizer.

The preceding scenario is now tested with the cost-based optimizer. The cost-based optimizer is turned on by analyzing the s_employee_test table with the following command:

```
ANALYZE TABLE s_employee_test COMPUTE STATISTICS;
```

Once the table is analyzed, the employee_first_name index is deleted and the preceding query is re-executed.

Output (7_33.sql)

```
real: 160

Execution Plan
-----------------------------------------------------------
   0       SELECT STATEMENT Optimizer=CHOOSE (Cost=153 Card=42 Bytes=23
           52)

   1    0    TABLE ACCESS (FULL) OF 'S_EMPLOYEE_TEST' (Cost=153 Card=42
             Bytes=2352)
```

The Explain Plan for cost-based reveals the employee_last_name index is not used to retrieve the result set. This exemplifies the differences between the optimizers because the cost-based optimizer determines the execution plan with the knowledge of statistical information related to the distribution of data, whereas rule-based is strictly determined by rule precedence.

However, if the employee_first_name column index is re-created and the index is analyzed, the execution plan for cost-based matches that of rule-based.

Output (7_33.sql)

```
real: 440

Execution Plan
-----------------------------------------------------------
   0       SELECT STATEMENT Optimizer=CHOOSE (Cost=67 Card=42 Bytes=235
           2)

   1    0    AND-EQUAL (Cost=67 Card=42 Bytes=2352)
   2    1      INDEX (RANGE SCAN) OF 'S_EMPLOYEE_TEST_IDX4' (NON-UNIQUE
               )

   3    1      INDEX (RANGE SCAN) OF 'S_EMPLOYEE_TEST_IDX3' (NON-UNIQUE
               )
```

If an index can completely satisfy a query, the execution plan will not include a step to go back to the table. Therefore, if indexes in your application contain most of the column data (with the exception of one column) to satisfy SQL statements, re-creating the index with the additional column may be advantageous. The benefits of eliminating the need to access the table data will increase performance.

The following example illustrates the technique of expanding the index to contain columns to satisfy queries. The first step is to remove the employee_last_name and employee_first_name indexes. The next step is to create one index, which is a concatenated index containing both columns. The statements to modify the indexes are illustrated in the following code segment.

```
DROP INDEX s_employee_test_idx3;
DROP INDEX s_employee_test_idx4;
CREATE INDEX s_employee_test_idx3
   ON s_employee_test (employee_last_name, employee_first_name);
```

The result of executing the preceding SQL statement illustrates the benefit by eliminating the requirement of accessing the table. The following execution plan reveals the query is entirely satisfied by the index. The SELECTed columns and the predicate clause are contained in the index.

Output (7_33.sql)

```
real: 50

Execution Plan
------------------------------------------------------------
   0       SELECT STATEMENT Optimizer=CHOOSE (Cost=1 Card=42 Bytes=2352
           )

   1    0    INDEX (RANGE SCAN) OF 'S_EMPLOYEE_TEST_IDX3' (NON-UNIQUE)
           (Cost=1 Card=42 Bytes=2352)
```

The preceding result is using cost-based optimization and illustrates the improvement in performance (.44 down to .05 seconds). If the scenario is tested in rule-based, the resulting execution plan is the same.

TIP
Take care with adding indexes: not only should this be a consideration for potential degradation of DML operations because of added overhead of updating more indexes, it could also alter the execution plan of existing SQL statements, which may be disastrous.

TIP
It is much more efficient if the entire SQL statement (columns selected and the predicate clause) can be satisfied by an index, eliminating the need to access the database table.

Improve Subquery Execution

Using a correlated subquery when a subquery is involved in a SQL statement is generally more efficient. Additionally, when multiple tables are joined in a SQL statement and a table in the join is only used in the predicate clause and not in the SELECT clause, the statement can be converted to a subquery. This method of transforming a SQL statement provides another method of rewriting a statement in the quest to improve performance.

When a subquery is correlated, the outer query executes first, followed by the inner query executing for each record returned from the outer query. When a subquery is non-correlated, the inner query executes first (the result set is treated similarly as a set of values from an IN condition), and then the outer query is executed.

When subqueries are used, using the EXISTS operator versus the IN operator is more efficient. The EXISTS operator terminates the inner query fetching when one matching record in the query is found, whereas the IN operator continues until all matching records are found.

The following illustrates the improvements when executing a correlated subquery versus a noncorrelated subquery. Each following query uses the rule-based optimizer, as both the s_employee and s_employee_test tables have not been analyzed and an index exists on the employee_last_name column.

The following query is a noncorrelated query.

File: 7_34.sql

```
SELECT employee_last_name, employee_first_name
FROM   s_employee
WHERE  employee_last_name IN
(SELECT employee_last_name
FROM    s_employee_test);
```

Output (7_34.sql)

```
real: 3350

Execution Plan
-----------------------------------------------------------
   0        SELECT STATEMENT Optimizer=CHOOSE
   1    0    MERGE JOIN
   2    1      SORT (JOIN)
   3    2        TABLE ACCESS (FULL) OF 'S_EMPLOYEE'
   4    1      SORT (JOIN)
   5    4        VIEW
   6    5          SORT (UNIQUE)
   7    6            TABLE ACCESS (FULL) OF 'S_EMPLOYEE_TEST'
```

When the statement is modified to a correlated subquery with an EXISTS as illustrated in the following example, the increased performance is evident.

File: 7_35.sql

```
SELECT employee_last_name, employee_first_name
FROM    s_employee a
WHERE   EXISTS
(SELECT 'X'
FROM    s_employee_test
WHERE   employee_last_name = a.employee_last_name);
```

Output (7_35.sql)

```
real: 990

Execution Plan
-----------------------------------------------------------
   0        SELECT STATEMENT Optimizer=CHOOSE
   1    0    FILTER
   2    1      TABLE ACCESS (FULL) OF 'S_EMPLOYEE'
   3    1      INDEX (RANGE SCAN) OF 'S_EMPLOYEE_TEST_IDX3' (NON-UNIQUE
                )
```

The output execution plan reveals the use of the employee_last_name index and increased efficiency.

TIP

Using EXISTS with a subquery can make queries dramatically faster, depending on the data being retrieved from each part of the query.

Beware of the Optimizer and Distribution of Data

Understanding that the rule-based optimizer only follows a set of rules to determine the execution plan is important. In rule-based, if an index exists, it will use the index, independent of the data distribution. To stress the importance of knowing the data distribution and the differences in the optimizer, pay particular attention to the following example. This example illustrates the large performance improvement of knowing the distribution of data and using the cost-based optimizer.

To create the scenario, the following PL/SQL program is executed to increase the salary of all employees with a salary greater than $1,100 by $10,000 (updates all 25,000 records except 61 records).

File: 7_36.sql

```
DECLARE
   CURSOR cur_emp_sal IS
      SELECT ROWID
      FROM   s_employee_test
      WHERE  salary > 1100;
   lv_counter_num PLS_INTEGER := 0;
BEGIN
   FOR cur_emp_sal_rec IN cur_emp_sal LOOP
      lv_counter_num := lv_counter_num + 1;
      UPDATE s_employee_test
      SET    salary = salary + 10000
      WHERE  ROWID = cur_emp_sal_rec.ROWID;
      IF MOD(lv_counter_num,500) = 0 THEN
         DBMS_APPLICATION_INFO.SET_MODULE(lv_counter_num, NULL);
         COMMIT;
      END IF;
   END LOOP;
   DBMS_APPLICATION_INFO.SET_MODULE(lv_counter_num, NULL);
END;
/
```

Note the execution of the DBMS_APPLICATION_INFO.SET_MODULE to log the commit every 500 records to the V$SESSION view. Refer to Chapter 12 for further information on monitoring the record logging in the V$SESSION view and on using the DBMS_APPLICATION_INFO package.

The following creates an index on the salary column.

```
CREATE INDEX s_employee_test_idx5 ON s_employee_test(salary);
```

The following illustrates the use of the salary column index by the optimizer:

File: 7_37.sql

```
SELECT employee_last_name, employee_first_name, salary
FROM   s_employee_test
WHERE  salary > 10000;
```

Output (7_37.sql)

```
24939 rows selected.

 real: 6090

Execution Plan
----------------------------------------------------------
    0      SELECT STATEMENT Optimizer=CHOOSE (Cost=153 Card=9128 Bytes=
           492912)
    1    0   TABLE ACCESS (FULL) OF 'S_EMPLOYEE_TEST' (Cost=153 Card=91
             28 Bytes=492912)
```

The cost-based optimizer overrides the use of the index (because the optimizer knows that greater than 5 percent of the rows are retrieved).

The following example shows the problem with using the rule-based optimizer by adding a RULE HINT. Hints are described later in this chapter.

File: 7_38.sql

```
SELECT /*+ RULE */ employee_last_name, employee_first_name, salary
FROM   s_employee_test
where  salary > 10000;
```

Output (7_38.sql)

```
24939 rows selected.

 real: 184830

Execution Plan
----------------------------------------------------------
    0      SELECT STATEMENT Optimizer=HINT: RULE
    1    0   TABLE ACCESS (BY ROWID) OF 'S_EMPLOYEE_TEST'
    2    1     INDEX (RANGE SCAN) OF 'S_EMPLOYEE_TEST_IDX5' (NON-UNIQUE
             )
```

The performance difference of going directly to the table versus using an index in this scenario is massive (6.09 seconds versus 184.83 seconds).

TIP
Knowledge of the data distribution is very beneficial and considered one of the top key items to have in your arsenal when optimizing SQL statements. Understanding the difference between the optimizers is also an important aspect to tuning.

TIP
Because the cost-based optimizer will be used when at least one of the tables in a multitable SQL statement (assuming the init.ora optimizer_mode parameter is set to CHOOSE) is executed, make sure all tables in a multitable join are analyzed. When a table that is part of a cost-based execution plan is not analyzed, the optimizer makes a best guess of the data distribution of that table. Eliminate guessing by analyzing the table.

TIP
The optimizer estimates the number of rows that will be returned for inequalities (the results are not always those desired). By understanding the true distribution of data (versus that estimated by the optimizer), the execution plan can be re-directed to return better performance than the optimizer can.

Understand UPDATE/DELETE (SELECT First)

Any UPDATE or DELETE statement executed in programs should be treated as a potential candidate for optimization. UPDATE and DELETE statements perform a SELECT first to retrieve the record prior to performing the operation. Therefore, Oracle creates an execution plan for UPDATE and DELETE statements and, thus, these may need performance improvements. Think of the predicate clause of an UPDATE or DELETE as if it is part of a SELECT statement.

To optimize UPDATE or DELETE statements, change the beginning portion of the statement to a SELECT and optimize the SELECT statement. Once the SELECT statement is optimized, the predicate clause of the SELECT statement can be placed back into the original UPDATE or DELETE.

The following UPDATE illustrates that an execution plan is created.

File: 7_39.sql

```
UPDATE s_employee
SET    salary = salary;
```

Output (7_39.sql)

```
25 rows updated.

 real: 490

Execution Plan
----------------------------------------------------------
   0      UPDATE STATEMENT Optimizer=CHOOSE
   1   0     TABLE ACCESS (FULL) OF 'S_EMPLOYEE'
```

TIP
Performance tuning should extend beyond SELECT statements and include UPDATE and DELETE statements because the first step (internally by Oracle) of an UPDATE and DELETE is a SELECT.

Force the Driving Table

The execution plan chosen by Oracle determines a driving table based on the order of the table names when a join condition is involved and no predicate condition exists that leads the optimizer to choose one table over the other.

When using the rule-based optimizer and Oracle resorts to the order of the table names in the FROM clause, the last table listed in the FROM clause is used as the driving table. This is illustrated in the following example, by the query joining the s_employee and s_department tables by the department_id column. When the s_department table is the last table in the FROM clause, the s_department is the driving table. When the table order is reversed, the driving table also changes.

The driving table order is shown in the following two queries:

File: 7_40.sql

```
SELECT employee_last_name, employee_first_name, department_name
FROM   s_employee emp, s_department dept
WHERE  emp.department_id = dept.department_id;
```

Output (7_40.sql)

```
Execution Plan
----------------------------------------------------------
   0      SELECT STATEMENT Optimizer=CHOOSE
   1   0     NESTED LOOPS
   2   1       TABLE ACCESS (FULL) OF 'S_DEPARTMENT'
   3   1       TABLE ACCESS (BY ROWID) OF 'S_EMPLOYEE'
   4   3         INDEX (RANGE SCAN) OF 'S_EMPLOYEE_DEPT' (NON-UNIQUE)
```

The preceding example shows the s_department table is the driving table.

File: 7_41.sql

```
SELECT employee_last_name, employee_first_name, department_name
FROM   s_department dept, s_employee emp
WHERE  emp.department_id = dept.department_id;
```

Output (7_41.sql)

```
Execution Plan
-------------------------------------------------------------
   0        SELECT STATEMENT Optimizer=CHOOSE
   1    0     NESTED LOOPS
   2    1       TABLE ACCESS (FULL) OF 'S_EMPLOYEE'
   3    1       TABLE ACCESS (BY ROWID) OF 'S_DEPARTMENT'
   4    3         INDEX (UNIQUE SCAN) OF 'S_DEPARTMENT_ID_PK' (UNIQUE)
```

The preceding example shows the s_employee table is the driving table.

The s_employee and s_department tables are then analyzed to force the use of the cost-based optimizer. As illustrated, the driving table changes when working with the cost-based optimizer. Cost-based uses the first table in the FROM clause as the driving table when all conditions are the same as the preceding example. This is illustrated in the following statement.

File: 7_42.sql

```
SELECT employee_last_name, employee_first_name, department_name
FROM   s_employee emp, s_department dept
WHERE  emp.department_id = dept.department_id;
```

Output (7_42.sql)

```
Execution Plan
-------------------------------------------------------------
   0        SELECT STATEMENT Optimizer=CHOOSE (Cost=26 Card=500 Bytes=40
            500)
   1    0     NESTED LOOPS (Cost=26 Card=500 Bytes=40500)
   2    1       TABLE ACCESS (FULL) OF 'S_EMPLOYEE' (Cost=1 Card=25 Byte
            s=1025)

   3    1       TABLE ACCESS (BY ROWID) OF 'S_DEPARTMENT'
   4    3         INDEX (UNIQUE SCAN) OF 'S_DEPARTMENT_ID_PK' (UNIQUE)
```

The preceding example shows the s_employee table is the driving table.

TIP
When the rule-based optimizer looks at the FROM clause to determine the driving table, the last table in the FROM clause will be the driving table. The cost-based optimizer works exactly the opposite. Therefore, depending on the optimizer in use, it is always recommended to take care when ordering SQL statement FROM clauses. Order them with the smallest table last for the rule-based optimizer (order them with the smallest table first for the cost-based optimizer).

Use Hints to Alter the Plan

The cost-based optimizer includes the capability to alter the execution plan with the use of hints. *Hints* are embedded in the SELECT portion of a SELECT statement to force the optimizer to create a different execution plan. Remember the optimizer follows a logical algorithm to determine the execution plan. If you do not like the execution plan or know of some reason why the optimizer should execute a different path, hints are a convenient mechanism to accomplish this redirection.

Why do hints exist with the cost-based optimizer? Although the cost-based optimizer considers more criteria, including data distribution and statistics, it is still not perfect and a way must exist to tell the optimizer to choose a different path. If you ever view the contents of the V$SQLAREA view, all SQL statements—including Oracle internal SQL statements—are contained and periodically you will notice Oracle's internal statements using hints.

All hints force the optimizer to use cost-based optimization, even if the tables being referenced are not analyzed. The only hint that will not cause the optimizer to cost-base is the RULE hint. The following is an example of a statement executing with the execution plan provided, followed by the same statement using the RULE hint to change the execution plan.

File: 7_43.sql

```
SELECT employee_last_name, employee_first_name, department_name
FROM   s_employee emp, s_department dept
WHERE  emp.department_id = dept.department_id;
```

Output (7_43.sql)

```
real: 1920

Execution Plan
-------------------------------------------------------------
   0       SELECT STATEMENT Optimizer=CHOOSE (Cost=4 Card=25 Bytes=1550
           )
   1    0    HASH JOIN (Cost=4 Card=25 Bytes=1550)
   2    1      TABLE ACCESS (FULL) OF 'S_DEPARTMENT' (Cost=1 Card=12 By
                tes=252)
   3    1      TABLE ACCESS (FULL) OF 'S_EMPLOYEE' (Cost=1 Card=25 Byte
                s=1025)
```

The example changed with the RULE hint is illustrated in the following script.

File: 7_44.sql

```
SELECT /*+RULE*/employee_last_name, employee_first_name,
       department_name
FROM    s_employee emp, s_department dept
WHERE   emp.department_id = dept.department_id;
```

Output (7_44.sql)

```
real: 1540

Execution Plan
-------------------------------------------------------------
   0       SELECT STATEMENT Optimizer=HINT: RULE
   1    0    NESTED LOOPS
   2    1      TABLE ACCESS (FULL) OF 'S_DEPARTMENT'
   3    1      TABLE ACCESS (BY ROWID) OF 'S_EMPLOYEE'
   4    3        INDEX (RANGE SCAN) OF 'S_EMPLOYEE_DEPT' (NON-UNIQUE)
```

Note the reference of using the RULE hint is included in the 1st line of the Explain Plan in the preceding output.

A hint can also be specified with the second comment command, namely two hyphens '--'. The following SELECT statement illustrates the use of a hint with the second comment command. This statement results in the same execution plan and output of the previous example (7_44.sql).

Establishing the Developer
Tuning Checklist

```
SELECT  --+RULE
        employee_last_name, employee_first_name,
        department_name
FROM    s_employee emp, s_department dept
WHERE   emp.department_id = dept.department_id;
```

TIP
*The two-hyphen comment method of specifying a
hint is very strict: the hint must be on its own line and
if any SELECT columns are specified, they are ignored;
there must be no spaces between the two hyphens
and the hint, otherwise the hint will be ignored and
treated as a comment.*

Several other available hints are outlined in the following descriptions:

- **FULL**   Used to force the optimizer to perform a full table scan on a
  specified table; generally helpful when a large portion of the table will be
  returned or the index should not be used (SELECT /*+ FULL(s_employee) */).

- **RULE**   Used to force the optimizer to use the rule-based optimizer to
  determine the execution plan (SELECT /*+ RULE */).

- **FIRST_ROWS**   Used to force the optimizer to determine an execution plan
  that will return the first row the fastest; generally helpful for small
  transaction result sets; generally not recommended when returning large
  transaction sets (SELECT /*+ FIRST_ROWS */).

- **ALL_ROWS**   Used to force the optimizer to determine an execution plan
  that will retrieve the entire result set the fastest; generally helpful for large
  transaction result sets; generally not recommended when returning small
  transaction sets (SELECT /*+ ALL_ROWS */).

- **INDEX**   Used to force the optimizer to use an index on a specified table by
  specifying the table name and the index name (SELECT /*+ INDEX
  (s_employee_test s_employee_test_idx3) */).

TIP
*To specify more than one hint, separate the hints
with spaces. If the hint is not specified correctly, the
hint will be ignored and treated as a comment.
Therefore, make sure the hint is recognized by
viewing the Explain Plan.*

TIP
Hints are not case-sensitive. When using table name aliases in a SQL statement, a reference to a table name in a hint with an alias defined must reference the alias, not the table name. If the table name is referenced in the hint with an alias, the hint will be ignored.

TIP
When prefixing table names with the schema (plsql_user.s_employee) in a SQL statement, a reference to a table name with a hint with the schema prefix included must reference the table name only, not the schema and table name. If the schema and table name are referenced in the hint, the hint will be ignored.

For a complete listing of hints and use of each, refer to *Oracle Performance Tuning Tips and Techniques,* by Richard J. Niemiec (Oracle Press).

Watch Out for Database Links

Database links are a valuable mechanism to share information between instances and distribute information between application environments (remote systems). However, database links should be understood in terms of the means in which data is processed. This is extremely important if joins are between tables on a remote database because these joins can severely impact performance. The key to remember is information is processed based on the setup of the query.

If the tables joined are solely on the remote database, then a major performance impact occurs if the tables are referred to through database links from a remote database. The difference is each of the tables (all records from each table) will be transferred to the calling database and then the records will be joined, resulting in a tremendous amount of overhead of transferring the records and possible space problems on the calling system. The method to eliminate the transfer of the data to the calling database and force the join condition on the remote database is to create a view on the remote database for the condition and then query the view.

Limit Dynamic SQL Statements

I am a firm believer in reusability and maintainability of applications. However, when building reusability and flexibility into your application, make sure the cost of the flexibility does not cause the demise of the application in terms of performance.

To illustrate this fact, consider the following PL/SQL procedure.

File: 7_45.sql

```
CREATE OR REPLACE PROCEDURE select_emp
   (p_emp_id_num NUMBER DEFAULT NULL,
    p_last_name_txt VARCHAR2 DEFAULT NULL,
    p_first_name_txt VARCHAR2 DEFAULT NULL,
    p_start_date DATE DEFAULT NULL,
    p_dept_num NUMBER DEFAULT NULL) IS
   CURSOR cur_emp IS
      SELECT employee_last_name, employee_first_name, salary
      FROM   s_employee_test
      WHERE  employee_id        LIKE p_emp_id_num    || '%'
      AND    employee_last_name LIKE p_last_name_txt  || '%'
      AND    employee_first_name LIKE p_first_name_txt || '%'
      AND    start_date         LIKE p_start_date     || '%'
      AND    department_id      LIKE p_dept_num       || '%';

   lv_last_name_txt  s_employee.employee_last_name%TYPE;
   lv_first_name_txt s_employee.employee_first_name%TYPE;
   lv_salary_num     s_employee.salary%TYPE;
BEGIN
   OPEN cur_emp;
   FETCH cur_emp INTO lv_last_name_txt, lv_first_name_txt,
                      lv_salary_num;
   CLOSE cur_emp;
   -- Processing Logic
END;
/
```

On the surface, the preceding procedure seems dynamic and flexible by accepting a number of parameters. However, the SQL statement in the procedure is passed with each of the predicate segments being passed with a bind variable. The content of the input to this procedure is irrelevant; the SQL statement will be re-used each time, with the first execution establishing the execution plan. Every execution thereafter will use the same execution plan independent of the input.

This is a potential performance tuning nightmare. Optimizing the query one way if the employee_last_name was entered and another way if the employee_id was entered would be ideal. This level of performance tuning is impossible the way this SQL statement was written. It is dynamic, but it will not be efficient in many cases. Therefore, I strongly recommend adding more logic in the preceding procedure to evaluate the input and conditionally execute different pre-created SQL statements, depending on the input. This allows for a more granular level of performance tuning and more control over the execution plan.

TIP
Be careful with using the LIKE operator and wildcard (%) in SQL statements to make PL/SQL program units dynamic because optimizing these SQL statements is nearly impossible. Rather, use PL/SQL logic to determine input and to direct the execution to the correct SQL statement.

Fine-Tune Web-Based Application SQL Statements

Performance tuning is important in all applications, but with the expansion of the Internet and Internet-based applications, performance tuning becomes even more important. A larger number of users are typically accessing Web-based applications. If you are developing Web-based applications interfacing with Oracle, you should adopt the following guidelines:

- Think beyond the normal client-server architecture and modularize functionality into smaller functions, in a succession of events.

- Functional modules must ensure the interaction to the database is in short bursts of processing, targeting execution time of one second or less.

- The generated Web pages should be kept small, less than 30K because the audience accessing the application is normally using modems.

- Tune every SQL statement in the application because one poorly optimized statement will be magnified even more in a Web-based application.

Modify NOT EQUAL Operators to Use an Index

Indexes can only be used to find data existing within a table. Whenever the NOT EQUAL operators (!= or <>) are used in the predicate clause, indexes on the columns being referenced cannot be used. Changing a NOT EQUAL operator to an OR of < and > conditions would allow the use of an index on the column with the rule-based optimizer, but not the cost-based optimizer.

TIP
*By replacing a NOT EQUAL operator with an OR
condition, an index can be used to eliminate a full
table scan when using the rule-based optimizer. Ensure
that the result set retrieved is still less than 5 percent of
the records for optimal performance.*

Determine Selectivity of a SQL Statement

Oracle offers several ways to determine the value of using an index, which depends
upon the SQL statement and the data distribution. One of the first ways is to
determine the number of unique or distinct keys in the index. This can be
accomplished by analyzing the table or the index, and then retrieving the
distinct_keys column from the USER_INDEXES view. By comparing the number of
distinct keys to the number of rows in the table, you can determine the selectivity of
the index. The greater the selectivity, the better the index would be for returning
small amounts of data.

TIP
*The selectivity of an index is what helps the cost-based
optimizer determine an execution plan. The more
selective, the fewer number of rows will be returned.
You can improve the selectivity by creating
concatenated/composite indexes, but if the additional
columns added to the index do not improve the
selectivity greatly, then the cost of the additional
columns may outweigh the gain.*

Cache Small Tables in Memory

The more data cached in memory, the more efficient the application will execute.
As evidenced earlier in this chapter, SQL statement execution is often faster the
second and subsequent times executed, mainly because the data is cached in
memory. What if all application tables were cached in memory? One problem is
every table cannot be cached in memory because of system memory limitations,
therefore focus should be placed on the smaller and most often used tables.

The following example caches the s_department table into memory.

```
ALTER TABLE s_department CACHE;
```

All queries to the s_department table are now faster, regardless of the condition used on the table. A cached table is pinned into memory and will be placed at the most recently used end of the cache. It will be pushed out of memory only after other full table scans to tables that are not cached are pushed out. Running a query multiple times places the data in memory so subsequent queries are faster. Only caching a table ensures the data is not later pushed out of memory.

TIP

Cache often-used, relatively small tables to ensure the data is not pushed out of memory by other data. Be careful: cached tables can alter the execution plan normally chosen by the optimizer, leading to an unexpected execution order for the query.

Use the Most Selective Index When Multiple Indexes Can Be Used

Having multiple indexes on a table can cause performance problems, especially when using the rule-based optimizer. The rule-based optimizer will attempt to use as many indexes as it can. In most cases, it is more efficient only to use one index per table. When using the cost-based optimizer, the execution plan considers the statistical data stored and version of Oracle used. I have seen the optimizer use the most efficient index, the wrong index, no index at all, or a merge of multiple indexes. The correct choice is to force the use of the correct index and the correct index is the most restrictive. Rewrite the query to force the use of the most restrictive index. Hints help force the optimizer to use an index and are described earlier in this chapter.

TIP

When multiple indexes on a single table are used within a query, use the most restrictive index. While Oracle's cost-based optimizer will generally force the use of the most restrictive index, variations will occur based on the version of Oracle used and the structure of the query. Forcing the use of the most restrictive index will guarantee the best performance.

Understand the Overhead Associated with Large Transactions

When performing large DML operations, such as INSERTs, UPDATEs, or DELETEs, these operations not only apply to manipulation to the database table, but also to any indexes affected by the operation. The more indexes affected by an operation, the more overhead involved; thus, the slower the complete execution. The more indexes existing on a database table, the slower the transactions will be.

If large DML operations are performed on a regular basis, it is often much more efficient to drop the index(es) prior to the operation(s) and then re-create the index(es) after the DML operation completes. I have used this technique on many occasions and the overall time savings far outweigh the extra steps to drop and re-create the index(es).

Summary

SQL performance tuning is not an exact science, so to become good at performance tuning takes knowledge and experience. This chapter focused on building the knowledge base necessary for optimizing SQL statements. The chapter concentrated on the entire process of SQL statement tuning. SQL performance tuning is critical to every application and has become even more important and visible in Web-based applications. Remember, 80 percent of most performance improvements in applications are a result of optimizing poorly written SQL statements.

This chapter provided a solid starting point for SQL statement tuning. To take the next step in SQL tuning, refer to *Oracle Performance Tuning Tips & Techniques,* by Richard J. Niemiec (Oracle Press).

Tips Review

■ Application users are a good source of identifying areas where performance problems exist in an application.

■ The V$SQLAREA view is a valuable area to monitor to pinpoint the top SQL statements that need to be optimized.

■ Turning TRACE on at the database level is generally not recommended because the logging of statistics for every SQL statement executed in the system introduces overhead per statement that can result in noticeable overall performance degradation.

■ The TRACEONLY option of AUTOTRACE is ideal for tuning because it does not display the result set to the screen, but it does include the number of records retrieved.

■ When optimizing SQL statements, remove the ORDER BY clause because the ORDER BY is performed once the result set is retrieved, and no SQL tuning can be performed to enhance the performance of an ORDER BY.

■ Use Explain Plan natively when a statement takes a long time to execute and only the execution plan is desired. The TRACE/TKPROF and AUTOTRACE will not provide an Explain Plan until the statements complete execution.

■ When a query is run multiple times in succession, it becomes faster because you have now cached the data in memory (full table scans are aged out of memory quicker than indexed scans). At times, people are tricked into believing they have made a query faster when they actually are accessing data stored in memory.

■ Any modification to a column in a predicate clause will eliminate the use of an index on that column. The predicate clause can often be rewritten to allow for the optimizer to use the index if desired. If index suppression is desired, add 0 to a numeric column and concatenate a NULL string to a character column.

■ Be careful of Oracle internally adding a function to a column to convert a column to compare the same data types. Always compare the same data types in predicate clauses to eliminate the hidden Oracle internal conversion.

■ For a concatenated index to be used in full or in part, the leading edge of the index must be present in the predicate clause. If any column contained in the index is not present in the predicate clause, then all columns of the index following that column cannot use the index.

■ When you want to use the cost-based optimizer, tables must be analyzed in your application. By analyzing the tables, the indexes are also analyzed. If you add an index of an already analyzed table, make sure to analyze the index. It is unnecessary to re-analyze the table when an index is added; the index can be analyzed separately.

■ Take care with adding indexes. It not only should be a consideration for potential degradation of DML operations because of added overhead of updating more indexes, it could also alter existing SQL statements execution plan, which may be disastrous.

Tips Review

- If the entire SQL statement (columns selected and the predicate clause) can be satisfied by an index, also eliminating the need to access the database table, this is much more efficient.

- Using EXISTS with a subquery can make queries dramatically faster, depending on the data being retrieved from each part of the query.

- Knowledge of the data distribution is very beneficial and considered one of the top key items to have in your arsenal when optimizing SQL statements. Understanding the difference between the optimizers is also an important aspect to tuning.

- The cost-based optimizer will be used when at least one of the tables in a multitable SQL statement (assuming the init.ora optimizer_mode parameter is set to CHOOSE) is executed; therefore, make sure all tables in a multitable join are analyzed. When a table that is part of a cost-based execution plan is not analyzed, the optimizer makes a best guess of the data distribution of that table. Eliminate guessing by analyzing the table.

- The optimizer estimates the number of rows that will be returned for inequalities; the results are not always those desired. By understanding the true distribution of data (versus that estimated by the optimizer), the execution plan can be re-directed to return better performance than the optimizer can.

- Performance tuning should extend beyond SELECT statements and include UPDATE and DELETE statements because the first step (internally by Oracle) of an UPDATE and DELETE is a SELECT.

- When the rule-based optimizer looks at the FROM clause to determine the driving table, the last table in the FROM clause will be the driving table. The cost-based optimizer works exactly the opposite. Therefore, depending on the optimizer in use, it is always recommended to take care when ordering SQL statement FROM clauses. Order them with the smallest table last for the rule-based optimizer (order them with the smallest table first for the cost-based optimizer).

- The two-hyphen comment method of specifying a hint is very strict: the hint must be on its own line, and if any SELECT columns are specified, they are ignored; there must be no spaces between the two hyphens and the hint, otherwise the hint will be ignored and treated as a comment.

■ To specify more than one hint, separate the hints with spaces. If the hint is not specified correctly, the hint will be ignored and treated as a comment. Therefore, make sure the hint is recognized by viewing the Explain Plan.

■ Hints are not case-sensitive. When using table name aliases in a SQL statement, a reference to a table name in a hint with an alias defined must reference the alias, not the table name. If the table name is referenced in the hint with an alias, the hint will be ignored.

■ When prefixing table names with the schema (plsql_user.s_employee) in a SQL statement, a reference to a table name with a hint with the schema prefix included must reference the table name only, not the schema and table name. If the schema and table name are referenced in the hint, the hint will be ignored.

■ Be careful with using the LIKE operator and wildcard (%) in SQL statements to make PL/SQL program units dynamic because optimizing these SQL statements is nearly impossible. Instead, use PL/SQL logic to determine input and direct the execution to the correct SQL statement.

■ By replacing a NOT EQUAL operator with an OR condition, an index can be used to eliminate a full table scan when using the rule-based optimizer. Ensure that the result set retrieved is still less than 5 percent of the records for optimal performance.

■ The selectivity of an index is what helps the cost-based optimizer determine an execution plan. The more selective, the fewer number of rows will be returned. You can improve the selectivity by creating concatenated/composite indexes, but if the additional columns added to the index do not improve the selectivity greatly, then the cost of the additional columns may outweigh the gain.

■ Cache often-used, relatively small tables to ensure the data is not pushed out of memory by other data. Be careful: cached tables can alter the execution plan normally chosen by the optimizer, leading to an unexpected execution order for the query.

■ When multiple indexes on a single table are used within a query, use the most restrictive index. While Oracle's cost-based optimizer generally forces the use of the most restrictive index, variations occur, based on the version of Oracle used and the structure of the query. Forcing the use of the most restrictive index guarantees the best performance.

Tips Review

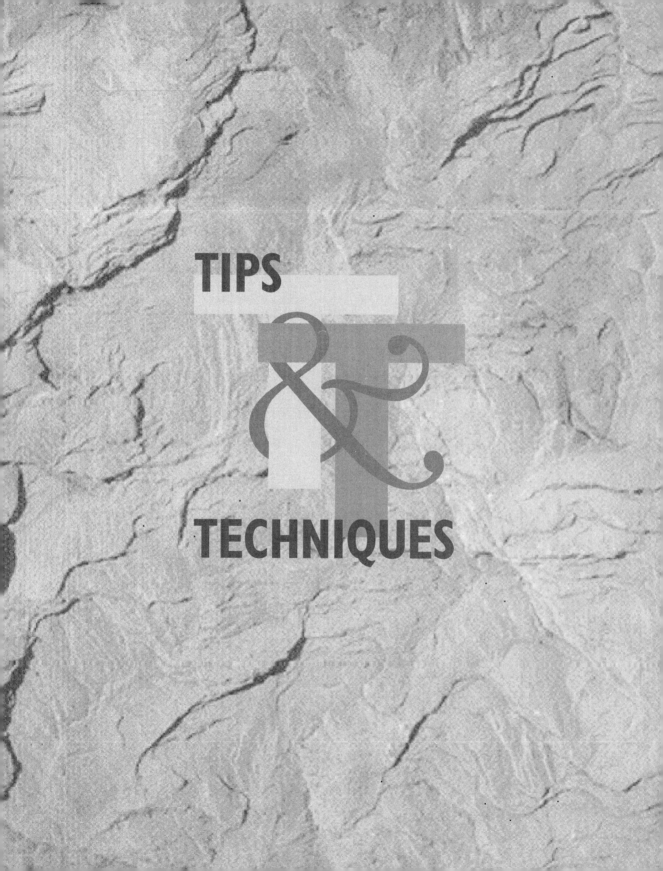

TIPS
&
TECHNIQUES

CHAPTER
8

Maximizing PL/SQL by Optimizing PL/SQL (Developer and DBA)

P L/SQL performance tuning is extremely important to the overall success of an application. A variety of areas can be optimized when developing in PL/SQL. Ensuring a PL/SQL program unit is optimized should be treated with the same priority as ensuring the source code executes accurately. Therefore, PL/SQL optimization should be considered an integral part of application development, taking place throughout the development and testing phase.

When focusing on performance improvements, the SQL statements in a PL/SQL program unit should be a main concern. SQL statement tuning is explored in further detail in Chapter 7, and I strongly recommend reviewing that chapter prior to advancing into PL/SQL optimization. One poor performing SQL statement in a PL/SQL program unit can mean the difference between the success and failure of an application. The PL/SQL performance tips and techniques covered in this chapter can help improve performance: some tips will result in huge performance improvements, while others will result in more incremental improvements, which, when combined, can produce a significant improvement in performance.

The PL/SQL areas covered in this chapter focus on language techniques, as well as configuration techniques. The more these techniques are integrated into your standard programming techniques, the more optimized your PL/SQL program units will be by default. The goal of this chapter is to cover a variety of areas that play a part in the overall performance improvements of PL/SQL program units. The amount of performance improvement realized in your environment by deploying these tips and techniques depends on the use of PL/SQL, the Oracle version in use, and the environment configuration. The tips and techniques covered in this chapter include:

- Identify the ranking of PL/SQL tuning impact
- Create a PL/SQL performance testing environment
- Use DBMS_APPLICATION_INFO for real-time monitoring
- Log timing information in a database table
- Reduce PL/SQL program unit iterations and iteration time
- Use PL/SQL tables to improve performance
- Use ROWID for iterative processing
- Reduce the calls to SYSDATE
- Standardize on data types, IF statement order, and PLS_INTEGER
    - Ensure the same data types in comparison operations
    - Order IF conditions based on the frequency of the condition
    - Use the PLS_INTEGER PL/SQL data type for integer operations

- Reduce the use of the MOD function

- Understand the PL/SQL engine handling of bind variables

- Use explicit versus implicit cursors

- Find similar SQL statements and SQL NOT using bind variables

- Store PL/SQL program units in the database

- Review added PL/SQL performance related considerations

  - Increase the Shared Pool to increase performance

  - Identify PL/SQL objects that need to be pinned

  - Pin/Cache PL/SQL objects

  - Modify the sql.bsq file to reduce data dictionary fragmentation

  - Execute PL/SQL program units on the server-side

  - Use temporary database tables for increased performance

  - Integrate a user tracking mechanism to pinpoint execution location

  - Create a timing and tracing mechanism to turn on/off conditionally

  - Use rollback segments when processing large transaction sets

  - Limit the use of dynamic SQL

  - Learn the Oracle supplied PL/SQL Packages that assist in performance tuning

Identify the Ranking of PL/SQL Tuning Impact

This chapter identifies a number of important areas to be reviewed to improve performance in your system as it relates to PL/SQL. Many of the techniques should be understood and become part of a developer's standard coding, where other techniques should be added to your arsenal of tips and techniques to be used when performance problems exist.

With the abundance of topics outlined in this chapter and the time limitations developers and DBAs generally have, determining which technique is going to result in the largest performance improvement is often difficult. Therefore, I created the following table listing each of the PL/SQL areas covered in this chapter with an Impact Rating and Role Responsibility assignment to assist developers and DBAs.

The Impact Rating designates the potential impact of concentrating your tuning efforts in each tuning area; remember, the rankings are generalized and depend on a variety of environment, configuration, and application variables. The Impact Rating system is based on a 1 (large potential for improvement, if not correct), 2 (potential for noticeable improvement), or 3 (smaller improvement, but helps, especially if repetitive iterations or recursion occurs). I call this squeezing the blood out of the turnip; however, many of these techniques should become standard programming techniques. The Role Responsibility is Developer, DBA, or both. Some of the PL/SQL areas are designated as 'N/A' for the Impact Rating to signify the area is more a technique that can help in the performance effort than an actual technique that can result in any performance improvement.

Identifying the Ranking of PL/SQL Tuning Impact

Performance Tuning Area	Rating Impact	Role Responsibility
SQL Tuning (covered in Chapter 7)	1	Developer & DBA
Create a PL/SQL Performance Testing Environment	N/A	Developer & DBA
Use DBMS_APPLICATION_INFO for Real-time Monitoring	N/A	Developer & DBA
Log Timing Information in a Database Table	N/A	Developer & DBA
Reduce PL/SQL Program Unit Iterations and Iteration Time	1	Developer
Use PL/SQL Tables to Improve Performance	1	Developer
Use ROWID for Iterative Processing	2	Developer
Reduce the Calls to SYSDATE	3	Developer
Standardize on Data Types, IF Statement Order, and PLS_INTEGER	3	Developer
Ensure the Same Data Types in Comparison Operations	3	Developer
Order IF Conditions Based on the Frequency of the Condition	3	Developer
Use the PLS_INTEGER Data Type for Integer Operations	3	Developer
Reduce the Use of the MOD Function	3	Developer

Performance Tuning Area	Rating Impact	Role Responsibility
Understand the PL/SQL Engine Handling of Bind Variables	N/A	Developer & DBA
Use Explicit versus Implicit Cursors	2	Developer
Find Similar SQL Statements and SQL NOT Using Bind Variables	2	Developer & DBA
Store PL/SQL Program Units in the Database	1	Developer & DBA
Review Added PL/SQL Performance Related Considerations	N/A	Developer & DBA
Increase the Shared Pool to Increase Performance	1	DBA
Identify PL/SQL Objects that Need to Be Pinned	2	DBA
Pin/Cache PL/SQL Objects	2	DBA
Modify the sql.bsq File to Reduce Data Dictionary Fragmentation	1	DBA
Execute PL/SQL Program Units on the Server-Side	1	Developer & DBA
Use Temporary Database Tables for Increased Performance	2	Developer & DBA
Integrate a User Tracking Mechanism to Pinpoint Execution Location	N/A	Developer & DBA
Create a Timing and Tracing Mechanism to Turn On/Off Conditionally	N/A	Developer & DBA
Use Rollback Segments When Processing Large Transaction Sets	2	Developer & DBA
Limit the Use of Dynamic SQL	1	Developer
Learn the Oracle Supplied PL/SQL Packages That Assist in Performance Tuning	N/A	Developer & DBA

Identifying the Ranking of PL/SQL Tuning Impact

Create a PL/SQL Performance Testing Environment

When testing PL/SQL program units for potential performance improvements, creating an environment to test the programs is important. A variety of products on the market assists in this effort, including Oracle's Procedure Builder, SQL*Navigator, TOAD, and SQL*Station. SQL*Plus also provides a solid testing environment. SQL*Plus is used for the performance testing outlined in this chapter.

Notice the main table used for testing in this chapter is the s_employee_test. This table was created from the s_employee table in Chapter 7 and contains 25,000 employee records.

A SQL*Plus timing function can be turned on to display the overall time of each PL/SQL program unit execution, with the following command:

```
SET TMINING ON
```

The preceding command is covered in further detail in Chapter 2, with other timing functions available in SQL*Plus.

The following lists several important techniques to follow during the performance enhancement effort in SQL*Plus:

- Create a baseline and ensure the tests are performed while comparing results accurately. This can be accomplished by testing the original program first and obtaining the results prior to changing any source code.

- Introduce and test only one source code modification at a time. This ensures the performance test enables you to monitor the improvement per modification.

- Log (spool) the entire session to a file to ensure all testing is available for review when complete.

- Make sure the testing is performed on a solid set of test data with the same distribution of data as the production environment.

- Make sure the testing is performed with a consistent load (or no load) on the system to eliminate variables that can distort the results.

- Remember the first execution of PL/SQL source code and SQL statements within a PL/SQL program unit will result in the SQL statements being parsed and loaded into the SQL Area (viewable in the V$SQLAREA view). For PL/SQL program units, if the source code is an anonymous block, it is loaded into the SQL Area. For stored PL/SQL program units, they are loaded into the object cache (viewable in the V$DB_OBJECT_CACHE view).

Additional overhead is apparent with the first execution, but subsequent executions should be faster due to caching. Execute statements more than once to ensure true timing is obtained; I often execute the same code 3+ times to ensure I get a true reading (the execution time should be fairly consistent after the 2nd execution, thus the 3+ executions to make sure).

For all the testing and timings in this chapter, the preceding list of techniques were followed. In addition, because I was on a standalone system, I granted the PLSQL_USER schema ALTER SYSTEM privilege and prior to each new timing of a source code modification, I flushed the Shared Pool with the following command:

```
ALTER SYSTEM FLUSH SHARED_POOL;
```

Developers typically are not granted this privilege, and this command should only be executed by a DBA in a test environment unless it is necessary in production as outlined in Chapter 9 and Chapter 12. This command deletes the contents of several Shared Pool caches and statistics, including the object cache (V$DB_OBJECT_CACHE view), the SQL Area (V$SQLAREA view), and the library cache (V$LIBRARYCACHE view).

Prior to performing any testing, the DBMS_UTILITY.GET TIME function can be called to log the starting time. During the PL/SQL program unit execution, the DBMS_UTILITY.GET_TIME function can be called to track execution time throughout the program sequence. To ease the use of this Oracle supplied function, the following scripts create a package containing procedures for starting and stopping a timer. This timer is used throughout this chapter to capture the execution timing of PL/SQL program units.

File: 8_1.sql

```
CREATE OR REPLACE PACKAGE stop_watch AS
   pvg_start_time_num      PLS_INTEGER;
   pvg_stop_time_num       PLS_INTEGER;
   pvg_last_stop_time_num  PLS_INTEGER;

-- This procedure creates a starting point for the timer routine and
-- is usually called once at the beginning of the PL/SQL program unit.
PROCEDURE start_timer;

-- This procedure retrieves a point in time and subtracts the current
-- time from the start time to determine the elapsed time. The
-- interval elapsed time is logged and displayed. This procedure is
-- usually called repetitively for each iteration or a specified
-- number of iterations.
PROCEDURE stop_timer;
END stop_watch;
/
```

File: 8_1a.sql

```
CREATE OR REPLACE PACKAGE BODY stop_watch AS
PROCEDURE start_timer AS
BEGIN
    pvg_start_time_num       := DBMS_UTILITY.GET_TIME;
    pvg_last_stop_time_num := pvg_start_time_num;
END start_timer;

PROCEDURE stop_timer AS
BEGIN
    pvg_stop_time_num := DBMS_UTILITY.GET_TIME;
    DBMS_OUTPUT.PUT_LINE('Total Time Elapsed: ' ||
        TO_CHAR((pvg_stop_time_num - pvg_start_time_num)/100,
        '999,999.99') || ' sec   Interval Time: ' ||
        TO_CHAR((pvg_stop_time_num - pvg_last_stop_time_num)/100,
        '99,999.99') || ' sec');
    pvg_last_stop_time_num := pvg_stop_time_num;
END stop_timer;
END;
/
```

The timing procedures in the preceding package can be easily integrated into any PL/SQL program unit. The following is a small example of the integration:

File: 8_2.sql

```
BEGIN
    stop_watch.start_timer;
    FOR lv_count_num IN 1..5 LOOP
        DBMS_LOCK.SLEEP(5);
        stop_watch.stop_timer;
    END LOOP;
END;
/
```

The Oracle supplied procedure DBMS_LOCK.SLEEP pauses processing for the specified amount of seconds. In the following case, the process is paused for five seconds for each iteration to illustrate the use of the stop_watch package. The output of the execution of this PL/SQL code segment follows:

Output (8_2.sql)

```
Total Time Elapsed:      5.01 sec   Interval Time:      5.01 sec
Total Time Elapsed:     10.03 sec   Interval Time:      5.02 sec
Total Time Elapsed:     15.04 sec   Interval Time:      5.01 sec
Total Time Elapsed:     20.05 sec   Interval Time:      5.01 sec
```

```
Total Time Elapsed:         25.06 sec    Interval Time:        5.01 sec

PL/SQL procedure successfully completed.
```

The DBMS_UTILITY.GET_TIME function and DBMS_LOCK.SLEEP procedure are covered in further detail in Chapters 11 and 12. The DBMS_OUTPUT.PUT_LINE used in the stop_watch package is adequate for quick debugging and timing; remember, the DBMS_OUTPUT.PUT_LINE procedure only displays the statements when the PL/SQL program unit completes, not when DBMS_OUTPUT.PUT_LINE is called. In the preceding example, the display did not return for 25 seconds. Chapters 4, 11, and 12 cover the DBMS_OUTPUT.PUT_LNE procedure in further detail.

To enhance the timing function, the DBMS_OUTPUT.PUT_LINE calls can be replaced with calls to the UTL_FILE, DBMS_APPLICATION_INFO, or DBMS_PIPE package procedures. The Oracle supplied package best suitable for the purpose of logging information depends on the application logic and logging (amount of information and frequency) desired.

To log information for review during processing or when complete, the UTL_FILE package can be used to log the results to an operating system file. For specific point-in-time information (only the recent point in time), the DBMS_APPLICATION_INFO package can be used to log the current point in time to the V$SESSION view for up-to-date execution information. For monitoring activity real-time to see all the results, the DBMS_PIPE package can be used to send the results to a pipe that can be polled by other sessions to read the pipe for real-time results. Each of these packages is detailed in Chapters 11 and 12.

One other common method of logging information to be reviewed or analyzed at a later time is to INSERT the results into a database table with a unique identifier and date and time of execution, providing the capability of logging of multiple executions. Several of the methods mentioned in this section are covered in subsequent sections in this chapter.

TIP
Always execute a PL/SQL program unit more than once when testing because the first execution typically takes longer due to the loading and parsing. The larger the program unit, the longer the initial overhead.

TIP
The DBMS_OUTPUT.PUT_LINE procedure does not display information to the screen until the procedure completes. It does not display at the time the procedure is called. If the PL/SQL program unit takes two hours to execute, the DBMS_OUTPUT.PUT_LINE information will not display for two hours.

Creating a PL/SQL Performance Testing Environment

TIP

For any PL/SQL program unit that executes for more than ten minutes, build a mechanism into the program unit to log the information to some location. This will enable you to know how long it has run and how long it has to go. This will save you a tremendous amount of time. Use the DBMS_APPLICATION_INFO, DBMS_PIPE, or UTL_FILE package to accomplish this, do not use DBMS_OUTPUT.PUT_LINE procedure.

Use **DBMS_APPLICATION_INFO** for Real Time Monitoring

The DBMS_APPLICATION_INFO package provides a powerful mechanism for communicating point-in-time information about the execution in an environment. This is illustrated in the following example enabling a long-running PL/SQL program unit to provide information on the progress of the routine every 1,000 records. The PL/SQL code segment updates the progress information with the number of records processed and the elapsed time every 1,000 records.

The following is an example illustrating the update of all employees' salary.

File: 8_3.sql

```
DECLARE
   CURSOR cur_employee IS
      SELECT employee_id, salary, ROWID
      FROM   s_employee_test;
   lv_new_salary_num NUMBER;
   lv_count_num       PLS_INTEGER := 0;
   lv_start_time_num PLS_INTEGER;
BEGIN
   lv_start_time_num := DBMS_UTILITY.GET_TIME;
   FOR cur_employee_rec IN cur_employee LOOP
      lv_count_num := lv_count_num + 1;
      -- Determination of salary increase Logic goes here
      lv_new_salary_num := cur_employee_rec.salary;
      UPDATE s_employee_test
      SET    salary  = lv_new_salary_num
      WHERE  rowid   = cur_employee_rec.ROWID;
      IF MOD(lv_count_num, 1000) = 0 THEN
         DBMS_APPLICATION_INFO.SET_MODULE('Records Processed: ' ||
            lv_count_num, 'Elapsed: ' || (DBMS_UTILITY.GET_TIME -
            lv_start_time_num)/100 || ' sec');
      END IF;
```

```
  END LOOP;
  COMMIT;
    DBMS_APPLICATION_INFO.SET_MODULE('Records Processed: ' ||
        lv_count_num, 'Elapsed: ' || (DBMS_UTILITY.GET_TIME -
        lv_start_time_num)/100 || ' sec');
END;
/
```

To monitor the progress, the V$SESSION view can be queried, as shown in the following example.

File: 8_4.sql

```
SELECT username, sid, serial#, module, action
FROM   v$session
WHERE  username = 'PLSQL_USER';
```

The following is the output from the V$SESSION view, when queried three different times. The last is when the PL/SQL program unit (8_3.sql) was completed.

Output (8_4.sql)

```
USERNAME    SID SERIAL# MODULE                    ACTION
----------- --- ------- ------------------------- ------------------
PLSQL_USER   7       4 SQL*Plus
PLSQL_USER  10      10 Records Processed: 1000    Elapsed: 4.37 sec
```

Output (8_4.sql)

```
USERNAME    SID SERIAL# MODULE                    ACTION
----------- --- ------- ------------------------- ------------------
PLSQL_USER   7       4 SQL*Plus
PLSQL_USER  10      10 Records Processed: 3000    Elapsed: 12.99 sec
```

Output (8_4.sql)

```
USERNAME    SID SERIAL# MODULE                    ACTION
----------- --- ------- ------------------------- ------------------
PLSQL_USER   7       4 SQL*Plus
PLSQL_USER  10      10 Records Processed: 25000   Elapsed: 126.66 sec
```

Note: to view the V$SESSION view information, SELECT must be granted on the V_$SESSION view. The reason for the two records being returned in the preceding output is that both the execution of the PL/SQL program unit to update employees' salary (8_3.sql) and the SQL statement to monitor the progress via the V$SESSION view (8_4.sql) are executed under the PLSQL_USER schema in two different SQL*Plus sessions. The preceding example illustrates a valuable technique to deploy in an environment and provides a real-time monitoring mechanism. It becomes easier to accurately determine how long a program has been running and to estimate how long a program has to complete. The DBMS_APPLICATION_INFO Oracle supplied package is detailed in Chapter 11 and Chapter 12.

If DBAs do not want users querying V$SESSION view information for all users, they can create a view on the V$SESSION view to limit the retrieval to only the executing user's session information. This can be accomplished by executing the following commands under the SYS user.

The following syntax creates the new view (session_log was used for the new view name, but any name could have been used).

File: 8_5.sql

```
CREATE VIEW session_log AS
SELECT *
FROM   v$session
WHERE  username = USERNAME;
```

The following syntax creates a public synonym.

File: 8_6.sql

```
CREATE PUBLIC SYNONYM session_log FOR session_log;
```

The following syntax grants SELECT permission to all users.

File: 8_7.sql

```
GRANT SELECT ON session_log TO PUBLIC;
```

Once the session_log view is set up, as shown in the preceding statements, the preceding V$SESSION view query (8_4.sql) can be changed to SELECT from the session_log view, as in the following query, to limit the output to only the user executing the query.

File: 8_8.sql

```
SELECT username, sid, serial#, module, action
FROM   session_log;
```

TIP
Use the Oracle supplied package DBMS_APPLICATION_INFO package to log point-in-time information to the V$SESSION view to enable monitoring of long-running processes.

Log Timing Information in a Database Table

Monitoring performance is an on-going process. Many variables in an environment can change and affect performance over time; therefore, performance should be monitored continuously. Some of the variables include user growth, data growth, reporting growth, application modification/enhancement deployment, and additional load on the system from other applications. With this in mind, an Oracle system must be regularly monitored to ensure performance remains at, or above, an acceptable level.

One method of monitoring the system performance is to create a mechanism for logging timing statistics for certain aspects of an application. Batch programs are good candidates for this monitoring procedure. The monitoring procedure can be accomplished by inserting timing statistics into a database table. The following example provides the database table logging method by creating a database table, and then integrating INSERT statements for the timing of the process into the table. The important information to log in the database table are the program identifier (some unique method of identifying the program), the date and time the program is executed, and the elapsed time of the execution. One column has been added for this application, namely, the number of records updated. This additional column is important for this application to monitor the growth of employee records being processed. When creating a timing log table for your application, add columns to store additional important processing information that may affect your timing results. Therefore, the following table can be created to log the timing information.

File: 8_9.sql

```
CREATE TABLE process_timing_log
    (program_name       VARCHAR2(30),
     execution_date     DATE,
     records_processed  NUMBER,
     elapsed_time_sec   NUMBER);
```

Once the table is created, PL/SQL program units can be enhanced to log the timing information into the process_timing_log table as illustrated in the following program.

File: 8_10.sql

```
CREATE OR REPLACE PROCEDURE update_salary AS
   CURSOR cur_employee IS
      SELECT employee_id, salary, ROWID
      FROM   s_employee_test;
   lv_new_salary_num NUMBER;
   lv_count_num      PLS_INTEGER := 0;
   lv_start_time_num PLS_INTEGER;
   lv_total_time_num NUMBER;
BEGIN
   lv_start_time_num := DBMS_UTILITY.GET_TIME;
   FOR cur_employee_rec IN cur_employee LOOP
      lv_count_num := lv_count_num + 1;
      -- Determination of salary increase
      lv_new_salary_num := cur_employee_rec.salary;
      UPDATE s_employee_test
      SET    salary      = lv_new_salary_num
      WHERE  rowid = cur_employee_rec.ROWID;
   END LOOP;
   lv_total_time_num := (DBMS_UTILITY.GET_TIME -
      lv_start_time_num)/100;
   INSERT INTO process_timing_log
      (program_name, execution_date, records_processed,
       elapsed_time_sec)
   VALUES
      ('UPDATE_SALARY', SYSDATE, lv_count_num,
       lv_total_time_num);
   COMMIT;
END update_salary;
/
```

As shown in the preceding code segment, the timer is started at the beginning of the program unit, and then the timer is stopped at the end of the program unit. The difference between the start and ending timer is logged into the process_timing_log for each execution of the update_salary program. If the update_salary program unit is executed three times, as shown in the following syntax, then three timing records will be inserted into the process_timing_log table.

```
EXECUTE update_salary
EXECUTE update_salary
EXECUTE update_salary
```

The following script retrieves the information from the process_timing_log table.

File: 8_11.sql

```
SELECT program_name,
       TO_CHAR(execution_date,'MM/DD/YYYY HH24:MI:SS') execution_time,
       records_processed, elapsed_time_sec
FROM   process_timing_log
ORDER BY 1,2;
```

Output (8_11.sql)

PROGRAM_NAME	EXECUTION_TIME	RECORDS_PROCESSED	ELAPSED_TIME_SEC
UPDATE_SALARY	06/19/1999 02:49:15	25000	99.35
UPDATE_SALARY	06/19/1999 02:51:45	25000	125.33
UPDATE_SALARY	06/19/1999 02:54:23	25000	141.51

As seen in the preceding output, a difference exists in the elapsed time for the same program execution. If the difference increases over time, this may indicate a need to analyze the program unit further or the application to determine what caused the execution time increase. With logging mechanisms in place, the elapsed time can be monitored at any point in time because the timing information is being logged to a database table.

In the preceding example, the time logged was per program unit. If the program is complex and executed for an extended period of time, it may be desirable to change the logging of timing statistics from once in the program. The INSERT into the process_timing_log table could be performed after a certain number of iterations or to log timing for certain functionality in a program unit.

TIP

Log (INSERT) execution timing information into a database table for long-running PL/SQL program units to integrate a proactive performance monitoring mechanism into your system. The database table can be reviewed at any point in time to determine if performance has decreased over time.

TIP

System load in terms of number of active sessions can have a large impact on the performance of program execution; therefore, it would be helpful to modify the database table logging method to include a column for the number of active sessions. This column can be filled by adding one additional query to the program unit being executed to retrieve the count from the V$SESSION view.

Logging Timing Information in a Database Table

Reduce PL/SQL Program Unit Iterations and Iteration Time

Any PL/SQL program unit involving looping logic is a strong candidate for performance improvements. Potential improvements for these types of programs can be accomplished two ways. The first is to reduce the number of iterations by restructuring the logic to accomplish the same functional result. The second is to reduce the time per iteration. Either reduction often improves performance dramatically.

To bring this point into perspective, think of the following scenario: We need to process 9,000 employee records in a PL/SQL routine and to process each employee takes two seconds. This equates to 18,000 seconds, which equates to five hours. If the processing per employee is reduced to one second, the time to process the 9,000 employees is reduced by 9,000 seconds or 2.5 hours . . . quite a difference!

The following example shows a minor restructuring of a PL/SQL program unit to illustrate a basic example of restructuring source code to reduce per loop processing and overall processing time. The program unit processes a loop 1,000,000 times. Each iteration adds to the incremental counter used to display a message each 100,000 iterations and adds to the total counter used to check for loop exiting.

File: 8_12.sql

```
DECLARE
    lv_counter_num        PLS_INTEGER := 0;
    lv_total_counter_num PLS_INTEGER := 0;
BEGIN
    stop_watch.start_timer;
    LOOP
        lv_counter_num         := lv_counter_num + 1;
        lv_total_counter_num := lv_total_counter_num + 1;
        IF lv_counter_num >= 100000 THEN
            DBMS_OUTPUT.PUT_LINE('Processed 100,000 Records. ' ||
                'Total Processed ' || lv_total_counter_num);
            lv_counter_num := 0;
            EXIT WHEN lv_total_counter_num >= 1000000;
        END IF;
    END LOOP;
    stop_watch.stop_timer;
END;
/
```

Output (8_12.sql)

```
Processed 100,000 Records. Total Processed 100000
Processed 100,000 Records. Total Processed 200000
Processed 100,000 Records. Total Processed 300000
Processed 100,000 Records. Total Processed 400000
Processed 100,000 Records. Total Processed 500000
Processed 100,000 Records. Total Processed 600000
Processed 100,000 Records. Total Processed 700000
Processed 100,000 Records. Total Processed 800000
Processed 100,000 Records. Total Processed 900000
Processed 100,000 Records. Total Processed 1000000
Total Time Elapsed:       4.98 sec    Interval Time:       4.98 sec

PL/SQL procedure successfully completed.
```

By changing the program to only add to the lv_total_counter_num variable each time the incremental counter reaches 100,000, the overall execution time is reduced.

File: 8_13.sql

```
DECLARE
   lv_counter_num        PLS_INTEGER := 0;
   lv_total_counter_num PLS_INTEGER := 0;
BEGIN
   stop_watch.start_timer;
   LOOP
      lv_counter_num        := lv_counter_num + 1;
      IF lv_counter_num >= 100000 THEN
         DBMS_OUTPUT.PUT_LINE('Processed 100,000 Records. Total ' ||
            'Processed ' || lv_total_counter_num);
         lv_total_counter_num := lv_total_counter_num +
            lv_counter_num;
         lv_counter_num := 0;
         EXIT WHEN lv_total_counter_num >= 1000000;
      END IF;
   END LOOP;
   stop_watch.stop_timer;
END;
/
```

The DBMS_OUTPUT.PUT_LINE output for the record processed numbers was not included in the following output.

Output (8_13.sql)

```
Total Time Elapsed:          3.66 sec    Interval Time:         3.66 sec

PL/SQL procedure successfully completed.
```

The preceding example illustrates the performance difference by changing the iteration logic to reduce the timing per iteration. The example is basic and shows a 26 percent increase on 1,000,000 iterations. Based on the restructuring and the iterations, this improvement can make a large difference.

TIP

When a PL/SQL program unit involves extensive looping or recursion, concentrate on reducing the execution time per iteration. This adds up fast, and it is easy to do the math to determine the overall improvement potential. The looping or recursion should also be reviewed for restructuring to reduce the number of iterations, while keeping the same functionality. With the extreme flexibility of PL/SQL and SQL, typically a variety of ways exists to accomplish the same result. If a PL/SQL program unit is not performing optimally, sometimes you have to rewrite the logic another way.

Use PL/SQL Tables to Improve Performance

PL/SQL tables are similar to arrays in other programming languages. PL/SQL tables are advantageous for temporary storage or repeated lookups of small code tables. PL/SQL tables should not be viewed as a mechanism for loading entire database tables into memory, unless these database tables contain a limited amount of records. PL/SQL tables require memory per PL/SQL table to store the information. Therefore, PL/SQL tables can be extremely helpful when attempting to increase performance, but they must be used appropriately or the performance improvement will not be realized.

The following example illustrates the use of PL/SQL tables to improve performance. The following code segment retrieves each employee record and for each employee, the department name is retrieved from the s_department table.

File: 8_14.sql

```
DECLARE
    CURSOR cur_dept (p_dept_num PLS_INTEGER) IS
        SELECT department_name
        FROM   s_department
        WHERE  department_id = p_dept_num;
    CURSOR cur_employee IS
        SELECT employee_id, department_id, salary
        FROM   s_employee_test;
    lv_dept_name_txt s_department.department_name%TYPE;
BEGIN
    stop_watch.start_timer;
    FOR cur_employee_rec IN cur_employee LOOP
        OPEN cur_dept(cur_employee_rec.department_id);
        FETCH cur_dept INTO lv_dept_name_txt;
        CLOSE cur_dept;
        -- Main Logic goes here
    END LOOP;
    stop_watch.stop_timer;
END;
/
```

Output (8_14.sql)

```
Total Time Elapsed:        44.38 sec   Interval Time:        44.38 sec

PL/SQL procedure successfully completed.
```

The department name retrieval can be modified to retrieve the department name from a PL/SQL table. This involves additional source code to accomplish the modification. The PL/SQL table is created and loaded with the s_department table records. For each employee record, the PL/SQL table is searched sequentially for the department_id value (the pointer is placed at the beginning of the PL/SQL table and each record in the table is checked one by one until a match is found). The following source code illustrates the use of PL/SQL tables.

File: 8_15.sql

```
DECLARE
    TYPE type_dept_table IS TABLE OF s_department%ROWTYPE
        INDEX BY BINARY_INTEGER;
    lv_dept_table type_dept_table;
```

```
    CURSOR cur_dept IS
        SELECT department_id, department_name
        FROM    s_department;
    CURSOR cur_employee IS
        SELECT employee_id, department_id, salary
        FROM    s_employee_test;
    lv_dept_name_txt s_department.department_name%TYPE;
    lv_index_num       PLS_INTEGER := 0;
    lv_match_bln       BOOLEAN := FALSE;
BEGIN
    stop_watch.start_timer;
    FOR cur_dept_rec IN cur_dept LOOP
        lv_index_num := lv_index_num + 1;
        lv_dept_table(lv_index_num).department_id
            := cur_dept_rec.department_id;
        lv_dept_table(lv_index_num).department_name
            := cur_dept_rec.department_name;
    END LOOP;
    FOR cur_employee_rec IN cur_employee LOOP
        lv_index_num := lv_dept_table.FIRST;
        lv_match_bln := FALSE;
        LOOP
            IF lv_dept_table(lv_index_num).department_id =
                cur_employee_rec.department_id THEN
                lv_match_bln := TRUE;
                lv_dept_name_txt :=
                    lv_dept_table(lv_index_num).department_name;
            END IF;
            EXIT WHEN (lv_index_num = lv_dept_table.LAST) OR
                lv_match_bln;
            lv_index_num := lv_dept_table.NEXT(lv_index_num);
        END LOOP;
        -- Main Logic goes here
    END LOOP;
    stop_watch.stop_timer;
END;
/
```

As seen in the following output, the savings in time (44.38 seconds reduced to 17.93 seconds) is worth the extra coding.

Output (8_15.sql)

```
Total Time Elapsed:        17.93 sec    Interval Time:        17.93 sec

PL/SQL procedure successfully completed.
```

Many developers will stop at this point; however, one more modification can be made to improve performance even further when using PL/SQL tables. This modification is possible in the preceding example, and in many other cases, but it relies on the search key being an integer. In this example, the search key (department_id) can be loaded into the PL/SQL table and, additionally, the search key can be used as the PL/SQL table index. The search for the department_name can be performed by the PL/SQL index versus a sequential scan through the PL/SQL table record by record, as illustrated in the following example.

File: 8_16.sql

```
DECLARE
   TYPE type_dept_table IS TABLE OF s_department%ROWTYPE
      INDEX BY BINARY_INTEGER;
   lv_dept_table type_dept_table;
   CURSOR cur_dept IS
      SELECT department_id, department_name
      FROM   s_department;
   CURSOR cur_employee IS
      SELECT employee_id, department_id, salary
      FROM   s_employee_test;
   lv_dept_name_txt s_department.department_name%TYPE;
BEGIN
   stop_watch.start_timer;
   FOR cur_dept_rec IN cur_dept LOOP
      lv_dept_table(cur_dept_rec.department_id).department_id
         := cur_dept_rec.department_id;
      lv_dept_table(cur_dept_rec.department_id).department_name
         := cur_dept_rec.department_name;
   END LOOP;
   FOR cur_employee_rec IN cur_employee LOOP
      lv_dept_name_txt :=
         lv_dept_table(cur_employee_rec.department_id).department_name;
      -- Main Logic goes here
   END LOOP;
   stop_watch.stop_timer;
END;
/
```

As displayed in the following output, the savings in time are a magnitude higher.

Output (8_16.sql)

```
Total Time Elapsed:        10.58 sec    Interval Time:        10.58 sec

PL/SQL procedure successfully completed.
```

Each of the timings recorded in this section was the second execution of the code segment to eliminate the overhead of the initial loading and parsing. A flush of the Shared Pool was also performed prior to each different code segment execution.

TIP

When using PL/SQL tables, the performance gain realized would increase as the size of the PL/SQL table increases (assuming the system has the memory to allocate for the PL/SQL tables).

TIP

Beware that the benefit of using PL/SQL tables may not be fully realized on certain versions of Oracle 8.0 and Oracle 8.1 on certain platforms because some bugs related to PL/SQL tables exist. As always, it is best to test your application in a test environment on a new release or platform prior to production deployment for both functional execution and performance.

TIP

PL/SQL table functionality and flexibility was greatly enhanced in PL/SQL version 2.3 and is covered in further detail in Chapter 4.

The question often asked is whether Oracle allocates memory to PL/SQL tables based on actual bytes needed or based on the number of records and length of records. Oracle allocates space to PL/SQL tables in chunks when the PL/SQL tables are populated and every record is fixed length, set to the maximum width of the record.

TIP

PL/SQL tables allocate memory based on the fixed length of the record size and the number of records loaded into the PL/SQL table. Memory is allocated to PL/SQL tables in chunks. Be EXTREMELY cognizant of the definition of your PL/SQL tables. DO NOT assign the contents of the PL/SQL table to %ROWTYPE unless this is needed. Oracle allocates the maximum total length of the database table record if the %ROWTYPE is referenced and allocates this much memory per PL/SQL table record.

The following example demonstrates the allocation of memory for PL/SQL tables.

The example creates a PL/SQL table that contains a record of ten characters in length and stores 200 records, each initialized to *A*. Prior to executing the code segment, the User Global Area (UGA) and Program Global Area (PGA) are retrieved to display the current memory requirements for the session. The following script displays the current usage of these two memory structures.

File: 8_17.sql

```
SELECT c.name, b.value
FROM   v$session a, v$sesstat b, v$statname c
WHERE  a.sid       = b.sid
AND    b.statistic# = c.statistic#
AND    b.value     != 0
AND    a.username  = 'PLSQL_USER'
AND    c.name       IN ('session uga memory', 'session pga memory');
```

The following results are from a session just logged into SQL*Plus.

Output (8_17.sql)

```
NAME                                VALUE
-------------------------------- ----------
session uga memory                  31764
session pga memory                  76592
```

The following PL/SQL program unit creating the PL/SQL table is now executed.

File: 8_18.sql

```
DECLARE
   TYPE type_temp_table IS TABLE OF VARCHAR(100)
      INDEX BY BINARY_INTEGER;
   lv_temp_table type_temp_table;
BEGIN
   FOR lv_count_num IN 1..200 LOOP
      lv_temp_table(lv_count_num) := 'A';
   END LOOP;
END;
/
```

As illustrated in the following output, the UGA is unaffected, but the PGA memory requirement is increased for the use of the PL/SQL table.

Output (8_17.sql)

NAME	VALUE
session uga memory	31764
session pga memory	111840

We need to create the baseline for the next code segment (8_19.sql). The following results are from a session that just logged into SQL*Plus.

Output (8_17.sql)

NAME	VALUE
session uga memory	31512
session pga memory	76592

The PL/SQL code segment is modified to increase the length of the record of the PL/SQL table to 10,000 from 100 with no modification to the number of records or values loaded into the PL/SQL table.

File: 8_19.sql

```
DECLARE
   TYPE type_temp_table IS TABLE OF VARCHAR(10000)
      INDEX BY BINARY_INTEGER;
   lv_temp_table type_temp_table;
BEGIN
   FOR lv_count_num IN 1..200 LOOP
      lv_temp_table(lv_count_num) := 'A';
   END LOOP;
END;
/
```

When the UGA and PGA are retrieved this time, the UGA remains constant again, but the PGA is increased significantly. The only change was the length of the PL/SQL table record.

Output (8_17.sql)

NAME	VALUE
session uga memory	31512
session pga memory	2088244

TIP

Be aware of the memory allocation and requirements of PL/SQL tables, outlined in the preceding example. PL/SQL tables have tremendous advantages, but they do come at a cost, which must be analyzed to understand the impact and appropriateness of using them. For a method of de-allocating memory allocated to PL/SQL tables when the memory is no longer needed for a session, refer to the DBMS_SESSION. FREE_UNUSED_USER_MEMORY procedure in Chapter 12.

Use ROWID for Iterative Processing

The ROWID variable can help improve PL/SQL programs that retrieve records from the database, perform manipulation on the column values, and then complete with an UPDATE to the retrieved record. When retrieving each record, the ROWID can be added to the selected column list. When updating each record, the ROWID can be used in the predicate clause. The ROWID is the fastest access path to a record in a table, even faster than a unique index reference.

The performance improvement of using the ROWID is illustrated in the following example. The example retrieves each of the 25,000 employee records, calculates a new salary for each employee, and then updates the employees' salary. The actual salary calculation is not shown in this example. The first PL/SQL code segment shows the timing results with the UPDATE using the employee_id column, which has a unique index on the column.

File: 8_20.sql

```
DECLARE
   CURSOR cur_employee IS
      SELECT employee_id, salary
      FROM   s_employee_test;
   lv_new_salary_num NUMBER;
BEGIN
   stop_watch.start_timer;
   FOR cur_employee_rec IN cur_employee LOOP
      -- Determination of salary increase goes here
      lv_new_salary_num := cur_employee_rec.salary;
      UPDATE s_employee_test
      SET    salary      = lv_new_salary_num
      WHERE  employee_id = cur_employee_rec.employee_id;
   END LOOP;
   COMMIT;
   stop_watch.stop_timer;
END;
/
```

The following output shows the timing of two executions of the preceding code segment.

Output (8_20.sql)

```
Total Time Elapsed:       152.63 sec    Interval Time:       152.63 sec

PL/SQL procedure successfully completed.

Total Time Elapsed:       128.50 sec    Interval Time:       128.50 sec

PL/SQL procedure successfully completed.
```

The same functionality is maintained while changing the UPDATE to perform the UPDATE based on the ROWID. This involves adding the ROWID in the SELECT statement and changing the UPDATE predicate clause.

File: 8_21.sql

```
DECLARE
   CURSOR cur_employee IS
      SELECT employee_id, salary, ROWID
      FROM   s_employee_test;
   lv_new_salary_num NUMBER;
BEGIN
   stop_watch.start_timer;
   FOR cur_employee_rec IN cur_employee LOOP
      -- Determination of salary increase
      lv_new_salary_num := cur_employee_rec.salary;
      UPDATE s_employee_test
      SET    salary = lv_new_salary_num
      WHERE  rowid  = cur_employee_rec.ROWID;
   END LOOP;
   COMMIT;
   stop_watch.stop_timer;
END;
/
```

The following output shows the timing of two executions of the preceding code segment.

Output (8_21.sql)

```
Total Time Elapsed:       135.54 sec    Interval Time:       135.54 sec

PL/SQL procedure successfully completed.
```

Using ROWID for Iterative Processing

```
Total Time Elapsed:        114.29 sec    Interval Time:        114.29 sec

PL/SQL procedure successfully completed.
```

As evidenced from the timings, the execution is faster by using the ROWID. The first PL/SQL code segment UPDATE statement retrieves the result by using the index on employee_id to get the ROWID, and then goes to the table to search by ROWID. The second PL/SQL code segment UPDATE statement goes, however, directly to the table to search by ROWID, thus eliminating the index search. The performance improvement would increase when more records are involved and when the index use is not referring to a unique index. The ROWID variable is described in further detail in Chapter 2.

TIP
Use the ROWID variable to enhance performance
when SELECTing a record in a PL/SQL program unit.
The record needs to be manipulated in the same
PL/SQL program unit.

Reduce the Calls to SYSDATE

The SYSDATE variable is a convenient method of retrieving the current date and time. Calls to SYSDATE involve some overhead; therefore, if this variable is needed to log the date of certain processing, the call to this variable should be made once at the start of the program versus each iteration. This technique of calling SYSDATE once at the start of the program assumes the date logging is desired at the point in time the program started.

The reduction of SYSDATE calls is illustrated in the following example. The example loops through 10,000 iterations, calling SYSDATE (only the date portion of the variable since the TRUNC function is used to truncate the time portion) every iteration.

File: 8_22.sql

```
DECLARE
    lv_current_date        DATE;
BEGIN
    stop_watch.start_timer;
    FOR lv_count_num IN 1..10000 LOOP
        lv_current_date := TRUNC(SYSDATE);
    END LOOP;
    stop_watch.stop_timer;
END;
/
```

The following output shows the timing of two executions of the preceding code segment.

Output (8_22.sql)

```
Total Time Elapsed:         4.80 sec    Interval Time:         4.80 sec

PL/SQL procedure successfully completed.

Total Time Elapsed:         3.31 sec    Interval Time:         3.31 sec

PL/SQL procedure successfully completed.
```

The following PL/SQL code segment is modified to retrieve only the SYSDATE once at the beginning of the program and set to another variable each iteration.

File: 8_23.sql

```
DECLARE
    lv_current_date     DATE := TRUNC(SYSDATE);
    lv_final_date       DATE;
BEGIN
    stop_watch.start_timer;
    FOR lv_count_num IN 1..10000 LOOP
        lv_final_date := lv_current_date;
    END LOOP;
    stop_watch.stop_timer;
END;
/
```

The following output shows the timing of two executions of the preceding code segment.

Output (8_23.sql)

```
Total Time Elapsed:          .06 sec    Interval Time:          .06 sec

PL/SQL procedure successfully completed.

Total Time Elapsed:          .06 sec    Interval Time:          .06 sec

PL/SQL procedure successfully completed.
```

As evident in the preceding example, overhead is associated with the SYSDATE call, and the number of calls to SYSDATE should be reduced, if possible.

The preceding example for SYSDATE was executed under Oracle 7.3.2. When the same two PL/SQL code segments were executed under Oracle 8.0.4 and Oracle 8.1.5, the timings were quite different than what might be expected. The following table shows the execution timing differences between Oracle versions of the previous two examples.

PL/SQL Code Segment	Oracle 7.3.2 Timing	Oracle 8.0.4 Timing	Oracle 8.1.5 Timing
File: 8_22.sql	4.80 sec/3.31 sec	.30 sec/.30 sec	2.98 sec/2.97 sec
File: 8_23.sql	.06 sec/.06 sec	.02 sec/.02 sec	.01 sec/.01 sec

It appears some optimization of the SYSDATE execution was introduced in Oracle 8.0.4; however, it does not appear to be integrated into Oracle 8.1.5. The table illustrates the improvement with limiting the SYSDATE calls in each Oracle version.

As mentioned in the introduction to this chapter, differences exist between Oracle versions, hardware platforms, and operating systems, which can result in different timing results than shown in this book. Therefore, always create a test environment where timings can be monitored accurately and consistently to ensure performance enhancements introduced in the test environment will be realized in production.

TIP
Attempt to limit the calls to SYSDATE in iterative or recursive loops because overhead is associated with this variable. Set a PL/SQL DATE variable to SYSDATE in the declaration, and reference the PL/SQL variable to eliminate the overhead.

Standardize on Data Types, IF Statement Order, and PLS_INTEGER

Several minor programming modifications can be introduced into your standard PL/SQL development that can improve performance. Three of these techniques are outlined in this section.

- Ensure the same data types in comparison operations

- Order IF conditions based on the frequency of the condition

- Use the PLS_INTEGER PL/SQL data type for integer operations

Ensure the Same Data Types in Comparison Operations

When variables or constant values are compared, they should have the same data type definition. If the comparison does not involve the same data types, then Oracle implicitly converts one of the values, thus introducing undesired overhead. Any time values are compared in a condition, the values should be the same data type. This should be a standard used when developing PL/SQL program units and is good programming style.

The following procedure illustrates the cost of comparing different data types, namely a numeric data type to a character value in an IF statement.

File: 8_24.sql

```
CREATE OR REPLACE PROCEDURE test_if (p_condition_num NUMBER) AS
   lv_temp_num           NUMBER := 0;
   lv_temp_cond_num      NUMBER := p_condition_num;
BEGIN
   stop_watch.start_timer;
   FOR lv_count_num IN 1..100000 LOOP
      IF lv_temp_cond_num = '1' THEN
         lv_temp_num := lv_temp_num + 1;
      ELSIF lv_temp_cond_num = '2' THEN
         lv_temp_num := lv_temp_num + 1;
      ELSIF lv_temp_cond_num = '3' THEN
         lv_temp_num := lv_temp_num + 1;
      ELSIF lv_temp_cond_num = '4' THEN
         lv_temp_num := lv_temp_num + 1;
      ELSIF lv_temp_cond_num = '5' THEN
         lv_temp_num := lv_temp_num + 1;
      ELSIF lv_temp_cond_num = '6' THEN
         lv_temp_num := lv_temp_num + 1;
      ELSIF lv_temp_cond_num = '7' THEN
         lv_temp_num := lv_temp_num + 1;
      ELSE
         lv_temp_num := lv_temp_num + 1;
      END IF;
   END LOOP;
   stop_watch.stop_timer;
END;
/
```

The following illustrates the execution of the test_if procedure.

```
EXECUTE test_if(8)
```

The following output is the execution result of the test_if procedure.

Output (8_24.sql)

```
Total Time Elapsed:        8.68 sec   Interval Time:       8.68 sec

PL/SQL procedure successfully completed.
```

Unnecessary overhead is introduced with the different data types. If the procedure is changed to the same data type comparisons, the following execution is much faster.

File: 8_25.sql

```
CREATE OR REPLACE PROCEDURE test_if (p_condition_num NUMBER) AS
   lv_temp_num          NUMBER := 0;
   lv_temp_cond_num     NUMBER := p_condition_num;
BEGIN
   stop_watch.start_timer;
   FOR lv_count_num IN 1..100000 LOOP
      IF lv_temp_cond_num = 1 THEN
         lv_temp_num := lv_temp_num + 1;
      ELSIF lv_temp_cond_num = 2 THEN
         lv_temp_num := lv_temp_num + 1;
      ELSIF lv_temp_cond_num = 3 THEN
         lv_temp_num := lv_temp_num + 1;
      ELSIF lv_temp_cond_num = 4 THEN
         lv_temp_num := lv_temp_num + 1;
      ELSIF lv_temp_cond_num = 5 THEN
         lv_temp_num := lv_temp_num + 1;
      ELSIF lv_temp_cond_num = 6 THEN
         lv_temp_num := lv_temp_num + 1;
      ELSIF lv_temp_cond_num = 7 THEN
         lv_temp_num := lv_temp_num + 1;
      ELSE
         lv_temp_num := lv_temp_num + 1;
      END IF;
   END LOOP;
   stop_watch.stop_timer;
END;
/
```

The following illustrates the execution of the new test_if procedure:

```
EXECUTE test_if(8)
```

Output (8_25.sql)

```
Total Time Elapsed:         3.22 sec    Interval Time:         3.22 sec

PL/SQL procedure successfully completed.
```

As shown in the preceding examples, the execution takes less than half the time. The improvement increases as the frequency of execution increases.

TIP
Ensure all conditional comparisons compare the same data types. Additionally, it helps to ensure the data types within the numeric family are comparing the same subtype. Therefore, in the preceding example (8_25.sql), the comparison in the IF statement to a 1,2,3, and so forth is comparing a NUMBER to a PLS_INTEGER. There is still some internal Oracle conversion overhead taking place. To eliminate this overhead, the 1,2,3... should be changed to 1.0, 2.0, 3.0.... When this change is made to the preceding example (8_25.sql), the timing is reduced to 2.10 seconds.

Order IF Conditions Based on the Frequency of the Condition

The natural programming method when developing an IF statement with multiple conditions is to order the conditional checks based on some sequential order. This order is typically alphabetical or numerically sequenced, to create a more readable segment of code, which usually is not the most optimal. Especially, when using the ELSIF condition several times in an IF statement, the most frequently met condition should appear first, followed by the next frequent match, and so forth.

In the previous section, the execution of the procedure was always carried out by passing an 8, which meant every loop had to check all eight conditional operations of the IF logic to satisfy the condition. If we pass a 1, which is equivalent to saying the first condition satisfies all IF executions, we get a more optimized result, as shown in the following example.

```
EXECUTE test_if(1)
```

Output (8_25.sql)

```
Total Time Elapsed:          1.18 sec    Interval Time:         1.18 sec

PL/SQL procedure successfully completed.
```

The preceding output illustrates a performance improvement from the preceding section with the correct ordering of IF conditions. Therefore, take the extra step of analyzing IF condition order before coding them.

TIP
Ensure the string of PL/SQL IF conditions appears in the order of most frequently satisfied, not a sequential order based numerically or alphanumerically.

Use the PLS_INTEGER PL/SQL Data Type for Integer Operations

The typical standard for declaring a numeric data type is to use the data type of NUMBER. In PL/SQL release 2.2, Oracle introduced the PLS_INTEGER data type. This data type can be used in place of any numeric family data type declaration, as long as the content of the variable is an integer and remains within the bounds of –2147483647 and +2147483647. Therefore, most counters and operations with integers can use this data type. The PLS_INTEGER involves fewer internal instructions to process, thus increasing performance when using this numeric data type. The more references to this variable, the more improvement realized.

This improvement is illustrated in the following PL/SQL code segment. The code segment is the same example as the previous two sections, with the data type declarations being changed to PLS_INTEGER from NUMBER.

File: 8_26.sql

```
CREATE OR REPLACE PROCEDURE test_if (p_condition_num PLS_INTEGER) AS
    lv_temp_num          PLS_INTEGER := 0;
    lv_temp_cond_num     PLS_INTEGER := p_condition_num;
BEGIN
    stop_watch.start_timer;
    FOR lv_count_num IN 1..100000 LOOP
        IF lv_temp_cond_num = 1 THEN
            lv_temp_num := lv_temp_num + 1;
        ELSIF lv_temp_cond_num = 2 THEN
```

```
            lv_temp_num := lv_temp_num + 1;
        ELSIF lv_temp_cond_num = 3 THEN
            lv_temp_num := lv_temp_num + 1;
        ELSIF lv_temp_cond_num = 4 THEN
            lv_temp_num := lv_temp_num + 1;
        ELSIF lv_temp_cond_num = 5 THEN
            lv_temp_num := lv_temp_num + 1;
        ELSIF lv_temp_cond_num = 6 THEN
            lv_temp_num := lv_temp_num + 1;
        ELSIF lv_temp_cond_num = 7 THEN
            lv_temp_num := lv_temp_num + 1;
        ELSE
            lv_temp_num := lv_temp_num + 1;
        END IF;
    END LOOP;
    stop_watch.stop_timer;
END;
/
```

The following illustrates the execution of the test_if procedure.

```
EXECUTE test_if(1)
```

The following performance improvement is evident based on the results of the execution.

Output (8_26.sql)

```
Total Time Elapsed:          .61 sec    Interval Time:          .61 sec

PL/SQL procedure successfully completed.
```

TIP
Use the PLS_INTEGER when processing integers to improve performance.

TIP
If a number with precision (decimals) is assigned to a PLS_INTEGER variable, the value will be rounded to a whole number as if the ROUND function was performed on the number.

Reduce the Use of the MOD Function

Certain PL/SQL functions are more costly to use than others. MOD is one function that is better to be performed with additional PL/SQL logic to improve the overall performance. This is illustrated in the following example. The MOD function is covered in more detail in Chapter 6. This is a useful function but, if executed in an IF statement as illustrated in the following example, additional overhead is introduced.

File: 8_27.sql

```
BEGIN
   stop_watch.start_timer;
   FOR lv_count_num IN 1..10000 LOOP
      IF MOD(lv_count_num, 1000) = 0 THEN
         DBMS_OUTPUT.PUT_LINE('Hit 1000; Total: ' || lv_count_num);
      END IF;
   END LOOP;
   stop_watch.stop_timer;
END;
/
```

The following output shows the timing of two executions of the preceding code segment (the DBMS_OUTPUT.PUT_LINE output is only displayed once).

Output (8_27.sql)

```
Hit 1000; Total: 1000
Hit 1000; Total: 2000
Hit 1000; Total: 3000
Hit 1000; Total: 4000
Hit 1000; Total: 5000
Hit 1000; Total: 6000
Hit 1000; Total: 7000
Hit 1000; Total: 8000
Hit 1000; Total: 9000
Hit 1000; Total: 10000
Total Time Elapsed:          .58 sec   Interval Time:        .58 sec

PL/SQL procedure successfully completed.

Total Time Elapsed:          .43 sec   Interval Time:        .43 sec

PL/SQL procedure successfully completed.
```

The preceding PL/SQL code segment is modified to eliminate the MOD function use and perform the same check with additional PL/SQL logic, as illustrated in the following code segment.

File: 8_28.sql

```
DECLARE
    lv_count_inc_num PLS_INTEGER := 0;
BEGIN
    stop_watch.start_timer;
    FOR lv_count_num IN 1..10000 LOOP
        lv_count_inc_num := lv_count_inc_num + 1;
        IF lv_count_inc_num = 1000 THEN
            DBMS_OUTPUT.PUT_LINE('Hit 1000; Total: ' || lv_count_num);
            lv_count_inc_num := 0;
        END IF;
    END LOOP;
    stop_watch.stop_timer;
END;
/
```

Output (8_28.sql)

```
Hit 1000; Total: 1000
Hit 1000; Total: 2000
Hit 1000; Total: 3000
Hit 1000; Total: 4000
Hit 1000; Total: 5000
Hit 1000; Total: 6000
Hit 1000; Total: 7000
Hit 1000; Total: 8000
Hit 1000; Total: 9000
Hit 1000; Total: 10000
Total Time Elapsed:        .11 sec    Interval Time:        .11 sec

PL/SQL procedure successfully completed.

Total Time Elapsed:        .05 sec    Interval Time:        .05 sec

PL/SQL procedure successfully completed.
```

As shown from the two preceding examples, the MOD function adds overhead and is better performed with PL/SQL IF statements. The preceding example for MOD was executed under Oracle 7.3.2. When the same two PL/SQL code segments were executed under Oracle 8.0.4 and Oracle 8.1.5, the timings were quite different than what might be expected. The following table shows the timing differences between versions of the previous two examples.

PL/SQL Code Segment	Oracle 7.3.2 Timing	Oracle 8.0.4 Timing	Oracle 8.1.5 Timing
File: 8_27.sql	.58 sec/.43 sec	.41 sec/.42 sec	.09 sec/.09 sec
File: 8_28.sql	.11 sec/.05 sec	.03 sec/.03 sec	.02 sec/.02 sec

Some optimization of the MOD execution appears to be introduced in Oracle 8.1.5. The table illustrates the improvement of eliminating the MOD function in each Oracle version.

TIP
The MOD function is one function that is faster to perform with additional PL/SQL logic. While this is minor, it is a standard technique to introduce into your PL/SQL standard programming techniques.

Understand the PL/SQL Engine Handling of Bind Variables

The Oracle Developer product suite contains several modules, each of which contains a PL/SQL Engine that is independent of the database server-side PL/SQL Engine. The client-side PL/SQL Engine will attempt to process all PL/SQL program units embedded in the application logic of the development products. Any calls to server-side stored PL/SQL program units or any SQL statements will be passed to the server side PL/SQL and SQL Engines, respectively, for execution. The purpose of this behavior is to increase performance by limiting network communications when the PL/SQL source code can be entirely processed on the client-side. If the local PL/SQL Engine is incapable of processing the PL/SQL program unit on its own, then the code, or portions of it, will be passed to the PL/SQL Engine on the server-side.

To achieve maximum performance, when this transfer from client-side to server-side occurs, two things are imperative: the communication between the client and server components must be kept to a minimum, and bind variables must be used. Therefore, no literal strings should be used in program units. Contrary to popular belief, directly referencing form fields does not hardcode a literal value when passed to the server; a bind value is still used when references are made to form fields. This fact is illustrated by monitoring the V$SQLAREA view content when different PL/SQL program unit methods are deployed in a form screen.

An example form screen was created to display employee information by basing the Form on the s_employee table. For each employee, the department_id is displayed and the department_name must be retrieved from the s_department table via a POST-QUERY trigger on the base s_employee block. Five methods of developing PL/SQL source code to implement this logic follow. These five methods illustrate the flexibility of the PL/SQL language and the actual location of the PL/SQL source code. As for the standard to follow, refer to Chapter 5 and Chapter 14 for further detail. The point of this section is to demonstrate that Oracle's internal processing of the SQL cursor on the server-side is the same in all cases.

The first method was to create the SELECT INTO statement directly into the POST-QUERY trigger, as illustrated in the following script (directly referencing the form fields for the department_id and nbt_department_name).

File: 8_29.sql

```
SELECT  department_name
INTO    :nbt_department_name
FROM    s_department
WHERE   department_id = :department_id;
```

The second method was to create a PL/SQL anonymous block with an explicit cursor in the POST-QUERY trigger, as illustrated in the following script (directly referencing the form fields for the department_id and nbt_department_name).

File: 8_30.sql

```
DECLARE
   CURSOR cur_department IS
      SELECT department_name
      FROM   s_department
      WHERE  department_id = :department_id;
BEGIN
   OPEN cur_department;
   FETCH cur_department INTO :nbt_department_name;
   CLOSE cur_department;
END;
```

The third method was to create a program unit in the form that is called from the POST-QUERY trigger, as illustrated in the following script (passing the form fields for the department_id and nbt_department_name as parameters).

```
fill_department(:department_id, :nbt_department_name);
```

The following is the fill_department procedure created as a form PL/SQL program unit.

File: 8_31.sql

```
PROCEDURE fill_department(p_department_id_num NUMBER,
   p_department_name_txt OUT VARCHAR2) IS
   CURSOR cur_department IS
      SELECT department_name
      FROM    s_department
      WHERE   department_id = p_department_id_num;
BEGIN
   OPEN cur_department;
   FETCH cur_department INTO p_department_name_txt;
   CLOSE cur_department;
END;
```

The fourth method was to create a program unit in the form that is called from the POST-QUERY trigger, as illustrated in the following script (passing the form fields for the department_id and nbt_department_name as parameters and using these passed in variables as cursor variable parameters).

```
fill_department(:department_id, :nbt_department_name);
```

The following is the fill_department procedure created as a form PL/SQL program unit.

File: 8_32.sql

```
PROCEDURE fill_department(p_department_id_num NUMBER,
   p_department_name_txt OUT VARCHAR2) IS
   CURSOR cur_department(lv_department_id_num NUMBER) IS
      SELECT department_name
      FROM    s_department
      WHERE   department_id = lv_department_id_num;
BEGIN
   OPEN cur_department(p_department_id_num);
   FETCH cur_department INTO p_department_name_txt;
   CLOSE cur_department;
END;
```

The fifth method is identical to the fourth method, with one change: the fill_department procedure was changed from a local form PL/SQL program unit to a database server-side stored PL/SQL program unit. The source code is not shown because it is the same as method four. The Oracle Developer product suite provides a convenient mechanism for moving a PL/SQL program unit from the client side to

Understanding the PL/SQL Engine Handling of Bind Variables

the server side. Both local and stored PL/SQL program units are visible in the Object Navigator of the Forms product; therefore, the program unit can be dragged and dropped to the desired location.

Each method was developed and the Form was executed, followed by the execution of the following V$SQLAREA script on the server side. The V$SQLAREA script retrieves any records in the SQL Area that contain the literal text 'DEPARTMENT' in a SQL cursor. Each time the script was executed the result was the same. Each time, the SQL statement was passed to the server-side SQL Engine for processing with the use of a bind variable.

File: 8_33.sql

```
SELECT sql_text
FROM   v$sqlarea
WHERE  INSTR(UPPER(sql_text), 'DEPARTMENT') > 0;
```

The following is the output retrieved for each execution.

Output (8_33.sql)

```
SQL_TEXT
------------------------------------------------------------------------
SELECT DEPARTMENT_NAME   FROM S_DEPARTMENT  WHERE DEPARTMENT_ID = :b1
SELECT ROWID,EMPLOYEE_ID,EMPLOYEE_LAST_NAME,DEPARTMENT_ID FROM S_EMPLO
YEE
select sql_text from v$sqlarea where instr(upper(sql_text), 'DEPARTMEN
T') > 0
```

From the preceding output, it is evident the first statement is the cursor we continually changed, but was processed the same. The second statement is the cursor for the execution of the query of the Form to return the employee information (this is internally created by the Oracle Form product when the EXECUTE QUERY key is pressed). The third statement is the cursor of the V$SQLAREA script.

TIP

Oracle Developer Forms internally creates cursors based on the Query conditions entered in the screen when the EXECUTE QUERY key is pressed. Note the column ROWID in the second line of the V$SQLAREA result set (Output 8_33.sql). The ROWID pseudo column is retrieved for every record queried and is used by Oracle to perform any UPDATE or DELETE operations. The ROWID is covered in further detail earlier in this chapter, as well as in Chapter 2 and Chapter 4.

Use Explicit versus Implicit Cursors

In the case of a code table lookup, when retrieving one record from a table, the SELECT statement can be created using an explicit or implicit cursor. The two types are illustrated in the following examples.

The following is the implicit cursor code segment for retrieving the department_name for each employee.

File: 8_34.sql

```
DECLARE
    CURSOR cur_employee IS
        SELECT *
        FROM    s_employee_test;
    lv_department_txt s_department.department_name%TYPE;
BEGIN
    FOR cur_employee_rec IN cur_employee LOOP
        -- Processing Logic goes here
        SELECT department_name
        INTO    lv_department_txt
        FROM    s_department
        WHERE   department_id = cur_employee_rec.department_id;
        -- Processing Logic
    END LOOP;
END;
/
```

The following script is the explicit cursor code segment for retrieving the department_name for each employee.

File: 8_35.sql

```
DECLARE
    CURSOR cur_employee IS
        SELECT *
        FROM    s_employee_test;
    CURSOR cur_department
        (p_department_num s_department.department_id%TYPE) IS
        SELECT department_name
        FROM    s_department
        where   department_id = p_department_num;
    lv_department_txt s_department.department_name%TYPE;
BEGIN
    FOR cur_employee_rec IN cur_employee LOOP
        -- Processing Logic goes here
        OPEN cur_department(cur_employee_rec.department_id);
```

```
        FETCH cur_department INTO lv_department_txt;
        CLOSE cur_department;
        -- Processing Logic goes here
    END LOOP;
END;
/
```

Using explicit cursors is more efficient, although more coding is involved. Oracle internally creates a cursor for every SQL statement executed. Explicit cursors embed the logic in the source code versus internally handled by Oracle. The performance improvement of explicit cursors becomes evident when frequent single row SELECTs are executed.

An implicit cursor always performs two fetches per SELECT INTO (the first fetch is to retrieve the record, the second fetch is to determine if the TOO_MANY_ROWS exception should be raised), whereas explicit cursors only perform the number of fetches coded in the source code. In the case of single row SELECTs, you would only execute one FETCH. The benefit is further magnified when PL/SQL program executions are from a client-side application front end because more network communication is necessary.

 TIP
Use explicit cursors over implicit cursors to reduce fetching and improve performance. This improvement will increase in any client-side application interface the more frequently single SELECTs are used.

Find Similar SQL Statements and SQL NOT Using Bind Variables

SQL statements created in PL/SQL program units should always reference a bind variable versus a constant value. To view SQL statements being executed in your application environment, the V$SQLAREA view can be queried. This view can be used to monitor all SQL statements executed in your system for a particular object or to highlight SQL statements not using bind variables. The V$SQLAREA view provides access to the current contents of the Shared SQL Area (part of the Shared Pool) at a specific point in time. Objects in the SQL Area are aged out over time depending on the LRU algorithm. An object residing in the SQL Area will not be aged out if it is currently in use by a session.

Many times PL/SQL code is identical to previously developed PL/SQL code in your system *except* for a variable or value that changes from one statement to another. These cases are difficult to track. Educating developers to use bind variables versus hard coding constants into a statement will eliminate this undesired overhead.

Likewise, developers often develop source code to create the same business logic, but with slight variations, causing the SQL statements to be treated as separate cursors. The easy answer is to make sure code is reused when possible but, in reality, this does not always happen.

The following script is one way to find the two types of statements. By varying the length of the matching sql_text column, you can find similar statements that may be candidates for bind variables or may be candidates for consolidating statements. You can also vary the HAVING clause to set the number of occurences that must exist to return the statement.

File: 8_36.sql

```
SELECT SUBSTR(UPPER(sql_text), 1, 55) sql_text, COUNT(*)
FROM   v$sqlarea
GROUP BY SUBSTR(UPPER(sql_text), 1, 55)
HAVING COUNT(*) > 1;
```

Output (8_36.sql)

```
SQL_TEXT                                                         COUNT(*)
--------------------------------------------------------------- ----------
DECLARE     LV_LAST_NAME_TXT   S_EMPLOYEE.EMPLOYEE_LAST_N            4
SELECT EMPLOYEE_ID,EMPLOYEE_LAST_NAME,EMPLOYEE_FIRST_NA              2
```

The result set returns a PL/SQL anonymous block and a SELECT statement. We can now zero in on the SELECT statement cursor to identify possible reuse. The V$SQLAREA query is restructured, as shown in the following script.

File: 8_37.sql

```
SELECT sql_text
FROM   v$sqlarea
WHERE  SUBSTR(UPPER(sql_text), 1, 55) =
   'SELECT EMPLOYEE_ID,EMPLOYEE_LAST_NAME,EMPLOYEE_FIRST_NA';
```

Output (8_37.sql)

```
SQL_TEXT
----------------------------------------------------------------------
SELECT EMPLOYEE_ID,EMPLOYEE_LAST_NAME,EMPLOYEE_FIRST_NAME,DEPARTMENT_I
D   FROM S_EMPLOYEE  WHERE EMPLOYEE_FIRST_NAME = :b1   AND EMPLOYEE_LAS
T_NAME = :b2
```

```
SELECT EMPLOYEE_ID,EMPLOYEE_LAST_NAME,EMPLOYEE_FIRST_NAME,DEPARTMENT_I
D   FROM S_EMPLOYEE  WHERE EMPLOYEE_LAST_NAME = :b1  AND EMPLOYEE_FIRS
T_NAME = :b2
```

The result set indicates the two cursors are identical, with the predicate clause conditions being ordered differently. One of the cursors can be modified by changing the order of the predicate clause to ensure the cursors are reused.

To search the SQL Area for cursors not using bind variables, the following query can be executed. This will retrieve all cursors with a single quote in the statement.

File: 8_38.sql

```
SELECT sql_text
FROM   v$sqlarea
WHERE  INSTR(sql_text, '''') > 0;
```

Output (8_38.sql)

```
SQL_TEXT
----------------------------------------------------------------------
SELECT employee_id, employee_last_name, employee_first_name from   s_e
mployee where  employee_last_name = 'PATEL'
select sql_text from v$sqlarea where  instr(sql_text, '''') > 0
select sql_text from v$sqlarea where instr(upper(sql_text), 'DEPARTMEN
T') > 0
```

From the result set, the s_employee table cursor can be further reviewed to determine if the statement should have been using a bind variable.

For further details on the complete processing of the PL/SQL Engine, SQL Engine, and PL/SQL program units, refer to Chapter 14.

Store PL/SQL Program Units in the Database

I generally recommend storing PL/SQL objects on the server-side for many of the obvious reasons. The server is usually more powerful, and objects are reused much more often (especially when pinned in the Shared Pool). The security methods employed are also more straightforward. Keeping the PL/SQL processing on the client side can be dependent on the power of the client and can lessen the number of round trips from client to server. When written correctly, the calls may be limited back to the server (see the following section for further information regarding this topic). There is certainly a continuing debate on the best location to store PL/SQL source code but, with the evolving thin client, the server will probably be the only place to store the PL/SQL. The exact execution of PL/SQL program units (server-side and client-side) is detailed in Chapter 14. The following list contains some compelling reasons for storing PL/SQL code on the server-side:

- Improves performance because the code is already compiled (p-code)
- Allows the capability to pin objects in the Shared Pool
- Enables transaction-level security at the database level
- Reduces redundant code and version-control issues
- Allows the PL/SQL source to be queried online because it is stored in the data dictionary
- Provides a mechanism to determine impact analysis because object dependencies are stored in the data dictionary
- Requires less memory because only one copy of the code is in memory
- Enhances load times when PL/SQL packages are used because the entire package is loaded into memory upon the first reference to any package element

Refer to Chapter 5 for further information related to compiling and storing PL/SQL source code in the database.

Review Added PL/SQL Performance Related Considerations

A variety of additional areas can improve the performance of PL/SQL source code execution. The following areas are briefly described with a reference to other areas in this book for further detail.

- Increase the Shared Pool to increase performance
- Identify PL/SQL objects that need to be pinned
- Pin/Cache PL/SQL objects
- Modify the sql.bsq file to reduce data dictionary fragmentation
- Execute PL/SQL program units on the server-side
- Use temporary database tables for increased performance

- Integrate a user tracking mechanism to pinpoint execution location

- Create a timing and tracing mechanism to turn on/off conditionally

- Use rollback segments when processing large transaction sets

- Limit the use of dynamic SQL

- Learn the Oracle supplied PL/SQL packages that assist in performance tuning

Increase the Shared Pool to Increase Performance

The Shared Pool is one of the top two most critical memory structures of an Oracle database. If this memory structure is not sized correctly for the database instance, the overall performance will suffer. The size of the Shared Pool is controlled by the init.ora parameter shared_pool_size. The Shared Pool contains several memory structures, many of which affect the caching of PL/SQL and cursor objects, which directly effects the overall performance of PL/SQL execution. The Shared Pool is covered in further detail in Chapter 9, with several methods discussed on monitoring the size and performance of the Shared Pool.

Identify PL/SQL Objects that Need to Be Pinned

Stored PL/SQL program units can be pinned or cached in the Shared Pool. The V$DB_OBJECT_CACHE view provides a window into the current PL/SQL objects loaded in the Shared Pool. Cached PL/SQL objects are shared among Oracle sessions, thus the more objects cached, the better the performance. Typically, the stored PL/SQL program units executed the most should be pinned. The larger PL/SQL program units meeting this criterion are the most critical to pin because the allocation in the Shared Pool memory must be contiguous and this space can become fragmented, thus potentially introducing memory allocation problems for larger PL/SQL program units.

The size of the Shared Pool memory needed to load the PL/SQL program unit can be viewed by looking at the sharable_mem column of the V$DB_OBJECT_CACHE view. This is covered in further detail in Chapter 9 and Chapter 12.

Pin/Cache PL/SQL Objects

The previous section describes the PL/SQL program units that are candidates for pinning in the Shared Pool to increase performance. The method of pinning the PL/SQL program units is provided through the Oracle supplied PL/SQL package DBMS_SHARED_POOL. This package is detailed in Chapter 12, and a procedure for pinning PL/SQL objects at database startup is outlined in Chapter 9.

Modify the sql.bsq File to Reduce Data Dictionary Fragmentation

The more PL/SQL source code stored in the database, the more important it becomes to monitor the table structures that store these objects for correct space allocation. The data dictionary is no different than any other Oracle application. The space allocation of the underlying data dictionary tables should be treated with more attention and care because the Oracle data dictionary tables are accessed more frequently by Oracle internally than any application.

The method for monitoring the data dictionary tables storing the PL/SQL source code and the method of defragmenting these tables are covered in Chapter 13. Database object space fragmentation can cause significant overall system performance degradation.

Execute PL/SQL Program Units on the Server-Side

PL/SQL has become a standard language for developing complex, functional, and detailed processes for Oracle applications. Often these PL/SQL program units take a considerable amount of time to complete execution. A good example of this type of program unit is nightly data transfer routines either to or from an external application system. These programs usually create or process large volumes of records by interfacing through data file extracts.

Often a choice must be made by a developer for the location to execute the process. When the choice is presented, always execute the process on the server, unless some compelling, special case exists not to do so. The elimination of network traffic and communication overhead inherent in the client-side and server-side communication is logarithmic in most cases.

TIP
Long-running or intensive PL/SQL program unit processes should always be executed directly on the server side, if possible. This eliminates the network and communication overhead.

Use Temporary Database Tables for Increased Performance

PL/SQL tables are great for specific cases, especially when repeated iterations are involved and the amount of data is relatively small. As outlined earlier in this chapter, the memory cost (per session) can add up fast if not used properly. When a temporary storage area is needed to house large volumes of records for a short period of time, the method of creating, indexing, and querying a temporary database table should be viewed as a viable and useful option. I have seen far too many developers abandon the common method of temporary database tables after the introduction and expansion of PL/SQL tables; remember, PL/SQL tables is not the preferred method in all cases.

Integrate a User Tracking Mechanism to Pinpoint Execution Location

Oracle-developed applications continue to become increasingly more complicated from a development standpoint, with all the products available and being used, as well as the location flexibility of PL/SQL program unit source code. When users express their displeasure over performance or inform the DBA that they are stuck, it is important to know what the users were executing at that point in time and the location in the source code of the actual processing logic.

The Oracle supplied DBMS_APPLICATION_INFO package, described earlier in this chapter and in Chapter 12, provides a mechanism for logging the location of processing logic execution. Developers can integrate calls to this package to log the current location of the process executing. A standard can be deployed to call the DBMS_APPLICATION_INFO.SET_MODULE procedure to identify the product the user is currently executing (for example, this can be accomplished in a startup trigger of Oracle Forms by logging the fact the user is in Forms and including the Form name, and upon exiting the Form by nulling these values). In procedures or functions, the DBMS_APPLICATION_INFO.SET_MODULE procedure can be called to identify the procedure name and, optionally, the time—down to the second—of when they entered the procedure. Upon exiting the procedures or functions, the same procedure can be called to NULL these values.

Create a Timing and Tracing Mechanism to Turn On/Off Conditionally

When an application is being deployed in production, the debugging and testing commands are typically removed or commented out of the PL/SQL program units. While in production, when a user expresses problems encountered, one method of analyzing the problem involves testing in the development or testing environment. If performance is the issue, often the production instance holds the key to the reason why something is causing performance degradation. With this in mind, we have deployed a technique in the past that enables a production PL/SQL program unit to be traced (turn TRACE on) conditionally, based on the user executing the program unit. We created a separate account for use for this reason only. If any performance monitoring needed to be performed, the special account user would execute the PL/SQL program unit in production.

The PL/SQL program unit contained an IF statement at the beginning of the routine that would check the username of the current user. If the username matched the special account, TRACE would be turned on via a call to the

DBMS_SESSION.SET_SQL_TRACE procedure. This TRACE procedure is covered in Chapter 12.

This method of conditionally turning on TRACE can also be deployed with timing logic, to enable logging of certain timing conditions. This method becomes increasingly important as more Web applications are deployed because Web interfaces are usually stateless (the user logs on, processes the PL/SQL program unit(s), creates the Web page, displays the Web page, and logs off). Therefore, tracking Oracle sessions and being able to TRACE desired sessions becomes increasingly difficult and more complex. The method of embedding logic directly into the production PL/SQL source code to turn TRACE or timing ON can be extremely beneficial.

Use Rollback Segments When Processing Large Transaction Sets

When large transactions are processed in a PL/SQL program unit, making sure the rollback segment allocated to the process can accommodate the size of the transaction is important. I have seen far too many long-running processes abort because of exceeding the rollback segment space. Oracle does not analyze the process prior to executing the process, to determine which rollback segment to assign. The responsibility of analyzing programs and processes is left to the developer and the DBA. It is important to assign a large transaction to an appropriately sized rollback segment. This is typically only necessary when large transactions are involved.

Oracle provides a mechanism for assigning a transaction to a rollback segment. The allocation of a transaction to a rollback segment is not based on the process or session; it is transaction-based. Therefore, if intermittent COMMITs are performed, then after each COMMIT, the transaction must be assigned to the rollback segment. The command to assign a transaction to a rollback segment is the SET TRANSACTION command. Oracle also provides the supplied procedure DBMS_TRANSACTION.USE_ROLLBACK_SEGMENT to perform this operation within a PL/SQL program unit. This technique is covered in Chapter 4 and the procedure DBMS_TRANSACTION.USE_ROLLBACK_SEGMENT is covered in Chapter 12.

Limit the Use of Dynamic SQL

Oracle provides the Oracle supplied package DBMS_SQL enabling the creation of dynamic SQL and PL/SQL commands. This is an extremely powerful feature, but also dangerous if not used appropriately. When designing and developing Oracle applications, one of the hardest decisions that must be made is where to draw the line on building in dynamic capabilities and flexibility. Developing dynamic and flexible applications is extremely helpful from a functional perspective. However, the more dynamic and flexible an application, the more potential for performance degradation.

A completely accurate and functional application is considered a failure if it does not perform at acceptable levels. Users will reject an application if they have to wait to do their job. I am not advocating the elimination of dynamic or flexible applications, but a balance must exist. Build flexibility into applications when necessary, not just to make every application module more flexible for the future, just in case business rules may change. Only build flexibility into applications when you are sure the flexibility is needed and the performance impact will be negligible.

The DBMS_SQL package provides the dynamic and flexible means in PL/SQL program units. Use this package when needed, but do not abuse it, unless you want to set yourself up for failure.

TIP

If you integrate the DBMS_SQL package into a PL/SQL program unit to create SQL statements dynamically for a production application, remember optimizing the generated SQL statements will be difficult.

TIP

Oracle 8.1 introduces a more efficient implementation of executing dynamic SQL and PL/SQL statements with the EXECUTE IMMEDIATE PL/SQL command. For further detail on this command, refer to Chapter 16. The previous tip, however, still applies to this new PL/SQL command.

Learn the Oracle Supplied PL/SQL Packages That Assist in Performance Tuning

With each new release of Oracle, the PL/SQL language continues to be enhanced, with major enhancements in the Oracle supplied PL/SQL packages. These packages introduce many capabilities not available outside these packages or more easily developed using these packages. Many of these packages contain procedures and/or functions that assist in the performance tuning capability. Chapter 12 covers the Oracle supplied packages. The packages should be reviewed to expand your arsenal of PL/SQL tuning techniques.

Summary

This chapter identified critical areas and covered each with examples to illustrate the improvements that can be realized with concentrated tuning efforts. The chapter highlighted the PL/SQL tuning techniques more likely to return the larger performance improvements and noted the techniques that should be part of a developer's standard coding techniques to increase performance on a smaller scale. In many applications, overall performance is increased by improving several areas. Often, several small improvements combined result in large overall improvements.

PL/SQL tuning can be accomplished by efforts from both the developer and the DBA. Each has the capability to make a tremendous impact on the success or failure of an application, specifically in the performance of an application. This chapter finished with a review of some additional areas resulting in performance improvements covered in detail in other sections in this book. For a complete list of performance tuning tips and techniques that extends well beyond the coverage in this chapter and Chapter 7, see *Oracle Performance Tuning Tips & Techniques,* by Richard J. Niemiec (Oracle Press).

Tips Review

- Always execute a PL/SQL program unit more than once when testing because the first execution typically takes longer due to the loading and parsing. The larger the program unit, the longer this initial overhead.

- DBMS_OUTPUT.PUT_LINE does not display the information from this procedure until the procedure completes. It does not display at the time the procedure is called. If the PL/SQL program unit takes two hours to execute, the DBMS_OUTPUT.PUT_LINE information will not display for two hours.

- For any PL/SQL program unit that executes for more than ten minutes, build a mechanism into the program unit to log the information to some location. This will enable you to know how long it has run and how long it has to go. This will save you a tremendous amount of time. Use the DBMS_APPLICATION_INFO, DBMS_PIPE, or UTL_FILE package to accomplish this, do not use DBMS_OUTPUT.PUT_LINE procedure.

- Use the Oracle supplied package DBMS_APPLICATION_INFO package to log point-in-time information to the V$SESSION view to enable monitoring of long-running processes.

- Log (INSERT) execution timing information into a database table for long-running PL/SQL program units to integrate a proactive performance monitoring mechanism into your system. This database table can then be reviewed at any point in time to determine if performance has decreased over time.

- System load in terms of number of active sessions can have a large impact on the performance of program execution; therefore, it would be helpful to modify the database table logging method to include a column for the number of active sessions. This column can be filled by adding one additional query to the program unit being executed to retrieve the count from the V$SESSION view.

■ When a PL/SQL program unit involves extensive looping or recursion, concentrate on reducing the execution time per iteration. This adds up fast, and it is easy to do the math to determine the overall improvement potential. The looping or recursion should also be reviewed for restructuring to reduce the number of iterations, while keeping the same functionality. With the extreme flexibility of PL/SQL and SQL, a variety of ways typically exists to accomplish the same result. If a PL/SQL program unit is not performing optimally, sometimes you have to rewrite the logic another way.

■ When using PL/SQL tables, the performance gain realized would increase as the size of the PL/SQL table increases (assuming the system has the memory to allocate for the PL/SQL tables).

■ Beware that the benefit of using PL/SQL tables may not be fully realized on certain versions of Oracle 8.0 and Oracle 8.1 on certain platforms because some bugs related to PL/SQL tables exist. As always, testing your application in a test environment on a new release or platform, prior to production deployment, is best for both functional execution and performance.

■ PL/SQL tables allocate memory based on the fixed length of the record size and the number of records loaded into the PL/SQL table. Memory is allocated to PL/SQL tables in chunks. Be EXTREMELY cognizant of the definition of your PL/SQL tables. DO NOT assign the contents of the PL/SQL table to %ROWTYPE unless this is needed. Oracle will allocate the maximum total length of the database table record if the %ROWTYPE is referenced and allocates this much memory per PL/SQL table record.

■ Be aware of the memory allocation and requirements of PL/SQL tables. PL/SQL tables have tremendous advantages, but they do come at a cost, which must be analyzed to understand the impact and appropriateness of using PL/SQL tables. For a method of deallocating memory allocated to PL/SQL tables when the memory is no longer needed for a session, refer to the DBMS_SESSION. FREE_UNUSED_USER_MEMORY procedure in Chapter 12.

■ Use the ROWID variable to enhance performance when SELECTing a record in a PL/SQL program unit; then the record needs to be manipulated in the same PL/SQL program unit.

■ Attempt to limit the calls to SYSDATE in iterative or recursive loops because overhead is associated with this variable. Set a PL/SQL DATE variable to SYSDATE in the declaration and reference the PL/SQL variable to eliminate the overhead.

■ Ensure all conditional comparisons compare the same data types. Additionally, it helps to ensure the data types within the numeric family are comparing the same subtype. Therefore, in example (8_25.sql), the comparison in the IF statement to a 1,2,3, and so forth is comparing a NUMBER to a PLS_INTEGER. There is still some internal Oracle conversion overhead taking place. To eliminate this overhead, the 1,2,3... should be changed to 1.0, 2.0, 3.0.... When this change is made to example (8_25.sql), the timing is reduced even further.

■ Ensure the string of PL/SQL IF conditions appears in the order of most frequently satisfied, not a sequential order based numerically or alphanumerically.

■ Use the PLS_INTEGER when processing integers to improve performance.

■ If a number with precision (decimals) is assigned to a PLS_INTEGER variable, the value will be rounded to a whole number, as if the ROUND function was performed on the number.

■ The MOD function is one function that is faster to perform with additional PL/SQL logic. While this is minor, it is a standard technique to introduce into your PL/SQL standard programming techniques.

■ Oracle Developer Forms internally creates cursors based on the Query conditions entered in the screen when the EXECUTE QUERY key is pressed. The ROWID pseudo column is retrieved for every record queried and is used by Oracle to perform any UPDATE or DELETE operations. The ROWID is covered in more detail earlier in this chapter, as well as in Chapter 2 and Chapter 4.

■ Use explicit cursors over implicit cursors to reduce fetching and improve performance. This improvement increases in any client-side application interface and the more frequently single SELECTs are used.

■ Long-running or intensive PL/SQL program unit processes should always be executed directly on the server side, if possible. This eliminates the network and communication overhead.

■ If you integrate the DBMS_SQL package into a PL/SQL program unit to create SQL statements dynamically for a production application, remember, optimizing the generated SQL statements will be difficult.

■ Oracle 8.1 introduces a more efficient implementation of executing dynamic SQL and PL/SQL statements with the EXECUTE IMMEDIATE PL/SQL command. For further detail on this command, refer to Chapter 16. The previous tip, however, still applies to this new PL/SQL command.

Tips Review

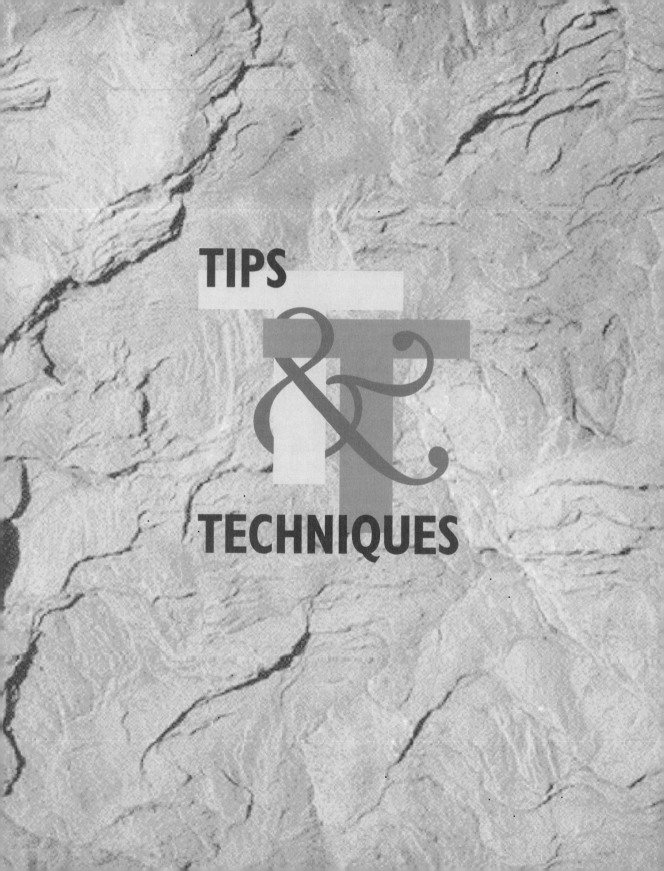

TIPS

&

TECHNIQUES

CHAPTER

9

Examining DBA-Related PL/SQL Issues (DBA)

The PL/SQL language is often thought of as a development language, which requires only that a developer understand it, to ensure applications are functional and accurate. Equally and often more important, however, is the DBA's knowledge of PL/SQL, specifically, how PL/SQL affects the overall success of a system. To ensure the overall success of a system, the DBA must understand and take responsibility for each area that PL/SQL affects as it relates to the overall configuration and efficiency of a system. PL/SQL has an impact in most of the areas that DBAs are responsible for. The more DBAs are aware of this effect, the easier their job will become.

This chapter focuses on several of the important areas in which DBAs must be knowledgeable and take some form of action. No new responsibilities are added to the DBAs; rather, there is an increase in the scope of their current responsibilities to ensure the PL/SQL effects are accounted for. The goal of this chapter is to highlight and examine several of the PL/SQL areas that can seriously affect the DBA's responsibilities.

Many of the topics covered are detailed in other chapters; however, these topics are mentioned here to enforce the criticality and to stress the importance of the DBA-related PL/SQL areas. The areas covered do not duplicate other areas of this book. Instead, they focus on providing additional information on a topic or providing a summary of the topic and then referring to another section in the book for further detail.

The following is a list of tips and techniques covered in this chapter.

- Review the creation of the PL/SQL components

- Examine the change of source code storage with PL/SQL

- Review the PL/SQL source code storage size

- Build a solid security model for PL/SQL objects

- Explore the Oracle supplied packages for the DBA

- Know when to encrypt PL/SQL source code

- Understand the PL/SQL versus SQL Engine

- Evaluate impact analysis at a detailed level

- Pinpoint invalid PL/SQL objects

- Identify disabled database triggers

- Review PL/SQL related init.ora parameters

- Monitor the Shared Pool use to determine optimization

- Monitor memory and use of PL/SQL program units

- Monitor PL/SQL-related information with the V$ views
  - Monitor the library cache (V$LIBRARY_CACHE)
  - Monitor the dictionary cache (V$ROWCACHE)
  - Evaluate I/O per user (V$SESS_IO)
  - Evaluate each user's resource consumption (V$SESSTAT)
  - Highlight open cursors per user (V$OPEN_CURSOR)
  - Identify current session SQL execution (V$SQLTEXT)
  - Determine object access at a point in time (V$ACCESS)
  - Pinpoint lock contention (V$LOCK)
    - Identify the locked user(s)
    - Identify the locking user(s)
  - Monitor rollback segment use (V$ROLLSTAT and V$TRANSACTION)
- Build a DBA monitoring system with DBMS_JOB, DBMS_PIPE, and DBMS_ALERT
- Pin PL/SQL objects and cursors
- Provide experienced developers with additional access
  - Provide developers with READ privilege on Oracle supplied PL/SQL files
  - Provide experienced developers with SELECT privilege on selected V$ views
- Learn PL/SQL yourself to take your DBA skills to the next level

Review the Creation of the PL/SQL Components

The PL/SQL language has been one of the core components of Oracle since the release of version 6. Originally, PL/SQL came as an option to the database. This was quickly eliminated as Oracle began to use the language internally as part of the core of the Oracle Engine. Many of the new features introduced in the recent versions of Oracle are created with PL/SQL extensions. When the database is originally created, the PL/SQL components that comprise the PL/SQL language are created by default.

Reviewing the Creation of the
PL/SQL Components

The PL/SQL components—namely data dictionary tables and views, core Oracle PL/SQL packages (STANDARD and DBMS_STANDARD), the Oracle supplied packages—are created through a set of SQL scripts. These scripts are executed in a series of calls originating in the catproc.sql file. When the creation scripts are complete, the PL/SQL language is set up and all the previously outlined components are created. Access is dependent on the schema privileges, the particular data dictionary view, and the Oracle supplied package. Many of the views are available to users and follow the same model as the standard Oracle data dictionary in terms of USER_*, ALL_*, and DBA_*. Some PL/SQL-related components are not created in the standard default installation, like replication, and must be created manually by executing the necessary scripts. Likewise, privileges on the PL/SQL component objects can be added beyond the default installation.

The PL/SQL-related script files are typically located under the rdbms/admin directory (ORACLE_HOME/rdbmsXXX/admin on UNIX, where XXX is the version). To obtain specific information for each file and to learn an invaluable amount of information, look in each of these files. This is well worth the time invested. These files vary between Oracle versions and some of these files vary per platform, so do not treat the review of these files as a one-time responsibility. Instead, treat it as a regular occurrence when new versions or new platforms are introduced.

For a more detailed description of the creation of the PL/SQL components, including the process and files, refer to Chapter 13.

TIP

Treat the SQL files that create the PL/SQL components like user documentation. It truly is a supplement to this documentation and is online.

Examine the Change of Source Code Storage with PL/SQL

With the advances of technology and, specifically, with the architecture of Oracle applications today—including storing PL/SQL source code in the database—a new level of space management has been introduced. This new level centers around the space management of stored PL/SQL program units in the form of packages, procedures, functions, and database triggers. Therefore, a DBA must monitor the database objects that store the PL/SQL source code and ensure efficiency by properly configuring these objects.

This responsibility becomes more difficult because the database objects that store the PL/SQL information are the underlying data dictionary tables and indexes. The underlying data dictionary tables and indexes are not like standard application database objects that can be reconfigured easily. These objects must be treated with much more care and adhere to more restrictions related to them. These data dictionary tables and views are created in the sql.bsq file, and the sql.bsq file is executed by default when a database is created. Therefore, these database objects will only be created if the database is rebuilt. The sizing of these database objects is also hardcoded in the sql.bsq file.

Two methods assist in space management of these database objects as the following will outline, both of which assume fragmentation is introduced in the database objects and the intent is to eliminate this fragmentation:

- **Quick Solution**   Increase the NEXT EXTENT value to limit the amount of further fragmentation.

- **Complete Solution**   Rebuild the database but, prior to the rebuild, modify the sql.bsq file for the fragmented database objects to increase the INITIAL EXTENT (large enough to store at least the current size) and the NEXT EXTENT (to limit the amount of fragmentation over time).

Remember these database objects are stored in the SYSTEM tablespace. For complete details on the main data dictionary database objects affected and the steps to solve this problem with extreme care, refer to Chapter 13.

With the default Oracle settings, several of the PL/SQL database objects are fragmented when the database is created. The more stored PL/SQL in your database, the higher level of fragmentation will occur, unless it is addressed.

TIP
Object storage fragmentation can cause performance degradation, and the data dictionary should be considered in your defragmentation efforts. Handle this defragmentation with extreme caution and ensure you have performed complete backups prior to defragmenting the data dictionary.

Review the PL/SQL Source Code Storage Size

Oracle contains a data dictionary view to provide a window into one component of memory related to the stored PL/SQL program units. The view actually stores information beyond stored PL/SQL objects, but the focus of this section will be limited to the PL/SQL specific objects.

This USER_OBJECT_SIZE (DBA_OBJECT_SIZE) view identifies three important memory components to each of these stored PL/SQL program units.

■ **Source size (SOURCE_SIZE)**   Size of source code in bytes (loaded during compilation)

■ **Parsed size (PARSED_SIZE)**   Size of memory in bytes loaded into memory when an object is compiling that references this object

■ **Code size (CODE_SIZE)**   Size of p-code in bytes (loaded during execution)

The following script illustrates this information retrieval for PL/SQL-related objects only.

File: 9_1.sql

```
SELECT name, type, source_size, parsed_size, code_size
FROM   user_object_size
WHERE  type IN ('PACKAGE', 'PACKAGE BODY',
       'PROCEDURE', 'FUNCTION', 'TRIGGER')
ORDER BY type, name;
```

Output (9_1.sql)

NAME	TYPE	SOURCE_SIZE	PARSED_SIZE	CODE_SIZE
VALIDATE_DATE_FORMAT	FUNCTION	354	880	669
GLOBAL	PACKAGE	45	206	77
GLOBAL	PACKAGE BODY	58	0	111
LOG_EXTENTS	PROCEDURE	454	1181	563
LOG_SOURCE	PROCEDURE	1978	3875	2474

Additional information relating to this data dictionary view is provided in Chapter 13 and Appendix C.

TIP
The parsed_size for all package body types will be 0, because objects referencing any package contents look at the package specification during compilation, not the package body. This is covered in further detail in Chapter 5.

Build a Solid Security Model for PL/SQL Objects

PL/SQL introduces a new layer of responsibility for the DBA, but also a powerful mechanism allowing a different security architecture that was previously unavailable in Oracle. An entire chapter is devoted in this book to security; refer to Chapter 10 for detailed information regarding PL/SQL security.

PL/SQL security is not hard to establish, but a DBA must understand how the PL/SQL security model works. The PL/SQL security model is slightly different than just granting access on an object. The concept is fundamentally different. If you remember the following, applying the necessary security will be easy.

- **Creating Stored PL/SQL Program Units**   When a developer creates a stored package, procedure, or function, the schema that is creating the program unit must have the necessary access to any operations performed in the program unit (Oracle system privileges: ALTER SESSION, CREATE TABLE, and so forth; Object privileges: SELECT, INSERT, UPDATE, or DELETE; Stored Object Privilege: EXECUTE).

  Example: If an UPDATE is performed on the s_employee table in the program unit, then the schema creating the PL/SQL program unit must have UPDATE privilege on s_employee.

- **Executing Stored PL/SQL Program Units**   Once a stored PL/SQL program unit is created and compiled in the database, it is accessible to any schema that has been granted EXECUTE privilege on the stored PL/SQL unit. This is extremely important to understand: The schema that has been granted EXECUTE *does not* have to have any other privileges on the underlying objects referenced in the stored PL/SQL program unit. The reason is the execution of the stored program unit executes with the PL/SQL program unit creator's privilege, *not the calling schema's privilege.*

  Example: If user JOE was executing the program unit that updates the s_employee table, the UPDATE would be successful as long as JOE has been granted EXECUTE on the program unit, even though JOE does not have UPDATE privilege on s_employee.

■ **Referencing Stored PL/SQL Program Units**   When referencing a stored PL/SQL program unit, it is the same as a table or view with regards to prefixing the object with the username. Therefore, it is recommended to treat these program units the same as tables and views and to create PUBLIC synonyms on these program units with the same name as the program unit name.

■ **Caveat 1: Creating Stored PL/SQL Program Units**   When a stored PL/SQL program unit is being created, the schema creating the program unit must have all the required privileges to the referenced objects through a DIRECT GRANT to their schema. If privilege has been granted to the schema through a *role, it will not succeed because privilege must be direct, not through a role.*

Example: If an UPDATE is performed on the s_employee table in the PL/SQL program unit, and the schema creating the program unit has UPDATE privilege on s_employee through a role, the creation and compilation of the program unit will fail.

■ **Caveat 2: Executing Oracle Supplied Packages**   When a schema executes an Oracle supplied package (actually a procedure or function within one of the packages), the package is executed with the calling schema's privilege, not the creator of the package.

Example: If user JOE attempts to execute the procedure DBMS_SESSION.SET_SQL_TRACE, then JOE must have EXECUTE privilege on the DBMS_SESSION package, and JOE must also have ALTER SESSION privilege.

■ **Caveat 3: Executing Oracle Supplied Packages**   Even though a schema may have access to execute one of the Oracle supplied packages, it does not mean they will be able to execute the command successfully. The schema must still have the proper access to the DDL, DML, or other operations in addition to privilege on the package.

Example: If user JOE attempts to execute the procedure DBMS_SESSION.SET_SQL_TRACE, even though JOE has EXECUTE privilege on the DBMS_SESSION package, because JOE does not have ALTER SESSION privilege, the execution will fail.

PL/SQL security needs to be enforced as part of the standard security model. With the method of security authentication that Oracle implements with stored PL/SQL program units, tremendous flexibility exists when designing your security model. Make sure you have a thorough understanding of this area. Refer to

Chapter 10 on security, Chapter 11 on Oracle supplied package security, and Chapter 13 for valuable scripts that provide information related to PL/SQL security.

TIP
Stored PL/SQL program units provide an additional security method that should be understood prior to architecting a security scheme. The importance of solid security is monumental, although I have yet to meet an Oracle DBA who feels his or her system is completely secure.

TIP
A new option in Oracle 8.1 on stored PL/SQL program unit creation provides additional flexibility in PL/SQL security as outlined in Chapter 16.

Explore the Oracle Supplied Packages for the DBA

Oracle has continued to expand the arsenal of supplied packages with each new version. Many of these packages contain valuable procedures and functions that are specifically focused on DBA-related commands for carrying out DBA responsibilities. Most of these commands can be executed from within SQL*Plus, but having knowledge of them—even if you are unable to program in PL/SQL—is extremely important when working with developers to diagnose problem areas in their PL/SQL code. If you can program in PL/SQL, then these Oracle supplied packages will immediately be of greater value to you.

Take the time to read (or at least scan) Chapter 11 and Chapter 12. This will be worth the time you invest. I have found the Oracle supplied packages are the most underused and unknown component of PL/SQL. Part of this is due to limited emphasis on the functionality, flexibility, and power these packages provide. More recently, these packages have gained more attention, but still, far too many developers and DBAs are truly unaware of this tremendous gift Oracle has provided.

The following is a list of some of the powerful capabilities that can be performed with these packages:

- Build an alerting, monitoring, and/or history logging system that is either synchronous or asynchronous (transaction or nontransaction based).

- Schedule procedures to execute once or at a regularly scheduled interval.

- Log information to a file that contains information about activity in the database or special conditions.

- Integrate logging information into long executing processes to reveal how long an operation has been executing and how many records have been processed.

- Turn SQL TRACE ON for the current session when a certain condition is reached or for a specific user who executes the process. Or turn on TRACE for any session in the system based on certain conditions such as resource usage.

- Dynamically execute SQL statements, DML, DDL, or PL/SQL commands to perform complex logic based on the user or application.

- Expand SQL tuning by setting timers in PL/SQL code and by uniquely identifying SQL statements for viewing in the V$SQLAREA view.

- Pin PL/SQL objects and cursors in the Shared Pool to increase performance.

- Review used and unused free space for database objects.

- Compute statistics for an object, schema, or database.

- Compile objects or schema objects.

- Modify session specific conditions and transaction specific conditions.

This list only scratches the surface of the overall functionality provided in these supplied packages.

Know When to Encrypt PL/SQL Source Code

Oracle stores PL/SQL program unit source code in the data dictionary, namely in the underlying USER_SOURCE (ALL_SOURCE and DBA_SOURCE) view tables. Being able to view and query this information online is very helpful, providing the capability to recreate the SQL creation scripts for stored PL/SQL objects. However, herein lie three reasons for potential danger.

1. Confidential or proprietary business rules or functionality can be embedded in the PL/SQL source code, accessible to Oracle users by querying the data dictionary.

2. PL/SQL stored packages, procedures, and functions typically contain the major complexity of the applications. Modification of this logic by someone could damage the core of the application, thus causing major problems. Because the logic is in the data dictionary, it provides the capability to

rebuild the PL/SQL stored objects in a SQL script, modify the logic, and then re-create the object. This re-creation of the object would require certain privileges, but it is still a potential problem.

3. Many Oracle development environments follow standard development methodologies with a version control mechanism. This mechanism controls the access to the source code; however, if the version control mechanism is not used and is bypassed, major problems can arise. If someone modifies a stored PL/SQL object, as outlined in the previous point, and implements the changes in production, the next time the proper steps are followed (that is, using the version control) to make changes to the module, it will nullify the previous, nonstandard changes.

When reviewing your PL/SQL development environment, take the necessary steps to reduce the risk of the potential danger previously noted. Two methods can be deployed to minimize this risk, outside the normal Oracle standard security capabilities. First, in the data dictionary views, USER_SOURCE, ALL_SOURCE and DBA_SOURCE, access can be limited to only certain Oracle schema. Second, the PL/SQL stored objects can be encrypted through Oracle's WRAP facility. The WRAP facility is covered in more detail in Chapter 5.

TIP

Use the WRAP facility to convert a stored PL/SQL module creation script into a "wrapped" version, disallowing curious minds from attaining source code access. This type of security is usually not needed because the basic Oracle security forces users to be granted rights to another schema's objects. If confidential business logic or critical core functionality is involved, "wrapping" the source code is the only way to be sure the logic is unreadable.

TIP

An additional step is to back up the DBA_SOURCE view on a regular interval (only new or changed source code). This technique is outlined in further detail in Chapter 3 and is accomplished with one PL/SQL procedure. The submission of this procedure for regular execution is detailed in Chapter 12 with the DBMS_JOB package. This is not a cure-all, but it is a great means of providing another level of backup that can even be hidden from developers.

Understand the PL/SQL Versus SQL Engine

It is extremely important for a DBA to understand the difference between the PL/SQL Engine and the SQL Engine. This understanding extends to the knowledge of the Oracle product sets that come standard with a PL/SQL Engine. Chapter 14 provides a detailed explanation of the difference between the PL/SQL Engine and the SQL Engine, as well as highlighting the difference between PL/SQL Engine processing on the client-side versus the server-side.

The method in which the PL/SQL Engine processes SQL statements is far different than many advocate and should be understood in detail, especially by the DBA, and especially when dealing with performance optimization.

Evaluate Impact Analysis at a Detailed Level

As the number of stored PL/SQL program units and database objects increases in an application, performing impact analysis when a modification or enhancement is needed becomes increasingly difficult. However, Oracle has dependency data dictionary views that provide a dependency mapping between database objects. This provides a powerful mechanism to determine the impact a PL/SQL program unit or database table change will have in your system. The more stored PL/SQL program unit code in your application, the more useful and more complete the dependency analysis can be performed. In Chapter 13, information is provided on obtaining dependency information, which concentrates on querying the USER_DEPENDENCY (ALL_DEPENDENCY and DBA_DEPENDENCY) views. The information provided in Chapter 13 is a high-level (actually one level) look at dependencies.

For a more complete dependency-mapping tree, the following PL/SQL program unit will return a complete dependency mapping for a specific object. This package contains the find_dep procedure that traverses the dependency map either top-down or bottom-up, depending on the parameter passed. The three input variables are

- **p_direction_txt**   Enter **T** for top-down traversal or **B** for bottom-up traversal.
- **p_object_name_txt**   Enter the name of the object to show the dependency tree (for packages, both the specification and body are traversed).
- **p_owner_txt**   Enter the user that owns the object (defaults to the current user).

The complete dependency_tree package is shown in the following scripts:

File: 9_2.sql

```
CREATE OR REPLACE PACKAGE dependency_tree AS
   - This package will traverse top-down (p_direction_txt = T) or
   - bottom-up (p_direction_txt = B)
   PROCEDURE find_dep
      (p_direction_txt   IN VARCHAR2,
      p_object_name_txt IN VARCHAR2,
      p_owner_txt       IN VARCHAR2 :=USER);
   PROCEDURE get_dep
      (p_direction_txt   IN VARCHAR2,
      p_direction_msg2   IN VARCHAR2,
      p_object_owner_txt IN VARCHAR2,
      p_object_name_txt  IN VARCHAR2,
      p_object_type_txt  IN VARCHAR2,
      p_index_num        IN PLS_INTEGER);
   FUNCTION repeat_char
      (p_repeat_num IN PLS_INTEGER,
      p_repeat_txt  IN VARCHAR2 := '-') RETURN VARCHAR2;
END dependency_tree;
/
```

File: 9_2a.sql

```
CREATE OR REPLACE PACKAGE BODY dependency_tree AS
----------------------------------------------------
PROCEDURE find_dep
   (p_direction_txt   IN VARCHAR2,
   p_object_name_txt IN VARCHAR2,
   p_owner_txt       IN VARCHAR2 :=USER) AS
   CURSOR cur_objects IS
      SELECT owner, object_name, object_type
      FROM   dba_objects
      WHERE  object_name = UPPER(p_object_name_txt)
      AND    owner       = UPPER(p_owner_txt);
   lv_count_num      PLS_INTEGER := 0;
   lv_string_txt     VARCHAR2(60);
   lv_direction_txt  VARCHAR2(1);
   lv_direction_msg  VARCHAR2(10);
   lv_direction_msg2 VARCHAR2(25);
BEGIN
   lv_direction_txt := UPPER(p_direction_txt);
   IF lv_direction_txt = 'B' THEN
```

```
          lv_direction_msg   := 'BOTTOM-UP';
          lv_direction_msg2 := 'Referenced by Object ';
      ELSE
          lv_direction_msg   := 'TOP-DOWN';
          lv_direction_msg2 := 'References Object ';
          lv_direction_txt   := 'T';
      END IF;
      lv_string_txt := repeat_char(55, '-');
      DBMS_OUTPUT.PUT_LINE(lv_string_txt);
      DBMS_OUTPUT.PUT_LINE('START OF DEPENDENCY TREE LISTING (' ||
          lv_direction_msg || ')');
      FOR cur_objects_rec IN cur_objects LOOP
          lv_count_num := lv_count_num + 1;
          DBMS_OUTPUT.PUT_LINE(lv_string_txt);
          DBMS_OUTPUT.PUT_LINE('Dependencies for ' ||
              cur_objects_rec.object_type || ' ' ||
              cur_objects_rec.owner || '.' ||
              cur_objects_rec.object_name);
          DBMS_OUTPUT.PUT_LINE(lv_string_txt);
          get_dep(lv_direction_txt, lv_direction_msg2,
              cur_objects_rec.owner,
              cur_objects_rec.object_name,
              cur_objects_rec.object_type, 0);
      END LOOP;
      IF lv_count_num = 0 THEN
          DBMS_OUTPUT.PUT_LINE(lv_string_txt);
          DBMS_OUTPUT.PUT_LINE('Object ' || p_owner_txt ||
              '.' || p_object_name_txt || ' does not exist.');
      END IF;
      DBMS_OUTPUT.PUT_LINE('');
      DBMS_OUTPUT.PUT_LINE(lv_string_txt);
      DBMS_OUTPUT.PUT_LINE('END OF DEPENDENCY TREE LISTING (' ||
          lv_direction_msg || ')');
      DBMS_OUTPUT.PUT_LINE(lv_string_txt);
  END find_dep;
  ---------------------------------------------------
  PROCEDURE get_dep
      (p_direction_txt    IN VARCHAR2,
       p_direction_msg2   IN VARCHAR2,
       p_object_owner_txt IN VARCHAR2,
       p_object_name_txt  IN VARCHAR2,
       p_object_type_txt  IN VARCHAR2,
       p_index_num        IN PLS_INTEGER) AS
      CURSOR cur_dep_objects_down IS
          SELECT referenced_owner owner, referenced_name name,
                 referenced_type type
          FROM   dba_dependencies
          WHERE  owner              = p_object_owner_txt
```

```
      AND    name                = p_object_name_txt
      AND    type                = p_object_type_txt
      AND    referenced_type  != 'NON-EXISTENT'
--    AND    referenced_owner <> 'SYS'   - Eliminate SYS objects
      ORDER BY referenced_owner, referenced_type, referenced_name;
  CURSOR cur_dep_objects_up IS
    SELECT owner, name, type
    FROM   dba_dependencies
    WHERE  referenced_owner = p_object_owner_txt
    AND    referenced_name = p_object_name_txt
    AND    referenced_type = p_object_type_txt
--    AND    owner             <> 'SYS'   - Eliminate SYS objects
      ORDER BY referenced_owner, referenced_type, referenced_name;
  lv_call_level_num    PLS_INTEGER := 0;
  lv_loop_index_num    PLS_INTEGER := 0;
  lv_object_owner_txt  VARCHAR2(30);
  lv_object_name_txt   VARCHAR2(100);
  lv_object_type_txt   VARCHAR2(20);
  lv_object_owner_txt2 VARCHAR2(30);
  lv_object_name_txt2  VARCHAR2(100);
  lv_object_type_txt2  VARCHAR2(20);
  lv_repeat_string_txt VARCHAR2(500) := '-';
BEGIN
  lv_call_level_num    := p_index_num + 1;
  lv_repeat_string_txt := repeat_char(lv_call_level_num, '-');
  lv_object_owner_txt  := p_object_owner_txt;
  lv_object_name_txt   := p_object_name_txt;
  lv_object_type_txt   := p_object_type_txt;
    IF p_direction_txt = 'T' THEN
      FOR cur_dep_objects_rec IN cur_dep_objects_down LOOP
        lv_loop_index_num    := lv_loop_index_num + 1;
        lv_object_owner_txt2 := cur_dep_objects_rec.owner;
        lv_object_name_txt2  := cur_dep_objects_rec.name;
        lv_object_type_txt2  := cur_dep_objects_rec.type;
        DBMS_OUTPUT.PUT_LINE(lv_repeat_string_txt || '> ' ||
          p_direction_msg2 || lv_object_owner_txt2 || '.' ||
        lv_object_name_txt2 || ' <' || lv_object_type_txt2 || '>');
        -- Recurse each branch for all relationships
        get_dep(p_direction_txt, p_direction_msg2,
              lv_object_owner_txt2, lv_object_name_txt2,
              lv_object_type_txt2, lv_call_level_num);
      END LOOP;
    ELSE
      FOR cur_dep_objects_rec IN cur_dep_objects_up LOOP
        lv_loop_index_num := lv_loop_index_num + 1;
        lv_object_owner_txt2 := cur_dep_objects_rec.owner;
        lv_object_name_txt2  := cur_dep_objects_rec.name;
        lv_object_type_txt2  := cur_dep_objects_rec.type;
```

```
                    DBMS_OUTPUT.PUT_LINE(lv_repeat_string_txt || '> ' ||
                        p_direction_msg2 || lv_object_owner_txt2 || '.' ||
                        lv_object_name_txt2 || ' <' ||
                        lv_object_type_txt2 || '>');
                    -- Recurse each branch for all relationships
                    get_dep(p_direction_txt, p_direction_msg2,
                            lv_object_owner_txt2, lv_object_name_txt2,
                            lv_object_type_txt2, lv_call_level_num);
            END LOOP;
        END IF;
    IF lv_loop_index_num = 0 AND lv_call_level_num = 1 THEN
        DBMS_OUTPUT.PUT_LINE('Object ' ||
            p_object_owner_txt || '.' ||
            lv_object_name_txt || ' has no dependencies.');
    END IF;
END get_dep;
-------------------------------------------------------
FUNCTION repeat_char
    (p_repeat_num IN PLS_INTEGER,
    p_repeat_txt  IN VARCHAR2 := '-')
    RETURN VARCHAR2 IS
    lv_string_txt VARCHAR2(500) := '-';
BEGIN
    FOR lv_num IN 0..p_repeat_num LOOP
        lv_string_txt := lv_string_txt || '-';
    END LOOP;
RETURN lv_string_txt;
END repeat_char;
-------------------------------------------------------
END dependency_tree;
/
```

To illustrate the dependency tree, five procedures that are dependent on one another are created in the following script.

File: 9_3.sql

```
CREATE PROCEDURE E AS
BEGIN
    NULL;
END;
/
CREATE PROCEDURE D AS
BEGIN
    E;
```

```
END;
/
CREATE PROCEDURE C AS
BEGIN
    D;
END;
/
CREATE PROCEDURE B AS
BEGIN
    C;
END;
/
CREATE PROCEDURE A AS
BEGIN
    B;
END;
/
```

The following output illustrates the execution of the dependency tree for the five procedures previously created in the top-down map (the *T* stands for top-down and the *A* signifies the dependency map for procedure *A* is desired).

Output (9_2.sql)

```
SET SERVEROUTPUT ON SIZE 1000000
EXECUTE dependency_tree.find_dep('T','A');


--------------------------------
START OF DEPENDENCY TREE LISTING (TOP-DOWN)
--------------------------------
Dependencies for PROCEDURE PLSQL_USER.A
--------------------------------
----> References Object PLSQL_USER.B <PROCEDURE>
----> References Object PLSQL_USER.C <PROCEDURE>
------> References Object PLSQL_USER.D <PROCEDURE>
-------> References Object PLSQL_USER.E <PROCEDURE>
------------------------------------------------------
END OF DEPENDENCY TREE LISTING (TOP-DOWN)
------------------------------------------------------

PL/SQL procedure successfully completed.
```

The following output illustrates the execution of the dependency tree for the five procedures previously created in the bottom-up map (the *B* stands for bottom-up and the *E* signifies the dependency map for procedure *E* is desired).

Output (9_2.sql)

```
EXECUTE dependency_tree.find_dep('B', 'E');


------------------------------------------------------
START OF DEPENDENCY TREE LISTING (BOTTOM-UP)
------------------------------------------------------
Dependencies for PROCEDURE PLSQL_USER.E
------------------------------------------------------
----> Referenced by Object PLSQL_USER.D <PROCEDURE>
-----> Referenced by Object PLSQL_USER.C <PROCEDURE>
------> Referenced by Object PLSQL_USER.B <PROCEDURE>
-------> Referenced by Object PLSQL_USER.A <PROCEDURE>
------------------------------------------------------
END OF DEPENDENCY TREE LISTING (BOTTOM-UP)
------------------------------------------------------

PL/SQL procedure successfully completed.
```

Note that in the preceding output, each level of the tree is indented with one more hyphen ('-').

Pinpoint Invalid PL/SQL Objects

Developers and DBAs must ensure that all stored PL/SQL objects are compiled successfully when any object is created or modified. If this is not verified, your system may not function properly. This can be very damaging to an environment and must be corrected immediately.

When a stored PL/SQL object is created, Oracle inserts the source code into the database and attempts to compile the source code. If the compilation is successful, then the status is set to VALID. When compilation is performed on an existing stored PL/SQL object that is referenced by another stored PL/SQL object, the stored object that references the object becomes INVALID. If any object becomes INVALID in this manner, it should be recompiled immediately.

The following script demonstrates the method of determining which objects are INVALID:

File: 9_4 .sql

```
SELECT    owner, object_type, object_name, status,
          TO_CHAR(created, 'MM/DD/YY HH24:MI:SS') created,
          TO_CHAR(last_ddl_time, 'MM/DD/YY HH24:MI:SS') modified
FROM      dba_objects
```

```
WHERE object_type IN ('PROCEDURE', 'FUNCTION', 'PACKAGE',
                      'PACKAGE BODY', 'TRIGGER')
AND    status = 'INVALID'
AND    owner  = 'PLSQL_USER'
ORDER BY owner, object_type, object_name;
```

Output (9_4.sql)

```
OBJECT_TYPE   OBJECT_NAME    STATUS   CREATED             MODIFIED
------------  -------------- -------  ------------------  ---------
PACKAGE       CLOSE          INVALID  03/06/99 13:53:20  03/06/99 14:12:53
PACKAGE BODY  CLOSE          INVALID  03/06/99 13:55:04  03/06/99 14:12:53
PROCEDURE     ADJUST_SALARY  INVALID  10/13/98 15:22:02  02/15/99 12:21:18
```

To ensure an uninterrupted system, the following guidelines should be integrated as a standard into your Oracle production environment:
– All stored PL/SQL object creations and modifications are performed during off hours.
– After creating or modifying any database object, the 9_4.sql script file must be executed and return no records. If any records exist, the objects should be recompiled immediately.
Oracle will attempt to recompile INVALID objects when the object is called for execution and, often this results in a successful compilation and execution. The process of compiling the object when called takes time and the exact time is dependent on the size of the object. Even more important are the consequences if the compilation fails: potential disaster if it's during production hours.

The impact of not following these guidelines is directly related to the size and architecture of your environment, specifically centering around the number of users, the volume of transactions, and the stored PL/SQL object design and configuration. The larger your system, the more chance for locking and contention-related problems for compiling PL/SQL objects. The larger your application, the larger the number of PL/SQL stored objects and object dependencies and, thus, the larger problems with dependent object recompilation. The main impact can be measured in downtime and user frustration, which is a common result of not following the preceding guidelines.

Pinpointing Invalid PL/SQL Objects

For more information related to stored PL/SQL compilation, refer to Chapter 5 (PL/SQL object re-compilation procedure) and Chapter 10.

TIP
Always execute the INVALID script (9_4.sql) after object modification and always manually recompile all objects prior to production hours (or use the re-compilation procedure provided in Chapter 5) .

Identify Disabled Database Triggers

Disabled database triggers are companions to invalid objects. In some respects, a disabled trigger is far more dangerous than an invalid object because it doesn't fail; *it just doesn't execute!* This can have severe consequences for applications (and, consequently, for business processes) that depend on business logic stored within procedural code in database triggers. For this reason, you MUST execute the following script on a daily basis:

File: 9_5.sql

```
SELECT owner, trigger_name, trigger_type,
       triggering_event, table_owner||'.'||table_name
FROM   dba_triggers
WHERE  status <> 'ENABLED'
AND    owner = 'PLSQL_USER'
ORDER BY owner, trigger_name;
```

Output (9_5.sql)

```
Trigger Name          Type             Event  Owner/Table
--------------------- ---------------- ------ ---------------------
BEFORE_INSERT_CUSTOMER BEFORE EACH ROW INSERT PLSQL_USER.S_CUSTOMER
```

Once the triggers are identified, they can be enabled manually or a dynamic SQL or PL/SQL script can be created to build the SQL statements to ENABLE the triggers. For more information on enabling and disabling triggers, refer to Chapter 13.

TIP
Always ensure database triggers are enabled since database triggers are the database gatekeepers and the last line of defense. Database triggers should always be monitored and enabled. If this DISABLE script (9_5.sql) is not executed, no message will be displayed to indicate the database trigger is disabled. The longer the database trigger remains disabled, the larger the problem that must be corrected.

Review PL/SQL Related init.ora Parameters

Several init.ora parameters can be set and modified, which have an effect on PL/SQL-related areas. The correct settings for each of these variables is dependent on your system and application, but the most important aspect of these parameters is to know what they affect and the general guideline for setting each. This section limits the scope to only the main PL/SQL related init.ora parameters.

Remember, the init.ora parameters available change from version to version. The following script illustrates the means for viewing the init.ora parameters on your system.

File: 9_6.sql

```
SELECT name, value, isdefault,
       isses_modifiable, issys_modifiable
FROM   v$parameter
ORDER BY name;
```

Output (9_6.sql)

NAME	VALUE	ISDEFAULT	ISSES_MOD	ISSYS_MOD
cursor_space_for_time	FALSE	TRUE	FALSE	FALSE
job_queue_interval	60	TRUE	FALSE	FALSE
job_queue_processes	1	FALSE	FALSE	FALSE

open_cursors	250	FALSE	FALSE	FALSE
optimizer_mode	CHOOSE	FALSE	FALSE	FALSE
session_cached_cursors	0	TRUE	FALSE	FALSE
shared_pool_reserved_min_alloc	5000	TRUE	FALSE	FALSE
shared_pool_reserved_size	0	TRUE	FALSE	FALSE
shared_pool_size	3500000	TRUE	FALSE	FALSE
sort_area_size	65536	TRUE	FALSE	FALSE
utl_file_dir		TRUE	FALSE	FALSE

The preceding query can be modified to view any parameters that have been changed by default or to view any parameters that can be changed per session (ALTER SESSION command) and for the entire system (ALTER SYSTEM command). The parameters with the columns, isses_modifiable, and issys_modifiable that are not set to FALSE, indicate the parameters that can be changed with an ALTER command, without shutting down the instance for the parameter modification to take effect. The preceding listing does not show any parameters can be modified. This listing is from version 7.3 (and is only PL/SQL-related parameters; several other parameters in version 7.3 can be changed with the ALTER command). The parameter listing is shown later in this section for version 8.0 and shows several of these parameters that are now changeable with the ALTER command. Each release of Oracle continues to expand the number of parameters that are changeable with the ALTER command. The preceding query can be executed on your system to determine the changeable parameters with your release.

TIP

Changing the init.ora parameters without stopping and restarting the instance can be extremely helpful for a short-term fix until the next instance shutdown (make sure to change the init.ora parameter because the ALTER SYSTEM result only remains in effect until the next instance startup). This can also be helpful when an init.ora parameter is a per-session value, one process requires a higher value for one of the parameters, and you cannot afford to set it for all sessions (in this case, the ALTER SESSION is a nice solution). A good example of altering a session parameter is the sort_area_size for a session that is executing a large program.

TIP
Do not rely on your knowledge of which init.ora parameters are changeable, as previously outlined. Execute the previous query to ensure because the number of init.ora parameters that can be modified real-time continues to grow tremendously with each new version.

Following is a list of each of the PL/SQL-related init.ora parameters with a description for each (Oracle 7.3).

Name	Default Value	Description
cursor_space_ for_time	FALSE	Specifies that more space will be allocated to cursor management of open cursors; this should only be set if the Shared Pool has been optimized and additional memory is available to handle more cursors; set dependent on your system and application
job_queue_ interval	60	Specifies the time interval at which the background job processes wake up to process awaiting jobs in the job queue that were submitted from the DBMS_JOB package (parameter is measured in seconds; the range is 1-3600); set dependent on the frequency of job executions; specific to the DBMS_JOB package use
job_queue_ processes	0	Specifies the number of background processes to create to process the job queue (if 0, no jobs will be processed; the range is 0-36); set dependent on the number of jobs executing in the job queue at any point in time; specific to the DBMS_JOB package use
open_cursors	50	Specifies the maximum number of cursors that can be opened per session; set dependent on application use of cursors (there is no overhead if this value is set higher than actually needed and the maximum is operating system dependent)

Name	Default Value	Description
optimizer_mode	choose	Specifies the default SQL optimization mode used; CHOOSE: uses cost-based optimizer if one of the database tables in the statement has been analyzed; FIRST_ROWS: uses cost-based optimizer with the execution plans determined based on minimizing initial response time; ALL_ROWS: uses cost-based optimizer with the execution plans determined based on minimizing overall retrieval time; RULE: uses rule-based optimizer unless hints are used; set dependent on the optimization method desired for SQL execution
session_cached_ cursors	0	Specifies the number of session cursors to cache; allows parsed calls to the same SQL statements to be cached and eliminates the need to reopen cursors; set based on the maximum number of cursors per session to keep in the cursor cache
shared_pool_size	3500000	This is an EXTREMELY IMPORTANT parameter that affects the overall performance of your system and ranks in the top three init.ora parameters that can affect your system the most; specifies the size of the Shared Pool that contains the library cache, dictionary cache, shared object cache, shared SQL cache (SQL Area), and other memory structures; refer to the section later in this chapter that focuses on monitoring the Shared Pool; set dependent on your system and application and monitor each cache regularly to ensure proper setting
shared_pool_ reserved_min_ alloc	5000	Specifies the minimum memory size of an object that will be able to use the Shared Pool space reserved with the shared_pool_reserved_size init.ora parameter; set dependent on the reserved size setting and the application module sizes as viewed in V$DB_OBJECT_CACHE and V$SQLAREA views (this parameter is eliminated in Oracle 8.1)

Name	Default Value	Description
shared_pool_ reserved_size	0	Specifies the size of the Shared Pool size reserved for larger objects that use the Shared Pool; in recent versions, this value defaults to 5 percent of the Shared Pool and can be set as high as 50 percent of the Shared Pool; the goal is to optimize the Shared Pool size and pin appropriate objects and reduce the need for reserving space; set dependent on your system and application modules
sort_area_size	65536	Specifies the maximum amount of operating system memory that can be used per session for large sorts; this is outside the SGA and is per session; therefore, be careful with this setting because it is per session; if the sort cannot be performed in the sort_area_size, then it will be performed inside the database in the temporary space segments
utl_file_dir	NULL	Specifies the operating system directories the UTL_FILE package can read from and write to; multiple directories can be specified and when a directory is specified, it enables read and write access to all files in this directory via the UTL_FILE package; this privilege overrides the operating system privilege on these directories; set dependent on specific directories that are set aside for these files and make sure these directories should be accessible to all Oracle users via the UTL_FILE package; if no files are specified, then the UTL_FILE package cannot be used; it is not recommended to specify wildcards as in '*'; specific to the UTL_FILE package

The default values, and whether the values are changeable real-time, change significantly from version to version (especially when looking at all init.ora parameters). The following output is from Oracle 8.0 to illustrate some of the differences between versions. The values shown for the changeable state of parameters is the same for Oracle 8.0 and 8.1 with the shared_pool_reserved_min_alloc parameter being eliminated in 8.1.

Reviewing PL/SQL Related init.ora Parameters

Output (9_6.sql)

NAME	VALUE	ISDEFAULT	ISSES_MOD	ISSYS_MOD
cursor_space_for_time	FALSE	TRUE	FALSE	FALSE
job_queue_interval	60	FALSE	FALSE	FALSE
job_queue_processes	2	FALSE	FALSE	IMMEDIATE
open_cursors	500	FALSE	FALSE	FALSE
optimizer_mode	CHOOSE	TRUE	TRUE	FALSE
session_cached_cursors	0	TRUE	TRUE	FALSE
shared_pool_reserved_min_alloc	4K	TRUE	FALSE	FALSE
shared_pool_reserved_size	900000	TRUE	FALSE	FALSE
shared_pool_size	18000000	FALSE	FALSE	FALSE
sort_area_size	65536	FALSE	TRUE	DEFERRED
utl_file_dir	d:\tusc_output	FALSE	FALSE	FALSE

The list of changeable parameters has grown between versions and the control of certain Oracle system areas has increased.

TIP

The init.ora parameters vary based on the Oracle options installed on your system. With each new version of Oracle, review the init.ora parameters in the new version; Oracle not only adds new init.ora parameters, Oracle also eliminates certain parameters. Many parameters have been eliminated by Oracle in version 8.1, some of which were introduced in version 8.0.

TIP

The V$PARAMETER view displays all init.ora parameters; however, a set of undocumented and hidden parameters is also available and usable. These parameters are not supported by Oracle and should only be used in a limited set of cases or as a last resort in a crisis situation. These parameters should only be used by an experienced DBA. Remember, use of these are at your own risk. The list can be found by executing the following query:

File: 9_7.sql

```
SELECT  indx, ksppinm
FROM    x$ksppi
WHERE   SUBSTR(ksppinm,1,1) = '_';
```

Output (9_7.sql)

```
INDX     KSPPINM
-------- -----------------------------
    20  _debug_sga
    32  _trace_buffers_per_process
    33  _trace_block_size
    34  _trace_archive_start
    38  _trace_archive_dest
    39  _trace_file_size
    94  _log_buffers_debug
    99  _disable_logging
   115  _allow_resetlogs_corruption
   126  _log_space_errors
   135  _corrupted_rollback_segments
   179  _init_sql_file
   239  _oracle_trace_events
   240  _oracle_trace_facility_version
```

Once again, these undocumented init.ora parameters should only be used with extreme caution and with the guidance of someone who has previously used them. These parameters can be helpful and they can also be disastrous. They provide a means for setting certain conditions in the database that provides another layer of information or recovery capability. Knowing these exist is important, but be careful. This script should only be executed when you are told to run this by a DBA who has previously modified these parameters.

TIP
In Oracle 8.0, any undocumented init.ora parameter that is modified will display in the query from the V$PARAMETER view.

Monitor the Shared Pool Use to Determine Optimization

A significant impact of moving PL/SQL application code to the database in the form of stored packages, procedures, functions, and database triggers is the impact of the size of the application code on the Shared Pool. When a procedure or function contained within a package is referenced through an application call, the entire package is loaded into the Shared Pool. This reality dictates an organized approach to application development. Rather than singularly organizing application code into packages based on application requirements, you must also consider the reusability of code across all applications. This requires a more significant DBA role in application design, ideally before application coding begins. The DBA can provide vital insight and awareness to designers who, ultimately, will rely on the DBA for guidance and support when an application is introduced into the production environment. The DBA, on the other hand, can anticipate the impact of the new application on the production system and address resource demands ahead of time.

Look for opportunities to build utility or service packages that provide the same functionality and, consequently, can be shared by all applications operating within the same database. The DBA should periodically check and record the growth in the Shared Pool. Applications change frequently; their space requirements in the Shared Pool (and data dictionary) often grow over time. Use the following query to identify the space occupied by stored application code in the SGA. The space used by 'SYS' owned packages should remain relatively constant over time, unless additional Oracle supplied packages are installed to enable additional features.

To increase the size of the Shared Pool, increase the shared_pool_size init.ora parameter. The value of this parameter is expressed in bytes and should be entered in the form *shared_pool_size = value* . The default value is 3500000 on most systems and the upper bound of this parameter is operating system dependent.

To view the contents of the Shared Pool, query the V$SGASTAT view as indicated in the following example. These results are selected from an Oracle 8.0.4 instance at startup with a shared_pool_size parameter of 18000000 bytes.

File: 9_8.sql

```
SELECT pool, name, bytes
FROM   v$sgastat
ORDER BY pool, name;
```

The output is only a subset of the 33 records that exist in the V$$GASTAT view.

Output: (9_8.sql)

```
POOL        NAME                              BYTES
----------- ------------------------------- -------
shared pool PL/SQL DIANA                    2660060
shared pool PL/SQL MPCODE                   1399220
shared pool PLS non-lib hp                     2096
shared pool dictionary cache               3468400
shared pool free memory                    2435956
shared pool library cache                  3633416
shared pool sql area                       2992288
            db_block_buffers               6553600
            fixed_sga                        47788
            log_buffer                      163840
```

The V$SGASTAT view details the amount of memory allocated to the various memory structures of the SGA. In Oracle 8.0, a new column called pool was added to enable the new feature of segmenting the Shared Pool. As shown, the last three memory structures are not part of the Shared Pool memory, but relate to other memory structures in the SGA that are set by other init.ora parameters. The following is a high-level breakdown of the SGA, as seen by querying the V$SGA view.

File: 9_9.sql

```
SELECT *
FROM   v$sga;
```

Output (9_9.sql)

```
NAME                      VALUE
--------------------  ---------
Fixed Size                47788
Variable Size          19755008
Database Buffers        6553600
Redo Buffers             172032
```

The variable size in the V$SGA view is the memory structure that needs to be viewed further by going to the V$SGASTAT. The mappings of V$SGA to V$SGASTAT are shown in the following table:

Fixed Size (V$SGA)	fixed_sga (V$SGASTAT)
Database Buffers (V$SGA)	db_block_buffers (V$SGASTAT)
Redo Buffers (V$SGA)	log_buffer (V$SGASTAT) + 1 Block
Variable Size (V$SGA)	30 Other Records (V$SGASTAT)

Of particular importance in the V$SGASTAT result set is the free memory value, which is an indicator of the free contiguous memory in the Shared Pool. If this value is constantly low (less than 500K) or if it is reduced in a short period of time after database startup, this is a good indicator your Shared Pool should be increased. If free memory is low, a stored package or procedure may result in an error because enough contiguous memory may not exist to load the object into the Shared Pool. The preceding script (9_8.sql) should be executed on a regular basis to determine the free memory on your system.

TIP
The allocation of the Shared Pool to the different memory structures within is controlled internally by Oracle. The important aspect is to monitor the different components and determine if the hit ratios (finding the objects in the caches) and free memory are at acceptable levels. Queries to view hit ratios are outlined later in this chapter.

An alternative and indication of Shared Pool allocation can be viewed through the DBMS_SHARED_POOL.SIZES procedure. This procedure call accepts a MINIMUM SIZE (in Kilobytes) parameter and displays all cursors and objects within the Shared Pool of a size greater than the MINIMUM SIZE input parameter. The actual statement issued to retrieve this information follows:

File: 9_10.sql

```
SELECT  TO_CHAR(SHARABLE_MEM / 1000 ,'999999') SZ,
        DECODE(KEPT_VERSIONS,0,'        ',
        RPAD('YES(' || TO_CHAR(KEPT_VERSIONS) || ')' ,6)) KEEPED,
        RAWTOHEX(ADDRESS) || ',' || TO_CHAR(HASH_VALUE)  NAME,
        SUBSTR(SQL_TEXT,1,354) EXTRA, 1 ISCURSOR
FROM    V$SQLAREA
WHERE   SHARABLE_MEM > &min_ksize * 1000
UNION
SELECT  TO_CHAR(SHARABLE_MEM / 1000 ,'999999') SZ,
        DECODE(KEPT,'YES','YES    ','        ') KEEPED,
        OWNER || '.' || NAME ||
        LPAD(' ',29 - (LENGTH(OWNER) + LENGTH(NAME) ) ) ||
        '(' || TYPE || ')'  NAME, NULL  EXTRA, 0 ISCURSOR
FROM    V$DB_OBJECT_CACHE V
WHERE   SHARABLE_MEM > &min_ksize * 1000
ORDER BY 1 DESC;
```

The preceding query can be placed into a procedure/package of your own construction to display a formatted view of cursors and objects within the Shared Pool.

 TIP
The DBMS_SHARED_POOL.SIZES procedure underlying query combines the sharable memory of the object cache (V$DB_OBJECT_CACHE view) and the SQL area (V$SQLAREA view).

Finally, a query against the V$SHARED_POOL_RESERVED view provides an additional indication of the appropriateness of the size of the Shared Pool. Ideally, the value of request_misses column should be zero, indicating that all objects are retained within the Shared Pool. Alternatively, and more realistically, when physical memory resources are limited, the value of request_failures column should be zero or at the very least constant, indicating requests for allocations of space within the Shared Pool are always successful.

Monitor Memory and Use of PL/SQL Program Units

Evaluating memory requirements of PL/SQL code requires a thorough understanding of the Shared Pool within the System Global Area (SGA). Oracle caches compiled PL/SQL code within the Shared Pool. This code remains in memory in a compiled state, even if the original caller session terminates. In this way, the code can be reused by all users, avoiding parsing and recompilation of the code upon each execution.

Three major areas comprise the Shared Pool:

- The library cache
- The data dictionary cache
- Control Structures

As indicated previously, the total size of the Shared Pool is determined by the init.ora parameter shared_pool_sizes. Increasing this parameter increases the total space reserved for the library and dictionary cache and the control structures for shared SQL Area.

Knowledge of the library cache component of the Shared Pool is key to understanding the memory requirements of PL/SQL program units, and the SQL statements they contain. The library cache is composed of:

- Shared SQL Areas
- Private SQL Areas
- PL/SQL Program Units
- Locks and Library Cache Handles (control structures)

Each SQL statement and PL/SQL program unit within the library cache contains both a shared area and a private area. This architecture enables multiple users to share portions of a program unit or SQL statement and maintain a separate copy of the program unit or statement's private area, at the same time. Oracle allocates a shared area to hold the parsed, compiled form of a program unit (pseudocode or p-code) and a shared SQL Area contains the execution plan and parse tree for a SQL statement, including DML statements that contain bind variable references.

A private area is allocated for each program unit, which contains local and global (package) variables and buffers for executing SQL statements. A private SQL Area is maintained for each execution of a SQL statement by a session and contains a persistent area maintained across multiple executions of the same SQL statement and a runtime area that contains information about the statement during execution. The size of the private area of a program unit is determined by the size and quantity of variables unique to each session executing the unit, while the size of a private SQL Area's persistent area is determined by the number of columns and binds contained in the SQL statement. A SQL statement's private area also contains information about required data type conversions and state information, such as recursive and/or remote cursor numbers or the state of a parallel operation.

The size of the private SQL Area's runtime area is determined by the type and complexity of the SQL statement executed and the combined width of the records. Generally speaking, DML statements require less runtime memory than queries.

When evaluating memory requirements of PL/SQL program units, the DBA must examine the characteristics of the SQL statements contained within the program code in addition to the memory required for calculations or database-independent logic. These SQL statements are interpreted in the same fashion as any other SQL statement issued.

In summary, when a PL/SQL program unit is executed, it follows these steps:

1. The Shared Pool library cache is checked for the existence of the program unit

2. If not found, the statement is parsed and memory for a shared SQL Area is allocated based on the type and complexity of the statement

3. If the entire Shared Pool is already allocated, areas are de-allocated using an LRU (Least Recently Used) algorithm until enough free space is available for the statement's shared SQL Area

4. Oracle issues an execute call on the SQL statement and a (private SQL Area) runtime area is allocated first, followed by allocation of a (private SQL Area) persistent area. The limit on the number of (private SQL Area) runtime areas is limited by the per session init.ora parameter open_cursors, which has a default setting of 50.

5. Upon each execution of a DML statement, Oracle allocates and de-allocates the SQL statement (private SQL Area) runtime area. For each execution of a SELECT statement, the (private SQL Area) runtime area remains allocated until all rows of the query are fetched or the query is canceled.

6. The (private SQL Area) persistent area remains allocated until the statement cursor is closed or the SQL statement handle is freed.

The preceding statement execution has major implications to the application developer and, consequently, to the DBA looking to maximize Shared Pool memory use:

■ All statement cursors should be explicitly opened and closed to guarantee deallocation of the (private SQL Area) persistent area memory. Persistent areas will continue to exist as long as the cursor associated with the statement remains open.

■ Likewise, combining two successive statements into a single statement will avoid unnecessary allocations and deallocations of (private SQL Area) runtime memory.

The amount of shared and private (persistent and runtime memory) can be retrieved from the V$SQL or V$SQLAREA views. The following table illustrates the differences in the amount of memory allocated for a simple SQL statement validation step. Notice the significant amount of additional memory required to parse a 'SELECT *...' statement versus a column reference or constant.

Statement	Sharable Memory	Persistent Memory	Runtime Memory
Select 'x' from dba_tables where table_name = 'NLS_MESSAGE'	47957	548	8376
Select table_name from dba_tables where table_name = 'NLS_MESSAGE'	47980	548	8376
Select * from dba_tables where table_name = 'NLS_MESSAGE'	64571	2424	12264

Monitoring PL/SQL Program Units

Based on the memory required for columns specified in the SELECT column list as outlined in the previous table, SQL statements should only contain the columns in the SELECT column list that are necessary for the statement.

Taking this one step further, SELECT statements often appear in PL/SQL program units using a cursor record type as illustrated in the following example.

File: 9_11.sql

```
CREATE OR REPLACE PROCEDURE example_proc1(p_table_txt IN VARCHAR2) AS
   CURSOR cur_tables IS
      SELECT *
      FROM   dba_tables
      WHERE  table_name = p_table_txt;
   lv_cur_tables_rec    cur_tables%rowtype;
BEGIN
   OPEN cur_tables;
   FETCH cur_tables INTO lv_cur_tables_rec;
   DBMS_OUTPUT.PUT_LINE('The indicator is: '||
      lv_cur_tables_rec.table_name);
   CLOSE cur_tables;
EXCEPTION
 WHEN OTHERS THEN
    DBMS_OUTPUT.PUT_LINE(p_table_txt||' was not found');
END example_proc1;
/
```

The persistent and runtime memory requirements for the preceding procedure are the same, even if this cursor was fetched into a single data variable (as in 'SELECT INTO...') versus the record type illustrated.

The following illustrates the impact of bind variable references on the size of persistent areas within the Shared Pool. An additional 20 bytes are required for a single bind variable reference in the where clause. Also note, the statement was converted to uppercase automatically during compilation. This allows for a greater chance of matching a shared SQL Area in the library cache when SQL statements compiled within stored program units are executed.

Statement	Sharable Memory	Persistent Memory	Runtime Memory
SELECT * FROM DBA_TABLES WHERE TABLE_NAME = :b1	64571	2444	12264

Oracle uses the shared SQL Area for recursive statements issued implicitly on behalf of user statements.

Shared areas are not always flushed from the Shared Pool. For example, if you execute a stored PL/SQL procedure and subsequently modify and recompile the procedure, the shared memory associated with the prior execution of that stored procedure remains in memory, while the persistent and runtime memory is released. Similarly, a shared SQL Area can be flushed from the Shared Pool even if it corresponds to an inactive open cursor. The init.ora parameter cursor_space_for_time can be used to control when a statement within the Shared Pool can be flushed. The default setting for this parameter is set to FALSE, enabling Oracle to flush statements when space is required, even if cursors associated with a shared SQL Area are open. If this parameter is set to TRUE, Oracle does not search the Shared Pool first prior to issuing an execute call. Only use this parameter when enough physical memory is available to size the Shared Pool to hold all application and recursive cursors.

TIP

*Convert any SQL statement 'SELECT *' or unused column references contained within PL/SQL program units to specific constant or column references. This reduces persistent and runtime memory use.*

TIP

When running dedicated server, the private SQL Area is allocated from the session's PGA. When running multithreaded server (MTS), the private SQL Area is allocated from the SGA.

Use the following statement to examine the library cache:

File: 9_12.sql

```
SELECT SUBSTR(USERNAME,1,10) "User",
       SUBSTR(machine,1,10) "Machine",
       sharable_mem, persistent_mem,
       runtime_mem, executions, v$sql.module,
       SUBSTR(v$sql.sql_text,1,60) "Statement"
FROM   v$session, v$sql, v$open_cursor
WHERE  v$open_cursor.saddr   = v$session.saddr
AND    v$open_cursor.address = v$sql.address
--AND   users_executing        > 0
--AND   v$session.username      = UPPER('&username')
ORDER BY SUBSTR(USERNAME,1,10), SUBSTR(machine,1,10);
```

The preceding code provides information about memory allocated to the library cache. Only PL/SQL program units and open SQL statement cursors associated with existing sessions are displayed. If you wish to see only currently executing PL/SQL program units and/or SQL statements, uncomment the line 'AND users_executing > 0'. Likewise, uncomment the line 'AND v$session.username = UPPER('&username')' to view information about a single user. When using the preceding script for Shared Pool sizing, remember, if you are running under multithreaded server, the persistent and runtime memory values are allocated from the SGA versus the PGA under dedicated server.

Use the following statement to examine object cache:

File: 9_13.sql

```
SELECT owner, name, type, loads,
       executions, locks, pins, kept
FROM   v$db_object_cache
ORDER BY executions DESC;
```

The preceding query shows how frequently objects are hit (executed) and very importantly, how frequently they are reloaded because they have been aged out. The query also provides information on pins and keeps. The preceding query illustrates the frequency of Oracle's use of the Oracle supplied packages, such as STANDARD and DBMS_APPLICATION_INFO.

Monitor PL/SQL Related Information with the V$ Views

Oracle provides a tremendous window into the real-time activity in the database. This real-time information is seen in the V$ views. The following is an arsenal of V$ scripts that help DBAs window into real-time activity and make educated decisions based on the output from these scripts. All these scripts are limited to PL/SQL-related issues. Each script is displayed with a brief description of what the script provides and information related to what to look for to determine if any action is required.

Monitor the Library Cache (V$LIBRARY_CACHE)

The following script provides a means of identifying the hit ratio of the library cache. The library cache is a component of the Shared Pool and, therefore, if the library hit ratios are inadequate, the overall system performance will suffer.

File: 9_14.sql

```
SELECT SUM(pins) pins, SUM(pinhits) pinhits,
       ((SUM(pinhits) / SUM(pins)) * 100) phitrat,
       SUM(reloads) reloads,
       ((SUM(pins) / (SUM(pins) + SUM(reloads))) * 100) rhitrat
FROM   v$librarycache;
```

Output (9_14.sql)

```
     PINS     PINHITS    PHITRAT    RELOADS    RHITRAT
---------- ----------- ---------- ---------- ----------
  19213071   18367177  95.5972994      45889 99.7617265
```

The goal of this statement is to provide statistics on the library cache to determine if the Shared Pool needs to be increased. There is an execution (pin) hit ratio (PHITRAT) and a reload hit ratio (RHITRAT). The recommended hit ratio for both is greater than 99 percent. If either of the hit ratios falls below this percentage, it indicates the Shared Pool can be increased to improve overall performance. In this example, the reload hit ratio is adequate, but the execution hit ratio is below the recommended ratio; therefore, increasing the Shared Pool can help in this system. This script should be executed regularly to determine the performance of the library cache and should be used as an indicator to increase your Shared Pool.

Monitor the Dictionary Cache (V$ROWCACHE)

The following script provides a means of identifying the dictionary cache effectiveness. Every time a statement is processed by Oracle, it uses the dictionary cache to find required information to execute the statement. The dictionary cache is a component of the Shared Pool, so if the dictionary hit ratio is inadequate, the overall system performance will suffer.

File: 9_15.sql

```
SELECT SUM(gets), SUM(getmisses),
       (1 - (SUM(getmisses) / (SUM(gets) +
       SUM(getmisses)))) * 100 hitrat
FROM   v$rowcache;
```

Output (9_15.sql)

```
SUM(GETS) SUM(GETMISSES)      HITRAT
--------- -------------- ----------
 0548694         344889 96.8340169
```

The goal of the preceding script is to provide statistics on the data dictionary cache to determine if the Shared Pool needs to be increased. The recommended minimum hit ratio is 90 percent. If the hit ratio falls below this percentage, it indicates that the Shared Pool can be increased to improve overall performance. In the preceding example, the hit ratio is adequate. The dictionary cache is made up of several components that relate to the caching of dictionary information; however, there is no means in the current release of Oracle to increase only one of these cache parameters. The preceding script should be executed regularly to determine the performance of the dictionary cache and be used as an indicator to increasing your Shared Pool.

Evaluate I/O per User (V$SESS_IO)

The following script provides a means of viewing all sessions to analyze the physical disk and memory activity. This is helpful when testing new versions of source code prior to production implementation to determine system resource requirements for execution or when tracking down performance degradation.

File: 9_16.sql

```
SELECT a.username, b.block_gets, b.consistent_gets,
       b.physical_reads
FROM   v$session a, v$sess_io b
WHERE  a.sid = b.sid
ORDER BY a.username;
```

Output (9_16.sql)

USERNAME	BLOCK_GETS	CONSISTENT_GETS	PHYSICAL_READS
SCOTT	42	346	0
PLSQL_USER	44885	2535	104
PLSQL_USER2	126314	4780893	321139

The goal of the preceding script is to highlight the physical disk and memory hits for each session. If a new version of an application module is being tested, this script can be executed to view the fetching activity to get an indication if the application module performance can be improved in terms of logical versus physical reads. This script should be executed when testing new application modules for performance and periodically to view session logical versus physical reads.

TIP
When using PL/SQL, the amount of flexibility in terms of programming logic increases and, therefore, some of the logic can be shifted from the SQL statements into PL/SQL logic for better performance.

Evaluate Each User's Resource Consumption (V$SESSTAT)

The following script provides a method for analyzing user statistics. When a new or updated application module is being tested to determine the overhead, this is extremely valuable. This also is a window into a user who is having performance problems because it provides statistics on a variety of areas for each user.

File: 9_17.sql

```
SELECT a.username, c.name, b.value
FROM   v$session a, v$sesstat b, v$statname c
WHERE  a.sid        = b.sid
AND    b.statistic# = c.statistic#
AND    b.value      != 0;
```

Output (9_17.sql)

USERNAME	NAME	VALUE
PLSQL_USER	logons cumulative	1
PLSQL_USER	opened cursors cumulative	14
PLSQL_USER	session uga memory max	31508
PLSQL_USER	table fetch by rowid	10
PLSQL_USER	SQL*Net roundtrips to/from client	64
PLSQL_USER	bytes received via SQL*Net from client	5441
PLSQL_USER	bytes sent via SQL*Net to client	2632
PLSQL_USER	db block changes	53
PLSQL_USER	physical reads	11
PLSQL_USER	consistent gets	72
PLSQL_USER	db block gets	39
PLSQL_USER	enqueue requests	2
PLSQL_USER	session pga memory max	76592

```
PLSQL_USER       session pga memory                  76592
PLSQL_USER       session uga memory                  31508
PLSQL_USER       recursive calls                        69
PLSQL_USER       user calls                             57
PLSQL_USER       opened cursors current                  1
PLSQL_USER       logons current                          1
```

The preceding script provides detailed statistics per user on his or her current session. This information can be used to determine if problem areas exist with the session or possibly with the application modules the user is executing. The example is limited to one user, but it provides information for all users, if desired. In addition, the script limits the statistics only to areas that have a value (b.value != 0). In this summary fashion, a DBA can get an all-encompassing view of the resources used since logging on and also the resources currently in use. This script should be executed when testing a new application module to determine overhead or to view user statistics when problems are noted by a user.

Highlight Open Cursors per User (V$OPEN_CURSOR)

The following script identifies the open cursors per user. This provides insight into what users are executing and enables a DBA to determine if cursors are being closed properly.

File: 9_18.sql

```
SELECT oc.user_name, s.sql_text
FROM   v$open_cursor oc, v$sqltext s
WHERE  oc.address    = s.address
AND    oc.hash_value = s.hash_value
ORDER BY oc.user_name, s.piece;
```

Output (9_18.sql)

```
USER_NAME   SQL_TEXT
----------  ------------------------------------------------------------
PLSQL_USER  update s_employee set salary = '10000'
SCOTT       begin DBMS_APPLICATION_INFO.SET_MODULE(:1,NULL); end;
SYS         select * from v$open_cursor
SYSTEM      select  oc.user_name, s.sql_text from  v$open_cursor
               oc, v$sqlte
SYSTEM      xt s where oc.address    = s.address and
```

```
           oc.hash_value  =       s.hash
SYSTEM     _value order by oc.user_name, s.piece
```

The goal of the preceding script is to highlight the open cursors per user in your system. It provides identification of current activity in your system and highlights if and when cursors are not being closed properly. If a user is identified from this statement with a large number of open cursors, it may signify that an application module or modules are not closing cursors when complete. As a general rule, cursors should be closed when they are no longer needed to eliminate system overhead (this is often a commonly overlooked PL/SQL coding area). This script should be executed regularly to determine if new applications are being introduced to your system that have not been coded properly.

Identify Current Session SQL Execution (V$SQLTEXT)

The following script displays the SQL statement currently being executed by each session. This is extremely useful when a DBA is trying to determine what is happening in the system at a point in time.

File: 9_19.sql

```
SELECT a.sid, a.username, s.sql_text
FROM   v$session a, v$sqltext s
WHERE  a.sql_address    = s.address
AND    a.sql_hash_value = s.hash_value
ORDER BY a.username, a.sid, s.piece;
```

Output (9_19.sql)

```
SID USERNAME    SQL_TEXT
--- ---------- -------------------------------------------------------------
 11 PLSQL_USER update s_employee set salary = 10000
  9 SYS        select  a.sid, a.username, s.sql_text from  v$session a, v$sqlte
  9 SYS        xt s where a.sql_address  = s.address and  a.sql_hash_value  = s
  9 SYS        .hash_value order by a.username, a.sid, s.piece
  4            select f.file#, f.block#, f.ts#, f.length from fet$ f, ts$ t whe
  4            re t.ts#=f.ts# and t.dflextpct!=0
  5            select local_tran_id, global_tran_fmt, global_oracle_id, global_
  5            foreign_id,        state, status, heuristic_dflt,        session
  5            _vector, reco_vector, 3600*24*(sysdate-reco_time),      3600*2
  5            4*(sysdate-nvl(heuristic_time,fail_time)), global_commit#   from
  5            pending_trans$  where session_vector != '00000000'
  6            BEGIN sys.dbms_ijob.remove(:job); END;
```

The goal of the preceding script is to display the SQL statements that each session is executing at the time this script is executed. In this example, the SYS user displays the SELECT statement of the script because the SYS user is executing the script. The records for SID 4, 5, and 6 are the Oracle background processes, so no username is displayed. The SQL_TEXT column displays the entire SQL statement, but the statement is stored in the V$SQLTEXT view as a VARCHAR2(2000) data type (in version 8.0, the length is increased to 4000) and, therefore, can span multiple records. The piece column is used to order the statement output. This script should be executed whenever the SQL statement for each session currently running is needed.

Determine Object Access at a Point in Time (V$ACCESS)

The following script provides a method for determining what database objects are being accessed at the current time. This is valuable if an application modification needs to be made during business hours versus off-hours or in a 24×7 environment, and the DBA needs to determine if the object being modified is currently in use.

File: 9_20.sql

```
SELECT a.sid, a.username, b.owner, b.object, b.type
FROM   v$session a, v$access b
WHERE  a.sid = b.sid;
```

Output (9_20.sql)

SID	USERNAME	OWNER	OBJECT	TYPE
8	SCOTT	SYS	DBMS_APPLICATION_INFO	PACKAGE
9	SYS	SYS	DBMS_APPLICATION_INFO	PACKAGE
9	SYS	SYS	X$BH	TABLE
10	SYSTEM	PUBLIC	V$ACCESS	SYNONYM
10	SYSTEM	PUBLIC	V$SESSION	SYNONYM
10	SYSTEM	SYS	DBMS_APPLICATION_INFO	PACKAGE
10	SYSTEM	SYS	V$ACCESS	VIEW
10	SYSTEM	SYS	V$SESSION	VIEW
10	SYSTEM	SYS	V_$ACCESS	VIEW

The preceding script helps identify the object access at a point in time on a system. Modifications to a production application should be performed off-hours, but this is not always an option. In such a case, the DBA needs to identify all users accessing the object(s) that must be modified. This script identifies these users and allows a DBA to notify the users to log off at the current time. As evidenced in the preceding example, the script displays all objects being accessed, including synonyms, views, stored source code, and so forth. This script should be executed when the need arises to identify the objects being accessed by each user.

Pinpoint Lock Contention (V$LOCK)

PL/SQL program units contain a major portion of the SQL logic deployed in many Oracle applications. Therefore, lock contention can be caused by PL/SQL program unit logic. The following locking sections provide a means for identifying critical information concerning the locked and locking users to help make an informed decision on resolving the lock contention. In Chapter 4, a method was outlined to help eliminate some of the locking issues that can be caused by using the FOR SHARE UPDATE attribute of the SQL command in PL/SQL programs.

Identify the Locked User(s)

The following script provides a means of identifying users currently locked in the system. This enables DBAs to ensure if an Oracle-related process is truly locking the user. It also identifies the current statement the locked user(s) are currently executing.

File: 9_21.sql

```
SELECT b.username, b.serial#, d.id1, a.sql_text
FROM   v$session b, v$lock d, v$sqltext a
WHERE  b.lockwait   = d.kaddr
AND    a.address    = b.sql_address
AND    a.hash_value = b.sql_hash_value;
```

Output (9_21.sql)

```
USERNAME SERIAL#    ID1 SQL_TEXT
-------- -------  ------ -----------------------------------------------
SCOTT         53 393242 update plsql_user.s_employee set salary = 5000
```

The goal of this statement is to view the locked user(s) and identify what statement(s) they are currently executing. Often, the user is not being locked within Oracle. The next step to resolving the locked user, if they show in this output, is to execute the next script to identify who the locking user is and what he or she is executing. In the preceding example, the user SCOTT is executing an UPDATE statement. This script should be executed whenever a user reports he or she is being locked.

Identify the Locking User(s)

The following script provides a means of identifying the user in the system that is locking another user. This enables DBAs to take the proper action based on the locked user, the locking user, and the statements being executed by both. It also identifies the current statement the locking user(s) are currently executing.

File: 9_22.sql

```
SELECT a.serial#, a.sid, a.username, b.id1, c.sql_text
FROM    v$session a, v$lock b, v$sqltext c
WHERE   b.id1 IN
(SELECT DISTINCT e.id1
FROM    v$session d, v$lock e
WHERE   d.lockwait   = e.kaddr)
AND     a.sid        = b.sid
AND     c.hash_value = a.sql_hash_value
AND     b.request    = 0;
```

Output (9_22.sql)

```
SERIAL#    SID USERNAME       ID1 SQL_TEXT
-------  ------ -----------  ------ ---------------------------------------
     18     11 PLSQL_USER  393242 update s_employee set salary = 10000
```

The goal of the preceding script is to view the locking user(s) and to identify what statement(s) they are currently executing. This script goes hand-in-hand with the previous script. In this example, the user PLSQL_USER is executing an UPDATE statement that is locking the user SCOTT as displayed from the previous script. The ID1 column links the two users. The DBA would now have the information to resolve the contention issue. This script should be executed whenever a user reports he or she is being locked.

Monitor Rollback Segment Use (V$ROLLSTAT and V$TRANSACTION)

The following script provides a means to identify the activity in the rollback segments and to determine if any contention exists. It provides a window into the current activity of each rollback segment, including the username, sid, serial number, and statement being executed. Often, a statement is being executed that needs to be aborted. This script provides the DBA with the necessary information to abort the process, if necessary.

File: 9_23.sql

```
SELECT a.name, b.xacts tr, c.sid, c.serial#, c.username, d.sql_text
FROM   v$rollname a, v$rollstat b, v$session c,
       v$sqltext d,v$transaction e
WHERE  a.usn            = b.usn
AND    b.usn            = e.xidusn
AND    c.taddr          = e.addr
AND    c.sql_address    = d.address
AND    c.sql_hash_value = d.hash_value
ORDER BY a.name, c.sid, d.piece;
```

Output (9_23.sql)

```
NAME   TR SID SERIAL# USERNAME    SQL_TEXT
-----  -- --- ------- ------------------------------------------------------
RB3    1  11       18 PLSQL_USER update s_employee set salary = '10000'
```

The goal of the preceding script is to identify the current statements executing in each rollback segment. If the system load is uncharacteristically slow, this is a means to view the DML operations taking place on your system. This also becomes a valuable tool for identifying runaway processes or long-running DML statements that need to be aborted. As evidenced in this example, the user PLSQL_USER is performing an UPDATE statement. If desired, the operation can be aborted by issuing the ALTER SYSTEM KILL SESSION command. This command needs the sid and serial#. If the preceding operation needed to be aborted, the following statement could be executed:

```
ALTER SYSTEM KILL SESSION '11,18';
```

Note, the order of the parameters is sid, then serial#. This script should be executed whenever system performance degrades or a user indicates that a DML operation is taking longer than expected.

Build a DBA Monitoring System with DBMS_JOB, DBMS_PIPE, and DBMS_ALERT

The goal of DBAs is to be proactive in their responsibilities to ensure the database executes efficiently and consistently. Many DBAs have an arsenal of SQL scripts that they execute on a regular basis to assist in this proactive role. However, if the DBA gets

Building a DBA Monitoring System

preoccupied, then the scripts do not get executed and the potential for failure increases. Oracle has provided three packages that allow DBAs to create a mechanism to schedule monitoring and alerting. These three packages are the DBMS_JOB, DBMS_PIPE, and DBMS_ALERT packages.

The DBMS_JOB package provides the capability to execute a stored PL/SQL object at a specified time or on a regular interval. The DBMS_PIPE (sent asynchronously, when encountered) and DBMS_ALERT (sent synchronously, when a successful COMMIT is processed) packages provide the capability to send a message to a waiting session when a certain condition occurs.

Therefore, the DBA's arsenal of scripts can be slightly modified into stored PL/SQL program units that are executed on a regular basis and look for certain conditions. If the conditions occur, the programs can send a message to a waiting session that receives the message and displays the message on the waiting terminal. This allows the DBA to have a proactive monitoring and alert system that can be viewed throughout the day for problem resolution.

The DBMS_JOB, DBMS_PIPE, and DBMS_ALERT packages are detailed in Chapter 11 and Chapter 12.

Pin PL/SQL Objects and Cursors

Since Oracle uses an LRU algorithm for the caching of objects in the Shared Pool, objects can be flushed out of the Shared Pool. If the objects are large, this will cause degradation in performance and possible errors because objects are loaded into the Shared Pool in contiguous segments. Heavily executed or large stored PL/SQL program units should be cached or pinned in the Shared Pool. Stored PL/SQL program units get pinned in the object cache and cursors get pinned in the SQL Area.

Oracle provides a procedure in the DBMS_SHARED_POOL package to pin these objects. More information on the DBMS_SHARED_POOL package can be found in Chapter 11 and Chapter 12. The following is a pinning mechanism that allows stored PL/SQL program units to be pinned or unpinned by inserting or deleting the name of the program unit from a database table. The database startup script must be modified to call the pin_objects procedure created in the following code segment.

The following command creates the table to store the names of the stored PL/SQL program units to pin. This should be created under a user with DBA privilege.

File: 9_24.sql

```
CREATE TABLE objects_to_pin
   (owner    VARCHAR2(30) NOT NULL,
    object   VARCHAR2(128) NOT NULL);
```

The following is a basic method of inserting objects into the objects-to-pin table. This can be modified to be more robust, and often a Forms front-end interface is created to streamline this function.

File: 9_25.sql

```
INSERT INTO objects_to_pin
   (owner, object)
VALUES
   (UPPER('&owner'), UPPER('&object'));
```

The following is a sample query to display the contents of the table.

File: 9_26.sql

```
SELECT owner, object
FROM    objects_to_pin
ORDER BY owner, object;
```

Output (9_26.sql)

```
OWNER                    OBJECT
-------------------      --------------------
PLSQL_USER               LOG_SOURCE
SYS                      DBMS_APPLICATION_INFO
SYS                      DBMS_OUTPUT
SYS                      DBMS_SHARED_POOL
SYS                      DBMS_STANDARD
SYS                      STANDARD
```

The following procedure accepts one parameter to signify if the objects in the objects-to-pin table should be pinned or unpinned. The default is to pin the objects. A *U* as input will unpin the objects in the table.

File: 9_27.sql

```
CREATE OR REPLACE PROCEDURE pin_objects
   (p_pin_flag_txt IN VARCHAR2 := 'P') IS
   -- The p_pin_flag_txt is either 'P' for pin
   -- or 'U' for unpin.
   CURSOR cur_pin_objects IS
     SELECT owner || '.' owner,
            object
```

```
      FROM    objects_to_pin
      ORDER BY owner, object;
BEGIN
   FOR cur_pin_objects_rec IN cur_pin_objects LOOP
      IF p_pin_flag_txt = 'U' THEN
         DBMS_SHARED_POOL.UNKEEP(cur_pin_objects_rec.owner ||
            cur_pin_objects_rec.object, 'P');
         DBMS_OUTPUT.PUT_LINE('Object Unpinned: ' ||
            cur_pin_objects_rec.owner ||
            cur_pin_objects_rec.object);
      ELSE
         DBMS_SHARED_POOL.KEEP(cur_pin_objects_rec.owner ||
            cur_pin_objects_rec.object, 'P');
         DBMS_OUTPUT.PUT_LINE('Object Pinned: ' ||
            cur_pin_objects_rec.owner ||
            cur_pin_objects_rec.object);
      END IF;
   END LOOP;
END pin_objects;
/
```

TIP
The pin_objects procedure should be called from the startup script to make certain the PL/SQL objects are pinned immediately, which will ensure the Shared Pool space is contiguously allocated in memory.

TIP
In Oracle 8.1, the pin_objects procedure can be moved from the database startup script to the new STARTUP database trigger.

The following illustrates the execution of the procedure that pins the objects.

Output (9_27.sql)

```
SET SERVEROUTPUT ON SIZE 1000000
EXECUTE pin_objects

Object Pinned: PLSQL_USER.LOG_SOURCE
Object Pinned: SYS.DBMS_APPLICATION_INFO
Object Pinned: SYS.DBMS_OUTPUT
```

```
Object Pinned: SYS.DBMS_SHARED_POOL
Object Pinned: SYS.DBMS_STANDARD
Object Pinned: SYS.STANDARD

PL/SQL procedure successfully completed.
```

The following query displays the stored PL/SQL program units currently pinned.

File: 9_28.sql

```
SELECT owner, name, type, kept
FROM   v$db_object_cache
WHERE  kept = 'YES';
```

Output (9_28.sql)

OWNER	NAME	TYPE	KEPT
SYS	STANDARD	PACKAGE	YES
SYS	STANDARD	PACKAGE BODY	YES
SYS	DBMS_SHARED_POOL	PACKAGE	YES
SYS	DBMS_SHARED_POOL	PACKAGE BODY	YES
PLSQL_USER	LOG_SOURCE	PROCEDURE	YES
SYS	DBMS_APPLICATION_INFO	PACKAGE	YES
SYS	DBMS_APPLICATION_INFO	PACKAGE BODY	YES
SYS	DBMS_STANDARD	PACKAGE	YES
SYS	DBMS_STANDARD	NON-EXISTENT	YES
SYS	DBMS_OUTPUT	PACKAGE	YES
SYS	DBMS_OUTPUT	PACKAGE BODY	YES

TIP
The previous query can be executed to list the sharable memory (sharable_mem column) required for the object and the number of times the object was loaded and executed (loads and executions columns) to determine which objects should be pinned.

TIP
Pinning frequently executed Oracle objects and application objects is recommended but, remember, adequate space must still exist in the Shared Pool for the objects that are not pinned.

The following illustrates the execution of the procedure to unpin the objects.

Output (9_27.sql)

```
SET SERVEROUTPUT ON SIZE 1000000
EXECUTE pin_objects('U');

Object Unpinned: PLSQL_USER.LOG_SOURCE
Object Unpinned: SYS.DBMS_APPLICATION_INFO
Object Unpinned: SYS.DBMS_OUTPUT
Object Unpinned: SYS.DBMS_SHARED_POOL
Object Unpinned: SYS.DBMS_STANDARD
Object Unpinned: SYS.STANDARD

PL/SQL procedure successfully completed.
```

The Shared Pool can be flushed at any time by issuing an ALTER SYSTEM command. Two of the components of the Shared Pool are the library cache and the SQL Area. Stored PL/SQL program units and SQL statements are stored in these memory areas and remain until aged out. An error can occur if an attempt is made to load a stored PL/SQL program unit and there is not enough contiguous space to load the object. If this happens, the ALTER SYSTEM FLUSH command should be executed. This command will not flush any pinned PL/SQL program units or cursors.

The following example illustrates the affect of the ALTER SYSTEM command to flush the Shared Pool.

The following query displays the number of records (cursors) in the SQL Area.

File: 9_29.sql

```
SELECT COUNT(*)
FROM   v$sqlarea;
```

Output (9_29.sql)

```
COUNT(*)
----------
       183
```

The following query displays the number of records (object) in the object cache.

File: 9_30.sql

```
SELECT COUNT(*)
FROM   v$db_object_cache;
```

Output (9_30.sql)

```
COUNT(*)
----------
       128
```

Upon flushing the Shared Pool with the following command, the SQL Area and object cache records and information is deleted. This is shown in the two queries that follow the flush command.

```
ALTER SYSTEM FLUSH SHARED_POOL;
System altered.
```

The number of records now in the SQL Area is shown below by executing the 9_29.sql script.

Output (9_29.sql)

```
  COUNT(*)
----------
         3
```

The number of records now in the object cache is shown below by executing the 9_30.sql script.

Output (9_30.sql)

```
COUNT(*)
----------
        15
```

TIP

All pinning should occur immediately after the startup of the instance, preferably in the instance startup script. The table to control the pinned objects should be owned by a DBA, and the execution of the procedure to pin the objects should be executed by the SYS user.

TIP

In addition to pinning stored PL/SQL objects, cursors can be pinned in the SQL Area by referencing the address and hash_value. Therefore, pinning cursors of the pinned PL/SQL program units for further efficiency would be helpful. One technique would be to use the DBMS_APPLICATION_INFO package to uniquely identify the cursors being loaded in the SQL Area, so a procedure can read through the SQL Area (V$SQLAREA view) and pin the desired cursors.

TIP

The address and hash_value of a cursor changes each time the cursor is loaded into the SQL Area, so a mechanism must be created to provide the capability to identify the desired cursor.

Provide Experienced Developers with Additional Access

A struggle of power has existed between the DBA and developer for a long time. One important fact we often forget is we are a **TEAM**. Remember, **T**ogether **E**veryone **A**ccomplishes **M**ore. The success or failure of an application is directly attributable to the team—not to you, not to me—it always needs to be WE. We have to stop falling into the **WIIFM** principle, **W**hat's **I**n **I**t **F**or **M**e. So, when developers have expanded their knowledge into the performance-tuning arena and ask for certain permission to view the SQL creation files for the Oracle supplied packages or for access to the V$ views like V$SQLAREA, V$SESSION, and so forth, *give them access.*

Provide Developers with READ Privilege on Oracle Supplied PL/SQL Files

All developers should have READ privilege on the SQL scripts Oracle provides to create the Oracle supplied packages. These creation files are typically located in the ORACLE_HOME/rdbms/admin directory. Valuable information, including examples, limitations, tips, and more that cannot be found elsewhere is included in these files. No harm comes from providing this access. It helps the developer become more knowledgeable and, in turn, this can help you, the DBA, in the long run. As Oracle continues to progress, it is extremely evident that the role of the DBA is not being reduced. To the contrary, the DBA role is being expanded. The DBA role is expanding to the next level with Oracle8i; therefore, any time that can be saved by experienced developers performing more (as long as it is still in the developer realm), the better.

As outlined in Chapter 1, no standard definition exists of the developer responsibilities and the DBA responsibilities. This typically varies by company, so read my general recommendations and allow the developer to expand into certain areas.

Additional information related to viewing these important SQL files is in Chapter 11.

Provide Experienced Developers with SELECT Privilege on Selected V$ Views

The second area of providing developers access is to specific V$ views that can help the developer with viewing real-time information related to performance optimization. Several references to the V$ views are included throughout this book. Most references are for the DBA; however, the more experienced a developer is, the more he or she can assist in the overall success.

DBAs often are reluctant to provide access to the V$ views because of the following two reasons:

- Fear the developer will attempt to modify data in these views

- Fear the developer will constantly be referencing these views and performance will suffer

The first fear can be eliminated with the knowledge that the V$ views and the underlying tables—namely the X$ tables—are not modifiable, even if you want to modify them, even if you are the SYS user. I have tried; it does not allow you to modify them.

The second fear is valid. The larger your system, the more resource-intensive queries against these views. If you follow the next five rules (or a portion of them), this fear should be reduced and you can accomplish the desired goal of making the developer more productive:

- Provide access only to the V$ views that will be of value to the developer (a short list follows).

- Educate developers on the importance of limiting queries against these views to only when they are truly required because they are resource-intensive.

- Caution the developers tactfully: If they abuse the privilege, it will be revoked.

- Provide access only to these views on a development or test system.

- Alternatively, create views on top of the V$ views that limit the result set to only their usernames or a select set of usernames.

The following definitions outline the recommended V$ views. The recommended views should only be granted to experienced developers and will vary per environment, depending on the developer's responsibilities. The following is the recommended list of V$ views with a description of the value each view provides to the developer:

- **V$PARAMETER**   Enables a developer to view certain PL/SQL parameters, including UTL_FILE settings, DBMS_JOB settings, and so forth

- **V$SESSION**   Enables a developer to view information for a session; helpful when optimizing SQL (also required for SET AUTOTRACE ON in SQL*Plus)

- **V$SESSTAT**   Enables a developer to view information for a session; helpful when optimizing SQL (also required for SET AUTOTRACE ON in SQL*Plus)

- **V$SESS_IO**   Enables a developer to view memory information for a session; helpful when optimizing SQL

- **V$SQLAREA**   Enables a developer to pinpoint the SQL statements that are the most resource-intensive and, more than likely, the problem areas in your system

- **V$SQLTEXT**   Enables a developer to view the entire SQL statement versus the many other views that only show the first 1000 characters (the 1000 is dependent on the version)

■ **V$STATNAME** Needed to join to the V$SESSTAT view to provide the descriptive name of the session statistic; helpful when optimizing SQL (also required for SET AUTOTRACE ON in SQL*Plus)

Access to these views can be provided with the following command:

```
GRANT SELECT ON v_$session TO plsql_user;
```

Remember, a view is created on each V$ view that eliminates the underscore, and a public synonym is also created for each view.

Learn PL/SQL Yourself to Take Your DBA Skills to the Next Level

The list of DBAs responsibilities covers a variety of areas. Many of the DBA's responsibilities rely on some form of monitoring, whether this be the data dictionary views or the V$ views. This monitoring is often accomplished through a set of scripts developed by the DBA to relay critical information about all aspects of the database. Some of the scripts are for information only, others are for providing optimization statistics, and others are for alerting the DBA of certain exceeded thresholds. I am a firm believer in these scripts, but why not take this monitoring to the next level?

The next level is to apply the PL/SQL language to your SQL scripts. This provides the next level in analysis capability and provides a more detailed control of results, which is more granular. I have expanded many of the standard SQL scripts I have used over the years with PL/SQL capabilities, and I have found this tremendously valuable. Remember, PL/SQL is similar to most other programming languages, so learning the basics of the language is fairly simple. The following is an example of taking a standard script and fueling the script with PL/SQL.

The following illustrates an example of turning the TRACE facility ON for the top three resource-intensive processes.

File: 9_31.sql

```
DECLARE
   CURSOR cur_trace IS
      SELECT a.username, a.sid, a.serial#, b.physical_reads,
             b.block_gets, b.consistent_gets
      FROM   v$session a, v$sess_io b
      WHERE  a.sid = b.sid
```

Taking Your DBA Skills to the Next Level

```
        AND    NVL(a.username,'XX') NOT IN ('SYS', 'SYSTEM', 'XX')
        ORDER BY b.physical_reads DESC;
     lv_count_num PLS_INTEGER := 0;
BEGIN
   FOR cur_trace_rec IN cur_trace LOOP
      lv_count_num := lv_count_num + 1;
      IF lv_count_num = 4 THEN
         EXIT;
      END IF;
      DBMS_SYSTEM.SET_SQL_TRACE_IN_SESSION(cur_trace_rec.sid,
         cur_trace_rec.serial#, TRUE);
      DBMS_OUTPUT.PUT_LINE('Sessions Traced--Username: ' ||
         RPAD(cur_trace_rec.username,20) || ' Sid: '      ||
         RPAD(cur_trace_rec.sid,8) || ' Serial#: ' ||
         cur_trace_rec.serial#);
   END LOOP;
END;
/
```

Output (9_31.sql)

```
Sessions Traced--Username: PLSQL_USER          Sid: 10      Serial#: 45
Sessions Traced--Username: SCOTT               Sid: 7       Serial#: 149
Sessions Traced--Username: JCT                 Sid: 8       Serial#: 12

PL/SQL procedure successfully completed.
```

With my previous approach, I would have executed the script in the preceding example and then executed three separate ALTER SESSION commands to accomplish the same result.

Take the challenge and advance to the next level of DBA monitoring by learning PL/SQL.

Summary

This chapter concentrated on important DBA-related PL/SQL issues that must be understood and addressed to ensure a solid application. DBAs have a large responsibility in terms of the PL/SQL language and must be handled in a proactive manner. DBAs should learn as much as possible about the PL/SQL language. I know many DBAs who execute SQL scripts to monitor certain aspects of their database. SQL scripts work, but if DBAs want to take the next step in database monitoring, they need to start using PL/SQL to add a finer level of manipulation layer. The use of PL/SQL greatly enhances the overall functionality and flexibility of DBAs.

Tips Review

■ Treat the SQL files that create the PL/SQL components like user documentation. It truly is a supplement to this documentation and is online.

■ Object storage fragmentation can cause performance degradation, and the data dictionary should be considered in your defragmentation efforts. Handle this defragmentation with extreme caution and ensure you have performed complete backups prior to defragmenting the data dictionary.

■ Stored PL/SQL program units provide an additional security method that should be understood prior to designing a security scheme. The importance of solid security is monumental, although I have yet to meet an Oracle DBA who feels his or her system is completely secure.

■ A new option in Oracle 8.1 on stored PL/SQL program unit creation provides additional flexibility in PL/SQL security as outlined in Chapter 16.

■ Use the WRAP facility to convert a stored PL/SQL module creation script into a "wrapped" version, disallowing curious minds from attaining source code access. This type of security is usually not needed because the basic Oracle security forces users to be granted rights to another schema's objects. If confidential business logic or critical core functionality is involved, "wrapping" the source code is the only way to be sure the logic is unreadable.

■ An additional step is to back up the DBA_SOURCE view on a regular interval (only new or changed source code). This technique is outlined in further detail in Chapter 3 and is accomplished with one PL/SQL procedure. The submission of this procedure for regular execution is detailed in Chapter 12 with the DBMS_JOB package. While this is not a cure-all, it is a great means of providing another level of backup that can even be hidden from the developers.

■ To ensure an uninterrupted system, the following guidelines should be integrated as a standard into your Oracle production environment:

   ■ All PL/SQL-stored object creations and modifications are performed during off-hours.

   ■ After creating or modifying any database object, the 9_4.sql script file must be executed and return no records. If any records exist, the objects should be recompiled immediately. Oracle will attempt to recompile INVALID objects when the object is called for execution and, often, this results in a successful compilation and execution. The process of compiling the object when called takes time, and the exact time is dependent on the size of the object. More important are the

Tips Review

consequences if the compilation fails: potential disaster if it's during production hours.

■ Always execute the INVALID script (9_4.sql) after object modification and always manually recompile all objects prior to production hours (or use the re-compilation procedure provided in Chapter 5).

■ Always ensure database triggers are enabled. Because database triggers are the database gatekeepers and the last line of defense, they should always be monitored and enabled. If the DISABLE script (9_5.sql) is not executed, no indication will tell you the database trigger is disabled. The longer the database trigger remains disabled, the larger the problem that must be corrected.

■ Changing the init.ora parameters without stopping and restarting the instance can be extremely helpful for a short-term fix until the next instance shutdown (make sure to change the init.ora parameter because the ALTER SYSTEM result will only remain in effect until the next instance startup). This can also be helpful when an init.ora parameter is a per session value and one process requires a higher value for one of the parameters, and you cannot afford to set it for all sessions (in this case, the ALTER SESSION is a nice solution). A good example of altering a session parameter is the sort_area_size for a session that is executing a large program.

■ Do not rely on your knowledge of which init.ora parameters are changeable. Execute the 9_5.sql query to ensure because the number of init.ora parameters that can be modified real-time continues to grow tremendously with each new version.

■ The init.ora parameters vary based on the Oracle options installed on your system. With each new version of Oracle, review the init.ora parameters in the new version: Oracle not only adds new init.ora parameters, Oracle also eliminates certain parameters. Many parameters have been eliminated by Oracle in version 8.1, some of which were introduced in version 8.0.

■ The V$PARAMETER view displays all init.ora parameters; however, a set of undocumented and hidden parameters is also available and usable. These are not supported by Oracle and should only be used in a limited set of cases or as a last resort in a crisis situation. They should only be used by an experienced DBA and, remember, use of these is at your own risk.

■ In Oracle 8.0, any undocumented init.ora parameter that is modified will display in the query from the V$PARAMETER view.

■ The allocation of the Shared Pool to the different memory structures within is controlled internally by Oracle. The important aspect is to monitor the different components and determine if the hit ratios (finding the objects in the caches) and free memory are at acceptable levels.

■ The DBMS_SHARED_POOL.SIZES underlying query combines the sharable memory of the object cache (V$DB_OBJECT_CACHE view) and the SQL Area (V$SQLAREA view).

■ Convert any SQL statement 'SELECT *' or unused column references contained within PL/SQL program units to specific constant or column references. This reduces persistent and runtime memory use.

■ When running dedicated server, the private SQL Area is allocated from the session's PGA. When running multithreaded server (MTS), the private SQL Area is allocated from the SGA.

■ When using PL/SQL, the amount of flexibility in terms of programming logic increases and, therefore, some of the logic can be shifted from the SQL statements into PL/SQL logic for better performance.

■ This pin_objects procedure (9_27.sql) should be called from the startup script to make certain the PL/SQL objects are pinned immediately to ensure the Shared Pool space will be contiguously allocated in memory.

■ In Oracle 8.1, the pin_objects procedure can be moved from the database startup script to the new STARTUP database trigger.

■ The V$DB_OBJECT_CACHE query (9_28.sql) can be executed to list the sharable memory (sharable_mem column) required for the object and the number of times the object was loaded and executed (loads and executions columns) to determine which objects should be pinned.

■ Pinning frequently executed Oracle objects and application objects is recommended, but remember, adequate space must still exist in the Shared Pool for the objects that are not pinned.

■ In addition to pinning stored PL/SQL objects, cursors can be pinned in the SQL Area by referencing the address and hash_value. Therefore, pinning cursors of the pinned PL/SQL program units for further efficiency would be helpful. One technique would be to use the DBMS_APPLICATION_INFO package to uniquely identify the cursors being loaded in the SQL Area, so a procedure can read through the SQL Area (V$SQLAREA view) and pin the desired cursors.

■ The address and hash_value of a cursor changes each time the cursor is loaded into the SQL Area; therefore, a mechanism must be created to provide the capability to identify the desired cursor.

Tips Review

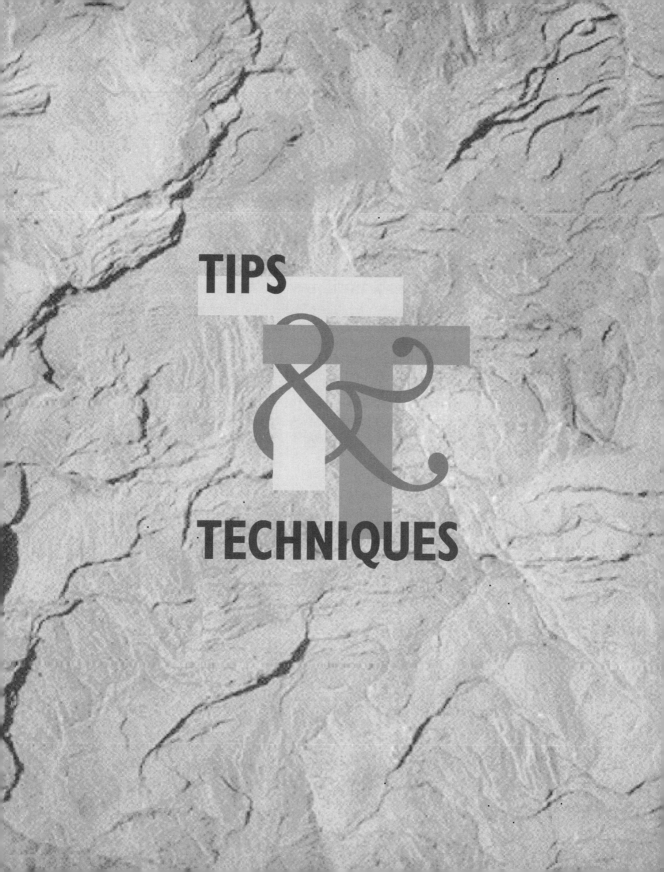

TIPS
&
TECHNIQUES

CHAPTER
10

Unlocking
PL/SQL Security
(Developer and DBA)

S ecurity in any system is a critical component and an issue that should be reviewed and analyzed for every application deployment to ensure the application is secure and only the necessary privilege has been granted to each user accessing the application. Security is often assumed, ignored, or misunderstood, but it is rarely analyzed to ensure the proper security is set up for a system. When people think about security, they tend to get scared by the term. I have asked this question in many presentations: "How many people feel their environment is 100 percent secured?" I have yet to have one person raise his or her hand, and this question has been asked of more than 5,000 people, mostly of Oracle DBAs with over three years' experience!

Oracle security has a number of areas that must be understood to ensure proper security. When stored PL/SQL objects and database triggers were first introduced, the security aspect of PL/SQL added another layer of responsibility for DBAs, but it also provided some avenues for implementing and enforcing tighter security. An entirely new security model can be deployed by using the inherent security integrated into stored PL/SQL objects and database triggers.

This chapter concentrates on Oracle security issues that must be understood regarding Oracle system and object privilege, and focuses on the aspects of PL/SQL security. The goal of this chapter is to highlight the various security issues related to Oracle systems and outline techniques to ensure necessary security measures are established to secure your environment. Although security is generally thought of as a DBA's responsibility, it is important for developers to understand in order to develop more effectively. The chapter covers the following tips and techniques:

- Establish security for an Oracle environment
  - Provide Oracle system privileges
    - Necessary for application developer
    - Necessary for application user
  - Provide application object privileges
- Understand security for creation of stored PL/SQL objects
  - Grant necessary system privilege to create PL/SQL stored objects
  - Grant necessary object privilege to create PL/SQL stored objects
  - Grant necessary privilege for users to execute PL/SQL stored objects
  - Understand early binding
- Understand Oracle supplied PL/SQL package privileges
- Ensure application portability through the use of PUBLIC synonyms

- Review system and object privileges in your system
- Lock application account after production
- Additional PL/SQL related security
  - Permission for Web-based applications
  - Encrypt source code
  - Limit SQL*Plus access
  - Provide Forms security on login
  - Provide additional security with database triggers
  - New PL/SQL security feature in Oracle 8i

Establish Security for an Oracle Environment

When beginning Oracle development, it is important to establish the application development environment in terms of the user schemas, object creation, and security. The recommended approach is to create one schema per application to be designated as the development account for all objects, including tables, indexes, views, sequences, PL/SQL stored objects (packages, procedures, functions, database triggers), synonyms, grants, and so forth. This technique allows centralized development of all objects, ensuring ease of development, maintenance, production implementation, and portability. The application development environment established as outlined in this section should be followed when creating the application production environment. If any components of an application will be considered service or utility modules that will be shared between applications, these modules should be created and placed in a separate Oracle user schema.

   The sample application created in this book follows this methodology. The tables, indexes, sequences, and synonyms were created under the schema PLSQL_USER. All stored PL/SQL stored objects (packages, procedures, functions, and database triggers) in this book are created as PLSQL_USER to ensure proper privileges when creating the stored PL/SQL objects and when creating the proper privileges to application users on the tables, views, and stored objects. Application object privileges should also be granted from the centralized schema account for ease of maintenance and documentation. PUBLIC synonyms should be created under the same account for all objects (tables, views, sequences, packages, procedures, functions) to ensure ease of production implementation, reduce coding (no need to specify the user name prior to referencing objects), and ease of portability. I strongly recommended you create PUBLIC synonyms (the same name as the object name) to eliminate confusion.

The typical order of application object creation is

1. Create tables/views/sequences

2. Create indexes

3. Create stored PL/SQL objects

4. Create PUBLIC synonyms

5. Grant privileges

Two types of privileges are needed for application development and deployment. The first is Oracle system privileges, creating an application developer account for developers to create Oracle objects (tables, indexes, packages, procedures, and so forth) and providing application users the ability to log into Oracle. The second is application object privileges, allowing users to access the application objects to enable them to perform their required functions.

Provide Oracle System Privileges

Two groups of Oracle system privileges are required when developing an application, namely, the developer group and user group. There are 86 privileges (Oracle 7.3) available in Oracle and these can be viewed by executing the following query:

File: 10_1.sql

```
SELECT *
FROM   system_privilege_map;
```

The result (only a subset) of the 86 privileges follows:

Output (10_1.sql)

```
NAME
----------------------------
CREATE USER
BECOME USER
ALTER USER
DROP USER
CREATE TABLE
CREATE ANY TABLE
ALTER ANY TABLE
DROP ANY TABLE
SELECT ANY TABLE
INSERT ANY TABLE
```

```
UPDATE ANY TABLE
DELETE ANY TABLE
CREATE ANY INDEX
ALTER ANY INDEX
DROP ANY INDEX
CREATE SYNONYM
CREATE ANY SYNONYM
DROP ANY SYNONYM
CREATE PUBLIC SYNONYM
DROP PUBLIC SYNONYM
CREATE VIEW
CREATE ANY VIEW
DROP ANY VIEW
CREATE SEQUENCE
CREATE ANY SEQUENCE
ALTER ANY SEQUENCE
DROP ANY SEQUENCE
SELECT ANY SEQUENCE
CREATE DATABASE LINK
CREATE PUBLIC DATABASE LINK
DROP PUBLIC DATABASE LINK
CREATE ROLE
DROP ANY ROLE
GRANT ANY ROLE
ALTER ANY ROLE
CREATE PROCEDURE
CREATE ANY PROCEDURE
ALTER ANY PROCEDURE
DROP ANY PROCEDURE
EXECUTE ANY PROCEDURE
CREATE TRIGGER
CREATE ANY TRIGGER
ALTER ANY TRIGGER
DROP ANY TRIGGER
CREATE PROFILE
ALTER PROFILE
DROP PROFILE
GRANT ANY PRIVILEGE
```

Oracle system privileges can be granted directly to a schema (user) or granted to a role. If granted to a role, then the desired schema can be granted to the role. By default, when an Oracle database is created, four roles are created, namely, the PUBLIC, CONNECT, RESOURCE, and DBA roles.

Prior to the concept of roles, which was introduced in Oracle7, these same four roles were the only groups of Oracle system privileges that could be granted to a user. There was no method of granting the 86 system privileges individually to a user.

Establishing Security for an Oracle Environment

Following is a segment of the sql.bsq file that displays the creation of these four roles (refer to Chapters 9 and 13 for more information on the sql.bsq file):

```
create user sys identified by change_on_install
/
create role public
/
create role connect
/
grant create session,alter session,create synonym,create view,
 create database link,create table,create cluster,create sequence
 to connect
/
create role resource
/
grant create table,create cluster,create sequence,create trigger,
 create procedure to resource
/
create role dba
/
grant all privileges to dba with admin option
/
grant dba to system with admin option
/
```

The standard conventions outlined in Chapter 3 are not followed in the preceding segment of code because it is copied directly from the sql.bsq file.

The following table describes these four default roles in more detail.

Role Name	Description and Recommendations of Role Usage
PUBLIC	Assigned by default to all users. When you need to make something accessible to all users, grant it to this role.
CONNECT	Grant to an application user account.
RESOURCE	Grant to an application development account.
DBA	Grant to a user account that needs to perform database administration tasks. This should only be granted to a select number of user accounts.

If a user schema is granted to the RESOURCE role, it must also be granted to the CONNECT role. Oracle will not grant this by default. The SYSTEM user is assigned to the DBA role upon database creation. If an account assigned to the RESOURCE role needs a system privilege that is not assigned to them, then that privilege should be granted explicitly to the account. Do not automatically grant them the DBA role. . . *this could be very dangerous.* The CONNECT role is granted privileges beyond the CREATE SESSION privilege. I recommend changing this role's privilege to CREATE SESSION and ALTER SESSION only. This can be accomplished with the following statements under a DBA user.

File: 10_2.sql

```
REVOKE CREATE TABLE, CREATE CLUSTER, CREATE SYNONYM, CREATE VIEW,
   CREATE SEQUENCE, CREATE DATABASE LINK FROM CONNECT;
```

This allows a schema to connect to Oracle and to modify the session characteristics, which may be required for certain applications. The remainder of the scope of activity that can be performed by a user with CONNECT relies on the object privileges granted to this schema. If the CONNECT privilege is changed as previously shown, I would change the RESOURCE role to include the CONNECT role privileges. This can be accomplished with the following statements under a DBA user.

File: 10_3.sql

```
GRANT CREATE SYNONYM, CREATE VIEW, CREATE DATABASE LINK,
   CREATE PUBLIC SYNONYM, DROP PUBLIC SYNONYM TO RESOURCE;
```

The CONNECT and RESOURCE role, as previously defined, ensure developer and application user accounts have the system privileges they should have. With the system privileges of the RESOURCE role, a schema can be created and assigned to the RESOURCE role to be used as a development account. This account would be able to fulfill the needs of a development account and execute the five steps previously outlined to create tables, views, sequences, indexes, stored PL/SQL objects, PUBLIC synonyms, and grant access to all objects they create. The CREATE PUBLIC SYNONYM and DROP PUBLIC SYNONYM were added to the RESOURCE role, even though this was not in the CONNECT or RESOURCE role by default. These SYNONYM privileges were added to allow a development schema to create and drop PUBLIC synonyms. All the CREATE system privileges provide the schema with the capability to DROP the object, with the exception of the CREATE PUBLIC SYNONYM. For this reason, the DROP PUBLIC SYNONYM was also provided to the system privilege set. If the user created the object, the explicit DROP system privilege does not need to be granted.

TIP
When the RESOURCE role is granted to a user, the UNLIMITED TABLESPACE system privilege is also granted to the user. This system privilege does not show in the sql.bsq file listing for the RESOURCE role and is granted internally by Oracle. It does not show in the data dictionary as a system privilege assigned to the RESOURCE role either. However, once the RESOURCE role is assigned to a user, the UNLIMITED TABLESPACE system privilege shows in the SESSION_PRIVS data dictionary view, as illustrated in script 10_7.sql later in this chapter.

TIP
When Oracle parses a SQL statement, it must determine whether the object reference is to a table, private synonym, or public synonym; there can be one of each with the same name. Oracle must determine which object to use by checking for object existence in the following order: First, Oracle checks to see if the current user owns a table with the object name; second, Oracle checks to see if the current user has a private synonym with the name of the object; and, third, Oracle checks to see if a PUBLIC synonym exists with the name of the object. When an object name match is found, then that object is used to execute the SQL statement. If an object name match is not found, then an error results. This parsing precedence extends to any object references, including views, sequences, packages, procedures, and functions.

Necessary for Application Developer

The development schema/account should be created and assigned to the CONNECT and RESOURCE role. This privilege allows all the development needs previously outlined (1-5 under "Establishing Security for an Oracle Development Environment") to be accomplished. The statements to create a user and assign the user to the CONNECT and RESOURCE role are shown in the following statements and must be executed under a DBA user:

File: 10_4.sql

```
CREATE USER tempc IDENTIFIED BY tempc;
GRANT CONNECT, RESOURCE to tempc;
```

The modified system privileges for the CONNECT and RESOURCE roles previously created are described in the following table:

Role	System Privilege	Description
CONNECT	CREATE SESSION	Enables a user to log into Oracle.
CONNECT	ALTER SESSION	Enables a user to alter his or her session with the ALTER SESSION command.
RESOURCE	CREATE TABLE	Enables a user to create/drop tables in his or her own schema.
RESOURCE	CREATE VIEW	Enables a user to create/drop views in his or her own schema.
RESOURCE	CREATE SEQUENCE	Enables a user to create/drop sequences in his or her own schema.
RESOURCE	CREATE PROCEDURE	Enables a user to create/drop stored PL/SQL objects of type packages, procedures, and functions in his or her own schema.
RESOURCE	CREATE TRIGGER	Enables a user to create/drop database triggers in his or her own schema.
RESOURCE	CREATE SYNONYM	Enables a user to create/drop private synonyms in his or her own schema.
RESOUCE	CREATE DATABASE LINK	Enables a user to create/drop database links in his or her own schema.
RESOURCE	CREATE CLUSTER	Enables a user to create/drop clusters in his or her own schema.
RESOURCE	CREATE PUBLIC SYNONYM	Enables a user to create public synonyms.
RESOURCE	DROP PUBLIC SYNONYM	Enables a user to drop public synonyms.

After all the application objects are created under the development schema and are ready for testing, user schema can be created with the system privilege, as shown in the following section. Once the user schema is created, then the application object privilege must be granted to the proper user schema.

Necessary for Application User

The application user schemas/accounts should be created and assigned to the CONNECT role. This privilege enables all users to log into the system to create a session and to alter session characteristics. Access to the application is granted based on the user's responsibilities in the system. This access is granted by providing user schema with the correct object privileges.

The statements to apply the necessary system privileges are shown in the following statements and must be executed under a DBA user:

File: 10_5.sql

```
CREATE USER tempb IDENTIFIED BY tempb;
GRANT CONNECT TO tempb;
```

At this point, the TEMPB schema has the system privilege of creating and altering a session only. The next step is to authorize the correct application object privilege.

Provide Application Object Privileges

Once an application is developed, tested, and ready for production implementation, the application user schemas are created with the proper Oracle system privilege, as previously detailed, followed by the proper application object privilege that encompasses the following objects:

- Tables
- Sequences
- Views
- Packages, Procedures, Functions

The question that must be answered is "What type of object privilege is necessary?" This usually depends on the application interface, namely, the screens, reports, and programs that must be executed and by which application users. Based on further analysis of the issues outlined, what usually becomes apparent is different types or groups of users will need access to the system. Some require access to different modules (screens, reports, programs) and some require different type of access for different modules. Therefore, the types of users are broken into groups. These groups are created in Oracle as roles, the necessary object privileges for each role are identified and created, and the users are assigned to the appropriate role.

The typical object privileges required for the various objects are shown in the following table:

Object Type	Typical Access Granted
Table, View	SELECT, INSERT, UPDATE, DELETE
Sequence	SELECT

Object Type	Typical Access Granted
Package, Procedure, Function	EXECUTE
Database Trigger	No Privilege Required, Implicit Execution

A database trigger containing a call to execute a stored PL/SQL object, such as a procedure or function, must have EXECUTE privilege on the specific stored PL/SQL object. The "Typical Access Granted" provided in the preceding table for database triggers assumes the procedural logic is coded directly in the database trigger creation statement.

The developer or DBA is responsible for determining the object privileges (for each object type previously outlined) necessary for each group of users for each screen, report, and program module. Once this is determined, the roles can be created, the proper object privileges can be assigned to the roles, and the users can be assigned to the proper role.

Assume the application analysis determined the following groups, users, and object privileges were needed:

Group:	**Entry**
Users:	Joe, Lori
Tables:	Query and Enter employees
	Query and Enter customers
Group:	**Maintenance**
Users:	Rich, Brad
Tables:	Query and Update employees
	Query and Update customers
Procedures:	Execute validate_salary
Group:	**Manager**
Users:	Regina, Kristen
Tables:	Query, Enter, Update, and Delete employees
.	Query, Enter, Update, and Delete customers
Procedures:	Execute validate_salary
	Execute adjust_salary

The following SQL statements would create the necessary security for this application, assuming a PUBLIC synonym was created for every table and procedure previously outlined:

File: 10_6.sql

```
-- Create the 3 roles
CREATE ROLE entry;
CREATE ROLE maintenance;
CREATE ROLE manager;

-- Assign object privileges to roles
GRANT SELECT, INSERT ON s_employee TO entry;
GRANT SELECT, INSERT ON s_customer TO entry;
GRANT SELECT, UPDATE ON s_employee TO maintenance;
GRANT SELECT, UPDATE ON s_customer TO maintenance;
GRANT EXECUTE ON validate_salary TO maintenance;
GRANT SELECT, INSERT, UPDATE, DELETE ON s_employee TO manager;
GRANT SELECT, INSERT, UPDATE, DELETE ON s_customer TO manager;
GRANT EXECUTE ON validate_salary TO manager;
GRANT EXECUTE ON adjust_salary TO manager;

-- Create users (object privilege) and assign to appropriate role

-- Joe and Lori are entry level users
CREATE USER joe identified by joe;
CREATE USER lori identified by lori;
GRANT CONNECT TO joe, lori;
GRANT entry TO joe, lori;

-- Rich and Brad are maintenance level users
CREATE USER rich identified by rich;
CREATE USER brad identified by brad;
GRANT CONNECT TO rich, brad;
GRANT maintenance TO rich, brad;

-- Regina and Kristen are manager level users
CREATE USER regina identified by regina;
CREATE USER kristen identified by kristen;
GRANT CONNECT TO regina, kristen;
GRANT manager TO regina, kristen;
```

Understand Security for Creation of Stored PL/SQL Objects

Creating stored PL/SQL objects relies on the correct business and functional definitions, as well as an experienced developer to develop and test the modules for correctness. Once this is completed, providing proper access on these objects is necessary. Unfortunately, this is one area of PL/SQL that is often misunderstood. The goal of this section is to educate developers and DBAs on what is necessary for an application developer account to create stored PL/SQL objects and the necessary privilege to grant application users the ability to execute these stored PL/SQL objects. The application developer account must first have the proper Oracle system privilege to create a stored PL/SQL object. The application developer account must then be granted the proper object privilege on the objects referenced in the stored PL/SQL object and, finally, the application developer account must grant the proper privilege to application users to allow them to execute each PL/SQL stored object.

Grant Necessary System Privilege to Create PL/SQL Stored Objects

Four types of Oracle system privilege are related to the creation of stored PL/SQL objects and database triggers. These four types are outlined in the following table with the description of each privilege.

Object Type	System Privilege	Description
Package, Procedure, Function	CREATE PROCEDURE	Enables the user to create these object types *under his or her* account.
Package, Procedure, Function	CREATE ANY PROCEDURE	Enables the user to create these object types *under any* account.
Database Trigger	CREATE TRIGGER	Enables the user to create this object type *under his or her* account.
Database Trigger	CREATE ANY TRIGGER	Enables the user to create this object type *under any* account.

To see if the user has the necessary Oracle system privilege, the following query can be executed in SQL*Plus:

File: 10_7.sql

```
SELECT *
FROM   session_privs;
```

The following output displays the Oracle system privileges for the current session:

Output (10_7.sql)

```
PRIVILEGE
----------------------------------------
```

```
CREATE SESSION
ALTER SESSION
UNLIMITED TABLESPACE
CREATE TABLE
CREATE CLUSTER
CREATE SYNONYM
CREATE PUBLIC SYNONYM
CREATE VIEW
CREATE SEQUENCE
CREATE DATABASE LINK
CREATE PROCEDURE
CREATE TRIGGER
12 rows selected.
```

This user has the necessary object privilege to create stored PL/SQL objects and database triggers.

Grant Necessary Object Privilege to Create PL/SQL Stored Objects

To create a stored PL/SQL object, the user schema that attempts to create the stored PL/SQL object must have the proper object privileges for all references in the PL/SQL source code granted directly to the user. *Object privilege cannot be granted through a role.* The object must either be owned by the user or the correct privilege must have been granted directly to the user schema.

This is best illustrated by the following example. This example creates a procedure that will update all salaries by a specified percentage.

File: 10_8.sql

```
CREATE OR REPLACE PROCEDURE adjust_salary
   (p_percent_increase_num NUMBER) AS
   lv_percent_input_num NUMBER;
BEGIN
   lv_percent_input_num := p_percent_increase_num;
   DBMS_OUTPUT.PUT_LINE('Salaries Increased by: ' ||
      p_percent_increase_num);
   lv_percent_input_num := 1 + lv_percent_input_num/100;
   DBMS_OUTPUT.PUT_LINE('Multiplier: ' || lv_percent_input_num);
   UPDATE s_employee
   SET    salary = NVL(salary,0) * lv_percent_input_num;
   COMMIT;
END;
/
```

The following scenarios highlight the cases when a user can and cannot create the adjust_salary procedure (the owner of the s_employee table is PLSQL_USER and a PUBLIC synonym exists for the s_employee table that mirrors the table name):

1. If the PLSQL_USER attempted to execute this segment of code to create this procedure, the creation would succeed because the PLSQL_USER schema created the s_employee table and, therefore, has explicit UPDATE access on this table.

2. If the user TEMPC attempted to execute this segment of code without explicit UPDATE privilege on the s_employee table, the creation would fail with the following error: *PLS-00201: identifier 'S_EMPLOYEE' must be declared.*

3. If the user TEMPC attempted to execute this segment of code and was explicitly granted UPDATE privilege on the PLSQL_USER s_employee table as shown in the following statement, the creation would succeed.

   ```
   GRANT UPDATE ON s_employee TO tempc;
   ```

4. If the user TEMPC was granted UPDATE privilege on the PLSQL_USER s_employee table through a role, as the following statements show, the creation would fail with the following error: *PLS-00201: identifier 'S_EMPLOYEE' must be declared.* This is the same error encountered when no privilege was granted on the s_employee table.

File:10_9.sql

```
CREATE ROLE temp_emp;
GRANT UPDATE ON s_employee TO temp_emp;
GRANT temp_emp TO tempc;
```

TIP
To create a stored PL/SQL object, the schema must contain CREATE PROCEDURE/CREATE TRIGGER system privilege, as well as direct object privilege for any objects referenced in the PL/SQL source code.

Access granted through a role does not suffice for the object privilege. Oracle enforces this condition to ensure efficiency is maintained during execution of PL/SQL stored objects. Object privilege grants are maintained through explicit commands of GRANT and REVOKE; therefore, these commands adjust the data dictionary and invalidate a stored PL/SQL object if privilege is changed on referenced objects for a user who created an object. Roles can be changed with the SET ROLE command, which is per session and not reflected in the data dictionary. Therefore, because this role manipulation is unchanged in the data dictionary and is only at the session level, the stored PL/SQL object remains VALID when a SET ROLE command is executed, even though it affects the privilege of referenced objects in a stored PL/SQL object. If the calling user attempts to execute the stored PL/SQL object, a run-time error occurs.

To illustrate this, assume the 3rd scenario outlined in the preceding example is executed, the TEMPC user has UPDATE privilege on the s_employee table, and the TEMPC user has successfully created the adjust_salary procedure. If UPDATE privilege were subsequently removed from the TEMPC user on the s_employee table, then the adjust_salary procedure would be INVALIDated. Any time the privileges are revoked from a user that affects a stored PL/SQL object; the object will become INVALID (as seen in the USER_OBJECTS data dictionary view and illustrated in Chapter 9 and Chapter 13). The SET ROLE command would effectively revoke privilege from a user, the stored PL/SQL object would remain VALID for the session, and a run-time error would be encountered. Oracle has eliminated this problem by enforcing direct privilege for referenced objects.

Grant Necessary Privilege for Users to Execute PL/SQL Stored Objects

Once stored PL/SQL objects are created, the only privilege that must be granted to a user or role to execute the stored PL/SQL object is EXECUTE.

TIP
When a user executes a stored PL/SQL object on which he or she has been granted EXECUTE privilege, the stored PL/SQL object source code is executed with the object privileges of the user who created the stored PL/SQL object. The calling user does not have to possess any object privileges, with relation to the objects referenced in the stored PL/SQL object. This is a major advantage of stored PL/SQL objects in relation to security.

The following example highlights this extremely important fact. Assume the adjust_salary procedure was created under the PLSQL_USER account and a PUBLIC synonym was created for this procedure that mirrored the procedure name. Assume the TEMPC user does not have any privilege on the s_employee table. By issuing the following command(s):

```
GRANT EXECUTE ON adjust_salary TO tempc;
```

or

```
CREATE ROLE temp_salary;
GRANT EXECUTE ON adjust_salary TO temp_salary;
GRANT temp_salary TO tempc;
```

The TEMPC user can now execute the adjust_salary procedure by calling the procedure in SQL*Plus as the following statement illustrates:

```
EXECUTE adjust_salary(10)
```

The TEMPC user *does not* have to possess UPDATE privilege on the s_employee table: the adjust_salary procedure will be executed with the privileges of the PLSQL_USER user because the PLSQL_USER user created the stored PL/SQL object. This applies to all PL/SQL objects created by Oracle users, excluding the Oracle supplied packages (security for the Oracle supplied packages is discussed later in this chapter).

TIP
The only privilege that must be granted to a user to execute a stored PL/SQL object is EXECUTE. The user does not need object privilege on objects referenced in the stored PL/SQL object source code.

TIP
Refer to the last section in this chapter and in Chapter 16 for information on a new feature in Oracle 8i that adds flexibility to the security architecture of stored PL/SQL objects.

Understand Early Binding

Understanding how Oracle compiles a stored PL/SQL object is important. Early binding is a key concept in understanding how Oracle stored PL/SQL objects execute when called. When a stored PL/SQL object is created, it is syntactically parsed, the objects in the PL/SQL source code are bound (this is referred to as *early binding*), object privileges in the PL/SQL source code are checked, the source code is inserted into the database (viewable in USER_SOURCE, ALL_SOURCE, and DBA_SOURCE), and the object is either successfully or unsuccessfully compiled (the status column in the USER_OBJECTS, ALL_OBJECTS, and DBA_OBJECTS is set to VALID or INVALID and errors are logged if unsuccessful).

Early binding encompasses the object binding of each object referenced in the PL/SQL source code. Remember, PL/SQL source code can reference any object, including tables, views, sequences, and other stored PL/SQL objects. Once the binding takes place, the call to execute a stored PL/SQL object is bound to the objects that are determined during compilation.

Early binding can be illustrated by referring to the preceding adjust_salary procedure. If we grant explicit UPDATE access to TEMPC on the PLSQL_USER s_employee table and create the adjust_salary procedure under the TEMPC user, subsequent calls to the adjust_salary procedure will update the PLSQL_USER s_employee table.

If an s_employee table is now created under the TEMPC user and the adjust_salary procedure is executed by user TEMPC…, what table would be updated: the PLSQL_USER or the TEMPC s_employee table? The TEMPC table.

The reason is, upon original creation of the adjust_salary procedure under the TEMPC user, Oracle implicitly creates a dependency between the object being compiled and the nonexistence of the referred object in the TEMPC schema. This happens because a PUBLIC synonym is used for the s_employee table. Once the TEMPC user created its own s_employee table, the adjust_salary procedure became INVALID (status in the USER_OBJECTS view) because a dependency existed in the data dictionary. When the adjust_salary was then executed, Oracle recompiled the adjust_salary procedure with the new reference to the s_employee table of the TEMPC user. Now, if the s_employee table created under the TEMPC user had a different structure than the table under the PLSQL_USER and caused the implicit compilation of the adjust_salary procedure to be unsuccessful, then an error would have resulted when the adjust_salary procedure was executed.

Because using PUBLIC synonyms for all objects is recommended, as outlined in this chapter, the preceding caveat can be avoided by creating all stored PL/SQL objects under the owner of the objects referenced in the PL/SQL source code. This guideline not only centralizes the objects, it also avoids problems that can be introduced by this and other caveats that exist when working with stored PL/SQL objects.

 TIP

Early binding occurs when a PL/SQL object is stored in the database and ensures that any objects referenced in the stored PL/SQL object source code refer to one and only one specific object.

Understand Oracle Supplied PL/SQL Package Privileges

Oracle supplied packages are created during database creation. These packages are created under the SYS user. Most of these packages are created with a PUBLIC synonym defined for the package mirroring the name of the package, and EXECUTE privilege is granted to PUBLIC. There are a few of the packages that EXECUTE is not granted by default to PUBLIC. These packages that do not grant EXECUTE by default typically are related to DBA-specific procedures, which should be restricted to DBAs. For a list of Oracle-supplied packages and more details on these powerful packages, refer to Chapter 11 and Chapter 12.

The last distinction in terms of security with these packages relates to the execution of these package procedures and/or functions when called. *When calling an Oracle supplied package procedure or function, the execution is not executed with the SYS user privilege (even though SYS created the Oracle-stored packages), it is executed with the object privilege of the calling user. This execution difference is true for any package procedure or function providing functionality, which involves a command that can be performed separately in SQL.* When the TEMPC user executes the Oracle supplied packages, it looks at the TEMPC Oracle system and object privileges. Run-time errors can occur if the proper privileges do not exist for the attempted operation that is called by the package. To help you become more familiar with the Oracle system privileges necessary to execute the Oracle supplied packages, the comments in the package specifications SQL script files normally define these requirements.

Ensure Application Portability Through the Use of PUBLIC Synonyms

When you create your application development environment, eliminating any hardcoded usernames in your application setup or source code files is important. Creating PUBLIC synonyms for objects that mirror the name of the object can eliminate references to usernames. This allows for all references to objects to reference the object name; if it is decided later to change the name of the user account that owns all the objects, then the SQL scripts to create the objects can be executed under the new user without modification. This applies to all objects: tables, views, sequences, packages, procedures, functions, and so forth.

Ensuring Application Portability

This method should also be followed when deploying an application into production.

Review System and Object Privileges in Your System

Depending on your environment and security setup, keeping track of the privileges granted at the Oracle system and application object level can become cumbersome. Being able to review all privileges at all levels is necessary. Oracle has provided the infrastructure for reviewing this information by storing all Oracle system privileges, application object privileges, users, and roles in the data dictionary. The list of the corresponding data dictionary views is shown in the following tables:

Information on profiles, roles, and privileges granted to each user and role:

ROLE_ROLE_PRIVS	ROLE_SYS_PRIVS	ROLE_TAB_PRIVS
SESSION_PRIVS	SESSION_ROLES	USER_RESOURCE_LIMITS
DBA_PROFILES	DBA_ROLES	
USER_SYS_PRIVS		DBA_SYS_PRIVS
USER_ROLE_PRIVS		DBA_ROLE_PRIVS

Information on tables and column access:

COLUMN_PRIVILEGES	TABLE_PRIVILEGES	
USER_COL_PRIVS	ALL_COL_PRIVS	DBA_COL_PRIVS
USER_COL_PRIVS_MADE	ALL_COL_PRIVS_MADE	
USER_COL_PRIVS_RECD	ALL_COL_PRIVS_RECD	
USER_TAB_PRIVS	ALL_TAB_PRIVS	DBA_TAB_PRIVS
USER_TAB_PRIVS_MADE	ALL_TAB_PRIVS_MADE	
USER_TAB_PRIVS_RECD	ALL_TAB_PRIVS_RECD	

The following scripts can be used to retrieve information to provide the capability to review, analyze, and understand the current privileges in your system (users executing the following scripts must possess SELECT privilege on the data dictionary views referenced):

The following script provides a list of Oracle system privileges to users.

File: 10_10.sql

```
-- Oracle System Privilege Grants to Users
SELECT b.privilege what_granted,
       b.admin_option, a.username
FROM   sys.dba_users a, sys.dba_sys_privs b
WHERE  a.username = b.grantee
ORDER BY 1,2;
```

Output (10_10.sql)

```
Granted Privilege                 Admin Username
--------------------------------- ----- ---------------
ALTER SESSION                     NO    PLSQL_USER
ALTER SESSION                     NO    TEMP_USER
ALTER SESSION                     NO    TEST2
CREATE ANY TABLE                  NO    PLSQL_USER
CREATE ANY TABLE                  NO    TEST2
```

The following script provides a list of Oracle system privileges to roles.

File: 10_11.sql

```
-- Oracle System Privilege Grants to Roles
SELECT privilege what_granted,
       admin_option, grantee
FROM   sys.dba_sys_privs
WHERE  NOT EXISTS
(SELECT 'x'
FROM    sys.dba_users
WHERE   username = grantee)
ORDER BY 1,2;
```

Output (10_11.sql)

```
Granted Privilege     Admin  Grantee
--------------------- ------ -------------
ALTER ANY PROCEDURE   YES    DBA
ALTER ANY ROLE        YES    DBA
ALTER ANY SEQUENCE    YES    DBA
ALTER SESSION         NO     CONNECT
CREATE SEQUENCE       NO     RESOURCE
```

	YES	DBA
CREATE TABLE	NO	RESOURCE
	YES	DBA

The following script provides a list of application object grants to users.

File: 10_12.sql

```
-- Object Grants to Users
SELECT b.owner || '.' || b.table_name obj,
       b.privilege what_granted, b.grantable,
       a.username
FROM   sys.dba_users a, sys.dba_tab_privs b
WHERE  a.username = b.grantee
ORDER BY 1,2,3;
```

Output (10_12.sql)

Object	Granted Priv	Admin Option	Username
PLSQL_USER.CORE_PROCESS	EXECUTE	NO	SCOTT
PLSQL_USER.LOG_EXTENTS	EXECUTE	NO	TEMP1
PLSQL_USER.NAME_PKG	EXECUTE	NO	TEMP
PLSQL_USER.OBJECTS_TO_PIN	SELECT	NO	SYS

The following script provides a list of application object grants to roles.

File: 10_13.sql

```
-- Object Grants to Roles
SELECT owner || '.' || table_name obj,
       privilege what_granted, grantable, grantee
FROM   sys.dba_tab_privs
WHERE  NOT EXISTS
(SELECT  'x'
FROM     sys.dba_users
WHERE    username = grantee)
ORDER BY 1,2,3;
```

Output (10_13.sql)

Object	Granted Priv	Admin Option	Grantee

PLSQL_USER.LOG_SOURCE	EXECUTE	NO	PUBLIC
PLSQL_USER.SOURCE_LOG	INSERT	NO	PUBLIC
PLSQL_USER.SOURCE_LOG	SELECT	NO	PUBLIC
SYS.ALL_CATALOG	SELECT	YES	PUBLIC
SYS.DBMS_DESCRIBE	EXECUTE	NO	PUBLIC
SYS.DUAL	SELECT	YES	PUBLIC
SYS.USER_TAB_PRIVS	SELECT	YES	PUBLIC

The following script provides a list of direct role grants to users.

File: 10_14.sql

```
-- Direct Role Grants to Users
SELECT b.granted_role ||
       DECODE(admin_option, 'YES',
       ' (With Admin Option)',
       NULL) what_granted, a.username
FROM   sys.dba_users a, sys.dba_role_privs b
WHERE  a.username = b.grantee
ORDER BY 1;
```

Output (10_14.sql)

```
Granted Roles                         Username
------------------------------        ------------
CONNECT                               PLSQL_USER
CONNECT                               JCT
CONNECT (With Admin Option)          SYS
DBA                                   PLSQL_USER
DBA                                   TUSC
DBA (With Admin Option)              SYS
DBA (With Admin Option)              SYSTEM
RESOURCE                              PLSQL_USER
RESOURCE                              JCT
RESOURCE (With Admin Option)         SYS
```

The following script provides a list of direct role grants to roles.

File: 10_15.sql:

```
-- Direct Role Grants to Roles
SELECT granted_role ||
       DECODE(admin_option, 'YES',
       ' (With Admin Option)', NULL) what_granted,
       grantee
FROM   sys.dba_role_privs
```

Reviewing System and Object
Privileges in Your System

```
WHERE   NOT EXISTS
(SELECT 'x'
FROM    sys.dba_users
WHERE   username = grantee)
ORDER BY 1;
```

Output (10_15.sql):

Granted Roles	Grantee
DBA	IOUG
EXP_FULL_DATABASE	DBA
IMP_FULL_DATABASE	DBA

The following script provides a list of user privileges granted by user of all granted roles, Oracle system privileges, and application object privileges.

File: 10_16.sql

```
SELECT a.username,
       b.granted_role || DECODE(admin_option,'YES',
       ' (With Admin Option)',NULL) what_granted
FROM   sys.dba_users a, sys.dba_role_privs b
WHERE  a.username = b.grantee
UNION
SELECT a.username,
       b.privilege || DECODE(admin_option,'YES',
       ' (With Admin Option)', NULL) what_granted
FROM   sys.dba_users a, sys.dba_sys_privs b
WHERE  a.username = b.grantee
UNION
SELECT a.username,
       b.table_name || ' - ' || b.privilege
       || DECODE(grantable,'YES',
       ' (With Grant Option)',NULL) what_granted
FROM   sys.dba_users a, sys.dba_tab_privs b
WHERE  a.username = b.grantee
ORDER BY 1;
```

Output (10_16.sql)

Username	Granted Role or Privilege
PLSQL_USER	CONNECT
PLSQL_USER	CREATE ANY TABLE

```
PLSQL_USER            DBA
PLSQL_USER            DBA_SOURCE - SELECT
PLSQL_USER            DBMS_JOB - EXECUTE
PLSQL_USER            RESOURCE
PLSQL_USER            UNLIMITED TABLESPACE
PLSQL_USER            V_$ACCESS - SELECT
SYS                   CHECK_IN - EXECUTE (With Grant Option)
SYS                   CONNECT (With Admin Option)
SYS                   DBA (With Admin Option)
```

Lock Application Account After Production

Once an application goes into production, there is a period of postproduction. This period of time is spent making any modifications/enhancements necessary for the production application to operate correctly and efficiently. Once this postproduction phase of an application implementation is complete, it is often desirable to lock the main production account down. A method of accomplishing this exists, without changing the password or other major modifications to the account. This method eliminates direct logging onto the account without affecting any objects that exist under the schema.

To accomplish this, the CREATE SESSION privilege must be removed from the user. If the privilege was granted directly, the privilege can be revoked from a DBA account with the following statement:

```
REVOKE CREATE SESSION FROM plsql_user;
```

If the CREATE SESSION privilege was granted through a role, then the role(s) must be identified for this user that have been granted to the user. This can be accomplished by executing the following statement:

File: 10_17.sql

```
SELECT *
FROM   role_sys_privs
WHERE  privilege = 'CREATE SESSION';
```

The output follows for the PLSQL_USER:

Output (10_17.sql)

```
ROLE                              PRIVILEGE                          ADM
--------------------------------  ---------------------------------  ---
```

CONNECT	CREATE SESSION	NO
DBA	CREATE SESSION	YES

Once the roles have been identified, they must be revoked from the user. These roles can be revoked from a DBA account with the following statement:

```
REVOKE CONNECT, DBA FROM plsql_user;
```

The preceding script would disable connecting to this user. The objects still exist and can be referenced, but the user account cannot be directly logged into. If the account needs to be enabled for login, then the CREATE SESSION privilege, or a role with this privilege, could be granted to this user.

Additional PL/SQL Related Security

Additional areas are related to PL/SQL security that are worth mentioning. The following sections provide a brief explanation of these areas.

Permission for Web-Based Applications

When developing applications for the Web, whether for the intranet or the Internet, the interface can be completely controlled via stored PL/SQL program units, which are called and executed with actions from an HTML page. Web-based applications create an environment that allows for security to be entirely encapsulated and controlled through stored PL/SQL program units. This translates to access and processing that is entirely controlled through the stored PL/SQL program unit functionality. In this environment, there is no need to grant access to the underlying database tables. The application users only required CONNECT privilege as outlined previously and EXECUTE on the necessary stored PL/SQL objects. Refer to Chapter 15 for more information on PL/SQL for the Web.

Encrypt Source Code

To add another layer of security for stored PL/SQL program unit source code, these objects can be encrypted to hide the view of source code in the data dictionary source views (USER_SOURCE, ALL_SOURCE, and DBA_SOURCE). Oracle provides a facility for WRAPping packages, procedures, and functions prior to creating these objects in the database. The WRAP facility is covered in more detail in Chapter 5. WRAPping should be considered in environments where source code security is needed or confidential information is embedded in the source code.

Additional PL/SQL Related Security

Limit SQL*Plus Access

SQL*Plus often provides a back door that circumvents security because application users are typically provided access to objects based on the application interface. Access to the underlying objects remains in existence even if the application user logs into SQL*Plus. Therefore, if DELETE privilege was granted on the s_employee table to user SCOTT by user PLSQL_USER, based on the need for the SCOTT user to be able to delete employee records based on verification in a Form, a potential security risk is introduced. If user SCOTT has access to SQL*Plus and logs into SQL*Plus, then SCOTT can issue a DELETE command against the s_employee table. This could be devastating!

One method to eliminate the SQL*Plus access is to use the Oracle Product User Profile introduced in Oracle version 6. This facility allows for SQL*Plus access to be limited by telling Oracle what operations you do not want certain users to perform in SQL*Plus. The information is logged in SYSTEM tables referenced by every user logging into SQL*Plus (excluding SYSTEM). The Product User Profile tables are created with the pupbld.sql script and, if this script has not been executed in your Oracle environment, then the message "Warning: Product user profile information not loaded" appears every time a user logs into SQL*Plus. Once the pupbld.sql script is executed, this message no longer appears when logging into SQL*Plus.

The Product User Profile facility allows SQL and SQL*Plus commands to be limited in SQL*Plus. Refer to the *Oracle SQL*Plus Users Guide and Reference* documentation for further details.

Provide Forms Security on Login

There has been a long-standing security concern when using the Oracle Developer Forms product and other products to develop application interfaces. This security problem is introduced when the necessary object privilege is granted to application users. The Forms interface is robust and allows for a controlled interface to the underlying data; however, the object privileges are provided at the database level to application users, not at the Forms level. Therefore, even though the application controls the access and functionality, what happens if the user connects to Oracle in SQL*Plus or from another product through an ODBC driver? Once this login occurs in one of these products, the object privilege is still valid in these products for the application user. This can be devastating!

One technique for securing applications of this nature is to provide the necessary object privileges at the time of login into a Form. In the startup of the Form, the application user can be granted the proper role(s) for access while in the

Form through the DDL SET ROLE command or DBMS_SESSION.SET_ROLE procedure. When the application user logs out of the Form, the object privileges are no longer valid. The privileges of the role(s) assigned in this manner are only valid while the session is logged on, not at the database level.

Provide Additional Security with Database Triggers

Database triggers are created on database tables at the database level. This allows for functional control at the database level, which is the lowest level available to build logic. If a BEFORE INSERT database trigger is created on the s_employee table, then no matter what product is used on the front end to create the INSERT into the s_employee table, this BEFORE INSERT trigger will execute when the INSERT is attempted.

This introduces the capability to build security logic at the database level, which can verify desired conditions of data manipulation on any table. Remember, database triggers execute implicitly and, therefore, do not have to be called to execute.

New PL/SQL Security Feature in Oracle8i

For years, many developers have sought for the mechanism of creating stored PL/SQL objects that executed with the invokers privilege (similar to the method Oracle deploys for several of the Oracle provided packages) on the objects referenced in the PL/SQL source code. In Oracle 8i, Oracle has introduced this mechanism by adding an argument in the CREATE command for creating a stored PL/SQL object. For more details on this new feature, refer to Chapter 16.

This feature can be beneficial in certain situations, but it should not be thought of as the standard method to deploy. Remember the discussion on stored PL/SQL objects and how compilation and execution of these objects work. If this method is deployed, additional object privileges have to be granted, and overhead will be introduced for compilation when the stored PL/SQL object is called for execution.

Summary

Oracle security is an extremely critical, but often overlooked and/or misunderstood, area of application deployment. It is usually easy to implement security, making sure all users who should have access to the application do have access. More difficult and more important is also to ensure the security given to users does not allow unauthorized access. Far too many Oracle environments deal with security through ignorance. This chapter outlined the necessary areas of Oracle security for development and deployment of applications from a general overview and a more specific analysis of the PL/SQL security issues.

Tips Review

■ When the RESOURCE role is granted to a user, the UNLIMITED TABLESPACE system privilege is also granted to the user. This system privilege does not show in the sql.bsq file listing for the RESOURCE role and is granted internally by Oracle. It does not show in the data dictionary as a system privilege assigned to the RESOURCE role either. However, once the RESOURCE role is assigned to a user, the UNLIMITED TABLESPACE system privilege shows in the SESSION_PRIVS data dictionary view.

■ When Oracle parses a SQL statement, it must determine whether the object reference is to a table, private synonym, or public synonym; there can be one of each with the same name. Oracle must determine which object to use by checking for object existence in the following order: first, Oracle checks to see if the current user owns a table with the object name; second, Oracle checks to see if the current user has a private synonym with the name of the object; and, third, Oracle checks to see if a PUBLIC synonym exists with the name of the object. When an object name match is found, then that object is used to execute the SQL statement. If an object name match is not found, then an error results. This parsing precedence extends to any object references, including views, sequences, packages, procedures, and functions.

■ To create a stored PL/SQL object, the schema must contain create PROCEDURE/CREATE TRIGGER system privilege, as well as direct object privilege for any objects referenced in the PL/SQL source code.

■ When a user executes a stored PL/SQL object on which he or she has been granted EXECUTE privilege, the stored PL/SQL object source code is executed with the object privileges of the user who created the stored PL/SQL object. The calling user does not have to possess any object privileges, with relation to the objects referenced in the stored PL/SQL object. This is a major advantage of stored PL/SQL objects in relation to security.

■ Early binding occurs when a PL/SQL object is stored in the database and ensures that any objects referenced in the stored object source code refer to one and only one specific object.

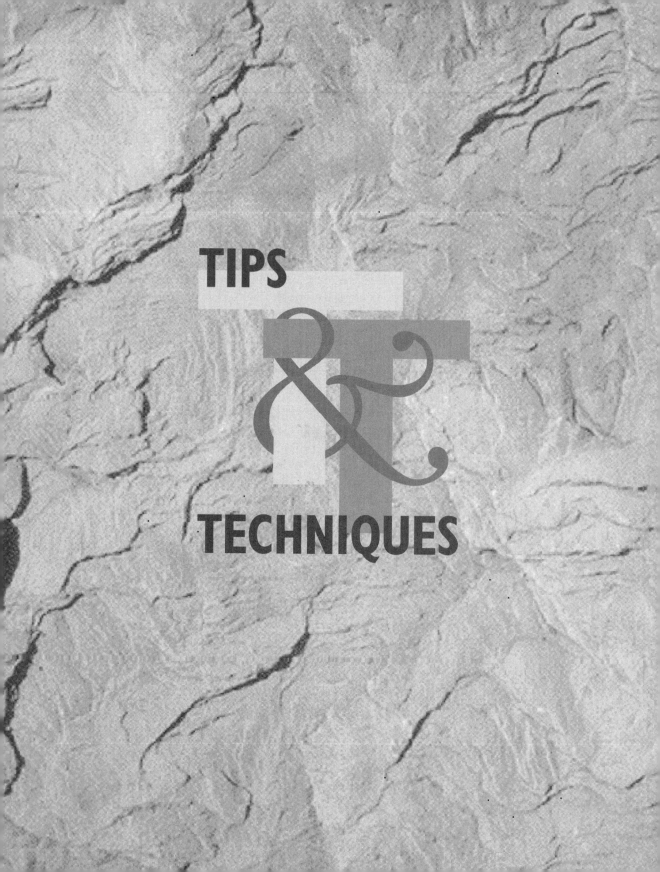

CHAPTER
11

Exploring the
Oracle Supplied
PL/SQL Packages
(Developer and DBA)

How many times have you heard the phrase "Our goal is to not re-invent the wheel"? This saying seems to be used more frequently now and with good reason. The general nature of Oracle developers and DBAs is to focus on completing a task or carrying out a responsibility with the knowledge they have and, in the Oracle world, this often means building a SQL script or PL/SQL program unit on the fly to accomplish the task or need. In addition, when the task is complete, people typically do not have the time to document what they did or create a nice canned routine (PL/SQL package, procedure, or function) to perform the task or function in the future. Oracle has provided the means of creating subroutines or stored PL/SQL program units in the form of procedures, functions, and groups of program units in packages. The storage of program units in the database allows for a central repository of these subroutines.

Furthermore, Oracle has assisted in the task of proceduralizing several developer and DBA routines and functions into stored PL/SQL packages that are standard with Oracle. These packages are helpful when developing an application or administering a database. These packages provide robust functionality, greatly enhancing the PL/SQL language and providing a wealth of DBA functions to assist in administering the database from transaction monitoring to controlling of the Shared Pool. Developers and DBAs should review this gift provided by Oracle to become familiar with these packages and their capabilities. Also advantageous would be to take Oracle's lead in this area and continue to build packaged subroutines and procedures in a similar manner to ease development and administration of Oracle based systems.

The goal of this chapter is to outline the Oracle-supplied PL/SQL packages and to build a reference framework of these packages that can be combined with Chapter 12 to ensure this Oracle gift is used effectively. This chapter outlines the Oracle supplied PL/SQL packages and provides the following tips and techniques.

- Understand the scope of the Oracle supplied packages

- Explore the structure of Oracle supplied packages

- View the script files at the Operating System

- Create the Oracle supplied packages

- Identify the Oracle supplied packages in your system

- Execute the Oracle supplied packages

- Provide a detailed reference of the Oracle supplied packages

Understand the Scope of the Oracle Supplied Packages

Oracle has supplied a gift to developers and DBAs, yet few take advantage of these powerful packages. The main reason for the lack of use of these packages resides in the lack of knowledge regarding this functionality. I have asked numerous PL/SQL developers if they have ever used the Oracle supplied PL/SQL packages. The response by many is they have not used them at all or to a limited extent. Actually, when I mention the DBMS_OUTPUT package is one of these Oracle supplied packages, the response changes. Knowledge of the Oracle supplied PL/SQL packages is extremely important when developing and/or administering Oracle systems because some useful procedures and functions are in these packages, which extend the PL/SQL language and overall functionality. Oracle has already done a great deal of work for us by creating these modules as standard PL/SQL routines. Do not re-invent the wheel; use what Oracle has spent a long time creating. This functionality should be treated the same as any of the standard PL/SQL language commands.

This chapter focuses on several of the most useful packages for the majority of developers and DBAs. The chapter provides the framework and an understanding of these packages and the packages' content. As each new release of Oracle comes out, take some of the suggestions and routines outlined in this chapter to help you gain a better understanding of what's new to your environment. One of the main areas of growth with each new version of Oracle is the introduction of new packages and the expansion of existing packages. Most of the packages created contain procedures and functions that are wrapped and not viewable to developers and DBAs. Some of these procedures and functions are written in native PL/SQL; however, most of these are stub routines to C programs. Therefore, attempting to get around a bug fix or to integrate new functionality into your existing version of Oracle by installing a package from a later release generally will install (because of limited installation checking), but will not work because of the underlying C execution calls.

Many of these packages are used heavily by Oracle internally, so you must never modify any of these packages. If you need a slightly modified version of the package, create your own.

Explore the Structure of Oracle Supplied Packages

The main Oracle supplied packages are core packages to the PL/SQL language. These are the STANDARD package (specification and body creation in file standard.sql) and the DBMS_STANDARD package (specification creation in file dbmsstdx.sql). The STANDARD package is extremely lengthy and contains all the

PL/SQL commands, including operands, data type definitions, standard exceptions, and so forth. The standard PL/SQL language commands are typically created as functions, and all data types and standard exceptions are defined, as shown in the following segment of the standard.sql file (these are only selected lines of this file and some of the lines have been reformatted because of space limitations; this was from Oracle 7.3—note that the following code listing does not conform to the standards identified in Chapter 3 and used throughout this book because this code was copied directly from one of Oracle's SQL files).

```
create or replace package STANDARD is
   type BOOLEAN is (FALSE, TRUE);
   type DATE is DATE_BASE;
   subtype BINARY_INTEGER is INTEGER range '-2147483647'..2147483647;
   -- used to be -2147483648 - less than MAXSB4MINVAL

NO_DATA_FOUND exception;
   pragma EXCEPTION_INIT(NO_DATA_FOUND, 100);
VALUE_ERROR exception;
   pragma EXCEPTION_INIT(VALUE_ERROR, '-6502');

function SQLERRM return varchar2;
   pragma FIPSFLAG('SQLERRM', 1452);

function '=' (LEFT BOOLEAN, RIGHT BOOLEAN) return BOOLEAN;
function '||' (LEFT VARCHAR2, RIGHT VARCHAR2) return VARCHAR2;

function UPPER(ch VARCHAR2) return varchar2;
   pragma FIPSFLAG('UPPER', 1452);

function ADD_MONTHS(LEFT DATE, RIGHT NUMBER) return DATE;
   pragma BUILTIN('ADD_MONTHS',39, 12, 13);
   -- PEMS_DATE, DATE_ADD_MONTHS1
   pragma FIPSFLAG('ADD_MONTHS', 1450);
function ADD_MONTHS(LEFT NUMBER, RIGHT DATE) return DATE;
   pragma BUILTIN('ADD_MONTHS',39, 12, 14);
   -- PEMS_DATE, DATE_ADD_MONTHS2
   pragma FIPSFLAG('ADD_MONTHS', 1450);

function 'LIKE' (str varchar2, pat varchar2) return boolean is
  begin
    return peslik(str, pat);
  end;

function USER return varchar2 is
  c varchar2(255);
  begin
```

```
    select user into c from sys.dual;
    return c;
end;
```

The DBMS_STANDARD package contains extensions to the STANDARD package and serves a similar purpose. This file is much shorter than the STANDARD package file and is a stub routine that references *C* programs.

All PL/SQL package content, Oracle supplied packages and user created packages, including variables, procedures, and functions, must be referenced by preceding the package element with the package name. However, the STANDARD and DBMS_STANDARD package elements do not follow this rule and can be referenced without preceding the element with the package name. This is illustrated in the following script:

File: 11_1.sql (Does not use the STANDARD package prefix with the SUBSTR function)

```
DECLARE
  lv_temp_txt VARCHAR2(30) := 'Hello Joe';
BEGIN
    lv_temp_txt := SUBSTR(lv_temp_txt, 1,5);
    DBMS_OUTPUT.PUT_LINE(lv_temp_txt);
END;
/
```

Output (11_1.sql)

```
Hello

PL/SQL procedure successfully completed.
```

File: 11_2.sql (Uses the STANDARD package prefix with the SUBSTR function)

```
DECLARE
    lv_temp_txt VARCHAR2(30) := 'Hello Joe';
BEGIN
    lv_temp_txt := STANDARD.SUBSTR(lv_temp_txt, 1,5);
    DBMS_OUTPUT.PUT_LINE(lv_temp_txt);
END;
/
```

Output (11_2.sql)

Exploring the Structure of Oracle Supplied Packages

```
Hello

PL/SQL procedure successfully completed.
```

Most of the other Oracle supplied packages have been created to extend the PL/SQL functionality and to make the language more robust. Review these packages and determine which procedures and functions within them are of value to you as a developer or DBA.

The Oracle supplied PL/SQL packages are typically a combination of procedures and functions and are created and stored in the database. There are two parts of a package, namely a specification and body section. Each section is created separately with a CREATE (or CREATE OR REPLACE) statement and stored separately in the database. Package bodies are typically stored in the database in compiled format.

View the Script Files at the Operating System

The best source of information related to the Oracle supplied packages is found in the actual script files at the operating system for each of these packages. These creation files are typically located in the ORACLE_HOME/rdbms/admin directory. Most Oracle supplied packages are named with a prefix of DBMS, but a few exist that do not follow this naming convention. Many of these are for internal use by Oracle only and are not callable. The packages intended for server-side execution only are prefixed with a DBMS, whereas, the server-side packages not prefixed with DBMS were intended as generic packages that someday might be expanded to client-side execution.

Many package creations are in their own files and follow the convention of placing the package specification creation, PUBLIC synonym creation (if one is to be created), and execution access commands in a file beginning with DBMS followed by an abbreviation of the package name and suffix of sql. The package body is located in a separate file that is wrapped. The body filename begins with PRVT followed by the same abbreviation used in the filenaming of the package specification file and a suffix of plb. The dbmsutil.sql and prvtutil.plb vary from this convention by containing several Oracle supplied packages.

These script files contain valuable comments providing a solid background of most of the packages and their elements. The files often contain descriptions of the program units, exceptions that can be raised, limitations, access information, and example code showing the use. If your environment prohibits you from accessing these files, you may want to ask your DBA or system administrator for READ ONLY access on these files.

The following shows a sample segment of the dbmssql.sql file. (Note that the following code listing does not conform to the standards identified in Chapter 3 and used throughout this book because this code was copied directly from one of Oracle's SQL files.)

```
Rem     dbmssql.sql - DBMS package for dynamic SQL
Rem   DESCRIPTION
Rem     This package provides a means to use dynamic SQL to access
Rem     the database.
REM   ***********************************************************
REM   THIS PACKAGE MUST NOT BE MODIFIED BY THE CUSTOMER.  DOING SO
REM   COULD CAUSE INTERNAL ERRORS AND CORRUPTIONS IN THE RDBMS.
REM   ***********************************************************


REM   *************************************
REM   THIS PACKAGE MUST BE CREATED UNDER SYS.
REM   *************************************


REM   ***********************************************************
REM   PROCEDURES AND FUNCTIONS IN THIS PACKAGE ARE EXECUTED UNDER
REM   THE CURRENT CALLING USER, NOT UNDER THE PACKAGE OWNER SYS.
REM   ***********************************************************


create or replace package dbms_sql is


   -----------
   -- OVERVIEW
   --
   -- This package provides a means to use dynamic SQL to access the
   -- database.
   --

   ------------------------
   -- RULES AND LIMITATIONS
   --
   -- Bind variables of a SQL statement are identified by their names.
   -- When binding a value to a bind variable, the string identifying
   -- the bind variable in the statement may optionally contain the
   -- leading colon. For example, if the parsed SQL statement is
   -- "SELECT ENAME FROM EMP WHERE SAL > :X", on binding the variable
   -- to a value,it can be identified using either of the strings ':X'
   -- and 'X'.
   --
   -- Columns of the row being selected in a SELECT statement are
   -- identified by their relative positions (1, 2, 3, ...) as they
   -- appear on the select list from left to right.
   --
```

```
--   Privileges are associated with the caller of the
--   procedures/functions in this package as follows:
--     If the caller is an anonymous PL/SQL block, the
--     procedures/functions are run using the privileges of the
--     current user.
--     If the caller is a stored procedure, the procedures/functions
--     are run using the privileges of the owner of the stored
--     procedure.
--
--   WARNING: Using the package to dynamically execute DDL statements
--   can results in the program hanging. For example, a call to a
--   procedure in a package will result in the package being locked
--   until the execution returns to the user side. Any operation that
--   results in a conflicting lock, such as dynamically trying to
--   drop the package, before the first lock is released will result
--   in a hang.
--
--   The flow of procedure calls will typically look like this:
--
--
--                           -----------
--                          | open_cursor |
--                           -----------
--                               |
--                               |
--                               v
--                             -----
--            ------------->| parse |
--            |               -----
--            |                 |
--            |                 |----------
--            |                 v         |
--            |              --------------  |
--            |-------->| bind_variable | |
--            |      ^     --------------   |
--            |      |        |            |
--            |    -----------|            |
--            |                |<--------
--            |                v
--            |            query?---------- yes ---------
--            |                |                        |
--            |               no                        |
--            |                |                        |
--            |                v                        v
--            |             -------                -------------
--            |-------->| execute |         ->| define_column |
--            |             -------         |   -------------
--            |                |------------|          |
--            |                |            |     -----------|
```

```
--        |                    v            |              v
--        |             ---------------     |           -------
--        |      ->| variable_value |       |  ------>| execute |
--        |      |   ---------------        |  |        -------
--        |      |          |               |  |           |
--        |      ----------|                |  |           |
--        |                 |               |  |           v
--        |                 |               |  |        ----------
--        |              |<-----------      |----->| fetch_rows |
--        |                 |               |           ----------
--        |                 |               |              |
--        |                 |               |              v
--        |                 |               |        ------------------
--        |                 |               |   | column_value       |
--        |                 |               |   | variable_value     |
--        |                 |               |        ------------------
--        |                 |               |              |
--        |              |<------------------------
--        |                 |
--        |    ------------------|
--        |                 |
--        v                 v
--               -------------
--              | close_cursor |
--               -------------
```

The preceding code segment from the DBMS_SQL package script file is a selected subset only. Any of the comment lines found after the statement CREATE OR REPLACE PACKAGE DBMS_SQL IS could be found in the data dictionary USER_SOURCE (ALL_SOURCE, and DBA_SOURCE) view. Scripts to retrieve this information are found in Chapter 13. The package body for each of these packages is wrapped and, therefore, the information retrieved from the data dictionary views also displays in wrapped format.

Create the Oracle Supplied Packages

The Oracle supplied packages are typically created upon database creation. The file that executes all the necessary scripts for the PL/SQL language setup and Oracle supplied packages creation is the catproc.sql script file, which is located in the ORACLE_HOME/rdbms/admin directory. The content of this file with some of the comments removed is displayed in the following script. This file will look slightly different, depending on the platform and version of Oracle in your environment. The following file is from a 7.3.2 version of Oracle under Windows 95.

```
Rem  catproc.sql
Rem     DESCRIPTION
Rem     Run all sql scripts for the procedural option
Rem        This script must be run while connectd as SYS or INTERNAL.
Rem basic procedural views
@@catprc
@@catjobq
@@catsnap

Rem Remote views
@@catrpc

Rem Views and tables for deferred RPC
@@catdefer

Rem Setup for pl/sql
@@standard
@@dbmsstdx
@@pipidl
@@pidian
@@diutil
@@pistub
@@plitblm
Rem packages implementing PL/SQL file data type
@@utlfile
@@prvtfile.plb

Rem pl/sql packages used for rdbms functionality
@@dbmsutil
@@prvtutil.plb
@@dbmssyer
@@prvtsyer.plb
@@dbmslock
@@prvtlock.plb
@@dbmspipe
@@prvtpipe.plb
@@dbmsalrt
@@prvtalrt.plb
@@dbmsotpt
@@prvtotpt.plb
@@dbmsdesc
@@prvtdesc.plb
@@dbmssql
@@prvtsql.plb
@@dbmspexp
@@prvtpexp.plb
@@dbmsjob
@@prvtjob.plb
```

```
Rem dbmsdfrd is replaced by dbmsdefr for the replication option
@@dbmsdfrd
@@prvtdfrd.plb
@@dbmssnap
@@prvtsnap.plb
```

Notice the catproc.sql file must be executed by the SYS user and needs to be executed when a database is created. Several of the files are necessary for the internal core of Oracle, and many other files are necessary to use certain PL/SQL functionality. The comments in the catproc.sql file describe the main groupings of PL/SQL script files executed.

The files executed from the catproc.sql script create PL/SQL specific data dictionary tables and views, the Oracle supplied packages, PUBLIC synonyms, and EXECUTE privilege on these packages. Most packages create PUBLIC synonyms and provide EXECUTE to PUBLIC, but not all packages. These exceptions are noted later in this chapter when each package is outlined in greater detail. Additionally, this may be slightly different with the Oracle version and platform in your environment.

TIP
Because all stored PL/SQL program units, including the Oracle supplied packages source code, are stored in the data dictionary, the default storage allocation of these data dictionary tables becomes fragmented quickly. Space fragmentation can be a cause of performance degradation. This initial storage allocation of data dictionary tables for PL/SQL stored objects can be modified. The technique of modifying the initial allocation is detailed in Chapter 13.

Execute the Oracle Supplied Packages

The Oracle supplied PL/SQL package program units are always executed on the database server, regardless of the location of the execution call to the stored package program unit. Therefore, a client-side PL/SQL program that executes an Oracle supplied package program unit will be executed on the database server. This method of execution is the same process of execution for any stored PL/SQL program unit, as detailed in Chapter 14.

A distinct difference exists in the execution of an Oracle supplied package program unit. Oracle supplied PL/SQL package program units are executed with the privileges of the calling schema, not the creator of the Oracle supplied package. This is unlike user created (non-Oracle supplied packages) PL/SQL package program unit execution, which executes with the privilege of the program unit creator. This is done by Oracle with good reason, because the owner of all the Oracle supplied packages is the SYS user.

For further detail on security, refer to Chapter 10 and Chapter 16.

Identify the Oracle Supplied Packages in Your System

Depending on the Oracle version and platform on which your system resides, the Oracle supplied PL/SQL packages will vary slightly. Therefore, being able to determine which packages are available on your system is important. The following script can be executed to list all Oracle supplied packages installed on your system. If you have further questions, I would again recommend viewing the contents of the operating system files that created these packages.

File: 11_3.sql

```
SELECT object_name
from   dba_objects
WHERE  owner = 'SYS'
AND    object_type = 'PACKAGE'
ORDER BY object_name;
```

The following output only lists a subset of the Oracle supplied packages returned from the preceding query.

Output (11_3.sql)

```
OBJECT_NAME
--------------------
DBMS_ALERT
DBMS_APPLICATION_INFO
DBMS_DDL
DBMS_OUTPUT
DBMS_PIPE
DBMS_STANDARD
DIANA
DIUTIL
PIDL
PLITBLM
STANDARD
UTL_FILE
```

The following script enables you to display more detailed information for each package, including the procedures and functions for each package, the parameters, and whether the parameter is an input, output, or input/output argument.

File: 11_4.sql

```
SET PAGESIZE 58
BREAK ON object SKIP 1 ON overload SKIP 1
COLUMN object         FORMAT A32 HEADING 'Package.Procedure(Function)'
COLUMN argument_name FORMAT A20 HEADING 'Parameter'
COLUMN data_type      FORMAT A15 HEADING 'Data Type'
COLUMN in_out         FORMAT A6  HEADING 'In/Out'
COLUMN overload       NOPRINT
SPOOL 11_4.lis
SELECT package_name || '.' || object_name object, argument_name,
       DECODE(data_type, 'FLOAT', 'INTEGER', data_type) data_type,
       in_out, overload
FROM   all_arguments
WHERE  owner = 'SYS'
AND    package_name = UPPER('&package')
AND    (package_name LIKE 'DBMS%'
OR     package_name  LIKE 'UTL%')
AND    package_name  <> 'DBMS_STANDARD'
ORDER BY package_name || '.' || object_name, overload, position;
SPOOL OFF
```

The preceding script prompts for the package to retrieve. If all packages are desired, the predicate line "package_name = UPPER('&package')" can be removed. The following output only lists the DBMS_OUTPUT package resulting from this script.

Output (11_4.sql)

Package.Procedure(Function)	Parameter	Data Type	In/Out
DBMS_OUTPUT.ENABLE	BUFFER_SIZE	INTEGER	IN
DBMS_OUTPUT.GET_LINE	LINE	VARCHAR2	OUT
	STATUS	INTEGER	OUT
DBMS_OUTPUT.GET_LINES	LINES	PL/SQL TABLE	OUT
	NUMLINES	INTEGER	IN/OUT
DBMS_OUTPUT.PUT	A	VARCHAR2	IN

	A	NUMBER	IN
	A	DATE	IN
DBMS_OUTPUT.PUT_LINE	A	VARCHAR2	IN
	A	NUMBER	IN
	A	DATE	IN

The predicate line that prompts for the package is extremely helpful when attempting to determine all the elements of a package.

If the procedure name is known, then the following SQL*Plus DESCRIBE command can be used to list the contents of the procedure similar to the previous.

```
DESCRIBE DBMS_OUTPUT.PUT_LINE
```

The output follows:

```
PROCEDURE DBMS_OUTPUT.PUT_LINE

Argument Name                       Type                    In/Out Default?
------------------------------      ---------------------   ------ --------
A                                   VARCHAR2                IN

PROCEDURE DBMS_OUTPUT.PUT_LINE
Argument Name                       Type                    In/Out Default?
------------------------------      ---------------------   ------ --------
A                                   NUMBER                  IN

PROCEDURE DBMS_OUTPUT.PUT_LINE
Argument Name                       Type                    In/Out Default?
------------------------------      ---------------------   ------ --------
A                                   DATE                    IN
```

Notice that the DESCRIBE lists a default column, which is to identify if a default parameter is defined for the parameter. This column will not display the actual default value if one exists; it will only list the word DEFAULT as the following illustrates.

```
DESCRIBE DBMS_DDL.ANALYZE_OBJECT
```

The output follows:

```
PROCEDURE DBMS_DDL.ANALYZE_OBJECT
Argument Name                       Type                       In/Out Default?
```

```
--------------------------------   ------------------------   ------  --------
TYPE                              VARCHAR2                   IN
SCHEMA                           VARCHAR2                   IN
NAME                             VARCHAR2                   IN
METHOD                           VARCHAR2                   IN
ESTIMATE_ROWS                    NUMBER                     IN      DEFAULT
ESTIMATE_PERCENT                 NUMBER                     IN      DEFAULT
METHOD_OPT                       VARCHAR2                   IN      DEFAULT
```

The actual default for values for each of these previous parameters is NULL. This can be determined from looking at the source code file or the actual source code for this package in the USER_SOURCE (ALL_SOURCE and DBA_SOURCE) view.

TIP
The query from the previous ALL_ARGUMENTS view does not include the default_value column because the value is never set. The reason the value is never set is the underlying join that creates this view does not use the proper column. One of the underlying data dictionary tables for the ALL_ARGUMENTS view is argument$, and the column that stores whether a default value exists is the default# column. This value is set to 1 when a default value is defined, but this column is not included in the ALL_ARGUMENTS view. The query from argument$ to view the default value (default#) column is included in the following script.

File: 11_5.sql

```
SELECT  procedure$, argument, default#
FROM    argument$
where   procedure$ = 'ANALYZE_OBJECT';
```

Output (11_5.sql)

PROCEDURE$	ARGUMENT	DEFAULT#
ANALYZE_OBJECT	METHOD_OPT	1
ANALYZE_OBJECT	ESTIMATE_PERCENT	1
ANALYZE_OBJECT	ESTIMATE_ROWS	1
ANALYZE_OBJECT	METHOD	
ANALYZE_OBJECT	NAME	

| ANALYZE_OBJECT | SCHEMA |
| ANALYZE_OBJECT | TYPE |

SELECT privilege must be granted to the argument$ table to view this information.

Provide a Detailed Reference of the Oracle Supplied Packages

As previously indicated in this chapter, the Oracle supplied packages are not readily used by most Oracle developers and DBAs. Since there are so many elements provided in these packages, it becomes overwhelming at times, especially when first learning them. The feeling is the same as when first learning the data dictionary views and the abundance of information contained in these valuable views. For these massive areas, I have always found it extremely helpful to reference a document or chart that outlines these areas. Often, the name of the element gives you valuable insight into the package element. Oracle has attempted to name these packages and package elements with this in mind.

Therefore, I have provided a quick reference for several of the Oracle supplied PL/SQL packages. This reference concentrates on packages that are used or can be used by most developers and DBAs. For each Oracle supplied package, the following are included:

Information Provided	Description
Package Name	Name of the Oracle package
Script Filenames	Name of the operating system files that create the package
Description	Brief description of the package use and contents
Public Synonym	Defines if a PUBLIC synonym is created for the package
Access Granted	Defines if EXECUTE privilege is granted to PUBLIC
Extra Processing	Specifies if additional objects are created for this package
Oracle8 Differences	Briefly describes changes to the package in Oracle8
Package Elements	Lists the package elements (procedures and functions)

Notice that there is a section for each package that defines the Oracle8 differences to these packages.

The packages contain procedures, overloaded procedures, and functions. An overloaded procedure is identifiable when a break in the parameter list exists. The procedure name is not duplicated for overloaded procedures (DBMS_OUTPUT.PUT_LINE is an example). Any procedure listed with only one line, no arguments listed, and the IN/OUT set to IN signifies the procedure requires no input parameters (DBMS_PIPE.RESET_BUFFER is an example). Functions can be identified when one of the records listed for the program unit has IN/OUT set to OUT and a parameter name (DBMS_PIPE.CREAT_PIPE is an example) does not exist.

All Oracle supplied packages are created by the SYS user. Although many of the scripts have been granted EXECUTE privilege on the package, this does not mean your attempt to execute the package will be successful. Remember, the Oracle schema that executes the Oracle supplied packages will execute with the current schema's Oracle privileges. Notice this is different from executing stored PL/SQL program units created by other schema. (For further detailed information regarding security and privilege, refer to Chapter 10 and Chapter 16.)

For those packages where access has not been granted to PUBLIC, privilege can be granted to those where you deem necessary. Likewise, PUBLIC or private synonyms can also be granted as desired on these packages.

The following Oracle supplied packages are described next. The "Package Elements" section was created by executing script 11_4.sql for each package.

DBMS_ALERT	DBMS_APPLICATION_INFO	DBMS_DDL
DBMS_JOB	DBMS_OUTPUT	DBMS_PIPE
DBMS_SESSION	DBMS_SHARED_POOL	DBMS_SPACE
DBMS_SQL	DBMS_SYSTEM	DBMS_TRANSACTION
DBMS_UTILITY	UTL_FILE	

Package Name: DBMS_ALERT
Script Filenames: Specification—dbmsalrt.sql, Body—prvtalrt.plb
Description: This package provides the capability to support asynchronous notification of database events. Alerts are transaction based and, therefore, are sent via a COMMIT. The waiting session does not receive the alert until the transaction signaling the alert commits. If a COMMIT fails or the transaction is rolled back, the alert is not sent. This package uses one database pipe and two locks for each alert that a session has registered. The maximum time to wait for an alert is set to unlimited (1,000 days).
Public Synonym: Created in body script
Access Granted: None
Extra Processing: Table dbms_alert_info is created in the body script.
Oracle8 Differences: None

Providing a Detailed Reference of the Oracle Supplied Packages

Package Elements:

Package.Procedure(Function)	Parameter	Data Type	In/Out
DBMS_ALERT.REGISTER	NAME	VARCHAR2	IN
DBMS_ALERT.REMOVE	NAME	VARCHAR2	IN
DBMS_ALERT.REMOVEALL			IN
DBMS_ALERT.SET_DEFAULTS	SENSITIVITY	NUMBER	IN
DBMS_ALERT.SIGNAL	NAME	VARCHAR2	IN
	MESSAGE	VARCHAR2	IN
DBMS_ALERT.WAITANY	NAME	VARCHAR2	OUT
	MESSAGE	VARCHAR2	OUT
	STATUS	INTEGER	OUT
	TIMEOUT	NUMBER	IN
DBMS_ALERT.WAITONE	NAME	VARCHAR2	IN
	MESSAGE	VARCHAR2	OUT
	STATUS	INTEGER	OUT
	TIMEOUT	NUMBER	IN

Package Name: DBMS_APPLICATION_INFO
Script Filenames: Specification—dbmsutil.sql, Body—prvtutil.plb
Description: This package provides a mechanism for registering application information in certain V$ views. This registered information can be monitored by a DBA to determine how the system is being used and to conduct performance analysis and resource accounting based on the registration scheme set up. The information registered through this package will appear in the module and action columns of the V$SESSION and V$SQLAREA views.
Public Synonym: Created in specification script
Access Granted: PUBLIC
Extra Processing: None
Oracle8 Differences: The overloaded procedure SET_SESSION_LONGOPS was added to support long operations.
Package Elements:

Package.Procedure(Function)	Parameter	Data Type	In/Out
DBMS_APPLICATION_INFO.READ_CLIENT_INFO	CLIENT_INFO	VARCHAR2	OUT
DBMS_APPLICATION_INFO.READ_MODULE	MODULE_NAME	VARCHAR2	OUT

	ACTION_NAME	VARCHAR2	OUT
DBMS_APPLICATION_INFO.SET_ACTION	ACTION_NAME	VARCHAR2	IN
DBMS_APPLICATION_INFO.SET_CLIENT_INFO	CLIENT_INFO	VARCHAR2	IN
DBMS_APPLICATION_INFO.SET_MODULE	MODULE_NAME	VARCHAR2	IN
	ACTION_NAME	VARCHAR2	IN

Package Name: DBMS_DDL
Script Filenames: Specification—dbmsutil.sql, Body—prvtutil.plb
Description: This package provides the capability to compile objects and analyze objects for a specified schema.
Public Synonym: Created in specification script
Access Granted: PUBLIC
Extra Processing: None
Oracle8 Differences: The ALTER_TABLE_NOT_REFERENCEABLE and ALTER_TABLE_REFERENCEABLE procedures were added.
Package Elements:

Package.Procedure(Function)	Parameter	Data Type	In/Out
DBMS_DDL.ALTER_COMPILE	TYPE	VARCHAR2	IN
	SCHEMA	VARCHAR2	IN
	NAME	VARCHAR2	IN
DBMS_DDL.ANALYZE_OBJECT	TYPE	VARCHAR2	IN
	SCHEMA	VARCHAR2	IN
	NAME	VARCHAR2	IN
	METHOD	VARCHAR2	IN
	ESTIMATE_ROWS	NUMBER	IN
	ESTIMATE_PERCENT	NUMBER	IN
	METHOD_OPT	VARCHAR2	IN

Package Name: DBMS_JOB
Script Filenames: Specification—dbmsjob.sql, Body—prvtjob.plb
Description: This package provides support for scheduling stored PL/SQL procedure execution in a job queue. There is a variety of settings for manipulating the execution of this job queue.
Public Synonym: Created in both the specification and body script
Access Granted: PUBLIC
Extra Processing: catjobq.sql is executed in catproc.sql to create the job queue data dictionary views, which stores the information for the job queue.
Oracle8 Differences: None
Package Elements:

Package.Procedure(Function)	Parameter	Data Type	In/Out
DBMS_JOB.BROKEN	JOB	BINARY_INTEGER	IN
	BROKEN	PL/SQL BOOLEAN	IN
	NEXT_DATE	DATE	IN
DBMS_JOB.CHANGE	JOB	BINARY_INTEGER	IN
	WHAT	VARCHAR2	IN
	NEXT_DATE	DATE	IN
	INTERVAL	VARCHAR2	IN
DBMS_JOB.CHECK_PRIVS	JOB	BINARY_INTEGER	IN
DBMS_JOB.INTERVAL	JOB	BINARY_INTEGER	IN
	INTERVAL	VARCHAR2	IN
DBMS_JOB.ISUBMIT	JOB	BINARY_INTEGER	IN
	WHAT	VARCHAR2	IN
	NEXT_DATE	VARCHAR2	IN
	INTERVAL	VARCHAR2	IN
	NO_PARSE	PL/SQL BOOLEAN	IN
DBMS_JOB.NEXT_DATE	JOB	BINARY_INTEGER	IN
	NEXT_DATE	DATE	IN
DBMS_JOB.REMOVE	JOB	BINARY_INTEGER	IN
DBMS_JOB.RUN	JOB	BINARY_INTEGER	IN
DBMS_JOB.SUBMIT	JOB	BINARY_INTEGER	OUT
	WHAT	VARCHAR2	IN
	NEXT_DATE	DATE	IN
	INTERVAL	VARCHAR2	IN
	NO_PARSE	PL/SQL BOOLEAN	IN
DBMS_JOB.USER_EXPORT	JOB	BINARY_INTEGER	IN
	MYCALL	VARCHAR2	IN/OUT
DBMS_JOB.WHAT	JOB	BINARY_INTEGER	IN
	WHAT	VARCHAR2	IN

Package Name: DBMS_OUTPUT
Script Filenames: Specification—dbmsotpt.sql, Body—prvtotpt.plb
Description: This package provides the capability to log information in a message
buffer, so it can be retrieved later and displayed to the screen. If this package is not
enabled, then all calls to this package are ignored. This package is useful for
debugging PL/SQL source code, especially in SQL*Plus. The default buffer size is

20,000 bytes. The minimum is 2,000 and the maximum is 1,000,000. Refer to Chapter 4 for further details regarding this package.
Public Synonym: Created in specification script
Access Granted: PUBLIC
Extra Processing: None
Oracle8 Differences: None
Package Elements:

Package.Procedure(Function)	Parameter	Data Type	In/Out
DBMS_OUTPUT.DISABLE			IN
DBMS_OUTPUT.ENABLE	BUFFER_SIZE	INTEGER	IN
DBMS_OUTPUT.GET_LINE	LINE	VARCHAR2	OUT
	STATUS	INTEGER	OUT
DBMS_OUTPUT.GET_LINES	LINES	PL/SQL TABLE	OUT
	NUMLINES	INTEGER	IN/OUT
DBMS_OUTPUT.NEW_LINE			IN
DBMS_OUTPUT.PUT	A	VARCHAR2	IN
	A	NUMBER	IN
	A	DATE	IN
DBMS_OUTPUT.PUT_LINE	A	VARCHAR2	IN
	A	NUMBER	IN
	A	DATE	IN

Package Name: DBMS_PIPE
Script Filenames: Specification—dbmspipe.sql, Body—prvtpipe.plb
Description: This package provides the capability to send messages between sessions asynchronously. Pipes operate independently of transactions, which is different from the DBMS_ALERT package. They also operate asynchronously. There can be multiple readers and writers of the same pipe. Pipes only operate between sessions in the same instance and use the Shared Pool for the message communication.
Public Synonym: Created in specification script
Access Granted: None
Extra Processing: None

Oracle8 Differences: None
Package Elements:

Package.Procedure(Function)	Parameter	Data Type	In/Out
DBMS_PIPE.CREATE_PIPE		INTEGER	OUT
	PIPENAME	VARCHAR2	IN
	MAXPIPESIZE	INTEGER	IN
	PRIVATE	PL/SQL BOOLEAN	IN
DBMS_PIPE.NEXT_ITEM_TYPE		INTEGER	OUT
DBMS_PIPE.PACK_MESSAGE	ITEM	VARCHAR2	IN
	ITEM	NUMBER	IN
	ITEM	DATE	IN
DBMS_PIPE.PACK_MESSAGE_RAW	ITEM	RAW	IN
DBMS_PIPE.PACK_MESSAGE_ROWID	ITEM	ROWID	IN
DBMS_PIPE.PURGE	PIPENAME	VARCHAR2	IN
DBMS_PIPE.RECEIVE_MESSAGE		INTEGER	OUT
	PIPENAME	VARCHAR2	IN
	TIMEOUT	INTEGER	IN
DBMS_PIPE.REMOVE_PIPE		INTEGER	OUT
	PIPENAME	VARCHAR2	IN
DBMS_PIPE.RESET_BUFFER			IN
DBMS_PIPE.SEND_MESSAGE		INTEGER	OUT
	PIPENAME	VARCHAR2	IN
	TIMEOUT	INTEGER	IN
	MAXPIPESIZE	INTEGER	IN
DBMS_PIPE.UNIQUE_SESSION_NAME		VARCHAR2	OUT
DBMS_PIPE.UNPACK_MESSAGE	ITEM	VARCHAR2	OUT
	ITEM	NUMBER	OUT
	ITEM	DATE	OUT
DBMS_PIPE.UNPACK_MESSAGE_RAW	ITEM	RAW	OUT

DBMS_PIPE.UNPACK_MESSAGE_ROWID ITEM		ROWID	OUT

Package Name: DBMS_SESSION
Script Filenames: Specification—dbmsutil.sql, Body—prvtutil.plb
Description: This package provides access to several SQL ALTER SESSION commands to assist in modifying the operation of a session within PL/SQL.
Public Synonym: Created in specification script
Access Granted: None
Extra Processing: None
Oracle8 Differences: The IS_SESSION_ALIVE function was added.
Package Elements:

Package.Procedure(Function)	Parameter	Data Type	In/Out
DBMS_SESSION.CLOSE_DATABASE_LINK	DBLINK	VARCHAR2	IN
DBMS_SESSION.FREE_UNUSED_USER_MEMORY			IN
DBMS_SESSION.IS_ROLE_ENABLED		PL/SQL BOOLEAN	OUT
	ROLENAME	VARCHAR2	IN
DBMS_SESSION.RESET_PACKAGE			IN
DBMS_SESSION.SET_CLOSE_CACHED_OPEN_CURSORS	CLOSE_CURSORS	PL/SQL BOOLEAN	IN
DBMS_SESSION.SET_LABEL	LBL	VARCHAR2	IN
DBMS_SESSION.SET_MLS_LABEL_FORMAT	FMT	VARCHAR2	IN
DBMS_SESSION.SET_NLS	PARAM	VARCHAR2	IN
	VALUE	VARCHAR2	IN
DBMS_SESSION.SET_ROLE	ROLE_CMD	VARCHAR2	IN
DBMS_SESSION.SET_SQL_TRACE	SQL_TRACE	PL/SQL BOOLEAN	IN
DBMS_SESSION.UNIQUE_SESSION_ID		VARCHAR2	OUT

Package Name: DBMS_SHARED_POOL
Script Filenames: Specification—dbmspool.sql, Body—prvtpool.plb
Description: This package provides access to the Shared Pool, including pinning/unpinning stored PL/SQL objects and cursors and viewing the PL/SQL objects in the Shared Pool over a certain size. This package is not created during the

installation because catproc.sql does not reference these files. To use this package, it must be created by logging into the SYS user and executing the dbmspool.sql and prvtpool.plb script files.

Public Synonym: None

Access Granted: None

Extra Processing: The DBA_KEEPSIZES view is created in the body script.

Oracle8 Differences: None

Package Elements:

Package.Procedure(Function)	Parameter	Data Type	In/Out
DBMS_SHARED_POOL.ABORTED_REQUEST _THRESHOLD	THRESHOLD_SIZE	NUMBER	IN
DBMS_SHARED_POOL.KEEP	NAME	VARCHAR2	IN
	FLAG	CHAR	IN
DBMS_SHARED_POOL.SIZES	MINSIZE	NUMBER	IN
DBMS_SHARED_POOL.UNKEEP	NAME	VARCHAR2	IN
	FLAG	CHAR	IN

Package Name: DBMS_SPACE

Script filenames: Specification—dbmsutil.sql, Body—prvtutil.plb

Description: This package provides segment space information not currently viewable through the standard data dictionary views.

Public Synonym: Created in specification script

Access Granted: PUBLIC

Extra Processing: None

Oracle8 Differences: A parameter was added to each of the procedures enabling the space to be limited to a table partition.

Package Elements:

Package.Procedure(Function)	Parameter	Data Type	In/Out
DBMS_SPACE.FREE_BLOCKS	SEGMENT_OWNER	VARCHAR2	IN
	SEGMENT_NAME	VARCHAR2	IN
	SEGMENT_TYPE	VARCHAR2	IN
	FREELIST_GROUP_ID	NUMBER	IN
	FREE_BLKS	NUMBER	OUT
	SCAN_LIMIT	NUMBER	IN
DBMS_SPACE.UNUSED_SPACE	SEGMENT_OWNER	VARCHAR2	IN
	SEGMENT_NAME	VARCHAR2	IN
	SEGMENT_TYPE	VARCHAR2	IN

TOTAL_BLOCKS	NUMBER	OUT
TOTAL_BYTES	NUMBER	OUT
UNUSED_BLOCKS	NUMBER	OUT
UNUSED_BYTES	NUMBER	OUT
LAST_USED_EXTENT_FILE_ID	NUMBER	OUT
LAST_USED_EXTENT_BLOCK_ID	NUMBER	OUT
LAST_USED_BLOCK	NUMBER	OUT

Package Name: DBMS_SQL

Script Filenames: Specification—dbmssql.sql, Body—prvtsql.plb

Description: This package provides a means to create dynamic SQL and PL/SQL for use in PL/SQL. This package is extremely important to know because it basically removes certain SQL limitations and allows for PL/SQL program units to be extremely flexible and dynamic.

Public Synonym: Created in Specification script

Access Granted: PUBLIC

Extra Processing: None

Oracle8 Differences: The BIND_ARRAY, DEFINE_ARRAY, DESCRIBE_COLUMNS procedures were added. Several procedures were overloaded to add support for BLOB, CLOB, and BFILE types including BIND_VARIABLE, COLUMN_VALUE, DEFINE_COLUMN, and VARIABLE_VALUE. The PARSE procedure was also overloaded.

Package Elements:

Package.Procedure(Function)	Parameter	Data Type	In/Out
DBMS_SQL.BIND_VARIABLE	C	INTEGER	IN
	NAME	VARCHAR2	IN
	VALUE	NUMBER	IN
	C	INTEGER	IN
	NAME	VARCHAR2	IN
	VALUE	VARCHAR2	IN
	C	INTEGER	IN
	NAME	VARCHAR2	IN
	VALUE	VARCHAR2	IN
	OUT_VALUE_SIZE	INTEGER	IN
	C	INTEGER	IN
	NAME	VARCHAR2	IN
	VALUE	DATE	IN
	C	INTEGER	IN
	NAME	VARCHAR2	IN
	VALUE	MLSLABEL	IN

DBMS_SQL.BIND_VARIABLE_CHAR	C	INTEGER	IN
	NAME	VARCHAR2	IN
	VALUE	CHAR	IN
	C	INTEGER	IN
	NAME	VARCHAR2	IN
	VALUE	CHAR	IN
	OUT_VALUE_SIZE	INTEGER	IN
DBMS_SQL.BIND_VARIABLE_RAW	C	INTEGER	IN
	NAME	VARCHAR2	IN
	VALUE	RAW	IN
	C	INTEGER	IN
	NAME	VARCHAR2	IN
	VALUE	RAW	IN
	OUT_VALUE_SIZE	INTEGER	IN
DBMS_SQL.BIND_VARIABLE_ROWID	C	INTEGER	IN
	NAME	VARCHAR2	IN
	VALUE	ROWID	IN
DBMS_SQL.CLOSE_CURSOR	C	INTEGER	IN/OUT
DBMS_SQL.COLUMN_VALUE	C	INTEGER	IN
	POSITION	INTEGER	IN
	VALUE	NUMBER	OUT
	C	INTEGER	IN
	POSITION	INTEGER	IN
	VALUE	VARCHAR2	OUT
	C	INTEGER	IN
	POSITION	INTEGER	IN
	VALUE	DATE	OUT
	C	INTEGER	IN
	POSITION	INTEGER	IN
	VALUE	MLSLABEL	OUT
	C	INTEGER	IN
	POSITION	INTEGER	IN
	VALUE	NUMBER	OUT
	COLUMN_ERROR	NUMBER	OUT
	ACTUAL_LENGTH	INTEGER	OUT
	C	INTEGER	IN

	POSITION	INTEGER	IN
	VALUE	VARCHAR2	OUT
	COLUMN_ERROR	NUMBER	OUT
	ACTUAL_LENGTH	INTEGER	OUT
	C	INTEGER	IN
	POSITION	INTEGER	IN
	VALUE	DATE	OUT
	COLUMN_ERROR	NUMBER	OUT
	ACTUAL_LENGTH	INTEGER	OUT
	C	INTEGER	IN
	POSITION	INTEGER	IN
	VALUE	MLSLABEL	OUT
	COLUMN_ERROR	NUMBER	OUT
	ACTUAL_LENGTH	INTEGER	OUT
DBMS_SQL.COLUMN_VALUE_CHAR	C	INTEGER	IN
	POSITION	INTEGER	IN
	VALUE	CHAR	OUT
	C	INTEGER	IN
	POSITION	INTEGER	IN
	VALUE	CHAR	OUT
	COLUMN_ERROR	NUMBER	OUT
	ACTUAL_LENGTH	INTEGER	OUT
DBMS_SQL.COLUMN_VALUE_LONG	C	INTEGER	IN
	POSITION	INTEGER	IN
	LENGTH	INTEGER	IN
	OFFSET	INTEGER	IN
	VALUE	VARCHAR2	OUT
	VALUE_LENGTH	INTEGER	OUT
DBMS_SQL.COLUMN_VALUE_RAW	C	INTEGER	IN
	POSITION	INTEGER	IN
	VALUE	RAW	OUT
	C	INTEGER	IN
	POSITION	INTEGER	IN
	VALUE	RAW	OUT
	COLUMN_ERROR	NUMBER	OUT
	ACTUAL_LENGTH	INTEGER	OUT
DBMS_SQL.COLUMN_VALUE_ROWID	C	INTEGER	IN
	POSITION	INTEGER	IN
	VALUE	ROWID	OUT

	C	INTEGER	IN
	POSITION	INTEGER	IN
	VALUE	ROWID	OUT
	COLUMN_ERROR	NUMBER	OUT
	ACTUAL_LENGTH	INTEGER	OUT
DBMS_SQL.DEFINE_COLUMN	C	INTEGER	IN
	POSITION	INTEGER	IN
	COLUMN	NUMBER	IN
	C	INTEGER	IN
	POSITION	INTEGER	IN
	COLUMN	VARCHAR2	IN
	COLUMN_SIZE	INTEGER	IN
	C	INTEGER	IN
	POSITION	INTEGER	IN
	COLUMN	DATE	IN
	C	INTEGER	IN
	POSITION	INTEGER	IN
	COLUMN	MLSLABEL	IN
DBMS_SQL.DEFINE_COLUMN_CHAR	C	INTEGER	IN
	POSITION	INTEGER	IN
	COLUMN	CHAR	IN
	COLUMN_SIZE	INTEGER	IN
DBMS_SQL.DEFINE_COLUMN_LONG	C	INTEGER	IN
	POSITION	INTEGER	IN
DBMS_SQL.DEFINE_COLUMN_RAW	C	INTEGER	IN
	POSITION	INTEGER	IN
	COLUMN	RAW	IN
	COLUMN_SIZE	INTEGER	IN
DBMS_SQL.DEFINE_COLUMN_ROWID	C	INTEGER	IN
	POSITION	INTEGER	IN
	COLUMN	ROWID	IN
DBMS_SQL.EXECUTE		INTEGER	OUT
	C	INTEGER	IN
DBMS_SQL.EXECUTE_AND_FETCH		INTEGER	OUT
	C	INTEGER	IN
	EXACT	PL/SQL BOOLEAN	IN
DBMS_SQL.FETCH_ROWS		INTEGER	OUT

	C	INTEGER	IN
DBMS_SQL.IS_OPEN		INTEGER	OUT
	C	INTEGER	IN
DBMS_SQL.LAST_ERROR_POSITION		INTEGER	OUT
DBMS_SQL.LAST_ROW_COUNT		INTEGER	OUT
DBMS_SQL.LAST_ROW_ID		ROWID	OUT
DBMS_SQL.LAST_SQL_FUNCTION_CODE		INTEGER	OUT
DBMS_SQL.OPEN_CURSOR		INTEGER	OUT
DBMS_SQL.PARSE	C	INTEGER	IN
	STATEMENT	VARCHAR2	IN
	LANGUAGE_FLAG	INTEGER	IN
DBMS_SQL.VARIABLE_VALUE	C	INTEGER	IN
	NAME	VARCHAR2	IN
	VALUE	NUMBER	OUT
	C	INTEGER	IN
	NAME	VARCHAR2	IN
	VALUE	VARCHAR2	OUT
	C	INTEGER	IN
	NAME	VARCHAR2	IN
	VALUE	DATE	OUT
	C	INTEGER	IN
	NAME	VARCHAR2	IN
	VALUE	MLSLABEL	OUT
DBMS_SQL.VARIABLE_VALUE_CHAR	C	INTEGER	IN
	NAME	VARCHAR2	IN
	VALUE	CHAR	OUT
DBMS_SQL.VARIABLE_VALUE_RAW	C	INTEGER	IN
	NAME	VARCHAR2	IN
	VALUE	RAW	OUT
DBMS_SQL.VARIABLE_VALUE_ROWID	C	INTEGER	IN
	NAME	VARCHAR2	IN
	VALUE	ROWID	OUT

Package Name: DBMS_SYSTEM
Script Filenames: Specification—dbmsutil.sql, Body—prvtutil.plb

Providing a Detailed Reference of the Oracle Supplied Packages

Description: This package provides several system level utilities. The only procedure that should be executed is the SET_SQL_TRACE_IN_SESSION. This allows for a session to be traced by only knowing the SID and SERIAL#. This is helpful for a DBA attempting to monitor a session that is currently executing more closely, by tracing the session. The SID and SERIAL# can be found in several V$ views including V$SESSION.
Public Synonym: None
Access Granted: None
Extra Processing: None
Oracle8 Differences: The KCFRMS, KSDDDT, KSDFLS, KSDIND, and KSDWRT procedures were added.
Package Elements:

Package.Procedure(Function)	Parameter	Data Type	In/Out
DBMS_SYSTEM.DIST_TXN_SYNC	INST_NUM	NUMBER	IN
DBMS_SYSTEM.READ_EV	IEV	BINARY_INTEGER	IN
	OEV	BINARY_INTEGER	OUT
DBMS_SYSTEM.SET_EV	SI	BINARY_INTEGER	IN
	SE	BINARY_INTEGER	IN
	EV	BINARY_INTEGER	IN
	LE	BINARY_INTEGER	IN
	NM	VARCHAR2	IN
DBMS_SYSTEM.SET_SQL_TRACE_IN_SESSION	SID	NUMBER	IN
	SERIAL#	NUMBER	IN
	SQL_TRACE	PL/SQL BOOLEAN	IN

Package Name: DBMS_TRANSACTION
Script Filenames: Specification—dbmsutil.sql, Body—prvtutil.plb
Description: This package provides SQL transaction commands through PL/SQL. Some of the commands are SET commands, ALTER SESSION commands, and others are included for completeness. It also provides functions for monitoring transaction activities (transaction IDs and ordering of steps of transactions).
Public Synonym: Created in specification script
Access Granted: PUBLIC
Extra Processing: None
Oracle8 Differences: None
Package Elements:

Package.Procedure(Function)	Parameter	Data Type	In/Out
DBMS_TRANSACTION.ADVISE_COMMIT			IN
DBMS_TRANSACTION.ADVISE_NOTHING			IN
DBMS_TRANSACTION.ADVISE_ROLLBACK			IN
DBMS_TRANSACTION.BEGIN_DISCRETE_ TRANSACTION			IN
DBMS_TRANSACTION.COMMIT			IN
DBMS_TRANSACTION.COMMIT_COMMENT	CMNT	VARCHAR2	IN
DBMS_TRANSACTION.COMMIT_FORCE	XID	VARCHAR2	IN
	SCN	VARCHAR2	IN
DBMS_TRANSACTION.LOCAL_TRANSACTI ON_ID		VARCHAR2	OUT
	CREATE_TRANS ACTION	PL/SQL BOOLEAN	IN
DBMS_TRANSACTION.PURGE_LOST_DB_E NTRY	XID	VARCHAR2	IN
DBMS_TRANSACTION.PURGE_MIXED	XID	VARCHAR2	IN
DBMS_TRANSACTION.READ_ONLY			IN
DBMS_TRANSACTION.READ_WRITE			IN
DBMS_TRANSACTION.ROLLBACK			IN
DBMS_TRANSACTION.ROLLBACK_FORCE	XID	VARCHAR2	IN
DBMS_TRANSACTION.ROLLBACK_SAVEPO INT	SAVEPT	VARCHAR2	IN
DBMS_TRANSACTION.SAVEPOINT	SAVEPT	VARCHAR2	IN
DBMS_TRANSACTION.STEP_ID		NUMBER	OUT
DBMS_TRANSACTION.USE_ROLLBACK_SE GMENT	RB_NAME	VARCHAR2	IN

Providing a Detailed Reference of the Oracle Supplied Packages

Package Name: DBMS_UTILITY

Script Filenames: Specification—dbmsutil.sql, Body—prvtutil.plb

Description: This package provides various utilities. These utilities include analyzing and compiling schemas or the entire database, using a timing function, and retrieving information from the database.

Public Synonym: Created in Specification script

Access Granted: PUBLIC

Extra Processing: The ORDER_OBJECT_BY_DEPENDENCY and DBA_ANALYZE views are created in the body script.

Oracle8 Differences: The ANALYZE_PART_OBJECT (allows for analyzing a table partition), DB_VERSION, and EXEC_DDL_STATEMENT procedures were added. The GET_PARAMETER_VALUE function was added.

Package Elements:

Package.Procedure(Function)	Parameter	Data Type	In/Out
DBMS_UTILITY.ANALYZE_DATABASE	METHOD	VARCHAR2	IN
	ESTIMATE_ROWS	NUMBER	IN
	ESTIMATE_PERCENT	NUMBER	IN
	METHOD_OPT	VARCHAR2	IN
DBMS_UTILITY.ANALYZE_SCHEMA	SCHEMA	VARCHAR2	IN
	METHOD	VARCHAR2	IN
	ESTIMATE_ROWS	NUMBER	IN
	ESTIMATE_PERCENT	NUMBER	IN
	METHOD_OPT	VARCHAR2	IN
DBMS_UTILITY.COMMA_TO_TABLE	LIST	VARCHAR2	IN
	TABLEN	BINARY_INTEGER	OUT
	TAB	PL/SQL TABLE	OUT
DBMS_UTILITY.COMPILE_SCHEMA	SCHEMA	VARCHAR2	IN
DBMS_UTILITY.DATA_BLOCK_ADDRESS_BLOCK		NUMBER	OUT
	DBA	NUMBER	IN
DBMS_UTILITY.DATA_BLOCK_ADDRESS_FILE		NUMBER	OUT
	DBA	NUMBER	IN
DBMS_UTILITY.FORMAT_CALL_STACK		VARCHAR2	OUT
DBMS_UTILITY.FORMAT_ERROR_STACK		VARCHAR2	OUT

DBMS_UTILITY.GET_HASH_VALUE		NUMBER	OUT
	NAME	VARCHAR2	IN
	BASE	NUMBER	IN
	HASH_SIZE	NUMBER	IN
DBMS_UTILITY.GET_TIME		NUMBER	OUT
DBMS_UTILITY.IS_PARALLEL_SERVER		PL/SQL BOOLEAN	OUT
DBMS_UTILITY.MAKE_DATA_BLOCK_ADDRESS		NUMBER	OUT
	FILE	NUMBER	IN
	BLOCK	NUMBER	IN
DBMS_UTILITY.NAME_RESOLVE	NAME	VARCHAR2	IN
	CONTEXT	NUMBER	IN
	SCHEMA	VARCHAR2	OUT
	PART1	VARCHAR2	OUT
	PART2	VARCHAR2	OUT
	DBLINK	VARCHAR2	OUT
	PART1_TYPE	NUMBER	OUT
	OBJECT_NUMBER	NUMBER	OUT
DBMS_UTILITY.NAME_TOKENIZE	NAME	VARCHAR2	IN
	A	VARCHAR2	OUT
	B	VARCHAR2	OUT
	C	VARCHAR2	OUT
	DBLINK	VARCHAR2	OUT
	NEXTPOS	BINARY_INTEGER	OUT
DBMS_UTILITY.PORT_STRING		VARCHAR2	OUT
DBMS_UTILITY.TABLE_TO_COMMA	TAB	PL/SQL TABLE	IN
	TABLEN	BINARY_INTEGER	OUT
	LIST	VARCHAR2	OUT

Package Name: UTL_FILE
Script Filenames: Specification—utlfile.sql, Body—prvtfile.plb
Description: This package provides the capability to read and write operating system files. This package can only be used to manipulate files on the database server. Many of Oracle's client tools provide a similar package to allow for client-side file I/O named TEXT_IO.
Public Synonym: Created in body script
Access Granted: PUBLIC
Extra Processing: None

Oracle8 Differences: None
Package Elements:

Package.Procedure(Function)	Parameter	Data Type	In/Out
UTL_FILE.FCLOSE	FILE	PL/SQL RECORD	IN/OUT
	ID	BINARY_INTEGER	IN/OUT
UTL_FILE.FCLOSE_ALL			IN
UTL_FILE.FFLUSH	FILE	PL/SQL RECORD	IN
	ID	BINARY_INTEGER	IN
UTL_FILE.FOPEN		PL/SQL RECORD	OUT
	ID	BINARY_INTEGER	OUT
	LOCATION	VARCHAR2	IN
	FILENAME	VARCHAR2	IN
	OPEN_MODE	VARCHAR2	IN
UTL_FILE.GET_LINE	FILE	PL/SQL RECORD	IN
	ID	BINARY_INTEGER	IN
	BUFFER	VARCHAR2	OUT
UTL_FILE.IS_OPEN		PL/SQL BOOLEAN	OUT
	FILE	PL/SQL RECORD	IN
	ID	BINARY_INTEGER	IN
UTL_FILE.NEW_LINE	FILE	PL/SQL RECORD	IN
	ID	BINARY_INTEGER	IN
	LINES	BINARY_INTEGER	IN
UTL_FILE.PUT	FILE	PL/SQL RECORD	IN
	ID	BINARY_INTEGER	IN
	BUFFER	VARCHAR2	IN
UTL_FILE.PUTF	FILE	PL/SQL RECORD	IN
	ID	BINARY_INTEGER	IN
	FORMAT	VARCHAR2	IN
	ARG1	VARCHAR2	IN
	ARG2	VARCHAR2	IN
	ARG3	VARCHAR2	IN
	ARG4	VARCHAR2	IN
	ARG5	VARCHAR2	IN
UTL_FILE.PUT_LINE	FILE	PL/SQL RECORD	IN
	ID	BINARY_INTEGER	IN
	BUFFER	VARCHAR2	IN

Summary

In this chapter, the Oracle supplied PL/SQL packages were outlined. These packages are used by Oracle internally and should become a standard tool for developers and DBAs. Reviewing these packages and understanding when and where they can be used is extremely important. They have continued to expand over the years; this expansion continues with Oracle8 as highlighted in this chapter. The framework of the Oracle supplied packages is identified to provide the necessary knowledge for using these packages. Chapter 12 advances with the Oracle supplied packages by providing more detail on these packages and example programs that use these powerful packages. Refer to Chapter 16 for information specific to the new Oracle supplied packages in Oracle 8.0 and 8.1.

Tips Review

- Because all stored PL/SQL program units, including the Oracle supplied packages source code, are stored in the data dictionary, the default storage allocation of these data dictionary tables becomes fragmented quickly. Space fragmentation can be a cause of performance degradation. This initial storage allocation of data dictionary tables for PL/SQL stored objects can be modified. The technique of modifying the initial allocation is detailed in Chapter 13.

- The query from the ALL_ARGUMENTS view does not include the default_value column because the value is never set. The reason it is never set is that the underlying join that creates this view does not use the proper column. One of the underlying data dictionary tables for the ALL_ARGUMENTS view is argument$, and the column that stores whether a default value exists is the default# column. This value is set to 1 when a default value is defined, but this column is not included in the ALL_ARGUMENTS view.

Tips Review

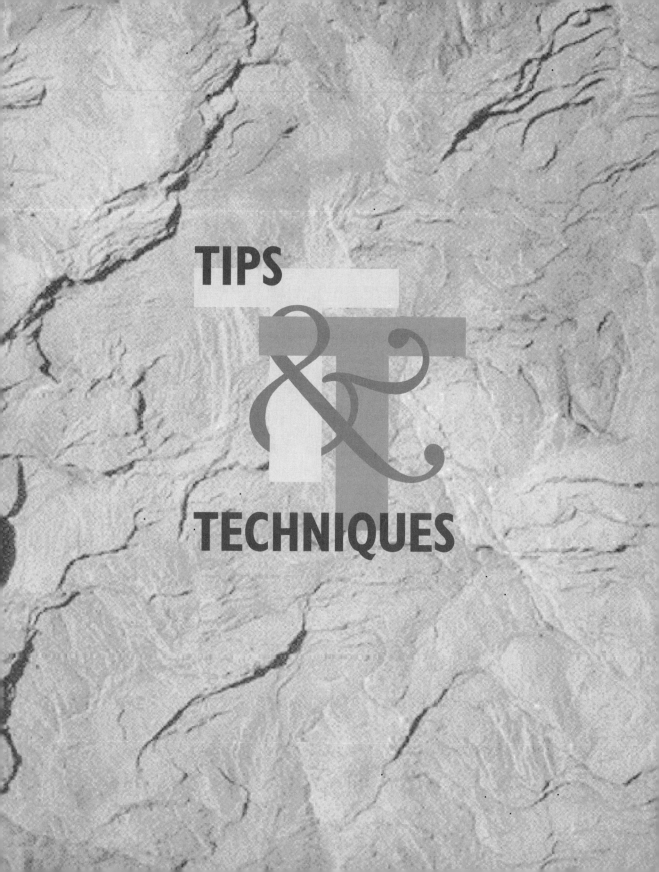

TIPS & TECHNIQUES

CHAPTER
12

Understanding the
Power of the
Oracle Supplied
PL/SQL Packages
(Developer and DBA)

C reating a stored PL/SQL package has a tremendous amount of advantages when developing real-world applications. The advantages are numerous, as outlined in Chapter 5, and Oracle's assistance in this area should be known and used. Oracle has provided several stored PL/SQL packages that come standard with the Oracle RDBMS. Many of these packages are created during the installation. The specifics of many of these packages are outlined in Chapter 11, including the creation, access, purpose, Oracle8 differences, and content (procedures and functions). This chapter takes the next step in the explanation of these powerful Oracle supplied PL/SQL packages by providing examples of several of the packages to highlight the usefulness and power Oracle has provided to us.

The examples are limited to the procedures and functions within the packages that will be most valuable to developers and DBAs. Some of the packages contain standalone procedures and functions, while others contain procedures and functions dependent on other procedures and functions to make full use of the package. Each of the packages is identified as either containing standalone contents (procedures or functions that can be executed independent of other procedures or functions within the package being executed to perform a complete action), or dependent contents (procedures or functions that cannot be executed independent of other procedures or functions within the package being executed to perform a complete action). Each of the packages is identified as for whom the package is primarily provided, whether a developer and/or a DBA. Lastly, each section in this chapter provides a list of possible uses of each package.

The goal of this chapter is to expand the understanding of the Oracle supplied PL/SQL packages through a set of examples demonstrating the power of these packages. This chapter provides tips and techniques on the following Oracle supplied PL/SQL packages:

- Build an alert system into your environment (DBMS_ALERT)

- Create an application registration and asynchronous communication vehicle (DBMS_APPLICATION_INFO)

- Compile and analyze objects (DBMS_DDL)

- Use the Oracle job scheduler (DBMS_JOB)

- Provide an easy debugging facility (DBMS_OUTPUT)

- Create an asynchronous message facility (DBMS_PIPE)

- Enhance session control and identification (DBMS_SESSION)

- Control the caching of PL/SQL objects (DBMS_SHARED_POOL)

- Retrieve free space information (DBMS_SPACE)

- Extend PL/SQL by dynamically creating SQL and PL/SQL (DBMS_SQL)

- Turn on the TRACE facility for any session (DBMS_SYSTEM)

- Specify the rollback segment to use for large processing (DBMS_TRANSACTION)

- Expand the PL/SQL language with a set of utilities (DBMS_UTILITY)

- Read and write server-side operating system files (UTL_FILE)

- Pause execution for a specified amount of time (DBMS_LOCK)

Build an Alert System into Your Environment (DBMS_ALERT)

The DBMS_ALERT package provides the capability to build a monitoring system into your environment and to raise alerts when certain conditions occur. This monitoring system can be integrated into a number of areas, including application threshold alerting (order quantity falls below threshold, need to order more), and DBA resource monitoring (scripts are executed and a log file is created with resource areas that exceed a threshold). The possibilities are endless, and the DBMS_ALERT package provides a set of procedures and functions to enable this capability.

The DBMS_ALERT package provides a communication vehicle to multiple database sessions. Each session must register to be able to receive an alert. Then when an alert is signaled, all registered database sessions are sent the alert message. DBMS_ALERT is transaction-based, meaning the signal does not occur until a COMMIT occurs. The alert information, as well as the registration list, is kept in internal database tables and the DML resulting from the alert changing or being signaled needs to be committed. Therefore, when a database event occurs, with alert functionality attached (identical to a database trigger), each registered user receives notification.

The DBMS_ALERT package is a dependent package and is useful to both developers and DBAs. The most used procedures and functions are outlined in the following subsections.

Register Sessions

The REGISTER procedure adds the current session into the registration list for the specified alert. A database session can register for multiple alerts at any time. Also, the REGISTER procedure performs an implicit COMMIT, because the session is being added to the internal registration table.

Procedure Syntax

```
DBMS_ALERT.REGISTER(name IN VARCHAR2);
```

Example

```
DBMS_ALERT.REGISTER('REORDER_THRESHOLD_ALERT');
```

Signal an Alert

The SIGNAL procedure implements the signaling functionality; the alert name and message are specified and sent to all sessions registered for the alert. Remember, the alert message is only signaled after a COMMIT occurs. A ROLLBACK voids any uncommitted alert signals. Alert names are not case-sensitive and have a maximum of 30 bytes. In addition, the maximum message length is 1,800 bytes.

Procedure Syntax

```
DBMS_ALERT.SIGNAL(name IN VARCHAR2, message IN VARCHAR2);
```

Example

```
DBMS_ALERT.SIGNAL('REORDER_THRESHOLD_ALERT',
   'Need to Re-order Inventory.');
```

Wait for Alerts

The WAITONE procedure implements the message capturing functionality. The procedure waits for an alert to be signaled for a specified amount of time. If no alert message is captured within the specified time span, the procedure times out. The WAITONE procedure returns the status of alert request and message, if any. The status codes (0 - Alert Occurred, 1 - Timed Out) are used to determine whether the message was successfully captured. The time-out parameter values are measured in seconds.

The WAITANY procedure implements generic alert processing, waiting for all alerts for which the session is currently registered. The alert name of the message captured is an OUT parameter, which is different than the WAITONE procedure. All other functionality is identical to the WAITONE procedure.

Procedure Syntax

```
DBMS_ALERT.WAITONE(name IN VARCHAR2, message OUT VARCHAR2,
   status OUT NUMBER, timeout IN NUMBER DEFAULT MAXWAIT);
```

```
DBMS_ALERT.WAITANY(name OUT VARCHAR2, message OUT VARCHAR2,
   status OUT NUMBER, timeout IN NUMBER DEFAULT MAXWAIT);
```

The maxwait default in the DBMS_ALERT package is set to a constant of 86400000 (seconds), which equates to approximately 1,000 days.

Example

```
DBMS_ALERT.WAITONE('REORDER_THRESHOLD_ALERT', lv_message_txt,
   lv_status_num);
DBMS_ALERT.WAITANY(lv_alert_name_txt, lv_message_txt, lv_status_num);
```

Remove User Session from Registry

The REMOVE procedure removes the current session from the specified alerts registration lists. The REMOVEALL procedure deletes the current session from all alert registration lists. Both the REMOVE and REMOVEALL procedures perform implicit COMMITs.

Procedure Syntax

```
DBMS_ALERT.REMOVE(name IN VARCHAR2);
DBMS_ALERT.REMOVEALL;
```

Example

```
DBMS_ALERT.REMOVE('REORDER_THRESHOLD_ALERT');
DBMS_ALERT.REMOVEALL;
```

Raise an Alert When Inventory Reaches the Reorder Point

The Example database has an inventory table (s_inventory) containing a column that stores the amount in stock (amount_in_stock) and the reorder threshold point (reorder_point). Therefore, once the amount in stock falls below the reorder threshold point, more products should be ordered in the given warehouse. Therefore, an alert can be used to signal the reorder point and automatically create an order to the supplier for more inventory of the given product.

The following example illustrates how this scenario would be created using the DBMS_ALERT package. The automatic creation of an order from the supplier is replaced by a message to the screen for simplicity.

The s_inventory table in the Example database has the following structure:

Building DBMS_ALERT into Your Environment

```
Name                                  Null?     Type
-----------------------------------   --------- ----
PRODUCT_ID                            NOT NULL  NUMBER(7)
WAREHOUSE_ID                          NOT NULL  NUMBER(7)
AMOUNT_IN_STOCK                                 NUMBER(9)
REORDER_POINT                                   NUMBER(9)
MAX_IN_STOCK                                    NUMBER(9)
OUT_OF_STOCK_EXPLANATION                        VARCHAR2(255)
RESTOCK_DATE                                    DATE
```

A database trigger is placed on the s_inventory table to signal automatically for each product when the amount in stock falls below the reorder threshold point. The AFTER UPDATE trigger for the s_inventory table is illustrated in the following code.

File: 12_1.sql

```
CREATE OR REPLACE TRIGGER au_inventory
   -- This database trigger executes for each record that the
   -- amount_in_stock falls below the reorder_point and is
   -- performed after the update
   AFTER UPDATE of amount_in_stock
   ON s_inventory
   FOR EACH ROW
   WHEN (new.amount_in_stock < new.reorder_point)
BEGIN
   -- If inventory for a product falls below the reorder point
   -- an alert is sent out and contains the warehouse, product,
   -- amount in stock, and reorder point.
   DBMS_ALERT.SIGNAL('REORDER_THRESHOLD_ALERT', 'Warehouse: ' ||
      :new.warehouse_id || '  Product: ' || :new.product_id ||
      '  Current Stock: ' || :new.amount_in_stock ||
      '  Reorder Point: ' || :new.reorder_point);
END au_inventory;
/
```

An Oracle session executes the following PL/SQL program unit to receive each alert as it is created. In this example, the alert is displayed to the screen using the DBMS_OUTPUT.PUT_LINE procedure. This session is executed in SQL*Plus as the following illustrates.

File: 12_2.sql

```
SET SERVEROUTPUT ON SIZE 1000000
DECLARE
   lv_message_txt VARCHAR2(1800);
   lv_status_num  PLS_INTEGER;
```

```
BEGIN
   -- Registers the alert for the session.
   DBMS_ALERT.REGISTER('REORDER_THRESHOLD_ALERT');
   -- Processes the first 10 alerts and then ends and displays alerts.
   FOR lv_count_num IN 1..10 LOOP
      -- Catches each of the alerts.
      DBMS_ALERT.WAITONE('REORDER_THRESHOLD_ALERT',
         lv_message_txt, lv_status_num);
      -- Status of 0 means successful alert capture, otherwise it is
      -- unsuccessful.
      IF lv_status_num = 0 THEN
         DBMS_OUTPUT.PUT_LINE(lv_message_txt);
      ELSE
         DBMS_OUTPUT.PUT_LINE('Alert Failed.');
      END IF;
   END LOOP;
END;
/
```

Oracle sessions continue to update the amount in stock, and the database trigger executes each time the amount is updated. Once there are ten updates of the amount in stock where the amount in stock falls below the reorder point, the PL/SQL program unit completes and displays to the screen the following output.

Output (12_2.sql)

```
Warehouse: 10501   Product: 20510   Current Stock: 49    Reorder Point: 50
Warehouse: 301     Product: 41050   Current Stock: 36    Reorder Point: 40
Warehouse: 301     Product: 41080   Current Stock: 37    Reorder Point: 40
Warehouse: 401     Product: 40422   Current Stock: 37    Reorder Point: 40
Warehouse: 401     Product: 50417   Current Stock: 117   Reorder Point: 120
Warehouse: 10501   Product: 20512   Current Stock: 49    Reorder Point: 50
Warehouse: 10501   Product: 41010   Current Stock: 138   Reorder Point: 140
Warehouse: 101     Product: 30421   Current Stock: 1799  Reorder Point: 1800
Warehouse: 101     Product: 10011   Current Stock: 617   Reorder Point: 625
Warehouse: 101     Product: 41020   Current Stock: 438   Reorder Point: 450
```

Possible Uses of DBMS_ALERT

The following is a list of possible uses of the DBMS_ALERT package:

Developer

- When certain application conditions occur in the application

- When threshold parameters are built into an application and these thresholds are exceeded

- When selected errors are encountered in the application

DBA

- When certain critical thresholds are reached (data dictionary or V$ views)
  - Extreme amount of disk reads or memory reads for a statement/session
  - An object is nearing (within 15 extents of) the object maximum extent setting
  - Not enough space available in tablespace for next object extension
- When specific conditions occur in the system that should not occur
  - Number of sessions for one user exceeds a threshold
  - Objects are being created in the SYSTEM tablespace
  - SYSTEM tablespace is being used for temporary sorting

Create an Application Registration and Asynchronous Communication Vehicle (DBMS_APPLICATION_INFO)

The DBMS_APPLICATION_INFO package provides a powerful real-time mechanism for building asynchronous application information registration and logging into your system. This package can be used in a variety of ways. Several methods are described in the following subsections.

The DBMS_APPLICATION_INFO package is a standalone package, which is useful to DBAs primarily and advanced developers.

Register or Log Session Information

The main component of the DBMS_APPLICATION_INFO package is the SET_MODULE procedure. This procedure allows two columns in the V$SESSION and V$SQLAREA views to be set. By calling this procedure and providing two input parameters, these two columns are set immediately. This package updates the V$ views; therefore, it does not require a COMMIT for these columns to be set.

Procedure Syntax

```
DBMS_APPLICATION_INFO.SET_MODULE(module_name IN VARCHAR2,
   action_name IN VARCHAR2);
```

The module_name parameter is limited to 48 characters and the action_name parameter is limited to 32 characters (module column defined as VARCHAR2(48) and action column defined as VARCHAR2(32) in the V$SESSION view).

The two views updated with this information are detailed in the following bullets:

- **View: V$SESSION**

The V$SESSION view contains one record for each Oracle session currently logged in. The SET_MODULE procedure sets two V$SESSION columns for the calling session as the following script illustrates.

The current session user is identified with the following SQL*Plus command.

```
SHOW USER
user is "PLSQL_USER"
```

File: 12_3.sql

```
SELECT sid, serial#, username, module, action
FROM   v$session
WHERE  USERNAME = 'PLSQL_USER';
```

Output (12_3.sql)

```
       SID    SERIAL# USERNAME         MODULE                   ACTION
---------- ---------- ---------------- ------------------------ -------
         7          7 PLSQL_USER       SQL*Plus
```

```
EXECUTE DBMS_APPLICATION_INFO.SET_MODULE('Package: TEST',
  'Procedure: MAIN');
```

Output (12_3.sql)

```
   SID    SERIAL# USERNAME         MODULE                   ACTION
------ ---------- ---------------- ------------------------ ----------------
     7          7 PLSQL_USER       Package: TEST            Procedure: MAIN
```

Any time a user logs into SQL*Plus, the DBMS_APPLICATION_INFO.SET_ MODULE procedure is executed internally by Oracle and the module column is set to SQL*Plus. This is illustrated in the preceding example, when the V$SESSION view was first queried for the user PLSQL_USER. The module and action columns can be set to any values desired and should be used as a registering mechanism to identify specific information to aid in pinpointing current session activity. The value of module and action remain set in the V$SESSION view for the session until the values are changed again by the SET_MODULE procedure (or other DBMS_APPLICATION_INFO procedure) or the session terminates. It is recommended to set these values upon entering a form, procedure, or other source code segment, and then set these values to NULL when exiting the form, procedure, or other source code segment. The SET_MODULE technique ensures the registration of information is current and accurate at all times. The use of this procedure can be adopted as a standard in your environment to provide invaluable tracking of users throughout application execution.

■ View: V$SQLAREA

The V$SQLAREA view contains one record for each SQL statement or PL/SQL program unit execution since the last database startup. Once the SET_MODULE procedure is executed for a session, the module and action columns of the V$SQLAREA view are set for each SQL statement or PL/SQL program unit inserted in this view as illustrated in the following code:

File: 12_4.sql

```
SELECT sql_text, module, action
FROM    v$sqlarea
WHERE   INSTR(UPPER(sql_text), 'INVENTORY') > 0;
```

Output (12_4.sql)

```
SQL_TEXT                                MODULE              ACTION
--------------------------------------- ------------------- -----------------
SELECT * FROM s_inventory               SQL*Plus
SELECT sql_text, module, action FRO     Package: TEST       Procedure: MAIN
M    v$sqlarea  WHERE   INSTR(UPPER(s
ql_text), 'INVENTORY') > 0
```

As the preceding output illustrates, the module and action values are still set from the preceding SET_MODULE call.

File: 12_5.sql

```
SELECT product_id
FROM    s_inventory
WHERE   ROWNUM < 5;
```

Output (12_5.sql)

```
PRODUCT_ID
----------
     10011
     10012
     10013
     10021
```

Output (12_4.sql)

```
SQL_TEXT                              MODULE            ACTION
------------------------------------- ----------------- ----------------
SELECT * FROM s_inventory             SQL*Plus
SELECT sql_text, module, action FRO   Package: TEST     Procedure: MAIN
M   v$sqlarea  WHERE  INSTR(UPPER(s
ql_text), 'INVENTORY') > 0
SELECT product_id FROM s_inventory    Package: TEST     Procedure: MAIN
WHERE ROWNUM < 5
```

The value of module and action is set for each new SQL statement or PL/SQL program unit executed to the current setting of the module and action. The module and action values for a session do not change for the session operations until the values are changed again by the SET_MODULE procedure (or other DBMS_APPLICATION_INFO procedure) or the session terminates. It is recommended to set these values upon entering a form, procedure, or other source code segment, and then set these values to NULL when exiting the form procedure or other source code segment. The SET_MODULE technique ensures the registration of information is current and accurate at all times. Otherwise, SQL statement and PL/SQL program unit executions can be logging inaccurate module and action information and can lead to more complex debugging. The use of this procedure can be adopted as a standard in your environment to provide invaluable tracking of users throughout application execution.

Change Only the Action Column Value

Oracle provides the means of only updating the action column without affecting the module column. Accomplished with the SET_ACTION procedure, the following syntax illustrates this procedure.

Procedure Syntax

```
DBMS_APPLICATION_INFO.SET_ACTION(action_name IN VARCHAR2);
```

The SET_ACTION procedure operates identically to the SET_MODULE procedure, but only changes the action column.

Read the Current Setting of the Action and Module Columns

Oracle provides a means of reading the current values of the module and action columns. This is accomplished with the READ_MODULE procedure, illustrated in the following syntax:

Procedure Syntax

```
DBMS_APPLICATION_INFO.READ_MODULE(module_name OUT VARCHAR2,
    action_name OUT VARCHAR2);
```

File: 12_6.sql

```
SET SERVEROUTPUT ON SIZE 1000000
DECLARE
    lv_module_txt VARCHAR2(48);
    lv_action_txt VARCHAR2(32);
BEGIN
    -- Read Original Values and Display
    DBMS_APPLICATION_INFO.READ_MODULE(lv_module_txt, lv_action_txt);
    DBMS_OUTPUT.PUT_LINE('Before  Module: ' || lv_module_txt ||
        CHR(9) || ' Action: ' || lv_action_txt);
    DBMS_APPLICATION_INFO.SET_MODULE('PL/SQL BLock',
        'Testing DBMS_APPLICATION_INFO');
    -- Read Changed Values and Display
    DBMS_APPLICATION_INFO.READ_MODULE(lv_module_txt, lv_action_txt);
    DBMS_OUTPUT.PUT_LINE('After  Module: ' || lv_module_txt ||
        CHR(9) || ' Action: ' || lv_action_txt);
END;
/
```

Output (12_6.sql)

```
Before  Module: SQL*Plus       Action:
After   Module: PL/SQL BLock    Action: Testing DBMS_APPLICATION_INFO

PL/SQL procedure successfully completed.
```

Communicating Information with
DBMS_APPLICATION_INFO

In the preceding example, the CHR(9) used in the DBMS_OUTPUT.PUT_LINE command, adds a literal TAB between the two column values to ensure the output is correctly aligned in the screen display.

Set and Read Additional Information in V$SESSION

One additional column, client_info, can be used in the V$SESSION view. Again, this value is set and read similarly to the SET_MODULE procedure. The two procedures are SET_CLIENT_INFO and READ_CLIENT_INFO:

Procedure Syntax

```
DBMS_APPLICATION_INFO.SET_CLIENT_INFO(client_info IN VARCHAR2);
DBMS_APPLICATION_INFO.READ_CLIENT_INFO(client_info OUT VARCHAR2);
```

File: 12_7.sql

```
DECLARE
   lv_client_info_txt VARCHAR2(64);
BEGIN
   -- Read Original Value
   DBMS_APPLICATION_INFO.READ_CLIENT_INFO(lv_client_info_txt);
   DBMS_OUTPUT.PUT_LINE('Before  Client Info: ' ||
      NVL(lv_client_info_txt, 'NULL'));
   DBMS_APPLICATION_INFO.SET_CLIENT_INFO
      ('Testing DBMS_APPLICATION_INFO');
   -- Read Changed Value
   DBMS_APPLICATION_INFO.READ_CLIENT_INFO(lv_client_info_txt);
   DBMS_OUTPUT.PUT_LINE('After   Client Info: ' ||
      NVL(lv_client_info_txt, 'NULL'));
END;
/
```

Output (12_7.sql)

```
Before  Client Info: NULL
After   Client Info: Testing DBMS_APPLICATION_INFO

PL/SQL procedure successfully completed.
```

File: 12_8.sql

```
SELECT client_info
FROM   v$session
WHERE  username = 'PLSQL_USER';
```

Output (12_8.sql)

```
CLIENT_INFO
-----------------------------
Testing DBMS_APPLICATION_INFO
```

The client_info parameter is limited to 64 characters because the client_info column is defined as VARCHAR2(64).

Possible Uses of DBMS_APPLICATION_INFO

The following is a list of possible uses of the DBMS_APPLICATION_INFO package:

Developer

- Log the name of the Form the user is in (column: client_info or column: module)

- Log the name of the package (column: module) and procedure executing (column: action)

- Log the main description location of the session (column: module) and a checkpoint (column: action) (useful for identifying the location of source code execution)

- Log the number of records processed (column: action) and the elapsed time since the process started (column: action)

- Log a unique identifier of the client system (column: client_info) (read the registry and log the machine)

DBA

- Read V$SQLAREA and V$SESSION columns module and action to determine location or state of statements and sessions

- Read V$SESSION column client_info to determine location of system execution

Compile and Analyze Objects (DBMS_DDL)

The DBMS_DDL package provides two procedures enabling you to specify database objects to be compiled and analyzed. PL/SQL program units can call these procedures and execute the compilation or analysis prior to the execution of other PL/SQL commands.

The DBMS_DDL package is a standalone package and is useful to both developers (compile objects) and DBAs (analyze objects).

These procedures are outlined in the following sections.

Compile an Object

The ALTER_COMPILE procedure provides the same capability as the following SQL command:

```
ALTER PROCEDURE|FUNCTION|PACKAGE [<schema>.]<name> COMPILE [BODY];
```

The ALTER_COMPILE procedure syntax follows:

Procedure Syntax

```
DBMS_DDL.ALTER_COMPILE(type IN VARCHAR2, schema IN VARCHAR2,
    name IN VARCHAR2);
```

TIP
The type is not case-sensitive; however, the schema and name of the object are case-sensitive.

Procedures, functions, package specifications, and package bodies can be re-compiled with the ALTER_COMPILE procedure, but database triggers cannot. If the schema is set to NULL, then it assumes the current schema. Since the ALTER_COMPILE procedure is the same as the preceding SQL ALTER command, the same system privileges are required for the successful execution of this procedure.

Examples

```
-- Re-compiles the reset_ship_date procedure for the current schema.
DBMS_DDL.ALTER_COMPILE('PROCEDURE', NULL, 'RESET_SHIP_DATES');
-- Re-compiles the global package specification and package body
-- for the current schema.
DBMS_DDL.ALTER_COMPILE('package', NULL, 'GLOBAL');
```

```
-- Re-Compiles the global package specification for the current schema
DBMS_DDL.ALTER_COMPILE('package specification', null, 'GLOBAL');
-- Re-Compiles the global package body for the current schema
DBMS_DDL.ALTER_COMPILE('package body', null, 'GLOBAL');
```

Analyze an Object

The ANALYZE_OBJECT procedure provides the same capability as the following command:

```
ANALYZE TABLE|CLUSTER|INDEX [<schema>.]<name> [<method>] STATISTICS
   [SAMPLE <n> [ROWS|PERCENT]];
```

The ANALYZE_OBJECT procedure syntax follows.

Procedure Syntax

```
DBMS_DDL.ANALYZE_OBJECT(type IN VARCHAR2, schema IN VARCHAR2,
   name IN VARCHAR2, method IN VARCHAR2,
   estimate_rows IN NUMBER DEFAULT NULL,
   estimate_percent IN NUMBER DEFAULT NULL,
   method_opt IN VARCHAR2 DEFAULT NULL);
```

TIP
The type is not case-sensitive; however, the schema and name of the object are case-sensitive.

The type can be table, cluster, or index. The method should be set to COMPUTE to compute statistics, set to ESTIMATE to estimate statistics, and set to DELETE to delete statistics. The estimate_rows is used when the method is set to ESTIMATE. It should be set if a certain number of rows will be used to create the statistics (if the estimate is to be based on a percentage of rows, this column should be set to NULL, which is the default). The estimate_percent is used when the method is set to ESTIMATE and should be set if a certain percentage of rows will be used to create the statistics (if the estimate is to be based on a number of rows, this column should be set to NULL, which is the default). The method_opt is optional and by default it is set to NULL, which specifies all components of the object should be analyzed. The method_opt can be set to FOR TABLE to indicate statistics for only the table; to FOR ALL INDEXES to indicate statistics for all indexes; to FOR ALL COLUMNS [SIZE *n*] to indicate statistics for all columns with a maximum of *n* partitions in the histogram; and to FOR ALL INDEXED COLUMNS [SIZE *n*] to indicate statistics for all indexed columns with a maximum of *n* partitions in the histogram (the default for *n* is 75 and the maximum is 254).

Examples

```
-- Analyzes complete statistics on all components of the s_employee
-- table of the current schema.
DBMS_DDL.ANALYZE_OBJECT('TABLE', NULL, 'S_EMPLOYEE', 'COMPUTE');
-- Analyzes estimated statistics on 75 percent of the records on all
-- components of the s_employee table of the current schema.
DBMS_DDL.ANALYZE_OBJECT('TABLE', NULL, 'S_EMPLOYEE', 'ESTIMATE',
   NULL, 75);
-- Analyzes estimated statistics on 50,000 of the records for only the
-- table of the s_employee table of the current schema.
DBMS_DDL.ANALYZE_OBJECT('TABLE', NULL, 'S_EMPLOYEE', 'ESTIMATE',
   50000, NULL, 'FOR TABLE');
```

Possible Uses of DBMS_DDL

The following is a list of possible uses of the DBMS_DDL package.

Developer

■ Create PL/SQL program unit to find invalidated objects automatically and to compile these objects, allowing for more complex re-compilation techniques to be applied

DBA

■ Create PL/SQL program unit to analyze objects, allowing for more complex analyze statistics techniques to be applied

Use the Oracle Job Scheduler (DBMS_JOB)

The DBMS_JOB package provides support for scheduling the execution of PL/SQL program units in a job queue. This is similar to operating system batch schedulers (such as the UNIX cron facility) and is completely controlled by the DBMS_JOB procedures. The scheduler is flexible and functional.

The DBMS_JOB package is a dependent package and is useful to both developers and DBAs.

Two main init.ora parameters relate to the DBMS_JOB package, three data dictionary views can be viewed to assist in monitoring and manipulating the job queue, and several procedures can manipulate the job queue. A brief description of each component and several examples are provided outlining the init.ora parameters, data dictionary views, and procedures of this powerful package, in the following sections.

The following examples focus on monitoring and manipulating the PL/SQL source code logging procedure called log_source. This procedure was described at the end of Chapter 3. The procedure reads the DBA_SOURCE and DBA_OBJECTS views to identify any PL/SQL new or modified objects, and then inserts the source code into the source_log table. This logging mechanism is beneficial by providing an additional backup mechanism of your stored PL/SQL source code. The backup interval must be determined to set up how often the log_source procedure is executed. I would recommend once an hour as a baseline. The execution interval can be modified based on the activity of changes taking place in your environment.

Modify the init.ora Parameters

The job_queue_processes and job_queue_interval init.ora parameters can change the DBMS_JOB functionality. These settings will directly impact the functionality of the DBMS_JOB package and both settings should be set dependent on the size and activity in your system. The following query illustrates the method of viewing the settings of these parameters.

File: 12_9.sql

```
SELECT name, value, isdefault, isses_modifiable, issys_modifiable
FROM   v$parameter
WHERE  UPPER(name) IN ('JOB_QUEUE_PROCESSES','JOB_QUEUE_INTERVAL')
ORDER BY NAME;
```

Output (12_9.sql)

NAME	VALUE	ISDEFAULT	ISSES	ISSYS_MOD
job_queue_interval	60	TRUE	FALSE	FALSE
job_queue_processes	0	TRUE	FALSE	FALSE

The isses_modifiable column indicates if the parameter is modifiable with the ALTER SESSION command, and the issys_modifiable column indicates if the parameter is modifiable with the ALTER SYSTEM command.

TIP
The V$PARAMETER query in the preceding example reveals that neither of the job queue parameters are modifiable without changing the parameter in the init.ora. In the release of Oracle 8.0, the job_queue_processes parameter is changed to allow for the ALTER SYSTEM command to change this parameter.

TIP
In the release of Oracle 8.0 and Oracle 8.1, an abundance of init.ora parameters is now modifiable with either the ALTER SYSTEM or ALTER SESSION command. To determine on your system which init.ora parameters are changeable in this manner, execute the preceding query with the predicate (WHERE) clause removed.

job_queue_processes
The job_queue_processes parameter controls the number of Oracle processes created to process the job queue. The default is set to 0; therefore, it must be set to at least 1, for any processes to be executed through DBMS_JOB. The maximum number for this parameter is 36.

job_queue_interval
The job_queue_interval parameter controls the interval (specified in seconds) between the job queue processes polling for queued jobs to execute. The default is set to 60; it indicates the job queue processes wake up every 60 seconds and reads the DBA_JOBS view to determine if any jobs should be executed. The maximum for this parameter is 3600 seconds or one hour.

TIP
The more processes executing in your environment in the job queue, the higher the job_queue_processes should be. The increased frequency (shorter time frame) of your processes in the job queue, the smaller the job_queue_interval should be.

View the Job Queue and Jobs Executing
The following three data dictionary views provide the capability to monitor the job queue and any jobs executing at the current time.

- **DBA_JOBS**   Contains a list of all jobs in the queue for all users
- **USER_JOBS**   Contains a list of all jobs for the current user
- **DBA_JOBS_RUNNING**   Contains a list of all jobs currently executing

The following two scripts show the useful information that can be obtained from these views.

Using the Oracle Job Scheduler
(DBMS_JOB)

File: 12_10.sql

```
SELECT what, job, priv_user,
       TO_CHAR(last_date, 'MM/DD/YYYY HH24:MI:SS') last,
       DECODE(this_date, NULL, 'NO', 'YES') running,
       TO_CHAR(next_date, 'MM/DD/YYYY HH24:MI:SS') next,
       interval, total_time, broken
FROM   dba_jobs
ORDER BY what;
```

Output (12_10.sql)

Process	Job #	User Privilege	Last Execution
Currently Executing	Next Execution	Execution Interval	Time to Exe in secs	Disabled
LOG_SOURCE;		5 PLSQL_USER	05/02/1999 08:07:36
NO	05/02/1999 08:08:06	sysdate+30/86400	38	N

The information presented in the preceding query provides important details about the current state of the PL/SQL program unit and information related to when it was placed in the job queue. The columns in the preceding output are outlined in the following:

- **Process** Identifies the process (PL/SQL Program unit) in the job queue

- **Job#** Identifies the unique job number assigned to the process by Oracle. This is extremely important to know because all the DBMS_JOB procedures require the process to be identified by this unique number.

- **User Privilege** Identifies the user privilege to be used when the process is executed

- **Last Execution** Identifies the last time the process was executed

- **Currently Executing** Identifies if the process is executing at the current time (NO or YES)

- **Next Execution** Identifies the next time this process will execute

- **Execution Interval** Identifies the interval used between each execution

- **Time to Exe in secs** Identifies the total clock time this process has used to execute (this is the total time for all executions, not the last execution only)

- **Disabled** Identifies if the process is disabled (N for No or Y for Yes)

File: 12_11.sql

```
SELECT a.job, what,
       TO_CHAR(SYSDATE, 'mm/dd/yyyy hh24:mi:ss') now,
       TO_CHAR(a.this_date, 'mm/dd/yyyy hh24:mi:ss') this
FROM   dba_jobs_running a, dba_jobs b
WHERE  a.job = b.job;
```

Output (12_11.sql)

```
Job # Process               Current Time         Start of Execution
----- --------------------- -------------------- -------------------
    5 LOG_SOURCE;            05/02/1999 08:34:47 05/02/1999 08:34:37
```

The information presented in the preceding query indicates what processes are currently executing and when each process started executing, as well as the current time. The preceding process has been executing for ten seconds.

Submit a Job (DBMS_JOB.SUBMIT)

The SUBMIT procedure provides the capability to submit a job and specify the significant pieces of information required to execute the process, namely, the name of the process to execute, the date of next execution, and the execution interval. Each job submitted is assigned a unique job number. The job number is the only method to uniquely identify a process.

Procedure Syntax

```
DBMS_JOB.SUBMIT (job OUT BINARY_INTEGER, what IN VARCHAR2,
   next_date IN DATE DEFAULT SYSDATE,
   interval  IN  VARCHAR2 DEFAULT 'NULL',
   no_parse  IN  BOOLEAN DEFAULT FALSE);
```

File: 12_12.sql

```
DECLARE
   lv_job_num PLS_INTEGER;
BEGIN
   DBMS_JOB.SUBMIT(lv_job_num, 'LOG_SOURCE;', SYSDATE,
      'SYSDATE + 1/24', NULL);
   DBMS_OUTPUT.PUT_LINE('Assigned Job #: ' || lv_job_num);
END;
/
```

Output (12_12.sql)

```
Assigned Job #: 8

PL/SQL procedure successfully completed.
```

The preceding example submitted the log_source procedure to execute every hour. The following equality information can be used to determine the interval desired.

1 Day = 24 Hours = 1440 Minutes = 86400 seconds

Therefore, depending on the interval desired, the calculation is made easy by referring to the previous equality. Several examples are shown in the following table:

Interval Desired	Value for Interval
Every Week	SYSDATE + 7
Every Day	SYSDATE + 1
Every 2 Hours	SYSDATE + 2/24
Every 15 Minutes	SYSDATE + 15/1440
Every 90 Seconds	SYSDATE 90/86400

TIP
When specifying the WHAT variable in this procedure, you must include a ";" included at the end of the procedure you are executing, otherwise an error will occur.

TIP
Setting the interval of execution becomes confusing quickly, unless you have an easy mechanism to convert your desired interval into a value. The preceding equality information provides this easy translation formula. Try it, it's easy!

TIP
For the interval, any of the date functions outlined in Chapter 6 can also be used to introduce more flexibility in setting the time interval.

TIP
If no interval is specified, the process executes at the specified time and then is removed from the job queue. After each execution of the process, the next date is determined as calculated from the interval. The process will not execute exactly on the next date/time setting, it will execute the next time the job processes wake up to execute processes in the job queue. Therefore, the actual execution time may be off slightly and typically not by more than the init.ora parameter job_queue_interval.

Modify a Submitted Job

Several DBMS_JOB procedures can change the attributes of a submitted job. The CHANGE procedure provides the capability to alter what process is executing, the next execution date, and the interval. The WHAT, NEXT_DATE, and INTERVAL procedures are used to change each one of these values individually. Specifying a NULL value for any of the values in the CHANGE procedure will leave the value unchanged, as illustrated in the following example.

Procedure Syntax

```
DBMS_JOB.CHANGE(job IN BINARY_INTEGER, what IN VARCHAR2,
    next_date IN DATE, interval IN VARCHAR2);
```

Example

```
DBMS_JOB.CHANGE(8, NULL, NULL, 'SYSDATE + 2/24');
```

The preceding example modifies the process with unique job identification of 8 by changing the execution interval to execute every two hours.

Remove a Submitted Job from the Job Queue

Once a job is submitted with an interval, the job will execute indefinitely. A process in the job queue can be removed at any time with the REMOVE procedure. Once the job is removed, it will not longer be executed. If it's already executing when the request is made, it will complete its current execution.

Procedure Syntax

```
DBMS_JOB.REMOVE(job IN BINARY_INTEGER);
```

Example

```
DBMS_JOB.REMOVE(8);
```

The preceding example removes the process with unique job identification of 8 from the job queue.

Disable a Submitted Job and Keep in the Job Queue

Once a job is submitted with an interval, the job will execute indefinitely. A process in the job queue can be disabled at any time with the BROKEN procedure. When a job is disabled, it remains in the queue, but does not execute. Once disabled, the job can either be executed or removed from the queue. If the job is executed, then the job is enabled from that point forward.

Procedure Syntax

```
DBMS_JOB.BROKEN(job IN BINARY_INTEGER, broken IN BOOLEAN,
    next_date IN DATE DEFAULT SYSDATE);
```

Example

```
DBMS_JOB.BROKEN(8, TRUE, NULL);
```

The preceding example disables the process with unique job identification of 8 in the job queue. We can execute the script 12_10.sql to see job # 8 is disabled by viewing the disabled column. This is illustrated in the following output.

Output (12_10.sql)

```
Process                          Job # User Privilege  Last Execution
-------------------------------- ------ --------------- ---------------
Currently                        Execution            Time to Exe
Executing Next Execution         Interval               in secs Disabled
--------- ---------------------- ---------------- ------------- --------
LOG_SOURCE;                          8 PLSQL_USER
NO        01/01/4000 00:00:00 SYSDATE + 2/24                   0 Y
```

To enable the process again, the BROKEN procedure is executed with the broken value set to FALSE.

Execute a Submitted Job in the Job Queue Immediately

Once a job is submitted with an interval, the job will execute indefinitely. A process in the job queue can be forced to execute immediately at any time with the RUN procedure. The following procedure forces this operation.

Procedure Syntax

```
DBMS_JOB.RUN(job IN BINARY_INTEGER);
```

Example

```
DBMS_JOB.RUN(8);
```

The preceding example forces the execution of the process with unique job identification of 8 in the job queue.

TIP
When the DBMS_JOB.RUN procedure is executed, the process will execute immediately. It also forces a disabled (broken) process in the job queue to become enabled. If a process is enabled when the DBMS_JOB.RUN is executed, the next date is recalculated.

Possible Uses of DBMS_JOB

The following is a list of possible uses of the DBMS_JOB package:

Developer

- Schedule application threshold verification programs
- Schedule periodic application programs (daily, weekly, monthly, and so forth)
- Schedule summary or roll-up programs

DBA

- Schedule DBA script execution and alerting routines

Using the Oracle Job Scheduler (DBMS_JOB)

- Identify free space getting low

- Identify object(s) becoming too fragmented

- Identify rollback segment contention

- Execute V$ view or data dictionary view scripts

- Schedule DBA monitoring activities

- Schedule DBA maintenance activities

TIP
Any processes submitted to the job queue and executed at regular intervals will remain when the database is shut down and restarted.

TIP
Manipulating the job queue with the DBMS_JOB procedures and executing scripts to view the data dictionary views can become tedious if the amount of job queue processes is large. We (at TUSC) have built a front-end in Oracle Developer Forms to the DBA_JOBS and DBA_JOBS_RUNNING views. The Form also provides a set of push buttons that execute the procedures in the DBMS_JOB package to allow easier monitoring and manipulation of the job queue.

Provide an Easy Debugging Facility (DBMS_OUTPUT)

The DBMS_OUTPUT package is useful for debugging PL/SQL program units being tested in SQL*Plus by displaying information to the terminal. However, the display to the terminal does not take place until the entire PL/SQL program unit has completed. Contrary to popular belief, it does not display the message to the screen when the DBMS_OUTPUT.PUT_LINE procedure is executed. This procedure writes information to the message buffer only; therefore, it still needs to be read from this message buffer and displayed to the screen. When in SQL*Plus, executing the following SQL*Plus command forces the message buffer to be read to display the message buffer contents to the screen once the PL/SQL program unit completes execution.

```
SET SERVEROUTPUT ON SIZE 1000000
```

If the program unit takes four hours to complete, the first message displayed to the screen from the DBMS_OUTPUT.PUT_LINE procedure will be in four hours. If the message buffer is not large enough, then the PL/SQL program unit will abort when the message buffer is filled and display the contents of the message buffer to the screen upon the abort.

When in SQL*Plus, I recommend using the DBMS_OUTPUT.PUT_LINE only when all display messages can be displayed when the PL/SQL program unit completes. I also recommend turning the SERVEROUTPUT ON in SQL*Plus with the previous SQL*Plus command.

When your PL/SQL code is integrated into other source code, executed in a form, report, or other product environment, then the DBMS_OUTPUT.PUT_LINE will never be logged to the message buffer or displayed, as long as the DBMS_OUTPUT.ENABLE procedure is not executed. DBMS_OUTPUT.ENABLE enables the message buffer only. It does not retrieve the messages from the buffer when the PL/SQL block completes. The GET_LINE and GET_LINES procedures must be used for this.

A risk of overflowing the message buffer always exists when using the DBMS_OUTPUT.ENABLE and DBMS_OUTPUT.PUT_LINE procedures. I recommend using the DBMS_OUTPUT.PUT_LINE for debugging only, and once the PL/SQL source code is tested and fully debugged, these statements can be left in the source code for future use, if necessary. The PL/SQL program unit can be placed in production and if ever enhanced, the program unit can be moved to SQL*Plus with SERVEROUTPUT ON to see all the debugging messages again. This enables a developer to leave all debugging statements in the source code for later use without effect when executed in production.

For more details on the DBMS_OUTPUT package refer to Chapter 4. The DBMS_OUTPUT.PUT_LINE is an overloaded procedure and enables the input parameter to be a number, date, or character value. If more interactive display is necessary for a PL/SQL program unit or a program unit runs for an extended period of time, I recommend using the DBMS_PIPE, DBMS_APPLICATION_INFO, or UTL_FILE packages, or a temporary table.

The DBMS_OUTPUT package is a dependent package and is useful to both developers and DBAs.

TIP
*If the DBMS_OUTPUT.ENABLE procedure is executed in a PL/SQL program unit and the program unit is not being executed in SQL*Plus, then DBMS_OUTPUT.PUT_LINE procedure executions will fill the message buffer. If the DBMS_OUTPUT.GET_LINE or DBMS_OUTPUT.GET_LINES procedures are not executed, then the message buffer can overflow and cause an error that is difficult to locate.*

Providing an Easy Debugging Facility

TIP
I recommend keeping DBMS_OUTPUT.PUT_LINE procedure calls in PL/SQL program units for debugging and testing in SQL*Plus. This allows for only turning on the message buffer and receiving these messages by the SET SERVEROUTPUT ON SIZE 1000000 command in SQL*Plus. This is the preferred method versus using the DBMS_OUTPUT.ENABLE in PL/SQL program units. The disadvantage of leaving in the DBMS_OUTPUT.PUT_LINE procedure calls is that the overhead of the procedure call still exists. Adding conditional logic around these commands can eliminate this overhead.

Possible Uses of DBMS_OUTPUT

The DBMS_OUTPUT package should be limited to display in SQL*Plus only. If a message buffer is desired for messaging, it would be better to use a PL/SQL table to enable the capability of controlling the storage and retrieval, even when errors occur. The use of PL/SQL tables eliminates the size limitation that exists within the DBMS_OUTPUT package message buffer.

Create an Asynchronous Message Facility (DBMS_PIPE)

The DBMS_PIPE package provides a means for communication between different sessions through a piped message. This package serves a similar purpose as the DBMS_ALERT package with the main difference being messages are sent asynchronously and are not dependent on a successful commit point. Messages are packed or logged into a pipe to be received and unpacked or read at another time, usually by another database session. So, multiple sessions can read or write to public pipes. Each user session must receive and unpack the message to be read. These messages are stored in the Shared Global Area (SGA) and the transport vehicle between sessions is through the SGA.

The DBMS_PIPE package is similar to electronic mail systems, remote component. The remote user creates a number of messages and buffers them on their machine and then, at a desired time, they dial up to the server and send all the buffered messages. These messages are then available to other users and uniquely identified by username. The users to whom the mail was sent can read each mail message one at a time.

With the DBMS_PIPE package, messages are packed in the session's private buffer until sent to the SGA memory to wait in the pipe.

The following is an illustration of the general flow of the DBMS_PIPE package:

- **User Sending Message(s)**   Creates Pipe/Packs Message(s)/Sends Message

- **User Receiving Message(s)**   Receives Message(s)/Unpacks Message(s)

Messages are packed and sent at logical locations in a PL/SQL Program Unit. Once messages are received, they are processed by the appropriate action (logging the information, displaying the information, triggering execution of other programs, and so forth).

The DBMS_PIPE package is a dependent package and is useful for both developers and DBAs. The following sections provide detailed information on the main procedures and functions that make up the DBMS_PIPE package.

Create a Pipe

A pipe must be named for the receiving session to identify from which pipe to read the messages. The CREATE_PIPE function enables a pipe to be created explicitly; however, a pipe can be created implicitly with the SEND_MESSAGE procedure. The CREATE_PIPE function returns a status code of 0 if the pipe is created or already exists.

TIP
I recommend creating a pipe explicitly as a standard to ensure easier procedural standards and more structured programming. I also recommend creating a pipe as public, unless a special need exists to keep it private. Public pipes can be seen by all users, whereas private pipes are only seen by sessions of the same username of the creator of the pipe.

The following syntax illustrates the CREATE_PIPE function:

Function Syntax

```
DBMS_PIPE.CREATE_PIPE(pipename IN VARCHAR2,
   maxpipesize IN INTEGER DEFAULT 8192,
   private IN BOOLEAN DEFAULT TRUE) RETURN INTEGER;
```

File: 12_13.sql

```
DECLARE
   lv_status_num PLS_INTEGER;
BEGIN
   lv_status_num := DBMS_PIPE.CREATE_PIPE('TEST 1');
   DBMS_OUTPUT.PUT_LINE('Status: ' || lv_status_num);
END;
/
```

Output (12_13.sql)

```
Status: 0

PL/SQL procedure successfully completed.
```

The V$DB_PIPES view provides a list of each pipe created in the database and indicates the type of pipe, private or public. Once the preceding code segment has been executed, the pipe can be seen with the following query.

File: 12_14.sql

```
SELECT *
FROM   v$db_pipes;
```

Output (12_14.sql)

```
OWNERID    NAME                    TYPE      SIZE
---------- ------------------- ------- ----------
        19 TEST 1                  PRIVATE    479
```

Remove a Pipe

Once a pipe is no longer needed, it is important to delete the pipe explicitly. Remember, a pipe takes up space in the SGA, so it is important to treat a pipe like a cursor: when the use of the pipe is complete, remove it. The REMOVE_PIPE function enables a pipe to be removed explicitly. This function returns a status code of 0 if the pipe is removed successfully or if the pipe does not exist.

TIP

I recommend removing the pipe explicitly as a standard to ensure easier procedural standards and more structured programming.

The following syntax illustrates the REMOVE_PIPE function:

Function Syntax

```
DBMS_PIPE.REMOVE_PIPE(pipename IN VARCHAR2) RETURN INTEGER;
```

File: 12_15.sql

```
DECLARE
   lv_status_num PLS_INTEGER;
BEGIN
   lv_status_num := DBMS_PIPE.REMOVE_PIPE('TEST 1');
   DBMS_OUTPUT.PUT_LINE('Status: ' || lv_status_num);
END;
/
```

Output (12_15.sql)

```
Status: 0

PL/SQL procedure successfully completed.
```

Once the preceding statement has been executed, the pipe is deleted as seen by executing the query against the V$DB_PIPES view again.

TIP
The pipes are created in the SGA and require space; therefore, take care to size the pipes based on the messaging volume. When a pipe is no longer needed, remove the pipe to free the space in the SGA.

Package a Piped Message

The PACK_MESSAGE procedure packs data into the message buffer. Packing of a series of data items, even with different data types, into the message buffer is allowed. This procedure is overloaded for VARCHAR2, DATE, and NUMBER data types as the following syntax illustrates.

Procedure Syntax

```
DBMS_PIPE.PACK_MESSAGE(item IN VARCHAR2);
DBMS_PIPE.PACK_MESSAGE(item IN NUMBER);
DBMS_PIPE.PACK_MESSAGE(item IN DATE);
```

Creating an Asynchronous Message Facility

Example

```
DBMS_PIPE.PACK_MESSAGE('Message 1');
DBMS_PIPE.PACK_MESSAGE('Message 2');
```

The preceding two calls to the DBMS_PIPE.PACK_MESSAGE procedure sends the two literal text strings into the message buffer. These messages continue to fill the message buffer until a DBMS_PIPE.SEND_MESSAGE call is encountered. Once this call is encountered, the current content of the message buffer is forwarded to the SGA into the pipe specified in the DBMS_PIPE.SEND_MESSAGE call and the message buffer is flushed.

TIP

Even though the PACK_MESSAGE procedure enables differing data types to be sent to the message buffer, I would limit a pipe to one data type, unless there is a standard pattern of the messages. This will eliminate the need for additional coding to evaluate the data type on the receiving end. If data types are intermixed, the NEXT_ITEM_TYPE function has to be used to determine the data type of the current message in the message stack.

Send a Piped Message

The SEND_MESSAGE function sends the contents of the message buffer (all messages packed or logged in the pipe into the specified pipe). If the pipe does not yet exist, it will be implicitly created as a public pipe. The SEND_MESSAGE function returns a status code of the sent pipe (0 – successful, 1 - timed out trying to send pipe, or 3 - pipe was interrupted). Identical to the DBMS_ALERT, the time-out parameter is in seconds and the default maximum timeout is 86400000 seconds or 1,000 days.

Function Syntax

```
DBMS_PIPE.SEND_MESSAGE(pipename IN VARCHAR2,
    timeout IN INTEGER DEFAULT MAXWAIT,
    maxpipesize IN INTEGER DEFAULT 8192) RETURN NUMBER;
```

File: 12_16.sql

```
DECLARE
    lv_status_num PLS_INTEGER;
BEGIN
    lv_status_num := DBMS_PIPE.SEND_MESSAGE('TEST 1');
    DBMS_OUTPUT.PUT_LINE('Status: ' || lv_status_num);
END;
/
```

Output (12_16.sql)

```
Status: 0

PL/SQL procedure successfully completed.
```

The preceding call to SEND_MESSAGE forwards the contents of the message buffer to the 'TEST 1' pipe in the SGA and flushes the message buffer. The 'TEST 1' pipe in the SGA retains the contents of the buffer until the message is received by a session. Additional messages can be sent to the 'TEST 1' pipe, and will be stored in the order of submission in the SGA until each message is received with the RECEIVE_MESSAGE function call.

Process Mixed Data Types When Reading a Piped Message

The NEXT_ITEM_TYPE function returns the data type of the next item in message buffer. This function is necessary if the pipe involves intermixed data types. The return codes are as follows: 0 - no more items in the pipe; 6 - NUMBER, 9 - VARCHAR2, 11 - ROWID, 12 - DATE, and 23 - RAW. These codes enable the program to determine the data type of the next message on the stack.

Function Syntax

```
DBMS_PIPE.NEXT_ITEM_TYPE RETURN NUMBER;
```

Flush the Contents of the Current Message Buffer

Each PACK_MESSAGE call sends a message to the message buffer. If you want to reset this buffer at any time without sending the message to the pipe with the SEND_MESSAGE call, the RESET_BUFFER procedure can be called. The following command syntax executes this procedure:

Procedure Syntax

```
DBMS_PIPE.RESET_BUFFER;
```

Receive a Piped Message

The RECEIVE_MESSAGE function receives a message from the named pipe and loads the message into a local message buffer of the current session. It returns a status code of the pipe being received (0 – successful, 1 - timed out, or 3 - pipe was interrupted). The time-out parameter is measured in seconds. This command is the counterpart of the SEND_MESSAGE function and receives the current message from

the pipe in the SGA. If no messages exist in the named pipe in the SGA, then the
session calling the RECEIVE_MESSAGE function is placed in a wait cycle and
remains in a wait cycle until another message is sent to the named pipe. The session
will wait up to the maximum of 86400000 seconds or 1,000 days by default.

Function Syntax

```
DBMS_PIPE.RECEIVE_MESSAGE(pipename IN VARCHAR2, timeout IN NUMBER)
   RETURN INTEGER;
```

File: 12_17.sql

```
DECLARE
   lv_status_num PLS_INTEGER;
BEGIN
   lv_status_num := DBMS_PIPE.RECEIVE_MESSAGE('TEST 1');
   DBMS_OUTPUT.PUT_LINE('Status: ' || lv_status_num);
END;
/
```

Output (12_17.sql)

```
Status: 0

PL/SQL procedure successfully completed.
```

The preceding command reads the pipe 'TEST 1' and returns the next message
in the pipe. This message is read into the current session's message buffer for
processing with the UNPACK_MESSAGE procedure. The messages are read
sequentially from the pipe in FIFO (First In First Out) order. No method exists to
override the way messages are read.

Unpack and Read a Piped Message

The UNPACK_MESSAGE procedure unpacks data from the message buffer. This
procedure is overloaded for VARCHAR2, DATE, and NUMBER data types. Errors
occur when no more items are in the buffer or when data types do not match. The
error encountered when no more messages are in the message buffer and the
UNPACK_MESSAGE procedure is called is shown in the following.

```
ORA-06556: the pipe is empty, cannot fulfill the unpack_message request
```

This error can be handled with an EXCEPTION when unpacking messages.

Procedure Syntax

```
DBMS_PIPE.UNPACK_MESSAGE(item OUT VARCHAR2);
DBMS_PIPE.UNPACK_MESSAGE(item OUT NUMBER);
DBMS_PIPE.UNPACK_MESSAGE(item OUT DATE);
```

Manage Pipes

The PURGE procedure clears all data from the pipe. However, the pipe itself will still exist, until a point where it is pushed out of the SGA or the REMOVE_PIPE function is called.

Procedure Syntax

```
DBMS_PIPE.PURGE(pipename IN VARCHAR2);
```

Example of DBMS_PIPE Being Implemented in a Database Trigger

The following example demonstrates the use of pipes in a database trigger to perform a global messaging alert to all current sessions, indicating an order has been filled. This example demonstrates the capability to create pipes dynamically based on certain conditions at a point in time.

File: 12_18.sql

```
CREATE OR REPLACE TRIGGER bu_order
   BEFORE UPDATE of order_filled ON s_order
   REFERENCING OLD AS OLD NEW AS NEW
   FOR EACH ROW
   WHEN (NEW.order_filled = 'Y')
DECLARE
   CURSOR cur_user IS
     SELECT DISTINCT username
     FROM   v$session
     WHERE  NVL(username,'*') NOT IN ( 'SYS', 'SYSTEM', '*');
   lv_pipe_status_num PLS_INTEGER;
BEGIN
   -- If an order has been filled, notify all sessions with ORDER_ID
   -- and TOTAL. For all non-system users, send the piped message
   FOR cur_user_rec IN cur_user LOOP
     DBMS_PIPE.PURGE (cur_user_rec.username);
```

```
        DBMS_PIPE.PACK_MESSAGE (:NEW.order_id);
        DBMS_PIPE.PACK_MESSAGE (:NEW.total);
        lv_pipe_status_num := DBMS_PIPE.SEND_MESSAGE
           (cur_user_rec.username);
     END LOOP;
END bu_order;
/
```

The preceding example creates a pipe for each current user. All users in the system would have a process in the application to monitor the pipe of their name to view each order filled. The example was used for a specific application where it was necessary to alert current users of filled orders. Typically, the amount of pipes needs to be limited. In the example application, the number of users was small.

Example of DBMS_PIPE to Monitor Long-running Processes

The DBMS_OUTPUT package flushes the message buffer at completion or interruption of the program executing; therefore, the output is only sent to the screen after completion of the program unit. In summary, information cannot be seen during processing.

In most complex production environments, the PL/SQL processing is usually harder to follow and debug. This also applies to commonly executed PL/SQL routines that take long periods of time to execute. When routines are executing over long periods of time, knowing how long the process has been executing is helpful to determine the remaining time to completion. In this type of PL/SQL program unit, the DBMS_OUTPUT package will not fulfill this need and the DBMS_PIPE package can be used. This could allow a PL/SQL developer to "pipe" output from the processing session to another, reading the piped information upon demand.

The following package creation script provides modules that can be implemented as debugging techniques in any piece of PL/SQL code. The PIPE_OUTPUT package uses a global package variable as a switch, to determine whether to pipe messages, similar to setting SERVEROUTPUT ON. The following PUT_LINE procedure could be used to replace any previous calls to the DBMS_OUTPUT.PUT_LINE procedure. Lastly, the GET_LINE procedure can be called from any session to view the current output stored in the pipe.

File: 12_19a.sql

```
CREATE OR REPLACE PACKAGE pipe_output IS
   pvg_pipe_on_bln BOOLEAN := FALSE;
PROCEDURE set_pipeoutput_on;
PROCEDURE put_line (p_message_txt VARCHAR2);
PROCEDURE get_line (p_waittime_num NUMBER := 1);
END pipe_output;
/
```

Creating an Asynchronous Message Facility

File: 12_19b.sql

```
CREATE OR REPLACE PACKAGE BODY pipe_output IS
PROCEDURE set_pipeoutput_on IS
-- Opens the communication pipe
BEGIN
   pvg_pipe_on_bln := TRUE;
END set_pipeoutput_on;

PROCEDURE put_line (p_message_txt VARCHAR2) IS
-- Sends the username of the executing user and a message to the pipe
  lv_status_num PLS_INTEGER;
BEGIN
   IF (pvg_pipe_on_bln) THEN
      DBMS_PIPE.PACK_MESSAGE(USER);
      DBMS_PIPE.PACK_MESSAGE(p_message_txt);
      lv_status_num := DBMS_PIPE.SEND_MESSAGE('OUTPUT');
   END IF;
END put_line;

PROCEDURE get_line (p_waittime_num NUMBER := 1) IS
-- Monitors the pipe based on a specified wait time, reading and
-- displaying the username and messages as they are sent from the
-- executing process.
   lv_status_num            PLS_INTEGER;
   lv_username_txt          VARCHAR2(30);
   lv_message_txt           VARCHAR2(2000);
   lv_message_processed_bln BOOLEAN := FALSE;
BEGIN
   LOOP
      lv_status_num := DBMS_PIPE.RECEIVE_MESSAGE('OUTPUT',
         p_waittime_num);
      EXIT WHEN (lv_status_num != 0);
      lv_message_processed_bln := TRUE;
      DBMS_PIPE.UNPACK_MESSAGE(lv_username_txt);
      DBMS_PIPE.UNPACK_MESSAGE(lv_message_txt);
      DBMS_OUTPUT.PUT_LINE(RPAD('USER: '||lv_username_txt,30)||
                           'MESSAGE: '||lv_message_txt);
   END LOOP;
   IF NOT lv_message_processed_bln THEN
      DBMS_OUTPUT.PUT_LINE('No output in pipe.');
   END IF;
END get_line;
END pipe_output;
/
```

The preceding packaged procedures created provide a powerful and real-time mechanism for monitoring PL/SQL routine processing.

Creating an Asynchronous Message Facility

The following example shows the steps for placing output into the new output pipe. The SET_PIPEOUTPUT_ON procedure is called to start placing output into the pipe, followed by subsequent calls to the PUT_LINE procedure to place messages into the pipe.

File: 12_20.sql

```
BEGIN
   pipe_output.set_pipeoutput_on;
   FOR lv_loop_num IN 1..5 LOOP
      pipe_output.put_line('Currently in iteration: ' ||
         TO_CHAR(lv_loop_num) || '.' );
   END LOOP;
END;
/
```

Lastly, the following code segment uses the GET_LINE procedure to read all the output currently stored in the pipe. A parameter exists specifying how long to wait for a pipe before exiting the program. The output is displayed with the user who created the output, followed by the output message itself.

File: 12_21.sql

```
SET SERVEROUTPUT ON
EXECUTE pipe_output.get_line
```

Output (12_21.sql)

```
USER: PLSQL_USER     MESSAGE: Currently in iteration: 1.
USER: PLSQL_USER     MESSAGE: Currently in iteration: 2.
USER: PLSQL_USER     MESSAGE: Currently in iteration: 3.
USER: PLSQL_USER     MESSAGE: Currently in iteration: 4.
USER: PLSQL_USER     MESSAGE: Currently in iteration: 5.

PL/SQL procedure successfully completed.
```

EXECUTE privilege must be granted by SYS on the DBMS_PIPE package to users who need to use this package.

Possible Uses of DBMS_PIPE

The following is a list of possible uses of the DBMS_PIPE package:

Developer

■ When certain application conditions occur within an application

- When certain threshold parameters are built into an application and are then exceeded
- When selected errors are encountered within an application
- When monitoring PL/SQL program execution progress
- To interface with external services
- To communicate with programs/systems outside the database

DBA

- When certain critical thresholds are reached (data dictionary or V$ views)
    - Extreme amount of disk reads or memory reads for a statement/session
    - An object is nearing (within 15 extents of) the object maximum extent setting
    - Not enough space available in a tablespace for next object extension
- When specific conditions occur in the system that should not occur
    - Number of Sessions for one user exceeds a certain number
    - Objects are being created in the SYSTEM tablespace
    - SYSTEM tablespace is being used for temporary sorting

Enhance Session Control and Identification (DBMS_SESSION)

The DBMS_SESSION package enables session-specific parameters and characteristics to be changed. Many of these changes can be made through DDL commands; however, a select few cannot be performed through DDL commands. Each of these commands has unique instances when it would be helpful. The following is a list of procedures and functions covered in this section:

- IS_ROLE_ENABLED
- SET_ROLE
- SET_NLS
- SET_SQL_TRACE
- RESET_PACKAGE
- FREE_UNUSED_USER_MEMORY

The name of each procedure and function is descriptive of the function it performs. In the following subsections, these procedures and functions are briefly described with an example of each. The DBMS_SESSION package is a standalone package and is useful to DBAs primarily and advanced developers.

Work with Roles via IS_ROLE_ENABLED and SET_ROLE

The IS_ROLE_ENABLED function allows a program unit to check if a certain role is enabled, and the SET_ROLE procedure provides the capability to enable and disable roles.

The syntax of the IS_ROLE_ENABLED function is illustrated in the following:

Function Syntax

```
DBMS_SESSION.IS_ROLE_ENABLED(rolename VARCHAR2) RETURN BOOLEAN;
```

The IS_ROLE_ENABLED function will return a Boolean of either TRUE or FALSE. The IS_ROLE_ENABLED can be used to determine the level of user executing a PL/SQL program unit. The following PL/SQL program unit illustrates this logic.

File: 12_22.sql

```
BEGIN
    IF DBMS_SESSION.IS_ROLE_ENABLED('ADMINSTRATOR') THEN
        DBMS_OUTPUT.PUT_LINE('Current Role Administrator');
        -- Process Administrator Logic
    ELSIF DBMS_SESSION.IS_ROLE_ENABLED('MANAGER') THEN
        DBMS_OUTPUT.PUT_LINE('Current Role Manager');
        -- Process Manager Logic
    ELSE
        DBMS_OUTPUT.PUT_LINE('Current Role Operator');
        -- Process Operator Logic
    END IF;
END;
/
```

TIP
The IS_ROLE_ENABLED input parameter is case-sensitive; therefore, it is important to ensure the role variable is passed as uppercase (unless explicit lowercase roles were defined).

To display a list of the current schema role assignments, the following query can be executed:

File: 12_23.sql

```
SELECT username, granted_role, default_role
FROM   user_role_privs
ORDER BY granted_role;
```

Output (12_23.sql)

```
USERNAME                          GRANTED_ROLE                      DEF
------------------------------    ------------------------------    ---
PLSQL_USER                        CONNECT                           YES
PLSQL_USER                        DBA                               YES
PLSQL_USER                        RESOURCE                          YES
PLSQL_USER                        TEMP_EMP                          YES
```

To receive a list of currently enabled role assignments in a PL/SQL program unit, use the following code segment.

File: 12_24.sql

```
DECLARE
   CURSOR cur_roles IS
      SELECT granted_role
      FROM   user_role_privs
      ORDER BY granted_role;
BEGIN
   FOR cur_roles_rec IN cur_roles LOOP
      IF DBMS_SESSION.IS_ROLE_ENABLED(cur_roles_rec.granted_role) THEN
         DBMS_OUTPUT.PUT_LINE('Role Enabled: ' ||
            cur_roles_rec.granted_role);
      END IF;
   END LOOP;
END;
/
```

Output (12_24.sql)

```
Role Enabled: CONNECT
Role Enabled: DBA
Role Enabled: RESOURCE
Role Enabled: TEMP_EMP
PL/SQL procedure successfully completed.
```

The SET_ROLE procedure is shown in the following.

Enhancing Session Control and Identification

Procedure Syntax

```
DBMS_SESSION.SET_ROLE(role_cmd VARCHAR2);
```

The SET_ROLE procedure performs the same operation as the GRANT ROLE command, enabling all roles to be revoked or role(s) to be assigned in a PL/SQL program unit. The following examples illustrate the removal of all roles, except CONNECT, in a session for PLSQL_USER, followed by the assignment of CONNECT, RESOURCE, and DBA roles through the SET_ROLE procedure. After each command, the preceding PL/SQL program unit will be executed and the output displayed.

Example 1: CONNECT role granted

```
EXECUTE DBMS_SESSION.SET_ROLE('CONNECT')
```

Example 1 Output (12_24.sql)

```
Role Enabled: CONNECT

PL/SQL procedure successfully completed.
```

Example 2: CONNECT, RESOURCE, DBA roles granted

```
EXECUTE DBMS_SESSION.SET_ROLE('CONNECT, RESOURCE, DBA')
```

Example 2 Output (12_24.sql)

```
Role Enabled: CONNECT
Role Enabled: DBA
Role Enabled: RESOURCE

PL/SQL procedure successfully completed.
```

Setting roles becomes increasingly useful when a complex security architecture is required based on the application and environment characteristics.

TIP
The SET_ROLE procedure cannot be called from database triggers or stored PL/SQL program units.

Modify NLS Parameters via SET_NLS

A number of NLS parameters are set at the database level through the init.ora parameters. These parameters can be modified at the session level for a particular session with the SET_NLS procedure. A list of these NLS properties can be displayed by executing the following command:

File: 12_25.sql

```
SELECT parameter, value
FROM   v$nls_parameters
ORDER BY parameter;
```

Output (12_25.sql)

```
PARAMETER                          VALUE
---------------------------------  -------------
NLS_CALENDAR                       GREGORIAN
NLS_CHARACTERSET                   WE8ISO8859P1
NLS_CURRENCY                       $
NLS_DATE_FORMAT                    DD-MON-YY
NLS_DATE_LANGUAGE                  AMERICAN
NLS_ISO_CURRENCY                   AMERICA
NLS_LANGUAGE                       AMERICAN
NLS_NUMERIC_CHARACTERS             .,
NLS_SORT                           BINARY
NLS_TERRITORY                      AMERICA
```

The parameter name and new value are required parameters of the SET_NLS procedure. The following is the syntax of the SET_NLS procedure.

Procedure Syntax

```
DBMS_SESSION.SET_NLS(param VARCHAR2, value VARCHAR2);
```

The following is an example of changing the standard date format for a session.

Example

```
DBMS_SESSION.SET_NLS('NLS_DATE_FORMAT', '''MM/DD/YYYY''');
```

The preceding example changes the standard date format for a session. Notice the value must be surrounded in three single quotes to work properly. The three single quotes equate to one literal quote on each end of the value. This is required based on how Oracle internally processes the parameter value of this procedure. The date format in the current session is now changed, as shown in the following example.

File: 12_26.sql

```
SELECT SYSDATE
FROM    DUAL;
```

Output (12_26.sql)

```
SYSDATE
----------
05/23/1999
```

Conditionally Turning on TRACE via SET_SQL_TRACE

PL/SQL program units are becoming more complex, and optimization of these program units has become more difficult. The Oracle TRACE facility can be a helpful mechanism for pinpointing problematic SQL statements hidden within PL/SQL program units. The SET_SQL_TRACE enables the current session to be traced. The Oracle TRACE facility is described in further detail in Chapter 7.

The SET_SQL_TRACE is merely a toggle that turns tracing on or off by passing a Boolean value of TRUE or FALSE to the procedure. This procedure can be extremely beneficial when testing, as well as when in a production environment and tracing is necessary. TRACE can be turned on conditionally and, in a production environment, one method is to turn TRACE on when the PL/SQL program unit is executed by a specific user (possibly the owner of the PL/SQL program unit). The program unit can be traced in production without turning TRACE on for all executions of the same program unit.

The SET_SQL_TRACE procedure is shown in the following.

Procedure Syntax

```
DBMS_SESSION.SET_SQL_TRACE(sql_trace BOOLEAN);
```

The following is an example of the logic of user-dependent tracing in a PL/SQL program unit.

File: 12_27.sql

```
CREATE OR REPLACE PROCEDURE core_process IS
BEGIN
   IF USER = 'PLSQL_USER' THEN
      DBMS_SESSION.SET_SQL_TRACE(TRUE);
      DBMS_OUTPUT.PUT_LINE('Tracing is turned on...');
   END IF;
   -- Main Logic
   DBMS_SESSION.SET_SQL_TRACE(FALSE);
   DBMS_OUTPUT.PUT_LINE('Tracing is turned off.');
END;
/
```

In the preceding procedure, to execute the command successfully, the PLSQL_USER must have ALTER SESSION system privilege.

Reset the State of All Package Values via RESET_PACKAGE

Any reference to a package will load the entire content of the package—including the specification and body—therefore, all global variables are initialized and loaded in memory. However, if restarting a current session's package state to when it was originally loaded ever becomes necessary, Oracle has provided the RESET_PACKAGE procedure. Care should be taken when executing this procedure because it will reset the state of all packages for the current session, which is analogous to the first time all packages were loaded.

The RESET_PACKAGE procedure is shown in the following.

Procedure Syntax

```
DBMS_SESSION.RESET_PACKAGE;
```

The following example illustrates the resetting of all package variables. The following package specification contains a global counter for the number of operations in a session.

File: 12_28.sql

```
CREATE OR REPLACE PACKAGE GLOBAL_MAIN IS
   pvg_operation_counter_num PLS_INTEGER:=0;
END global_main;
/
```

The following PL/SQL program unit illustrates the calling of this variable and adding one to it.

File: 12_29.sql

```
SET SERVEROUTPUT ON SIZE 1000000
BEGIN
   global_main.pvg_operation_counter_num :=
      global_main.pvg_operation_counter_num + 1;
   DBMS_OUTPUT.PUT_LINE('Global Value: ' ||
      global_main.pvg_operation_counter_num);
END;
/
```

The following output is displayed when the preceding program unit is executed twice.

Output (12_29.sql)

```
Global Value: 1
PL/SQL procedure successfully completed.

Global Value: 2
PL/SQL procedure successfully completed.
```

The following illustrates the execution of the RESET_PACKAGE procedure to reset the state of all packages.

```
EXECUTE DBMS_SESSION.RESET_PACKAGE
```

The previous PL/SQL program unit (12_29.sql) is executed and, as expected, because all package states were re-initialized, the counter again begins at 0.

Output (12_29.sql)

```
Global Value: 1
PL/SQL procedure successfully completed.

Global Value: 2
PL/SQL procedure successfully completed.
```

The preceding execution of the PL/SQL program unit needs to execute the SET SERVEROUTPUT command because the RESET_PACKAGE execution resets the

DBMS_OUTPUT package, which the SET SERVEROUTPUT command implicitly executes (DBMS_OUTPUT.ENABLE procedure).

Free Unused Session Memory via FREE_UNUSED_USER_MEMORY

Each session requires memory resources in various locations, and the amount of memory required varies depending on the programs executed. Memory is required in the Shared Pool, which is part of the SGA, outlined in further detail in Chapter 9. The UGA (User Global Area) and the PGA (Program Global Area) are allocated per session, depending on the programs executed. At the operating system process level two types of memory physically exist—PGA and SGA. Logically, three memory pools exist, namely the PGA, SGA, and UGA. Irrespective of the server mode (dedicated or shared MTS), the logical PGA always maps to the physical PGA and the logical SGA always maps to the physical SGA.

The UGA and PGA are memory requirements per session. When the MTS configuration is used, the UGA memory is no longer memory allocated outside of the Shared Pool. With MTS, the UGA memory is allocated in the Shared Pool, thus requiring a larger SGA. The UGA memory is mapped to the SGA with MTS because the user information must persist for the entire session. However, within one session, each request may be processed by a different process, so the session information must remain accessible in memory to all MTS server processes. Hence, the UGA is mapped to the SGA. In the dedicated server mode, one server serves a user (session) for the entire session; therefore, the user information can be kept in the PGA.

The UGA and the PGA are memory structures allocated for user variable space, PL/SQL tables, sort area, and so forth. If a session is executing programs consuming a large amount of memory (>200K) and memory is at a premium, then it can be advantageous to return unused memory once it is no longer needed. Oracle automatically returns memory for a session when the session ends. However, if large operations are performed and the session continues processing, the unused memory will not be de-allocated. The FREE_UNUSED_FREE_MEMORY procedure provides the capability of returning free unused memory.

The following is the syntax for the FREE_UNUSED_FREE_MEMORY procedure.

Procedure Syntax

```
DBMS_SESSION.FREE_UNUSED_FREE_MEMORY;
```

The following query displays the current memory allocated to the UGA and PGA for the current session.

File: 12_30.sql

```
SELECT  c.name, b.value
FROM    v$session a, v$sesstat b, v$statname c
WHERE   a.sid       = b.sid
AND     b.statistic# = c.statistic#
AND     b.value      != 0
AND     a.username   = 'PLSQL_USER'
AND     c.name       IN ('session uga memory', 'session pga memory');
```

Output (12_30.sql)

NAME	VALUE
session uga memory	29076
session pga memory	215240

The following executes the FREE_UNUSED_USER_MEMORY procedure,

```
EXECUTE DBMS_SESSION.FREE_UNUSED_USER_MEMORY
```

followed by a second look at the UGA and PGA again.

Output (12_30.sql)

NAME	VALUE
session uga memory	29076
session pga memory	85104

In the preceding example, the UGA did not decrease, but the PGA decreased by 130K. The amount it reduces is dependent on the type of operations performed by the session. Large compilations, large sorts, and use of large PL/SQL tables result in more memory use, thus a larger decrease in memory allocated when this procedure is executed.

The following example illustrates the memory allocation of PL/SQL tables. The following procedure is executed from Chapter 4 to load the s_product table into a PL/SQL table.

```
EXECUTE process_products.populate_prod_table
```

Output (12_30.sql)

NAME	VALUE
session uga memory	67960
session pga memory	193932

The preceding output shows the UGA increased by 38K and the PGA increased by 108K. The following executes the FREE_UNUSED_USER_MEMORY procedure again:

```
EXECUTE DBMS_SESSION.FREE_UNUSED_USER_MEMORY
```

The UGA once again remains constant, but the PGA is reduced by 74K, as the following output shows.

Output (12_30.sql)

```
NAME                                 VALUE
------------------------------- ----------
session uga memory                   67960
session pga memory                  119152
```

The populate_prod_table procedure is part of the package process_products; therefore, additional overhead from the package remains in memory.

Possible Uses of DBMS_SESSION

The following is a list of possible uses of the DBMS_SESSION package:

Developer

- To change the default date format
- To TRACE a session
- To change roles for a particular program to ensure proper privileges
- To free memory when an unusually large PL/SQL table or other memory-intensive operation is performed
- To reset the state of all package variables and restart a program unit

DBA

- To TRACE a session
- To change roles for a particular program to ensure proper privileges
- To free memory when an unusually large PL/SQL table or other memory-intensive operation is performed

Enhancing Session Control and Identification

Control the Caching of PL/SQL Objects (DBMS_SHARED_POOL)

The DBMS_SHARED_POOL package provides an extremely powerful and useful feature for PL/SQL performance. PL/SQL objects are loaded into the Shared Pool upon execution. These objects are aged out based on an LRU (Least Recently Used) algorithm. The DBMS_SHARED_POOL package enables PL/SQL objects to be pinned or kept in the Shared Pool, signifying it is not considered in the LRU algorithm.

PL/SQL objects used frequently in applications should be pinned in memory upon database startup. The database startup script can be modified to execute the pinning of the desired PL/SQL objects. The DBMS_SHARED_POOL package contains procedures to pin objects, unpin objects, and view the size of objects in the Shared Pool. The DBMS_SHARED_POOL package is a standalone package and is primarily useful to DBAs.

The following sections outline the DBMS_SHARED_POOL procedures.

Pin PL/SQL Objects

Pinning objects reduces the potential of fragmentation causing the Shared Pool to run out of space when an object is attempting to be placed in the Shared Pool. Objects placed in the Shared Pool must have enough contiguous space; otherwise an error will occur.

The pinned PL/SQL objects can be viewed in the V$DB_OBJECT_CACHE view. The following query displays all packages and procedures in this view.

File: 12_31.sql

```
SELECT owner, name, type, sharable_mem, kept
FROM   v$db_object_cache
WHERE  type like 'P%'
ORDER BY owner, name;
```

Output (12_31.sql)

OWNER	NAME	TYPE	SHARABLE_MEM	KEP
PLSQL_USER	LOG_SOURCE	PROCEDURE	21,337	NO
SYS	DBMS_APPLICATION_INFO	PACKAGE	11,569	NO
SYS	DBMS_APPLICATION_INFO	PACKAGE BODY	4,577	NO
SYS	DBMS_JOB	PACKAGE	15,220	NO
SYS	DBMS_JOB	PACKAGE BODY	10,924	NO
SYS	DBMS_OUTPUT	PACKAGE	13,059	NO
SYS	DBMS_OUTPUT	PACKAGE BODY	9,031	NO
SYS	STANDARD	PACKAGE	118,416	NO
SYS	STANDARD	PACKAGE BODY	26,752	NO

The preceding output is only a subset of the result set. As illustrated in the preceding output, no objects are pinned at the current time.

The following is the syntax for the KEEP procedure.

Procedure Syntax

```
DBMS_SHARED_POOL.KEEP(name IN VARCHAR2, flag IN CHAR DEFAULT 'P');
```

Example

```
DBMS_SHARED_POOL.KEEP('LOG_SOURCE', 'P');
```

The preceding example illustrates the pinning of the log_source procedure. Once the V$DB_OBJECT_CACHE query (12_31.sql) is executed, after pinning the log_source procedure (limiting the result to the first record), the kept column is set to YES.

Output (12_31.sql)

OWNER	NAME	TYPE	SHARABLE_MEM	KEP
PLSQL_USER	LOG_SOURCE	PROCEDURE	21,337	YES

In addition to pinning PL/SQL objects in the object cache of the Shared Pool, you can also pin cursors in the SQL Area of the Shared Pool with this procedure. The address and hash_value of the cursor must be known, which can be retrieved from the V$SQLAREA view. The following illustrates the method to pin a cursor with this procedure. The following query displays the pinned cursors in the SQL Area.

File: 12_32.sql

```
SELECT sql_text, address, hash_value,
       sharable_mem, kept_versions
FROM   v$sqlarea
WHERE  kept_versions != 0;
```

The following output shows there are currently no pinned cursors.

Output (12_32.sql)

```
no rows selected
```

To pin cursors, the cursors, address and hash_value must be known. The following query displays the cursors in the SQL Area that reference the DBA_JOBS_RUNNING view.

File: 12_33.sql

```
SELECT  sql_text, address, hash_value,
        sharable_mem, kept_versions
FROM    v$sqlarea
WHERE   INSTR(UPPER(sql_text), 'DBA_JOBS_RUNNING') > 0;
```

Output (12_33.sql)

```
SQL_TEXT                        ADDRESS   HASH_VALUE SHARABLE_MEM KEPT_VERSIONS
------------------------------- --------- ---------- ------------ -------------
SELECT a.job, what,      TO_CHA 019FA10C -1.506E+09        2,882             0
R(a.this_date, 'mm/dd/yyyy hh24:m
i:ss') this FROM    dba_jobs_runni
ng a, dba_jobs b WHERE   a.job = b
.job

SELECT a.job, what, TO_CHAR(a.thi 01A090FC 1361526073       53,586             0
s_date, 'mm/dd/yyyy hh24:mi:ss')
FROM    dba_jobs_running a, dba_jo
bs b WHERE   a.job = b.job
```

The following example shows the pinning of the last cursor in the preceding query.

```
EXECUTE DBMS_SHARED_POOL.KEEP('01A090FC 1361526073','C');
```

This time, when the V$SQLAREA query is executed, the pinned cursor is returned.

Output (12_32.sql)

```
SQL_TEXT                        ADDRESS   HASH_VALUE SHARABLE_MEM KEPT_VERSIONS
------------------------------- --------- ---------- ------------ -------------
SELECT a.job, what, TO_CHAR(a.thi 01A090FC 1361526073       53,586             1
s_date, 'mm/dd/yyyy hh24:mi:ss')
FROM    dba_jobs_running a, dba_jo
bs b WHERE   a.job = b.job
```

Unpin PL/SQL Objects

If a PL/SQL object or cursor that was pinned needs to be unpinned, the UNKEEP procedure should be executed. A list of pinned PL/SQL objects and cursors could be determined with slightly modified versions of the scripts in the previous section.

The following is the syntax for the UNKEEP procedure:

Procedure Syntax

```
DBMS_SHARED_POOL.UNKEEP(name IN VARCHAR2, flag IN CHAR DEFAULT 'P');
```

Example

```
DBMS_SHARED_POOL.UNKEEP('LOG_SOURCE', 'P');
```

The preceding example unpins the log_source procedure. The following illustrates the method to unpin the cursor that was pinned in the previous section.

```
EXECUTE DBMS_SHARED_POOL.UNKEEP('01A090FC 1361526073','C');
```

Identify Candidates for Pinning

Both PL/SQL objects and cursors can be pinned in the Shared Pool. PL/SQL objects are pinned by name and cursors are pinned by address and hash_value. The V$DB_OBJECT_CACHE and V$SQLAREA views can be queried to determine the objects and cursors with a large sharable memory size. The SIZES procedure provides a method of identifying objects in the V$DB_OBJECT_CACHE and V$SQLAREA, which require a sharable memory size that exceeds a specified threshold.

The lower limit of the sharable memory size (in kilobytes) is provided as an input parameter, and the result is all objects and cursors from these two views exceeding this threshold that may be candidates for pinning. The result set lists the sharable memory size of the PL/SQL object and cursor in thousand units (input value of 50 equates to 50K). The result set lists all the objects in these views and signifies whether the object has been pinned (KEPT). For records returned from the V$DB_OBJECT_CACHE view, the name of the object, the type of PL/SQL program unit, and pinned flag are returned. For records returned from the V$SQLAREA view, the actual cursor text, address and hash value, the literal identifier of a cursor, and pinned flag are returned.

The following is the syntax for the SIZES procedure:

Procedure Syntax

```
DBMS_SHARED_POOL.SIZES(minsize IN NUMBER);
```

Example

```
EXECUTE DBMS_SHARED_POOL.SIZES(50)
```

Example Output

```
SIZE(K) KEPT    NAME
------- ------  ------------------------------------------------------------
118     YES     SYS.STANDARD                    (PACKAGE)
54              SELECT a.job, what,         TO_CHAR(SYSDATE, 'mm/dd/yyyy hh24:mi
                i:ss') now,         TO_CHAR(a.this_date, 'mm/dd/yyyy hh24:mi
                :ss') this FROM   dba_jobs_running a, dba_jobs b WHERE  a.j
                ob = b.job
```

```
           (019CA308,-61945416)      (CURSOR)
54    YES(1) SELECT a.job, what, TO_CHAR(a.this_date, 'mm/dd/yyyy hh24:mi:ss
              s') FROM   dba_jobs_running a, dba_jobs b WHERE  a.job = b.
              job
           (01A090FC,1361526073)     (CURSOR)

PL/SQL procedure successfully completed.
```

Pinning PL/SQL objects and cursors reduces the fragmentation of the shared memory in the Shared Pool. The following error will result if an attempt is made to load a PL/SQL object or cursor and not enough contiguous free memory is available in the Shared Pool.

```
ORA-4031: unable to allocate XXX bytes of shared memory
```

(*XXX* is the number of bytes it is attempting to allocate.) In this case, the quick resolution is to issue the following command:

```
ALTER SYSTEM FLUSH SHARED_POOL;
```

The preceding command flushes the Shared Pool shared memory and the error will be eliminated. All PL/SQL objects and cursors are flushed from the Shared Pool with this command, so the system will be slower until the PL/SQL objects and cursors are reloaded. This error is an indication that your Shared Pool should be increased and you may want to start pinning large, often-used PL/SQL objects.

TIP

When the Shared Pool is flushed, any pinned objects remain pinned and are not flushed.

TIP

A cursor's address and hash_value are assigned when loaded into shared memory; therefore, you cannot hardcode these values.

Possible Uses of DBMS_SHARED_POOL

The following is a list of possible uses of the DBMS_SHARED_POOL package:

DBA

- To identify large objects that are candidates for pinning (caching)
- To pin and unpin PL/SQL objects

Retrieve Free Space Information (DBMS_SPACE)

The DBMS_SPACE package provides procedures indicating to a DBA how much unused space and how many free blocks are available in tables, indexes, and clusters. This package assists DBAs in their major responsibility of space management.

The DBMS_SPACE package is a standalone package and is primarily useful to DBAs.

List Space Not Used for Objects

The total space allocated to an object in blocks and bytes and the unused space in this allocation are extremely important for a DBA to know. This information assists in determining the space allocation necessary for objects and is helpful in identifying space availability in objects. Unused space refers to blocks not currently used (no records exist in the blocks). This enables a DBA to identify space that may be de-allocated from objects back to the database free list for use by other objects.

The following is the syntax for the UNUSED_SPACE procedure:

Procedure Syntax

```
DBMS_SPACE.UNUSED_SPACE(segment_owner IN VARCHAR2,
   segment_name IN VARCHAR2, segment_type IN VARCHAR2,
   total_blocks OUT NUMBER, total_bytes OUT NUMBER,
   unused_blocks OUT NUMBER, unused_bytes OUT NUMBER,
   last_used_extent_file_id OUT NUMBER,
   last_used_extent_block_id OUT NUMBER,
   last_used_block OUT NUMBER);
```

Listing Free Blocks for Objects

The total free block list assists in determining future space allocation for objects. The output from the FREE_BLOCKS procedure will be helpful in identifying objects that have blocks in use, but still contain free space. The result set may be an indicator to adjust the percent free and/or percent used storage parameters. A free block does not mean the block is not being used (no records exist in the blocks); instead, it means more records can be inserted into the block.

The following is the syntax for the FREE_BLOCKS procedure:

Procedure Syntax

```
DBMS_SPACE.FREE_BLOCKS(segment_owner IN VARCHAR2,
   segment_name IN VARCHAR2, segment_type IN VARCHAR2,
   freelist_group_id IN NUMBER, free_blks OUT NUMBER,
   scan_limit IN NUMBER);
```

Retrieving Free Space Information

File: 12_34.sql

```
DECLARE
   CURSOR cur_tables IS
      SELECT table_name
      FROM   user_tables
      ORDER BY table_name;
   lv_total_blocks_num            PLS_INTEGER;
   lv_total_bytes_num             PLS_INTEGER;
   lv_unused_blocks_num           PLS_INTEGER;
   lv_unused_bytes_num            PLS_INTEGER;
   lv_last_used_extent_file_num   PLS_INTEGER;
   lv_last_used_extent_block_num  PLS_INTEGER;
   lv_last_used_block_num         PLS_INTEGER;
BEGIN
   DBMS_OUTPUT.PUT_LINE(
   'Current                          Blocks                Bytes');
   DBMS_OUTPUT.PUT_LINE(
   'Schema         Table Name      Total Unused        Total' ||
   '      Unused');
   DBMS_OUTPUT.PUT_LINE('------------------' ||
   '-----------------------------------------------------------');
   FOR cur_tables_rec IN cur_tables LOOP
      DBMS_SPACE.UNUSED_SPACE(USER, cur_tables_rec.table_name,
         'TABLE', lv_total_blocks_num, lv_total_bytes_num,
         lv_unused_blocks_num, lv_unused_bytes_num,
         lv_last_used_extent_file_num,
         lv_last_used_extent_block_num,
         lv_last_used_block_num);
      DBMS_OUTPUT.PUT_LINE(RPAD(USER,15) ||
      RPAD(cur_tables_rec.table_name,15) ||
      TO_CHAR(lv_total_blocks_num, '999,999') ||
      TO_CHAR(lv_unused_blocks_num, '999,999') ||
      TO_CHAR(lv_total_bytes_num, '999,999,999') ||
      TO_CHAR(lv_unused_bytes_num, '999,999,999'));
   END LOOP;
END;
/
```

Output (12_34.sql)

Current		Blocks		Bytes	
Schema	Table Name	Total	Unused	Total	Unused
PLSQL_USER	PLAN_TABLE	5	1	10,240	2,048
PLSQL_USER	SOURCE_LOG	85	25	174,080	51,200

PLSQL_USER	S_CUSTOMER	5	2	10,240	4,096
PLSQL_USER	S_DEPARTMENT	5	3	10,240	6,144
PLSQL_USER	S_EMPLOYEE	5	3	10,240	6,144
PLSQL_USER	S_EMPLOYEE_TEMP	5	3	10,240	6,144
PLSQL_USER	S_EMPLOYEE_TEST	1,430	465	2,928,640	952,320

The preceding output is only a subset of the result set.

Possible Uses of DBMS_SPACE

The following is a list of possible uses of the DBMS_SPACE package:

DBA

■ To assist in space management of objects by identifying the allocated space to objects versus the current free space of the object

Extend PL/SQL by Dynamically Creating SQL and PL/SQL (DBMS_SQL)

Creating flexible and functional PL/SQL with embedded SQL is commonplace with the PL/SQL language and Oracle supplied packages. However, some SQL commands cannot be performed or performed easily with the PL/SQL language, namely, DDL statements. The DBMS_SQL package provides the capability to perform DDL statements and to create dynamic DML routines, dynamic SELECT statements, and dynamic PL/SQL routines. Dynamic PL/SQL routines execute and create PL/SQL program units based on input.

Therefore, the DBMS_SQL is the package enabling PL/SQL to be extended further as needed. Whether the need is to create a temporary table, to grant privileges, or to create a query dynamically, DBMS_SQL is the answer. The DBMS_SQL package can be used in many different ways by the PL/SQL developer and the DBA to provide desired results. This package was introduced in PL/SQL release 2.1.

The DBMS_SQL package is a dependent package and is useful to developers and DBAs.

The SQL statements are created as character strings, return columns and variables are defined, the SQL statement string is explicitly parsed and executed, and the SQL statement results are processed. Several different types of statements can be processed by the DBMS_SQL package: non-query DML statements (i.e., INSERTS, DELETES, and UPDATES), DCL statements (i.e., GRANT, REVOKE), DDL

Extending PL/SQL with DBMS_SQL

statements (i.e., DROP TABLE, CREATE TABLE, and so forth), query statements, and PL/SQL blocks.

Execute DML and DDL Statements

To perform DML or DDL statements, the steps for using DBMS_SQL are straightforward: Open the cursor, parse the DML (DDL) statement, and close the cursor. For DDL statements, the EXECUTE function is currently unnecessary because the PARSE statement actually performs the statement execution. The user performing the DDL statement must be granted the system privilege outside a database role assignment, like RESOURCE. To use DBMS_SQL to create a temporary table, the CREATE ANY TABLE privilege must be granted directly to the user.

Steps Necessary

1. Open cursor (OPEN_CURSOR)

2. Parse statement (PARSE)

3. Bind any input variables (BIND_VARIABLE)

4. Execute statement (EXECUTE)

5. Close cursor (CLOSE_CURSOR)

Opening a Cursor

The OPEN_CURSOR function returns a cursor ID to be used in subsequent procedure calls. A call to the OPEN_CURSOR function should always have an accompanying CLOSE_CURSOR call to free system resources. The following is the syntax for the OPEN_CURSOR function:

Function Syntax

```
DBMS_SQL.OPEN_CURSOR RETURN NUMBER;
```

Parse Statement

The PARSE procedure sends the statement to the server. In doing so, it verifies syntax and semantics of the statement and returns errors if they occur. Through this, an execution plan is determined. A database version/language must be specified (V6, V7, or NATIVE). Oracle8 behaves identically to Oracle7. In creating the statement, all trailing semicolons are excluded for DML and DDL statements.

Procedure Syntax

```
DBMS_SQL.PARSE(c IN INTEGER, statement IN VARCHAR2,
  language_flag IN NUMBER);
```

Valid Language Flag Parameter Values

The following is a list of valid language_flag parameter values:

- **DBMS_SQL.V6**   Version 6 behavior

- **DBMS_SQL.V7**   Version 7 behavior

- **DBMS_SQL.NATIVE**   Behavior for the database to which the program is connected

TIP
*I recommend using DBMS_SQL.NATIVE for the
language_flag parameter, making your PL/SQL
programs more flexible by ensuring they execute on
any version of Oracle.*

Bind Any Input Variables

The BIND_VARIABLE procedure associates place holders with variables. A colon often identifies the placeholders, but this syntax is optional. If no place holders are present, no bind variables are necessary. The BIND_VARIABLE procedure is overloaded for different data types and lengths. Using the out_value_size parameter is required for VARCHAR2 data types, so the bind variable is not initialized, as having no length, which would happen if the value passed in was NULL. Bind variables are illegal for DDL statements.

Procedure Syntax

```
DBMS_SQL.BIND_VARIABLE(c IN NUMBER, name IN VARCHAR2,
  value IN VARCHAR2);
DBMS_SQL.BIND_VARIABLE(c IN NUMBER, name IN VARCHAR2,
  value IN VARCHAR2, out_value_size IN NUMBER);
```

Execute Statement

The EXECUTE function returns the number of rows processed thus far. The call to the EXECUTE procedure is unnecessary for DDL statements, but causes no harm.

Function Syntax

```
DBMS_SQL.EXECUTE(c IN NUMBER) RETURN NUMBER;
```

Close Cursor

The CLOSE_CURSOR procedure simply frees resources allocated to the cursor. This procedure should be used with all open cursors, also being included in the exception handler.

Procedure Syntax

```
DBMS_SQL.CLOSE_CURSOR(c IN OUT NUMBER);
```

Example of DDL Functionality

The following procedure can be used to provide a generic interface to the DBMS_SQL package for executing DDL statements. A DDL statement needs to be passed as a character string to the exec_ddl procedure.

File: 12_35.sql

```
CREATE OR REPLACE PROCEDURE exec_ddl(p_statement_txt VARCHAR2) IS
-- This procedure provides a way to dynamically perform any DDL
-- statements from within your normal PL/SQL processing.
   lv_exec_cursor_num    PLS_INTEGER := DBMS_SQL.OPEN_CURSOR;
   lv_rows_processed_num PLS_INTEGER := 0;
BEGIN
   DBMS_SQL.PARSE(lv_exec_cursor_num, p_statement_txt,
      DBMS_SQL.NATIVE);
   lv_rows_processed_num := DBMS_SQL.EXECUTE(lv_exec_cursor_num);
   DBMS_SQL.CLOSE_CURSOR(lv_exec_cursor_num);
EXCEPTION
   WHEN OTHERS THEN
      IF DBMS_SQL.IS_OPEN(lv_exec_cursor_num) THEN
         DBMS_SQL.CLOSE_CURSOR(lv_exec_cursor_num);
      END IF;
      RAISE;
END exec_ddl;
/
```

Once the exec_ddl procedure is created, any DDL statement can be executed, as long as the necessary system privilege is granted directly to the schema user (not through a role) executing the exec_ddl procedure. Therefore, when the following statement is executed under the PLSQL_USER, an error will occur.

File: 12_36.sql

```
EXECUTE exec_ddl('CREATE TABLE temp_sql (column1 VARCHAR2(10))')
```

Output (12_36.sql)

```
ERROR at line 1:
ORA-01031: insufficient privileges
ORA-06512: at "PLSQL_USER.EXEC_DDL", line 17
ORA-06512: at line 1
```

Even though the PLSQL_USER possesses the CREATE ANY TABLE privilege, it does not suffice because this privilege was granted through a role. Once CREATE ANY TABLE is granted directly to PLSQL_USER from the SYS account, the DDL statement succeeds, as the following illustrates.

```
GRANT CREATE ANY TABLE TO plsql_user;
```

File: 12_36.sql

```
EXECUTE exec_ddl('CREATE TABLE temp_sql (column1 VARCHAR2(10))')
```

The table now exists:

```
DESCRIBE temp_sql

 Name                                      Null?    Type
 ----------------------------------------- -------- ----
 COLUMN1                                            VARCHAR2(10)
```

Execute SQL SELECT Statements

For dynamically creating SELECT statements with DBMS_SQL, a few more steps are involved than for DML or DDL statements. After the statement is parsed, bind variables can be declared and columns must be defined. Then the statement needs to be executed and rows fetched. Lastly, the column values must be accepted and processed.

Steps Necessary

    1. Open cursor (OPEN_CURSOR) **

    2. Parse statement (PARSE) **

3. Bind input variables (BIND_VARIABLE) **
4. Define output variables (DEFINE_COLUMN)
5. Execute statement (EXECUTE) **
6. Fetch rows (FETCH_ROWS)
7. Return results to variables (COLUMN_VALUE)
8. Close cursor (CLOSE_CURSOR) **

The '**' follows each step in the preceding list of steps that are also used for DML and DDL Statements. For these steps, their explanations will not be revisited.

Defining Output Variables

The DEFINE_COLUMN procedure is necessary for every column in the SELECT statement. The data type and length can be specified for a column by the column position in the SELECT statement.

Procedure Syntax

```
DBMS_SQL.DEFINE_COLUMN(c IN NUMBER, position IN NUMBER,
    column IN VARCHAR2);
DBMS_SQL.DEFINE_COLUMN(c IN NUMBER, position IN NUMBER,
    column IN VARCHAR2, column_size IN NUMBER);
```

Fetching Rows

The FETCH_ROWS function fetches rows associated with the result set of a defined query, one row at a time. It returns the number of rows fetched thus far. The function returns zero when all rows have been fetched. The FETCH_ROWS function is often used in loops to process one row at a time. If used within a loop to fetch all records, the EXIT condition should be used when the return value of FETCH_ROWS is equal to zero, not when the NO_DATA_FOUND exception is raised or when the %NOTFOUND cursor attribute is TRUE.

Function Syntax

```
DBMS_SQL.FETCH_ROWS(c IN NUMBER) RETURN NUMBER;
```

Alternative to EXECUTE & FETCH_ROWS Functions

The EXECUTE_AND_FETCH function can replace the EXECUTE function call and the first call to the FETCH_ROWS function, using only one network trip. This can improve performance on remote databases. The function returns the number of rows fetched thus far, identical to the FETCH_ROWS function. The program can specify if an error should occur if more than one row is returned. If the exact parameter is passed in as TRUE, the TOO_MANY_ROWS exception will be raised if the query returns more than one row. If passed in as FALSE, this exception is never raised.

Function Syntax

```
DBMS_SQL.EXECUTE_AND_FETCH(c IN NUMBER, exact IN BOOLEAN)
   RETURN NUMBER;
```

Return Results into Variables

The COLUMN_VALUE procedure moves the buffered data into PL/SQL variables. Typically, these are the same variables used with the DEFINE_COLUMN procedure. A COLUMN_VALUE procedure call should match every DEFINE_COLUMN procedure call. The COLUMN_VALUE procedure provides column-level errors and is overloaded for different data types. If the data type of the value parameter does not match the type used in the BIND_VARIABLE procedure, the DBMS_SQL.INCONSISTENT_TYPES *(ORA-6562: type of OUT argument must match type of column or bind variable)* exception is raised.

Procedure Syntax

```
DBMS_SQL.COLUMN_VALUE(c IN NUMBER, position IN NUMBER,
   value OUT VARCHAR2);
DBMS_SQL.COLUMN_VALUE(c IN NUMBER, position IN NUMBER,
   value OUT VARCHAR2, column_error OUT NUMBER,
   actual_length OUT NUMBER);
```

Example of SELECT Functionality

The following SHOW_ORDERS procedure illustrates how SELECT statements can be dynamically constructed. The following example enables the ORDER BY column to be passed into the procedure to dictate the result set order.

File: 12_37.sql

```
CREATE OR REPLACE PROCEDURE show_orders
   (p_order_by_txt IN VARCHAR2 := '1') IS
   -- This function outputs the order information to the terminal
   -- (using DBMS_OUTPUT), but orders the output, using the
   -- specified "ORDER BY" clause.
   lv_cursor_id_num PLS_INTEGER;
   lv_statement_txt VARCHAR2(500);
   lv_rowcount_num  PLS_INTEGER := 0;
   lv_ord_rec       s_order%ROWTYPE;
BEGIN
   -- Open a cursor to be used
   lv_cursor_id_num := DBMS_SQL.OPEN_CURSOR;
   -- Set up statement for first column
   lv_statement_txt := 'SELECT customer_id, total ' ||
                       'FROM   s_order ' ||
```

```
                         'ORDER BY ' || p_order_by_txt;
    DBMS_SQL.PARSE(lv_cursor_id_num, lv_statement_txt,DBMS_SQL.NATIVE);
    DBMS_SQL.DEFINE_COLUMN(lv_cursor_id_num, 1,lv_ord_rec.customer_id);
    DBMS_SQL.DEFINE_COLUMN(lv_cursor_id_num, 2,lv_ord_rec.total);
    lv_rowcount_num := DBMS_SQL.EXECUTE(lv_cursor_id_num);
    LOOP
       EXIT WHEN DBMS_SQL.FETCH_ROWS(lv_cursor_id_num) = 0;
       DBMS_SQL.COLUMN_VALUE(lv_cursor_id_num, 1,
          lv_ord_rec.customer_id);
       DBMS_SQL.COLUMN_VALUE(lv_cursor_id_num, 2, lv_ord_rec.total);
       -- Provide output, tab delimited, in specified order
       DBMS_OUTPUT.PUT_LINE(lv_ord_rec.customer_id || CHR(9) ||
          TO_CHAR(lv_ord_rec.total, '$999,999,999.99'));
    END LOOP;
    -- Close cursor when processing complete
    DBMS_SQL.CLOSE_CURSOR(lv_cursor_id_num);
EXCEPTION
    WHEN OTHERS THEN
       IF DBMS_SQL.IS_OPEN(lv_cursor_id_num) THEN
          DBMS_SQL.CLOSE_CURSOR(lv_cursor_id_num);
       END IF;
       RAISE_APPLICATION_ERROR(-20101, 'Error processing SQL ' ||
          'statement in SHOW_ORDERS procedure', FALSE);
END show_orders;
/
```

Once the show_orders procedure is created, the orders can be sorted by order_id or total. The following two executions show the output results of each.

Example execution of show_orders

```
SET SERVEROUTPUT ON SIZE 1000000
EXECUTE show_orders
```

Example output from executing show_orders

```
201            $84,000.00
202               $595.00
203             $7,707.00
204           $601,100.00
204             $2,770.00
205             $8,056.60
206             $8,335.00
208               $377.00
```

```
208             $32,430.00
209              $2,722.24
210             $15,634.00
210                $550.00
211            $142,171.00
212            $149,570.00
213          $1,020,935.00
214              $1,539.13

PL/SQL procedure successfully completed.
```

Example execution of show_orders

```
EXECUTE show_orders('2')
```

Example output from executing show_orders

```
208                $377.00
210                $550.00
202                $595.00
214              $1,539.13
209              $2,722.24
204              $2,770.00
203              $7,707.00
205              $8,056.60
206              $8,335.00
210             $15,634.00
208             $32,430.00
201             $84,000.00
211            $142,171.00
212            $149,570.00
204            $601,100.00
213          $1,020,935.00

PL/SQL procedure successfully completed.
```

Execute PL/SQL Blocks and Stored Code

For dynamically creating PL/SQL blocks with DBMS_SQL, one additional step must be added to the process outlined in the preceding section. The additional step is to retrieve values from the output variables, using the VARIABLE_VALUE procedure. This type of functionality can be used to perform nearly any type of PL/SQL logic, such as calling a database procedure or determining a value of a variable.

Steps Necessary

1. Open cursor (OPEN_CURSOR) **
2. Parse statement (PARSE) **
3. Bind input variables (BIND_VARIABLE) **
4. Execute statement (EXECUTE) **
5. Retrieve values of output variables (VARIABLE_VALUE)
6. Close cursor (CLOSE_CURSOR) **

The '**' follows each step in the preceding list of steps that are also used for DML and DDL Statements. For these steps, their explanations will not be revisited.

Retrieving Values of Output Variables

The VARIABLE_VALUE procedure is used after the EXECUTE statement to retrieve variable values from the local buffer. A matching call to the VARIABLE_VALUE procedure is unnecessary for every call to the BIND_VARIABLE procedure. This procedure is also overloaded for different data types. As with the COLUMN_VALUE procedure, if the data type of the value parameter does not match the type used in the BIND_VARIABLE procedure, the DBMS_SQL.INCONSISTENT_TYPES *(ORA-6562: type of OUT argument must match type of column or bind variable)* exception is raised.

Procedure Syntax

```
DBMS_SQL.VARIABLE_VALUE(c IN NUMBER, name IN VARCHAR2,
   value OUT VARCHAR2);
```

Example of PL/SQL Functionality

The math_calc function provides a generic interface for basic arithmetic logic. Provide a mathematical statement as a character string and the function returns the result with the desired precision.

File: 12_38.sql

```
CREATE OR REPLACE FUNCTION math_calc(p_statement_txt VARCHAR2,
   p_precision_num PLS_INTEGER := 2)
RETURN NUMBER IS
   -- This function uses a character string of arithmetic logic,
   -- selecting against the DUAL table to return a number value.
   lv_cursor_id_num    PLS_INTEGER;
   lv_statement_txt    VARCHAR2(500);
```

```
   lv_rowcount_num      PLS_INTEGER;
   lv_return_value_num NUMBER;
BEGIN
   -- Open a cursor to be used
   lv_cursor_id_num := DBMS_SQL.OPEN_CURSOR;
   -- Set up PL/SQL block to assign variable statement value
   lv_statement_txt :=
      'BEGIN ' ||
      '   :lv_value_num := ' || p_statement_txt || ';' ||
      'END;';
   -- Parse the PL/SQL block
   DBMS_SQL.PARSE(lv_cursor_id_num, lv_statement_txt,DBMS_SQL.NATIVE);
   -- Set up bind variable for usage
   DBMS_SQL.BIND_VARIABLE(lv_cursor_id_num, ':lv_value_num',
      lv_return_value_num);
   -- Execute the cursor
   lv_rowcount_num := DBMS_SQL.EXECUTE(lv_cursor_id_num);
   -- Retrieve variable value
   DBMS_SQL.VARIABLE_VALUE(lv_cursor_id_num, ':lv_value_num',
      lv_return_value_num);
   DBMS_SQL.CLOSE_CURSOR(lv_cursor_id_num);
   RETURN ROUND(lv_return_value_num, p_precision_num);
EXCEPTION
   WHEN OTHERS THEN
      IF DBMS_SQL.IS_OPEN(lv_cursor_id_num) THEN
         DBMS_SQL.CLOSE_CURSOR(lv_cursor_id_num);
      END IF;
      RAISE_APPLICATION_ERROR(-20101, 'Error processing SQL ' ||
         'statement in MATH_CALC procedure', FALSE);
END math_calc;
/
```

Once the math_calc function is created, math calculations can be performed as desired. The following two executions show the output results of two calculations.

File: 12_39.sql

```
SET SERVEROUTPUT ON SIZE 1000000
DECLARE
   lv_return_num NUMBER;
BEGIN
   lv_return_num := math_calc('4*5', 2);
   DBMS_OUTPUT.PUT_LINE('Value: ' || lv_return_num);
END;
/
```

Output (12_39.sql)

```
Value: 20

PL/SQL procedure successfully completed.
```

File: 12_40.sql

```
DECLARE
    lv_return_num  NUMBER;
    lv_value_num_1 NUMBER;
    lv_value_num_2 NUMBER;
BEGIN
    lv_value_num_1 := 100.002;
    lv_value_num_2 := 3.02;
    lv_return_num  := math_calc(TO_CHAR(lv_value_num_1) ||
        ' * ' || TO_CHAR(lv_value_num_2), 5);
    DBMS_OUTPUT.PUT_LINE('Value: ' || lv_return_num);
END;
/
```

Output (12_40.sql)

```
Value: 302.00604

PL/SQL procedure successfully completed.
```

DBMS_SQL Error Processing

The DBMS_SQL package contains several error-handling functions, providing the developer and user valuable information. The majority of these functions will only be used with SELECT statements, but they are not limited to these statements. The IS_OPEN function should be implemented in the exception handler to check if a cursor is being left open and closed, if necessary.

Available Error Functions

- **LAST_ERROR_POSITION** Returns the byte offset within the statement where the error occurred

- **LAST_ROW_COUNT** Returns the cumulative count of number of rows fetched

- **LAST_ROW_ID** Returns the ROWID of the last row processed

- **LAST_SQL_FUNCTION_CODE** Returns the function code for the SQL statement currently being executed

- **IS_OPEN** Returns TRUE if the cursor is already open, otherwise FALSE

Function Syntax

```
DBMS_SQL.LAST_ERROR_POSITION RETURN NUMBER;
DBMS_SQL.LAST_ROW_COUNT RETURN NUMBER;
DBMS_SQL.LAST_ROW_ID RETURN ROWID;
DBMS_SQL.LAST_SQL_FUNCTION_CODE RETURN NUMBER;
DBMS_SQL.IS_OPEN(c IN NUMBER) RETURN BOOLEAN;
```

TIP

DBMS_SQL logic is powerful, but not always necessary. Only use this package when necessary because the amount of source code required to accomplish the complete use of DBMS_SQL is extensive and prone to errors, as well as the extra overhead associated with using this package.

TIP

Reuse cursors whenever possible because each cursor requires resources. Only re-parse statements if they change. A statement is not considered changed when a different value is assigned to a bind variable. Remember, a parse is necessary for Oracle to verify security, syntax, and create an execution plan for the statement.

TIP

Any statement executed with DBMS_SQL requires the schema user executing the PL/SQL program unit to have the necessary privilege for the generated DBMS_SQL statement(s) directly granted. If the access is provided through a role, the program will result in an error.

TIP

DBMS_SQL cursors need to be explicitly closed to free memory. As a general rule, always close a cursor when it is no longer needed. In addition, always include close cursor logic in all exception handlers to ensure these cursors are closed when errors are encountered.

TIP
Functions that contain DBMS_SQL processing cannot be used as inline functions. This is a limitation of using the DBMS_SQL package.

TIP
Oracle 8.1 introduces a more efficient implementation of executing dynamic SQL and PL/SQL statements with the EXECUTE IMMEDIATE PL/SQL command. For further detail on this command refer to Chapter 16.

Possible Uses of DBMS_SQL

The following is a list of possible uses of the DBMS_SQL package:

Developer

- Create dynamic SELECT statements
- Create dynamic DML based on input
- Create dynamic PL/SQL: Output a PL/SQL program unit based on input

DBA

- Create dynamic SELECT statements
- Create dynamic DML based on input
- Create DDL statements to allow execution of DDL
- Change permissions based on executing user
- Create dynamic PL/SQL: Output a PL/SQL program unit based on input

Turn on the TRACE Facility for Any Session (DBMS_SYSTEM)

As outlined in several sections in this book, SQL tuning is extremely important to the overall success of an application. Additionally, the TRACE facility is one of the facilities available to assist in this tuning process. Oracle has provided a method of turning on the TRACE facility for a particular session. The sid and serial# of the session must be known. These values can be obtained from the V$SESSION view.

The DBMS_SYSTEM package is a standalone package and is primarily useful to DBAs.

A DBA typically reviews the V$ views to identify performance bottlenecks. Once a bottleneck is determined, the DBA can identify the user(s) primarily responsible for the performance degradation. Once these users are identified, the sessions can be viewed from the V$SESSION view and the sid and serial# determined.

The SET_SQL_TRACE_IN_SESSION can then be called and TRACE can be turned on for the session identified. This complements the capabilities of turning TRACE on system wide and for the current session.

Procedure Syntax

```
DBMS_SYSTEM.SET_SQL_TRACE_IN_SESSION (sid IN NUMBER,
    serial# IN NUMBER, SQL_TRACE IN BOOLEAN);
```

The following script provides a list of all sessions sorting by disk reads descending. The sessions that appear at the top can be TRACEd to identify what they are executing.

File: 12_41.sql

```
SELECT a.username, a.sid, a.serial#, b.physical_reads,
       b.block_gets, b.consistent_gets
FROM   v$session a, v$sess_io b
WHERE  a.sid = b.sid
AND    NVL(a.username,'XX') NOT IN ('SYS', 'SYSTEM', 'XX')
ORDER BY b.physical_reads DESC;
```

Output (12_41.sql)

USERNAME	SID	SERIAL#	PHYSICAL_READS	BLOCK_GETS	CONSISTENT_GETS
PLSQL_USER	8	283	56	194	562

This process can be automated by creating a PL/SQL program unit to retrieve the sessions with the highest disk reads and turning on TRACE for each. The following PL/SQL source code carries out this task by retrieving the top five sessions and turning on TRACE for each of these sessions. The TRACE remains on until the session terminates or the TRACE is turned off. To execute this program unit, SELECT access must be granted on V_$SESSION and V_$TRANSACTION and the user must have privilege to execute the ALTER SYSTEM statement.

Turning on the TRACE Facility for Any Session

File: 12_42.sql

```
DECLARE
   CURSOR cur_trace IS
      SELECT a.username, a.sid, a.serial#, b.physical_reads,
             b.block_gets, b.consistent_gets
      FROM   v$session a, v$sess_io b
      WHERE  a.sid = b.sid
      AND    NVL(a.username,'XX') NOT IN ('SYS', 'SYSTEM', 'XX')
      ORDER BY b.physical_reads DESC;
   lv_count_num PLS_INTEGER := 0;
BEGIN

   FOR cur_trace_rec IN cur_trace LOOP
      lv_count_num := lv_count_num + 1;
      IF lv_count_num = 6 THEN
         EXIT;
      END IF;
      DBMS_SYSTEM.SET_SQL_TRACE_IN_SESSION(cur_trace_rec.sid,
         cur_trace_rec.serial#, TRUE);
      DBMS_OUTPUT.PUT_LINE('Sessions Traced---Username: ' ||
         RPAD(cur_trace_rec.username,20) || ' Sid: '       ||
         RPAD(cur_trace_rec.sid, 8) || ' Serial#: ' ||
         cur_trace_rec.serial#);
   END LOOP;
END;
/
```

Output (12_42.sql)

```
Sessions Traced---Username: PLSQL_USER   Sid: 8  Serial#: 283

PL/SQL procedure successfully completed.
```

In the preceding example, overhead is associated with the TRACE facility because Oracle is spooling statistical information to an operating system file. The statistics file can then be converted to a readable file with the TKPROF command as outlined in Chapter 7, followed by a review of the statistics to assist in identifying SQL statements that may need to be optimized.

Possible Uses of DBMS_SYSTEM

The following is a list of possible uses of the DBMS_SYSTEM package:

DBA

- Create PL/SQL program units to identify resource-intensive sessions by analyzing the V$ views and turning on TRACE for these sessions, enabling for more flexible and robust analysis techniques to be applied

Specify the Rollback Segment to Use for Large Processing (DBMS_TRANSACTION)

When processing large transactions, having certain resources available to ensure the transactions complete successfully is important. When processing a large DML operation, such as an UPDATE, it is important to ensure the operation uses a large rollback segment to store the before image of the record (a snapshot of the record prior to modification) for read consistency and in case the transaction is rolled back. The USE_ROLLBACK_SEGMENT procedure enables the specification of a rollback segment prior to the start of a transaction. The rollback segment specified is used for the next transaction only. Once a COMMIT or ROLLBACK is performed, the next transaction will not automatically allocate the transaction to the rollback segment specified in the procedure call. Therefore, if intermittent commits are performed, then the USE_ROLLBACK_SEGMENT procedure needs to be called after each COMMIT.

On Oracle systems processing large (batch manipulation) and small (transaction-based processing) transactions, a combination of large and small rollback segments usually exists. The smaller rollback segments are created to be used for the transaction-based processing and the larger rollback segments are created to be used for the larger, batch-oriented processing. Any rollback segments that are online will be used by Oracle. The larger rollback segments are often brought online in the programs prior to specifying their use.

The DBMS_TRANSACTION package is a standalone package and is primarily useful to DBAs and advanced developers.

Procedure Syntax

```
DBMS_TRANSACTION.USE_ROLLBACK_SEGMENT (rb_name IN VARCHAR2);
```

The following script displays the current rollback segments with the status and size in bytes of the segment. If the status is not online, then the rollback segment needs to be altered to bring the segment online before it can be used.

Specifying the Rollback Segment for Large Processing

File: 12_43.sql

```
SELECT b.segment_name, status, sum(bytes) sum_bytes
FROM    dba_extents a, dba_rollback_segs b
WHERE   a.segment_name = b.segment_name
AND     a.segment_type = 'ROLLBACK'
GROUP BY b.segment_name, status
ORDER BY status DESC, b.segment_name;
```

Output (12_43.sql)

SEGMENT_NAME	STATUS	SUM_BYTES
RB1	ONLINE	6195200
RB2	ONLINE	2457600
RB3	ONLINE	307200
SYSTEM	ONLINE	204800
RB4	OFFLINE	2457600

To bring the RB4 rollback segment online for use, the following command must be executed:

```
ALTER ROLLBACK SEGMENT rbB4 ONLINE;
```

If we execute the preceding rollback segment script again, we see the rollback segment is now online and available for use.

Output (12_43.sql)

SEGMENT_NAME	STATUS	SUM_BYTES
RB1	ONLINE	6195200
RB2	ONLINE	2457600
RB3	ONLINE	307200
RB4	ONLINE	2457600
SYSTEM	ONLINE	204800

The following script lists each active rollback segment and the number of transactions currently using each rollback segment. If no records are returned, then no active or pending transactions are currently in any rollback segment. SELECT privilege on the V_$ROLLNAME and V_$TRANSACTION is required to execute the following script.

File: 12_44.sql

```
SELECT name, COUNT(*)
FROM   v$rollname a, v$transaction b
WHERE  a.usn = b.xidusn
GROUP BY name;
```

Output (12_44.sql)

```
no rows selected
```

The following PL/SQL program unit uses the USE_ROLLBACK_SEGMENT procedure to assign the UPDATE transaction to the RB4 rollback segment.

File: 12_45.sql

```
BEGIN
    DBMS_TRANSACTION.USE_ROLLBACK_SEGMENT('RB4');
    UPDATE s_employee
    SET    salary = NVL(salary, 0) * 1.1;
END;
/
```

Since there was no COMMIT or ROLLBACK performed in the preceding code segment, the UPDATE transaction assigned to the RB4 is viewable by executing the previous V$ script (12_44.sql), as illustrated in the following output.

Output (12_44.sql)

```
NAME                                   COUNT(*)
------------------------------------- ----------
RB4                                            1
```

Once the transaction is completed with a COMMIT or ROLLBACK, we can view the V$ view again to see the transaction is no longer assigned to the RB4 rollback segment.

Output (12_44.sql)

```
no rows selected
```

Possible Uses of DBMS_TRANSACTION

The following is a list of possible uses of the DBMS_TRANSACTION package:

Specifying the Rollback Segment for Large Processing

Developer

- Create PL/SQL program units to find certain rollback segments automatically to use for larger processing and assign the transactions in that process to these rollback segments

DBA

- Create PL/SQL program units to find certain rollback segments automatically to use for larger processing, bring these rollback segments online, and assign the transactions in that process to these rollback segments

Expand the PL/SQL Language with a Set of Utilities (DBMS_UTILITY)

The DBMS_UTILITY contains several procedures and functions that provide the capability to perform DDL commands with PL/SQL; however, this package also contains several useful procedures and functions that cannot be accomplished with standard DDL commands.

The DBMS_UTILITY package is a standalone package and is useful to both developers (all content with the exception of analyzing objects) and DBAs (analyzing objects).

The following procedures and functions are covered in this section.

- ANALYZE_DATABASE
- ANALYZE_SCHEMA
- COMPILE_SCHEMA
- FORMAT_ERROR_STACK
- FORMAT_CALL_STACK
- GET_TIME

Computing Statistics via ANALYZE_DATABASE and ANALYZE_SCHEMA

These two procedures are provided to enable computing statistics for cost-based optimization. These procedures can be embedded into stored PL/SQL program units and submitted to the DBMS_JOB scheduler at a specified interval or executed manually. Scheduling analyze routines through DBMS_JOB would ensure the database (all tables, indexes, and clusters in all schemas) or selected schema were analyzed on a regular basis. These two procedures provide the flexibility of computing all statistics, estimating statistics, or deleting statistics. The estimation can be performed by specifying the number of rows or the percentage of rows, and the ability to limit the estimation to only tables or indexes.

The following syntax contains both the ANALYZE_DATABASE and ANALYZE_SCHEMA procedures.

Procedure Syntax

```
PROCEDURE ANALYZE_DATABASE
   (method            VARCHAR2,
    estimate_rows     NUMBER    DEFAULT NULL,
    estimate_percent  NUMBER    DEFAULT NULL,
    method_opt        VARCHAR2  DEFAULT NULL);
PROCEDURE ANALYZE_SCHEMA
   (schema            VARCHAR2,
    method            VARCHAR2,
    estimate_rows     NUMBER    DEFAULT NULL,
    estimate_percent  NUMBER    DEFAULT NULL,
    method_opt        VARCHAR2  DEFAULT NULL);
```

Examples

```
-- Computes all schema object statistics in the database using all
-- the rows in every object
DBMS_UTILITY.ANALYZE_DATABASE ('COMPUTE');
-- Estimates all schema object statistics in the database based on
-- 100,000 of the rows per object
DBMS_UTILITY.ANALYZE_DATABASE ('ESTIMATE', 100000);
-- Estimates all schema object statistics in the database based on
-- 50 percent of the rows per object
DBMS_UTILITY.ANALYZE_DATABASE ('ESTIMATE', NULL, 50);
-- Deletes all schema object statistics in the database
DBMS_UTILITY.ANALYZE_DATABASE ('DELETE');

-- Computes statistics based on all the rows (Schema: SCOTT)
DBMS_UTILITY.ANALYZE_SCHEMA ('SCOTT', 'COMPUTE');
-- Estimates statistics based on 100,000 of the rows per object
DBMS_UTILITY.ANALYZE_SCHEMA ('SCOTT', 'ESTIMATE', 100000);
-- Estimates statistics based on 50 percent of the rows per object
DBMS_UTILITY.ANALYZE_SCHEMA ('SCOTT', 'ESTIMATE', NULL, 50);
-- Deletes all statistics (Schema: SCOTT)
DBMS_UTILITY.ANALYZE_SCHEMA ('SCOTT', 'DELETE');
```

Expanding the PL/SQL Language

The method parameter is not case-sensitive; however, for the ANALYZE_SCHEMA procedure, the schema parameter is case-sensitive and must be uppercase; otherwise, an error will occur, stating the user does not exist.

TIP
To compute complete statistics, the literal 'COMPUTE' must be used for the method parameter. The documentation (Oracle 7.3, corrected in subsequent Oracle releases) provided in the SQL creation file (dbmsutil.sql) states that to compute complete statistics, the method parameter should be NULL.

Compile Objects via COMPILE_SCHEMA

As outlined in Chapter 5, Chapter 9, and Chapter 13, when stored PL/SQL program units are modified, all INVALID objects should be re-compiled prior to production hours to ensure the modifications are placed into production properly. Scripts are shown in Chapter 5, Chapter 9, and Chapter 13 identifying INVALID objects that need to be re-compiled. The COMPILE_SCHEMA procedure provides the capability to provide a schema name as a parameter and all objects are then compiled for the schema.

Procedure Syntax

```
DBMS_UTILITY.COMPILE_SCHEMA(schema IN VARCHAR2)
```

Example

```
DBMS_UTILITY.COMPILE_SCHEMA('PLSQL_USER');
```

TIP
The schema name must be in uppercase and a valid user. If the schema name is not entered in uppercase or the schema name is typed incorrectly, no error will occur; the procedure call will return a successful operation. Therefore, always execute the INVALID object script to ensure the operation executed properly.

TIP
The COMPILE_SCHEMA procedure compiles all functions, procedures, and packages in alphabetical order. It does not attempt to compile triggers. This is evident by viewing the V$SQLAREA view. It does not perform the compile in dependency order.

The V$SQLAREA view is searched for the ALTER command as the following script illustrates.

File: 12_46.sql

```
SELECT sql_text
FROM   v$sqlarea
WHERE  INSTR(UPPER(sql_text), 'ALTER') > 0;
```

A subset of the result is displayed in the following output:

Output (12_46.sql)

```
SQL_TEXT
-----------------------------------------------------------------
alter FUNCTION "PLSQL_USER"."DATE_RANGE" compile
alter FUNCTION "PLSQL_USER"."VALIDATE_DATE_FORMAT" compile
alter FUNCTION "PLSQL_USER"."VALIDATE_TITLE" compile
alter PROCEDURE "PLSQL_USER"."A" compile
alter PROCEDURE "PLSQL_USER"."ABC1" compile
alter PROCEDURE "PLSQL_USER"."B" compile
alter PROCEDURE "PLSQL_USER"."C" compile
alter PROCEDURE "PLSQL_USER"."CORE_PROCESS" compile
alter PROCEDURE "PLSQL_USER"."LOAD_DATA" compile
alter PROCEDURE "PLSQL_USER"."LOG_EXTENTS" compile
alter PROCEDURE "PLSQL_USER"."LOG_SOURCE" compile
alter PROCEDURE "PLSQL_USER"."PIN_OBJECTS" compile
alter package "PLSQL_USER"."CLOSE" compile body
alter package "PLSQL_USER"."CLOSE" compile specification
alter package "PLSQL_USER"."DEPENDENCY_MAP" compile body
alter package "PLSQL_USER"."DEPENDENCY_MAP" compile specification
alter package "PLSQL_USER"."GLOBAL" compile body
alter package "PLSQL_USER"."GLOBAL" compile specification
select sql_text from v$sqlarea where instr(upper(sql_text), 'ALTER')
> 0
```

Process Errors via FORMAT_ERROR_STACK and FORMAT_CALL_STACK

Every application should have a tightly integrated error-control mechanism to ensure errors are trapped and handled appropriately. Some errors can be anticipated; however, no matter how much forethought is placed on specifically addressing each error, some errors will not be accounted for. These unaccounted errors need to be logged to a specific location whether a database table or an operating system file for further analysis. The FORMAT_ERROR_STACK and FORMAT_CALL_STACK functions provide the capability of reading the internal

Oracle calling and error stack. These functions are ideal for pinpointing errors and debugging complex PL/SQL source code. In Chapter 5, the use of these two functions is shown in more detail with the creation of a generic error logging mechanism.

The syntax for these two functions is illustrated in the following examples:

Function Syntax

```
FUNCTION FORMAT_ERROR_STACK RETURN VARCHAR2;
FUNCTION FORMAT_CALL_STACK RETURN VARCHAR2;
```

The results of using the two preceding functions are illustrated in the following examples. The first example (12_47.sql) creates two procedures with the second procedure referencing the first procedure when executed. The first example illustrates the propagation of errors to the outer loop to process errors encountered or exceptions raised. The second example (12_48.sql) extends the first example by adding more complete error and exception processing to illustrate the recommended approach to error handling.

File: 12_47.sql

```
CREATE OR REPLACE PROCEDURE error_test1 AS
BEGIN
   RAISE VALUE_ERROR;
END error_test1;
/
CREATE OR REPLACE PROCEDURE error_test2 AS
BEGIN
   error_test1;
EXCEPTION
   WHEN OTHERS THEN
      DBMS_OUTPUT.PUT_LINE(DBMS_UTILITY.FORMAT_CALL_STACK);
      DBMS_OUTPUT.PUT_LINE(DBMS_UTILITY.FORMAT_ERROR_STACK);
END error_test2;
/
```

Example execution of error_test2

```
EXECUTE error_test2
```

Example output from executing error_test2

```
----- PL/SQL Call Stack -----
  object      line  object
  handle    number  name
```

```
 18ff6d8           6   procedure PLSQL_USER.ERROR_TEST2
 1890b74           1   anonymous block

ORA-06502: PL/SQL: numeric or value error

PL/SQL procedure successfully completed.
```

File: 12_48.sql

```
CREATE OR REPLACE PACKAGE errors AS
   pu_failure_excep EXCEPTION;
   PRAGMA EXCEPTION_INIT (pu_failure_excep, -20000);
END errors;
/
CREATE OR REPLACE PROCEDURE error_test1 AS
BEGIN
   RAISE VALUE_ERROR;
EXCEPTION
   WHEN OTHERS THEN
      DBMS_OUTPUT.PUT_LINE(DBMS_UTILITY.FORMAT_CALL_STACK);
      DBMS_OUTPUT.PUT_LINE(DBMS_UTILITY.FORMAT_ERROR_STACK);
      RAISE errors.pu_failure_excep;
END error_test1;
/
CREATE OR REPLACE PROCEDURE error_test2 AS
BEGIN
   error_test1;
EXCEPTION
   WHEN errors.pu_failure_excep THEN
      DBMS_OUTPUT.PUT_LINE('Procedure error_test2 Failed.');
   WHEN OTHERS THEN
      DBMS_OUTPUT.PUT_LINE(DBMS_UTILITY.FORMAT_CALL_STACK);
      DBMS_OUTPUT.PUT_LINE(DBMS_UTILITY.FORMAT_ERROR_STACK);
      DBMS_OUTPUT.PUT_LINE('Procedure error_test2 Failed.');
END error_test2;
/
```

Example execution of error_test2

```
EXECUTE error_test2
```

Example output from executing error_test2

```
----- PL/SQL Call Stack -----
  object      line  object
```

```
 handle     number   name
18fff08          6   procedure PLSQL_USER.ERROR_TEST1
18ff6d8          3   procedure PLSQL_USER.ERROR_TEST2
1890b74          1   anonymous block

ORA-06502: PL/SQL: numeric or value error

Procedure error_test2 Failed.

PL/SQL procedure successfully completed.
```

The FORMAT_CALL_STACK and the FORMAT_ERROR_STACK should be called at the point of the error to ensure the call stack and error stack are returning at the point in time of the error. Propagating the error handling to the outermost program unit is not good practice. As evidenced in the two preceding examples, more information is present at the time of the error than at the outer loop. Further information on this approach to error handling is provided in Chapter 5.

Integrate Timing Routines to Monitor PL/SQL Performance via GET_TIME

Once all the application is programmatically correct and all functionality is working properly, the application needs to be stress tested (tested in a similar manner that will be as close to a production simulation as possible). This simulation will enable the performance and scalability of the application to be tested. The goal is to identify areas (PL/SQL program units or segments of source code, SQL statements, and so forth) in the application that are candidates for performance analysis for further optimization. Timers can be integrated in programs to monitor the timing of sections of PL/SQL source code and displayed or logged to a table or file. Refer to DBMS_OUTPUT, DBMS_PIPE, DBMS_ALERT, and UTL_FILE packages in this chapter or in Chapter 8 for further information on displaying and logging information in a PL/SQL program unit. The GET_TIME function provides the capability to capture timings down to one-hundredths of a second. If timing is only required down to the second, the SYSDATE variable can be used.

The GET_TIME function provides a point in time reference; therefore, the GET_TIME function is called at the beginning of the operation and then again at the end of the operation. The two values are then subtracted and divided by 100 to get the total time in seconds down to one-hundredths of a second.

The following is an example of the GET_TIME function syntax:

Function Syntax

```
DBMS_UTILITY.GET_TIME RETURN NUMBER;
```

The following example illustrates the use of the GET_TIME function.

File: 12_49.sql

```
DECLARE
    lv_temp_num          PLS_INTEGER := 0;
    lv_temp_cond_num     PLS_INTEGER := 5;
    lv_timer_start_num PLS_INTEGER;
    lv_timer_end_num     PLS_INTEGER;
BEGIN
    lv_timer_start_num := DBMS_UTILITY.GET_TIME;
    FOR lv_loop_num IN 1..10000 LOOP
        IF lv_temp_cond_num = 1 THEN
            lv_temp_num := lv_temp_num + 1;
        ELSIF lv_temp_cond_num = 2 THEN
            lv_temp_num := lv_temp_num + 1;
        ELSIF lv_temp_cond_num = 3 THEN
            lv_temp_num := lv_temp_num + 1;
        ELSIF lv_temp_cond_num = 4 THEN
            lv_temp_num := lv_temp_num + 1;
        ELSE
            lv_temp_num := lv_temp_num + 1;
        END IF;
    END LOOP;
    lv_timer_end_num := DBMS_UTILITY.GET_TIME;
    DBMS_OUTPUT.PUT_LINE((lv_timer_end_num - lv_timer_start_num)/100);
END;
/
```

Output (12_49.sql)

```
.2

PL/SQL procedure successfully completed.
```

In the preceding examples, two variables are used—first to get the starting point and then to get the ending point. This example is a small PL/SQL code segment repeated from Chapter 8 to illustrate a PL/SQL program unit that can be used for testing the timings of specific PL/SQL commands to determine the best PL/SQL commands to use for optimization.

TIP
The GET_TIME function as used in the preceding code segment will, at times, result in a negative number. The negative number is a result of the timer used for the GET_TIME function wrapping around and restarting at zero.

Expanding the PL/SQL Language

Possible Uses of **DBMS_UTILITY**

The following is a list of possible uses of the DBMS_UTILITY package:

Developer

- Develop routines to compile the schema if INVALID objects exist

- Create complete error handlers with the call and error stack capability

- Integrate timing logic in programs to monitor program execution and to locate slow problem areas

DBA

- Create programs to analyze the database or schema dependent on certain conditions

- Develop program to compile schema if INVALID objects exists

- Integrate timing logic in programs to monitor program execution and to locate slow problem areas

Read and Write Server-Side Operating System Files (UTL_FILE)

The UTL_FILE package is useful for both developers and DBAs who need to read or write operating system files on the database server. This package provides four basic functions of reading and writing to an operating system file on the server side, namely the capability to open a file, read or write to a file, and close a file. The power of this package lies in the PL/SQL language commands to process information prior to writing information out or after reading information in. This package was introduced in PL/SQL release 2.3.

The UTL_FILE package is a dependent package and is useful to both developers and DBAs.

The UTL_FILE package does not allow processing of client-side operating system files. Client-side operating system file processing is integrated into the Oracle Developer product with the TEXT_IO package as a standard Oracle supplied package in this product. The TEXT_IO package is covered in Chapter 14.

The UTL_FILE package should be considered a facility for processing data files, as well as logging process, error, or statistical information during PL/SQL program execution. The UTL_FILE package should not be considered a replacement for a report development product.

The typical order of events is that a file is opened for reading or writing, the opened file is read from or written to, and then the file is closed. Several characteristics are related to the processing of operating system files that are covered in more detail in the following sections.

INIT.ORA Parameter

For the UTL_FILE package to be enabled, the utl_file_dir parameter must be specified in the init.ora file (by default no directories are listed, essentially disabling the UTL_FILE package). Each directory to be accessed on the server must be specified separately with this parameter. If directories are specified here, later directory comparisons are always case-sensitive. In any case, all file I/O operations are performed by the ORACLE user and, therefore, the ORACLE user must have operating system permissions on the specified directories.

UNIX Example

```
UTL_FILE_DIR = /temp
UTL_FILE_DIR = /home/oracle/errors
UTL_FILE_DIR = /home/oracle/output
UTL_FILE_DIR = /loaders
```

Windows 95/NT Examples

```
UTL_FILE_DIR = c:\temp
UTL_FILE_DIR = c:\app\errors
UTL_FILE_DIR = c:\app\output
UTL_FILE_DIR = d:\loaders
```

To enable all directories in either UNIX or Windows NT

```
UTL_FILE_DIR = *
```

Caution should be taken in determining the directories to list for the utl_file_dir parameter. The "*" should never be used to ensure Oracle users cannot manipulate any files on the system. The utl_file_dir parameter essentially bypasses the operating system privilege on directories and, therefore, extra planning should be performed up-front when setting this parameter.

The use of this package should be determined for an application, and then the directories necessary for each type of file processed should be created to segment the operating system files logically. To view the directories defined for use with this parameter, the following script can be executed.

File: 12_50.sql

```
SELECT name, value, isses_modifiable, issys_modifiable
FROM    v$parameter
WHERE   name = 'utl_file_dir';
```

Output (12_50.sql)

```
NAME             VALUE                                  ISSES ISSYS_MOD
---------------  -------------------------------------  ----- ----------
utl_file_dir     c:\apps\output, c:\apps\error,  FALSE FALSE
                    c:\apps\statistics, c:\apps\l
                 oaders
```

SELECT privilege must be granted on the V_$PARAMETER view for the preceding script to complete successfully.

> **TIP**
> *When the UTL_FILE package will be used in your environment, take the time to define the types of use, create separate directories for each type of file use, and then set the init.ora parameter utl_file_dir to include each of these directories.*

> **TIP**
> *The UTL_FILE package does not look at the current schema account for operating system privilege in the directory specified in the PL/SQL program unit. It looks at the ORACLE user permissions, thus bypassing the standard operating system file access permissions.*

Declare the File Handle/Identifier

FILE_TYPE is a variable type declared in the UTL_FILE package that must be used as the declaration data type of a file handle for all file functions and procedures of the UTL_FILE package. A variable of FILE_TYPE is necessary for every implementation of UTL_FILE. In a stored procedure or package in which the UTL_FILE package is to be implemented, file handles must be declared. File handles are created/assigned when a file is opened. The following example illustrates this variable declaration.

File: 12_51.sql

```
DECLARE
   lv_file_id_num   UTL_FILE.FILE_TYPE;
BEGIN
   lv_file_id_num := UTL_FILE.FOPEN('c:\apps\loaders',
       'test4.dat', 'W');
   UTL_FILE.FCLOSE(lv_file_id_num);
END;
/
```

The preceding PL/SQL code segment opens and closes the file c:\apps\loaders\test4.dat, which creates the file, if the file did not exist, and flushes the contents of the file if it did exist. The file handle cannot be displayed with the DBMS_OUTPUT.PUT_LINE, as this will result in an error. The file handle must be used for all file operations. Once a PL/SQL program unit completes, the file handle is lost.

TIP
If a procedure terminates without closing a file that was opened, the file handle will not be known and, therefore, must be closed with the UTL_FILE.FCLOSE_ALL procedure call.

Open a File

The FOPEN function opens a file for input or output. The function returns the file handle or identifier with a UTL_FILE.FILE_TYPE data type. Files can be opened in Read (R), Write (W), or Append (A) modes. The IS_OPEN function is provided to enable the processing to check if a file is already opened. This function returns a Boolean to indicate if the file is currently opened.

Procedure Syntax

```
UTL_FILE.FOPEN(location IN VARCHAR2, filename IN VARCHAR2,
   open_mode IN VARCHAR2);
```

Function Syntax

```
UTL_FILE.IS_OPEN(file IN UTL_FILE.FILE_TYPE) RETURN BOOLEAN;
```

Up to ten files can be opened at any one time with the UTL_FILE package prior to Oracle 8.0.6. With Oracle 8.0.6 and later, you can open a maximum of 50 files at any one time.

Read from a File

The GET_LINE procedure reads one line of text from the specified file at a time. The new line character is not included in the return string. When the end of file is reached, the NO_DATA_FOUND exception is raised. If the file line does not fit into the buffer variable declared, the VALUE_ERROR exception is raised. If the file was not opened in read mode (R), the UTL_FILE.INVALID_OPERATION exception will be raised when the GET_LINE procedure is called. If an operating system error occurs while reading the file, the UTL_FILE.READ_ERROR exception will be raised.

Procedure Syntax

```
UTL_FILE.GET_LINE(file IN UTL_FILE.FILE_TYPE, buffer OUT VARCHAR2);
```

Write to a File

To write to a file, the file must be opened in an overwrite (W) or append (A) mode. The PUT procedure outputs a specified string to a file, without a new line character. The PUT_LINE procedure, outputs a specified string to a file, along with new line character following. The PUT_LINE procedure is equivalent to calling the PUT procedure followed by calling the NEW_LINE procedure. If the file was not opened in overwrite (W) or append (A) mode, the UTL_FILE.INVALID_OPERATION exception will be raised when the PUT or PUT_LINE procedures are executed. If an operating system error occurs while writing to the file, the UTL_FILE.WRITE_ERROR exception will be raised.

When the PUT or PUT_LINE procedures are executed, the information is actually written to a buffer, not directly to the file. Once the buffer is full, the buffered information is written to the file. When viewing a file during write operations, you will not see all lines written until the file is closed or the FFLUSH procedure is executed. If you are using a file to monitor progress of a process and you need up-to-date information, the FFLUSH procedure should be called after each PUT_LINE executed.

Procedure Syntax

```
UTL_FILE.PUT(file IN UTL_FILE.FILE_TYPE, buffer IN VARCHAR2);
UTL_FILE.PUT_LINE(file IN UTL_FILE.FILE_TYPE, buffer IN VARCHAR2);
UTL_FILE.FFLUSH(file IN UTL_FILE.FILE_TYPE);
```

Closing a File

The FCLOSE procedure closes the specified file. The FCLOSE_ALL procedure closes all currently opened files. The FCLOSE_ALL procedure should be used for cleanup within exception handling procedures. If the specified file was not open, the UTL_FILE.INVALID_FILEHANDLE exception will be raised when the FCLOSE procedure is called. If an operating system error occurs while closing files, the UTL_FILE.WRITE_ERROR exception will be raised. These close procedures free resources used for UTL_FILE package processing.

When files are no longer needed for reading or writing, they should be explicitly closed. Operating system files will remain locked until the file is closed or the session that opened the file is terminated successfully. If a file is not closed explicitly using the FCLOSE procedure or the FCLOSE_ALL procedure and the session is abnormally terminated, then a file lock will remain on the file. This file can then be rewritten to, but not deleted, until the database is shutdown and restarted.

Procedure Syntax

```
UTL_FILE.FCLOSE(file IN UTL_FILE.FILE_TYPE);
UTL_FILE.FCLOSE_ALL;
```

Handle Exceptions

When incorporating the UTL_FILE package functionality into PL/SQL program units, additional error handling must be integrated into the existing error process. Seven pre-defined exceptions can be raised in the UTL_FILE package:

- UTL_FILE.INTERNAL_ERROR

- UTL_FILE.INVALID_FILEHANDLE

- UTL_FILE.INVALID_MODE

- UTL_FILE.INVALID_OPERATION

- UTL_FILE.INVALID_PATH

- UTL_FILE.READ_ERROR

- UTL_FILE.WRITE_ERROR

Each UTL_FILE defined exception should be included into the exception-handling section to enable specific trapping of each error to ensure the proper error message is logged in your error handling routine. If one generic error handler is used, an unexplained exception will result. This provides no description of the error because these errors raised by the UTL_FILE package are created as user-defined exceptions in the declaration section of the UTL_FILE package specification (these declarations can be seen in the utlfile.sql file in the ORACLE_HOME/admin directory).

Example of a Procedure to Load a Data File and Search the File for a Character String

The UTL_FILE package functionality is illustrated in the following example. The process_products procedure processes a product data file with fixed-length fields and loads the data into the s_product table. The procedure also searches each product record loaded for a particular character string and writes this information to a separate log file, along with statistics of the processing.

File: 12_52.sql

```
CREATE OR REPLACE PROCEDURE process_products
   (p_directory_txt VARCHAR2 := 'c:\apps\loaders',
    p_filename_txt   VARCHAR2 := 'prodlist.dat',
    p_string_txt VARCHAR2) IS
-- DESCRIPTION: This package processes a product data file by
-- loading all product records into the s_product table. The
-- file loaded is scanned while loaded to log each line that
-- a specified string was found in. The statistics of the load
-- are also logged.
lv_file_id_num           UTL_FILE.FILE_TYPE;
lv_file_id_num_2         UTL_FILE.FILE_TYPE;
lv_output_filename_txt VARCHAR2(30);
lv_filename_txt          VARCHAR2(30);
lv_error_desc_txt        VARCHAR2(50);
lv_line_cnt_num          PLS_INTEGER := 0;
lv_error_cnt_num         PLS_INTEGER := 0;
lv_buffer_txt            VARCHAR2(2000);
lv_found_bln             BOOLEAN := FALSE;

-- This procedure reduces the code redundancy in the exception
-- handling process and is called by each exception condition.
PROCEDURE error_processing (p_file_num UTL_FILE.FILE_TYPE,
    p_line_num PLS_INTEGER, p_error_txt VARCHAR2) IS
BEGIN
   ROLLBACK;
   UTL_FILE.PUT_LINE(p_file_num, 'Line: ' ||
      p_line_num || ' Error: ' || p_error_txt);
   UTL_FILE.PUT_LINE(p_file_num, '----------------------------');
   UTL_FILE.PUT_LINE(p_file_num, 'File Process ABORTED');
```

```
        UTL_FILE.FCLOSE_ALL;
   END error_processing;
BEGIN
   -- Opens the input data file on the server for reading.
   lv_file_id_num := UTL_FILE.FOPEN(p_directory_txt,
      p_filename_txt, 'R');
   -- Creates the log file name by stripping the file
   -- extension and adding .log on the end.
   lv_output_filename_txt := SUBSTR(p_filename_txt, 1,
      INSTR(p_filename_txt, '.') - 1) || '.log';
   -- Opens the log file on the server for writing.
   lv_file_id_num_2 := UTL_FILE.FOPEN(p_directory_txt,
      lv_output_filename_txt, 'W');
   UTL_FILE.PUT_LINE(lv_file_id_num_2,
      'Processing Products Log File');
   UTL_FILE.PUT_LINE(lv_file_id_num_2,
      '----------------------------');
   UTL_FILE.PUT_LINE(lv_file_id_num_2, 'Directory:      ' ||
      p_directory_txt);
   UTL_FILE.PUT_LINE(lv_file_id_num_2, 'Input File:     ' ||
      p_filename_txt);
   UTL_FILE.PUT_LINE(lv_file_id_num_2, 'Output File:    ' ||
      lv_output_filename_txt);
   UTL_FILE.PUT_LINE(lv_file_id_num_2, 'Search String: ' ||
      p_string_txt);
   UTL_FILE.PUT_LINE(lv_file_id_num_2,
      '----------------------------');
LOOP
   lv_buffer_txt   := NULL;
   -- When end of file reached, the loop is terminated.
   BEGIN <<read_file>>
      UTL_FILE.GET_LINE(lv_file_id_num, lv_buffer_txt);
   EXCEPTION
      WHEN NO_DATA_FOUND THEN
         EXIT;
   END read_file;
   lv_line_cnt_num := lv_line_cnt_num + 1;
   -- If an error encountered on the insert, then the line
   -- and error are logged to the log file and processing
   -- continues.
   BEGIN <<insert_product>>
      -- When processing fixed length data files, if the spaces
      -- are not trimmed off the left and right side, the spaces
      -- will be part of the value inserted.
      INSERT INTO s_product
         (product_id, product_name, short_desc)
      VALUES
         (RTRIM(LTRIM(SUBSTR(lv_buffer_txt, 1, 7), ' '), ' '),
```

```
                    RTRIM(LTRIM(SUBSTR(lv_buffer_txt, 8, 50), ' '), ' '),
                    RTRIM(LTRIM(SUBSTR(lv_buffer_txt, 58), ' '), ' '));
         EXCEPTION
            WHEN OTHERS THEN
               UTL_FILE.PUT_LINE(lv_file_id_num_2,
                  'Line: ' || lv_line_cnt_num || ' Error: ' ||
                  SUBSTR(SQLERRM,1,200));
               lv_error_cnt_num := lv_error_cnt_num + 1;
         END insert_product;
         -- The line number is written to the log file every time
         -- the search string is found.
         IF INSTR(UPPER(lv_buffer_txt), UPPER(p_string_txt)) > 0 THEN
            UTL_FILE.PUT_LINE(lv_file_id_num_2,
               'String Found on Line: ' || lv_line_cnt_num);
            lv_found_bln := TRUE;
         END IF;
      END LOOP;
      COMMIT;   -- If the search string is not found in the file, a
      -- message is written to the log file to indicate this condition.
      IF NOT lv_found_bln THEN
         UTL_FILE.PUT_LINE(lv_file_id_num_2,
            'The string was not found in the file.');
      END IF;
      -- Final processing statistics are written to the log file.
      UTL_FILE.PUT_LINE(lv_file_id_num_2,
         '----------------------------');
      UTL_FILE.PUT_LINE(lv_file_id_num_2,
         'Number of Total Products Processed: ' ||
         TO_CHAR(lv_line_cnt_num, '999,999'));
      UTL_FILE.PUT_LINE(lv_file_id_num_2,
         'Number of Products Inserted:        ' ||
         TO_CHAR(lv_line_cnt_num - lv_error_cnt_num, '999,999'));
      UTL_FILE.PUT_LINE(lv_file_id_num_2,
         'Number of Products with Error:      ' ||
         TO_CHAR(lv_error_cnt_num, '999,999'));
      UTL_FILE.PUT_LINE(lv_file_id_num_2,
         '----------------------------');
      UTL_FILE.PUT_LINE(lv_file_id_num_2,
         'File Processed Successfully');
      UTL_FILE.FCLOSE_ALL;
EXCEPTION
   -- If any of the UTL_FILE exceptions are raised or any errors
   -- encountered, the entire process is rolled back, and the line
   -- number and error number are written to the log file.
   WHEN UTL_FILE.INTERNAL_ERROR THEN
```

```
            error_processing(lv_file_id_num_2, lv_line_cnt_num,
                'UTL_FILE.INTERNAL_ERROR encountered');
     WHEN UTL_FILE.INVALID_FILEHANDLE THEN
            error_processing(lv_file_id_num_2, lv_line_cnt_num,
                'UTL_FILE.INVALID_FILEHANDLE encountered');
     WHEN UTL_FILE.INVALID_MODE THEN
            error_processing(lv_file_id_num_2, lv_line_cnt_num,
                'UTL_FILE.INVALID_MODE encountered');
     WHEN UTL_FILE.INVALID_OPERATION THEN
            error_processing(lv_file_id_num_2, lv_line_cnt_num,
                'UTL_FILE.INVALID_OPERATION encountered');
     WHEN UTL_FILE.INVALID_PATH THEN
            error_processing(lv_file_id_num_2, lv_line_cnt_num,
                'UTL_FILE.INVALID_PATH encountered');
     WHEN UTL_FILE.READ_ERROR THEN
            error_processing(lv_file_id_num_2, lv_line_cnt_num,
                'UTL_FILE.READ_ERROR encountered');
     WHEN UTL_FILE.WRITE_ERROR THEN
            error_processing(lv_file_id_num_2, lv_line_cnt_num,
                'UTL_FILE.WRITE_ERROR encountered');
     WHEN OTHERS THEN
            error_processing(lv_file_id_num_2, lv_line_cnt_num,
                SUBSTR(SQLERRM,1,200));
END process_products;
/
```

Review the preceding example, as it provides a solid example of processing data files and working with the UTL_FILE package. The use of PL/SQL adds functionality and flexibility into this process. The procedure creates an output log file and creates the name of the file based on the input filename by changing the extension of the file. Separate PL/SQL blocks are embedded to enable more granular error trapping and more control of the processing. All important information is written to the log file as the process is executing. The procedure controls the transaction outcome by performing a COMMIT or ROLLBACK. The procedure logs the following information to the output file: The success or failure of the entire procedure, individual error records, file errors, and final statistics on the input file processing.

TIP

Use the power of PL/SQL to devise your naming of files manipulated with the UTL_FILE package. Unique names can be created by using the executing schema username, combined with the date and time. Be creative, but create a standard mechanism to identify files uniquely.

Reading/Writing Server-Side Operating System Files

TIP
When processing fixed-length records in a data file, always use the RTRIM and LTRIM functions to trim spaces on each side of the value. If you do not perform these functions prior to inserting the data, these will be included in the values inserted into the database. This makes it difficult when querying based on these columns with this type of value. The RTRIM and LTRIM functions are shown in the preceding PL/SQL example.

Once the preceding example procedure is created, the following data file can be processed.

File: c:\apps\loaders\product.dat

```
30011   BUNNY BOOT 2                        BEGINNERS SKI BOOT
30012   ACE SKI BOOT 2                      INTERMEDIATE SKI BOOT
30013   PRO SKI BOOT 2                      ADVANCED SKI BOOT
30021   BUNNY SKI POLE 2                    BEGINNERS SKI POLE
30022   ACE SKI POLE 2                      INTERMEDIATE SKI POLE
30023   PRO SKI POLE 2                      ADVANCED SKI POLE
40106   JUNIOR SOCCER BALL 2                JUNIOR SOCCER BALL
40108   WORLD CUP SOCCER BALL 2             WORLD CUP SOCCER BALL
40201   WORLD CUP NET 2                     WORLD CUP NET
40510   BLACK HAWK KNEE PADS 2              KNEE PADS, PAIR
40512   BLACK HAWK ELBOW PADS 2             ELBOW PADS, PAIR
```

The process_products procedure is called to process the preceding data file in SQL*Plus.

```
EXECUTE process_products('c:\apps\loaders', 'product.dat', 'pole')
```

The following example illustrates the log file output.

File: c:\apps\loaders\product.log

```
Processing Products Log File
---------------------------
Directory:      c:\apps\loaders
Input File:     product.dat
Output File:    product.log
Search String: pole
---------------------------
String Found on Line: 4
String Found on Line: 5
```

```
String Found on Line: 6
---------------------------
Number of Total Products Processed:      11
Number of Products Inserted:             11
Number of Products with Error:            0
---------------------------
File Processed Successfully
```

The following is the data inserted in the s_product table.

File: 12_53.sql

```
SELECT product_id, product_name, LENGTH(product_name)
FROM    s_product
WHERE   INSTR(product_name, '2') > 0
ORDER BY product_id;
```

Output (12_53.sql)

```
PRODUCT_ID PRODUCT_NAME                                LENGTH(PRODUCT_NAME)
---------- ------------------------------------------- --------------------
     30011 BUNNY BOOT 2                                                  12
     30012 ACE SKI BOOT 2                                                14
     30013 PRO SKI BOOT 2                                                14
     30021 BUNNY SKI POLE 2                                              16
     30022 ACE SKI POLE 2                                                14
     30023 PRO SKI POLE 2                                                14
     40106 JUNIOR SOCCER BALL 2                                          20
     40108 WORLD CUP SOCCER BALL 2                                       23
     40201 WORLD CUP NET 2                                               15
     40510 BLACK HAWK KNEE PADS 2                                        22
     40512 BLACK HAWK ELBOW PADS 2                                       23
```

The length column was included to illustrate the actual length of the product_name column value inserted. If the RTRIM and LTRIM functions were not used, the length value would display a 50 for each record.

TIP

Always explicitly close files when they are no longer needed. The best approach is to close each file by the file handle variable to ensure you are not closing files you want to remain open. If the entire process is complete, then the FCLOSE_ALL can be used without the possibility of closing an unwanted file.

Reading/Writing Server-Side Operating System Files

TIP

Exception handlers should include calls to close open files when using the UTL_FILE package because most UTL_FILE procedures and functions need the file handle. Once the PL/SQL program unit containing the file handle variable is completed, the file handle is lost. Thus, no more operations can be performed against the file. To close all files, use the FCLOSE_ALL procedure.

TIP

The maximum length of a line that can be written is 1022 bytes prior to Oracle release 8.0.3. In 8.03 and subsequent releases, the line length maximum of the UTL_FILE package is increased to 32K by calling a new overloaded FOPEN procedure.

Possible Uses of UTL_FILE

The following is a list of possible uses of the UTL_FILE package:

Developer

- Log to a file when certain application conditions occur in the application
- Log to a file when certain threshold parameters are built into an application and exceeded
- Log to a file when selected errors are encountered in the application
- Process data files by reading the files, processing the records, and then inserting them into a table

DBA

- Log to a file when certain critical thresholds are reached (data dictionary or V$ views)
  - Extreme amount of disk reads or memory reads for a statement/session
  - An object is nearing (within 15 extents of) the object maximum extent setting
  - Not enough space available in a tablespace for next object extension

- Log to a file when specific conditions occur in the system that should not occur
    - Number of sessions for one user exceeds a certain number
    - Objects are being created in the SYSTEM tablespace
    - SYSTEM tablespace is being used for temporary sorting

Pause Execution for a Specified Amount of Time (DBMS_LOCK)

The situation will arise when execution needs to pause in a PL/SQL program unit for a specified period of time or to pause in between iterations to enable a release of a resource or lock or to attempt an operation again in a highly transaction-oriented environment. This capability is provided with the SLEEP procedure.

The DBMS_LOCK package was not described in detail in Chapter 11, but is detailed in the dbmslock.sql file script file (package body located in prvtlock.plb). A public synonym is created, but no access is granted on this package; access is left to the DBA. Other procedures are included in the DBMS_LOCK package focusing on record locks, but this chapter limits the discussion only to the SLEEP procedure.

The SLEEP procedure is a standalone procedure and is useful to both developers and DBAs.

Procedure Syntax

```
DBMS_LOCK.SLEEP(seconds IN NUMBER);
```

File: 12_54.sql

```
SET TIMING ON
BEGIN
   DBMS_LOCK.SLEEP(5.7);
END;
/
```

Output (12_54.sql)

```
PL/SQL procedure successfully completed.

real: 5710
```

The real-time displayed in the preceding example output is in thousandths of seconds; therefore, the time this example executed in is 5.71 seconds (5710/1000). The time the example was programmed to pause for was 5.7 seconds. The other processing of the example accounts for the .01 second. The SLEEP procedure accepts values down to hundredths of seconds.

Possible Uses of DBMS_LOCK.SLEEP

The following is a list of possible uses of the DBMS_LOCK.SLEEP procedure:

Developer

- When there is a need for a time pause in application processing
- When a process is executing and fails due to resource contention, allow the process to pause and then attempt the operation again because the resource may be available in a short time (a good example is attempting to lock a record, in a highly transaction-oriented environment, the lock will probably free in a matter of seconds; rather than abort the process or attempt it immediately, build in a short delay)

DBA

- When identifying certain bottlenecks in your system from the V$ views (real-time views), rather than the system alerting you immediately, let the process pause for a short time and re-execute the process to ensure the bottleneck still exists:
  - Lock contention
  - Rollback segment contention
  - Session Maximum

Summary

In this chapter, we expanded the exploration into the powerful supplied Oracle packages by providing detailed examples and more real-world insight into each. The chapter focused on the more usable and helpful procedures and functions within these packages. Several examples were provided to ensure the true power of these Oracle supplied packages is understood and used to its fullest. Remember, these packages are also used by Oracle internally and they should be considered part of the PL/SQL language. Developers and DBAs should use these packages.

Reviewing these packages and understanding when and where they can be used is extremely important.

Tips Review

- The V$PARAMETER view signifies that neither of the job queue parameters (DBMS_JOB package) are modifiable without changing the parameter in the init.ora. In the release of Oracle 8, the job_queue_processes parameter is changed to enable the ALTER SYSTEM command to change this parameter.

- In the release of Oracle 8 and Oracle 8.1, an abundance of init.ora parameters are now modifiable with either the ALTER SYSTEM or ALTER SESSION command. To determine which init.ora parameters are changeable in this manner on your system, query the V$PARAMETER view for the isses_modifiable and issys_modifiable column values.

- The more processes executing in your environment in the job queue via the DBMS_JOB package, the higher the job_queue_processes should be. The increased frequency (shorter timeframe) of your processes in the job queue, the smaller the job_queue_interval should be.

- Setting the DBMS_JOB interval of execution becomes confusing quickly, unless you have an easy mechanism to convert your desired interval into a value. The equality information provides this easy translation formula (1 Day = 24 Hours = 1440 Minutes = 86400 seconds). Try it, it's easy!

- If no interval is specified for DBMS_JOB, the process executes at the specified time and then is removed from the job queue. After each execution of the process, the next date/time is determined as calculated from the interval. The process will not execute exactly on the next date setting; it will execute the next time the job processes wake up to execute processes in the job queue. Therefore, the actual execution time may be off slightly, but typically not by more than the init.ora parameter job_queue_interval.

- When the DBMS_JOB.RUN procedure is executed, the process will execute immediately, as well as force a disabled (broken) process in the job queue to become enabled. If a process is enabled when the DBMS_JOB.RUN is executed, the next date is re-calculated.

- If the DBMS_OUTPUT.ENABLE procedure is executed in a PL/SQL program unit and the program unit is not being executed in SQL*Plus, then DBMS_OUTPUT.PUT_LINE procedure executions will fill the message buffer. If the DBMS_OUTPUT.GET_LINE or DBMS_OUTPUT.GET_LINES procedures are not executed, then the message buffer can overflow and cause an error that is difficult to identify.

- I recommend keeping DBMS_OUTPUT.PUT_LINE procedure calls in PL/SQL program units for debugging and testing in SQL*Plus. This enables only turning on the message buffer and receiving these messages by the SET SERVEROUTPUT ON SIZE 1000000 command in SQL*Plus. This is the preferred method to using the DBMS_OUTPUT.ENABLE in PL/SQL program units.

- I recommend explicitly creating a pipe when using DBMS_PIPE as a standard to ensure easier procedural standards and more structured programming. I also recommend creating a pipe as public, unless a special need exists to keep it private. Public pipes can be seen by all users, whereas private pipes are only seen by sessions of the same username of the creator of the pipe.

- The pipes are created in the SGA and require space; therefore, take care to size the pipes based on the messaging volume. When a pipe is no longer needed, remove the pipe to free the space in the SGA.

- Pinning PL/SQL objects and cursors reduces the fragmentation of the shared memory in the Shared Pool.

- When the Shared Pool is flushed, any pinned objects remain pinned and are not flushed.

- I recommend using DBMS_SQL.NATIVE for the language_flag parameter, making your PL/SQL programs more flexible by ensuring they execute on any version of Oracle.

- DBMS_SQL logic is powerful, but not always necessary. Only use this package when necessary because the amount of source code necessary to accomplish the complete usage of DBMS_SQL is extensive and prone to errors. Extra overhead is also associated with using this package.

- Reuse cursors whenever possible because each cursor requires resources. Only re-parse statements if they change. A statement is not considered changed when a different value is assigned to a bind variable. Remember, a parse is necessary for Oracle to verify security and syntax, and to create an execution plan for the statement.

- Any statement executed with DBMS_SQL requires the schema user executing the PL/SQL program unit to have the necessary privilege for the generated DBMS_SQL statement(s) directly granted. If the access is provided through a role, the program will result in an error.

■ DBMS_SQL cursors need to be explicitly closed to free memory. Therefore, as a general rule, always close a cursor when it is no longer needed. In addition, always include close cursor logic in all exception handlers to ensure these cursors are closed when errors are encountered.

■ Oracle 8.1 introduces a more efficient implementation of executing dynamic SQL and PL/SQL statements with the EXECUTE IMMEDIATE PL/SQL command. For further detail on this command refer to Chapter 16.

■ To compute complete statistics with the DBMS_UTILITY package, the literal 'COMPUTE' must be used for the method parameter. The documentation (Oracle 7.3, corrected in later Oracle releases) provided in the SQL creation file (dbmsutil.sql) states that to compute complete statistics, the method parameter should be NULL.

■ The DBMS_UTILITY.COMPILE_SCHEMA procedure compiles all functions, procedures, and packages in alphabetical order. It does not attempt to compile triggers. This is evident by viewing the V$SQLAREA view. It does not perform the compile in dependency order.

■ The DBMS_UTILITY.GET_TIME function will, at times, result in a negative number. This negative number is a result of the timer used for the DBMS_UTILITY.GET_TIME function wrapping around and restarting at zero.

■ When the UTL_FILE package will be used in your environment, take the time to define the types of use, create separate directories for each type of file use, and then set the init.ora parameter utl_file_dir to include each of these directories.

■ The UTL_FILE package does not look at the current schema account for operating system privilege in the directory specified in the PL/SQL program unit. It looks at the ORACLE user permissions, thus bypassing the standard operating system file access permissions.

■ If a procedure ever terminates without closing a file that was opened, the file handle will not be known and, therefore, must be closed with the UTL_FILE.FCLOSE_ALL procedure call.

■ When processing fixed length records in a data file, always use the RTRIM and LTRIM functions to trim spaces on each side of the value. If you do not perform these functions prior to inserting the data, these will be included in the values inserted into the database. This makes it difficult when querying based on these columns with this type of value.

■ Always explicitly close files when they are no longer needed. The best approach is to close each file by the file handle variable to ensure you are

Tips Review

not closing files you wanted to remain open. If the entire process is complete, then the UTL_FILE.FCLOSE_ALL can be used without the possibility of closing an unwanted file.

■ Exception handlers should include calls to close open files when using the UTL_FILE package because most UTL_FILE procedures and functions need the file handle. Once the PL/SQL program unit that contains the file handle variable is completed, the file handle is lost. Thus, no more operations can be performed against the file. To close all files, use the UTL_FILE.FCLOSE_ALL procedure.

■ The maximum length of a line that can be written is 1022 bytes prior to Oracle release 8.0.3. In 8.03 and subsequent releases, the line length maximum of the UTL_FILE package is increased to 32K.

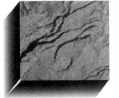

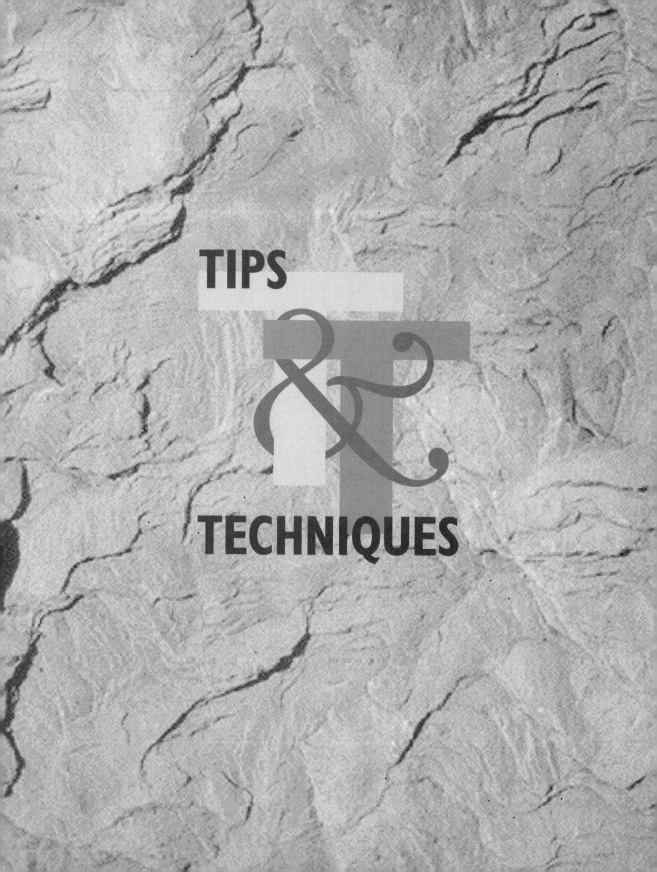

TIPS & TECHNIQUES

CHAPTER
13

Taking Advantage of the PL/SQL Data Dictionary (Developer and DBA)

Oracle has created an important and helpful application that is available to all developers and DBAs to assist in the development, deployment, analysis, administration, and configuration of Oracle-based systems. This application is a key element to the Oracle architecture; it is known as the *data dictionary.* Oracle stores information related to all database objects in its data dictionary. This repository is constantly queried and updated by Oracle. Every developer and DBA should use this powerful tool on a regular basis. The more this valuable tool is used and understood, the more value is gained. Constant use is necessary to realize the vast amount of information stored in the data dictionary and this information continues to be upgraded to support the growth of the Oracle product.

When Oracle introduced PL/SQL, an extended set of data dictionary tables and views was added to store PL/SQL object information. These additional tables and views are a gift from Oracle because they can be used by developers and DBAs to manage code development, deployment, administration, and configuration of stored PL/SQL objects. This chapter examines several areas that relate to the data dictionary from both a developer and a DBA perspective. Several of the DBA-focused sections should be left in the hands of the DBA to administer and concentrate on, but the background knowledge would be beneficial for developers to understand some of the DBA related responsibilities that center around the PL/SQL data dictionary. The following tips explain how to take advantage of these tables and views associated with the data dictionary and understand the contents:

- Execute catalog.sql and catproc.sql when re-creating a database
- Automate the SQL files executed upon database creation
- Understand Oracle file naming conventions
- Modify the sql.bsq file for optimal storage and speed
- Automate the process of checking space fragmentation
- Know the contents of the PL/SQL data dictionary
- Provide correct access to the PL/SQL data dictionary
- Determine access on stored PL/SQL program units
- Build online help for all PL/SQL data dictionary information
- View object creation and modification timestamps
- Verify all PL/SQL objects are valid upon creation or modification
- Re-create PL/SQL source code from the database
- Provide capability to enable/disable database triggers

■ Provide a facility to identify all stored PL/SQL object errors

■ Develop search engines for the PL/SQL object source code

■ Develop an impact analysis facility for database objects

■ Determine the object size loaded into memory

■ Use dynamic SQL on the data dictionary to build DDL scripts

Remember, the data dictionary is like any other application, and you should get to know this application, structure, and data. You will become a better developer or DBA if you use this valuable tool that Oracle provides. References exist to all three levels of data dictionary views, namely, USER_* (returns information on objects owned by the current user), ALL_* (returns information on objects owned by the current user and objects accessible to the current user), and DBA_* (returns information on all objects). All three are useful, but your system and object privilege will dictate which of these views you can query and the results that will be returned.

Execute catalog.sql and catproc.sql when Re-creating a Database

DBAs must understand the data dictionary and procedural option creation to gain valuable insight into the Oracle architecture and to become more proficient when creating or re-creating databases. During a standard Oracle installation, Oracle executes a script that creates the database (during the create database, the sql.bsq file is executed which creates the data dictionary tables) and executes the scripts which creates the data dictionary views (catalog.sql) and all components of the procedural option (catproc.sql). These files are generally located in the ORACLE_HOME/rdbms/admin directory on most UNIX platforms and in the ORACLE_HOME\rdbms73\admin directory on Windows 95 (assuming Oracle7.3). The procedural option consists of a set of scripts that build all the necessary components for the PL/SQL architecture and language. The build includes creating additional data dictionary tables and views specific to PL/SQL structures and PL/SQL packages for internal use by Oracle and external use by developers and DBAs. When a database is re-created with the CREATE DATABASE command, only the sql.bsq file is executed; therefore, the data dictionary tables are only created (not the views). When re-creating a database, after the installation, you must create the views and set up the procedural option by manually executing the catalog.sql and catproc.sql files. These files must be executed under the SYS user or while connected as INTERNAL. The catalog.sql and catproc.sql files call a number of other files that are executed. (See Figure 13-1 for an execution map of these files for Oracle 7.3.) The execution map is similar in Oracle8 and 8i and can be viewed by looking in the SQL script files outlined previously.)

Directory: d:\orawin95\rdbms73\admin

sql.bsq (data dictionary tables)	Executed by Oracle (creation/re-creation)
catalog.sql (data dictionary views)	Install (automatic)/Re-create (manual)

cataudit.sql (auditing views)	catexp.sql (import/export views)
catldr.sql (SQL*Loader views)	catsvrmg.sql (server manager views)

catproc.sql (main script for procedural option)	Install (automatic)/Re-create (manual)

catprc.sql (PL/SQL views)	catjobq.sql (job scheduling views)
catsnap.sql (snapshot views)	catrpc.sql (remote database views)
catdefer.sql	(deferred replication views)
standard.sql	(STANDARD package creation)
dbmsstdx.sql	(DBMS_STANDARD package creation)
pipidl.sql	(PIDL package creation)
pidian.sql	(DIANA package creation)
diutil.sql	(DIUTIL package creation)
pistub.sql	(STUBS package creation)
plitblm.sql	(PLITBLM package creation)
utlfile.sql, prvtfile.plb	(UTL_FILE package creation)
dbmsutil.sql, prvtutil.plb	(DBMS_* package creation)
dbmssyer.sql, prvtsyer.plb	(DBMS_SYS_ERROR package creation)
dbmslock.sql, prvtlock.plb	(DBMS_LOCK package creation)
dbmspipe.sql, prvtpipe.plb	(DBMS_PIPE package creation)
dbmsalrt.sql, prvtalrt.plb	(DBMS_ALERT package and table creation)
dbmsotpt.sql, prvtotpt.plb	(DBMS_OUTPUT package creation)
dbmsdesc.sql, prvtdesc.plb	(DBMS_DESCRIBE package creation)
dbmssql.sql, prvtsql.plb	(DBMS_SQL & DBMS_SYS_SQL package creation)
dbmspexp.sql, prvtpexp.plb	(DBMS_EXPORT_EXTENSION package creation)
dbmsjob.sql, prvtjob.plb	(DBMS_JOB package creation)
dbmsdfrd.sql, prvtdfrd.plb	(DBMS_DEFER* package creation)
dbmssnap.sql, prvtsnap.plb	(DBMS_SNAPSHOT & DBMS_REFRESH package creation)

FIGURE 13-1.   *Files executed to build the data dictionary tables, views, and Oracle supplied packages*

TIP

Read these Oracle creation file comments to gain valuable insights on the data dictionary tables and views, and Oracle-supplied packages not documented elsewhere. Information can also be found by querying the USER_SOURCE view, specifically the Oracle supplied package specifications.

TIP

Most of the Oracle creation files have been enhanced to include the new or enhanced features found in Oracle8 and 8i. If you have implemented or are upgrading to Oracle8 or Oracle8i, it's worth your time to re-examine these files. Oracle has maintained a similar directory and file structure in Oracle8 and 8i, so Figure 13-1 can be used as a guide for an execution map of Oracle creation files for Oracle8 and 8i. Note that some of these files have been modified and new files have been added, depending on the version of Oracle.

Automate the SQL Files Executed upon Database Creation

Proper files *must* be executed upon a database creation; this is critical. Automating this process can be helpful. The sql.bsq file is the only file executed upon creation of a database because by default the init.ora parameter _init_sql_file is set equal to the value of "sql.bsq" (this also will include the directory path to this file). As noted in the previous section, two other SQL files must be executed upon creation. You can ensure these SQL files are executed by using one of the following methods:

- **Manual method**   The DBA uses recall to determine which files need to be executed. This introduces a margin of error.

- **Script method**   The DBA builds an operating system script file to execute each time the database is rebuilt.

- **Automatic method**   The DBA alters the _init_sql_file parameter in the init.ora file to include the list of SQL files to be executed upon creation.

In the last method, there is no need to remember the scripts to be executed.

Re-creating a Database

To automate database recreation, the _init_sql_file parameter *must* be modified in the init.ora file (typically located in the ORACLE_HOME/dbs directory) as shown in the following script:

File: init.ora

```
_init_sql_file = (sql.bsq, catalog.sql, catproc.sql)
```

Note that users running Oracle 7.2 or previous releases must type init_sql_file as the parameter name not _init_sql_file.

TIP
When Oracle 7.3 was released, the name of the init_sql_file parameter was changed to _init_sql_file. The way to view the parameter's settings was also changed. Users could no longer use the V$PARAMETER view to check that the sql.bsq, catalog.sql, and catproc.sql files were being called for execution. This change left many users feeling they had lost a valuable tool. In fact, the users really didn't lose the ability to view the parameter; the method for viewing changed. In Oracle 7.3 and subsequent releases, users can view the _init_sql_file parameter by querying and joining the X$KSPPI and X$KSPPCV tables by the indx column as shown in the following 13_1.sql script.

File: 13_1.sql

```
SELECT     a.ksppinm, b.ksppstvl
FROM       x$ksppi a, x$ksppcv b
WHERE      a.indx  = b.indx
AND        ksppinm = '_init_sql_file';
```

Output (13_1.sql)

```
KSPPINM           KSPPSTVL
---------------   --------------------------
_init_sql_file    %RDBMS73%\ADMIN\SQL.BSQ
```

Note that this operation of changing the _init_sql_file parameter must be performed by an experienced DBA, and the 13_1.sql file must be executed by the user SYS.

TIP
Any values in the ksppinm column of the X$KSPPI
table preceded by a "_" are not viewable in the
V$PARAMETER view. While no problem exists with
modifying the previous parameter, changing most of
the other parameters that are not viewable in the
V$PARAMETER view is not recommended. Failure to
follow this guideline could result in your database
crashing or being severely damaged.

Understand Oracle Filenaming Conventions

Both the developer and the DBA must understand the naming conventions Oracle uses to segment their creation scheme. The creation files provided by Oracle *must not* be modified, except in the manner outlined in the following section, "Modify the sql.bsq File for Optimal Storage and Speed." Several of the PL/SQL packages are used internally by the Oracle kernal. If these package creation files are modified, the database can fail to function properly. If you talk to Oracle, modification of these scripts will nullify your technical support agreement on the product with Oracle.

While Oracle protects most of the script files from being modified by WRAPping the package body (encrypting it), understanding how Oracle uses file names and extensions can help you recognize the contents of the files and avoid potential disasters. The naming conventions are

■ **Data dictionary related files**   These files start with cat and contain an extension of sql. For example, catalog.sql, catproc.sql.

■ **Package specification related files**   These files start with dbms and contain an extension of sql (usually *unWRAPped* files with extensive comments and extreme value to review). For example, dbmsutil.sql, dbmspipe.sql.

■ **Package body related files**   These files start with prvt and contain the extension of plb (usually *WRAP*ped files with minimal value to review). For example, prvtutil.plb, prvtpipe.plb.

Oracle supplied PL/SQL package files are typically separated into two files: one for the package specification and one for the package body.

WRAPping is performed by Oracle with the WRAP facility they provide and is outlined in more detail in Chapter 5.

Understand Filenaming Conventions

Modify the sql.bsq File for Optimal Storage and Speed

Disclaimer: The method outlined in this section is for the advanced DBA and, if used, should be carried out with extreme caution. I have used this method previously on several systems and know of many others who have also used this method with success. It can be extremely advantageous to deploy. If you feel comfortable using this method, you are doing so at your own risk. Consult Oracle prior to making any modifications to the sql.bsq file.

For the DBA, eliminating database fragmentation is one of the keys to achieving optimal database performance. Oracle had always used the database to store data, while the source code was stored at the operating system level. The responsibility of the DBA was limited to forecasting data growth and dealing with data fragmentation. However, with the advent of Oracle7 and PL/SQL version 2.0, Oracle created a whole new paradigm that introduced the expansion of database storage to include PL/SQL source code. This paradigm has evolved over the years and now it has become much more efficient and effective to store source code, namely, PL/SQL objects in the database.

This database storage of source code adds a new dimension to the DBA's responsibility of fragmentation. A DBA must now consider the storage of this source code in the database and ensure fragmentation is addressed in this realm. As we have seen over the years, the client/server computing model has become more efficient by deploying this database source code storage model. Likewise, the Internet/intranet model is dependent on this database source code storage model, so a DBA must address the source code database storage and fragmentation on these objects.

To avoid fragmentation of the data dictionary tables that store the PL/SQL objects (see Table 13-1), enough storage space should be allocated when they are created.

By default, the sql.bsq file used to create the data dictionary tables sets the SYSTEM default storage to an INITIAL extent of 10K, the NEXT (incremental) extent

COL$[2]	DEPENDENCY$[2]	ERROR$[1]
IDL_CHAR$[1]	IDL_SB4$[1]	IDL_UB1$[1]
IDL_UB2$[1]	LINK$[1]	OBJ$[2]
OBJAUTH$[2]	SOURCE$[1]	SYSAUTH$[1]
TRIGGER$[2]	TRIGGERCOL$[1]	USER$[1]

[1]refers to a table with one index and [2]refers to a table with two indexes.

TABLE 13-1.   *Data Dictionary Tables Used to Store PL/SQL Program Units*

to 10K, and the PCTINCREASE (percent increase) to 50, as shown in the following code segment. This code segment was copied from a section of the sql.bsq file. (Note: the source code listing for the following steps does not conform to the standards identified in Chapter 3 and used throughout this book because this code was copied directly from one of Oracle's SQL files.)

```
create tablespace SYSTEM datafile "D_DBFN"
  default storage (initial 10K next 10K) online
/
  .       .     .      .      .      .
  .       .     .      .      .      .
create table source$                     /* source table */
( obj#          number not null,         /* object number */
  line          number not null,         /* line number */
  source        varchar2("M_VCSZ"))      /* source line */
/
```

Under Personal Oracle 7.3, when a new database is created with the default Oracle stored PL/SQL program units that are part of the PL/SQL packages, several data dictionary tables are allocated over five extents. (For example, the SOURCE$ table is created with 11 extents.)

Oracle inserts the source code into the data dictionary every time a PL/SQL program unit (packages, procedures, functions, and database triggers) is compiled; therefore the default values are typically too small. The following query reveals the storage allocation of the PL/SQL data dictionary tables:

File: 13_2.sql

```
SELECT    segment_name, segment_type, COUNT(*), SUM(bytes)
FROM      dba_extents
WHERE     segment_name IN
          ('COL$', 'DEPENDENCY$', 'ERROR$', 'IDL_CHAR$',
           'IDL_SB4$', 'IDL_UB1$', 'IDL_UB2$', 'LINK$', 'OBJ$',
           'OBJAUTH$', 'SOURCE$', 'SYSAUTH$', 'TRIGGER$',
           'TRIGGERCOL$', 'USER$')
GROUP BY  segment_name, segment_type
ORDER BY  segment_type, segment_name;
```

Output (13_2.sql)

SEGMENT_NAME	SEGMENT_TYPE	COUNT(*)	SUM(BYTES)
DEPENDENCY$	TABLE	4	71680
ERROR$	TABLE	1	10240

IDL_CHAR$	TABLE	3	40960
IDL_SB4$	TABLE	5	112640
IDL_UB1$	TABLE	8	399360
IDL_UB2$	TABLE	9	593920
LINK$	TABLE	1	10240
OBJ$	TABLE	5	112640
OBJAUTH$	TABLE	1	10240
SOURCE$	TABLE	12	1955840
SYSAUTH$	TABLE	1	10240
TRIGGER$	TABLE	1	10240
TRIGGERCOL$	TABLE	1	10240

The underlying data dictionary table storage is not modifiable; therefore, increasing the initial storage of these tables must be considered, especially when creating or re-creating a database that stores a large number of PL/SQL program units and source code. Typically, an object's storage can be compressed by exporting with the compress extents option set, followed by an import of the object. The data dictionary objects (tables and indexes) are created in the sql.bsq file, and therefore the storage of these objects cannot be compressed/changed with an export and import. The data dictionary objects are owned by SYS and are not exported, even during a full database export.

Prior to a full database import being performed, the data dictionary tables and indexes are created automatically with the CREATE DATABASE command as outlined in the earlier section, "Automate the SQL Files Executed Upon Database Creation." This object storage modification must be handled when the object is created, then modified in the sql.bsq file.

The sql.bsq file can be modified to increase the storage of these data dictionary tables and indexes by adding a STORAGE clause to each table and index creation statement. When the STORAGE clause is not included in the table and index creation statement, the data dictionary tables are created in the SYSTEM tablespace with the default storage values. The following is an example of how to modify one of these tables in the sql.bsq file, namely, the source$ table:

File: sql.bsq with a STORAGE clause added (the added clause is bolded)

```
create table source$                        /* source table */
( obj#          number not null,            /* object number */
  line          number not null,            /* line number */
  source        varchar2("M_VCSZ"))         /* source line */
STORAGE (INITIAL 3M NEXT 1M PCTINCREASE 50)
/
```

This method would be deployed for all PL/SQL-related data dictionary tables based on the 13_2.sql file output. As previously noted, indexes are associated with most of these tables, and it is equally important to adjust the storage of these objects.

The method for identifying fragmentation and adjusting the storage of indexes is the same as for tables as outlined previously.

TIP
Modify the storage parameters in the sql.bsq file as necessary based on your volume of stored PL/SQL objects to eliminate fragmentation. Make sure a backup copy of the sql.bsq file is created prior to modification. This operation should only be performed by an experienced DBA. Consult Oracle prior to making any modifications to the sql.bsq file.

TIP
Execute the 13_2.sql script on a weekly or monthly basis to monitor fragmentation to ensure your SYSTEM tablespace does not become fragmented by stored PL/SQL program units.

Automate the Process of Checking Space Fragmentation

A DBA can monitor and eliminate fragmentation in two ways: manually or automatically. As discussed in the previous section, you can execute the 13_2.sql file to monitor growth, or you can automate this process by setting up a table to log the growth automatically at a specified interval. The history log table can then be monitored on a periodic basis to forecast space needs. The following outlines the technique used to accomplish this technique:

1. Create a history log table (extents_log) with the columns the same as those returned from the 13_2.sql script and the addition of one more column, namely a date stamp (13_3.sql).

2. Create a stored PL/SQL procedure that will INSERT the 13_2.sql file output into this history log table on a specified interval (13_4.sql). The user who executes the 13_4.sql script must have been granted SELECT privilege to the DBA_EXTENTS view directly, not through a role. This can be granted by the SYS or SYSTEM user to the PLSQL_USER schema as follows:

   ```
   GRANT SELECT ON dba_extents TO PLSQL_USER;
   ```

3. Determine the INSERT interval and set up the stored procedure to be executed in the UNIX cron facility or to be executed in the Oracle batch

scheduler DBMS_JOB package at the desired interval (since the date is only being recorded, it is assumed the interval will be no more than once per day, more like weekly). More information on the Oracle supplied package DBMS_JOB can be found in Chapters 11 and 12.

4. Create a SQL script to provide a report on the contents of the history log table ordered by table and by date (13_5.sql).

5. Analyze the results from the 13_5.sql script periodically to determine the correct sizing based on the growth of these tables.

File: 13_3.sql

```
CREATE TABLE extents_log
(log_date              DATE,
segment_name          VARCHAR2(81),
segment_type          VARCHAR2(17),
count_extents         NUMBER,
bytes_extents         NUMBER);
```

File: 13_4.sql

```
CREATE OR REPLACE PROCEDURE log_extents AS
BEGIN
   INSERT INTO extents_log
   SELECT TRUNC(SYSDATE), segment_name, segment_type,
          COUNT(*), SUM(bytes)
   FROM   dba_extents
   WHERE  segment_name IN
          ('COL$', 'DEPENDENCY$', 'ERROR$', 'IDL_CHAR$',
           'IDL_SB4$', 'IDL_UB1$', 'IDL_UB2$', 'LINK$', 'OBJ$',
           'OBJAUTH$', 'SOURCE$', 'SYSAUTH$', 'TRIGGER$',
           'TRIGGERCOL$', 'USER$')
   GROUP BY   segment_name, segment_type;
END log_extents;
/
```

File: 13_5.sql

```
SELECT       segment_name, log_date, segment_type,
             count_extents, bytes_extents
FROM         extents_log
ORDER BY     segment_name, log_date;
```

Checking Space Fragmentation

TIP
The logging/monitoring process outlined in this section can and should be expanded to include the indexes on these tables.

TIP
When analyzing table and index sizing, do not size the objects according to the size 13_2.sql returns; instead, examine the growth and determine a size to accommodate additional growth.

Know the Contents of the PL/SQL Data Dictionary

Many developers and DBAs do not use the data dictionary in their daily activities. Others who say they use the data dictionary do not use it to the fullest. The fact of the matter is, the data dictionary is often intimidating because of its expansive size. This section details the contents of the seven main PL/SQL views and concentrates on the USER_* views, but realize each view also has an ALL_* and DBA_* view counterpart. These counterparts contain the same information with a slight variation, based upon the schema querying the information.

For each of the PL/SQL views, the following is provided:

- A general description of the content

- A description of when records are inserted into the underlying table(s) of the view

- A list of the underlying table(s) of the view

For more detail on each view, review catalog .sql and catproc .sql, located in the ORACLE\HOME\rdbms\admin directory.

- **USER_OBJECTS**   This view contains a list of all objects in the database and includes for each, the creation date of the object, modification date of the object, and the compiled status (INVALID: not currently compiled, VALID: currently compiled). The objects in this view consist of tables, indexes, clusters, views, synonyms, sequences, package specifications, package bodies, procedures, functions, and database triggers. Every time an object is created, a record is inserted into the underlying table(s) of this view.

TIP
Database triggers will only exist in this view in Oracle version 7.3 (PL/SQL version 2.3) and subsequent releases.

The underlying data dictionary tables for this view are OBJ$ and LINK$.

■ **USER_SOURCE**   This view contains the current version of source code for package specifications, package bodies, procedures, and functions. This also includes all comment lines embedded in the stored object creation statement. Every time an object is created, whether compiled successfully or not, records are inserted into the underlying table(s) of this view. The number of records depends on the size of the source code of the object.

TIP
The USER_SOURCE view does not contain the source code for database triggers. This source code is only stored in the underlying table(s) of the USER_TRIGGERS view.

TIP
When an error during compilation is encountered, the error specifies the line number of the error in the source code. This line number corresponds to the line of the source code in the USER_SOURCE view, not the line in the script file from which the PL/SQL object was created. When Oracle inserts the source code in this table, the lines may not correspond exactly to those in your script file used to create the stored object.

The underlying data dictionary tables for this view are OBJ$ and SOURCE$.

■ *USER_TRIGGERS*   This view contains all the information in the creation statement of a database trigger. This view also contains the status of the trigger (ENABLED: executed implicitly based on table manipulation, DISABLED: not executed until ENABLED). Every time a trigger is created, whether compiled successfully or not, one record is inserted into the underlying table(s) of this view.

NOTE
The actual source code of the trigger is stored in a LONG column; therefore, only one record is necessary (LONG datatype in Oracle8 stores up to 2G).

TIP
Database triggers are implicitly executed; therefore, no source code directly calls the execution of triggers. The execution depends entirely on the status of the database trigger being set to ENABLED. The only way to tell if a trigger is disabled is to query the USER_TRIGGERS view.

The underlying data dictionary tables for this view are OBJ$, TRIGGER$, and USER$.

- **USER_TRIGGER_COLS**   This view contains information that relates to database trigger column references. Every time a trigger is created, whether compiled successfully or not, one record is inserted into the underlying table(s) of this view for every column referenced.

The underlying data dictionary tables for this view are OBJ$, TRIGGER$, USER$, COL$, and TRIGGERCOL$.

- **USER_DEPENDENCIES**   This view contains information that shows the dependencies between objects in the database. The objects in this view consist of tables, indexes, clusters, views, synonyms, sequences, package specifications, package bodies, procedures, functions, and database triggers. This view only contains the object if it is dependent on another object or if another object is dependent on the object. For example, if a stored procedure was named *x* that calls stored procedure *y*, and stored procedure *y* calls procedure *z*, then there would be one record for the dependency of *x* on *y* and one record for the dependency of *y* on *z*. Every time an object is created, a record is inserted into the underlying table(s) of this view for every object upon which the new object is dependent.

The underlying data dictionary tables for this view are OBJ$, USER$, and DEPENDENCY$.

- **USER_ERRORS**   This view contains all current errors for stored PL/SQL object compilation, so it contains errors for package specifications, package bodies, procedures, functions, and database triggers. Every time an object is compiled unsuccessfully, one or more records are inserted into the underlying table(s) of this view. The number of records inserted into this view depends on the size and the number of the errors. If an object is compiled successfully, no records are inserted into this view. When an object that was compiled unsuccessfully in the past is then recompiled successfully, the records relating to the object are deleted from this view.

The underlying data dictionary tables for this view are OBJ$ and ERROR$.

■ **USER_OBJECT_SIZE** This view contains the size in bytes of the object that is loaded into memory when an object is compiled, executed (p-code), or referenced by another object during compilation. It also contains the size of the error loaded into the Shared Pool, if an error exists during compilation. The objects in this view consist of views, package specifications, package bodies, procedures, functions, and database triggers. Every time an object is created, whether compiled successfully or not, one record is inserted into the underlying table(s) of this view. The contents of this view are described in more detail later in this chapter in the section, "Determine the Object Size Loaded into the Memory."

The underlying data dictionary tables for this view are OBJ$, IDL_UB1$, IDL_UB2$, IDL_UB4$, IDL_CHAR$, SOURCE$, and ERROR$.

Provide Correct Access to the PL/SQL Data Dictionary

The information stored in the data dictionary repository is invaluable. Being able to access this information is critical, but not all of the information is accessible to all Oracle users by default. Oracle provides access to this information through a set of views built on top of the underlying data dictionary tables. For each segment of information, there is a USER_*, ALL_*, and DBA_* view.

Each view is created in a similar fashion. In the following, the view creation steps are outlined using the USER_SOURCE view as an example. (Note, the source code listing for the following steps does not conform to the standards identified in Chapter 3 and used throughout this book because this code was copied directly from one of Oracle's SQL files.)

1. View created

```
create or replace view USER_SOURCE
(NAME, TYPE, LINE, TEXT)
as
select o.name,
decode(o.type, 7, 'PROCEDURE', 8, 'FUNCTION', 9, 'PACKAGE',
11, 'PACKAGE BODY', 'UNDEFINED'),
```

```
s.line, s.source
from sys.obj$ o, sys.source$ s
where o.obj# = s.obj#
  and o.type in (7, 8, 9, 11)
  and o.owner# = userenv('SCHEMAID');
```

2. View and column comments created

```
comment on table USER_SOURCE is
'Source of stored objects accessible to the user';
comment on column USER_SOURCE.NAME is
'Name of the object';
comment on column USER_SOURCE.TYPE is
'Type of the object: "PROCEDURE", "FUNCTION", "PACKAGE"
   or "PACKAGE BODY"';
comment on column USER_SOURCE.LINE is
'Line number of this line of source';
comment on column USER_SOURCE.TEXT is
'Source text';
```

3. Public synonym with the same name as the view dropped

```
drop public synonym USER_SOURCE;
```

4. Public synonym with the same name as the view created

```
create public synonym USER_SOURCE for USER_SOURCE;
```

5. Access granted on the view to PUBLIC with the GRANT option (this is for all USER_* and ALL_* views only; DBA_* views do not contain this step. All DBA_* views are accessible only by users explicitly granted access to them or users in the DBA role.)

```
grant select on USER_SOURCE to public with grant option;
```

TIP
The "WITH GRANT OPTION" can be used on most SQL commands that pertain to system privileges. It extends the privilege granted to allow the granted user or role the ability to grant this privilege to others.

The following are the seven main PL/SQL data dictionary views related to stored PL/SQL objects:

USER_OBJECTS[1]	ALL_ OBJECTS[1]	DBA_OBJECTS[1]
USER_SOURCE	ALL_SOURCE	DBA_SOURCE
USER_TRIGGERS	ALL_TRIGGERS	DBA_TRIGGERS
USER_TRIGGER_COLS	ALL_TRIGGER_COLS	DBA_TRIGGER_COLS
USER_DEPENDENCIES	ALL_DEPENDENCIES	DBA_DEPENDENCIES
USER_ERRORS	ALL_ERRORS	DBA_ERRORS
USER_OBJECT_SIZE	ALL_OBJECT_SIZE	DBA_OBJECT_SIZE

[1]Indicates the views created in the catalog.sql file that relate to stored PL/SQL objects. All other views are created in the catprc.sql file. Note that this is not the entire list of PL/SQL related data dictionary views, but the main set. Other PL/SQL views are outlined in Appendix C.

These views provide developers and DBAs a wealth of information. The USER_* views provide access to all objects created by the current schema (user). The ALL_* views provide access to all objects created by the current schema and all objects to which the current schema has been granted access. The DBA_* views provide access to all objects in the database. The USER_* and ALL_* views are accessible to all Oracle users by default.

To provide access to the DBA_* views to a specific schema, execute the following command:

```
GRANT SELECT ON dba_source TO plsql_user;
```

You can use the GRANT SELECT command to extend access to the DBA_* views to users belonging to a role or by assigning that role to the user(s) desired as outlined in the following script:

```
CREATE ROLE select_plsql_dba_role;
GRANT select_plsql_dba_role TO plsql_user;
GRANT SELECT ON dba_source TO select_plsql_dba_role;
```

Note: The last SQL statement must be performed by the SYS user.

Determine Access on Stored PL/SQL Program Units

Oracle users must be provided the proper access on stored PL/SQL program units to allow the correct users to execute the stored PL/SQL objects. The privilege that must be granted for an Oracle user to execute a stored PL/SQL object is EXECUTE.

To determine the current privilege for stored PL/SQL objects, run the following queries:

File: 13_6.sql (schema privileges)

```
SELECT      b.owner || '.' || b.table_name object,
            b.privilege what_granted, b.grantable, a.username
FROM        dba_users a, dba_tab_privs b
WHERE       a.username = b.grantee
AND         privilege = 'EXECUTE'
ORDER BY    1,2,3;
```

Output (13_6.sql)

```
OBJECT                       WHAT_GRANTED      GRA USERNAME
---------------------------- ----------------- --- ----------
PLSQL_USER.LOG_EXTENTS       EXECUTE           NO  TEMP1
PLSQL_USER.VALIDATE_TITLE    EXECUTE           NO  TEMP1
```

File: 13_7.sql (role privileges)

```
SELECT      owner || '.' || table_name object,
            privilege what_granted, grantable, grantee
FROM        dba_tab_privs
WHERE       NOT EXISTS
(SELECT     'x'
FROM        dba_users
WHERE       username = grantee)
AND         privilege =  'EXECUTE'
ORDER BY    1,2,3;
```

Output (13_7.sql)

```
OBJECT                     WHAT_GRANTED      GRA GRANTEE
-------------------------- ----------------- --- -------
SYS.DBMS_APPLICATION_INFO  EXECUTE           NO  PUBLIC
SYS.DBMS_DDL               EXECUTE           NO  PUBLIC
SYS.DBMS_DESCRIBE          EXECUTE           NO  PUBLIC
SYS.DBMS_OUTPUT            EXECUTE           NO  PUBLIC
SYS.DBMS_SPACE             EXECUTE           NO  PUBLIC
SYS.DBMS_SQL               EXECUTE           NO  PUBLIC
```

The preceding queries need to be executed under a schema that has access to the DBA_* views.

TIP
You do not have to specify the names of the columns in an ORDER BY clause. You can reference the number position in the SELECT list of the columns, as shown in the previous queries.

For more details on privilege usage and security of PL/SQL objects, refer to Chapter 10.

Build Online Help for All PL/SQL Data Dictionary Information

Remembering the use of every view and column in the data dictionary is difficult, so having online help for view definitions and columns is important. For every Oracle data dictionary view created, Oracle provides a comment for the view and every column within the view. All comments are stored in the database and are accessible through the USER_TAB_COMMENTS (ALL_TAB_COMMENTS and DBA_TAB_COMMENTS) and USER_COL_COMMENTS (ALL_COL_COMMENTS and DBA_COL_COMMENTS) views. You can use the information contained in this online reference tool by using the following script to query the contents of a data dictionary view or column in that view:

File: 13_8.sql

```
SELECT      table_name, comments
FROM        all_tab_comments
WHERE       table_name = UPPER('&&table_name');
SELECT      column_name, comments
FROM        all_col_comments
WHERE       table_name = UPPER('&&table_name');
UNDEFINE table_name
```

Output (13_8.sql)

```
TABLE_NAME                           COMMENTS
----------------------------------   ----------------------------
USER_OBJECTS                         Objects owned by the user

COLUMN_NAME                          COMMENTS
----------------------------------   ----------------------------
OBJECT_NAME                          Name of the object
OBJECT_ID                            Object number of the object
OBJECT_TYPE                          Type of the object
CREATED                              Timestamp for the creation of
                                     the object
LAST_DDL_TIME                        Timestamp for the last DDL
                                     change (including GRANT and REVOKE)
                                     to the object
TIMESTAMP                            Timestamp for the specification
                                     of the object
STATUS                               Status of the object
```

The 13_8.sql file can be updated to allow for a search of the comments, if the table is unknown, by adding an additional predicate clause as shown in the following:

```
AND    UPPER(comments) LIKE '%CREAT%'
```

The method of commenting your table and view definitions can and should be extended to all tables created in any application. This can be accomplished with the following commands:

```
COMMENT ON TABLE s_customer IS
  'Customer table that stores customer related information';
COMMENT ON COLUMN s_customer.customer_id IS
  'Unique identifier for each customer';
```

The USER_TAB_COLUMNS and USER_COL_COMMENTS views contain information on all tables and columns in the database. To limit the online help to the data dictionary and overall view level comments, Oracle provides an additional view named DICTIONARY (or DICT synonym). The DICTIONARY view can be used to provide a brief description of every data dictionary view or to provide a facility to pinpoint the view name of interest by searching the contents of this view, as shown in the following query.

File: 13_9.sql

```
SELECT      *
FROM        DICTIONARY
WHERE       table_name LIKE '%DEPEND%';
```

Output (13_9.sql)

```
TABLE_NAME               COMMENTS
------------------------ ----------------------------------------
ALL_DEPENDENCIES         Dependencies to and from objects accessible
                         to the user
USER_DEPENDENCIES        Dependencies to and from a users objects
```

This script was executed from a user who did not have access to the DBA_* views; therefore the DBA_DEPENDENCIES view was not returned.

View Object Creation and Modification Timestamps

While developing or enhancing applications, the developer or DBA *must* be able to retrace specific events in the development life cycle, specifically when an object was last created or modified. Oracle has built-in date/time stamping for some of the objects in the database. Unfortunately, they only provide the creation and last modification dates, and not an audit trail of all the modification dates. The USER_OBJECTS view stores the creation date and last modification date for every object in the database. To view this information, run the following query:

File: 13_10.sql

```
SELECT      object_name, object_type,
            TO_CHAR(created, 'MM/DD/YY HH24:MI:SS') created,
            TO_CHAR(last_ddl_time, 'MM/DD/YY HH24:MI:SS') updated
FROM        dba_objects
WHERE       object_type IN ('PACKAGE','PACKAGE BODY', 'PROCEDURE',
                            'FUNCTION', 'TRIGGER')
AND         OWNER       = 'PLSQL_USER'
ORDER BY    object_name;
```

Output (13_10.sql)

```
OBJECT_NAME     OBJECT_TYPE     CREATED             UPDATED
--------------- --------------- ------------------- -------------------
A               PROCEDURE       05/07/99 16:57:31   05/24/99 09:57:06
ABC1            PROCEDURE       03/07/99 07:25:31   05/24/99 09:58:04
AU_INVENTORY    TRIGGER         04/19/99 09:44:06   05/26/99 09:17:25
DATE_RANGE      FUNCTION        03/13/99 14:13:26   05/24/99 09:57:59
DEPENDENCY_MAP  PACKAGE         05/07/99 13:15:17   05/24/99 09:57:05
DEPENDENCY_MAP  PACKAGE BODY    05/07/99 13:15:25   05/24/99 09:57:11
PIN_OBJECTS     PROCEDURE       05/08/99 07:08:25   05/24/99 09:57:48
```

This script limits the objects to the stored PL/SQL objects only. If the predicate clause was eliminated, all the objects would be returned.

Verify All PL/SQL Objects Are Valid upon Creation or Modification

Developers and DBAs must ensure all stored PL/SQL objects are compiled successfully when any object is created or modified. If this is not verified, your system may not function properly. This can be damaging to an environment and must be corrected immediately.

When a stored PL/SQL object is created, Oracle inserts the source code into the database and attempts to compile the source code. If the compilation is successful, the status is set to VALID. When compilation is performed on an existing stored PL/SQL object referenced by another stored PL/SQL object, the stored object that references the object becomes INVALID. If any object becomes INVALID in this manner, it should be recompiled immediately.

The following script demonstrates the method of determining which PL/SQL objects are INVALID:

File: 13_11.sql

```
SELECT    object_type, object_name, status, created, last_ddl_time
FROM      user_objects
WHERE     object_type IN ('PROCEDURE', 'FUNCTION', 'PACKAGE',
                          'PACKAGE BODY', 'TRIGGER')
AND       status = 'INVALID';
```

TIP
To ensure an uninterrupted system, the following guidelines should be integrated as a standard into your Oracle production environment:
   All PL/SQL stored object creations and modifications are performed during off-hours.
   After creating any database object, the 13_11.sql script file must be executed and return no records.

The impact of not following these guidelines is directly related to the size and architecture of your environment, specifically centering around the number of users, volume of transactions, and stored PL/SQL object design and configuration. The larger your system, the more chance for locking and contention related problems for compiling PL/SQL objects. The larger your application, the larger number of PL/SQL stored objects and object dependencies and, thus, the larger problems with dependent object recompilation. The main impact can be measured in downtime (lost revenue) and user frustration, which is a common result of not following the previous guidelines.

Re-create PL/SQL Source Code from the Database

In any environment, a backup mechanism and version control standard must be implemented. No matter how encompassing these mechanisms and standards may be, they are only as effective as their enforcement. Inevitably, no matter what your environment configuration, a time will come when the latest version of a source code module is indeterminate: It was not checked back into the version control system and several modifications were made and deployed in production; two developers somehow have the same file and have both made changes and deployed them into production; a developer modified the production source code and made changes that were deployed into production, but is not sure what copy of the file in their possession is the latest version. In these and other similar cases, the question always becomes "Where is the latest version of the source code?" Oracle inserts all stored PL/SQL object source code in the database—namely in the data dictionary—for each new version of the object; therefore, the latest production version of source code can always be found in the database, and, thus, re-created if necessary.

The USER_SOURCE (ALL_SOURCE, DBA_SOURCE) and USER_TRIGGERS (ALL_TRIGGERS, DBA_TRIGGERS) views can be used to re-create the source code files. The following scripts enable you to re-create stored PL/SQL objects, namely package specifications, package bodies, procedures, functions, and database triggers.

All these objects are re-created from the DBA_SOURCE view with the exception of database triggers because this source code is seen through the DBA_TRIGGERS view.

These script files do not create an output file in tabular format, but rather an output file that contains the CREATE statements for each object. These output files can serve as a backup of the stored PL/SQL objects or used to create the stored PL/SQL objects in another environment for analysis or testing needs.

Each script file below contains the following steps to re-create the source code:

1. Prompts for user input, namely, the schema owner of the objects and tablespace location for temporary table creation

2. Creates a temporary table to be used in the output file creation

3. Queries the DBA_SOURCE or DBA_TRIGGERS view and inserts the information into the temporary table

4. Queries the temporary table and spools to an output file once all records are inserted into the temporary table

5. Drops the temporary table

To execute these scripts, the user must have access to the DBA_* views. Access can be granted as outlined in an earlier section in this chapter, "Provide Correct Access to the PL/SQL Data Dictionary." The USER_* and ALL_* views can also be used for the source code re-creation.

File: 13_12.sql (packages, procedures, and functions)

```
SET TERMOUT ON
PROMPT Generating script to create:
PROMPT packages, procedures and functions...
PROMPT
DEFINE tablespace = &&tablespace
DEFINE owner = &&owner
PROMPT
SET TERMOUT OFF
SPOOL 13_12.log
CREATE TABLE migrate_procedures
(statement_sequence NUMBER NOT NULL,
 statement_text     VARCHAR2(2000))
TABLESPACE &&tablespace
STORAGE (INITIAL 1M NEXT 1M PCTINCREASE 0);
DECLARE
   lv_sequence_num PLS_INTEGER := 0;
   CURSOR cur_source IS
      SELECT  name, type, line, text
      FROM    dba_source
      WHERE   owner = UPPER('&&owner')
      AND     type IN ('PACKAGE', 'PACKAGE BODY',
                       'PROCEDURE', 'FUNCTION')
      ORDER BY DECODE(type, 'FUNCTION', '2', 'PROCEDURE', '3',
                     'PACKAGE', '1' || name || 'PA',
                     '1' || name || 'PB'), name, line;
BEGIN
   FOR cur_source_rec IN cur_source LOOP
      IF cur_source_rec.line = 1 THEN
         IF lv_sequence_num != 0 THEN
            lv_sequence_num := lv_sequence_num + 1;
            INSERT INTO migrate_procedures
            (statement_sequence, statement_text)
             VALUES
            (lv_sequence_num, '/');
         END IF;
```

```
           lv_sequence_num := lv_sequence_num + 1;
           INSERT INTO migrate_procedures
           (statement_sequence, statement_text)
           VALUES
           (lv_sequence_num, 'CREATE OR REPLACE ' ||
            cur_source_rec.text);
       ELSE
           lv_sequence_num := lv_sequence_num + 1;
           INSERT INTO migrate_procedures
           (statement_sequence, statement_text)
            VALUES
           (lv_sequence_num, cur_source_rec.text);
       END IF;
    END LOOP;
    lv_sequence_num := lv_sequence_num + 1;
    INSERT INTO migrate_procedures
    (statement_sequence, statement_text)
    VALUES
    (lv_sequence_num, '/');
EXCEPTION
    WHEN OTHERS THEN
       DBMS_OUTPUT.PUT_LINE('Program Error-Begin Error Message.');
       DBMS_OUTPUT.PUT_LINE(SQLERRM);
       RAISE_APPLICATION_ERROR(-20000, 'End of error message');
END;
/
SPOOL OFF
SET HEADING OFF
SET PAGESIZE 0
SET FEEDBACK OFF
SPOOL 13_12.lis
SELECT    statement_text
FROM      migrate_procedures
ORDER BY statement_sequence;
SPOOL OFF
DROP TABLE migrate_procedures;
UNDEFINE tablespace
UNDEFINE owner
```

File: 13_13.sql (database triggers)

```
SET TERMOUT ON
SET LONG 2000
PROMPT Generating script to create database triggers...
PROMPT
DEFINE tablespace = &&tablespace
DEFINE owner = &&owner
```

```
PROMPT
SET TERMOUT OFF
SPOOL 13_13.log
CREATE TABLE migrate_triggers
(statement_sequence NUMBER NOT NULL,
 statement_text     LONG)
TABLESPACE &&tablespace
STORAGE (INITIAL 1M NEXT 1M PCTINCREASE 0);
DECLARE
   lv_sequence_num  PLS_INTEGER := 0;
   CURSOR cur_triggers IS
      SELECT trigger_name, trigger_type, triggering_event,
             table_name, referencing_names, when_clause,
             trigger_body
      FROM   dba_triggers
      WHERE  table_owner = UPPER('&&owner')
      ORDER BY trigger_name;
BEGIN
   FOR cur_triggers_rec IN cur_triggers LOOP
      lv_sequence_num := lv_sequence_num + 1;
      INSERT INTO migrate_triggers
      (statement_sequence, statement_text)
      VALUES
      (lv_sequence_num, 'CREATE OR REPLACE TRIGGER ' ||
      cur_triggers_rec.trigger_name);
      lv_sequence_num := lv_sequence_num + 1;
      IF cur_triggers_rec.trigger_type LIKE 'BEFORE%' THEN
         INSERT INTO migrate_triggers
         (statement_sequence, statement_text)
         VALUES
         (lv_sequence_num, 'BEFORE ' ||
         cur_triggers_rec.triggering_event);
      ELSE
         INSERT INTO migrate_triggers
         (statement_sequence, statement_text)
         VALUES
         (lv_sequence_num, 'AFTER ' ||
         cur_triggers_rec.triggering_event);
      END IF;
      lv_sequence_num := lv_sequence_num + 1;
      INSERT INTO migrate_triggers
      (statement_sequence, statement_text)
      VALUES
      (lv_sequence_num, 'ON ' ||
      cur_triggers_rec.table_name);
      lv_sequence_num := lv_sequence_num + 1;
      INSERT INTO migrate_triggers
      (statement_sequence, statement_text)
```

```
      VALUES
       (lv_sequence_num, cur_triggers_rec.referencing_names);
      IF cur_triggers_rec.trigger_type LIKE '%EACH ROW' THEN
         lv_sequence_num := lv_sequence_num + 1;
         INSERT INTO migrate_triggers
         (statement_sequence, statement_text)
         VALUES
         (lv_sequence_num, 'FOR EACH ROW');
      END IF;
      IF cur_triggers_rec.when_clause IS NOT NULL THEN
         lv_sequence_num := lv_sequence_num + 1;
         INSERT INTO migrate_triggers
         (statement_sequence, statement_text)
         VALUES
         (lv_sequence_num, 'WHEN (' ||
         cur_triggers_rec.when_clause || ')');
      END IF;
      lv_sequence_num := lv_sequence_num + 1;
      INSERT INTO migrate_triggers
      (statement_sequence, statement_text)
      VALUES
      (lv_sequence_num, cur_triggers_rec.trigger_body);
      lv_sequence_num := lv_sequence_num + 1;
      INSERT INTO migrate_triggers
      (statement_sequence, statement_text)
      VALUES
      (lv_sequence_num, '/');
   END LOOP;
EXCEPTION
   WHEN OTHERS THEN
      DBMS_OUTPUT.PUT_LINE('Program Error-Begin Error Message.');
      DBMS_OUTPUT.PUT_LINE(SQLERRM);
      RAISE_APPLICATION_ERROR(-20000, 'End of error message');
END;
/
SPOOL OFF
SET HEADING OFF
SET PAGESIZE 0
SET FEEDBACK OFF
SPOOL 13_13.lis
SELECT  Statement_Text
FROM    migrate_triggers
ORDER BY Statement_Sequence;
SPOOL OFF
DROP TABLE migrate_triggers;
UNDEFINE tablespace
UNDEFINE owner
```

Re-creating PL/SQL Source Code

The output for the DBA_SOURCE view is written to 13_12.lis, and the output for the DBA_TRIGGERS view is written to 13_13.lis. These scripts can be used to create a backup of source code by setting them up in a batch facility to execute nightly or at any other interval.

TIP
Developers should always remember that the latest version of stored PL/SQL program units is stored in the database. If there is ever any confusion as to what is the latest source code in production, retrieve it from the database.

Providing Capability to Enable/Disable Database Triggers

Provide Capability to Enable/Disable Database Triggers

Database triggers can be a nightmare for developers and DBAs if they are not designed and implemented properly. The key to remember is they are implicitly executed and are associated with a DML (INSERT, UPDATE, and DELETE) operation on a specific database table. Database triggers are an integral component to the overall functionality and processing of a system. Once a database trigger is created and compiled successfully, it will always execute implicitly (assuming the status, set to ENABLED). But there are times—such as data loading or some nightly processing—that may introduce a need to turn off these triggers so the processing performed in the trigger is not executed. To turn off a database trigger, the trigger must be DISABLED. In many cases, forgetting to turn off triggers can be devastating and can possibly corrupt data. Likewise, forgetting to turn on triggers can be devastating and can possibly corrupt data.

A database trigger can be disabled at any time by executing the following command:

```
ALTER TRIGGER before_insert_customer DISABLE;
```

The following command allows you to disable all the triggers on a table:

```
ALTER TABLE s_customer DISABLE ALL TRIGGERS;
```

To enable database triggers, the previous two commands would be modified to change DISABLE to ENABLE. To disable all triggers under a schema, the following script can be used to build a disable script dynamically:

File: 13_14.sql

```
SET HEADING OFF
SET FEEDBACK OFF
SET PAGESIZE 0
SELECT    'ALTER TRIGGER ' || trigger_name || ' DISABLE;'
FROM      user_triggers
ORDER BY table_name;
```

Output (13_14.sql)

```
ALTER TRIGGER BEFORE_INSERT_CUSTOMER DISABLE;
ALTER TRIGGER BEFORE_UPDATE_CUSTOMER DISABLE;
```

The preceding script can be modified to change the word DISABLE to ENABLE and re-executed to dynamically build an enable script. The 13_14.sql script can also be modified to disable all triggers by table, as shown in the following script:

File: 13_15.sql

```
SET HEADING OFF
SET FEEDBACK OFF
SET PAGESIZE 0
SELECT    'ALTER TABLE ' || table_name || ' DISABLE ALL TRIGGERS;'
FROM      user_tables a
WHERE     EXISTS
(SELECT   'X'
FROM      user_triggers
WHERE     table_name = a.table_name)
ORDER BY table_name;
```

Output (13_15.sql)

```
ALTER TABLE S_CUSTOMER DISABLE ALL TRIGGERS;
```

Providing Capability to
Enable/Disable Database Triggers

The following script can be used to identify all triggers in your schema and/or system, the details of the triggers, what table they are on, what type of trigger they are, when they fire, and whether they are enabled.

File: 13_16.sql

```
SELECT     table_name, trigger_name, trigger_type type,
           triggering_event event, status
FROM       user_triggers
ORDER BY   table_name;
```

Output (13_16.sql)

```
TABLE_NAME  TRIGGER_NAME            TYPE             EVENT    STATUS
----------  ----------------------  ---------------  -------  -------
S_CUSTOMER  BEFORE_INSERT_CUSTOMER  BEFORE EACH ROW  INSERT   ENABLED
S_CUSTOMER  BEFORE_UPDATE_CUSTOMER  BEFORE EACH ROW  UPDATE   ENABLED
```

TIP
Prior to version 7.3 of Oracle (version 2.3 of PL/SQL), triggers were not stored in compiled format. This means every time the trigger was executed, the trigger was compiled and loaded into memory. This caused additional overhead when using database triggers. Therefore, many people kept certain functions outside of database triggers. If you have implemented Oracle 7.3 or subsequent releases, this consideration should be re-examined since the overhead is radically reduced.

Provide a Facility to Identify All Stored PL/SQL Object Errors

If you are a developer creating multiple stored PL/SQL program units, being able to retrieve the errors encountered for any objects that did not compile successfully is essential. Unsuccessful compilations log errors to the data dictionary ERROR$ table and can be viewed through the USER_ERRORS (ALL_ERRORS, DBA_ERRORS) view. For more information on the contents of this view, see the section, "Know the

Contents of the PL/SQL Data Dictionary." This view can return multiple errors for a single object with the line number of the error included. The line number corresponds to the line number in the USER_SOURCE view. The following query returns the errors in the USER_ERRORS view:

File: 13_17.sql

```
COLUMN    text FORMAT a30 word_wrapped
SELECT    name, type, line, text
FROM      user_errors
ORDER BY  name, type, sequence;
```

Output (13_17.sql)

```
NAME                         TYPE       LINE TEXT
---------------------------- ---------- ---- ----------------------------------
BEFORE_INSERT_CUSTOMER TRIGGER            2 PLS-00103: Encountered the
                                            symbol "=" when expecting one
                                            of the following:
                                            := . ( @ % ; indicator
                                            The symbol ":= was inserted
                                            before "=" to continue.
BEFORE_UPDATE_CUSTOMER TRIGGER            2 PLS-00201: identifier
                                            'NEW.DATE_MODIFIED' must be
                                            declared
BEFORE_UPDATE_CUSTOMER TRIGGER            2 PL/SQL: Statement ignored
```

TIP

The word_wrapped attribute on the COLUMN command in this script causes line breaks to occur on words, rather than splitting words.

TIP

Any stored PL/SQL objects with records in the USER_ERRORS view will have a status in the USER_OBJECTS view of INVALID. The reverse is not always true; do not rely on the USER_ERRORS view to determine objects that are not compiled; instead, refer to the USER_OBJECTS view to be sure.

Identifying All Stored PL/SQL Object Errors

The SHOW ERRORS command will return the errors encountered during the latest object compilation. If you are compiling multiple objects, therefore, only the last object's errors will be returned. To see all the errors for all objects compiled, the USER_ERRORS view must be used. The SHOW ERRORS is also session specific, so if you leave the session and return, the SHOW ERRORS command will not show you any errors previously encountered.

Develop Search Engines for the PL/SQL Object Source Code

How many times have you needed to know the location of a source code segment? More specifically, how many times have you needed to know the package or procedure in which the source code segment resides, or the package that contains a procedure or function? The need to locate certain modules or segments of code increases as your application source code grows and more developers are added to the development team. All these questions can be answered by building queries that allow for searching the data dictionary view that stores the source code, namely the USER_SOURCE view.

The following query shows three methods of searching the USER_SOURCE view to answer some of the previous questions:

File: 13_18.sql (procedure location: what package is that in?)

```
SELECT    DISTINCT name, type
FROM      all_source
WHERE     UPPER(text) LIKE '%SUBMIT%';
```

Output (13_18.sql)

```
NAME                          TYPE
----------------------------  ------------
DBMS_IJOB                     PACKAGE
DBMS_IJOB                     PACKAGE BODY
DBMS_IREFRESH                 PACKAGE
DBMS_IREFRESH                 PACKAGE BODY
DBMS_JOB                      PACKAGE
DBMS_JOB                      PACKAGE BODY
```

File: 13_19.sql (code logic: where is that segment of code or comment?)

```
COLUMN    text    FORMAT    a30 word_wrapped
SELECT    name, type, text
FROM      all_source
WHERE     UPPER(text) LIKE '%FREE BLOCKS%';
```

Output (13_19.sql)

```
NAME              TYPE       TEXT
----------------  ---------  ------------------------------
DBMS_SPACE        PACKAGE    --  Returns information about
                             free blocks in an object
                             (table, index,
DBMS_SPACE        PACKAGE    --     maximum number of free
                             blocks to read
DBMS_SPACE        PACKAGE    --     count of free blocks for
                             the specified group
```

File: 13_20.sql (line location: display the source code range of lines of a program unit)

```
COLUMN    text    FORMAT    a78
SELECT    text
FROM      all_source
WHERE     name = UPPER('&name')
AND       type = UPPER('&type')
AND       line BETWEEN &starting_line AND &ending_line;
```

Output (13_20.sql)

```
TEXT
----------------------------------------------------------------
PACKAGE dbms_job IS
  -- Parameters are:
  --
```

```
-- JOB is the number of the job being executed.
-- WHAT is the PL/SQL procedure to execute.
--   The job must always be a single call to a procedure. The
--     routine may take any number of hardcoded parameters.
--     Special parameter values recognized are:
--        job:    an in parameter, the number of the current job
```

The last query prompts for four values and these are listed below with the values entered for the output that was previously returned.

Object Name:	dbms_job
Object Type:	package
Starting Line:	1
Ending Line:	10

The database trigger source code is more difficult to search because the source code is stored in a column of datatype LONG. This eliminates the same method of searching this source code because no functions can be performed on LONG columns. To deploy the same searching mechanism as previously, the source code would be SELECTed into a PL/SQL VARCHAR2 column and this variable would have to be searched with PL/SQL functions. This method is detailed in Chapter 4.

Develop an Impact Analysis Facility for Database Objects

No matter what system is developed, there will be a need for change at some point, whether that change is due to a new or changing business need or an enhancement of a process. One of the critical steps in defining the magnitude of change to a system is to perform an impact analysis. Since Oracle determines object dependencies at object creation time and stores this information in the data dictionary, a means exists to analyze this information through the USER_DEPENDENCIES (ALL_DEPENDENCIES, DBA_DEPENDENCIES) view. If you have an object that will change, the following query will locate all the stored PL/SQL objects that depend on this object and need to be reviewed.

File: 13_21.sql

```
SELECT    name, type
FROM      user_dependencies
WHERE     referenced_name = UPPER('&object_name')
```

```
AND        referenced_type = UPPER('&object_type')
ORDER BY   name;
```

Output (13_21.sql: executed under SYS and entered object_name = dbms_standard and object_type = package)

```
NAME                      TYPE
----------------------    --------------
DBMS_ALERT                PACKAGE BODY
DBMS_DDL                  PACKAGE BODY
DBMS_DESCRIBE             PACKAGE BODY
DBMS_LOCK                 PACKAGE BODY
DBMS_OUTPUT               PACKAGE BODY
DBMS_SHARED_POOL          PACKAGE BODY
DBMS_SNAPSHOT             PACKAGE BODY
DBMS_UTILITY              PACKAGE BODY
```

For documentation purposes, the preceding script can be slightly modified to create a dependency mapping of all the objects in your architecture as shown in the following script:

File: 13_22.sql

```
BREAK ON    r_name SKIP 1
SET HEADING OFF
SELECT   DECODE(referenced_type, 'NON-EXISTENT', '.....',
         referenced_type) || ' ' || referenced_owner ||
         '.' || referenced_name r_name, '    is referenced by: ' ||
         type || ' ' || owner || '.' || name name,
         '     Referenced Link: ' || DECODE(referenced_link_name,
         NULL, 'none', referenced_link_name) r_link
FROM     dba_dependencies
WHERE    owner NOT IN ('SYS', 'SYSTEM')
ORDER BY 1,2;
```

Output (13_22.sql)

```
TABLE PLSQL_USER.S_CUSTOMER
    is referenced by: TRIGGER PLSQL_USER.BEFORE_INSERT_CUSTOMER
    Referenced Link: none
```

```
is referenced by: TRIGGER PLSQL_USER.BEFORE_UPDATE_CUSTOMER
Referenced Link: none
```

Each of the dependency mappings is helpful for impact analysis. The previous dependency mapping is limited to one level. To obtain a complete multilevel dependency hierarchy mapping, refer to Chapter 9.

Determine the Object Size Loaded into Memory

Database performance is one of the critical responsibilities of a DBA, and one of the key components is the database configuration—specifically when it comes to memory and the Shared Global Area (SGA). The Shared Pool (a memory structure in the SGA) is one of the top three memory structures considered in determining proper memory sizing and can severely impact the overall performance of a database. Stored PL/SQL objects that are compiled and executed are cached in the Shared Pool. The amount of memory is dependent on the size of the stored PL/SQL object(s). Oracle stores the size of memory (in bytes) required for certain operations for each stored object in the USER_OBJECT_SIZE (ALL_USER_OBJECT_SIZE, DBA_OBJECT_SIZE) view. The following query displays the memory required by each stored object for different operations on the PL/SQL object:

File: 13_23.sql

```
COLUMN    source_size FORMAT 999,999
COLUMN    parsed_size FORMAT 999,999
COLUMN    code_size   FORMAT 999,999
SELECT    name, type, source_size, parsed_size, code_size
FROM      user_object_size
ORDER BY  type, name;
```

Output (13_23.sql)

NAME	TYPE	SOURCE_SIZE	PARSED_SIZE	CODE_SIZE
DBMS_ALERT	PACKAGE	12,960	1,191	527
DBMS_APPLICATION_INFO	PACKAGE	2,905	753	347
DBMS_DDL	PACKAGE	2,518	741	194
DBMS_DESCRIBE	PACKAGE	8,894	1,131	211

The previous query lists three memory sizes loaded into memory based on the object use as outlined here:

source_size	Size loaded when the object is compiled
code_size	Size loaded when the object is being executed
parsed_size	Size loaded when another object is being compiled that references the object

Refer to Chapter 9 for a more detailed explanation of PL/SQL memory allocation and usage.

Use Dynamic SQL on the Data Dictionary to Build DDL Scripts

Creating or re-creating DDL statements to manipulate stored database objects is always necessary. This can be accomplished by typing the statements in manually or by taking advantage of dynamic SQL to streamline the creation of these statements. Dynamic SQL is nothing more than writing SELECT statements that embed constant text to every record returned to create DDL statements as output versus a standard tabular report as output. This method uses the data dictionary views for the information and can be an extremely powerful tool when several DDL statements need to be re-created. This method also reduces the margin for typographical errors.

Several dynamic SQL examples are illustrated in earlier sections of this chapter: "Re-create PL/SQL Source Code from the Database" and "Provide Capability to Enable/Disable Database Triggers."

The following is a set of scripts that further exemplify the usefulness of dynamic SQL :

File: 13_24.sql (drop all stored PL/SQL objects under a schema)

```
SET HEADING OFF
SET FEEDBACK OFF
SET PAGESIZE 0
SPOOL 13_24.log
SELECT    'DROP ' || object_type || ' ' || object_name || ';'
FROM      user_objects
WHERE     object_type IN ('PACKAGE','PACKAGE BODY','PROCEDURE',
```

```
                                'FUNCTION','TRIGGER')
ORDER BY  object_type;
SPOOL OFF
```

Output (13_24.sql)

```
DROP PROCEDURE LOG_EXTENTS;
DROP PROCEDURE VALIDATE_TITLE;
```

File: 13_25.sql (recompile all stored PL/SQL objects under a schema)

```
SET HEADING OFF
SET FEEDBACK OFF
SET PAGESIZE 0
SPOOL 13_25.log
SELECT      'ALTER ' || DECODE(object_type, 'PACKAGE
            BODY','PACKAGE',object_type) || '_' || object_name ||
            DECODE(object_type,'PACKAGE BODY','_COMPILE BODY;',
            '_COMPILE;')
FROM        user_objects
WHERE       object_type IN ('PACKAGE','PACKAGE BODY','PROCEDURE',
                        'FUNCTION','TRIGGER')
ORDER BY  object_type;
SPOOL OFF
```

Output (13_25.sql)

```
ALTER PROCEDURE ADJUST_SALARY COMPILE;
ALTER TRIGGER BEFORE_INSERT_CUSTOMER COMPILE;
ALTER TRIGGER BEFORE_UPDATE_CUSTOMER COMPILE;
```

File: 13_26.sql (granting access to all stored PL/SQL objects under a schema; prompts for schema or role)

```
SET HEADING OFF
SET FEEDBACK OFF
SET PAGESIZE 0
SPOOL 13_26.log
SELECT      'GRANT EXECUTE ON ' || object_name || ' TO ' ||
            UPPER('&user_role') || ';'
FROM        user_objects
WHERE       object_type IN ('PACKAGE','PROCEDURE','FUNCTION')
ORDER BY object_type, object_name;
SPOOL OFF
```

Output (13_26.sql: entered user_role=temp)

```
GRANT EXECUTE ON ADJUST_SALARY to TEMP;
GRANT EXECUTE ON LOG_EXTENTS to TEMP;
```

File: 13_27.sql (create public synonym for all stored PL/SQL objects under a schema)

```
SET HEADING OFF
SET FEEDBACK OFF
SET PAGESIZE 0
SPOOL 13_27.log
SELECT    'CREATE PUBLIC SYNONYM ' || object_name || ' FOR ' ||
          object_name || ';'
FROM      user_objects
WHERE     object_type IN ('PACKAGE','PROCEDURE','FUNCTION')
ORDER BY object_type, object_name;
SPOOL OFF
```

Output (13_27.sql)

```
CREATE PUBLIC SYNONYM ADJUST_SALARY FOR ADJUST_SALARY;
CREATE PUBLIC SYNONYM LOG_EXTENTS FOR LOG_EXTENTS;
```

Take advantage of using the data dictionary to create DDL statements. This is also extremely helpful when you are maintaining separate operating system SQL scripts for different objects creations and you are in question if the scripts still contain the latest modifications made to the database.

Summary

In this chapter, we explored the data dictionary and examined this extremely powerful tool that Oracle has provided for developers and DBAs. The key is to understand the details of the data dictionary to ensure you use this tool to its fullest extent. The PL/SQL data dictionary creation was outlined, and techniques for optimizing the storage of these objects were highlighted, along with the script files executed upon database creation. The seven main PL/SQL data dictionary views were reviewed and key information related to accessing the data dictionary and to executing stored PL/SQL objects was highlighted. The chapter ended with a variety of tips centered around taking advantage of the PL/SQL data dictionary information and applying various techniques that can be of great value to both developers and DBAs.

Building DDL Scripts

Far too often, developers and DBAs overlook the power of using the data dictionary information. Developers and DBAs need to harness this power and realize the potential benefits. This chapter has only targeted a small segment of the data dictionary and exemplifies the power that can be realized from this information. Use of the data dictionary should become an integral tool in your daily development and/or administration activities. And, remember, the data dictionary is another application.

Tips Review

- Read the Oracle creation SQL file comments to gain valuable insight on the data dictionary tables and views, and Oracle supplied packages not documented elsewhere. Information can also be found by querying the USER_SOURCE view, specifically the Oracle supplied package specifications.

- Most of the Oracle creation files have been enhanced to include the new or enhanced features found in Oracle8 and Oracle8i. If you have implemented or are upgrading to Oracle8 or Oracle8i, it's worth your time to re-examine these files.

- When Oracle 7.3 was released, the name of the init_sql_file parameter was changed to _init_sql_file.

- Any values in the ksppinm column of the X$KSPPI table preceded by a "_" are not viewable in the V$PARAMETER view. While no problem exists with modifying the _init_sql_file parameter, changing most of the other parameters that are not viewable in the V$PARAMETER view is not recommended. Failure to follow this guideline could result in your database crashing or being severely damaged.

- Modify the storage parameters in the sql.bsq file as necessary based on your volume of stored PL/SQL objects to eliminate fragmentation. Make sure a backup copy of the sql.bsq file is created prior to modification. This operation should only be performed by an experienced DBA. Consult Oracle prior to making any modifications to the sql.bsq file.

- When analyzing table and index sizing, do not size the objects according to the current size; instead, examine the growth and determine a size to accommodate additional growth.

- When an error during compilation is encountered, the error specifies the line number of the error in the source code. This line number corresponds to the line of the source code in the USER_SOURCE view, not the line in the script file from which the PL/SQL object was created.

- The "WITH GRANT OPTION" can be used on most SQL commands that pertain to system privileges. It extends the privilege granted to allow the granted user or role the ability to grant this privilege to others.

- You do not have to specify the names of the columns in an ORDER BY clause. You can reference the number position in the SELECT list of the columns.

- To ensure an uninterrupted system, the following guidelines should be integrated as a standard into your Oracle production environment:

  - All PL/SQL stored object creations and modifications are performed during off-hours.

  - After creating any database object, the invalid (13_11.sql) script file must be executed and return no records.

- Developers should always remember that the latest version of stored PL/SQL program units is stored in the database. If there is ever any confusion as to what is the latest source code in production, retrieve it from the database.

- Prior to version 7.3 of Oracle (version 2.3 of PL/SQL), triggers were not stored in compiled format. This means every time the trigger was executed, the trigger was compiled and loaded into memory. This caused additional overhead when using database triggers. Therefore, many people kept certain functions outside of database triggers. If you have implemented Oracle 7.3 or subsequent releases, this consideration should be re-examined since the overhead is radically reduced.

- The word_wrapped attribute on the COLUMN command causes line breaks to occur on words, rather than splitting words.

- Any stored PL/SQL objects with records in the USER_ERRORS view will have a status in the USER_OBJECTS view of INVALID. The reverse is not always true; do not rely on the USER_ERRORS view to determine objects that are not compiled; instead, refer to the USER_OBJECTS view to be sure.

Building DDL Scripts

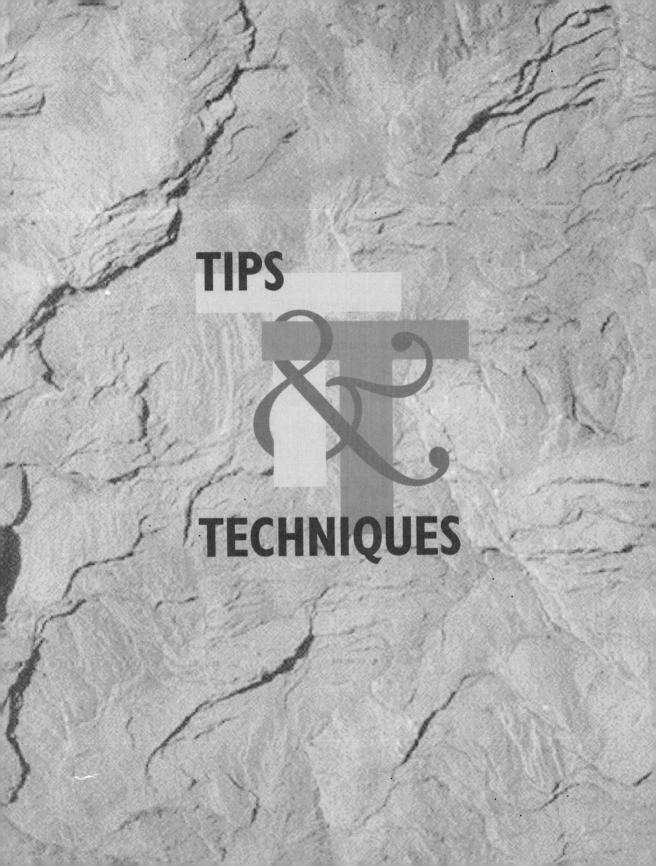

TIPS & TECHNIQUES

CHAPTER
14

Exploring PL/SQL
Product Integration
(Developer and DBA)

P L/SQL is not only a critical component on the database server; it also is the standard language and a fundamental element of any successfully developed and deployed application. Development products continue to advance at a rapid pace and, with each new release, come new and robust advances in the PL/SQL language. Likewise, with each new release, the role of PL/SQL in the overall product scheme of Oracle continues to increase in scope. Therefore, an expertise in PL/SQL has become essential. In addition, it is extremely important to understand the product integration of PL/SQL as it relates to each product, whether from Oracle or a third party.

As the Oracle development tools have advanced, so has the complexity of applications development. SQL*Forms 3.0, the prior release and nongraphical Forms product that is now part of the Oracle Developer product, was the first Oracle development tool to integrate PL/SQL into the development environment. This was only the start. PL/SQL is now integrated in Oracle Developer, Oracle Designer, and Oracle Discoverer products, previously named Developer 2000, Designer 2000, and Discoverer 2000, respectively. Other Oracle products and third-party products are not as tightly integrated, but they rely on and support the use of PL/SQL in its products.

This chapter explores the PL/SQL role and integration in these development products. It highlights the supplied PL/SQL components in these products and communication between these products and the database server. The Oracle Developer product is covered in more detail—specifically the Forms module—to provide further insight into the integration and role of PL/SQL in these products.

The goal of this chapter is to highlight the integration of PL/SQL in development products and outline the expansive realm of PL/SQL in the client-side and sever-side architecture. This chapter covers the following tips and techniques to explain the integration of PL/SQL in the Oracle development products and environment:

- Review the evolution of PL/SQL product integration

- Understand the integration of PL/SQL in the product set

- Use and understand the built-in PL/SQL packages in Oracle Developer

- Determine the best location for PL/SQL source code

- Understand PL/SQL program unit name resolution

- Share PL/SQL variables between forms

- Use explicit cursors versus implicit cursors

- Build communication between forms and stored PL/SQL program units

- Check the database error when responding to a form error

- Use the ON-ERROR trigger to capture interface errors in forms

- Use KEY- triggers to centralize code

- Base a form block on a stored procedure

Review the Evolution of PL/SQL Product Integration

PL/SQL was originally integrated into the database in the release of Oracle 6.0 and the SQL*Forms 3.0 product. This integration was in the form of a new architecture, which resulted in a PL/SQL Engine being integrated as a component in the Oracle database kernel, and a PL/SQL Engine being integrated in the SQL*Forms 3.0 product. Therefore, PL/SQL code developed in the SQL*Forms 3.0 product was first passed to the local product PL/SQL Engine for processing. The SQL*Forms 3.0 PL/SQL Engine would attempt to process the PL/SQL source code. If it could process the entire program unit, then it would complete the process and no interaction would take place between the SQL*Forms product and the database server. However, if any server side calls were in the PL/SQL program unit, such as data manipulation (SQL) or calls to database server stored PL/SQL program units, this portion of the program unit would be forwarded to the database server for processing. In addition to the SQL*Forms 3.0 PL/SQL Engine processing the standard PL/SQL language commands, this engine included PL/SQL extensions to process SQL*Forms specific functions integrated into the SQL*Forms product to increase the functionality of the SQL*Forms product.

The PL/SQL architecture has continued to expand as the Oracle RDBMS and product set has evolved over the years. A PL/SQL Engine is currently embedded in Oracle Developer (Forms, Reports, and Graphics), Oracle Designer, and Oracle Discoverer. In addition, Oracle has extended each of these products to include a set of built-in packages for many product-centric features. Over the years, Oracle has integrated the new built-in packages either in the client-side or server-side product, depending on the use and overall scope of the package. The Oracle built-in packages integrated into the database (server-side) are available to all products. The Forms built-in packages are for use in only the Forms product and contain specific functionality centered around Forms features. This is true of all built-in packages Oracle supplies with each product. The packages center around functionality specific to the product. Some Oracle supplied packages are available in more than one module, like the Oracle Developer product where several built-in packages are available to Forms, Reports, and Graphics.

Other products (including non-Oracle products that support PL/SQL) like SQL*Plus and the Pro Languages (i.e. Pro*C) do not contain their own PL/SQL Engine. Therefore, all PL/SQL source code is forwarded to the database PL/SQL

Engine for processing. Figure 14-1 represents this general processing and flow of PL/SQL language execution.

Oracle Developer, Oracle Designer, and Oracle Discoverer all contain their own PL/SQL Engine (client-side). A PL/SQL Engine also exists in the Oracle kernel (server-side). If a PL/SQL program unit can be executed by the PL/SQL Engine on the client, it will. Only SQL statements and stored PL/SQL program unit calls are passed to the server for execution. If a SQL statement is executed, the call is passed to the SQL Engine for processing. If a stored PL/SQL program unit is called, the call is passed to the server-side PL/SQL Engine and executed on the server.

In earlier versions of Forms, the PL/SQL Engine lagged behind the current version of the database PL/SQL Engine, so some consideration had to be taken when developing PL/SQL logic in terms of the location and versions. As of version 2.0 of Oracle Developer (Developer 2000), the PL/SQL Engine has been upgraded to support PL/SQL 2.X. The PL/SQL Engine contained in the products is now upgraded regularly to keep pace with the database version. Therefore, Oracle Developer version 6.0 supports PL/SQL version 8.0 (Oracle8 contains the PL/SQL Engine version 8.0).

Oracle development tools include PL/SQL as the programming language; therefore, developers have the capabilities of taking advantage of application

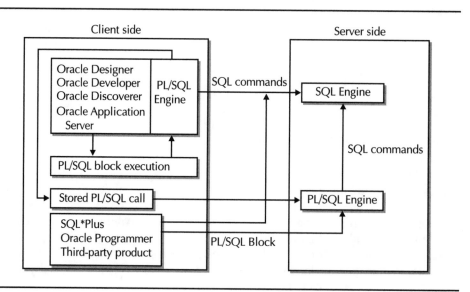

FIGURE 14-1. *PL/SQL Engine integration and execution in the database server and product toolset*

partitioning concepts, deciding where it is best to place the source code: server-side or client-side. Having a thorough understanding of how the PL/SQL Engines work on the client-side and server-side is essential to developing robust, efficient, and full-featured applications.

Understand the Integration of PL/SQL in the Product Set

This section is critical to understand. The execution of PL/SQL program units by the PL/SQL Engine is not fully understood, and this section outlines the detailed flow and processing of the PL/SQL Engine.

Oracle Developer contains a PL/SQL Engine for each module that processes all PL/SQL program units (anonymous blocks, procedures, and functions) on the client-side. When a PL/SQL program unit is executed, the code is passed to the local (client-side) PL/SQL Engine. The procedural statements are processed by the PL/SQL Engine on the client-side. The SQL statements and database server stored PL/SQL program unit calls are transferred to the server to be processed. The SQL statements passed are first modified by the PL/SQL Engine to convert the entire statement to uppercase with spaces removed (the conversion to uppercase does not take place on data values, for example, "where employee_name = 'smith'" gets converted to "WHERE EMPLOYEE_NAME = 'smith'").

The following outlines the execution of the client-side and server-side PL/SQL Engines for the different development products:

Execution in Products or Modules Containing a PL/SQL Engine

Oracle Developer (Forms, Reports, and Graphics)
Oracle Designer
Oracle Discoverer

- Module PL/SQL Program Unit or PL/SQL Library Program Unit Execution: Passed to the client-side PL/SQL Engine and processed. If the PL/SQL program unit does not contain calls to stored PL/SQL program units or contain any SQL statements, then it is processed entirely on the client-side and no communication occurs with the server-side. If the PL/SQL program unit contains a call to a database stored PL/SQL program unit, the call is passed to the PL/SQL Engine on the database sever-side and processed. If the PL/SQL program unit contains a SQL statement, then the SQL statement is reformatted to all uppercase with spaces removed and then passed directly to the SQL Engine on the server-side for processing.

- SQL Statement Execution (No PL/SQL source code present): Passed to the server-side SQL Engine and processed as is. The statement is sent directly as coded without any reformatting of the command.

Execution in Products or Modules *Not* Containing a PL/SQL Engine

> SQL*Plus
> Oracle Programmer (i.e.. Pro*C, Pro*Cobol)
> Third-Party Products (that support PL/SQL language)

- PL/SQL Program Unit Execution: Passed to the server-side PL/SQL Engine and processed. If the PL/SQL program unit does not contain calls to stored PL/SQL program units or contain any SQL statements, then it is processed entirely by the PL/SQL Engine. If the PL/SQL program unit contains a call to a stored PL/SQL program unit, and the program unit does not contain SQL statements, then the block is processed entirely by the PL/SQL Engine. If the PL/SQL program unit contains a SQL statement, then the SQL statement is reformatted to all uppercase with spaces removed, and then passed directly to the SQL Engine for processing.

- SQL Statement Execution (No PL/SQL source code present): Passed to server-side SQL Engine and processed as is. The statement is sent directly as coded without any reformatting of the command.

With the preceding PL/SQL Engine execution understood, the following five examples are provided to illustrate the PL/SQL Engine execution and the order of events that take place for different scenarios. Each example is outlined prior to the execution and identifies the location of the PL/SQL program unit. The SQL Area is viewed prior to and following the code execution, namely the V$SQLAREA view is queried to display the PL/SQL and SQL statements that are passed to the SQL Engine (you must have been granted SELECT privilege on the V$SQLAREA view to execute the following V$SQLAREA script). The V$SQLAREA script executed in each of the examples is shown below. The script searches for all SQL text with the key word "employee", including uppercase and lowercase. The starting point of the SQL Area for each scenario is shown below and is obtained by executing the V$SQLAREA script.

File: 14_1.sql

```
SELECT  sql_text
FROM    v$sqlarea
WHERE   INSTR(UPPER(sql_text), 'EMPLOYEE') > 0;
```

Output (14_1.sql) (starting contents of the V$SQLAREA prior to each PL/SQL execution)

```
SQL_TEXT
------------------------------------------------------------
SELECT sql_text FROM   v$sqlarea WHERE  INSTR(UPPER(sql_text
), 'EMPLOYEE') > 0 OR     INSTR(sql_text, 'employee') > 0
```

The preceding output reveals the starting point SQL Area only contains the V$SQLAREA query each time. To ensure the starting point is consistent, the Shared Pool, which includes the SQL Area, is flushed after each execution. The Shared Pool is flushed by executing the following command.

```
ALTER SYSTEM FLUSH SHARED_POOL;
```

The preceding command should only be performed by a DBA and only when absolutely necessary, as discussed in Chapter 9. It is used here in a test environment to illustrate the PL/SQL Engine execution. Use of the preceding command also provides a good way to test the execution to determine optimal SQL Area executions when testing for performance and a consistent starting point is needed. Finally, ALTER SYSTEM privilege is necessary to execute the previous command.

- **Scenario 1:** PL/SQL source code is created in an anonymous block in Forms. The code contains two identical cursors, with different case and spacing as shown in Figure 14-2.

  After execution of the preceding segment of PL/SQL code in the Form, the V$SQLAREA query returned the following output. Notice the same SQL statement was used to process the SQL statement on the server-side, even though the SQL statements differed in spacing and case (upper- and lower-case). The PL/SQL Engine on the client-side converted the entire SQL statement to uppercase and eliminated spaces. This extra processing by the SQL Engine allowed the same cursor to be used for the two SQL statements, thus improving performance.

Output (14_1.sql)

```
SQL_TEXT
----------------------------------------------------------
SELECT EMPLOYEE_FIRST_NAME,EMPLOYEE_LAST_NAME,TITLE    FROM S
_EMPLOYEE

SELECT sql_text FROM   v$sqlarea WHERE  INSTR(UPPER(sql_text
), 'EMPLOYEE') > 0 OR     INSTR(sql_text, 'employee') > 0
```

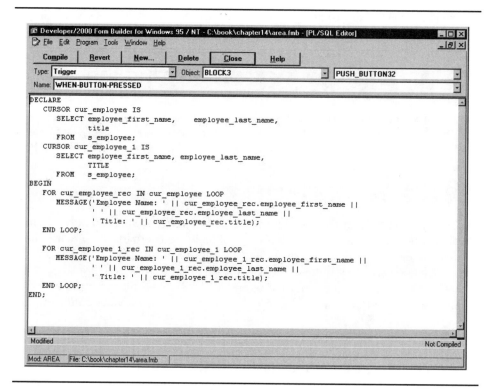

FIGURE 14-2. *The PL/SQL anonymous block that is executed*

■ **Scenario 2:** PL/SQL source code is created in a PL/SQL program unit in Forms. The same two cursors as in Scenario 1 are used as shown in Figure 14-3.

After execution of the preceding PL/SQL program unit in the Form, the V$SQLAREA query returned the following output. Notice the same result as in Scenario 1. This result illustrates that the processing of a client-side PL/SQL anonymous block and a client-side PL/SQL program unit are processed in an identical manner.

Output (14_1.sql)

```
SQL_TEXT
-----------------------------------------------------------
SELECT EMPLOYEE_FIRST_NAME,EMPLOYEE_LAST_NAME,TITLE    FROM S
_EMPLOYEE

SELECT sql_text FROM   v$sqlarea WHERE  INSTR(UPPER(sql_text
), 'EMPLOYEE') > 0 OR     INSTR(sql_text, 'employee') > 0
```

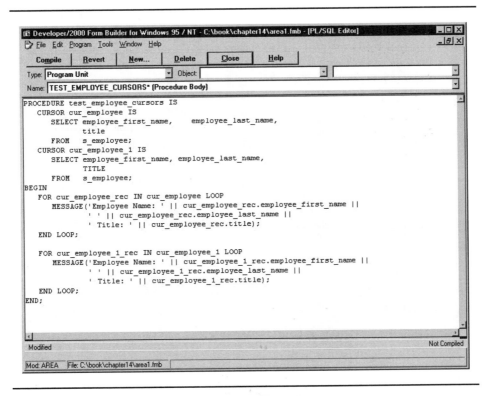

FIGURE 14-3. *The PL/SQL program unit that is executed*

■ **Scenario 3:** The same two cursors as in Scenario 1 are executed directly in SQL*Plus in the form of SELECT statements as shown in the following script.

File: 14_2.sql (both cursors executed one after another; the output of the queries is the same, but is not provided here)

```
SELECT employee_first_name,      employee_last_name,
       title
FROM   s_employee;

SELECT employee_first_name, employee_last_name,
       TITLE
FROM   s_employee;
```

After execution of the two preceding SQL statements in SQL*Plus, the V$SQLAREA query returned the following output. Notice the SQL statements were passed to the SQL Engine exactly the way they were entered in SQL*Plus and are processed by the SQL Engine as two different cursors, unlike the previous two scenarios. The difference between this scenario and Scenario 1 and 2 is that the SQL statements were not first passed through the PL/SQL Engine, since the statements were not embedded in a PL/SQL program unit. Remember, anytime SQL statements are embedded in a PL/SQL program unit, they are processed first by the PL/SQL Engine, which reformats SQL statements and then forwards them onto the SQL Engine. SQL statements not embedded in a PL/SQL program unit are sent "as is" directly to the SQL Engine, and no reformatting occurs prior to the SQL Engine receiving the SQL statements. Scenario 3 processes the same and is independent of whether the SQL*Plus product was on the client-side or server-side.

Output (14_1.sql)

```
SQL_TEXT
-----------------------------------------------------------------
SELECT employee_first_name,      employee_last_name,          ti
tle FROM    s_employee

SELECT employee_first_name, employee_last_name,          TITLE
 FROM    s_employee

SELECT sql_text FROM    v$sqlarea WHERE   INSTR(UPPER(sql_text
), 'EMPLOYEE') > 0 OR      INSTR(sql_text, 'employee') > 0
```

■ **Scenario 4:** The same PL/SQL anonymous block as in Scenario 1 is executed in SQL*Plus as shown in the following script.

File: 14_3.sql

```
DECLARE
   CURSOR cur_employee IS
      SELECT employee_first_name,      employee_last_name,
             title
      FROM    s_employee;
   CURSOR cur_employee_1 IS
      SELECT employee_first_name, employee_last_name,
             TITLE
      FROM    s_employee;
BEGIN
   FOR cur_employee_rec IN cur_employee LOOP
      NULL;
   END LOOP;
   FOR cur_employee_1_rec IN cur_employee_1 LOOP
```

```
      NULL;
   END LOOP;
END;
/
```

After execution of the preceding segment of PL/SQL code in SQL*Plus, the V$SQLAREA query returned the following output. Notice the same SQL statement was used to process the SQL statement on the server-side, which is identical to the processing in Scenario 1. The PL/SQL Engine on the server-side processed the preceding code segment and illustrates the identical reformatting of SQL statements prior to sending the SQL statement to the SQL Engine. The preceding example is slightly different regarding the processing of the PL/SQL block. The PL/SQL block is passed to the SQL Area, when the processing is performed by the server-side PL/SQL Engine as illustrated below.

Output (14_1.sql)

```
SQL_TEXT
-------------------------------------------------------------
DECLARE    CURSOR cur_employee IS       SELECT employee_firs
t_name,    employee_last_name,         title        FROM
   s_employee;    CURSOR cur_employee_1 IS       SELECT empl
oyee_first_name, employee_last_name,            TITLE
   FROM    s_employee; BEGIN    FOR cur_employee_rec IN cur_em
ployee LOOP         NULL;    END LOOP;    FOR cur_employee_1_r
ec IN cur_employee_1 LOOP         NULL;    END LOOP; END;


SELECT EMPLOYEE_FIRST_NAME,EMPLOYEE_LAST_NAME,TITLE    FROM S
_EMPLOYEE


SELECT sql_text FROM    v$sqlarea WHERE   INSTR(UPPER(sql_text
), 'EMPLOYEE') > 0 OR      INSTR(sql_text, 'employee') > 0
```

- **Scenario 5:** The same PL/SQL program unit as in Scenario 2 is executed in SQL*Plus as shown in the following script.

File: 14_4.sql

```
CREATE OR REPLACE PROCEDURE test_employee_cursors IS
   CURSOR cur_employee IS
      SELECT employee_first_name,    employee_last_name,
            title
      FROM    s_employee;
   CURSOR cur_employee_1 IS
      SELECT employee_first_name, employee_last_name,
            TITLE
```

```
        FROM    s_employee;
BEGIN
    FOR cur_employee_rec IN cur_employee LOOP
        NULL;
    END LOOP;
    FOR cur_employee_1_rec IN cur_employee_1 LOOP
        NULL;
    END LOOP;
END;
/
```

The following executes the stored PL/SQL program unit in SQL*Plus.

```
EXECUTE test_employee_cursors;
```

After execution of the preceding stored PL/SQL program unit in SQL*Plus, the V$SQLAREA query returned the following output. Notice the same SQL statement was used to process the SQL statement on the server-side (the same as in Scenario 4). The preceding example is slightly different from Scenario 4 regarding the processing of the PL/SQL block. The SQL statement is processed the same as in Scenario 4; however, the PL/SQL block that calls the stored PL/SQL program unit is passed to the SQL Area (not the stored PL/SQL program unit source code itself) as illustrated below.

Output (14_1.sql)

```
SQL_TEXT
---------------------------------------------------------------
SELECT EMPLOYEE_FIRST_NAME,EMPLOYEE_LAST_NAME,TITLE    FROM S
_EMPLOYEE

SELECT sql_text FROM   v$sqlarea WHERE  INSTR(UPPER(sql_text
), 'EMPLOYEE') > 0 OR     INSTR(sql_text, 'employee') > 0

begin test_employee_cursors; end;
```

TIP
If Scenario 5 is repeated with the procedure being WRAPped prior to creating the procedure, and the same steps were followed in Scenario 5, the result would be identical in terms of the output from the V$SQLAREA view. This result illustrates the fact that WRAPped PL/SQL program units stored in the database will still process and pass SQL statements through the SQL Area in the same manner as unWRAPped program units.

TIP
When the process of tuning PL/SQL code starts, an understanding of the processing of the PL/SQL Engines, whether client-side or server-side, provides further insight into the processing of the PL/SQL code and assists in the restructuring of PL/SQL and PL/SQL architecture. Remember that the PL/SQL Engine reformats SQL statements (converts the entire statement to uppercase, not including data values, and eliminates spaces) included in PL/SQL source code prior to passing these statements to the SQL Engine.

Understand and Use the Built-in PL/SQL Packages in Oracle Developer

Oracle Developer and all its components are shipped with several built-in packages containing many PL/SQL program units that can be used when developing applications. These packages enable the developer to extend the application to include complex functionality. To access the procedures and functions within these packages, specify the name of the package along with the name of the procedure or function. Many of these packages are specific to the Oracle Developer module, but many others contain standard procedures and functions also present on the server-side. Remember, the PL/SQL Engine uses many of the built-in packages to accomplish core PL/SQL functionality, so you will find these packages similar on the client-side in Oracle Developer product modules to the server-side packages stored in the database and created upon database creation. One particular example of this is the STANDARD package.

Become familiar with the packages, procedures, and functions Oracle provides. Do not re-invent the wheel. Oracle has provided a nice set of useful procedures and functions. Your responsibility is to learn them and be able to determine if a built-in package already exists to accomplish the required functionality. If it does, use it. Many procedures and functions are contained in some of these built-in packages. Many of the procedures are overloaded. Learn these products by reviewing the online and/or hard copy user documentation of the Oracle Developer or other product set.

Oracle Developer is comprised of several component modules, including the three main modules of Forms, Reports, and Graphics. The navigator of all three is similar, and most built-in packages are present and consistent across all three modules. Like all other facets of the PL/SQL language, these packages have been enhanced with each new version. It is imperative they are reviewed on a regular basis—especially when new versions are introduced—to ensure the components of each package is known. This saves time in the long run because Oracle has provided some very functional and flexible capabilities in these packages. The following are screen shots from each module listing the built-in packages. This section is provided as a reference point for the three modules to demonstrate further the capabilities Oracle provides with each of the products. Figure 14-4 shows all the built-in packages available in the Oracle Developer Forms module from Forms version 5.0.5.4.0. Figure 14-5 shows all the built-in packages available in the Oracle Developer Reports module from Reports version 3.0.4.6.3. Finally, Figure

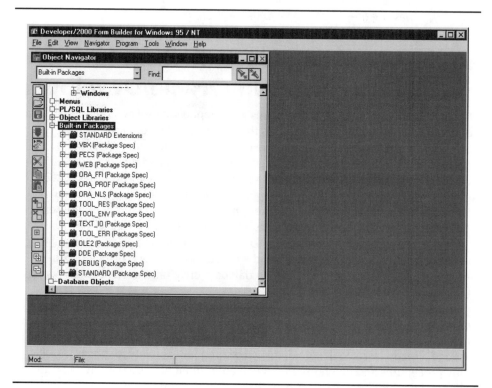

FIGURE 14-4. *Built-in packages available in the Oracle Developer Forms module from Forms version 5.0.5.4.0*

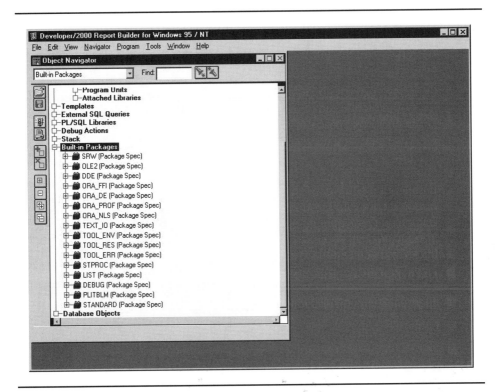

FIGURE 14-5. *Built-in packages available in the Oracle Developer Reports module from Reports version 3.0.4.6.3*

14-6 shows all the built-in packages available in the Oracle Developer Graphics module from Graphics version 3.0.3.2.0.

The following table outlines each of the built-in packages in the Oracle Developer product (Forms, Reports, and Graphics), namely, the module in which

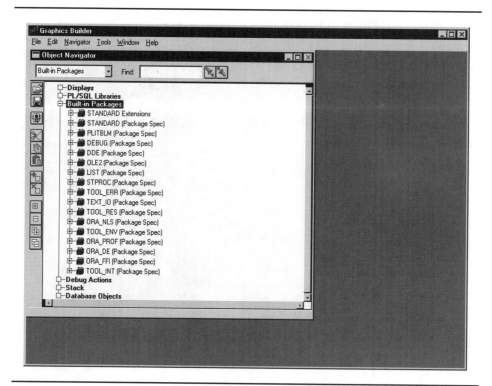

FIGURE 14-6. *Built-in packages available in the Oracle Developer Graphics module from Graphics version 3.0.3.2.0*

each built-in is available, the name of the built-in, and a brief description of each of the packages. The consistent components across all three modules are listed first (signified by "All" in the Oracle Developer Module column), followed by each of the modules and the specific packages unique to each module.

Oracle Developer Module	Oracle Built-In Package	Description of Package Contents
All	DDE	Provides Dynamic Data Exchange support within Oracle Developer components.

Oracle Developer Module	Oracle Built-In Package	Description of Package Contents
All	DEBUG	Provides debugging support within Oracle Developer program units, including creating triggers and setting breakpoints.
All	OLE2	Provides PL/SQL API support for OLE2 automation objects.
All	ORA_FFI	Provides an interface for calling C functions.
All	ORA_NLS	Provides the capability to access high-level information of the language in the current environment.
All	ORA_PROF	Provides support for timing functions to use when specific timing interval information is needed, such as optimizing PL/SQL program units.
All	STANDARD	Provides the core function support of the PL/SQL language (100+ functions).
All	TEXT_IO	Provides support to read and write operating system files on the client system.
All	TOOL_ENV	Provides an interface to the Oracle environment variables content.
All	TOOL_ERR	Provides an interface to the error stack, which is created when errors are encountered.
All	TOOL_RES	Provides support for manipulating resource files (text file format) to be used for Oracle*Terminal. Therefore, the resource files must be converted from and to the standard resource file format to text files before and after manipulation with this package. The utilities to convert resource files are included with the Oracle*Terminal module.

Oracle Developer Module	Oracle Built-In Package	Description of Package Contents
Forms Only	PECS	Provides the capability to define application specific events to the PECS system.
Forms Only	VBX	Provides VBX support.
Forms Only	WEB	Provides the capability to display a URL in a target window.
Reports Only	SRW	Provides SQL Report Writer (SRW) functionality for most Report specific controls and functions, including procedures, functions, and exceptions.
Graphics Only	TOOL_INT	Provides the capability to launch other Oracle products and also manipulate parameter lists for passing information between the products.
Forms and Graphics	STANDARD Extensions	Provides the core Forms Builder functionality for most of the Forms specific actions from window routines to key movements (contains several hundred procedures and functions).
Reports and Graphics	LIST	Provides support for arrays.
Reports and Graphics	ORA_DE	Should not be used because it contains constructs used by Oracle Developer for private PL/SQL services.
Reports and Graphics	PLITBLM	Provides support for PL/SQL tables.
Reports and Graphics	STPROC	Should not be used because it is used internally by Oracle Developer to call subprograms stored in the database. Calls to this package are automatically generated.

Determine the Best Location for PL/SQL Source Code

One critical aspect of PL/SQL programming when developing in product modules (that is, Oracle Developer) is where to place the source code: in the database as a stored program unit, in a PL/SQL library to be attached to other Forms, in a program unit in the Form, or as an anonymous block in the form. No one answer is correct for all PL/SQL code developed because it depends on the functionality of the code (Form specific code or field specific code), the contents of the code (SQL statements, calls to stored PL/SQL program units), and whether it is a code segment that will be used in other areas of your application.

The following are guidelines to which I adhere when I am trying to determine the location of PL/SQL source code.

- **Anonymous Block:** If I am only performing basic logic at a column or trigger level and the PL/SQL block will never be referenced elsewhere in the Form or application, I create an anonymous block to accomplish the logic. (Exception: If the PL/SQL code has database interaction and the block contains all generic PL/SQL—not Forms specific calls—then it is a candidate for database server-side storage. This would be important for processing optimization, and the code in question can easily be tested by turning the PL/SQL block into a program unit and creating it on the server-side.)

- **Forms PL/SQL Program Unit:** If I am only performing logic in one Form and the PL/SQL block will be referenced in more than one location in the Form and never be referenced elsewhere in the application, I create a PL/SQL program unit at the Form level of the Form. (Exception: The same exception applies as for an anonymous block.)

- **Forms PL/SQL Library Program Unit:** If I am performing logic in multiple Forms of an application and it contains Forms specific PL/SQL program unit calls, then I create a program unit and store it in a PL/SQL library, which can be attached to the Form(s) that references the program unit. Each PL/SQL Library should contain similar logic program units. Packages can further segment a library, especially if variables must be shared among program units. Once a library is created, it can be attached to a form, a menu, or another library module. The same library can be attached to multiple Oracle Developer modules. Libraries are saved in operating system files and are saved by default with a .pll file extension.

■ **Stored PL/SQL Program Unit in the Database:** If I am performing logic in multiple Forms or modules of an application and it does not contain Forms specific PL/SQL program unit calls, then I create a program unit and store it in the database, which then can be called from any PL/SQL module. Packages can further combine program units, especially if variables must be shared among program units. Refer to Chapter 5 for more detail on the advantages of packages. (Exception: If a PL/SQL program unit is called repetitively in a Form or other module and does not contain any calls to the database server, the program unit may be a candidate to keep on the client-side and placed in a PL/SQL library versus the database due to the overhead of the roundtrip to the database. This roundtrip time increases as the number of parameters passed to the program unit increases. Therefore, the more remote procedure calls (RPCs), the more overhead and potential performance degradation.)

■ **Location Segmentation:** If the decision is made to store a PL/SQL code segment in a PL/SQL library due to Forms or module specific program unit calls, and the PL/SQL code segment includes logic that can be further segmented into a separate program unit that would be callable in several other locations, then this further segmentation of program units should be performed. Typically, this program unit segmentation is performed to allow for storage of the program unit on the database server-side for optimization, efficiency, standardization, and ease of maintenance. Be careful about how far you granularize your program units, so they do not become too fragmented. You don't want to make it impossible either to locate the program unit or to modify it in the future.

■ **Location Modification:** PL/SQL code segments will be developed in the course of any Form developed, and many PL/SQL code segments will be developed for an entire application development effort. The location decision is often hard to make correctly 100 percent of the time, especially in the initial stages of the application development life cycle. If you are certain a segment of code will be used in many locations, then the PL/SQL program unit can be placed in the proper location up-front or if you know you have developed a PL/SQL program unit that will contain core functionality or business logic. However, you will develop several PL/SQL program units whose location you may change over time. If you generally end up reusing a code segment more than you originally thought you would, change the location. Communicate with other developers to ensure they are aware of both the PL/SQL libraries and the stored PL/SQL program units that you are creating. Maintenance will be much easier down the road.

■ **Think Dynamic:** As you develop be cognizant of reusability. Many PL/SQL code segments you develop can be altered slightly to become generic/dynamic modules that can be used throughout your application by using parameters to build this dynamic capability. In our company, we have built over a hundred PL/SQL program units offering this dynamic capability; many are generalized for all applications and many are specific to Forms and other modules.

TIP
Always think of the location the PL/SQL program unit would best serve the application. Always think of reusability. Always communicate and document PL/SQL Libraries and stored PL/SQL program units created to the development team.

Understand PL/SQL Program Unit Name Resolution

As outlined in the previous section, there are a number of locations to place PL/SQL program units. With all the locations available to place PL/SQL program units, understanding how the PL/SQL Engine performs program unit resolution is important. Understanding the order of precedence may play into your location decision and/or naming of PL/SQL program units.

The following illustrates this with a PL/SQL block executed in an Oracle Form trigger.

```
DECLARE
   lv_invoice_total_num NUMBER;
BEGIN
   lv_invoice_total_num := calculate_customer_total(:customer_id);
END;
```

How does the PL/SQL Engine resolve the reference to the function named calculate_customer_total in the preceding example? The PL/SQL Engine resolves the PL/SQL program unit reference in the following order:

■ Is the program unit defined in the current PL/SQL block?

■ Is the program unit a standard PL/SQL command?

■ Is the program unit a Forms built-in procedure or function?

■ Is the program unit a user-named procedure or function in the Form?

- Is the program unit a user-named procedure or function in an attached PL/SQL library?

- Is the program unit defined in the DBMS_STANDARD package on the server side?

- Is the program unit stored in the database and does the user have access it?

If the PL/SQL Engine finds a match at any point in the previous process (during compilation), it continues on to the program unit execution process. If the PL/SQL Engine does not find the program unit in any of the previous steps, an error is raised.

Share Variables Between Forms

Rarely is an application developed with only one form. When implementing multiple form applications, you may have the requirement to share data. The first inclination is to use global variables. This may not be the best choice. Excessive use of global variables can impede performance because they are 255 characters in length.

TIP

Because global variables are a fixed length of 255 characters, as a general rule, limit the number of global variables in any particular form to five.

If you should not use global variables, what should you use? There are two alternate options to share variables between forms, namely using database server stored PL/SQL packages and PL/SQL libraries.

Any variable declared in a package specification is in scope for the entire session. A package specification does not require a package body.

TIP

Package specifications can be used to create global variables that can be accessed by all programs during that session. Once the session is terminated or the package is recompiled, the variables will no longer be available.

In Forms, you are restricted from accessing server-side package variables directly within client-side PL/SQL. Therefore, you need to create functions and procedures that set and retrieve package variables. The following is a generic package that enables communication between server-side PL/SQL package variables and client-side PL/SQL. The package contains procedures and functions to set variables and retrieve the contents of the variables. The package provides the capability to process NUMBER, VARCHAR2, and DATE variables.

File: 14_5.sql

```
CREATE OR REPLACE PACKAGE pkg_vars AS
-- Purpose: This package can be used to process server-side package
-- global variables.  Each global variable can be declared below or
-- in any other PL/SQL package. Any variable in this section has a
-- scope of the current session. The set_pvar PROCEDURE is overloaded
-- and can accept either a NUMBER, VARCHAR2, OR DATE as the second
-- parameter. The first parameter should be in the format
-- package_name.variable_name.  The get_pnumber, get_pdate, and
-- get_pvarchar2 FUNCTIONs can be used to receive either a NUMBER,
-- DATE, and VARCHAR2, respectively.
   pvg_cursor_num PLS_INTEGER;
   pvg_temp_num    PLS_INTEGER;
   pvg_ord_num     NUMBER;
   pvg_cust_num    NUMBER;
   PROCEDURE set_pvar(p_varname_txt VARCHAR2, p_val NUMBER);
   PROCEDURE set_pvar(p_varname_txt VARCHAR2, p_val VARCHAR2);
   PROCEDURE set_pvar(p_varname_txt VARCHAR2, p_val DATE);
   FUNCTION get_pnumber(p_varname_txt VARCHAR2)
      RETURN NUMBER;
   FUNCTION get_pvarchar2(p_varname_txt VARCHAR2)
      RETURN VARCHAR2;
   FUNCTION get_pdate(p_varname_txt VARCHAR2)
      RETURN DATE;
END pkg_vars;
/
```

File: 14_5a.sql

```
CREATE OR REPLACE PACKAGE BODY pkg_vars IS
PROCEDURE set_pvar(p_varname_txt VARCHAR2, p_val NUMBER) IS
BEGIN
   pvg_cursor_num := DBMS_SQL.OPEN_CURSOR;
   DBMS_SQL.PARSE(pvg_cursor_num,
      'BEGIN ' ||p_varname_txt || ' := :the_value; END;',
      DBMS_SQL.NATIVE);
   DBMS_SQL.BIND_VARIABLE(pvg_cursor_num, ':the_value', p_val);
   pvg_temp_num := DBMS_SQL.EXECUTE(pvg_cursor_num);
   DBMS_SQL.CLOSE_CURSOR(pvg_cursor_num);
```

```
END set_pvar;
-------------------------------------------------------------------
PROCEDURE set_pvar(p_varname_txt VARCHAR2, p_val VARCHAR2) IS
BEGIN
   pvg_cursor_num := DBMS_SQL.OPEN_CURSOR;
   DBMS_SQL.PARSE(pvg_cursor_num,
      'BEGIN ' ||p_varname_txt || ' := :the_value; END;',
      DBMS_SQL.NATIVE);
   DBMS_SQL.BIND_VARIABLE(pvg_cursor_num, ':the_value', p_val,
      2000);
   pvg_temp_num := DBMS_SQL.EXECUTE(pvg_cursor_num);
   DBMS_SQL.CLOSE_CURSOR(pvg_cursor_num);
END set_pvar;
-------------------------------------------------------------------
PROCEDURE set_pvar(p_varname_txt VARCHAR2, p_val DATE) IS
BEGIN
   pvg_cursor_num := DBMS_SQL.OPEN_CURSOR;
   DBMS_SQL.PARSE(pvg_cursor_num,
      'BEGIN ' ||p_varname_txt || ' := :the_value; END;',
      DBMS_SQL.NATIVE);
   DBMS_SQL.BIND_VARIABLE(pvg_cursor_num, ':the_value', p_val);
   pvg_temp_num := DBMS_SQL.EXECUTE(pvg_cursor_num);
   DBMS_SQL.CLOSE_CURSOR(pvg_cursor_num);
END set_pvar;
-------------------------------------------------------------------
FUNCTION get_pnumber(p_varname_txt VARCHAR2)
   RETURN NUMBER IS
   lv_value_num NUMBER;
BEGIN
   pvg_cursor_num := DBMS_SQL.OPEN_CURSOR;
   DBMS_SQL.PARSE(pvg_cursor_num,
      'BEGIN :the_value := ' ||p_varname_txt || '; END;',
      DBMS_SQL.NATIVE);
   DBMS_SQL.BIND_VARIABLE(pvg_cursor_num, ':the_value', lv_value_num);
   pvg_temp_num := DBMS_SQL.EXECUTE(pvg_cursor_num);
   DBMS_SQL.VARIABLE_VALUE(pvg_cursor_num, ':the_value', lv_value_num);
   DBMS_SQL.CLOSE_CURSOR(pvg_cursor_num);
   RETURN lv_value_num;
END get_pnumber;
-------------------------------------------------------------------
FUNCTION get_pvarchar2 (p_varname_txt VARCHAR2)
   RETURN VARCHAR2 IS
   lv_value_txt VARCHAR2(2000);
BEGIN
   pvg_cursor_num := DBMS_SQL.OPEN_CURSOR;
   DBMS_SQL.PARSE(pvg_cursor_num,
```

```
            'BEGIN :the_value := ' ||p_varname_txt || '; END;',
         DBMS_SQL.NATIVE);
      DBMS_SQL.BIND_VARIABLE(pvg_cursor_num, ':the_value',
         lv_value_txt, 2000);
      pvg_temp_num := DBMS_SQL.EXECUTE(pvg_cursor_num);
      DBMS_SQL.VARIABLE_VALUE(pvg_cursor_num, ':the_value', lv_value_txt);
      DBMS_SQL.CLOSE_CURSOR(pvg_cursor_num);
      RETURN lv_value_txt;
END get_pvarchar2;
------------------------------------------------------------------
FUNCTION get_pdate(p_varname_txt VARCHAR2)
   RETURN DATE IS
   lv_value_date DATE;
BEGIN
   pvg_cursor_num := DBMS_SQL.OPEN_CURSOR;
   DBMS_SQL.PARSE(pvg_cursor_num,
         'BEGIN :the_value := ' ||p_varname_txt || '; END;',
         DBMS_SQL.NATIVE);
   DBMS_SQL.BIND_VARIABLE(pvg_cursor_num, ':the_value', lv_value_date);
   pvg_temp_num := DBMS_SQL.EXECUTE(pvg_cursor_num);
   DBMS_SQL.VARIABLE_VALUE(pvg_cursor_num, ':the_value',lv_value_date);
   DBMS_SQL.CLOSE_CURSOR(pvg_cursor_num);
   RETURN lv_value_date;
END get_pdate;
------------------------------------------------------------------
END pkg_vars;
/
```

Two simple examples to illustrate the preceding package are provided below.
The first example sets the pkg_vars.pvg_cust_num variable, followed by the second
example that retrieves the variable. The examples are executed in SQL*Plus, but are
the same when calling from other products.

```
EXECUTE pkg_vars.set_pvar('pkg_vars.pvg_cust_num', 10)
```

File: 14_6.sql

```
DECLARE
   lv_temp_cust_num NUMBER;
BEGIN
   lv_temp_cust_num := pkg_vars.get_pnumber('pkg_vars.pvg_cust_num');
   DBMS_OUTPUT.PUT_LINE('Customer Number: ' || lv_temp_cust_num);
END;
/
```

Output (14_6.sql)

```
Customer Number: 10

PL/SQL procedure successfully completed.
```

If specific variables are used, these procedures and functions can be greatly simplified by hardcoding the variable names. However, the Oracle supplied built-in package DBMS_SQL was used extensively to provide flexibility and to make this variable interface dynamic. The DBMS_SQL package is described in detail in Chapter 11 and Chapter 12. In addition, with Oracle 8i the previous source code can be modified/simplified using the new EXECUTE IMMEDIATE command to replace the DBMS_SQL calls. This Oracle 8i feature is covered in Chapter 16.

In Oracle Developer (Developer 2000) 2.0 and subsequent releases, Oracle introduced a new option that enables the sharing of library data. When invoking one form module from another, the developer can use the OPEN_FORM, CALL_FORM, and NEW_FORM built-in procedures. These built-in procedures have a new parameter that enables forms to share data between forms that have identical libraries attached at design time as shown below.

```
CALL_FORM('FORMA', HIDE, NO_REPLACE, NO_QUERY_ONLY, SHARE_LIBRARY_DATA)
NEW_FORM('FORMA', TO_SAVEPOINT, NO_QUERY_ONLY, SHARE_LIBRARY_DATA)
OPEN_FORM('FORMA', ACTIVATE, NO_SESSION, SHARE_LIBRARY_DATA)
```

TIP
Use the SHARE_LIBRARY_DATA parameter in the CALL_FORM, NEW_FORM, and OPEN_FORM built-in procedures to share library data between forms. The parameters are positional. Therefore, the parameters that precede SHARE_LIBRARY_DATA need to be passed.

Use Explicit Cursors Versus Implicit Cursors

In most forms, you will either be validating a value or displaying a description based on a code or ID value in several sections of a form. A good example is when a query is performed, a POST-QUERY trigger often is created on the block to fill the descriptions for all the foreign key references. Because the foreign key references should only return one record, the developer has the option to use an implicit cursor or an explicit cursor to accomplish this task.

I strongly recommend using an explicit cursor because this will result in half the number of fetches than if you use an implicit cursor. The implicit cursor will perform two fetches for every cursor because it must determine if the TOO_MANY_ROWS exception should be raised, whereas an explicit cursor fetch is controlled by the developer.

The following examples illustrate the difference between implicit and explicit cursors. Assume a customer form exists that displays the sales representative full name and the region name for each customer. If the form displays ten records at one time, then the following code for a POST-QUERY can be performed in one of two methods shown in the following scripts:

Method 1: Implicit Cursor Usage
File: 14_7.sql

```
BEGIN
   SELECT employee_first_name || ' ' employee_last_name
   INTO   :nbt_employee_name
   FROM   s_employee
   WHERE  employee_id = :sales_rep_id;

   SELECT region_name
   INTO   :nbt_region_name
   FROM   s_region
   WHERE  region_id = :region_id;
END;
/
```

Method 2: Explicit Cursor Usage
File: 14_8.sql

```
DECLARE
   CURSOR cur_employee IS
      SELECT employee_first_name || ' ' employee_last_name
      FROM   s_employee
      WHERE  employee_id = :sales_rep_id;
   CURSOR cur_region IS
      SELECT region_name
      FROM   s_region
      WHERE  region_id = :region_id;
BEGIN
   OPEN cur_employee;
   FETCH cur_employee INTO :nbt_employee_name;
   CLOSE cur_employee;
   OPEN cur_region;
```

```
    FETCH cur_region INTO :nbt_region_name;
    CLOSE cur_region;
END;
/
```

Error handling has been left out of these PL/SQL blocks to reduce the code segment size. Both methods will work, and from the code it may appear Method 1 would be preferred because it is less code. However, Method 1 requires 40 fetches to the database (two fetches per record for the employee cursor and two fetches per record for the region cursor; 4 * 10 records). Method 2 requires 20 fetches from the database (one fetch per record for the employee cursor and one fetch per record for the region cursor; 2 * 10 records). Therefore, explicit cursors are always recommended for optimization.

In older versions of PL/SQL (prior to version 2.3 of PL/SQL), a reference to the variable SYSDATE variable would cause a SELECT SYSDATE FROM dual. With the PL/SQL version 2.3 and subsequent releases, the SYSDATE function is included in the STANDARD package.

TIP

In PL/SQL versions prior to 2.3, instead of having multiple references to SYSDATE, consider using a CURSOR to select the value into a null-canvas item or a global variable.

Build Communication Between Forms and Stored PL/SQL Program Units

Proper communication between client-side PL/SQL program units and stored PL/SQL program units must be handled to ensure successful processing. When Form modules (client-side) execute stored PL/SQL program units (server-side), the communication of information is usually handled by procedure and function parameter lists and the RETURN from a function. However, the communication of error processing usually does not receive with the same level of care and detail. Error processing is a must. It should be handled with far greater detail because errors can occur at any time without warning. Granted, many of the errors can be anticipated, but what about harder-to-anticipate errors (out of space, constraint violations, and so forth)? When a stored PL/SQL program unit is called from the client-side PL/SQL, the client-side PL/SQL program waits for completion of the program unit processing. If the stored PL/SQL program unit has error handling that successfully handles the error, then upon return to the client-side PL/SQL program, the client-side views the execution of the stored PL/SQL program unit as a success. In many cases, this is not the desired result. Typically, you want to know about both the error and the processing of the PL/SQL logic in the form.

Learn to be proactive and to develop a generic error-handling routine that captures and logs all errors encountered throughout your application to an error table, which can be reviewed at any time. A generic error logging process is detailed in Chapter 5.

Two examples of handling the same error follow; both offer a means for communicating errors between the Form PL/SQL program unit and the stored PL/SQL program unit. The process involves validating an employee's title from a WHEN-VALIDATE_ITEM trigger. When a new value is entered, it is checked against the s_title table to ensure a valid title has been entered.

The first example illustrates the passing of an invalid value entry back to the Form via exception pragmas. Notice this program also handles unknown errors that could arise. This example begins by showing the Form PL/SQL anonymous block that calls the stored PL/SQL program unit.

File: 14_9.sql

```
DECLARE
    pu_failure_excep EXCEPTION;
    PRAGMA EXCEPTION_INIT(pu_failure_excep, -20000);
BEGIN
    validate_title(:title);
EXCEPTION
    WHEN pu_failure_excep THEN
        MESSAGE('Invalid Title. Re-enter a valid Title.');
        RAISE FORM_TRIGGER_FAILURE;
    WHEN OTHERS THEN
        MESSAGE('Error: UNKNOWN');
        RAISE FORM_TRIGGER_FAILURE;
END;
/
```

File: 14_10.sql

```
CREATE OR REPLACE PROCEDURE validate_title
    (p_title_txt VARCHAR2) IS
    CURSOR cur_title IS
        SELECT 'x'
        FROM   s_title
        WHERE  title = p_title_txt;
    lv_title_txt    VARCHAR2(1);
    pu_failure_excep EXCEPTION;
```

```
   PRAGMA EXCEPTION_INIT(pu_failure_excep, -20000);
BEGIN
   IF p_title_txt IS NOT NULL THEN
      OPEN cur_title;
      FETCH cur_title into lv_title_txt;
      IF cur_title%NOTFOUND THEN
         CLOSE cur_title;
         RAISE pu_failure_excep;
      END IF;
      CLOSE cur_title;
   END IF;
EXCEPTION
   WHEN pu_failure_excep THEN
      RAISE;
   WHEN OTHERS THEN
      -- The call to the error logging procedure would be inserted
      -- in this location.
      RAISE;
END validate_title;
/
```

The second example illustrates the passing of an invalid value entry back to the form via a RETURN from a function. Notice this program unit also handles unknown errors that could arise. The example begins by showing the form PL/SQL anonymous block that calls the stored PL/SQL program unit.

File: 14_11.sql

```
DECLARE
   lv_title_found_bln BOOLEAN := FALSE;
BEGIN
   lv_title_found_bln := validate_title(:title);
   IF NOT lv_title_found_bln THEN
      MESSAGE('Invalid Title. Re-enter a valid Title.');
      RAISE FORM_TRIGGER_FAILURE;
EXCEPTION
   WHEN FORM_TRIGGER_FAILURE THEN
      RAISE;
   WHEN OTHERS THEN
      MESSAGE('Error: UNKNOWN');
      RAISE FORM_TRIGGER_FAILURE;
END;
/
```

File: 14_12.sql

```
CREATE OR REPLACE FUNCTION validate_title
   (p_title_txt VARCHAR2) RETURN BOOLEAN IS
   CURSOR cur_title IS
      SELECT 'x'
      FROM    s_title
      WHERE   title = p_title_txt;
   lv_title_txt         VARCHAR2(1);
   lv_title_found_bln BOOLEAN := FALSE;
BEGIN
   IF p_title_txt IS NOT NULL THEN
      OPEN cur_title;
      FETCH cur_title into lv_title_txt;
      IF cur_title%NOTFOUND THEN
         lv_title_found_bln := FALSE;
      ELSE
         lv_title_found_bln := TRUE;
      END IF;
      CLOSE cur_title;
      RETURN lv_title_found_bln;
   END IF;
EXCEPTION
   WHEN OTHERS THEN
      -- The call to the error logging procedure would be inserted
      -- in this location.
      RAISE;
END validate_title;
/
```

TIP
Communication of errors between the client-side PL/SQL and server-side stored PL/SQL must be handled with care. Two methods can handle this communication. The function example in this section is helpful for quick validation checks; however, as the complexity of the code increases, using pragmas to communicate errors will be needed to create seamless integration between PL/SQL program units.

Communication Between Forms and Stored PL/SQL Program Units

Check the Database Error When Responding to a Form Error

Oracle Forms contains the following five variables that trap runtime error information:

- ERROR_CODE
- ERROR_TEXT
- ERROR_TYPE
- DBMS_ERROR_CODE
- DBMS_ERROR_TEXT

The first three variables record error information specific to the Forms environment, while the last two record error information returned by the Oracle database. For the purposes of this discussion, only the ERROR_CODE and DBMS_ERROR_CODE variables will be covered, as they contain the actual error codes returned by their respective products. The other three variables return additional information about the error codes. Often, only the ERROR_CODE variable is accommodated by user-defined error handling logic. To respond properly to a runtime error in Forms code, it is necessary to analyze both the ERROR_CODE and the DBMS_ERROR_CODE. The same error in the Forms product can be generated by multiple errors in the database.

For example, the Oracle Forms error *FRM-40508 (unable to INSERT record)* indicates a problem was encountered during an attempted insert into the database. This Forms error can be triggered by any number of database errors, including:

- *ORA-01400: mandatory (NOT NULL) column is missing or NULL during insert*
- *ORA-00001: unique constraint (constraint name) violated*
- *ORA-01031: insufficient privileges*
- *ORA-01401: inserted value too large for column*

The only way to determine the cause of the Oracle Forms error (*FRM-40508*) is to analyze the DBMS_ERROR_CODE variable. Only when both error variables are analyzed will the program be able to respond in the appropriate manner. If the error was caused by a NULL in a mandatory column or a constraint violation, the program might provide additional guidance to the user. If the error was caused by either insufficient privileges or a column-sizing problem, the program should log the appropriate information to be researched later by the Forms developer.

Use the On-Error Trigger to Capture Interface Errors in Forms

Any Oracle Forms form module, no matter how simple in design, can experience runtime errors when it is released to the user community. At the very least, the users may have not been given sufficient privileges to the underlying tables. This is a minor problem that should have been discovered during testing. Many other problems may be encountered at runtime, which may be difficult or impossible to discover during testing. One common problem is insufficient space to extend a table or index.

Furthermore, users generally have a bizarre way of using a form that a developer did not try during testing. The complexity of the Forms product, combined with that of the database, always leaves open an avenue for possible runtime errors. To assist in the identification and correction of these runtime errors, it is imperative that form modules be written with the same robustness as server-side PL/SQL code. Any custom PL/SQL code (triggers, program units, and libraries) that is added to a form must be written with proper exception handling and error processing.

What may not be so obvious is the form module itself could generate errors even if it does not contain custom PL/SQL code. These errors should be planned for, as well. For example, insufficient privileges on a base table would interfere with the form module's capability to perform standard block operations such as querying data. The form module itself, and not the custom PL/SQL code, would generate runtime errors of this nature.

Implementing form-level error handling is not difficult to design. With the PL/SQL libraries and property subclassing introduced in the more recent versions of Oracle Forms, implementing it for an entire application is a trivial task. First, we need to create two program units that will reside in a PL/SQL library.

The first procedure is called log_error. Its purpose is to create an error file on the file system. This procedure must accept the following arguments: a generic text string (for developer messages) and the five Oracle Forms error variables (previously outlined in the preceding section). The log_error procedure is illustrated in the following code segment. The following notes should make understanding this procedure easier.

- The sole purpose of this procedure is to record as much information as possible about a runtime error. The information recorded includes the following: The five Oracle Forms error variables, the names and values of all system variables, and additional programmer messages (such as the location within a PL/SQL routine where the error occurred).

- When working with error handlers in Oracle Forms, writing error logs to the file system, in lieu of the database, is often preferable. The Form module is executing external to the database and a lost connection to it would not prevent the recording of error messages.

■ By default, the error log file will be written to a directory specified by the global variable error_log_dir. This directory should be located on a file server, so all logs are written to the same location. The variable should have been initialized at application startup, perhaps from a control table in the database (refer to Chapter 4 for an outline of this type of structure).

■ The procedure will attempt to create a unique file name in the DOS 8.3 format based upon the current time. If an operating system supporting long filenames is used, then the procedure should be enhanced to include the username as part of the file name. This will decrease the likelihood of multiple users writing to the same error log file.

■ Realizing that the desired error log file may be currently unavailable, (because another form module may be writing to it or the needed file server is no longer available) this procedure will make repeated attempts to open the file. If the file does not become available within a specified time frame (usually seconds), then the procedure will default to a different file on the local machine.

■ Due to the generic nature of this procedure, it makes a perfect complement to the exception handling that should be present in custom PL/SQL code. When your custom code encounters an unhandled runtime error, use the log_error procedure to write error information to a log file.

File: 14_13.sql

```
PROCEDURE log_error
   (p_message_txt           IN VARCHAR2,  -- The programmer's message
    p_error_code_num        IN NUMBER,    -- Forms Error_Code value
    p_error_text_txt        IN VARCHAR2,  -- Forms Error_Text value
    p_error_type_txt        IN VARCHAR2,  -- Forms Error_Type value
    p_dbms_error_code_num   IN NUMBER,    -- Forms DBMS_Error_Code value
    p_dbms_error_text_txt   IN VARCHAR2)  -- Forms DBMS_Error_Text value
   IS
   lv_button_pressed_num NUMBER;
   lv_done_excep         EXCEPTION;
   lv_error_file_txt     VARCHAR2(100);
   lv_file_handle_num    TEXT_IO.FILE_TYPE; -- File handle used to
                                            -- write to the error log.
   lv_log_error_bln1     BOOLEAN; -- Used to track runtime errors that
                                  -- occur in this procedure.
   lv_log_error_bln2     BOOLEAN; -- Used to track runtime errors that
                                  -- occur in this procedure.
   lv_open_attempts_num  PLS_INTEGER := 0;
   lv_dir_txt            VARCHAR2(50);
```

```
BEGIN
  -- The following 4 lines can be uncommented if it is desired to
  -- ensure that a database connection has been established
  -- in order for this procedure to execute.
--   IF GET_APPLICATION_PROPERTY(DATASOURCE) <> 'ORACLE' THEN
--      MESSAGE('Not Connected to Database.', NO_ACKNOWLEDGE);
--      RAISE lv_done_excep;
--   END IF;
  -- Initialize variables.
  DEFAULT_VALUE('c:', 'global.error_log_dir');
  lv_dir_txt := NAME_IN('global.error_log_dir');
  lv_log_error_bln1 := FALSE;
  lv_log_error_bln2 := FALSE;
  -- Display the informational message.
  BEGIN
    MESSAGE('Recording application error...', NO_ACKNOWLEDGE);
    SYNCHRONIZE;
  EXCEPTION
    WHEN OTHERS THEN
        lv_log_error_bln2 := TRUE;
  END;
  -- Create the name of the error log file and then open it.
  WHILE lv_open_attempts_num < 100 LOOP
    IF lv_open_attempts_num <= 80 THEN
        lv_error_file_txt := lv_dir_txt || '\' ||
            TO_CHAR(SYSDATE, 'dddsssss')||'.rel';
    ELSE
        lv_error_file_txt := 'runform.rel';
    END IF;
    BEGIN
        lv_file_handle_num := TEXT_IO.FOPEN(lv_error_file_txt, 'A');
        EXIT;
    EXCEPTION
        WHEN OTHERS THEN
            lv_open_attempts_num := lv_open_attempts_num + 1;
            IF lv_open_attempts_num = 80 THEN
                -- Display an error indicating that the error file
                -- could not be opened,and a generic file will be used.
                NULL;
            END IF;
    END;
  END LOOP;
  IF lv_open_attempts_num >= 100 THEN
    -- Display an error indicating that the error file
    -- could not be opened.
    RAISE FORM_TRIGGER_FAILURE;
  END IF;
  -- Record the name of the log file.
```

```
COPY(lv_error_file_txt, 'global.last_rel_file');
-- If any errors occurred in this program unit while attempting
-- to log another error then write them to the file.
IF lv_log_error_bln1 THEN
   -- text_io statements...
   NULL;
END IF;
IF lv_log_error_bln2 THEN
   -- text_io statements...
   NULL;
END IF;
-- Write error information to the file.
TEXT_IO.PUT_LINE(lv_file_handle_num, USER);
TEXT_IO.PUT_LINE(lv_file_handle_num,
   TO_CHAR(SYSDATE, 'Mon DD, YYYY  HH24:MI:SS'));
TEXT_IO.PUT_LINE(lv_file_handle_num, ' ');
TEXT_IO.PUT_LINE(lv_file_handle_num,
   'Error Code: '||TO_CHAR(p_error_code_num));
TEXT_IO.PUT_LINE(lv_file_handle_num,
   'Error Text: '||p_error_text_txt);
TEXT_IO.PUT_LINE(lv_file_handle_num,
   'Error Type: '||p_error_type_txt);
TEXT_IO.PUT_LINE(lv_file_handle_num,
   'DBMS Error Code: '||TO_CHAR(p_dbms_error_code_num));
TEXT_IO.PUT_LINE(lv_file_handle_num,
   'DBMS Error Text: '||p_dbms_error_text_txt);
TEXT_IO.PUT_LINE(lv_file_handle_num, ' ');
TEXT_IO.PUT_LINE(lv_file_handle_num, p_message_txt);
TEXT_IO.PUT_LINE(lv_file_handle_num, ' ');
-- Use text_io to write the name and value of all system_variables.
TEXT_IO.PUT_LINE(lv_file_handle_num,
   'End of standard error report.');
TEXT_IO.PUT_LINE(lv_file_handle_num, ' ');
-- Close the error log file.
TEXT_IO.FCLOSE(lv_file_handle_num);
-- Display the informational message.
BEGIN
   MESSAGE('Application error has been recorded.', NO_ACKNOWLEDGE);
   SYNCHRONIZE;
EXCEPTION
   WHEN OTHERS THEN
      NULL;
END;
EXCEPTION
WHEN lv_done_excep THEN
   NULL;
WHEN FORM_TRIGGER_FAILURE THEN
   RAISE FORM_TRIGGER_FAILURE;
```

```
   WHEN OTHERS THEN
      MESSAGE('An error has occurred during the error logging ' ||
         'procedure.', NO_ACKNOWLEDGE);
      RAISE FORM_TRIGGER_FAILURE;
END;
```

A sample log file created by this procedure would appear as the following:

Output (14_13.sql)

```
TUSC
Aug 12, 1998  16:17:20
Error Code: 0
Error Text:
Error Type:
DBMS Error Code: -20000
DBMS Error Text: ORA-20000:
ORA-06512: at "TUSC.CONFIGURATION_MANAGER", line 166
ORA-01400: mandatory(NOT NULL) column is missing or NULL during insert
Unhandled exception in create_customer_questions procedure.
BLOCK_STATUS: CHANGED
COORDINATION_OPERATION:
CURRENT_BLOCK: CUSTOMER_STRUCTURES
CURRENT_DATETIME: 12-AUG-1998 16:17:20
CURRENT_ITEM:
CURRENT_FORM: CUSTSTRUC
CURRENT_VALUE:
CURSOR_BLOCK: CUSTOMER_STRUCTURES
CURSOR_ITEM: CUSTOMER_STRUCTURES.ATTACHMENT_POINT
CURSOR_RECORD: 1
CURSOR_VALUE: Y
CUSTOM_ITEM_EVENT:
CUSTOM_ITEM_EVENT_PARAMETERS:
DATE_THRESHOLD: 01:00
EFFECTIVE_DATE: 12-AUG-1998 16:16:17
EVENT_WINDOW:
FORM_STATUS: CHANGED
LAST_RECORD: TRUE
MESSAGE_LEVEL: 10
MODE: NORMAL
MOUSE_BUTTON_PRESSED:
MOUSE_BUTTON_SHIFT_STATE:
MOUSE_CANVAS:
MOUSE_FORM:
MOUSE_ITEM:
MOUSE_RECORD: 0
MOUSE_RECORD_OFFSET: 0
```

Capturing Interface Errors in Forms

```
MOUSE_X_POS: 0.000000
MOUSE_Y_POS: 0.000000
RECORD_STATUS: CHANGED
SUPPRESS_WORKING: FALSE
TRIGGER_BLOCK: CUSTOMER_STRUCTURES
TRIGGER_ITEM:
TRIGGER_RECORD: 1
End of standard error report.
```

The second procedure, analyze_error, shown below is used to process runtime errors generated by the form module itself and determines whether the writing of an error file is warranted. Many things can trigger the error event within a form, and writing to an error log file every time a runtime error was encountered would not be wise. This would flood the file system with error files for such problems as:

■ At first record

■ Field must be entered

■ Field must be entered completely

■ Query caused no records to be retrieved

■ You cannot delete this record

■ Hours must be between 0 and 23

Although these problems are actual errors, they do not warrant an error file; instead, a warning message to the user would be more appropriate. The analyze_error procedure is illustrated in the following script. The following notes should make this procedure easier to understand.

■ The following procedure assumes all errors are severe and the desired behavior is to create an error log file. Global variables are used to override this behavior. The variable names must have the format TLAECA_*xxxxxyyyy* where *xxxxx* is the five-digit ERROR_CODE value and *yyyyy* is the five-digit DBMS_ERROR_CODE value. If a variable with this name is found, then the action specified by its value will be carried out. The value must be a ten-character string of ones (1) and zeroes (0) that serve as bit switches. A one (1) in the first (leftmost) position will cause the error to be displayed to the user in a message line. A one (1) in the second position will write an error log file. These global variables should be loaded at application startup to be available when a run-time error occurs.

File: 14_14.sql

```
PROCEDURE analyze_error
   (p_error_code_num        IN NUMBER,   -- Forms Error_Code value
    p_error_text_txt        IN VARCHAR2, -- Forms Error_Text value
    p_error_type_txt        IN VARCHAR2, -- Forms Error_Type value
    p_dbms_error_code_num IN NUMBER,     -- Forms DBMS_Error_Code value
    p_dbms_error_text_txt   IN VARCHAR2) -- Forms DBMS_Error_Text value
IS
   lv_button_pressed_num       PLS_INTEGER;
   lv_control_actions_txt      VARCHAR2(10);
   lv_error_var_name_txt       VARCHAR2(24);
BEGIN
   -- Search the control array for the specific runtime error.
   lv_error_var_name_txt := 'global.TLAECA_'||
      LPAD(TO_CHAR(ABS(p_error_code_num)), 5, '0')||
      LPAD(TO_CHAR(ABS(p_dbms_error_code_num)), 5, '0');
   DEFAULT_VALUE('?', lv_error_var_name_txt);
   lv_control_actions_txt := NAME_IN(lv_error_var_name_txt);
   IF lv_control_actions_txt = '?' THEN
      ERASE(lv_error_var_name_txt);
      lv_error_var_name_txt := 'global.TLAECA_'||
         LPAD(TO_CHAR(ABS(p_error_code_num)), 5, '0')||'00000';
      DEFAULT_VALUE('?', lv_error_var_name_txt);
      lv_control_actions_txt := NAME_IN(lv_error_var_name_txt);
      IF lv_control_actions_txt = '?' THEN
         ERASE(lv_error_var_name_txt);
         lv_control_actions_txt := '1100000000';
      END IF;
   END IF;
   -- Process the error as detailed by the lv_control_actions_txt
   -- variable. Display a message to the user.
   IF SUBSTR(lv_control_actions_txt, 1, 1) = 1 THEN
      MESSAGE('Error Analyzer ' || p_error_text_txt, NO_ACKNOWLEDGE);
   END IF;
   -- Log the error in an external file.
   IF SUBSTR(lv_control_actions_txt, 2, 1) = 1 THEN
      log_error('Runtime error trap.', p_error_code_num,
                p_error_text_txt, p_error_type_txt,
                p_dbms_error_code_num, p_dbms_error_text_txt);
   END IF;

-- As a final step, raise a FORM-TRIGGER-FAILURE.
-- The FORM_TRIGGER_FAILURE exception must be raised so that program
-- blocks which are monitoring the FORM_SUCCESS variable will not be
-- fooled into thinking that a packaged procedure succeeded.
```

```
     RAISE FORM_TRIGGER_FAILURE;
EXCEPTION
   WHEN FORM_TRIGGER_FAILURE THEN
      RAISE FORM_TRIGGER_FAILURE;
   WHEN OTHERS THEN
      log_error('Unhandled exception tusc_lib.analyze_error.',
         p_error_code_num,
         p_error_text_txt,
         p_error_type_txt,
         p_dbms_error_code_num,
         p_dbms_error_text_txt);
      RAISE FORM_TRIGGER_FAILURE;
END;
```

We have a procedure to analyze runtime errors and a procedure to write error files as needed; all that remains is to trap the error event. Create a Form level ON-ERROR trigger and call the analyze_error procedure, as the following code illustrates:

```
analyze_error(error_code,
   error_text,
   error_type,
   dbms_error_code,
   dbms_error_text);
```

Use KEY-Triggers to Centralize Code

Each function key is mapped to a particular event in the Oracle Forms run-time process. For example, by default, F9 represents KEY-LISTVAL and F10 represents the COMMIT/SAVE process (on Windows-based clients).

One of the challenges every developer faces is controlling what the user can do while running his or her application. You need to be prepared for anything. Using the KEY-OTHERS trigger in conjunction with desired KEY- events allows you to control your runtime environment.

A KEY-OTHERS trigger is associated with all keys that can have key triggers associated with them, but are not currently defined by function key triggers (at any level). When developing an application, a good practice is to create a KEY-OTHERS trigger and add other KEY-triggers, as functionality is required. When deploying this method, immediately add the KEY-EXIT trigger to enable a form to be exited.

The following is a list of KEY-triggers that may be created in your form. For any key trigger that is not defined, the KEY-OTHERS trigger logic will execute.

Use KEY- Triggers to Centralize Code

Built-In	Key Trigger	Associated Function Key
ABORT_QUERY	KEY-EXIT	[Exit/Cancel]
BLOCK_MENU	KEY-MENU	[Block Menu]
CLEAR_BLOCK	KEY-CLRBLK	[Clear Block]
CLEAR_FORM	KEY-CLRFRM	[Clear Form]
CLEAR_RECORD	KEY-CLRREC	[Clear Record]
COMMIT_FORM	KEY-COMMIT	[Commit]
COUNT_QUERY	KEY-CQUERY	[Count Query Hits]
CREATE_RECORD	KEY-CREREC	[Insert Record]
DELETE_RECORD	KEY-DELREC	[Delete Record]
DOWN	KEY-DOWN	[Down]
DUPLICATE_ITEM	KEY-DUPITEM	[Duplicate Item]
DUPLICATE_RECORD	KEY-DUPREC	[Duplicate Record]
EDIT_TEXTITEM	KEY-EDIT	[Edit]
ENTER	KEY-ENTER	[Enter]
ENTER_QUERY	KEY-ENTQRY	[Enter Query]
EXECUTE_QUERY	KEY-EXEQRY	[Execute Query]
EXIT_FORM	KEY-EXIT	[Exit/Cancel]
HELP	KEY-HELP	[Help]
LIST_VALUES	KEY-LISTVAL	[List]
LOCK_RECORD	KEY-UPDREC	[Lock Record]
NEXT_BLOCK	KEY-NXTBLK	[Next Block]
NEXT_ITEM	KEY-NEXTITEM	[Next Item]
NEXT_KEY	KEY-NXTKEY	[Next Primary Key Fld]
NEXT_RECORD	KEY-NXTREC	[Next Record]
NEXT_SET	KEY-NXTSET	[Next Set of Records]
PREVIOUS_BLOCK	KEY-PRVBLK	[Previous Block]
PREVIOUS_ITEM	KEY-PREVITEM	[Previous Item]
PREVIOUS_RECORD	KEY-PRVREC	[Previous Record]
PRINT	KEY-PRINT	[Print]
SCROLL_DOWN	KEY-SCRDOWN	[Scroll Down]
SCROLL_UP	KEY-SCRUP	[Scroll Up]
UP	KEY-UP	[Up]

Use KEY- Triggers to Centralize Code

All key specific source code should be encapsulated in the appropriate key trigger. For example, all code necessary to exit a form should be included in the KEY-EXIT trigger. When you want to exit the form, you issue a DO_KEY ('EXIT_FORM') command. The following is an example of a WHEN-BUTTON-PRESSED trigger for a button that exits a form.

```
BEGIN
    DO_KEY('EXIT_FORM');
END;
```

Any code specific to exiting the form should be included in the KEY-EXIT trigger.

Base a Form Block on a Stored Procedure

With the release of Oracle Developer (Developer 2000), Oracle introduced several new features. One of the additions was the capability to base a Forms Block on a PL/SQL stored procedure. This new feature allows for the partitioning of the application to reduce the amount of database "round trips," which, in turn, improves performance. It also allows for better encapsulation and the capability to implement a more secure environment.

For a Form based on a stored procedure, authorized users would only have to be granted EXECUTE privilege on the stored procedure, versus the standard SELECT, INSERT, UPDATE, and DELETE on the underlying database tables of the form. Refer to Chapter 10 for more information on PL/SQL security.

The following is an example of a package that a forms block can use as its data source versus a database table. Note that the PL/SQL code required in the stored procedures replaces the functionality Oracle Forms provides by default when a block in a form is based on a database table. This includes the SELECT, INSERT, UPDATE, DELETE, and LOCK commands Oracle Forms creates by default behind the scenes in normal Oracle Forms execution.

File: 14_15.sql

```
CREATE OR REPLACE PACKAGE s_employee_pkg AS
   TYPE type_emp_rec IS RECORD
      (employee_id          s_employee.employee_id%TYPE,
       employee_last_name   s_employee.employee_last_name%TYPE,
       employee_first_name  s_employee.employee_first_name%TYPE,
       salary               s_employee.salary%TYPE,
       department_id        s_employee.department_id%TYPE,
       department_name      s_department.department_name%TYPE);
```

```
   TYPE type_emp_no_rec IS RECORD
      (employee_id          s_employee.employee_id%TYPE);
   TYPE type_emp_ref_cur  IS REF CURSOR RETURN type_emp_rec;
   TYPE type_emp_table    IS TABLE OF type_emp_rec
                             INDEX BY BINARY_INTEGER;
   TYPE type_emp_no_table IS TABLE OF type_emp_no_rec
                             INDEX BY BINARY_INTEGER;

   PROCEDURE empquery_refcur
      (p_block_data_rec IN OUT type_emp_ref_cur,
       p_deptno_num IN NUMBER);
   PROCEDURE empquery
      (p_deptno_num IN NUMBER,
       p_block_data_table IN OUT type_emp_table);
   PROCEDURE empinsert (p_block_data_table IN type_emp_table);
   PROCEDURE empupdate (p_block_data_table IN type_emp_table);
   PROCEDURE empdelete (p_block_data_table IN type_emp_no_table);
   PROCEDURE emplock   (p_block_data_table IN type_emp_no_table);
END s_employee_pkg;
/
```

File: 14_15a.sql

```
CREATE OR REPLACE PACKAGE BODY s_employee_pkg AS
PROCEDURE empquery_refcur
   (p_block_data_rec IN OUT type_emp_ref_cur,
    p_deptno_num IN NUMBER) IS
BEGIN
   OPEN p_block_data_rec FOR
   SELECT e.employee_id, e.employee_last_name, e.employee_first_name,
          e.salary, e.department_id, d.department_name
   FROM   s_employee e, s_department d
   WHERE  e.department_id = NVL(p_deptno_num, e.department_id)
   AND    e.department_id = d.department_id
   ORDER BY e.employee_id;
END empquery_refcur;
PROCEDURE empquery
   (p_deptno_num IN NUMBER,
    p_block_data_table IN OUT type_emp_table) IS

   lv_array_num NUMBER := 1;
   CURSOR cur_empselect IS
     SELECT e.employee_id, e.employee_last_name,
            e.employee_first_name, e.salary,
            e.department_id, d.department_name
     FROM   s_employee e, s_department d
```

```
        WHERE    e.department_id = NVL(p_deptno_num, e.department_id)
        AND      e.department_id = d.department_id
        ORDER BY e.employee_id;
BEGIN
   OPEN cur_empselect;
   LOOP
      FETCH cur_empselect INTO
         p_block_data_table(lv_array_num).employee_id,
         p_block_data_table(lv_array_num).employee_last_name,
         p_block_data_table(lv_array_num).employee_first_name,
         p_block_data_table(lv_array_num).salary,
         p_block_data_table(lv_array_num).department_id,
         p_block_data_table(lv_array_num).department_name;
      EXIT WHEN cur_empselect%NOTFOUND;
      lv_array_num := lv_array_num + 1;
   END LOOP;
END empquery;
PROCEDURE empinsert(p_block_data_table IN type_emp_table) IS
   lv_count_num   NUMBER;
BEGIN
   lv_count_num := p_block_data_table.COUNT;
   FOR lv_array_num IN 1..lv_count_num LOOP
      INSERT INTO s_employee( employee_id, employee_last_name,
                  employee_first_name, salary, department_id)
      VALUES (p_block_data_table(lv_array_num).employee_id,
              p_block_data_table(lv_array_num).employee_last_name,
              p_block_data_table(lv_array_num).employee_first_name,
              p_block_data_table(lv_array_num).salary,
              p_block_data_table(lv_array_num).department_id);
   END LOOP;
END empinsert;
PROCEDURE empupdate(p_block_data_table IN type_emp_table) IS
   lv_count_num NUMBER;
BEGIN
   lv_count_num := p_block_data_table.COUNT;
   FOR lv_array_num IN 1..lv_count_num LOOP
      UPDATE s_employee
      SET    employee_last_name  =
                p_block_data_table(lv_array_num).employee_last_name,
             employee_first_name =
                p_block_data_table(lv_array_num).employee_first_name,
             salary              =
                p_block_data_table(lv_array_num).salary,
             department_id       =
                p_block_data_table(lv_array_num).department_id
      WHERE  employee_id         =
                p_block_data_table(lv_array_num).employee_id;
```

```
   END LOOP;
END empupdate;
PROCEDURE empdelete(p_block_data_table IN type_emp_no_table) IS
   lv_count_num NUMBER;
BEGIN
   lv_count_num := p_block_data_table.COUNT;
   FOR lv_array_num IN 1..lv_count_num LOOP
      DELETE FROM s_employee
      WHERE employee_id =
              p_block_data_table(lv_array_num).employee_id;
   END LOOP;
END empdelete;
PROCEDURE emplock(p_block_data_table IN type_emp_no_table) IS
   lv_count_num NUMBER;
   lv_block_rec type_emp_rec;
BEGIN
   lv_count_num := p_block_data_table.COUNT;
   FOR lv_array_num IN 1..lv_count_num LOOP
      SELECT e.employee_id, e.employee_last_name,
             e.employee_first_name, e.salary,
             e.department_id, d.department_name
      INTO   lv_block_rec
      FROM   s_employee e, s_department d
      WHERE  e.employee_id   =
             p_block_data_table(lv_array_num).employee_id
      AND    e.department_id = d.department_id
      FOR UPDATE OF e.employee_last_name NOWAIT;
   END LOOP;
END emplock;
END s_employee_pkg;
/
```

Once the preceding package is created, a form can be created in the Oracle Forms module that is based on the s_employee_pkg stored package. There is a data block wizard in the Forms navigator to walk you through the creation of a form based on a stored program unit. The data block wizard will prompt you for all the procedures to execute for the basic operations in forms, including query, insert, update, delete, and lock. Including all these procedures is not required. If you omit any of the procedures, that particular action is not performed or available in the form.

When a form is based on a stored procedure, you can SELECT, INSERT, UPDATE, DELETE, and LOCK records. However, venturing down the path of basing forms on stored procedures versus database tables, you need to realize the amount of additional development required. This feature is beneficial, but only in selected cases.

Summary

This chapter examined the role of the PL/SQL language in the Oracle product set and third-party products. Over the years, Oracle has increased the integration of the PL/SQL language by incorporating a separate PL/SQL Engine in many of the products. This engine supports the PL/SQL language and PL/SQL extensions specific to each product. This integration knowledge becomes a requirement to developing and deploying successful Oracle-based applications. This chapter highlighted some of the built-in packages and specifics on the Oracle products, primarily the Forms product. The chapter then covered some strategies of PL/SQL development and use that can impact the overall development and continued maintenance.

Tips Review

- If a procedure is WRAPped prior to creating the procedure, the output from the V$SQLAREA view is identical. WRAPped PL/SQL program units stored in the database will still process and pass SQL statements through the SQL Area in the same manner as unWRAPped program units.

- When the process of tuning PL/SQL code starts, an understanding of the processing of the PL/SQL Engines, whether client-side or server-side, provides further insight into the processing of the PL/SQL code and assists in the restructuring of PL/SQL and PL/SQL architecture. Remember, the PL/SQL Engine reformats SQL statements (converts the entire statement to uppercase, not including data values, and eliminates spaces) included in PL/SQL source code prior to passing these statements to the SQL Engine.

- Always think of the location the PL/SQL program unit would best serve the application. Always think of reusability. Always communicate and document PL/SQL Libraries and stored PL/SQL program units created to the development team.

- As a general rule, because global variables are a fixed length of 255 characters, limit the number of global variables in any particular form to five.

- Package specifications can be used to create global variables, which can be accessed by all programs during that session. Once the session is terminated or the package is recompiled, the variables will no longer be available.

- Use the SHARE_LIBRARY_DATA parameter in the CALL_FORM, NEW_FORM, and OPEN_FORM built-in procedures to share library data between forms. The parameters are positional. Therefore, the parameters that precede SHARE_LIBRARY_DATA need to be passed.

■ In PL/SQL versions prior to 2.3, instead of having multiple references to SYSDATE, consider using a CURSOR to select the value into a null-canvas item or a global variable.

■ Communication of errors between the client-side PL/SQL and server-side stored PL/SQL must be handled with care. As the complexity of the code increases, using pragmas to communicate errors will be needed to create seamless integration between PL/SQL program units.

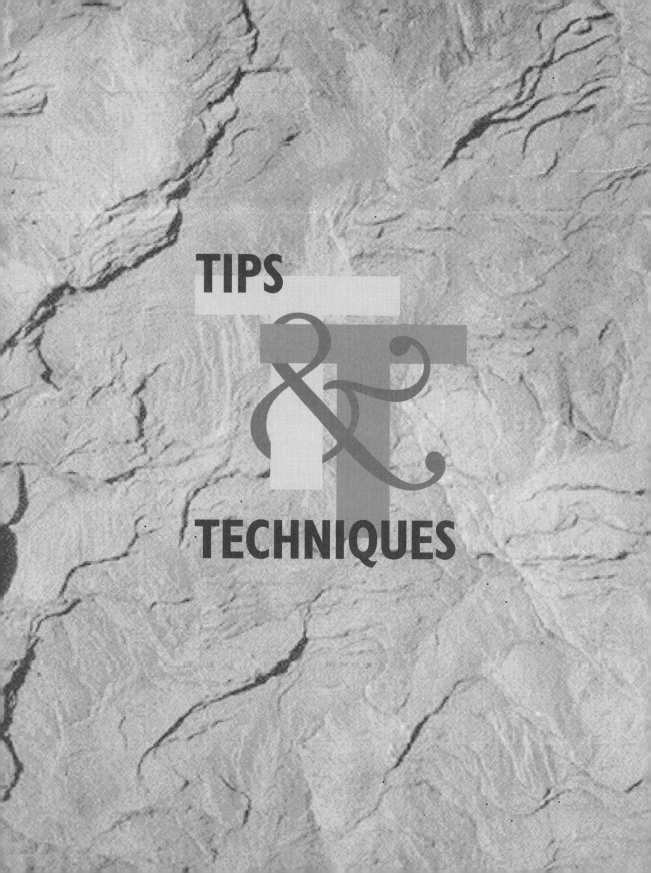

TIPS
& T
TECHNIQUES

CHAPTER
15

Understanding the
Critical Role of
PL/SQL in the Web
(Developer and DBA)

P L/SQL plays a critical role in Oracle's strategic move to the Web. From the initial version of Oracle (Web) Application Server to the current version, the role of PL/SQL has increased with each new version. This increased role has come in the form of enhanced functionality and flexibility through the expansion of new Web-based packages and procedures. The goal of this chapter is to introduce you to the integral role of PL/SQL in Oracle's Web product, namely Oracle Application Server. This chapter provides details on the various areas of this technology to jump-start your knowledge in the development and deployment of PL/SQL on the Web.

The Internet and the architecture on which it is based have developed over the years, as have the Oracle Web Server product and name. Versions 1 and 2 were called Oracle Web Server. Version 3 was renamed as Oracle Web Application Server, and version 4 removed Web from the name to make it Oracle Application Server. Why? Simply, Oracle's solution is not merely a Web Server; it is much, much more. The Oracle Application Server truly is an application server that uses "cartridges." In fact, more than 100 Web servers are available on the market, most of which are free, so why would anyone want to compete in that market? Oracle's product takes servicing Web applications to a new level, so this is not just another Web server.

PL/SQL is such an important and core part of Oracle Application Server, and your existing knowledge of PL/SQL allows you to leverage your experience and transition into this new area with ease. This chapter covers the following areas:

- Understanding cartridges and the PL/SQL cartridge

- Explaining how URLs execute applications

- Identifying the underlying operation when referencing URLs

- Detailing the PL/SQL Web toolkit

  - Outlining the components of the PL/SQL Web toolkit

  - Creating HTML tags not located in the PL/SQL Web toolkit

- Building Web pages with PL/SQL packages

  - Outlining PL/SQL toolkit considerations

  - Debugging parameters passed into PL/SQL procedures

- Writing Oracle PL/SQL for the Web

  - Using templates for code generation

  - Using WebAlchemy to convert HTML to PL/SQL

  - Setting standards when writing PL/SQL for the Web

■ Accessing stored procedures

   ■ Understanding transaction life

   ■ Viewing HTML output from SQL*Plus

   ■ Showing the source code of a stored PL/SQL program unit

   ■ Testing procedures with default values

■ Reviewing locking in a Web environment

   ■ Highlighting the best uses of transaction services

   ■ Maintaining state with optimistic locking

   ■ Preventing nontransactions

   ■ Creating a less than optimistic locking strategy

   ■ Using a last_update_date column locking strategy

   ■ Using the OWA_OPT_LOCK package

■ Including functional objects

   ■ Adding functional objects not supported by the PL/SQL toolkit

   ■ Including graphics

   ■ Including sound

   ■ Understanding the quality of MIDI sound files

   ■ Reviewing Java

   ■ Reviewing JavaScript

   ■ Reviewing form objects

■ Understanding the PL/SQL Agent use of environment variables

■ Passing parameters to PL/SQL

   ■ Getting parameters from the Web browser to the PL/SQL Agent

■ Most effective ways of using POST and GET

   ■ Passing parameters using an HTML form

   ■ Providing default parameter values

- Understanding the 5111 error message
- Understanding the numeric value error
  - Handling multivalued parameters
  - Understanding overloading procedures
- Understanding the PL/SQL Agent error handling
  - Handling application errors
  - Handling system errors
  - Integrating error pages

For more information on the PL/SQL cartridge and the Web PL/SQL toolkit, refer to *Oracle Application Server Web Toolkit Reference,* by Bradley D. Brown (Oracle Press).

Understanding Cartridges and the PL/SQL Cartridge

Cartridges are persistent processes that can be accessed from not only the Web, but also from the Oracle Database. One cartridge used in Oracle's Application Server is the PL/SQL cartridge. This cartridge began as a PL/SQL CGI (Common Gateway Interface) program as part of the Web toolkit in versions 1 and 2, and was actually re-engineered as a cartridge for version 3 of Oracle Application Server (Oracle Web Application Server).

The PL/SQL cartridge enables you to execute PL/SQL code through the Web. The results of the PL/SQL code can perform database operations (SELECT, INSERT, UPDATE, and DELETE), and they can return information back to the user's browser identical to other CGI programs. In this manner, the Web could refer to the Internet or your intranet, accessing PL/SQL through a URL. The URL is the text box where you specify a browser's address or location field.

Explaining How URLs Execute Applications

A *Universal Resource Locator* (URL) is the key to the Web and can be used to execute applications or programs. In short, the URL path is a virtual path the Web Listener maps to a physical file on the server. URLs contain the following four parts:

Cartridges and the PL/SQL Cartridge

- **Protocol** The standard or language used to transfer the information. In the case of the Web, the protocol is HyperText Transfer Protocol (HTTP). This protocol is usually followed by a colon and two forward slashes (that is, http://).

- **Domain** The virtual hostname maps to a specific IP address (a *hostname* is a unique character string that identifies exactly one computer on the Internet). For example: www.mountainbike.com might map to an IP address of 207.221.96.67. An optional component of the domain specification is the TCP/IP port. If no port number is specified, the default is port 80. The port number is separated from the virtual host name by a colon. For example, www.mountainbike.com:7777.

- **Virtual Path** The path name identifies the virtual path and a specific application (or program) to execute. This is an optional parameter. If it is not specified, the Web Listener will determine the virtual root for the virtual host specified. An example virtual path might be /cgi/runme.exe, specifying to execute the runme.exe program in the virtual directory called /cgi. With the Oracle Application Server, a virtual path can be handled by the Web Listener (servicing both CGI and file system requests) or the Web Request Broker (WRB, servicing cartridge requests).

- **Query String** Supplies parameter values to the requested application. This is also an optional parameter. The default is that no parameters will be passed to the application. An example of a query string might be first_name=Jeremy.

The combined syntax is as follows:

```
protocol://domain/virtual_path?query_string
```

A URL that invokes a PL/SQL Agent to access the database appears similar to the following:

```
http://www.mountainbike.com/biker/plsql/trails?skill_level=3
```

The substring http://www.mountainbike.com signals the Web browser to connect to the virtual host of www.mountainbike.com on the host's port 80 (the default port number because it was not specified explicitly in the URL) using the HTTP protocol.

When the Oracle Web Listener running on www.mountainbike.com receives the request, the virtual path substring */biker/plsql* cannot be resolved by the Web Listener, so it passes the information to the WRB. The WRB knows to connect to the PL/SQL cartridge for a specific PL/SQL Agent (the knowledge of what cartridge to pass the request to is identified in the setup configuration). A PL/SQL Agent logs into the database using a specific username and password specified in a Database Access Descriptor (DAD, in this case, the biker DAD), or requires the user specify a valid Oracle username/password to log into the database. The URL is processed as follows:

- The Web Listener is configured so the string */biker/plsql* is not a known virtual path, which causes it to invoke the WRB.

- The WRB understands */biker/plsql* to mean it should pass execution to a Web Request Broker Executable Engine (WRBX) interfaced to the PL/SQL cartridge in the form of CGI environment variables. (For the sake of compatibility, WRB can recognize CGI environment variables.)

- The string */biker/plsql* is passed as the environment variable SCRIPT_NAME. The PL/SQL Agent parses the SCRIPT_NAME to extract the PL/SQL Agent linked to a specific DAD. In this example, the DAD is *biker*. The PL/SQL Agent is passed as the directory name immediately preceding */plsql*, which is actually a file containing database connection information; *biker* is the name of the PL/SQL Agent itself.

- The string */trails* is passed as the environment variable PATH_INFO. This indicates *trails* is the specific application to be executed. The PL/SQL Agent executes the PL/SQL procedure called *trails* stored in the database.

- The question mark (?) denotes arguments are to follow.

- The string *skill_level=3* is passed as the environment variable QUERY_STRING. This indicates the value *3* (the most difficult level of mountain biking trails) is to be passed to the trails application (procedure) for the parameter skill_level. This corresponds in name, and is compatible in data type, to a PL/SQL parameter used in the application.

Identifying the Underlying Operation When Referencing URLs

When you reference a URL, the Web Listener and the WRB use the URL to determine the PL/SQL cartridge to run for a specific PL/SQL Agent by the virtual path you specify. The PL/SQL cartridge calls a stored procedure and passes in the appropriate values. The PL/SQL code facilitates the generation of HTML, which is sent back to the browser. Having your code execute within the database has performance, security, and portability benefits. These benefits are the main reason you want to design your dynamically generated Web pages to produce URLs that call PL/SQL procedures in response to user actions.

The advantages of storing application logic, namely PL/SQL packages, procedures, and functions, in the database are described in further detail in Chapter 5.

Detailing the PL/SQL Web Toolkit

The Oracle Application Server comes with a group of PL/SQL packages called the PL/SQL Web toolkit, which helps you communicate with the PL/SQL cartridge and send and receive information to and from the user's browser. Remember, all information displayed in your browser is translated to HTML for display.

Outlining the Components of the PL/SQL Web Toolkit

The PL/SQL Web toolkit contains three components, each with its own role in managing information displayed on your Web pages. Two of the packages facilitate the generation of the HTML: HyperText Procedures (HTP) and HyperText Functions (HTF). HTP sends HTML to the user's browser. HTF are typical PL/SQL functions that return data (HTML code) within PL/SQL as a string variable. The third major component in the toolkit is the OWA utilities. These are PL/SQL packages, each of which start with the letters OWA. OWA (Oracle Web Agent) is the original name for the PL/SQL CGI program. These utilities include a number of additional PL/SQL packages that assist in obtaining and sending various types of information. For example, OWA_COOKIE facilitates sending and reading cookies. A *cookie* is a string variable stored on the client's browser. The cookie can be set or read by the server upon any client request. OWA_UTIL contains a number of generic utilities to do everything from reading CGI variables to printing data in an HTML table. Utilities exist for locking records optimistically (OWA_OPT_LOCK), security (OWA_SEC), image processing (OWA_IMAGE), and more.

The following table lists the components according to versions of the toolkit:

Version 1.1+	Version 2.0+	Version 3.0+
HyperText Procedures (HTP)	Additional Oracle Web Agent (OWA) Utilities	OWA Security Utilities (OWA_SEC)
HyperText Functions (HTF)	OWA Pattern Utilities (OWA_PATTERN)	OWA Optimistic Locking Utilities (OWA_OPT_LOCK)

Version 1.1+	Version 2.0+	Version 3.0+
Oracle Web Agent (OWA) Utilities (OWA_UTIL)	OWA Text Utilities (OWA_TEXT) OWA Image Utilities (OWA_IMAGE) OWA Cookie Utilities (OWA_COOKIE)	

NOTE
Version 4.0 (Oracle Application Server) did not add any new packages or procedures to the toolkit.

The following example illustrates the use of these supplied Oracle packages. If you want to display a list of records from a database table, the following PL/SQL code would display a list of table names owned by the current DAD's users.

File: 15_1.sql

```
CREATE OR REPLACE PROCEDURE list_dads_tables IS
   CURSOR cur_tables IS
      SELECT table_name
      FROM   user_tables
      ORDER BY table_name;
BEGIN
  HTP.HTMLOPEN;
  HTP.HEADOPEN;
  -- The two single quotes ('') in the next command equates
  -- to one literal quote
  HTP.TITLE('Display a List of the Current DAD''s Tables');
  HTP.HEADCLOSE;
  HTP.BODYOPEN;
  HTP.ULISTOPEN;
     FOR cur_tables_rec IN cur_tables LOOP
        HTP.LISTITEM(cur_tables_rec.table_name);
     END LOOP;
  HTP.ULISTCLOSE;
  HTP.BODYCLOSE;
  HTP.HTMLCLOSE;
END list_dads_tables;
/
```

As illustrated in the preceding example, it is simple PL/SQL code with some PL/SQL Web toolkit package calls embedded within the code to generate the HTML displaying the table name list in a browser.

While the PL/SQL Web toolkit minimizes your need to know HTML syntax, you are still required to have a working knowledge of HTML. However, by using the PL/SQL Web toolkit, you will not be required to hardcode the exact HTML syntax (or tags) into your PL/SQL procedures.

Creating HTML Tags not Located in the PL/SQL Web Toolkit

If you find a specific HTML tag you use on a regular basis that is not part of the PL/SQL Web toolkit, you can write your own extended HTML package, extend the HTP and HTF packages, or use the print procedure of the HTP package to send data back to the user's browser (for example, HTP.PRINT('<SPAN ID=block1>')). I recommend you create your own package to store any extended HTML tags versus storing these extensions in the HTP and HTF packages. This method of extension eases upgrades to future versions of Oracle Application Server because your customized extension(s) will be created outside Oracle's packages.

Building Web Pages with PL/SQL Packages

You can approach the toolkit in two ways: Use HTP.PRINT for everything and embed your own HTML, or use the Web toolkit packages to their fullest extent. If you already know HTML, using HTP.PRINT with the PL/SQL cartridge may at first appear the easiest and the shortest learning curve. In the long run, using the toolkit provides for better long-term support and readability of your code. If you are familiar with Oracle Pro*Language products and Oracle Call Interface (OCI), this is a similar difference. Using the toolkit adds processing overhead by going to the database and executing the procedures that are translated into HTP.PRINT statements, but the development and future maintenance far outweigh this minimal overhead cost, in my opinion. Therefore, I strongly recommend using the PL/SQL toolkit provided by Oracle.

The preceding list_dads_tables procedure example demonstrates how to use the toolkit. The following example illustrates how to perform the same functionality with only the HTP.PRINT procedure.

File: 15_2.sql

```
CREATE OR REPLACE PROCEDURE list_dads_tables IS
    CURSOR cur_tables IS
        SELECT table_name
        FROM   user_tables
        ORDER BY table_name;
BEGIN
    HTP.PRINT('<HTML>');
    HTP.PRINT('<HEAD>');
    HTP.PRINT('<TITLE>Display a List of the Current DAD''s ' ||
        'Tables</TITLE>');
    HTP.PRINT('</HEAD>');
    HTP.PRINT('<BODY>');
    HTP.PRINT('<UL>');
        FOR cur_tables_rec IN cur_tables LOOP
            HTP.PRINT('<LI>' || cur_tables_rec.table_name);
        END LOOP;
    HTP.PRINT('</UL>');
    HTP.PRINT('</BODY>');
    HTP.PRINT('</HTML>');
END list_dads_tables;
/
```

Outlining PL/SQL Toolkit Considerations

When building Web pages, consider the forward compatibility of HTML, XML, or whatever new standards are introduced in the future. If you embed HTML into HTP.PRINT statements, you will be required to go back and change the HTML. If you use the PL/SQL toolkit as it is upgraded, you can take advantage of new HTML versions with little effort, thereby eliminating the need to be intimately familiar with World Wide Web technology. In addition, debugging the syntax of your code is more difficult when you use the HTP.PRINT procedure and concatenate your commands and attributes together because you must produce the HTML code, view it in the browser, and debug it. What happens if you forget a space? What if you misspelled the attributed name? What if your PL/SQL code uses IF, THEN, ELSE logic—will you test every possible HTML statement? By using the PL/SQL Web toolkit, the commands are checked for syntax at program unit compilation time. Again, I recommend the PL/SQL toolkit path. Whatever path you choose, it's critically important to pick a standard and stick with it.

Debugging Parameters Passed into PL/SQL Procedures

To assist with debugging, it may be helpful to display the parameters passed into your PL/SQL procedures. One option is to use the HTP.PRINT procedure to display each of your procedure variables. Another option is to use a database table, then insert values into the table. Unfortunately, using the database table method, if your procedure fails to execute, you will not see the values of these variables. You can always see each input parameter's value by looking in the PL/SQL Agent's log file (the name of this file is typically wrb.log, and it is located in the admin subdirectory under the Oracle Web Home directory). The wrb.log should be reviewed and understood because it logs important information regarding the WRB process. The log follows a standard format and is, therefore, easy to read and understand.

Writing Oracle PL/SQL for the Web

When writing PL/SQL for the Web, all your standard coding techniques should be followed (for further details regarding PL/SQL coding standards refer to Chapter 3). You will want to create a template (whether using HTML or PL/SQL), ensure you have standards in place, and run Explain Plan or TRACE your SQL for tuning (refer to Chapter 7 and Chapter 8 for more details on SQL and PL/SQL tuning). You also want to make sure you perform code reviews with your DBAs.

PL/SQL development should follow the same development methodology that you follow when developing PL/SQL for Oracle Developer or any other tool. Once the functionality is tested and perfected, then it can be modified for integration and deployment on the Web. Likewise, if you have already written a substantial amount of PL/SQL code, you can easily embed HTML commands within the PL/SQL to make it communicate with a browser.

Using Templates for Code Generation

You could develop a program (or even a PL/SQL procedure) that prompts a developer for answers to simple questions (like form or list query, SELECT statement, and so forth), then generates the code for the developer to use as a starting template. The template program, typically called a *template generator,* can also follow your standards. Developers can then use the template that is created to begin their coding efforts. The Oracle Government site (http://govt.us.oracle.com) contains a free application for download, which is made up of a set of packages called WebView, prompting a developer through a series of questions and resulting in the generation of the procedure. These procedures follow a set of standards, and your developers could use them as a starting point (or template).

Using WebAlchemy to Convert HTML to PL/SQL

You can convert static HTML pages to PL/SQL by using WebAlchemy, a free GUI tool written in Microsoft Visual C++. The Oracle Government site (http://govt.us.oracle.com) contains WebAlchemy free for download. Alan Hobbs, an Oracle consultant from Australia, developed this tool. WebAlchemy is not an official Oracle product, it is not supported by Oracle, and it is provided "as is." This utility converts HTML pages and Microsoft Active Server Pages (ASP) into PL/SQL procedures (containing HTP and HTF procedure calls). This tool is helpful for taking static HTML pages and converting the pages into a dynamic set of pages accessing an Oracle database. The most popular reasons for using this tool are

- To convert HTML designs and graphics from HTML generators, such as Macormedia Dreamweaver and Microsoft Frontpage

- To convert HTML code from another site

- To use as a learning tool of how to embed HTML into PL/SQL procedures to Web enable the information

Setting Standards When Writing PL/SQL for the Web

Setting standards when you write HTML and PL/SQL code for the Web is important. For example, although you don't have to start your HTML pages with the <HTML> or HTP.HTMLOPEN procedure call, this is a good standard to set for your HTML pages. In fact, you may find creating a procedure called *pageopen* worthwhile. Pageopen executes the HTP.HTMLOPEN, HTP.HEADOPEN, HTP.TITLE, HTP.HEADCLOSE, and HTP.BODYOPEN procedures as the following illustrates. You can pass as much information into this procedure as you like (for example, preferred background color and image) or pull most of the information from the user's profile in the database and pass in the title (which could be the same as the first level 1 header). Developing such a procedure can provide a consistent look and feel throughout your Web site. A complementary *pageclose* procedure can also save you some coding by producing the HTP.BODYCLOSE and HTP.HTMLCLOSE statements at the end of the page. Because JavaScript belongs in the HEAD section, you may also want to include a JavaScript parameter in your pageopen procedure.

File: 15_3.sql

```
CREATE OR REPLACE PROCEDURE pageopen
    (p_in_title_txt IN VARCHAR2) IS
BEGIN
    HTP.HTMLOPEN;
    HTP.HEADOPEN;
    HTP.TITLE (p_in_title_txt);
    HTP.HEADCLOSE;
    HTP.BODYOPEN;
    HTP.HEADER (1, p_in_title_txt, 'CENTER');
END pageopen;
/
```

Accessing Stored Procedures

As previously noted, stored procedures are accessed from the Web via standard URL resolutions. The Web Request Broker (WRB) is set up to run a PL/SQL Agent based on your URL specification. Standard input parameters are passed into the PL/SQL procedure. Procedures accept arguments for each unique parameter name submitted by the calling form. The URL will look similar to the following:

```
http://virtual_host:port/agent/plsql/package.proc?param1=value1&param2=value2
```

Where *agent* is the PL/SQL Web Agent name, *plsql* is the keyword the WRB uses to identify the call to the PL/SQL Agent (note, as of version 4.0 of the Oracle Application Server, such a "magic word" is no longer required). *Package* is the package name (if the procedure is not in a package, no package name would be supplied). *Proc* is the stored procedure name. *Param1* and *param2* are the parameters 1 and 2, respectively. *Value1* and *value2* are the respective values corresponding to parameters 1 and 2. Note: the parameter separator for parameters is the *&* character.

Understanding Transaction Life

Although cartridges are persistent, when using the PL/SQL cartridge, the connection to the database is not persistent. In other words, when you call a procedure or packaged procedure with a URL, the PL/SQL cartridge logs into the database using the username and password for the respective DAD, executes the procedure, and logs off the database. Prior to logging off, the database engine actually performs an implicit commit of your pending transactions. The life of the transaction is equal to the life of the procedure's completion.

The username and password can be prompted for each time a connection is made. The connection issue is an extremely important point to understand and remember when using the PL/SQL cartridge. This would be the same as starting SQL*Plus, executing a procedure, then immediately logging off SQL*Plus. Think of the issues that center on this type of scenario. This is how you need to think about PL/SQL in a Web environment and the execution therein.

Viewing HTML Output from SQL*Plus

To see the HTML output from SQL*Plus, you must enable output to the screen, execute a procedure, and then execute the OWA_UTIL.SHOWPAGE procedure, the following illustrates:

```
SET SERVEROUTPUT ON SIZE 1000000
EXECUTE get_customer_list ('12345')
EXECUTE OWA_UTIL.SHOWPAGE
```

Showing the Source Code of a Stored PL/SQL Program Unit

If OWA_UTIL.SHOWSOURCE is not disabled from direct browser access (this is accomplished by setting the "Protect PL/SQL Agent" to TRUE in your configuration of the PL/SQL Agent), you can easily show the source of a PL/SQL package or procedure by typing the following URL:

```
http://vitual_host:port/agent/plsql/owa_util.showsource?cname=package_or_procedure
```

If the PL/SQL Agent is protected, you can add an anchor within your procedure that displays the code listing when the link is selected. You could embed code in each procedure to do this, you could write your own generic procedure to handle this, or you can use OWA_UTIL.SIGNATURE to provide this type of functionality. The OWA_UTIL.SIGNATURE procedure produces a signature line and can provide a link to display the source code. You can also refer to Chapter 13 for more details on viewing stored PL/SQL source code by querying the data dictionary view USER_SOURCE (ALL_SOURCE, or DBA_SOURCE).

Testing Procedures with Default Values

Developers often test their code from within SQL*Plus or a PL/SQL editor. This is typically easy to do because you can call the procedure as previously demonstrated using the EXECUTE command. The following example illustrates the execution in SQL*Plus.

```
EXECUTE test_me ('a', 'b', 'c')
```

As you can see, the variables are passed into the procedure according to their relative positional order. But what if the parameters allowed default values if no value was passed for a parameter? For example, from a URL, the call to a procedure might look similar to the following:

```
http://virtual_host/bdb/plsql/test_me?p_param1_txt=a&p_param3_txt=c
```

The test_me procedure might be declared as such:

```
CREATE OR REPLACE PROCEDURE test_me
    (p_param1_txt IN VARCHAR2 DEFAULT 'x',
     p_param2_txt IN VARCHAR2 DEFAULT 'y',
     p_param3_txt IN VARCHAR2 DEFAULT 'z') IS
BEGIN
...
END;
/
```

How would you emulate this with the EXECUTE command? You can test your procedure to make sure it will work without the values being passed by using the "p_param1_txt => value1" syntax from SQL*Plus. For example, to emulate the preceding URL, you would type:

```
EXECUTE test_me (p_param1_txt => 'a', p_param3_txt => 'c')
```

Reviewing Locking in a Web Environment

As described in the preceding Transaction Life section, HTTP is a stateless protocol, which means managing record locks can be challenging. Remember that the PL/SQL cartridge logs into the database, performs its actions and logs off. If you have a procedure that performs a SELECT FOR UPDATE operation, the PL/SQL cartridge selects the record(s) and places a lock on the record(s) queried, and then, when the procedure finishes its execution, it unlocks the record(s)—most likely not the desired result. However, Transaction Services (available in the Advanced Edition of Oracle Application Server) can help automate application state management. When your application is going to perform a set of DML operations, such as INSERT, UPDATE, or DELETE over a span of time, you may wish to use Transaction Services.

Highlighting the Best Uses of Transaction Services

The best transactions for Transaction Services are those transactions that perform a set or group of operations spanning time, which are dependent upon each other. In other words, if you are developing a transaction that consists of one DML operation—say, an INSERT statement or multiple DMLs all in a single HTTP request—it is probably not worth using Transaction Services. However, if your transaction spans time and consists of multiple DML statements (for example, ten INSERT statements, three UPDATE statements, and one DELETE statement), then Transaction Services will simplify your development efforts. "Spans time" refers to the transaction consisting of a beginning, a middle, and an end, that the transaction is not capable of performing all in a single HTTP request but, rather, spans several HTTP requests; user interaction takes place at each stage (or state) of the transaction. An example of such a request could be as simple as a request from a user to UPDATE a record, which must be locked for that specific user.

Maintaining State with Optimistic Locking

If you are using the PL/SQL cartridge, you must describe your beginning, middle, and ending transaction components to the PL/SQL Agent's Transaction Services component. Using the PL/SQL Agent, your application must first call a procedure that indicates the user is beginning a transaction (Begin Transaction URI). Subsequent procedures that are members of the transaction (those within the transactional boundaries) may be called that perform database operations. Finally, when the user finishes the transaction, your application must call a procedure that indicates the transaction is complete. The completed transaction can either commit (Commit Transaction URI) or roll back (Rollback Transaction URI) the previous DML operations. State is automatically maintained across each of the transactions.

Here's how this is accomplished. When the beginning transaction has been noted, a timer is started. If additional transactions are not performed within the transactional boundaries in the set timeout period (Transaction Timeout), then the transaction is considered dead, operations that have been performed are rolled back, and all locks are freed. In other words, the connection to the database is persistent through the life of the transaction. This is almost certain to drive up your concurrent database user count, which is something that must be considered when using Transaction Services.

These components are defined at the PL/SQL Agent level, which is where you transaction-enable your package. In fact, your "transaction" (each of its procedures) should be contained within one package. This is accomplished through the Cartridge Administration page for PL/SQL cartridge and for a specific PL/SQL Agent. This information is at the bottom of the PL/SQL Agent Configuration Page (only if you have the Advanced Edition). These fields on the Transaction Services page list any transactions already defined for the agent and also allow the creation of new transactions.

Transaction Services actually follows the industry standard XA interface for implementing distributed transactions. Behind the scenes, the Transaction Service uses a number of cookies to manage the transaction. The cookies include OWS_VERSION, OWS_TXNAME, OWS_XID, and OWS_KEY.

Preventing Nontransactions

If you do not call the Begin Transaction URI (the procedure that begins the transaction) prior to calling a procedure within the package that performs DML operations, they are treated as nontransaction-based events. In other words, the COMMIT occurs immediately after the procedure completes. To prevent this, check for the existence (or absence) of one of the cookies previously described. If the cookie does not exist, you may wish to call the Begin Transaction procedure first.

Creating a Less than Optimistic Locking Strategy

Remember, when a user runs a procedure, the PL/SQL cartridge logs into the database, runs the procedure, and logs out. Because the Web does not maintain state (the Web doesn't know or care whether you're still connected), when the requested procedure specified in the URL is complete, the connection to the database is severed. If two users, USERA and USERB, update information at the same time, the user who presses Submit (assuming the form action is to update the database) last would have his or her information stored in the database. This is a poor locking strategy. If your procedure logic allows the described actions to occur, then you are assuming no two users will ever maintain the same record simultaneously, which may be a bit too optimistic.

Using a Last_Update_Date Column Locking Strategy

A slightly less optimistic locking strategy (which is the most common) implements a solution to the user overwriting situation previously outlined in one of two ways. First, each table in your system should include a column that stores the last_update_date. You can, optionally, include a username column to store the person who last updated the record. When the record is requested (for update), the last_update_date column is placed on the maintenance form as a hidden column. This date is used as part of the WHERE clause, and the last_update_date column is set to current date and time (SYSDATE) at the time of update (for example, "WHERE last_update_date = in_last_update_date"). This way, if another user updates the record prior to the time that another user submits the form, the second user's update would fail. The last_update_date column would no longer match the last_update_date column value the second user had stored in the hidden column.

One way to handle this conflict is for the second user to re-query the record and identify who changed the record by also storing the username of the person who last updated the value. If you want to take it further, you can display the content that existed before the user changes to help the user determine how to handle the concurrent update of the same record (this approach would require more columns to be added and updated).

Using the OWA_OPT_LOCK Package

The second method is similar, but it uses the OWA_OPT_LOCK package provided by Oracle. This package generates a checksum for the record, and this checksum is sent to each user's browser and stored in a hidden field. Before updating the record, the checksum is regenerated for the record and compared to the prior checksum. If the checksum is different, another user changed the record, which can be handled as you like. The advantage of this method is it doesn't require you to have a last_update_date column in every table. The disadvantage is you don't have any additional information at your disposal, such as the name of the person who made the change, the date, and the time the update was performed, and so on.

Including Functional Objects

HTML supports a number of functional objects. Functional objects include Graphics, Sound, Java, JavaScript (or other scripting language, such as VB Script, and so forth), and Form Objects (for example, variables, radio buttons, checkboxes, and drop-down list boxes).

Adding Functional Objects not Supported by the PL/SQL Toolkit

Some functional objects may not be directly supported by the PL/SQL Web toolkit (such as video, plug-ins, and new scripting languages). Remember, anything that is not supported can be generated with HTP.PRINT procedure calls, such as Java and JavaScript prior to version 3.0 of the Oracle Application Server, as shown in the examples in following sections.

Including Graphics

Graphics are an important part of a graphical user interface (GUI). If your application will be used on the Internet where bandwidth is an issue, small and compressed image formats are essential. Graphics or images are supported by the PL/SQL Web toolkit with the HTP.IMG procedure. A PL/SQL example of the HTP.IMG procedure call is illustrated below.

```
HTP.IMG('/ows-img/dbbrtbvw.gif');
```

The virtual path (/ows-img) and image file (dbbrtbvw.gif) are specified.

Including Sound

Sound is another functional object supported on the Web. Internet Explorer (IE) supports something Microsoft calls background sound, while the PL/SQL Web toolkit supports background sound as a functional object with the HTP.BGSOUND procedure. A PL/SQL example of the HTP.BGSOUND procedure call is illustrated below.

```
HTP.BGSOUND('blues.mid', '1');
```

The sound file (blues.mid) and number of times it loops (one) are specified. Another way sound can be included is as a standard hyperlink or anchor, as shown in the following example:

```
HTP.PRINT('Here is a sample of some ' ||
   HTF.ANCHOR('blues.mid','Blues Music'));
```

In the preceding example, the blues.mid link is called when the user selects the Blues Music link displayed on the browser, as shown in the following example:

```
Here is a sample of some Blues Music
```

Understanding the Quality of MIDI Sound Files

MIDI sound files are small because they are simple digital sound files that use a MIDI player containing preprogrammed musical instruments. However, MIDI sound quality depends greatly on the quality of the MIDI player. Whatever sound file type you select, your user's browser must have a corresponding helper to play the sound.

Reviewing Java

Oracle Application Server provides the HTP.APPLET and HTP.PARAM procedures to direct the browser to the correct applet code and parameters. The following segment of code illustrates the use of these two PL/SQL procedures to set up the browser environment:

File: 15_4.sql

```
HTP.APPLET('ScrollingText.class','40','500','ALIGN=center,
    BACKGROUND=slbackgd.gif');
HTP.PARAM('name',scrolling_text);
HTP.PARAM('width','500');
HTP.PARAM('size','36');
HTP.PARAM('height','40');
HTP.PARAM('color','blue');
HTP.PARAM('font','TimesRoman');
HTP.PARAM('format','bold');
HTP.PARAM('speed','1');
HTP.PARAM('background','black');
HTP.APPLETCLOSE;
```

Prior to version 3.0, Oracle Web server did not support Java applets with the PL/SQL Web toolkit commands. You had to use the HTP.PRINT procedure to embed the Java tags. For example:

```
HTP.PRINT('<Java Code>');
```

The PL/SQL syntax that would perform the same function as the preceding PL/SQL code (that used HTP.APPLET and HTP.PARAM) in version 3.0 is illustrated in the following example:

File: 15_5.sql

```
HTP.PRINT('<applet code="ScrollingText.class"
    ALIGN="center" WIDTH="500" HEIGHT="40"
    BACKGROUND="slbackgd.gif">
    <param name="name" value="'||scrolling_text||'">
    <param name="width" value="500">
    <param name="size" value="36">
    <param name="height" value="40">
    <param name="color" value="blue">
    <param name="font" value="TimesRoman">
    <param name="format" value="bold">
    <param name="speed" value="1">
    <param name="background" value="black"></applet>');
```

TIP

Free Java applets can be found on sites around the world—just surf the Web. A site for good free Java code can be found at www.shareware.com.

Reviewing JavaScript

Oracle Application Server provides the HTP.SCRIPT procedure to direct the browser to the correct scripting language (such as JavaScript or VB Script). The following line of PL/SQL code illustrates the use of the HTP.SCRIPT procedure to direct the browser to use the JavaScript language:

```
HTP.SCRIPT('window.alert("Cool pop up alert!")','JavaScript');
```

Prior to version 3.0, Oracle Application Server did not support JavaScript with the PL/SQL Web toolkit commands. You had to use the HTP.PRINT procedure to embed the code. For example:

```
HTP.PRINT('<JavaScript Code...>');
```

The following PL/SQL syntax would perform the same function as the preceding PL/SQL code (that used HTP.SCRIPT) in version 3.0:

```
HTP.PRINT('<script language="JavaScript">');
HTP.PRINT('window.alert("Cool pop up alert!");');
HTP.PRINT('</script>');
```

TIP

JavaScript is a powerful language that is effective for handling events HTML does not offer (for example, mouse events, timers, and so forth).

Reviewing Form Objects

Form objects are fully supported in the PL/SQL Web toolkit. They provide an effective method to enable users to INSERT or UPDATE data in the database. In the following example, users are prompted to enter their employment applications online. The example starts with some background information and then prompts the user for a name, address, and other important information. Upon submission, the register_emp procedure is called to pass in the information users entered:

Including Functional Objects

File: 15_6.sql

```
HTP.HTMLOPEN;
   HTP.BODYOPEN('bg_image.gif', ' TOPMARGIN=5 LEFTMARGIN=5
      BGPROPERTIES=FIXEDBGCOLOR=#FFFFFF TEXT=#000000');
   HTP.PARA;
   HTP.PRINT('If you're interested in employment opportunities ' ||
      'with ' || HTF.BOLD('TUSC') || ', please contact our ' ||
      'Technical Recruiter in one of the following ways:');
   HTP.ULISTOPEN;
      HTP.LISTITEM('Attach your resume to ' ||
         HTF.ANCHOR2('mailto:recruiter@tusc.com', 'Email', NULL,
         NULL, 'TITLE="Potential Employee"') || 'for the ' ||
         HTF.BOLD( 'TUSC') || ' Technical Recruiter');
      HTP.LISTITEM('Fax your resume to ' || HTF.BOLD('TUSC') ||
         '''s fax number below');
      HTP.LISTITEM('Mail your resume to ' || HTF.BOLD('TUSC') ||
         '''s address below');
      HTP.LISTITEM('Call ' || HTF.BOLD('TUSC') ||
         ' for more information');
      HTP.LISTITEM( 'Complete and submit the ' ||
         HTF.BOLD( 'On-Line Application Form') || 'below ');
   HTP.ULISTCLOSE;
   HTP.FONTCLOSE;
   HTP.PARA;
   HTP.HR;
   HTP.FONTOPEN(NULL, 'arial');
   HTP.BOLD('On-Line Application Form');
   HTP.BR;
   HTP.PRINT('Please tell us who you are and how you would like ' ||
      'us to make contact. When you have completed the form, ' ||
      'press the ' || HTF.ITALIC( 'Apply') ||
      ' button to send your application to ' ||
      HTF.BOLD( 'TUSC') || '. A ' || HTF.BOLD('TUSC') ||
      'representative will contact you at the first possible ' ||
      'convenience.');
   HTP.BR;
   HTP.FONTCLOSE;
   HTP.FORMOPEN( 'http://www.tusc.com/emp/plsql/register_emp',
      'POST');
   HTP.PREOPEN;
   HTP.PRINT( 'Name: ' );
   HTP.PRINT('<INPUT NAME="Name" SIZE="50" MAXLEN="50">');
   HTP.PRINT('Address: ' );
   HTP.PRINT('<INPUT NAME="Address" SIZE=30 MAXLEN="30">');
   HTP.PRINT('<INPUT NAME="Address" SIZE=30 MAXLEN="30">');
   HTP.PRINT('City State Zip: ' );
```

```
   HTP.PRINT('<INPUT NAME="City" SIZE=20  MAXLEN="20">');
   HTP.PRINT('<INPUT NAME="State" SIZE="2" MAXLEN="2" >');
   HTP.PRINT('<INPUT NAME="Zip" SIZE="10" MAXLEN="10">');
   HTP.PRINT('Email Address: ' );
   HTP.PRINT('<INPUT NAME="Email" SIZE="30" MAXLEN="30">');
   HTP.PRINT('Home Page: ' );
   HTP.PRINT('<INPUT NAME="Email" SIZE="30" MAXLEN="30">');
   HTP.PRINT('Day Phone: ' );
   HTP.PRINT('<INPUT NAME="Day Phone" SIZE="20" MAXLEN="20">');
   HTP.FORMCHECKBOX('Call Day Phone');
   HTP.PRINT('Call During Day? Night Phone: ');
   HTP.PRINT('<INPUT NAME="Night Phone" SIZE="20" MAXLEN="20">');
   HTP.FORMCHECKBOX('Call Night Phone');
   HTP.PRINT('Call During Night? Who Told You About ');
   HTP.BOLD('TUSC');
   HTP.PRINT('? Referral: ');
   HTP.PRINT('<INPUT NAME="Name" SIZE="50" MAXLEN="50">');
   HTP.PRECLOSE;
   HTP.FORMHIDDEN('Form Name', 'On-Line Application');
   HTP.CENTEROPEN;
   HTP.FORMSUBMIT(NULL, 'Apply');
   HTP.FORMRESET('Clear');
   HTP.CENTERCLOSE;
   HTP.FORMCLOSE;
   HTP.HR;
   HTP.CENTEROPEN;
   HTP.BOLD('TUSC');
   HTP.BR;
   HTP.PRINT('377 E. Butterfield Road, Suite 100');
   HTP.BR;
   HTP.PRINT('Lombard, IL 60148');
   HTP.BR;
   HTP.PRINT('Phone: (630) 960-2909');
   HTP.BR;
   HTP.PRINT('Fax: (630) 960-2938');
   HTP.BR;
   HTP.PRINT('Toll Free: 1-800-755-');
   HTP.ITALIC('TUSC');
   HTP.BR;
   HTP.FONTOPEN(NULL, NULL, '1');
   HTP.PRINT('Equal Opportunity Employer');
   HTP.FONTCLOSE;
   HTP.BR;
   HTP.CENTERCLOSE;
   HTP.HR;
   HTP.BODYCLOSE;
HTP.HTMLCLOSE;
```

Including Functional Objects

The preceding PL/SQL code generates the following HTML code:

File: 15_7.htm

```
<HTML>
<body background=bg_image.gif TOPMARGIN=5 LEFTMARGIN=5
   BGPROPERTIES=FIXED BGCOLOR=#FFFFFF TEXT=#000000>
<P>
If you're interested in employment opportunities with <b>TUSC</b>,
please contact our Technical Recruiter in one of the following ways:
</P>
<UL>
<LI>Attach your resume to <A HREF="mailto:recruiter@tusc.com"
TITLE="Potential Employee">Email</A>
for the <B>TUSC</B> Technical Recruiter
<LI>Fax your resume to <B>TUSC</B>'s fax number below
<LI>Mail your resume to <B>TUSC</B>'s address below
<LI>Call <b>TUSC</b> for more information
<LI>Complete and submit the <b>On-Line Application Form</B>
below
</UL>
</FONT>
<P>
<HR>
<FONT FACE=arial>
<B>On-Line Application Form</B><BR>
Please tell us who you are and how you would like us to make contact.
When you have completed the form, press the <I>Apply</I> button to
send your application to <B>TUSC</B>.
A <B>TUSC</B> representative will contact you at the first possible convenience.<BR>
</FONT>
<FORM ACTION=" http://www.tusc.com/emp/plsql/register_emp"
METHOD="POST">
<PRE>
Name: <INPUT NAME="Name" SIZE="50" MAXLEN="50">
Address: <INPUT NAME="Address" SIZE=30 MAXLEN="30">
<INPUT NAME="Address" SIZE=30 MAXLEN="30">
City State Zip: <INPUT NAME="City" SIZE=20 MAXLEN="20">
<INPUT NAME="State" SIZE="2" MAXLENGTH="2" >
<INPUT NAME="Zip" SIZE="10" MAXLENGTH="10">
Email Address: <INPUT NAME="Email" SIZE="30" MAXLEN="30">
Home Page: <INPUT NAME="Email" SIZE="30" MAXLEN="30">
Day Phone: <INPUT NAME="Day Phone" SIZE="20" MAXLEN="20">
<INPUT TYPE=CHECKBOX NAME="Call Day Phone" > Call During Day?
Night Phone: <INPUT NAME="Night Phone" SIZE="20" MAXLEN="20">
<INPUT TYPE=CHECKBOX NAME="Call Night Phone" > Call During Night?
Who Told You About <b>TUSC</b>?
Referral: <INPUT NAME="Name" SIZE="50" MAXLEN="50">
</PRE>
<INPUT TYPE="HIDDEN" NAME="Form Name" VALUE="On-Line Application">
<CENTER>
<INPUT TYPE="SUBMIT" VALUE="Apply"> <INPUT TYPE="RESET"
VALUE="Clear">
</CENTER>
</FORM>
</P>
<HR>
```

```
<CENTER>
<B>TUSC</B><BR>
377 E. Butterfield Road, Suite 100<BR>
Lombard, IL 60148<BR>
Phone: (630) 960-2909<BR>
Fax: (630) 960-2938<BR>
<BR>
Toll Free: 1-800-755-<I>TUSC</I>
<BR>
<FONT SIZE=1>Equal Opportunity Employer</font><br>
</CENTER>
<hr>
</BODY>
</HTML>
```

The preceding HTML output would be passed to the browser to display a Web page. The preceding example can be tested by saving the previous HTML generated code into a file (15_7.htm) and then starting a browser and opening the HTML file. The Web page seen in the browser is shown in Figure 15-1.

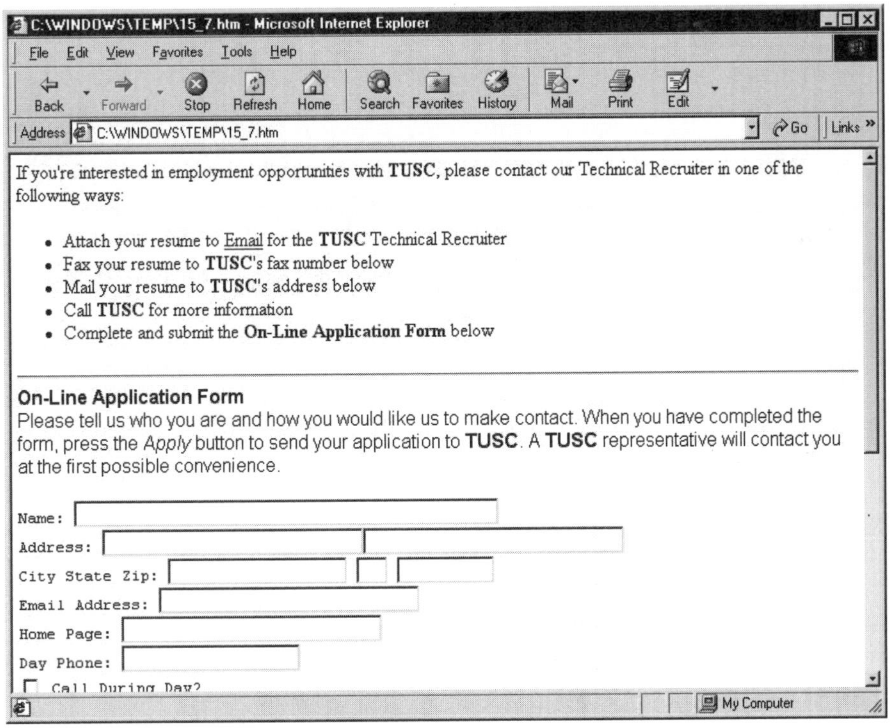

FIGURE 15-1.   *Web page generated by the preceding HTML code in the file 15_7.htm*

Understanding the PL/SQL Agent Usage of Environment Variables

The PL/SQL Agent can use environment variables and can be invoked through a CGI or the WRB. These variables can be useful to do the following:

- Determine if the user called this CGI with a GET or POST method (REQUEST_METHOD).

- Obtain the name of procedure called by the PL/SQL Agent (PATH_INFO).

- Obtain the DAD called to get to this procedure (SCRIPT_NAME).

- Obtain the parameter list passed in the URL (QUERY_STRING).

- Gather additional pieces of information. You can use OWA_UTIL.GET_CQI_ENV to determine the IP address of the remote user (for example, REMOTE_ADDR).

Passing Parameters to PL/SQL

A PL/SQL procedure usually requires parameters to execute and generate the appropriate HTML document. The following sections discuss several key concepts and provide tips a PL/SQL developer should understand with respect to how parameters get passed to the specified PL/SQL procedure.

Getting Parameters from the Web Browser to the PL/SQL Agent

Depending upon the REQUEST_METHOD (that is, GET or POST) used, parameters are passed from the Web browser to the Web Listener and then to the PL/SQL Agent in one of two ways:

- **GET** Through the QUERY_STRING environment variable. If the GET method is used by the Web browser, the Web Listener passes the parameters to the PL/SQL Agent in this environment variable.

- **POST** Through standard input. If the POST method is used, the Web Listener passes the parameters to the PL/SQL Agent using standard input.

The PL/SQL procedure is neither aware of the method used to pass the parameters from the Web Listener to the PL/SQL Agent nor concerned with which protocol (the WRB or CGI) is used. This is an important feature of the Oracle

PL/SQL Agent because it means the PL/SQL developer doesn't need to know whether GET or POST is used and the developer does not have to be concerned with parsing either the QUERY_STRING environment variable or standard input. Thus, PL/SQL developers can concentrate on what they know best: developing the functional logic to extract data from the Oracle database, based on previously parsed parameters passed by the Oracle PL/SQL Agent. However, the method (that is, GET or POST) and parameter list (QUERY_STRING) environmental parameters are available to the PL/SQL developer if needed.

Most Effective Ways of Using POST and GET

Use POST whenever possible. GET is the method automatically used for hyperlinks (anchors) and URLs to sites without forms. For HTML forms you have a choice. The GET method uses operating system environment variables; limits exist on the length of the QUERY_STRING. Some operating systems limit the command line to 255 characters. If you need to determine whether the user called your procedure using GET or POST, use the OWA_UTIL.GET_CGI_ENV procedure with a parameter of REQUEST_METHOD. Another issue with the GET method exists, in particular the Spyglass listener (the listener Oracle uses as its underlying HTTP listener) is known to crash with strings longer than 1024 characters. After considerable testing of other listeners, we found other listeners (Netscape and Microsoft) appear to have the same issue.

The GET method can be effective for testing your procedures because it is easy to see the actual URL (and parameters) being called. Because GET passes the parameter as a part of the URL, users can accurately bookmark a GET page, but they are unable to bookmark a POSTed page. This can be an effective security measure.

Passing Parameters Using an HTML Form

The following HTML example uses an HTML form that deploys the POST REQUEST_METHOD:

File: 15_8.sql

```
<FORM METHOD="POST"
ACTION="http://www.nhl.com/nhl/owa/hockey_pass">
Please type the name of the person you wish to search for:
<INPUT TYPE="text" NAME="p_person_txt"><P>
To submit the query, press this button:
<INPUT TYPE="submit" VALUE="Submit Query">. <P>
</FORM>
```

For this form, if you were to enter "Gretzky" in the textbox field called person, the browser would send "p_person_txt=Gretzky" to standard input. Note: the name of the HTML input variable, in this case "p_person_txt", must be the same as the PL/SQL parameter it is to match. The PL/SQL procedure, which is the recipient of the parameters, follows:

File: 15_9.sql

```
CREATE OR REPLACE PROCEDURE hockey_pass (p_person_txt IN VARCHAR2) IS
    lv_assists_num PLS_INTEGER;
BEGIN
    SELECT  num_assists
    INTO    lv_assists_num
    FROM    hockey_stats
    WHERE   name = p_person_txt;
    HTP.PRINT(p_person_txt || ' has ' || to_char(lv_assists_num) ||
        ' assists this season');
END hockey_pass;
/
```

Providing Default Parameter Values

If you cannot guarantee a value will be passed from a Web browser for a particular PL/SQL procedure parameter, then define the parameter with a default value. The following example illustrates the creation of a procedure that accepts two input values and displays the values:

File: 15_10.sql

```
CREATE OR REPLACE PROCEDURE showvals
    (p_a_txt IN VARCHAR2 DEFAULT NULL,
     p_b_txt IN VARCHAR2 DEFAULT NULL) IS
BEGIN
    HTP.PRINT('a = '|| p_a_txt || HTF.BR);
    HTP.PRINT('b = '|| p_b_txt || HTF.BR);
END showvals;
/
```

The two input variables are defined with a default value, which will be used if a parameter is not passed for either variable. Therefore, if the PL/SQL Agent receives a request to call procedure showvals with no value for input parameter "p_a_txt" and the value of 'Hello' for input parameter "p_b_txt", the procedure would display a NULL for "p_a_txt" and 'Hello' for "p_b_txt". If a default was not defined in this procedure, then the same call would generate an error and the following message would display:

```
OWS-05111: Agent : no procedure matches this call
OWA SERVICE: test_service
PROCEDURE: showvals
PARAMETERS: ===========
P_B_TXT: Hello
```

By "defaulting" the parameters, the request would properly output the HTML code:

```
a = <BR>
b = Hello<BR>
```

The output to the end user would appear as:

```
a =
b = Hello
```

Understanding the 5111 Error Message

The error message 5111 can be misleading because it does not accurately describe the true nature of the problem. Whenever you get this error, make certain you are passing the correct number of variables, the correct variable names (check for spelling errors), and so on.

Understanding the Numeric or Value Error

Another common error is the "numeric or value error" shown in the following example. (This error message would exist in the error file for the PL/SQL Agent.)

```
OWS-05101: Agent : execution failed due to Oracle error 6502
ORA-6502: PL/SQL: numeric or value error
ORA-6512: at "www_user.problem_procedure", line 20
ORA-6512: at line 1
```

The preceding error can be misleading. Most people look first to their input parameters and their respective data types, only to find they are all the same data types. Then they examine their program code looking for a place they assigned mismatched data types (for example, they may have placed a character in a number field), once again only to find nothing. The most important thing to note about this error is the line number (in our example, 20). If you look at line 20 in the problem procedure, you should find the source of the problem.

Usually, the problem is you do not have a numeric or value error; instead, you assigned a number to a variable that exceeds the maximum length defined or a text string to a variable that is too long for the variable defined. For example:

```
lv_screen_title_txt := 'This is the screen title for this Web page.';
```

Where the lv_screen_title_txt variable is declared as VARCHAR2(20). If the value being assigned is longer than 20 characters, you get this error message:

```
OWS-05101: Agent : execution failed due to Oracle error 6502
ORA-6502: PL/SQL: numeric or value error
ORA-6512: at line 1
```

This error can also be caused by attempting to pass a text string as an input variable to a procedure looking for a numeric value.

Handling Multivalued Parameters

Generally, you do not need to be concerned with the order in which the Oracle PL/SQL Agent receives parameters from a URL. The only case that might be relevant is when passing multiple values for the same form field. In this case, all the values for that form field should be together. If the order of the values in that field is significant, that order must be preserved in the URL.

You can have multiple values for the same HTML variable in a number of instances. The HTML tag SELECT enables users to select from a set of possible values for an HTML form field. If the MULTIPLE parameter of that SELECT tag exists or is set, the form allows multiple selections, and the user can choose to select more than one value. For example, if you ask a user to indicate his or her hobbies, the user may well have more than one. In this case, you pass the multiple values to a single PL/SQL parameter, which must be a PL/SQL table. A PL/SQL table is a data structure similar to an array (PL/SQL tables are covered in more detail in Chapter 4).

In the following example, a procedure called query_form prints an HTML page with all the columns for the specified database table. The procedure is invoked from a Web browser with a URL as the following illustrates:

```
http://virtual_host/agent/plsql/query_form?p_table_txt=s_employee
```

The query_form procedure might appear similar to the following example:

File: 15_11.sql

```
CREATE OR REPLACE PROCEDURE query_form
   (p_table_txt IN VARCHAR2) IS
   CURSOR cur_cols IS
   SELECT column_name
   FROM   user_tab_columns
   WHERE  table_name = UPPER(p_table_txt);
BEGIN
```

```
   HTP.HTMLOPEN;
   HTP.HEADOPEN;
   HTP.HTITLE('Query the ' || p_table_txt || ' table!');
   HTP.HEADCLOSE;
   HTP.BODYOPEN;
   -- Use owa_util.get_owa_service path to automatically retrieve
   HTP.FORMOPEN(OWA_UTIL.GET_OWA_SERVICE_PATH||'do_query');
   -- Put in the table as a hidden field to pass on to do_query
   HTP.FORMHIDDEN('p_table_txt', p_table_txt);
   -- Put in a dummy value, as we cannot DEFAULT NULL a PL/SQL
   -- table.
   HTP.FORMHIDDEN('COLS', 'dummy');
   FOR cur_cols_rec IN cur_cols LOOP
       -- Create a checkbox for each column. The form field name
       -- will be COLS and the value will be the given column name.
       -- Will need to use a PL/SQL table to retrieve a set of
       -- values like this. Can use the owa_util.ident_arr type
       -- since the columns are identifiers.
       HTP.FORMCHECKBOX('COLS', cur_cols_rec.column_name);
       HTP.PRINT(cur_cols_rec.column_name);
       HTP.NL;
   END LOOP;
   -- Pass a NULL field name for the Submit field; that way, a
   -- name/value pair is not sent in. Wouldn't want to do this
   -- if there were multiple submit buttons.
   HTP.FORMSUBMIT(NULL, 'Execute Query');
   HTP.FORMCLOSE;
   HTP.BODYCLOSE;
   HTP.HTMLCLOSE;
END query_form;
/
```

Invoking this procedure brings up a page that displays each of the columns in the table with a checkbox next to each column name. If the user were to query the empno, ename, job, and sal columns, the following procedure might be used to process this form submission:

File: 15_12.sql

```
-- DO_QUERY executes the query on the specified columns and table.
-- The OWA_UTIL.IDENT_ARR datatype is defined as:
-- type ident_arr is table of VARCHAR2(30) index by binary_integer
CREATE OR REPLACE PROCEDURE do_query
   (p_table_txt IN VARCHAR2,
   p_cols_rec  IN owa_util.ident_arr) IS
   lv_column_list_txt VARCHAR2(32000);
   lv_col_counter_num INTEGER;
```

```
    lv_ignore_bln        BOOLEAN;
BEGIN
    -- For PL/SQL tables, you have to loop through until you raise
    -- the NO_DATA_FOUND exception. Start the counter at 2 since we
    -- put in a dummy hidden field.
    lv_col_counter_num := 2;
    LOOP
        -- build a comma-delimited list of columns
        lv_column_list_txt := lv_column_list_txt ||
            p_cols_rec(lv_col_counter_num) || ',';
        lv_col_counter_num := lv_col_counter_num + 1;
    END LOOP;
EXCEPTION
    WHEN NO_DATA_FOUND THEN
        -- strip out the last trailing comma
        lv_column_list_txt := SUBSTR(lv_column_list_txt, 1,
            LENGTH(lv_column_list_txt) - 1);
        -- print the table - assumes HTML table support
        lv_ignore_bln := OWA_UTIL.TABLEPRINT(p_table_txt, 'BORDER',
                    OWA_UTIL.HTML_TABLE, lv_column_list_txt);
END do_query;
/
```

When the user selects the Execute Query button from the query_form procedure, the user sees the results of his query.

If you cannot guarantee that at least one value will be submitted to the PL/SQL table, use a hidden placeholder variable as the first value, as shown in the preceding code segment with the "dummy" value. A default NULL value cannot be provided for a PL/SQL table; a call to this procedure with just one argument (p_table_txt) would cause the PL/SQL Agent to generate an error.

TIP

The PL/SQL Agent can only pass parameters to PL/SQL tables that have a base type of VARCHAR2. This should not provide a significant limitation. The PL/SQL type VARCHAR2 is the largest PL/SQL data type, with a maximum length of 32K (32,767 bytes). The values can be explicitly converted to NUMBER, DATE, or LONG within the stored procedure (no conversion is needed for LONG values when using TO_NUMBER or TO_DATE).

TIP
PL/SQL table columns are referred to as variable(index #). A PL/SQL table operates the same as an array in most any other languages, but contains some of the same functionality as a database table. For this reason, if you refer to a record (or index) that does not exist (that is, one past the record set), you will raise a NO_DATA_FOUND exception error.

Understanding Overloading Procedures

PL/SQL enables you to overload procedures and functions in PL/SQL packages. In overloading, multiple procedures or functions contain the same name but are distinguished by different parameter definitions. The following is an example of creating an overloaded procedure:

File: 15_13.sql

```
CREATE OR REPLACE PACKAGE overload IS
    PROCEDURE proc1(p_charval_txt IN VARCHAR2);
    PROCEDURE proc1(p_numval_num  IN NUMBER);
END overload;
/
```

File: 15_13a.sql

```
CREATE OR REPLACE PACKAGE BODY overload IS
PROCEDURE proc1(p_charval_txt IN VARCHAR2) IS
BEGIN
    HTP.PRINT('The character value is ' || p_charval_txt);
END proc1;

PROCEDURE proc1(p_numval_num IN NUMBER) IS
BEGIN
    HTP.PRINT('The number value is '||p_numval_num);
END proc1;
END overload;
/
```

TIP
The PL/SQL Agent can use the capability of overloading procedures with the following restriction: If two procedures take the same number of parameters, those parameters must differ in name as well as data type. (Ordinarily, a difference in data types suffices to distinguish the parameters.) For example:

File: 15_14.sql

```
CREATE OR REPLACE PACKAGE overload IS
   PROCEDURE proc1(p_val IN VARCHAR2);
   PROCEDURE proc1(p_val IN NUMBER);
END overload;
/
```

If the preceding script is executed directly from SQL, this would be acceptable. When the PL/SQL Agent attempts to determine which procedure to call, it is unable to distinguish between the two procedures, generating an error. This limitation is imposed by the lack of HTML data types. Everything is essentially text. Therefore, when the PL/SQL Agent calls this overloaded procedure (proc1) in the package (overload), the PL/SQL agent package cannot distinguish which proc1 procedure to execute.

Understanding the PL/SQL Agent Error Handling

The Oracle PL/SQL Agent handles two types of errors:

- **Application Errors** These should be addressed and handled by the PL/SQL developer.

- **System Errors** These should be addressed by the Web server administrator and could include Application Errors if not handled properly at the PL/SQL application level.

Error handling is covered in further detail in the following section, along with the introduction of Error Pages for handling application and system errors.

Handling Application Errors

Application errors are specific to the PL/SQL application. All the PL/SQL procedures you develop should have their own exception handling, producing the appropriate output in HTML form (refer to Chapter 5 for further details regarding PL/SQL error handling).

The PL/SQL Agent does not read the HTML output to determine its content or whether it properly handles exceptions by generating error messages in HTML. As far as the PL/SQL Agent is concerned, if the PL/SQL code generates HTML output, the operation was successful, so handled exceptions are transparent. The user sees whatever handled exception message is generated by the PL/SQL procedure.

If you want a basic catchall exception handler, consider the following example (for a more detailed exception handler, refer to Chapter 5):

```
CREATE OR REPLACE PROCEDURE any_procedure IS

...procedure code here...

EXCEPTION
   WHEN OTHERS THEN
      DECLARE
         lv_error_code_num NUMBER          := SQLCODE;
         lv_error_msg_txt  VARCHAR2(300) := SQLERRM;
      BEGIN
         HTP.PRINT('Error #' || TO_CHAR(lv_error_code_num) ||
            ': ' || lv_error_msg_txt);
      END;
END any_procedure;
/
```

Make sure you want to use a catchall exception handler to process such exceptions. Do you really want to display generic error handling messages in production applications to the user? That's unlikely. Another way is to log exceptions in a table. The best way is to handle exceptions with a generic catchall error procedure. This way, you can easily enhance your error handling for your entire application by changing only one procedure. In this case, the preceding code could primarily become a black-box tool, which would be called as follows:

```
CREATE OR REPLACE PROCEDURE any_procedure IS

...procedure code here...
```

```
EXCEPTION
   WHEN OTHERS THEN
      DECLARE
         lv_error_code_num NUMBER        := SQLCODE;
         lv_error_msg_txt  VARCHAR2(300) := SQLERRM;
      BEGIN
         generic.error_procedure(lv_error_code_num, lv_error_msg_txt);
      END;
END any_procedure;
/
```

The generic.error_procedure would contain error-handling logic for all errors.

TIP

If you don't handle application errors, they escalate into system errors.

TIP

As of version 3.0 of Oracle Application Server, if you want to see these errors without going to the error log, you can set the error level for the PL/SQL Agent to 2. This is effective for debugging, but not the desired setting for a production environment.

Handling System Errors

System errors are detected when the PL/SQL Agent is unable to launch the PL/SQL procedure or when a PL/SQL exception is not handled by a PL/SQL procedure, causing the exception to be propagated back to the PL/SQL Agent as a system error. This causes a standard HTML error document to be returned to the browser.

For example, if the Oracle PL/SQL Agent cannot make a connection to the Oracle7 Server, the PL/SQL procedure cannot run and a system error occurs. The PL/SQL Agent then returns a default error message to the browser or returns a customized HTML error page (if an error page was previously configured as part of the DAD using the OWA_ERR_PAGE parameter).

TIP
System errors are written to the error log for the specific DAD or the PL/SQL Agent. You can get the specific Oracle error number from this error log file or from your own error procedure. Once you have the product the error relates to and the error number, you can use the error manual or the oerr utility (available only on UNIX) to find out more information about the specific error. Once you know the Oracle error number and the product name, the oerr utility provides quick access to the cause of the error and its potential resolution.

To use the oerr utility, type the following at the command line (in UNIX):

```
oerr {product} {error number}
```

For example, to find out more information about the ORA-100 error, type the following:

```
oerr ora 100
```

Integrating Error Pages

If the PL/SQL Agent fails from events such as the PL/SQL code receiving a run-time error, or if the Oracle database is down, you want to inform your users via an error page that the information they seek is unavailable. You have several options for handling errors:

- **Option 1:** For each PL/SQL Agent, you could assign one generic error page. If you want to have a custom error page for each form, you would be required to have a separate agent for each form page. This might be overkill.

- **Option 2:** You could develop a dynamic error page, which may be more useful, but it is an expensive alternative because the error page itself would fail if Oracle went down. It's best if the standard error page is static; however, if you are receiving run-time errors in your PL/SQL code, you should address these types of errors with an exception handler in your PL/SQL code. You can use this exception logic to generate a dynamic error page.

Whatever you do, don't let your PL/SQL Agent error message default to the following standard error message:

```
Request Failed—We were unable to process your request at this time.
Please try again later.
```

This message appears on a dismal gray background, with no graphics, and it is certainly not very descriptive. Therefore, you will want to develop some form of generic error page procedure at a minimum.

Summary

Oracle Application Server is a critical product in transforming your business to the Web, whether it is on an intranet or the Internet. PL/SQL plays a critical role in this product, and therefore, PL/SQL developers and DBAs have a head start with their knowledge of PL/SQL. This chapter provided a brief explanation of the Oracle Application Server, the world of the Web, and the role PL/SQL plays in this environment. When you are ready to explore the Web in more detail for deployment, you should obtain a thorough understanding of Oracle Application Server.

For more information on Oracle Application Server, the PL/SQL cartridge and the PL/SQL Web toolkit, see *Oracle Application Server Web Toolkit Reference*, by Bradley D. Brown (Oracle Press).

Tips Review

- Free Java applets can be found on sites around the world—just surf the Web. A site for some good free Java code can be found at www.shareware.com.

- JavaScript is a powerful language that is effective for handling events HTML does not offer (for example, mouse events, timers, and so forth).

- The PL/SQL Agent can only pass parameters to PL/SQL tables that have a base type of VARCHAR2. This should not provide a significant limitation. The PL/SQL type VARCHAR2 is the largest PL/SQL data type, with a maximum length of 32K (32,767 bytes). The values can be explicitly converted to NUMBER, DATE, or LONG within the stored procedure (no conversion is needed for LONG values when using TO_NUMBER or TO_DATE).

■ PL/SQL table columns are referred to as variable(index #). A PL/SQL table operates the same as an array in most other languages, but contains some of the same functionality as a database table. For this reason, if you refer to a record (or index) that does not exist (that is, one past the record set), you will raise a NO_DATA_FOUND exception error.

■ The PL/SQL Agent can use the capability of overloading procedures with the following restriction: If two procedures take the same number of parameters, those parameters must differ in name as well as data type. (Ordinarily, a difference in data types suffices to distinguish the parameters.)

■ If you don't handle application errors, they escalate into system errors.

■ As of version 3.0 of Oracle Application Server, if you want to see these errors without going to the error log, you can set the error level for the PL/SQL Agent to 2. This is effective for debugging, but not the desired setting for a production environment.

■ System errors are written to the error log for the specific DAD or the PL/SQL Agent. You can get the specific Oracle error number from this error log file or from your own error procedure. Once you have the product the error relates to and the error number, you can use the error manual or the oerr utility (available only on UNIX) to find out more information about the specific error. Once you know the Oracle error number and the product name, the oerr utility provides quick access to the cause of the error and its potential resolution.

Summary

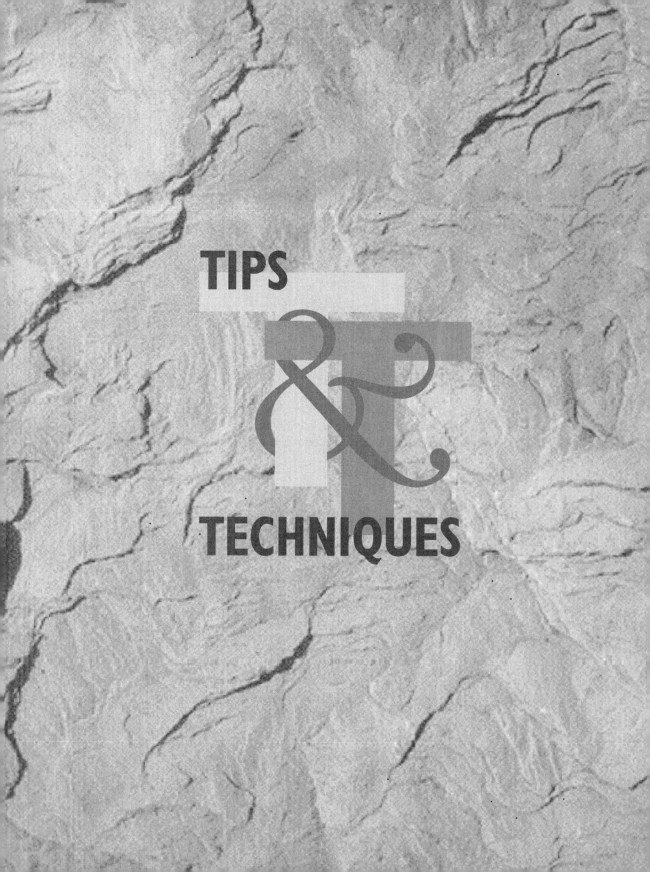

TIPS
&
TECHNIQUES

CHAPTER
16

New PL/SQL Related
Features in Oracle 8
and Oracle 8i
(Developer and DBA)

O racle 8.0 and Oracle 8i introduce several new features extending the flexibility and power of the PL/SQL language. Oracle 8i is version 8.1; therefore, for consistency in this chapter, I use Oracle 8.1. The PL/SQL extensions provide support for the large number of new database features. A combination of both developer and DBA extensions exists.

With any new release, knowing what is new and what has changed is extremely important as it provides the developer and the DBA with an awareness of the expanded functionality. The developer or DBA can then determine if the new features are useful to their responsibility. This chapter concentrates on identifying several of the new features in Oracle 8.0 and Oracle 8.1. The goal of this chapter is to provide awareness of the changes in these new versions with more emphasis placed on the PL/SQL features.

Each feature covered is identified as an Oracle 8.0 or Oracle 8.1 extension. The following features are covered throughout this chapter:

- Learn the new features of a release prior to deployment

- New PL/SQL commands and concepts

  - DDL commands, dynamic SQL, and PL/SQL made easier and faster with EXECUTE IMMEDIATE

  - Bulk binds with the FORALL statement

  - RETURNING clause of DML statements

  - NOCOPY parameter option

  - External procedure calls

  - Serially reusable packages

  - Autonomous transactions

  - Data dictionary changes

  - New database triggers

  - PL/SQL backward compatibility

- Performance improvements

- Oracle supplied packages

  - Advanced queuing (DBMS_AQ and DBMS_AQADM)

  - Large object support (DBMS_LOB)

  - Random number generator (DBMS_RANDOM)

- Block repair facility (DBMS_REPAIR)
- Process ROWIDs (DBMS_ROWID)
- Probe facility
    - DBMS_DEBUG
    - DBMS_PROFILER
    - DBMS_TRACE
- Extended security methodology
    - Stored PL/SQL program unit execution
    - Enhanced schema security
    - Addition of schema profiles
    - Password management facility
- Support for large object (LOB) data types
- New Objects types and concepts
    - Standard definitions and new object terms
    - Support of collections
        - VARRAY
        - NESTED TABLE
    - Support of object data types
- Database limitations
- New SQL related enhancements
    - ROWID changes
    - Function-based indexes
    - NO_INDEX hint
    - Index-organized tables
    - Drop column command
- Expanded Web integration into Oracle
    - Web development products (JDeveloper and Oracle Developer)

- Oracle Developer and Web-enabling

- Integration of Java with SQL (SQLJ & JDBC)

- Additional features of Oracle 8.0 and Oracle 8.1

Learn the New Features of a Release Prior to Deployment

When I receive a new release of Oracle, as with any software, the first thing I do is review the user documentation, release notes, and installation notes. I also talk to other contacts in the industry to increase my awareness of the advantages and disadvantages of the new version.

For release Oracle 8.0 and Oracle 8.1, Oracle has updated the documentation to provide information related to the new features. Oracle provides a readme.doc file for each release, to provide additional important information related to enhancements, bug fixes, functionality no longer available, and so forth. For Oracle 8.0 and Oracle 8.1, I have read the entire PL/SQL user manuals provided by Oracle to learn all of the new features and tested many of these features. At the time of a new release, I strongly recommend developers and DBAs spend time reviewing the complete manuals that apply to your responsibilities to increase your awareness and preparation for the new release. If you will be using any new features with the upgrade, I recommend testing those thoroughly.

TIP
The release of Oracle 8.1 contains a new manual providing documentation on the Oracle supplied packages called Oracle 8i Supplied Package Reference and is included on the CD-ROM documentation.

TIP
Upgrading or migrating to Oracle8 requires many steps prior to and after the installation. Ensure you read the entire installation and readme.doc documentation for your particular hardware and operating system.

New PL/SQL Commands and Concepts

The PL/SQL-related new features and concepts are covered in the following sections. The language has become more functional with a variety of new commands and new options on existing commands. For additional PL/SQL information refer to the *Oracle 8.0 PL/SQL User's Guide and Reference* and the *Oracle8i PL/SQL User's Guide and Reference* provided on CD-ROM with the Oracle release.

DDL Commands, Dynamic SQL, and PL/SQL Made Easier and Faster with EXECUTE IMMEDIATE

The EXECUTE IMMEDIATE command is introduced in Oracle 8.1. The EXECUTE IMMEDIATE eliminates much of the need for the DBMS_SQL package. This new PL/SQL command provides a simpler method of creating and executing DDL statements, dynamic SQL, and dynamic PL/SQL by enabling these commands to be executed with one statement versus the many statements necessary with the DBMS_SQL package.

The main advantages of this new command are reduction of source code (easier to read and maintain) and faster execution (command built into the PL/SQL Engine versus DBMS_SQL package calls). This command should replace the use of DBMS_SQL for all future development. For past development, it should only be changed from DBMS_SQL package calls if time permits or if the DBMS_SQL is a cause for current performance problems or issues.

The EXECUTE IMMEDIATE command can accept any SQL statement with the exception of SELECT statements retrieving multiple records. It also accepts bind variables with a USING clause.

The following example illustrates the execution of DDL commands to turn TRACE on and to increase the Sort Area Size for the current session. This example demonstrates the EXECUTE IMMEDIATE flexibility:

File:16_1.sql

```
DECLARE
   lv_sql_txt VARCHAR2(200);
BEGIN
   EXECUTE IMMEDIATE 'ALTER SESSION SET SQL_TRACE=TRUE';
   lv_sql_txt := 'ALTER SESSION SET SORT_AREA_SIZE = 1000000';
   EXECUTE IMMEDIATE lv_sql_txt;
END;
/
```

The following example illustrates the capability to build dynamic SQL to retrieve a count of records in all tables of the current schema.

New PL/SQL Commands and Concepts

File: 16_2.sql

```
DECLARE
   lv_count_num        PLS_INTEGER:=0;
   CURSOR cur_counts IS
      SELECT table_name
      FROM   user_tables
      ORDER BY table_name;
BEGIN
   FOR cur_counts_rec IN cur_counts LOOP
      EXECUTE IMMEDIATE 'SELECT COUNT(*) FROM ' ||
         cur_counts_rec.table_name INTO lv_count_num;
      DBMS_OUTPUT.PUT_LINE('Table Name: ' ||
         RPAD(cur_counts_rec.table_name, 15) ||
         ' Rows: ' || lv_count_num);
   END LOOP;
END;
/
```

Output (16_2.sql)

```
Table Name: S_CUSTOMER      Rows: 15
Table Name: S_DEPARTMENT    Rows: 12
Table Name: S_EMPLOYEE      Rows: 25
Table Name: S_IMAGE         Rows: 19
Table Name: S_INVENTORY     Rows: 114

PL/SQL procedure successfully completed.
```

In the preceding example, the result display was limited to five records.

The following example illustrates the use of bind variables to update all salaries by 10 percent.

File: 16_3.sql

```
DECLARE
   lv_salary_increase NUMBER := .10;
BEGIN
   EXECUTE IMMEDIATE 'UPDATE s_employee SET salary =
   NVL(salary, 0) * (1 + :increase)'
      USING lv_salary_increase;
END;
/
```

TIP
The EXECUTE IMMEDIATE command supersedes the DBMS_SQL command and is simpler and more efficient.

Bulk Binds with the FORALL Statement

The new FORALL statement is introduced in Oracle 8.1. This new PL/SQL command is specifically used for processing DML (INSERT, UPDATE, and DELETE) statements to improve performance by reducing the overhead of SQL processing. The FORALL statement enables bulk binding, providing the capability to issue DML statements in groups of DML statements versus a DML statement that manipulates one row at a time. Collecting the DML statement for intermittent or one execution eliminates the overhead of sending a SQL statement for each row to the SQL Engine for processing.

The FORALL statement follows the same structure as a FOR LOOP with a range. However, it does not contain an END LOOP statement, and it cannot contain any statements other than the index, lower and upper bound, and SQL statement that refers to the index.

The following is an example illustrating the use of the FORALL statement. The example collects a list of employees to be given a raise—in a PL/SQL table—and then the PL/SQL table is used for the bulk bind.

File: 16_4.sql

```
DECLARE
   TYPE lv_emp_tab IS TABLE OF PLS_INTEGER
      INDEX BY BINARY_INTEGER;
   lv_emp_tab_rec lv_emp_tab;
   lv_count_num    PLS_INTEGER := 0;
   -- Only department 41 is given raises
   CURSOR cur_emps IS
      SELECT employee_id, department_id, salary
      FROM   s_employee
      WHERE  department_id = 41;
BEGIN
   FOR cur_emps_rec IN cur_emps LOOP
      -- Processing Employee Logic goes here
      lv_count_num := lv_count_num + 1;
      lv_emp_tab_rec(lv_count_num) := cur_emps_rec.employee_id;
   END LOOP;
```

```
    FORALL lv_bulk_num IN 1..lv_emp_tab_rec.COUNT
        UPDATE s_employee
        SET salary = NVL(salary, 0) * 1.10
        WHERE employee_id = lv_emp_tab_rec(lv_bulk_num);
END;
/
```

The performance improvements come from sending the UPDATE statement to
the server one time for all employees, rather than the traditional method of moving
the UPDATE statement inside the cursor FOR loop. The traditional method would
have sent the UPDATE statement to the server for every iteration of the loop, thus
incurring more round trip and more processing overhead.

TIP
*The FORALL statement improves DML statements by
sending DML statements to the server less frequently,
thus reducing overhead and increasing performance.*

RETURNING Clause of DML Statements

Prior to the release of Oracle 8.0, when DML statements were executed in PL/SQL
natively, performing an additional SELECT was necessary to view the result set of a
row. If the DML manipulates only one record at a time, the result can be returned
into a PL/SQL variable or a PL/SQL record (to return multiple records, the BULK
COLLECT INTO clause can be used). The RETURNING clause can be used with an
INSERT, UPDATE, or DELETE statement.

The following example illustrates the RETURNING clause. The employee
with employee_id of 1 has a salary of $2,500. If the salary for this employee is
updated by 20 percent, we can retrieve the value updated in the database and
display the value:

File: 16_5.sql

```
DECLARE
    lv_new_salary_num s_employee.salary%TYPE;
BEGIN
    UPDATE s_employee
    SET     salary = NVL(salary, 0) * 1.2
    WHERE   employee_id = 1
    RETURNING salary INTO lv_new_salary_num;
    DBMS_OUTPUT.PUT_LINE('New Salary: ' ||
        lv_new_salary_num);
END;
/
```

Output (16_5.sql)

```
New Salary: 3000

PL/SQL procedure successfully completed.
```

The preceding method of displaying the employee's updated salary would have entailed an additional SELECT from the database table.

NOCOPY Parameter Option

The three types of parameter passing options to procedures and functions, prior to the release of Oracle 8.1, were IN (parameters passed by reference), OUT (copied out), and IN OUT (copied in and copied out). Oracle 8.1 adds an optional parameter that can be added to the OUT and IN OUT parameter types called NOCOPY. The NOCOPY follows the same method as IN parameters by passing parameters using references, which significantly reduces overhead associated with copying large data sets.

The current design of OUT and IN OUT parameters was created to ensure if exceptions were raised, then the changes could be rolled back. A copy of the parameter set was made; therefore, the rollback could be accomplished. With the NOCOPY, a reference is used; therefore, there is exposure because an exception causing a rollback cannot be performed.

TIP
The NOCOPY parameter option increases performance, especially on large parameter data sets; however, it introduces some exposure.

External Procedure Calls

Oracle 8.0 introduced the capability for PL/SQL programs to make calls to external (outside of the database) systems through DLLs or shared libraries. This provides PL/SQL the capability to interface with other systems to pass or receive data or use other languages, such as C, for more efficient complex number processing. Oracle 8.1 enhanced the performance of external calls, which can be realized by merely recompiling when migrating to Oracle 8.1.

Serially Reusable Packages

In the release of Oracle 8.0, Oracle added a new compiler directive with the SERIALLY_REUSABLE pragma for PL/SQL packages to change the default behavior of the package state. Once a package is referenced in a session, the entire package is loaded into the SGA memory, and the state of the package (global variables, constants, and so forth) is maintained in the session's UGA, until the session terminates. This is a tremendous benefit if the package is referenced repeatedly and the package state needs to be maintained. However, maintaining the package state requires UGA memory.

If a package is only referenced once in a session or the package state (global variables, constants, and so forth) is not necessary or desired for the implementation of the package, then the SERIALLY_REUSABLE pragma can be used in the creation of the package specification and the package body to eliminate the overhead of maintaining the package state.

The following is an example of this new pragma. This example creates a package variable and initializes the variable to zero. This package variable is called twice to illustrate the package state.

In the first example, the package is created without the new pragma.

File: 16_6.sql

```
CREATE OR REPLACE PACKAGE maintain_state IS
   pvg_base_count_num PLS_INTEGER := 0;
END;
/
```

The following PL/SQL program unit displays the value of the package variable, and then increments the value by ten and displays the variable.

File: 16_7.sql

```
BEGIN
   DBMS_OUTPUT.PUT_LINE('Original Value: ' ||
      maintain_state.pvg_base_count_num);
   maintain_state.pvg_base_count_num :=
      maintain_state.pvg_base_count_num + 10;
   DBMS_OUTPUT.PUT_LINE('New Value:       ' ||
      maintain_state.pvg_base_count_num);
END;
/
```

The preceding PL/SQL program unit is executed twice, and the variable is increased with each execution as the following illustrates.

Output (16_7.sql)

```
Original Value: 0
New Value:      10

PL/SQL procedure successfully completed.
```

Output (16_7.sql)

```
Original Value: 10
New Value:      20

PL/SQL procedure successfully completed.
```

Once the package is recreated with the SERIALLY_REUSABLE pragma, the results of calling the PL/SQL program unit are quite different.

File: 16_8.sql

```
CREATE OR REPLACE PACKAGE maintain_state IS
   PRAGMA SERIALLY_REUSABLE;
   pvg_base_count_num PLS_INTEGER := 0;
END;
/
```

As expected, when the PL/SQL program unit is executed twice again, the package variable begins at zero each time as the following illustrates.

Output (16_7.sql)

```
Original Value: 0
New Value:      10

PL/SQL procedure successfully completed.
```

Output (16_7.sql)

```
Original Value: 0
New Value:      10

PL/SQL procedure successfully completed.
```

TIP
The SERIALLY_REUSABLE pragma modifies the default behavior of the package state by eliminating the package state.

Autonomous Transactions

In the release of Oracle 8.1, Oracle added a new compiler directive through the AUTONOMOUS_TRANSACTION pragma for PL/SQL program units enabling program units to maintain their own transaction state. This enables transactions to be handled with more ease and finer granularity. Nested transactions can be committed or rolled back without affecting the other transactions.

The following example illustrates the new pragma. The first script creates the insert_product procedure, which inserts a product into the s_product table and then performs a COMMIT. The second script inserts a record into the s_inventory table, calls the insert_product procedure to insert the product 232, then rolls the transaction back.

File: 16_9.sql

```
CREATE OR REPLACE PROCEDURE insert_product
    (p_product_num VARCHAR2) IS
    PRAGMA AUTONOMOUS_TRANSACTION;
BEGIN
    INSERT INTO s_product
    (product_id, product_name)
    VALUES
    (p_product_num, 'NEW PRODUCT');
    COMMIT;
END;
/
```

File: 16_10.sql

```
BEGIN
    INSERT INTO s_inventory
        (warehouse_id, product_id)
    VALUES
        (10501, 10011);
    insert_product(232);
    ROLLBACK;
END;
/
```

As a result of the preceding script, the product 232 was inserted into the s_product table, and the s_inventory record was not inserted into the s_inventory table. Without the AUTONOMOUS_TRANSACTION pragma, the COMMIT that was performed in the insert_product procedure would have committed the s_inventory record.

Data Dictionary Changes

A variety of new views has been added to the data dictionary to provide storage for and access to the new features of Oracle 8.0 and Oracle 8.1. In addition, several of the existing views have been enhanced to support the latest features of the two versions. These enhancements include the addition of new columns to these views, as well as expansion of the object types displayed in these views.

The following is a table identifying the new PL/SQL related types supported in each of the PL/SQL-related views. For each data dictionary view, there is also an ALL_* and a DBA_* view.

Data Dictionary View	New Type Support Oracle 8.0	New Type Support Oracle 8.1
USER_OBJECTS	TYPE, TYPE BODY	JAVA SOURCE, JAVA CLASS, JAVA RESOURCE
USER_SOURCE	TYPE, TYPE BODY	JAVA SOURCE, JAVA CLASS
USER_ERRORS	TYPE, TYPE BODY	JAVA SOURCE, JAVA CLASS
USER_OBJECT_SIZE	TYPE, TYPE BODY	JAVA SOURCE, JAVA CLASS, JAVA RESOURCE
USER_TRIGGERS		STARTUP, SHUTDOWN, ERROR, LOGON, LOGOFF, CREATE, ALTER, DROP
USER_DEPENDENCIES	TYPE, TYPE BODY	JAVA SOURCE, JAVA CLASS

In addition, in Oracle 8.1, a new view was added to view internal triggers on a table named USER_INTERNAL_TRIGGERS (ALL_* and DBA_*).

New Database Triggers

Eight new database triggers have been added in the release of Oracle 8.1. These database triggers expand beyond the previous limitation of placing database triggers only on tables. These eight database triggers extend the powerful capability to database startup/shutdown, server-side errors, user logons/logoffs, and object creations/alterations/drops. The implicit execution process employed by previous database triggers is the same for these new triggers. Once the database trigger is created and enabled, it is executed based on database actions. No explicit calls are necessary to execute these database triggers.

The new database triggers provide an added level of independence and global coverage because they are implemented at the database level. The eight new triggers are outlined in the following table:

Database Trigger	BEFORE/AFTER Execution	Description
STARTUP	AFTER	Implicitly executes when the database is started
SHUTDOWN	BEFORE	Implicitly executes when the database is shut down
SERVERERROR	AFTER	Implicitly executes when a server-side error is encountered
LOGON	AFTER	Implicitly executes when a session connects to the database (logs on)
LOGOFF	BEFORE	Implicitly executes when a session disconnects from the database (logs off)
CREATE	AFTER	Implicitly executes when a database object is created; can be created based on schema or for the entire database
ALTER	AFTER	Implicitly executes when a database object is altered; can be created based on schema or for the entire database
DROP	AFTER	Implicitly executes when a database object is dropped; can be created based on schema or for the entire database

The eight new triggers are ideal for DBAs to build in mechanisms based on certain events. When the database is started, the objects that need to be pinned can now be moved from the startup SQL script to the STARTUP trigger. For further information about the object pinning routine, refer to Chapter 9. When the database is shutdown, statistics scripts can be executed to log information into monitoring tables with the SHUTDOWN trigger. Error trapping can be enhanced with the SERVERERROR trigger. Capturing user connect time can be handled through the LOGON and LOGOFF triggers. An object audit trail can be created through the CREATE, ALTER, and DROP triggers.

These triggers can be viewed in the USER_TRIGGERS (ALL_* and DBA_*) data dictionary view.

The following code segments create a logon statistics table and a LOGON and LOGOFF database trigger to capture the time when a user connects/disconnects to/from the database.

File: 16_11.sql

```
CREATE TABLE session_logon_statistics
(user_logged VARCHAR2(30),
start_time    DATE,
end_time      DATE);
```

File: 16_12.sql

```
CREATE OR REPLACE TRIGGER logon_log_trigger
AFTER LOGON
ON DATABASE
BEGIN
   INSERT INTO session_logon_statistics
   (user_logged, start_time)
   VALUES
   (USER, SYSDATE);
END;
/
```

File: 16_13.sql

```
CREATE OR REPLACE TRIGGER logoff_log_trigger
BEFORE LOGOFF
ON DATABASE
BEGIN
   UPDATE session_logon_statistics
   SET    end_time    = SYSDATE
   WHERE  user_logged = USER
   AND    end_time IS NULL;
END;
/
```

The following script retrieves the information from the session_logon_statistics table.

File: 16_14.sql

```
SELECT user_logged,
       TO_CHAR(start_time, 'MM/DD/YYYY HH24:MI:SS') "START TIME",
       TO_CHAR(end_time, 'MM/DD/YYYY HH24:MI:SS') "END TIME"
FROM   session_logon_statistics
order by user_logged, start_time;
```

Output (16_14.sql)

```
USER_LOGGED                    START TIME           END TIME
------------------------------ -------------------- --------------------
PLSQL_TEST                     07/10/1999 07:15:42
PLSQL_USER                     07/10/1999 07:12:55 07/10/1999 07:15:40
SYS                            07/10/1999 07:10:36 07/10/1999 07:12:53
```

TIP
The eight new database triggers expand the capability of database triggers and provide a method of performing new monitoring activities.

PL/SQL Backward Compatibility

In Oracle 8.0, the version number of PL/SQL has been changed from version 2 to version 8. Additionally, several minor changes were made to the PL/SQL Engine, disallowing certain conditions. If the PL/SQL version 2 Engine is a desired option, an init.ora parameter can be set as shown in the following.

```
PLSQL_V2_COMPATIBILITY = TRUE
```

The default of this parameter is FALSE, thus enabling PL/SQL version 8 handling. The compatibility parameter can also be set through the ALTER SYSTEM and ALTER SESSION commands.

TIP
In Oracle 8.0 and Oracle 8.1, many new init.ora parameters can be modified real-time through the ALTER SESSION and ALTER SYSTEM commands. The number of init.ora parameters that can be modified while the database is running continues to increase with each version. Query the isses_modifiable and issys_modifiable columns in the V$PARAMETER view to determine the init.ora parameters that can be changed real-time. Refer to Chapter 9 for further details related to the PL/SQL related init.ora parameters.

Performance Improvements

Oracle 8.0 and Oracle 8.1 introduced a variety of enhancements to PL/SQL specifically addressing performance improvements. Several of these are syntactical enhancements that can be used in specific areas to take advantage of the improvement. Other enhancements are internal to the PL/SQL Engine and transparent to most users. The internal PL/SQL improvements are important to be aware of so you realize performance can improve just by migrating to the new version.

The following is a list of the new PL/SQL features that improve performance, some of which have been covered previously in this chapter.

- **FORALL Command:** Bulk binds can be performed with the new FORALL command for DML statement processing to reduce transfer and processing overhead. (Oracle 8.1)

- **NOCOPY Parameter Option:** The NOCOPY parameter option on OUT and IN OUT parameters changes copies to references, which can result in large performance gains when parameters involve large data sets. (Oracle 8.1)

- **EXECUTE IMMEDIATE Command:** Dynamic SQL statements can now be created with the EXECUTE IMMEDIATE command versus DBMS_SQL package calls. It is faster and requires less source code. (Oracle 8.1)

- **Calls to External Procedures:** PL/SQL can communicate to systems outside Oracle through the external procedure interface, as well as perform complex, compute-intensive calculations with another (a compiled) language, such as C, which is faster than PL/SQL. (Oracle 8.0)

- **Internal Oracle PL/SQL Performance Improvements:** A variety of areas have been optimized to improve the performance of PL/SQL execution, including the STANDARD package, anonymous block execution, remote procedure call (RPC) parameter passing, PL/SQL records, PL/SQL tables, and SQL inline PL/SQL functions.

- **Internal Oracle PL/SQL Memory Improvements:** A variety of areas have been optimized for memory use, and the requirements of certain memory structures have been reduced. The memory reduction affects the server-side (SGA) memory and the client-side (UGA) memory. This includes the reduction of Shared Pool fragmentation due to modified handling of the compiled PL/SQL code when executing, the reduction of the SGA memory required for PL/SQL library compiled code (reduced by 20 percent), the reduction of the UGA memory required for SQL statements in PL/SQL source code due to an improved method of execution (40 percent reduction), and the reduction of memory required for processing LONG and LONG RAW data types because the model changed from pre-allocating the maximum potential length of these variables to allocating dynamically what is actually needed.

Oracle Supplied Packages

A tremendous number of Oracle supplied packages have been added in Oracle 8.0 and 8.1. To identify the packages installed by default, review the catproc.sql file. The catproc.sql file contains a description for each group of scripts executed during installation to identify the package contents' significance. Oracle introduced a new reference manual in Oracle 8.1, *Oracle 8i Supplied Package Reference*, covering 69 of the Oracle supplied packages. The following packages are listed, with the first list (ten packages) containing only a brief overview of the package in the reference, and the second list (59 packages) providing a detailed description of the package in the reference.

- Oracle Supplied Packages: Brief Description

CALENDAR②	SDO_ADMIN②
SDO_GEOM②	SDO_MIGRATE②
SDO_TUNE②	TIMESCALE②
TIMESERIES②	TSTOOLS②
UTL_PG②	VIR_PKG②

- Oracle Supplied Packages: Detailed Description

DBMS_ALERT	DBMS_APPLICATION_INFO
DBMS_AQ①	DBMS_AQADM①
DBMS_DDL	DBMS_DEBUG②
DBMS_DEFER	DBMS_DEFER_QUERY
DBMS_DEFER_SYS	DBMS_DESCRIBE
DBMS_DISTRIBUTED_TRUST_ADMIN②	DBMS_HS①
DBMS_HS_PASSTHROUGHS①	DBMS_IOT①
DBMS_JOB	DBMS_LOB①
DBMS_LOCK	DBMS_LOGMNR②
DBMS_LOGMNR_D②	DBMS_OFFLINE_OG
DBMS_OFFLINE_SNAPSHOT	DBMS_OLAP②
DBMS_ORACLE_TRACE_AGENT①	DBMS_ORACLE_TRACE_USER①

DBMS_OUTPUT	DBMS_PCLXUTIL②
DBMS_PIPE	DBMS_PROFILER②
DBMS_RANDOM①	DBMS_RECTIFIER_DIFF
DBMS_REFRESH	DBMS_REPAIR②
DBMS_REPCAT	DBMS_REPCAT_ADMIN
DBMS_REPCAT_INSTANTIATE②	DBMS_REPCAT_RGT②
DBMS_REPUTIL	DBMS_RESOURCE_MANAGER
DBMS_RESOURCE_MANAGER_PRIVS②	DBMS_RLS②
DBMS_ROWID①	DBMS_SESSION
DBMS_SHARED_POOL	DBMS_SNAPSHOT
DBMS_SPACE	DBMS_SPACE_ADMIN②
DBMS_SQL	DBMS_STATS②
DBMS_TRACE②	DBMS_TRANSACTION
DBMS_TTS②	DBMS_UTILITY
DEBUG_EXTPROC②	OUTLN_PKG②
UTL_COLL②	UTL_FILE
UTL_HTTP	UTL_RAW
UTL_REF②	

Oracle Supplied Packages

The list contains a ① for packages new in Oracle 8.0 and a ② for packages new in Oracle 8.1. No symbol signifies the package existence prior to Oracle 8.0.

To view the Oracle supplied packages installed in your database, execute the following script.

File: 16_15.sql

```
SELECT object_name, object_type
FROM   all_objects
WHERE  owner = 'SYS'
AND    object_type IN ('PACKAGE', 'PACKAGE BODY')
ORDER BY object_name, object_type;
```

Output (16_15.sql)

OBJECT_NAME	OBJECT_TYPE
DBMS_ALERT	PACKAGE
DBMS_ALERT	PACKAGE BODY
DBMS_APPLICATION_INFO	PACKAGE
DBMS_APPLICATION_INFO	PACKAGE BODY
DBMS_DDL	PACKAGE
DBMS_DDL	PACKAGE BODY

The preceding output only displays a subset of the full output. If a desired package does not appear in this list, contact your DBA and ask for access to the package or ask for the package to be created in the database.

The following sections are a brief outline of some of the Oracle supplied packages new to Oracle 8.0 and Oracle 8.1.

Advanced Queuing (DBMS_AQ and DBMS_AQADM)

Prior to Oracle 8.0, intersession communication processes—namely DBMS_PIPE and DBMS_ALERT packages—were introduced to establish methods of communication between processes within the database and its associated PL/SQL tool set. These packages provide a first glimpse of what would be a powerful, integrated communication system in Oracle8, known as *Advanced Queuing.*

The advanced queuing packages more closely resemble the transactional-based DBMS_ALERT package rather than the asynchronous DBMS_PIPE package. DBMS_AQ and DBMS_AQADM provide a more robust, structured, and reliable environment through which message objects can be passed. The message transfer routines are transactional (SQL) based; therefore, they can be depended upon to perform critical database functions.

Through advanced queuing, messages in the form of object structures or RAW data can be queued or stored in a queue by one process and de-queued, retrieved from the queue by another, different process. The message can be an actual object, so the message itself may be comprised of varying attributes that make up the object. The queue is actually a table structure created specifically for the queuing processes. The queue process requires one logical (NORMAL_QUEUE) queue to be established within a queue table. An additional logical queue (EXCEPTION_QUEUE) can also be created to maintain erroneous or stale messages within the queue table.

The two packages, DBMS_AQ and DBMS_AQADM, are used to perform functional and administrative operations, respectively. To use the advanced queuing system, permission (through the AQ_ADMINISTRATOR_ROLE role) to the administration package must be granted to the owner of the queue. In addition, the procedure DBMS_AQADM.GRANT_TYPE_ACCESS must also be executed for the queue owner.

The Timer Manager monitors the status of the queued messages and performs functions, such as moving stale messages (messages older than a set expiration time) to the exception queue and controlling delayed sending of messages. The AQ_TM_PROCESS is an optional parameter set in the init.ora controlling whether the manager can be started. To start this process, set the parameter to 1 and then invoke the manager by calling the DBMS_AQADM.START_TIME_MANAGER procedure.

The advanced queuing system is ideal for workflow applications, but it is also useful for module communication, as in the example of an order entry system interfacing to an accounts receivable system.

Advanced queuing provides a clean, autonomous approach to the life-long issue of integrating two dissimilar applications. Advanced Queuing enables the system of origin to run independently, even if the destination system to which it is interfacing is shutdown. When the destination system is brought online, all the messages from the origin system will be waiting to be processed.

TIP

Advanced Queuing is a more robust implementation of DBMS_PIPE and DBMS_ALERT providing a seamless communication method for independent systems.

Large Object Support (DBMS_LOB)

With the introduction of support for Large Objects (LOBs) in the release of Oracle 8.0, Oracle introduced the DBMS_LOB package to provide a mechanism for working with LOB data types. The DBMS_LOB package contains five functions, namely COMPARE, GETLENGTH, INSTR, READ, and SUBSTR. Six procedures are capable of manipulating the data within a large object, namely, APPEND, COPY, ERASE, LOADFROMFILE, TRIM, and WRITE. All these functions are overloaded to accommodate both the binary (BLOB and BFILE) and character (CLOB and NCLOB) objects. Lastly, the DBMS_LOB package contains six routines designed specifically to gain information about BFILE data types, namely, FILECLOSE, FILECLOSEALL, FILEEXITS, FILEGETNAME, FILEISOPEN, and FILEOPEN.

UTL_RAW complements DBMS_LOB by providing bit-wise manipulation functions used to manipulate binary objects. In the past, Oracle developers never had such powerful tools at their fingertips to aid in low-level program development.

TIP

Using DBMS_OUTPUT, DBMS_LOB, and UTL_RAW, a simple ASCII file viewer can be created displaying the contents of any character files from within SQL.

Oracle Supplied Packages

The introduction of large object types in Oracle 8.0 is reviewed later in this chapter.

Random Number Generator (DBMS_RANDOM)

Every developer at one time has a need to generate a random number. Prior to the release of Oracle 8.0, developers could either create their own random generator in PL/SQL or handle the task outside of the database, where standard random number generators abound. The DBMS_RANDOM package is implemented by accessing a generator internal to Oracle. This package is not installed by default and must be created by executing the catoctk.sql script under the SYS user. This script executes several scripts in succession to ensure the RANDOM function is available for use. The package is by default granted to PUBLIC.

The first step when using DBMS_RANDOM to generate random numbers is to initialize the generator using the INITIALIZE procedure. The parameter for this procedure identifies the seed number to be used as a basis for the generator. Using at least a five-digit value is recommended to ensure a well-randomized pattern. This seed value can be changed programmatically anytime thereafter by calling the SEED procedure directly.

To acquire a random number after initializing the generator, simply call the RANDOM function, which will return an integer of random value. Unlike more complex versions allowing the formatting of the returning number, RANDOM does not accept any parameters. As the following example demonstrates, the TERMINATE procedure should be called when completed to free any memory allocated for the random process. The following example generates five random numbers.

File: 16_16.sql

```
DECLARE
   lv_seed_num    PLS_INTEGER := 123456789;
   lv_random_num PLS_INTEGER;
BEGIN
   DBMS_RANDOM.INITIALIZE(lv_seed_num);
   FOR lv_loop_num IN 1..5 LOOP
      lv_random_num := DBMS_RANDOM.RANDOM;
      DBMS_OUTPUT.PUT_LINE('Loop: ' || lv_loop_num ||
         '    Random Number: ' || lv_random_num);
   END LOOP;
   DBMS_RANDOM.TERMINATE;
END;
/
```

Output (16_16.sql)

Oracle Supplied Packages

```
Loop: 1    Random Number: -1349346914
Loop: 2    Random Number: -1600794911
Loop: 3    Random Number: -1798261288
Loop: 4    Random Number: -1317260529
Loop: 5    Random Number: 190490462

PL/SQL procedure successfully completed.
```

Block Repair Facility (DBMS_REPAIR)

In Oracle 8.1, Oracle has made it easier for DBAs to find and repair block corruption without losing the entire corrupted database object. The DBMS_REPAIR package detects and repairs lost data, while making the object usable even when block corruption occurs. While some data (the corrupted data) may be lost, this feature enables you to skip the corrupted blocks without errors, thus making recovery from block corruption much easier. Additional reporting features are provided with this package. Prior to the introduction of this package, the recovery of an object with corrupted blocks was a manually intensive process.

The dbmsrepr.sql file contains the creation of the DBMS_REPAIR package and is created by default when the database is created. The DBMS_REPAIR is only accessible to the SYS user by default.

The following constants (all of data type BINARY INTEGER) are created in the declaration of the DBMS_REPAIR package and need to be used when passing these parameters.

- **Object Type Specification:** TABLE_OBJECT set to 1, INDEX_OBJECT set to 2, and CLUSTER_OBJECT set to 4

- **Flag Specification:** SKIP_FLAG set to 1, and NOSKIP_FLAG set to 2

- **Repair Table Action Specification:** CREATE_ACTION set to 1, PURGE_ACTION set to 2, and DROP_ACTION set to 3

- **Administration Table Type Specification:** REPAIR_TABLE set to 1 and ORPHAN_TABLE set to 2

The first step in executing the DBMS_REPAIR facility is to create a table storing the information about the corrupted blocks. The ADMIN_TABLES procedure provides the facility to create the table. The following illustrates the creation of this table.

```
EXECUTE DBMS_REPAIR.ADMIN_TABLES(table_name => 'REPAIR_S_EMPLOYEE',
    table_type => 1, action => 1)
```

The parameterized notation is used in the preceding example to provide the definition of the parameters.

TIP

The name of the table specified to be created for the DBMS_REPAIR package must begin with 'REPAIR_'; otherwise, an error will occur.

The table created from the preceding execution is described in the following code.

```
DESCRIBE repair_s_employee

 Name                                Null?      Type
 ---------------------------------   --------   ----
 OBJECT_ID                           NOT NULL   NUMBER
 TABLESPACE_ID                       NOT NULL   NUMBER
 RELATIVE_FILE_ID                    NOT NULL   NUMBER
 BLOCK_ID                            NOT NULL   NUMBER
 CORRUPT_TYPE                        NOT NULL   NUMBER
 SCHEMA_NAME                         NOT NULL   VARCHAR2(30)
 OBJECT_NAME                         NOT NULL   VARCHAR2(30)
 BASEOBJECT_NAME                                VARCHAR2(30)
 PARTITION_NAME                                 VARCHAR2(30)
 CORRUPT_DESCRIPTION                            VARCHAR2(2000)
 REPAIR_DESCRIPTION                             VARCHAR2(200)
 MARKED_CORRUPT                      NOT NULL   VARCHAR2(10)
 CHECK_TIMESTAMP                     NOT NULL   DATE
 FIX_TIMESTAMP                                  DATE
 REFORMAT_TIMESTAMP                             DATE
```

To check an object for corruption, the CHECK_OBJECT procedure is used. This is illustrated in the following example by checking the s_employee table of the PLSQL_USER.

File: 16_17.sql

```
DECLARE
   lv_blocks_corrupt_num BINARY_INTEGER;
BEGIN
   DBMS_REPAIR.CHECK_OBJECT(schema_name => 'PLSQL_USER',
      object_name => 'S_EMPLOYEE',
      repair_table_name => 'REPAIR_S_EMPLOYEE',
      corrupt_count => lv_blocks_corrupt_num);
   DBMS_OUTPUT.PUT_LINE('Corrupted_Blocks: ' ||
      lv_blocks_corrupt_num);
```

```
END;
/
```

Output (16_17.sql)

```
Corrupted_Blocks: 0

PL/SQL procedure successfully completed.
```

No corrupt blocks exist within the s_employee table. Four additional procedures are included with the DBMS_REPAIR package to assist with the repair of corrupted blocks.

TIP
The DBMS_REPAIR package provides a helpful method of identifying and repairing corrupted blocks in tables, indexes, and clusters. The example provided in this section could be modified to check every object in a schema.

Process ROWIDs (DBMS_ROWID)

With the new ROWID structure introduced in Oracle 8.0, Oracle has also provided a package to assist in conversions and other functions using ROWID. The DBMS_ROWID package is installed by dbmsutil.sql, called by catproc.sql, at database installation time. The following examples show some of the capabilities of the DBMS_ROWID package.

ROWID_TO_RESTRICTED—Displays the restricted V7 format of the ROWID.

File: 16_18.sql

```
SELECT ROWID "V8 ROWID",
       DBMS_ROWID.ROWID_TO_RESTRICTED(ROWID,0) "V7 ROWID",
       employee_id, employee_last_name
FROM   s_employee
WHERE  ROWNUM < 3;
```

Output (16_18.sql)

```
V8 ROWID            V7 ROWID                EMPLOYEE_ID EMPLOYEE_LAST_NAME
------------------- -------------------     ----------- --------------------
AAAGTxAABAAACqIAAA  00002A88.0000.0001                1 VELASQUEZ
AAAGTxAABAAACqIAAB  00002A88.0001.0001                2 NGAO
```

ROWID_BLOCK_NUMBER—Displays the block number of the row.

ROWID_ROW_NUMBER—Displays the row sequence number in the block. Multiple rows may exist per block and the sequence number starts at zero.

The following example illustrates the ROWID_BLOCK_NUMBER and ROWID_ROW_NUMBER functions.

File: 16_19.sql

```
SELECT  DBMS_ROWID.ROWID_BLOCK_NUMBER(ROWID) "Block Number",
        DBMS_ROWID.ROWID_ROW_NUMBER(ROWID) "Row in Block",
        employee_id
FROM    s_employee;
```

Output (16_19.sql)

```
Block Number Row in Block EMPLOYEE_ID
------------ ------------ -----------
       10888            0           1
       10888            1           2
       10888            2           3
       10888            3           4
       10888            4           5
       10888            5           6
       10888            6           7
       10888            7           8
```

Only a subset of 25 records in the s_employee table is displayed in the preceding example output.

The following example uses the same two functions to provide detailed statistics about the distribution of the s_employee table block distribution. This information is often helpful to DBAs when determining the data growth and database table sizing.

File: 16_20.sql

```
SELECT  COUNT(DISTINCT(DBMS_ROWID.ROWID_BLOCK_NUMBER(ROWID)))
        "Distinct Blocks",
        AVG(COUNT(DBMS_ROWID.ROWID_ROW_NUMBER(ROWID)))
        "Avg # Rows/Block",
```

```
      MIN(COUNT(DBMS_ROWID.ROWID_ROW_NUMBER(ROWID)))
      "Min # Rows/BLock",
      MAX(COUNT(DBMS_ROWID.ROWID_ROW_NUMBER(ROWID)))
      "Max # Rows/Block"
FROM   s_employee
GROUP  BY DBMS_ROWID.ROWID_BLOCK_NUMBER(ROWID);
```

Output (16_20.sql)

```
Distinct Blocks Avg # Rows/Block Min # Rows/BLock Max # Rows/Block
--------------- ----------------- ---------------- ----------------
              1                25               25               25
```

TIP
The DBMS_ROWID package provides a DBA with excellent information about the storage of data within the database. It can be used in lieu of the normal DBA tables and views for many operations.

Probe Facility

The Probe facility, a new feature in the release of Oracle 8.1, introduces three extremely powerful packages that enable developers to analyze and debug their PL/SQL program units with more ease. The three packages each provide a layer of analysis previously accomplished by manual coding techniques. The following lists the three packages and their purpose:

- **DBMS_DEBUG** Used to debug PL/SQL program units

- **DBMS_PROFILER** Used to analyze performance of PL/SQL program units

- **DBMS_TRACE** Used to trace the execution of PL/SQL program units

Each of these packages are PL/SQL APIs producing statistics and are implemented as server-side packages.

DBMS_DEBUG

The DBMS_DEBUG package is an API to the PL/SQL debugger layer. The DBMS_DEBUG package is created by default when the database is created and access is provided to PUBLIC. The creation files are dbmspb.sql and prvtpb.plb. The DBMS_DEBUG package works with one session executing the program unit to debug and another session monitoring the debugging information generated from the executing session.

The DBMS_DEBUG package functions similarly to the DBMS_PIPE package; one session is generating and sending information and the other session is reading the information.

A session command can be executed to switch on debug mode, as illustrated in the following code:

```
ALTER SESSION SET PLSQL_DEBUG = TRUE;
```

Once PLSQL_DEBUG is turned on, debug information will be generated for the remainder of the session or until the PLSQL_DEBUG is turned off with the ALTER SESSION command (set to FALSE).

If debug information is only desired for particular PL/SQL program units (package, procedure, function database trigger, or type) the desired program units can be compiled with a DEBUG option, as illustrated in the following example:

```
ALTER PACKAGE dependency_map COMPILE DEBUG;
ALTER PACKAGE dependency_map COMPILE DEBUG BODY;
```

For further information related to the DBMS_DEBUG package, refer to the *Oracle 8i Supplied Package Reference* or the comments in the dbmspb.sql script.

DBMS_PROFILER

The DBMS_PROFILER package is an API providing the capability to gather statistics related to the execution of PL/SQL program units to pinpoint performance problems. The DBMS_PROFILER package is not created by default when the database is created and must be created with the profload.sql script. The script should be executed under the SYS schema, and access is granted to PUBLIC. The profload.sql script calls the dbmspbp.sql and prvtpbp.plb scripts.

The DBMS_PROFILER is used as a component of the iterative performance improvement method. The process to be followed when using the DBMS_PROFILER is the same as outlined in Chapter 8. The only difference is the DBMS_PROFILER executes during the performance testing to provide more granular statistical information.

A typical profiler session follows the steps:

1. Start the profiler to collect statistics for a session.

2. Execute the PL/SQL program unit to profile.

3. Stop the profiler.

The DBMS_PROFILER execution logs statistics in memory structures that are flushed when the profiler is stopped. If the program execution is lengthy, flush the memory at regular intervals as recommended, which forces the statistics logged in memory to be written to database tables, followed by freeing the memory to log further statistics.

To use the DBMS_PROFILE package, database tables and other structures must be created through the proftab.sql script. This script can be executed under the schema executing the DBMS_PROFILER package or under a centralized schema (if centralized, create a PUBLIC synonym on the objects and grant SELECT and INSERT on the tables and sequence). The tables created are outlined in the following list:

- plsql_profiler_data

- plsql_profiler_units

- plsql_profiler_runs

The statistics gathered are extremely detailed, including the number of times each line was executed, the total execution time for each line, and the minimum and maximum execution time of each line. Once this information is logged in the database tables, the information can be retrieved with any report facility. Oracle has provided several routines that illustrate example methods of retrieving this information. These routines are provided in the form of two scripts located in the plsql/demo directory (under the ORACLE_HOME directory) called profrep.sql (creates several views and a package called PROF_REPORT_UTILITIES) and profsum.sql (executes profrep.sql and then provides various SQL statements to display profiler information and calls to the PROF_REPORT_UTILITIES package). Both these scripts should be reviewed in detail to understand the DBMS_PROFILER package statistics gathered, and how to create your own customized reports against these statistical tables.

For further information related to the DBMS_PROFILER package, refer to the *Oracle 8i Supplied Package Reference* or the comments in the dbmspbp.sql script.

DBMS_TRACE

The DBMS_TRACE package is an API that enables PL/SQL program unit execution tracing. The DBMS_TRACE package is created by default when the database is created and access is provided to PUBLIC. The creation files are dbmspbt.sql and prvtpbt.plb. The DBMS_TRACE is different from the TRACE facility that enables the tracing of SQL statements. The DBMS_TRACE package allows tracing of procedures, functions, and exceptions. The tracing information from the DBMS_TRACE package is written to a trace file, similar to the TRACE facility.

The DBMS_TRACE turns on and off PL/SQL tracing. Four levels of tracing can be set and are included in the package as constants as follows:

- **trace_all_calls** traces all PL/SQL program unit executions and exceptions (set to 1)

■ **trace_enabled_calls** traces only PL/SQL program unit executions and exceptions that have been set to DEBUG (set to 2)

■ **trace_all_exceptions** traces all exceptions (set to 4)

■ **trace_enabled_exceptions** traces only exception that have been set to DEBUG (set to 8)

When PL/SQL tracing is turned on, the level of tracing is specified. Tracing continues until the tracing is turned off or the session is terminated.

All PL/SQL program units and exceptions can be enabled by executing the DEBUG command that follows:

```
ALTER SESSION SET PLSQL_DEBUG = TRUE;
```

If TRACE information is only desired for particular PL/SQL program units (package, procedure, function database trigger, or type), the desired program units can be compiled with a DEBUG option, as illustrated in the following example:

```
ALTER PACKAGE dependency_map COMPILE DEBUG;
ALTER PACKAGE dependency_map COMPILE DEBUG BODY;
```

TIP
DBMS_TRACE does not work in a multithreaded server environment.

TIP
The DBMS_TRACE package is similar to the TRACE facility with respect to the volume of data that can be produced if set at the wrong level. Use caution when using the DBMS_TRACE package and limit the tracing to the desired areas.

For further information related to the DBMS_TRACE package, refer to the *Oracle 8i Supplied Package Reference* or the comments in the dbmspbt.sql script.

Extended Security Methodology

Oracle has added new security features, thus extending the capability of security in Oracle 8.0 and Oracle 8.1. These features have been integrated at the database level, and in PL/SQL.

Stored PL/SQL Program Unit Execution

In Oracle 8.1, a stored PL/SQL program unit can be created so when the program unit is executed, it is executed with the invoker's (schema executing) rights versus the definer's (creator of the object) rights. Prior to Oracle 8.1, when a stored PL/SQL program unit was created, the schema executing the stored PL/SQL program unit executed the program with the definer's (creator of the object) rights. The creation and execution privileges of stored PL/SQL program units, prior to the release of Oracle 8.1, is outlined in Chapter 10. This optional method of execution is the same as execution privilege in existence for Oracle supplied packages.

The new execution method is an option that can be added to the CREATE OR REPLACE command. The new AUTHID option controls the execution privilege used, whether definer (DEFINER) or invoker (CURRENT_USER). The default execution is DEFINER, which is the only method deployed prior to Oracle 8.1. This new option would be ideal if a stored PL/SQL program unit needed to be executed by multiple schemas to update different database objects. I like the addition of the option, but I still see limited use for the option with traditional stored PL/SQL program unit design.

The standard method of creating a stored procedure and granting access follows:

1. Create the stored PL/SQL program unit.

2. Create a PUBLIC synonym on the stored PL/SQL program unit.

3. Grant EXECUTE to the users or roles that should execute the stored PL/SQL program unit.

The following code segments illustrate the preceding steps with the new option used to force the use of the invoker's privilege.

File: 16_21.sql

```
CREATE OR REPLACE PROCEDURE display_customers
   AUTHID CURRENT_USER IS    -- AUTHID is the only change required
   CURSOR cur_cust IS
      SELECT customer_id, customer_name
      FROM   s_customer;
BEGIN
   FOR cur_cust_rec IN cur_cust LOOP
      DBMS_OUTPUT.PUT_LINE('Customer Id: ' ||
         cur_cust_rec.customer_id || CHR(9) ||
         ' Customer Name: ' || cur_cust_rec.customer_name);
   END LOOP;
END display_customers;
/
```

Extended Security Methodology

File: 16_22.sql

```
CREATE PUBLIC SYNONYM display_customers FOR display_customers;
GRANT EXECUTE ON display_customers TO plsql_test;
```

The preceding code segments were executed under the PLSQL_USER
schema. When the PLSQL_USER schema executes the procedure, the data
displayed is the data in the s_customer table owned by PLSQL_USER as shown
in the following output:

Output (16_21.sql)

```
EXECUTE display_customers

Customer Id: 201          Customer Name: UNISPORTS
Customer Id: 202          Customer Name: SIMMS ATHELETICS
Customer Id: 203          Customer Name: DELHI SPORTS
Customer Id: 204          Customer Name: WOMANSPORT
Customer Id: 205          Customer Name: KAM'S SPORTING GOODS
Customer Id: 206          Customer Name: SPORTIQUE

PL/SQL procedure successfully completed.
```

The preceding output only displays the first six records. The PLSQL_TEST
schema does not own an s_customer table; therefore, when the PLSQL_TEST user
attempts to execute the display_customers procedure, the following error occurs:

Output (16_21.sql)

```
EXECUTE display_customers

begin display_customers; end;

*
ERROR at line 1:
ORA-00942: table or view does not exist
ORA-06512: at "PLSQL_USER.DISPLAY_CUSTOMERS", line 4
ORA-06512: at "PLSQL_USER.DISPLAY_CUSTOMERS", line 7
ORA-06512: at line 1
```

If the PLSQL_TEST schema owned an s_customer table, the result would be
different. Therefore, I created an identical s_customer table (without the data) in the
PLSQL_TEST schema and inserted two customers. When the display_customers
procedure was executed, the result displayed the contents of the PLSQL_TEST
s_customer table data, as illustrated in the following output.

Output (16_21.sql)

```
EXECUTE display_customers

Customer Id: 100        Customer Name: SPORTS AUTHORITY
Customer Id: 101        Customer Name: SPORTSMART

PL/SQL procedure successfully completed.
```

The AUTHID option is available for procedures, functions, packages, and types. The definer (creator) of the stored program unit must possess the proper privilege to create the program unit, which means the program unit is compiled the same as if the AUTHID option were not present. The stored PL/SQL program unit is recompiled at runtime. This is a powerful feature, but should only be used when needed. The ideal environments would have the same table duplicated (same table name) under multiple schemas and only one stored PL/SQL program unit would be necessary in this case.

TIP

The AUTHID option provides the capability to create stored PL/SQL program units executed the same as Oracle supplied packages, namely, with the executor's (invoker's) privilege versus the creator's (definer's) privilege.

TIP

When the AUTHID option was introduced in Oracle 8.1, it required an additional parameter, namely, SQL_NAME_RESOLVE, which required the value to be set the same as AUTHID. As of Oracle 8.1.4, this parameter was eliminated because it was redundant.

Enhanced Schema Security

The Oracle security system has been enhanced in Oracle 8.0 with a variety of helpful options. The Oracle Security Server offers a single sign-on environment complete with the means for global roles and user setup, password expiration, minimum password lengths, shared database links, privileged database links, and encryption from OCI and PL/SQL. Many of the new security features are similar to several of the operating system security features.

The init.ora parameter dblink_encrypt_login specifies whether attempts to connect to other Oracle Servers through database links should use encrypted passwords. When you attempt to connect to a database using a password, Oracle encrypts the password before sending it to the database. If the dblink_encrypt_login parameter is TRUE, and the connection fails, Oracle does not re-attempt the connection. If this parameter is FALSE, Oracle re-attempts the connections using an unencrypted version of the password.

Several of the new security methods introduced new columns in the DBA_USERS, DBA_PROFILES, and DBA_DB_LINKS views as outlined in the following segment of code (an '*' identifies the new columns in Oracle 8.0).

```
DESCRIBE dba_users

Name                              Null?       Type
-------------------------------   --------    ----
USERNAME                          NOT NULL    VARCHAR2(30)
USER_ID                           NOT NULL    NUMBER
PASSWORD                                      VARCHAR2(30)
*ACCOUNT_STATUS                   NOT NULL    VARCHAR2(32)
*LOCK_DATE                                    DATE
*EXPIRY_DATE                                  DATE
DEFAULT_TABLESPACE                NOT NULL    VARCHAR2(30)
TEMPORARY_TABLESPACE              NOT NULL    VARCHAR2(30)
CREATED                           NOT NULL    DATE
PROFILE                           NOT NULL    VARCHAR2(30)
*EXTERNAL_NAME                                VARCHAR2(4000)
```

```
DESCRIBE dba_profiles

Name                              Null?       Type
-------------------------------   --------    ----
PROFILE                           NOT NULL    VARCHAR2(30)
RESOURCE_NAME                     NOT NULL    VARCHAR2(32)
*RESOURCE_TYPE                                VARCHAR2(8)
LIMIT                                         VARCHAR2(40)
```

```
DESCRIBE dba_db_links

Name                              Null?       Type
-------------------------------   --------    ----
OWNER                             NOT NULL    VARCHAR2(30)
DB_LINK                           NOT NULL    VARCHAR2(128)
USERNAME                                      VARCHAR2(30)
*HOST                                         VARCHAR2(2000)
CREATED                           NOT NULL    DATE
```

The following new roles have been created in Oracle 8.0.

```
SELECT_CATALOG_ROLE
EXECUTE_CATALOG_ROLE
DELETE_CATALOG_ROLE
AQ_USER_ROLE
AQ_ADMINISTRATOR_ROLE
RECOVERY_CATALOG_OWNER
HS_ADMIN_ROLE
```

TIP
New columns in DBA_USERS, DBA_PROFILES, and DBA_DB_LINKS offer new information concerning user account status and general security information.

Addition of Schema Profiles

Profiles are used in Oracle to prevent users from using inordinate amounts of resources and to enforce security regarding user passwords. The following options have been added in Oracle 8.0 to enhance security.

Option	Default Value	Description
FAILED_LOGIN_ATTEMPTS	5	Failed attempts allowed until the account is locked
PASSWORD_LIFE_TIME	60	Days the same password can be used
PASSWORD_REUSE_TIME	60	Days before a password can be reused
PASSWORD_REUSE_MAX	UNLIMITED	Password changes required before the current password can be reused
PASSWORD_VERIFY_FUNCTION	verify_function	Enables a PL/SQL password verification function to be passed as an argument to the PROFILE command
PASSWORD_LOCK_TIME	1/24 (1 hour)	Days an account will be locked after specified number of consecutive failed login attempts
PASSWORD_GRACE_TIME	10	Days after the grace period begins that a warning is issued and login is allowed

Extended Security Methodology

You can use fractions of days for all parameters with days as units. For example, one hour is 1/24 and one minute is 1/1440.

The VERIFY_FUNCTION function script (created in the script utlpwdmg.sql) is introduced in Oracle 8.0. The script must be run manually as SYS and is located in the ORACLE_HOME/rdbms/admin directory. It creates the VERIFY_FUNCTION function and an ALTER PROFILE command to set resource limits (the ALTER PROFILE command in this script sets the password_verify_function parameter to VERIFY_FUNCTION). The utlpwdmg.sql script can be customized. If you plan to change the VERIFY_FUNCTION function, follow these steps:

1. Make a copy of the utlpwdmg.sql script.

2. Change the name of the function to enable the original function to still be used.

3. Change the PL/SQL logic to perform your new algorithm.

4. Create the function under the SYS schema.

5. Alter or create a new profile to use the new PL/SQL function.

The VERIFY_FUNCTION function provides five simple password checks, as the following outlines:

- Ensures the password is not the same as the username

- Ensures the password is greater than four characters

- Ensures the password includes at least one character, one number, and one punctuation mark

- Ensures the password is not too simple by checking a list of simple words with an IN clause, which currently contains only eight words

- Ensures the password differs from the previous password by at least three characters

TIP
Use security profiles to manage user passwords and limits to user accounts. If profiles are not used, a single user could take the memory of the entire system for a given query. At times, the best performance improvement is often the elimination of potential performance degradations.

Password Management Facility

Several new options for managing password security are introduced in Oracle 8.0. Examples of expiring a password and locking a user out of the database are illustrated in this section.

The following expires a password immediately.

```
CONNECT system/manager
ALTER USER plsql_test PASSWORD EXPIRE;
```

When the PLSQL_TEST user attempts to log in, the following message is received, and the user will be forced to change his or her password immediately.

```
CONNECT plsql_test/plsql_test

ERROR:
ORA-28001: the account has expired
```

The following will lock a user account, thus disallowing any connection attempts (to unlock an account, the same command is used with the LOCK keyword changed to UNLOCK).

```
CONNECT system/manager
ALTER USER plsql_test ACCOUNT LOCK;
```

When PLSQL_TEST attempts to log in, the following message is received, and the user will be unable to connect to the database.

```
CONNECT plsql_test/plsql_test

ERROR:
ORA-28000: the account is locked
Warning: You are no longer connected to ORACLE.
```

TIP
Using the ALTER USER command enables you to expire and lock passwords.

Support for Large Object (LOB) Data Types

Oracle has introduced support for Large Objects in Oracle 8.0. The new Large Objects (LOBs) provide storage for large amounts of binary or ASCII data, as commonly found in document, audio, and video storage. The following four data types can be used to store large objects:

- **CLOB**   Stores single byte character data used for large character objects

- **BLOB**   Stores unstructured binary data used for large binary objects

- **NCLOB**   Stores multibyte character data (Japanese kanji implementation) used for large character objects (national character set)

- **BFILE**   Stores binary data in a file outside (in file system) the Oracle Database

Large objects are important to developers because, unlike the LONG and LONG RAW data types previously available, these can be manipulated through PL/SQL with the use of packages. The package DBMS_LOB can be used for standard manipulation and UTL_RAW for bit-wise manipulation of stored binary data, as discussed earlier in this chapter.

TIP
The LONG and LONG RAW data types can be replaced with the more functional BLOB, CLOB, NCLOB, and BFILE data types.

The structure of the LOB data types does not follow the rules of the conventional LONG and LONG RAW data types. An unlimited number of LOB data types are allowed within one table and each can store up to 4GB of information. Remember, only character (CLOB and NCLOB) LOBs can be displayed (selected) directly through SQL. Binary data must be translated or type cast into a character equivalent. By default, LOBs are stored offline in another table as an undefined object type with a column name similar to SYS_LOB[2 Byte Identifier]$ outside the originating table. They can be defined to be inline with the table upon creation, as long as they are not expected to exceed 4,000 bytes in size, at which point Oracle automatically moves them offline. Oracle controls the referencing (and de-referencing) from the originating table pointing to the appropriate record in the storage table. These references are assigned whenever a LOB is stored in the database, as long as the value is not NULL.

TIP
Always use the appropriate initializing function, either EMPTY_CLOB or EMPTY_BLOB, to initialize a LOB that would otherwise be NULL. This instantiation process enables these objects to be manipulated through PL/SQL. When initialized with NULL, no storage location is reserved for the object, which could cause errors if a direct reference is attempted.

Two methods are available to access the reference or locator of the LOB once stored in the database. Selecting the value of the column from the parent table returns its locator reference, but requires requerying after the value has been inserted. A simpler way from within PL/SQL to attain the locator of the LOB quickly during an INSERT statement is to use the new predicate RETURNING clause, as shown in the following example.

The first part of the example creates a table with a CLOB defined, followed by a PL/SQL code segment that retrieves the pointer to the CLOB.

File: 16_23.sql

```
CREATE TABLE test_clob
(clob_id    NUMBER,
clob_object CLOB);
```

File: 16_24.sql

```
DECLARE
     lv_clob_pointer_txt CLOB;
BEGIN
  INSERT INTO test_clob
   (clob_id, clob_object)
  VALUES
   (1, '1234567890')
  RETURNING clob_object INTO lv_clob_pointer_txt;
END;
/
```

In the preceding example, lv_clob_pointer_txt contains the locator where the clob_object is stored, thereby providing access to the object itself to subsequent routines.

BFILEs, as previously stated, are not stored in the database, but are maintained asynchronously outside the database. This is an important point because these transactions are not part of the standard Oracle transactional process; therefore, they cannot be committed or rolled back.

As with the other LOBs, manipulating BFILE objects takes place through the use of the DBMS_LOB package. Unlike the other LOBs, BFILE objects can only be read and cannot be modified (there is no UPDATE BFILE procedure). This is information outside the database, so additional setup is required.

TIP

SESSION_MAX_OPEN_FILES is the init.ora parameter identifying how many BFILE files can be open in one session at a time; the default is 10.

To save an object to the file system, the database must be aware of the file system. Specifically, Oracle requires a map of the directory structure in which the object will ultimately reside. To facilitate this process, Oracle can provide this information using the CREATE DIRECTORY command, as illustrated in the following code segment.

```
CREATE DIRECTORY home AS 'c:\';
```

The preceding segment of code illustrates the directory path and alias identifying the object's location. This directory path can be superseded during the FILEOPEN execution by entering a path with the filename itself. To view the directory(s) defined within a database, select from the ALL_DIRECTORIES and DBA_DIRECTORIES views.

To initialize a BFILE for use, the BFILENAME function is used, as illustrated in the following example. The first part of the example creates a table with a BFILE defined, followed by an INSERT statement to load a BFILE location.

File: 16_25.sql

```
CREATE TABLE test_bfile
(bfile_id    NUMBER,
bfile_object BFILE);
```

File: 16_26.sql

```
INSERT INTO test_bfile
(bfile_id, bfile_object)
VALUES
(1, BFILENAME('HOME', 'myfile.txt'));
```

New Objects Types and Concepts

With the release of Oracle 8.0, Oracle embraced object-oriented programming and offers several options in the area of objects. This section provides a brief overview of several of these new options, included in the following list:

- Standard Definitions of New Object Terms
- Support of Collections
    - VARRARY
    - NESTED TABLE
- Support of Object Data Types

To explain objects properly would require a complete book. The world of objects requires a whole new mindset, so the goal of this section is to concentrate on providing a brief, high-level overview of this expansive area.

Standard Definitions and New Object Terms

With the introduction of this expansive area comes the need to begin with the basics. This area introduces some major shifts in standard programming. The following is a list of some of the definitions related to objects.

- **Object** An entity or variable that can consist of entity and operational information, therefore, other objects.

- **Extensibility** The capability to conform to new requirements using existing structures. Oracle8 is extensible, enabling the assembly of new, abstract data types based on its pre-defined primitive types, such as NUMBER, VARCHAR2, DATE, and so forth.

- **VARRAY** An ordered list of data elements that is useful for nonsearchable finite data.

- **NESTED TABLE** An unordered set of data elements that is useful for searchable, indexable, unlimited data.

- **Method** Procedure or function that is part of the object type definition and can operate on the data attributes of the object type. Loosely defined, a trigger on a table could be looked at as a method for a table.

- **Object View** Enables the use of relational data in object-oriented applications.

- **Encapsulation** The mechanism through which data and their methods can be bound and protected. An *object* is a logical entity that encapsulates both the data and the code that manipulates the specified data.

- **Inheritance** The process by which one object can acquire the properties of another object.

- **Class** Related, hierarchical groupings or categorization of objects.

- **Polymorphism** An object's capability to react to or interface with a general class of actions achieved through overloading. With DBMS_OUTPUT.PUT_LINE it does not matter whether you send a character string, number, or date as parameters to the procedure.

- **Metadata** The data comprised of all the information about all the data on your system, how it is stored, where it is stored, and so forth. Metadata is "data about the data."

Support of Collections

A *collection* is a related group of data. A PL/SQL table is considered a collection. Two new object types introduced in Oracle 8.0 are VARRAYs and NESTED TABLEs. These can be created in the database and referenced in PL/SQL or they can be created in PL/SQL as user-defined types.

VARRAY

An additional member added to the primitive set is the VARRAY (short for VARYING ARRAY), exhibiting Oracle 8.0 capability to define lists known as collection object types. VARRAYs are ordered, fixed-length lists residing in a single column of a table or as a declared variable in PL/SQL. Through SQL, the list can only be selected as a whole. A VARRAY column in a database table can only be manipulated through the use of PL/SQL, where it can be read into a declared VARRAY variable for manipulation. Within PL/SQL, VARRAYs are implemented and function similarly to PL/SQL tables: their upper boundaries are defined and data is stored sequentially through an index. Unlike PL/SQL tables, VARRAYs are not stored as sparse arrays, whereby any element can be filled in any order. Assignments beyond the range (count) of the number of elements contained within a VARRAY will cause an *ORA-0653 Subscript beyond count* error.

TIP
To store data in a PL/SQL VARRAY past the (COUNT) number of elements, use the EXTEND command to enlarge the array by one element. This is different than the actual VARRAY size defined upon declaration, which cannot be extended.

A VARRAY can be used when a finite set of values is to be stored relating to a parent record. The VARRAY is actually a column stored as part of the corresponding row; therefore, no mechanism exists to index the values it contains within SQL. Physical allocation of the array is stored inline with the table as long as its size remains less than 4K. If this size is exceeded, Oracle will maintain the array as a BLOB data type.

A VARRAY type object is defined by identifying the number of elements it will contain, followed by the data type it will store. The creation and manipulation of a VARRAY is illustrated in the following PL/SQL code segment.

File: 16_27.sql

```
DECLARE
   TYPE lv_name_array IS VARRAY(5) OF VARCHAR2(10);
   lv_name_array_rec lv_name_array := lv_name_array('dave', 'pat',
```

```
        'bob');
BEGIN
    -- COUNT is currently at three
    FOR lv_loop_num in 1..lv_name_array_rec.COUNT LOOP
        DBMS_OUTPUT.PUT_LINE(lv_name_array_rec(lv_loop_num));
    END LOOP;
    -- Next Command: Pre-allocation necessary for subsequent statements
    lv_name_array_rec.EXTEND;
    lv_name_array_rec(lv_name_array_rec.COUNT) := 'tony';
    DBMS_OUTPUT.PUT_LINE(lv_name_array_rec(4));
END;
/
```

Output (16_27.sql)

```
dave
pat
bob
tony

PL/SQL procedure successfully completed.
```

A VARRAY type object can be used like any other type in object definitions. When a VARRAY is accessed from SQL*Plus, its index is used to insert and display the array information. Any manipulation of the VARRAY elements can only be accomplished through a programming tool, such as PL/SQL, which has the capability to index the elements individually as previously demonstrated.

NESTED TABLE

The second collection object type introduced in Oracle 8.0 is the NESTED TABLE, which is similar to a VARRAY. Both can be thought of as a set or list within a parenting table. VARRAYs are ordered lists residing in a single column, while a NESTED TABLE, as the name implies, is a table associated within another table. Oracle automatically handles the relationship between a parent table and its NESTED TABLE behind the scenes using a hidden 4-byte column called NESTED_TABLE_ID. This column is used to store a pointer back to the parenting record in a similar fashion as in the use of REFs. There is no need for an additional column for a VARRAY because a VARRAY is a fixed-length array existing within a single column of the related record.

The definition of a NESTED TABLE begins with an initial declaration of an object type. Oracle must be informed this type will be used as a NESTED TABLE. However, the relational model for a NESTED TABLE follows all the implicit rules of a traditional parent/child relationship, including data integrity. By virtue of the access mechanisms for nested tables, parent records cannot be removed leaving orphan children.

TIP
The access method itself implies parent/child integrity in the system. This is because the NESTED TABLE cannot be directly accessed.

The only way to access the information contained within a NESTED TABLE is through the parenting record. To design an object-oriented system properly, the designer must understand up-front how the data is to be accessed. For instance, consider the question "How many widgets were ordered today?" This question implies a count of the orders based upon a segment of items. In a NESTED TABLE environment, each order object would have to be selected and then its associated line items checked for every order. If the NESTED TABLE must be accessed directly without regard for the parenting object, NESTED TABLEs should not be used.

NESTED TABLEs should be used when an infinite, unordered set of records needs to be stored. In addition, if the object will require indexing and/or will be searchable, NESTED TABLEs should be used over a VARRAY object type.

TIP
NESTED TABLEs contain a hidden column called NESTED_TABLE_ID holding the REFerence back to the parent table. This column is used to look up child values by Oracle automatically. Oracle, on the other hand, does not create an index on this column automatically when the table is created. If the NESTED TABLE is going to store a substantial amount of data, it is highly recommended that this column be indexed.

TIP
Read NESTED TABLE queries by the sub-select first, picture a select set being returned to the outer query. This will make the statement easier to comprehend.

TIP
When working with objects, most commands require a table alias.

Support of Object Data Types

Object-type support is one of the expansive new features provided with the release of Oracle 8.0. New object types can be defined in the database to represent a business object used in a variety of locations in an application. An object type can possess a variety of attributes that may be of varying types, including scalar, another object type, a collection, a reference to an object type, and so forth. An object type can be defined to have multiple methods, including a constructor method, a MAP method, an ORDER method, and a user-defined method.

The SQL and the PL/SQL language have been greatly enhanced to support object types with a variety of new commands, options, and changes to the data dictionary.

Object-oriented programming introduces an entire new methodology to traditional OLTP programming. Take the time to understand and become proficient in this technology prior to developing any applications using these new object types.

Refer to the Oracle8 Database Reference manual set or the Oracle 8i Database Reference manual set for further information related to the new object types.

TIP
Remember to install Oracle8 with the objects option installed. Oracle did not include the objects option in their implementations of Personal Edition Oracle8 and Oracle Light.

Database Limitations

Everything continues to increase. Oracle has again expanded the limitations of many of the components of the database to ensure it is far beyond any system's full capacity. The following table highlights many of the limitations increased in Oracle 8.0.

Name	Oracle8 New Upper Limit
Database size	512PB (up from 32TB)
Maximum datafiles	65,533
Datafiles per tablespace	1,022
Blocks per datafile	4,000,000
Block size	32K
Maximum datafile size	128GB (4M*32K)
Maximum tablespace size	128TB (1022 *128GB)
db_block_buffers	Unlimited
SGA for 32-bit OS	4GB

Name	Oracle8 New Upper Limit
SGA for 64-bit OS	Beyond 4GB
User Population	10,000
Table columns	1,000 (up from 256)
B-tree Index columns	32 (up from 16)
Bitmap Index columns	30
VARCHAR2 column maximum length	4,000 (up from 2,000)

Oracle also increased support for very large databases (VLDB) with the addition of partitions and index-organized tables. The support of the 64-bit operating systems will provide increased performance. Version 8 executables are three times larger than version 7 executables, primarily because of new version 8 features. However, the actual size depends greatly on the features installed for Oracle8.

TIP
Stored PL/SQL program unit maximum size has increased with Oracle 8.1 from 32K bytes to 2^{26} bytes (basically unlimited).

New SQL-Related Enhancements

There are a variety of enhancements to the SQL language, as well as concepts, which are introduced in Oracle 8.0 and Oracle 8.1. This section outlines several of these new commands and concepts.

ROWID Changes

The format of Oracle's ROWID has completely changed. The expansion of the ROWID to a Base 64 encoding in Oracle 8.0 was necessary to support partitioned tables and indexes. This change has little effect on applications and systems that do not deploy the method of hardcoding ROWIDs. Hardcoding ROWIDs is never recommended because the ROWID changes when the database object is rebuilt. If ROWIDs were hardcoded into your application, pay careful attention to these locations when upgrading to Oracle8.

Oracle has introduced the DBMS_ROWID package providing procedures to convert between the two (pre-Oracle8 and post-Oracle8) ROWID formats. The formats of ROWIDs in Oracle7 and Oracle8 listed in the following table are different and are not interchangeable.

■ Oracle7 Restricted Format (BBBBBBBB.RRRR.FFFF)

BBBBBBBB	Block in Hex
RRRR	Row number within block
FFFF	File number

■ Oracle8 Extended Format (OOOOOOFFFBBBBBBSSS)

OOOOOO	Data object number identifying segment
FFF	Data file containing row
BBBBBB	Data block containing row
SSS	Row within block

Oracle8 can support more files per database and more blocks per file because of the extended format. Oracle can expand from Terabytes (TB) to Petabytes (PB) (1 Petabyte = 1,024 Terabytes = 1,048,576 Gigabytes).

Function-based Indexes

One of the largest problems with indexes is they are often unknowingly suppressed by developers. Developers using the UPPER function (or any function) can suppress an index on a column for a given query. In the release of Oracle 8.1, a way to combat this problem has been introduced. Function-based indexes enable the creation of an index based on a function or expression. The function or expression is specified when creating the index and is stored in the index. Function-based indexes can involve multiple columns, arithmetic expressions, or maybe a PL/SQL function or *C* callout. The following illustrates an example of a function-based index.

File: 16_28.sql

```
CREATE INDEX s_employee_idx2 ON s_employee(UPPER(employee_last_name));
```

File: 16_29.sql

```
SELECT employee_id, employee_last_name, employee_first_name
FROM   s_employee
WHERE  UPPER(employee_last_name) = 'NEWMAN';
```

The function-based index can be used for the preceding query. For large tables, where the condition retrieves a small amount of records, the query yields substantial performance gains. Function-based indexes should be thought of as part of the standard indexing methodology. If any predicate clause is repeated in several locations and can improve performance, it should be considered a candidate on which to create an index. As outlined in Chapter 7, when a column is modified in any manner in a predicate clause (with a function or expression), an index on the column will not be used, even if one exists, until now.

TIP

Function-based indexes add another dimension to the capability of indexing expressions, functions, and so forth.

TIP

Once a function-based index is created, it will only be considered an index that can be used if the init.ora parameter query_rewrite_enabled is set to TRUE. This parameter can be modified with the ALTER SYSTEM and ALTER SESSION commands.

NO_INDEX hint

The optimizer often uses undesirable indexes, despite efforts to override the use of the indexes. Oracle 8.1 introduces a hint specifically disallowing one or more indexes to be used by the optimizer, but does not suppress the use of all indexes (as with the FULL hint). The NO_INDEX hint requires a table to be supplied to specify for which table to suppress the indexes. The NO_INDEX hint will also accept specific indexes along with the table specified to be suppressed.

The following two examples illustrate the suppression of indexes with the NO_INDEX hint. The first example suppresses all indexes on the s_employee table, whereas the second example suppresses only one index on the s_employee table.

File: 16_30.sql

```
SELECT /*+ NO_INDEX (s_employee) */ employee_first_name,
       employee_last_name
FROM   s_employee
WHERE  employee_id = 25;
```

File: 16_31.sql

```
SELECT /*+ NO_INDEX (s_employee s_employee_id_pk) */
       employee_first_name, employee_last_name
FROM   s_employee
WHERE  employee_id = 25;
```

The two preceding scripts yield the same execution plan showing the suppression of the index by performing a full-table scan.

```
Execution Plan
------------------------------------------------------------
   0         SELECT STATEMENT Optimizer=CHOOSE (Cost=1 Card=1 Bytes=41)
   1     0     TABLE ACCESS (FULL) OF 'S_EMPLOYEE' (Cost=1 Card=1 Bytes=4
             1)
```

Index-Organized Tables

Index-organized tables were introduced in Oracle 8.0. An index-organized table combines the table and index creation into one object. The table data is stored in a b-tree structure. Only one database object is used to store both the data and the index. All the columns are stored as an index. B-tree indexes identify rows by primary keys, not by ROWIDs. A secondary index cannot be created on the table and, if updates are made, entire rows may be moved by the operation (costly). The performance gain is achieved when the data is accessed by the key in an exact match or range scan on the key.

Index-organized tables are advantageous when large lookup tables exist in your application.

Drop Column Command

In Oracle 8.1, Oracle introduced the DROP COLUMN command, which enables a column to be dropped from a table. While this may seem basic, developers and DBAs have wanted this new command for many years.

Examples of the DROP COLUMN command are illustrated in the following examples.

```
ALTER TABLE s_employee DROP COLUMN title;
ALTER TABLE s_employee DROP (userid);
ALTER TABLE s_employee DROP (salary, commision_pct);
```

The preceding statements display three variations of dropping columns. Each of the preceding columns dropped did not possess any cascading constraints.

To drop a column that is the parent of a parent-child (primary foreign key) relationship, the CASCADE CONSTRAINTS option can be added, as illustrated in the following command.

```
ALTER TABLE s_region DROP (region_id) CASCADE CONSTRAINTS;
```

In the preceding example, the region_id column was removed from the s_region table. The child (foreign) key relationship to the s_warehouse table is deleted and the region_id column remains in existence in the s_warehouse table. If the CASCADE CONSTRAINTS option is not supplied for a primary key column, an error will result that signifies the existence of the primary-foreign key condition.

TIP
The DROP COLUMN command has finally arrived. The DROP COLUMN command also contains an option for CASCADE CONSTRAINTS.

Expanded Web Integration into Oracle

Oracle has continued to demonstrate its strong commitment to the Web and Web-based products. Oracle has continued to expand integration with Java and, in Oracle 8.1, to enable the storage of stored Java program units. Oracle has also introduced new products (JDeveloper) and enhanced existing development products (Oracle Developer).

Web Development Products (JDeveloper and Oracle Developer)

JDeveloper is a product based on Borland's JBuilder technology. The original name for the effort was known as "Project Valhalla." JBuilder is similar in many ways to the look and feel of Oracle Developer. It has several wizards and contains an object navigator window to view dynamic HTML. The product includes an HTML-Java Wizard for building the Java that will generate the dynamic HTML. It has a Deployment Wizard that packages all files needed for given applications and consists of a PL/SQL Java Wizard for including calls to the database using PL/SQL. Wizards enable form creation and master detail forms as easily as Oracle Developer through the use of wizards. The JDBC driver is included with JBuilder and is hidden so connections to the database are made easily through "object navigator-like" windows. Oracle Developer currently runs on Windows 95 and NT.

JDeveloper is impressive in its early stages. It is a powerful tool geared toward the Java developer writing applications for the Oracle database. Oracle developers will find the transition from Oracle Developer to the look and feel of JDeveloper reasonably easy. Knowing how to write Java to generate dynamic HTML is the learning transition that must be made for the non-Java Oracle developers.

TIP

Currently, Oracle's JDeveloper is the 4GL Java tool for writing applications in Java that access an Oracle database.

Oracle Developer and Web-Enabling

Retraining your staff from Oracle Developer to JBuilder is reasonably simple, but an even faster way exists to Web-enable your current forms and reports. The answer is the latest version of the Oracle Developer suite of tools. Forms 5.x (Oracle Developer) and Reports 3.x (Oracle Reports) now have the capability to run as Web pages by using an applet viewer. The biggest advantage to using this method over the JBuilder solution is your application may already be written. With this tool, you can generate both Web-enabled and client-server versions of the application; users can use browsers or be in a typical PC client-server setup. I prefer the browser front-end for the reduction of PC maintenance. With this solution, the need to learn Java, HTML, or JavaScript is eliminated. The same .FMX runs on the browser or in a client-server setup.

The user's HTML page retrieves a Java applet, which is downloaded at run time from an application server to the user's Web browser. One issue that must be considered is the difference between how you write a screen when there is a constant connection (client-server) and the changes you make for performance in writing screens for a stateless interface (the Internet or intranet).

Now that I can develop applications with a 4GL Web tool, is there a faster way to get Internet commerce up and running without writing the whole thing myself? The answer is to integrate tools like Oracle's Internet Commerce Server (ICS) and others that can be used as a base for the development effort.

TIP

Oracle Forms and Oracle Reports have been the core products of Oracle for more than ten years. Memory and performance requirements for these products limit their usefulness on the Web to intranet-based deployment only. The day will come when Oracle Developer will be a viable solution for Internet deployment...it is just a matter of time.

Integration of Java with SQL (SQLJ and JDBC)

The two primary tools that enable Java to work with Oracle are JDBC and SQLJ. SQLJ is an integration of Oracle's SQL within Java code. JDBC is like ODBC for Java. JDBC is a call-level library interface, further enhanced by SQLJ's capability to access the database at compile time. Although both these methods allow the use of Java with Oracle, distinct differences and benefits exist. At times, when you use JDBC, it is both complementary and advantageous to use SQLJ.

SQLJ is perfect for simple SQL calls to the database and for embedding SQL within Java. The SQLJ preprocessor is written in Java and the pre-compiler changes the SQLJ to Java classes. Commonly used SQL statements that can be included in Java include:

- **Queries**   SELECT statements and expressions

- **Data Manipulation Language (DML)**   INSERT, UPDATE, and DELETE

- **Data Statements**   FETCH and SELECT INTO

- **Transaction control**   COMMIT, ROLLBACK, and so forth

- **Data Definition Language (DDL)**   CREATE, DROP, and so forth

- **Calls to stored procedures**   e.g., myproc(:x, :y, :z)

- **Calls to stored functions**   e.g., VALUES (myfun(:x))

Java Database Connectivity (JDBC) is a standard set of Java classes, specified by JavaSoft, so all vendors can access the database in the same manner. JDBC classes provide the standard features consistent with ODBC, such as transaction management, simple queries, manipulation of pre-compiled statements with bind variables, calls to stored procedures, access to the database dictionary, and other basic database access functionality. For the user, it is a matter of typing in the Web page desired and the necessary JDBC driver is downloaded to the browser from the Web server. There is no client-side installation. There is a thin JDBC driver that only works with TCP/IP, which is much faster. Both the Oracle JDBC and thin JDBC drivers are JDK (Java Development Kit) 1.0.2. and 1.1 compliant. These drivers work with SQL*Net along with firewalls certified with SQL*Net: Firewalls from Checkpoint, SunSoft, CISCO Systems, Milkyway Networks, Trusted Information Systems, Raptor, Secure Computing Corporation, and Global Internet.

Additional Features of Oracle 8.0 and Oracle 8.1

The following is a brief list of a number of the new features in Oracle 8.0 and Oracle 8.1 not covered in this chapter. Each new feature has an Oracle 8.0 or Oracle 8.1 designation.

- A complete recovery manager has been created called RMAN with several Oracle supplied packages created for this new feature. (Oracle 8.0)

- Table and index partitioning has been added to enable large tables and indexes to be segmented logically to increase performance. (Oracle 8.0)

- Net8 is replacing SQL*Net, and many of the original SQL*Net parameters are now obsolete. (Oracle 8.0)

- Parallel operations are expanded to DML statements. (Oracle 8.0)

- The star query processing algorithm is improved. (Oracle 8.0)

- Oracle's JDeveloper and Forms products can be used to generate Web-enabled applications running under Network Computing Architecture (NCA). (Oracle 8.1)

- A new ALTER SYSTEM option has been introduced enabling all database I/O to be suspended. This is provided with the keyword SUSPEND (RESUME provides the capability to resume normal database I/O activity). (Oracle 8.1)

- Materialized views provide assistance for data warehouse and other large applications that require data roll-ups and summary information, as well as data distribution. (Oracle 8.1)

- Oracle Call Interfase (OCI) cursor manager improvements were introduced to reduce memory and to increase performance by modifying connections to use a handle versus a cursor. (Oracle 8.0)

- Constraints can now be checked for a statement or for an entire transaction with new defer options. Additionally, constraints can be enabled with the new NOVALIDATE option enforcing all new data to meet the constraint condition. However, this eliminates the check of the existing data in the table (this is ideal to allow constraints to be in force for new data while existing data is corrected). (Oracle 8.0)

- Transportable tablespaces enable tablespaces to be copied to another database with the export and import utilities. (Oracle 8.1)

- Database statistics can now be exported through the export utility. (Oracle 8.1)

- Disk sorts can be enhanced to read multiple blocks through the sort_multiblock_read_count init.ora parameter. This improves large sort operations. (Oracle 8.1)

- Database buffer blocks (db_block_buffers) can be segmented to allow for optimizing blocks in the buffer cache. This can be accomplished by using the buffer_pool_keep and buffer_pool_recycle init.ora parameters, as well as new database object storage commands. (Oracle 8.0)

Summary

This chapter expanded on the PL/SQL language concepts by examining several of the new features and functionality added in Oracle 8.0 and Oracle 8.1. The PL/SQL language continues to increase in flexibility and functionality, so being aware of the version with which you are working and having a thorough understanding of the new features and capabilities in that version is crucial.

For further details on many of the topics in this chapter, refer to the *Oracle 8.0 PL/SQL User's Guide and Reference,* the *Oracle 8i PL/SQL User's Guide and Reference,* and the *Oracle 8i Supplied Packages Reference.*

Tips Review

- The release of Oracle 8.1 contains a new manual providing documentation on the Oracle supplied packages called *Oracle 8i Supplied Package Reference* and is included on the CD-ROM documentation.

- Upgrading or migrating to Oracle8 requires many steps prior to and after the installation. Ensure you read the entire installation and readme.doc documentation for your particular hardware and operating system.

- The EXECUTE IMMEDIATE command supersedes the DBMS_SQL command and is simpler and more efficient.

- The FORALL statement improves DML statements by sending DML statements to the server less frequently, thus reducing overhead and enchancing performance.

- The NOCOPY parameter option increases performance, especially on large parameter data sets; however, it does introduce some exposure.

- The SERIALLY_REUSABLE pragma modifies the default behavior of the package state by eliminating the package state.

- The eight new database triggers expand the capability of database triggers and provide a method of performing new monitoring activities.

- In Oracle 8.0 and Oracle 8.1, many new init.ora parameters can be modified real-time through the ALTER SESSION and ALTER SYSTEM commands. The number of init.ora parameters that can be modified while the database is running continues to increase with each version. Query the isses_modifiable and issys_modifiable columns in the V$PARAMETER view to determine the init.ora parameters that can be changed real-time.

- The name of the table specified to be created for the DBMS_REPAIR package must begin with 'REPAIR_'; otherwise, an error will occur.

- The DBMS_REPAIR package provides a helpful method of identifying and repairing corrupted blocks in tables, indexes, and clusters.

- The DBMS_ROWID package provides a DBA with excellent information about the storage of data within the database. It can be used in lieu of the normal DBA tables and views for many operations.

- DBMS_TRACE does not work in a multithreaded server environment.

- The DBMS_TRACE package is similar to the TRACE facility with respect to the volume of data that can be produced if set at the wrong level. Use caution when using the DBMS_TRACE package and limit the tracing to the desired areas.

- The AUTHID option provides the capability to create stored PL/SQL program units executed the same as Oracle supplied packages, namely, with the executor's (invoker's) privilege versus the creator's (definer's) privilege.

- When the AUTHID option was introduced in 8.1, it required an additional parameter—namely, SQL_NAME_RESOLVE—which required the value to be set the same as AUTHID. As of Oracle 8.1.4, this parameter was eliminated because it was redundant.

Tips Review

- New columns in DBA_USERS, DBA_PROFILES, and DBA_DB_LINKS offer new information concerning user account status and general security information.

- Use security profiles to manage user passwords and limits to user accounts. If profiles are not used, a single user could take the memory of the entire system for a given query. At times, the best performance improvement is often the elimination of potential performance degradation.

- Using the ALTER USER command enables you to lock and expire passwords.

- The LONG and LONG RAW data types can be replaced with the more functional BLOB, CLOB, NCLOB, and BFILE data types.

- Always use the appropriate initializing function, either EMPTY_CLOB or EMPTY_BLOB, to initialize a LOB that would otherwise be NULL. This instantiation process allows these objects to be manipulated through PL/SQL. When initialized with NULL, no storage location is reserved for the object, which can cause errors if a direct reference is attempted.

- SESSION_MAX_OPEN_FILES is the init.ora parameter that identifies how many BFILE files can be open in one session at a time. The default is 10.

- To store past the (COUNT) number of elements in a PL/SQL VARRAY, use the EXTEND command to enlarge the array by one element. This is different than the actual VARRAY size defined upon declaration, which cannot be extended.

- NESTED TABLEs contain a hidden column called NESTED_TABLE_ID holding the REFerence back to the parent table. This column is used to look up child values by Oracle automatically. Oracle, on the other hand, does not create an index on this column automatically when the table is created. That means if the NESTED TABLE is going to store a substantial amount of data, it is highly recommended that this column be indexed.

- Read NESTED TABLE queries by the sub-select first; picture a select set being returned to the outer query. This will make the statement easier to comprehend.

- Remember to install Oracle8 with the objects option installed. Oracle did not include the objects option in their implementations of Personal Edition Oracle8 and Oracle Light.

- Stored PL/SQL program unit maximum size has increased with Oracle 8.1 from 32K bytes to 2^{26} bytes (basically unlimited).

■ Function-based indexes add another dimension to the capability of indexing expressions, functions, and so forth.

■ Once a function-based index is created, it will only be considered an index that can be used if the init.ora parameter query_rewrite_enabled is set to TRUE. This parameter can be modified with the ALTER SYSTEM and ALTER SESSION.

■ The DROP COLUMN command is finally here. The DROP COLUMN command also contains an option for CASCADE CONSTRAINTS.

■ Oracle Forms and Oracle Reports have been the core products of Oracle for more than ten years. Memory and performance requirements for these products limit their usefulness on the Web to intranet-based deployment only. The day will come when Oracle Developer will be a viable solution for Internet deployment…it is just a matter of time.

Tips Review

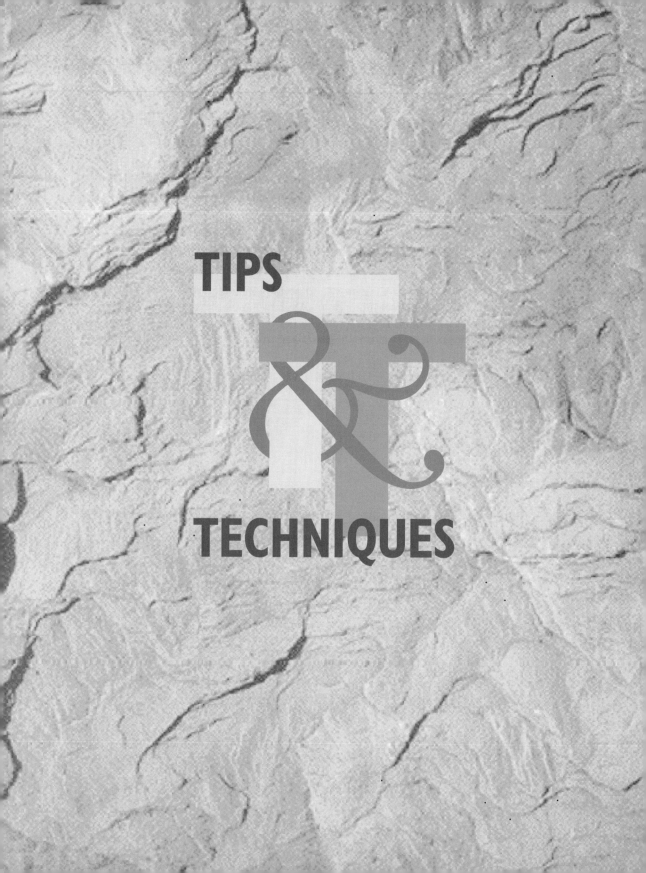

TIPS
&
TECHNIQUES

APPENDIX
A

The Example Database
(Developer and DBA)

The example database used throughout the book for most examples, was introduced in Chapter 1. Due to the length of the scripts and content, only the table definitions and content comments were included in Chapter 1. For further reference, the example database is included in its entirety in this appendix. These three scripts, namely plsqlusr.sql, plsqlobj.sql, and plsqlsyn.sql, can be downloaded from the Osborne McGraw-Hill Web site (www.osborne.com) or the TUSC Web site (www.tusc.com).

File: plsqlusr.sql

```
-- Program:     plsqlusr.sql
-- Creation:    09/01/97
-- Created By:  TUSC
-- Description: Creates the PL/SQL user named plsql_user to allow
--              for the plsqlobj.sql script to be executed.  This
--              script needs to be executed under a user with DBA
--              privileges.

SPOOL plsqlusr.log

CREATE USER plsql_user IDENTIFIED BY plsql_user;
GRANT CONNECT, RESOURCE TO plsql_user;

SPOOL OFF
```

File: plsqlobj.sql

```
-- Program:     plsqlobj.sql
-- Creation:    09/01/97
-- Created By:  TUSC
-- Description: Creates the sequences, tables, constraints, and
--              inserts the example data for the PL/SQL Tips and
--              Techniques Book.

SET ECHO OFF
SET FEEDBACK 1
SET TERMOUT ON

SPOOL plsqlobj.log

-- ***************************************************************
-- Creates sequence numbers for use in example database.
--
```

```
--      Sequence Number         Table
--      --------------------------------
--      s_customer_id           s_customer
--      s_department_id         s_department
--      s_employee_id           s_employee
--      s_image_id              s_image
--      s_longtext_id           s_longtext
--      s_order_id              s_order
--      s_product_id            s_product
--      s_region_id             s_region
--      s_warehouse_id          s_warehouse
-- ************************************************************

CREATE SEQUENCE s_customer_id
  MINVALUE 1
  MAXVALUE 9999999
  INCREMENT BY 1
  START WITH 216
  NOCACHE
  NOORDER
  NOCYCLE;

CREATE SEQUENCE s_department_id
  MINVALUE 1
  MAXVALUE 9999999
  INCREMENT BY 1
  START WITH 51
  NOCACHE
  NOORDER
  NOCYCLE;

CREATE SEQUENCE s_employee_id
  MINVALUE 1
  MAXVALUE 9999999
  INCREMENT BY 1
  START WITH 26
  NOCACHE
  NOORDER
  NOCYCLE;

CREATE SEQUENCE s_image_id
  MINVALUE 1
  MAXVALUE 9999999
  INCREMENT BY 1
  START WITH 1981
  NOCACHE
  NOORDER
  NOCYCLE;
```

plsqlobj.sql

```
CREATE SEQUENCE s_longtext_id
  MINVALUE 1
  MAXVALUE 9999999
  INCREMENT BY 1
  START WITH 1369
  NOCACHE
  NOORDER
  NOCYCLE;

CREATE SEQUENCE s_order_id
  MINVALUE 1
  MAXVALUE 9999999
  INCREMENT BY 1
  START WITH 113
  NOCACHE
  NOORDER
  NOCYCLE;

CREATE SEQUENCE s_product_id
  MINVALUE 1
  MAXVALUE 9999999
  INCREMENT BY 1
  START WITH 50537
  NOCACHE
  NOORDER
  NOCYCLE;

CREATE SEQUENCE s_region_id
  MINVALUE 1
  MAXVALUE 9999999
  INCREMENT BY 1
  START WITH 6
  NOCACHE
  NOORDER
  NOCYCLE;

CREATE SEQUENCE s_warehouse_id
  MINVALUE 1
  MAXVALUE 9999999
  INCREMENT BY 1
  START WITH 10502
  NOCACHE
  NOORDER
  NOCYCLE;
-- ************************************************************

-- ************************************************************
```

```
-- Creates tables and constraints for use in example database.
--
--    Table
--    -----------
--    s_customer
--    s_department
--    s_employee
--    s_image
--    s_inventory
--    s_item
--    s_longtext
--    s_order
--    s_product
--    s_region
--    s_title
--    s_warehouse
-- ****************************************************************
CREATE TABLE s_customer
(customer_id        NUMBER(7)
                    CONSTRAINT s_customer_id_nn NOT NULL,
 customer_name      VARCHAR2(50)
                    CONSTRAINT s_customer_name_nn NOT NULL,
 phone              VARCHAR2(15),
 address            VARCHAR2(400),
 city               VARCHAR2(35),
 state              VARCHAR2(30),
 country            VARCHAR2(30),
 zip_code           VARCHAR2(10),
 credit_rating      VARCHAR2(9),
 sales_rep_id       NUMBER(7),
 region_id          NUMBER(7),
 comments           VARCHAR2(255),
 preferred_customer VARCHAR2(1) DEFAULT 'N' NOT NULL,
 shipping_method    VARCHAR2(1) DEFAULT 'M' NOT NULL,
 CONSTRAINT s_customer_pref_cust CHECK
    (preferred_customer IN ('Y', 'N')),
 CONSTRAINT s_customer_ship_method CHECK
    (shipping_method IN ('M', 'F', 'U')),
 CONSTRAINT s_customer_id_pk PRIMARY KEY (customer_id),
 CONSTRAINT s_customer_credit_rating_ck CHECK
    (credit_rating IN ('EXCELLENT', GOOD', 'POOR')));

CREATE TABLE s_department
(department_id   NUMBER(7)
                 CONSTRAINT s_department_id_nn NOT NULL,
 department_name VARCHAR2(50)
                 CONSTRAINT s_department_name_nn NOT NULL,
 region_id       NUMBER(7),
```

```
   CONSTRAINT s_department_id_pk PRIMARY KEY (department_id),
   CONSTRAINT s_department_name_region_id_uk UNIQUE
      (department_name, region_id));

CREATE TABLE s_employee
(employee_id          NUMBER(7)
                      CONSTRAINT s_employee_id_nn NOT NULL,
 employee_last_name   VARCHAR2(25)
                      CONSTRAINT s_employee_last_name_nn NOT NULL,
 employee_first_name VARCHAR2(25),
 userid               VARCHAR2(8),
 start_date           DATE,
 comments             VARCHAR2(255),
 manager_id           NUMBER(7),
 title                VARCHAR2(25),
 department_id        NUMBER(7),
 salary               NUMBER(11, 2),
 commission_pct       NUMBER(4, 2),
 CONSTRAINT s_employee_id_pk PRIMARY KEY (employee_id),
 CONSTRAINT s_employee_userid_uk UNIQUE (userid),
 CONSTRAINT s_employee_commission_pct_ck CHECK
      (commission_pct IN (10, 12.5, 15, 7.5, 20)));

CREATE TABLE s_image
(image_id       NUMBER(7)   CONSTRAINT s_image_id_nn NOT NULL,
 format         VARCHAR2(25),
 use_filename   VARCHAR2(1),
 filename       VARCHAR2(255),
 image          LONG RAW,
 CONSTRAINT s_image_id_pk PRIMARY KEY (image_id),
 CONSTRAINT s_image_format_ck CHECK
      (format IN ('JFIFF', 'JTIFF')),
 CONSTRAINT s_image_use_filename_ck CHECK
      (use_filename IN ('Y', 'N')));

CREATE TABLE s_inventory
(product_id     NUMBER(7)
                      CONSTRAINT s_inventory_product_id_nn NOT NULL,
 warehouse_id   NUMBER(7)
                      CONSTRAINT s_inventory_warehouse_id_nn NOT NULL,
 amount_in_stock NUMBER(9),
 reorder_point  NUMBER(9),
 max_in_stock   NUMBER(9),
 out_of_stock_explanation VARCHAR2(255),
 restock_date   DATE,
 CONSTRAINT s_inventory_prod_id_whse_id_pk PRIMARY KEY
      (product_id, warehouse_id));
```

```
CREATE TABLE s_item
(order_id          NUMBER(7)
                   CONSTRAINT s_item_order_id_nn NOT NULL,
 item_id           NUMBER(7)
                   CONSTRAINT s_item_id_nn NOT NULL,
 product_id        NUMBER(7)
                   CONSTRAINT s_item_product_id_nn NOT NULL,
 price             NUMBER(11, 2),
 quantity          NUMBER(9),
 quantity_shipped  NUMBER(9),
 CONSTRAINT s_item_order_id_item_id_pk PRIMARY KEY
    (order_id, item_id),
 CONSTRAINT s_item_order_id_product_id_uk UNIQUE
    (order_id, product_id));

CREATE TABLE s_longtext
(longtext_id   NUMBER(7) CONSTRAINT s_longtext_id_nn NOT NULL,
 use_filename  VARCHAR2(1),
 filename      VARCHAR2(255),
 text          VARCHAR2(2000),
 CONSTRAINT s_longtext_id_pk PRIMARY KEY (longtext_id),
 CONSTRAINT s_longtext_use_filename_ck CHECK
    (use_filename in ('Y', 'N')));

CREATE TABLE s_order
(order_id      NUMBER(7)     CONSTRAINT s_order_id_nn NOT NULL,
 customer_id   NUMBER(7)
                   CONSTRAINT s_order_customer_id_nn NOT NULL,
 date_ordered  DATE,
 date_shipped  DATE,
 sales_rep_id  NUMBER(7),
 total         NUMBER(11, 2),
 payment_type  VARCHAR2(6),
 order_filled  VARCHAR2(1),
 CONSTRAINT s_order_id_pk PRIMARY KEY (order_id),
 CONSTRAINT s_order_payment_type_ck CHECK
    (payment_type IN ('CASH', 'CREDIT')),
 CONSTRAINT s_order_order_filled_ck CHECK
    (order_filled IN ('Y', 'N')));

CREATE TABLE s_product
(product_id    NUMBER(7)
                   CONSTRAINT s_product_id_nn NOT NULL,
 product_name  VARCHAR2(50)
                   CONSTRAINT s_product_name_nn NOT NULL,
 short_desc    VARCHAR2(255),
 longtext_id   NUMBER(7),
 image_id      NUMBER(7),
```

```
suggested_wholesale_price NUMBER(11, 2),
wholesale_units VARCHAR2(25),
CONSTRAINT s_product_id_pk PRIMARY KEY (product_id),
CONSTRAINT s_product_name_uk UNIQUE (product_name));

CREATE TABLE s_region
(region_id    NUMBER(7)     CONSTRAINT s_region_id_nn NOT NULL,
 region_name  VARCHAR2(50) CONSTRAINT s_region_name_nn NOT NULL,
 CONSTRAINT s_region_id_pk PRIMARY KEY (region_id),
 CONSTRAINT s_region_name_uk UNIQUE (region_name));

CREATE TABLE s_title
(title VARCHAR2(25)
 CONSTRAINT s_title_nn NOT NULL,
 CONSTRAINT s_title_pk PRIMARY KEY (title));

CREATE TABLE s_warehouse
(warehouse_id NUMBER(7)      CONSTRAINT s_warehouse_id_nn NOT NULL,
 region_id    NUMBER(7)
              CONSTRAINT s_warehouse_region_id_nn NOT NULL,
 phone        VARCHAR2(15),
 address      VARCHAR2(400),
 city         VARCHAR2(35),
 state        VARCHAR2(30),
 country      VARCHAR2(30),
 zip_code     VARCHAR2(10),
 manager_id   NUMBER(7),
 CONSTRAINT s_warehouse_id_pk PRIMARY KEY (warehouse_id));
-- ****************************************************************


-- ****************************************************************
-- Inserts data into each table for use in example database.
--
--      Table             Record Count
--      ----------------------------
--      s_customer        15
--      s_department      12
--      s_employee        25
--      s_image           19
--      s_inventory       114
--      s_item            62
--      s_longtext        34
--      s_order           16
--      s_product         33
--      s_region          5
--      s_title           8
--      s_warehouse       5
-- ****************************************************************
```

```
-- Customer Table
INSERT INTO s_customer VALUES
    (201, 'UNISPORTS', '55-2066101', '72 VIA BAHIA',
    'SAO PAOLO', NULL, 'BRAZIL', NULL, 'EXCELLENT',
    12, 2, 'Customer usually orders large amounts ' ||
    'and has a high order total.  This is okay as long ' ||
    'as the credit rating remains excellent.', 'N', 'M');
INSERT INTO s_customer VALUES
    (202, 'SIMMS ATHELETICS', '81-20101', '6741 TAKASHI BLVD.',
    'OSAKA', NULL, 'JAPAN', NULL, 'POOR', 14, 4,
    'Customer should always pay by cash until his credit ' ||
    'rating improves.', 'N', 'M');
INSERT INTO s_customer VALUES
    (203, 'DELHI SPORTS', '91-10351', '11368 CHANAKYA',
    'NEW DELHI', NULL, 'INDIA', NULL, 'GOOD', 14, 4,
    'Customer specializes in baseball equipment and is ' ||
    'the largest retailer in India.', 'N', 'M');
INSERT INTO s_customer VALUES
    (204, 'WOMANSPORT', '1-206-104-0103', '281 KING STREET',
    'SEATTLE', 'WASHINGTON', 'USA', '98101', 'EXCELLENT',
    11, 1, NULL, 'N', 'M');
INSERT INTO s_customer VALUES
    (205, 'KAM''S SPORTING GOODS', '852-3692888',
    '15 HENESSEY ROAD', 'HONG KONG', NULL, NULL,
    NULL, 'EXCELLENT', 15, 4, NULL, 'N', 'M');
INSERT INTO s_customer VALUES
    (206, 'SPORTIQUE', '33-2257201', '172 RUE DE RIVOLI',
    'CANNES', NULL, 'FRANCE', NULL, 'EXCELLENT', 15, 5,
    'Customer specializes in Soccer.  Likes to order ' ||
    'accessories in bright colors.', 'N', 'M');
INSERT INTO s_customer VALUES
    (207, 'SWEET ROCK SPORTS', '234-6036201', '6 SAINT ANTOINE',
    'LAGOS', NULL, 'NIGERIA', NULL, 'GOOD', NULL, 3, NULL,
    'N', 'M');
INSERT INTO s_customer VALUES
    (208, 'MUENCH SPORTS', '49-527454', '435 GRUENESTRASSE',
    'STUTTGART', NULL, 'GERMANY', NULL, 'GOOD', 15, 5,
    'Customer usually pays small orders by cash and large ' ||
    'orders on credit.', 'N', 'M');
INSERT INTO s_customer VALUES
    (209, 'BEISBOL SI!', '809-352689', '792 PLAYA DEL MAR',
    'SAN PEDRO DE MACON''S', NULL, 'DOMINICAN REPUBLIC',
    NULL, 'EXCELLENT', 11, 1, NULL, 'N', 'M');
INSERT INTO s_customer VALUES
    (210, 'FUTBOL SONORA', '52-404562', '3 VIA SAGUARO',
    'NOGALES', NULL, 'MEXICO', NULL, 'EXCELLENT', 12, 2,
    'Customer is difficult to reach by phone.  Try mail.',
    'N', 'M');
```

```
INSERT INTO s_customer VALUES
    (211, 'KUHN''S SPORTS', '42-111292', '7 MODRANY', 'PRAGUE',
    NULL, 'CZECHOSLOVAKIA', NULL, 'EXCELLENT', 15, 5, NULL,
    'N', 'M');
INSERT INTO s_customer VALUES
    (212, 'HAMADA SPORT', '20-1209211', '57A CORNICHE',
    'ALEXANDRIA', NULL, 'EGYPT', NULL, 'EXCELLENT', 13, 3,
    'Customer orders sea and water equipment.', 'N', 'M');
INSERT INTO s_customer VALUES
    (213, 'BIG JOHN''S SPORTS EMPORIUM', '1-415-555-6281',
    '4783 18TH STREET', 'SAN FRANCISCO', 'CA', 'USA', '94117',
    'EXCELLENT', 11, 1, 'Customer has a dependable credit ' ||
    'record.', 'N', 'M');
INSERT INTO s_customer VALUES
    (214, 'OJIBWAY RETAIL', '1-716-555-7171', '415 MAIN STREET',
    'BUFFALO', 'NY', 'USA', '14202', 'POOR', 11, 1,
    NULL, 'N', 'M');
INSERT INTO s_customer VALUES
    (215, 'SPORTA RUSSIA', '7-3892456', '6000 YEKATAMINA',
    'SAINT PETERSBURG', NULL, 'RUSSIA', NULL, 'POOR',
    15, 5, 'This customer is very friendly, but has ' ||
    'difficulty paying bills.  Insist upon cash.', 'N', 'M');

-- Department Table
INSERT INTO s_department VALUES (10, 'FINANCE', 1);
INSERT INTO s_department VALUES (31, 'SALES', 1);
INSERT INTO s_department VALUES (32, 'ACCOUNTING', 2);
INSERT INTO s_department VALUES (33, 'MARKETING', 3);
INSERT INTO s_department VALUES (34, 'SECURITY', 4);
INSERT INTO s_department VALUES (35, 'PAYROLL', 5);
INSERT INTO s_department VALUES (41, 'OPERATIONS', 1);
INSERT INTO s_department VALUES (42, 'HUMAN RESOURCES', 2);
INSERT INTO s_department VALUES (43, 'STRATEGIC PLANNING', 3);
INSERT INTO s_department VALUES (44, 'MAINTENANCE', 4);
INSERT INTO s_department VALUES (45, 'TECHNICAL WRITING', 5);
INSERT INTO s_department VALUES (50, 'ADMINISTRATION', 1);

-- Employee Table
INSERT INTO s_employee VALUES
    (1, 'VELASQUEZ', 'CARMEN', 'cvelasqu',
    to_date('03-MAR-90 8:30', 'dd-mon-yy hh24:mi'),
    NULL, NULL, 'PRESIDENT', 50, 2500, NULL);
INSERT INTO s_employee VALUES
    (2, 'NGAO', 'LADORIS', 'lngao', '08-MAR-90', NULL,
    1, 'VP, OPERATIONS', 41, 1450, NULL);
INSERT INTO s_employee VALUES
    (3, 'NAGAYAMA', 'MIDORI', 'mnagayam', '17-JUN-91',
    NULL, 1, 'VP, SALES', 31, 1400, NULL);
```

```
INSERT INTO s_employee VALUES
    (4, 'QUICK-TO-SEE', 'MARK', 'mquickto', '07-APR-90',
    NULL, 1, 'VP, FINANCE', 10, 1450, NULL);
INSERT INTO s_employee VALUES
    (5, 'ROPEBURN', 'AUDRY', 'aropebur', '04-MAR-90',
    NULL, 1, 'VP, ADMINISTRATION', 50, 1550, NULL);
INSERT INTO s_employee VALUES
    (6, 'URGUHART', 'MOLLY', 'murguhar', '18-JAN-91',
    NULL, 2, 'WAREHOUSE MANAGER', 41, 1200, NULL);
INSERT INTO s_employee VALUES
    (7, 'MENCHU', 'ROBERTA', 'rmenchu', '14-MAY-90',
    NULL, 2, 'WAREHOUSE MANAGER', 41, 1250, NULL);
INSERT INTO s_employee VALUES
    (8, 'BIRI', 'BEN', 'bbiri', '07-APR-90', NULL, 2,
    'WAREHOUSE MANAGER', 41, 1100, NULL);
INSERT INTO s_employee VALUES
    (9, 'CATCHPOLE', 'ANTOINETTE', 'acatchpo', '09-FEB-92',
    NULL, 2, 'WAREHOUSE MANAGER', 41, 1300, NULL);
INSERT INTO s_employee VALUES
    (10, 'HAVEL', 'MARTA', 'mhavel', '27-FEB-91', NULL, 2,
    'WAREHOUSE MANAGER', 41, 1307, NULL);
INSERT INTO s_employee VALUES
    (11, 'MAGEE', 'COLIN', 'cmagee', '14-MAY-90', NULL,
    3, 'SALES REPRESENTATIVE', 31, 1400, 10);
INSERT INTO s_employee VALUES
    (12, 'GILJUM', 'HENRY', 'hgiljum', '18-JAN-92', NULL,
    3, 'SALES REPRESENTATIVE', 31, 1490, 12.5);
INSERT INTO s_employee VALUES
    (13, 'SEDEGHI', 'YASMIN', 'ysedeghi', '18-FEB-91',
    NULL, 3, 'SALES REPRESENTATIVE', 31, 1515, 10);
INSERT INTO s_employee VALUES
    (14, 'NGUYEN', 'MAI', 'mnguyen', '22-JAN-92', NULL,
    3, 'SALES REPRESENTATIVE', 31, 1525, 15);
INSERT INTO s_employee VALUES
    (15, 'DUMAS', 'ANDRE', 'adumas', '09-OCT-91', NULL,
    3, 'SALES REPRESENTATIVE', 31, 1450, 17.5);
INSERT INTO s_employee VALUES
    (16, 'MADURO', 'ELENA', 'emaduro', '07-FEB-92', NULL,
    6, 'STOCK CLERK', 41, 1400, NULL);
INSERT INTO s_employee VALUES
    (17, 'SMITH', 'GEORGE', 'gsmith', '08-MAR-90',
    NULL, 6, 'STOCK CLERK', 41, 940, NULL);
INSERT INTO s_employee VALUES
    (18, 'NOZAKI', 'AKIRA', 'anozaki', '09-FEB-91', NULL,
    7, 'STOCK CLERK', 41, 1200, NULL);
INSERT INTO s_employee VALUES
    (19, 'PATEL', 'VIKRAM', 'vpatel', '06-AUG-91', NULL,
    7, 'STOCK CLERK', 41, 795, NULL);
```

```
INSERT INTO s_employee VALUES
    (20, 'NEWMAN', 'CHAD', 'cnewman', '21-JUL-91', NULL,
     8, 'STOCK CLERK', 41, 750, NULL);
INSERT INTO s_employee VALUES
    (21, 'MARKARIAN', 'ALEXANDER', 'amarkari', '26-MAY-91',
     NULL, 8, 'STOCK CLERK', 41, 850, NULL);
INSERT INTO s_employee VALUES
    (22, 'CHANG', 'EDDIE', 'echang', '30-NOV-90', NULL,
     9, 'STOCK CLERK', 41, 800, NULL);
INSERT INTO s_employee VALUES
    (23, 'PATEL', 'RADHA', 'rpatel', '17-OCT-90', NULL,
     9, 'STOCK CLERK', 41, 795, NULL);
INSERT INTO s_employee VALUES
    (24, 'DANCS', 'BELA', 'bdancs', '17-MAR-91', NULL,
     10, 'STOCK CLERK', 41, 860, NULL);
INSERT INTO s_employee VALUES
    (25, 'SCHWARTZ', 'SYLVIE', 'sschwart', '09-MAY-91',
     NULL, 10, 'STOCK CLERK', 41, 1100, NULL);

-- Image Table
INSERT INTO s_image VALUES
    (1001, 'JTIFF', 'Y', 'bunboot.tif', NULL);
INSERT INTO s_image VALUES
    (1002, 'JTIFF', 'Y', 'aceboot.tif', NULL);
INSERT INTO s_image VALUES
    (1003, 'JTIFF', 'Y', 'proboot.tif', NULL);
INSERT INTO s_image VALUES
    (1011, 'JTIFF', 'Y', 'bunpole.tif', NULL);
INSERT INTO s_image VALUES
    (1012, 'JTIFF', 'Y', 'acepole.tif', NULL);
INSERT INTO s_image VALUES
    (1013, 'JTIFF', 'Y', 'propole.tif', NULL);
INSERT INTO s_image VALUES
    (1291, 'JTIFF', 'Y', 'gpbike.tif', NULL);
INSERT INTO s_image VALUES
    (1296, 'JTIFF', 'Y', 'himbike.tif', NULL);
INSERT INTO s_image VALUES
    (1829, 'JTIFF', 'Y', 'safthelm.tif', NULL);
INSERT INTO s_image VALUES
    (1381, 'JTIFF', 'Y', 'probar.tif', NULL);
INSERT INTO s_image VALUES
    (1382, 'JTIFF', 'Y', 'curlbar.tif', NULL);
INSERT INTO s_image VALUES
    (1119, 'JTIFF', 'Y', 'baseball.tif', NULL);
INSERT INTO s_image VALUES
    (1223, 'JTIFF', 'Y', 'chaphelm.tif', NULL);
INSERT INTO s_image VALUES
    (1367, 'JTIFF', 'Y', 'grglove.tif', NULL);
```

```
INSERT INTO s_image VALUES
    (1368, 'JTIFF', 'Y', 'alglove.tif', NULL);
INSERT INTO s_image VALUES
    (1369, 'JTIFF', 'Y', 'stglove.tif', NULL);
INSERT INTO s_image VALUES
    (1480, 'JTIFF', 'Y', 'cabbat.tif', NULL);
INSERT INTO s_image VALUES
    (1482, 'JTIFF', 'Y', 'pucbat.tif', NULL);
INSERT INTO s_image VALUES
    (1486, 'JTIFF', 'Y', 'winbat.tif', NULL);

-- Inventory Table
INSERT INTO s_inventory VALUES
    (10011, 101, 650, 625, 1100, NULL, NULL);
INSERT INTO s_inventory VALUES
    (10012, 101, 600, 560, 1000, NULL, NULL);
INSERT INTO s_inventory VALUES
    (10013, 101, 400, 400, 700, NULL, NULL);
INSERT INTO s_inventory VALUES
    (10021, 101, 500, 425, 740, NULL, NULL);
INSERT INTO s_inventory VALUES
    (10022, 101, 300, 200, 350, NULL, NULL);
INSERT INTO s_inventory VALUES
    (10023, 101, 400, 300, 525, NULL, NULL);
INSERT INTO s_inventory VALUES
    (20106, 101, 993, 625, 1000, NULL, NULL);
INSERT INTO s_inventory VALUES
    (20108, 101, 700, 700, 1225, NULL, NULL);
INSERT INTO s_inventory VALUES
    (20201, 101, 802, 800, 1400, NULL, NULL);
INSERT INTO s_inventory VALUES
    (20510, 101, 1389, 850, 1400, NULL, NULL);
INSERT INTO s_inventory VALUES
    (20512, 101, 850, 850, 1450, NULL, NULL);
INSERT INTO s_inventory VALUES
    (30321, 101, 2000, 1500, 2500, NULL, NULL);
INSERT INTO s_inventory VALUES
    (30326, 101, 2100, 2000, 3500, NULL, NULL);
INSERT INTO s_inventory VALUES
    (30421, 101, 1822, 1800, 3150, NULL, NULL);
INSERT INTO s_inventory VALUES
    (30426, 101, 2250, 2000, 3500, NULL, NULL);
INSERT INTO s_inventory VALUES
    (30433, 101, 650, 600, 1050, NULL, NULL);
INSERT INTO s_inventory VALUES
    (32779, 101, 2120, 1250, 2200, NULL, NULL);
INSERT INTO s_inventory VALUES
    (32861, 101, 505, 500, 875, NULL, NULL);
```

```
INSERT INTO s_inventory VALUES
    (40421, 101, 578, 350, 600, NULL, NULL);
INSERT INTO s_inventory VALUES
    (40422, 101, 0, 350, 600, 'Phenomenal sales...', '08-FEB-93');
INSERT INTO s_inventory VALUES
    (41010, 101, 250, 250, 437, NULL, NULL);
INSERT INTO s_inventory VALUES
    (41020, 101, 471, 450, 750, NULL, NULL);
INSERT INTO s_inventory VALUES
    (41050, 101, 501, 450, 750, NULL, NULL);
INSERT INTO s_inventory VALUES
    (41080, 101, 400, 400, 700, NULL, NULL);
INSERT INTO s_inventory VALUES
    (41100, 101, 350, 350, 600, NULL, NULL);
INSERT INTO s_inventory VALUES
    (50169, 101, 2530, 1500, 2600, NULL, NULL);
INSERT INTO s_inventory VALUES
    (50273, 101, 233, 200, 350, NULL, NULL);
INSERT INTO s_inventory VALUES
    (50417, 101, 518, 500, 875, NULL, NULL);
INSERT INTO s_inventory VALUES
    (50418, 101, 244, 100, 275, NULL, NULL);
INSERT INTO s_inventory VALUES
    (50419, 101, 230, 120, 310, NULL, NULL);
INSERT INTO s_inventory VALUES
    (50530, 101, 669, 400, 700, NULL, NULL);
INSERT INTO s_inventory VALUES
    (50532, 101, 0, 100, 175, 'Wait for Spring.', '12-APR-93');
INSERT INTO s_inventory VALUES
    (50536, 101, 173, 100, 175, NULL, NULL);
INSERT INTO s_inventory VALUES
    (20106, 201, 220, 150, 260, NULL, NULL);
INSERT INTO s_inventory VALUES
    (20108, 201, 166, 150, 260, NULL, NULL);
INSERT INTO s_inventory VALUES
    (20201, 201, 320, 200, 350, NULL, NULL);
INSERT INTO s_inventory VALUES
    (20510, 201, 175, 100, 175, NULL, NULL);
INSERT INTO s_inventory VALUES
    (20512, 201, 162, 100, 175, NULL, NULL);
INSERT INTO s_inventory VALUES
    (30321, 201, 96, 80, 140, NULL, NULL);
INSERT INTO s_inventory VALUES
    (30326, 201, 147, 120, 210, NULL, NULL);
INSERT INTO s_inventory VALUES
    (30421, 201, 102, 80, 140, NULL, NULL);
INSERT INTO s_inventory VALUES
    (30426, 201, 200, 120, 210, NULL, NULL);
```

```
INSERT INTO s_inventory VALUES
    (30433, 201, 130, 130, 230, NULL, NULL);
INSERT INTO s_inventory VALUES
    (32779, 201, 180, 150, 260, NULL, NULL);
INSERT INTO s_inventory VALUES
    (32861, 201, 132, 80, 140, NULL, NULL);
INSERT INTO s_inventory VALUES
    (50169, 201, 225, 220, 385, NULL, NULL);
INSERT INTO s_inventory VALUES
    (50273, 201, 75, 60, 100, NULL, NULL);
INSERT INTO s_inventory VALUES
    (50417, 201, 82, 60, 100, NULL, NULL);
INSERT INTO s_inventory VALUES
    (50418, 201, 98, 60, 100, NULL, NULL);
INSERT INTO s_inventory VALUES
    (50419, 201, 77, 60, 100, NULL, NULL);
INSERT INTO s_inventory VALUES
    (50530, 201, 62, 60, 100, NULL, NULL);
INSERT INTO s_inventory VALUES
    (50532, 201, 67, 60, 100, NULL, NULL);
INSERT INTO s_inventory VALUES
    (50536, 201, 97, 60, 100, NULL, NULL);
INSERT INTO s_inventory VALUES
    (20510, 301, 69, 40, 100, NULL, NULL);
INSERT INTO s_inventory VALUES
    (20512, 301, 28, 20, 50, NULL, NULL);
INSERT INTO s_inventory VALUES
    (30321, 301, 85, 80, 140, NULL, NULL);
INSERT INTO s_inventory VALUES
    (30421, 301, 102, 80, 140, NULL, NULL);
INSERT INTO s_inventory VALUES
    (30433, 301, 35, 20, 35, NULL, NULL);
INSERT INTO s_inventory VALUES
    (32779, 301, 102, 95, 175, NULL, NULL);
INSERT INTO s_inventory VALUES
    (32861, 301, 57, 50, 100, NULL, NULL);
INSERT INTO s_inventory VALUES
    (40421, 301, 70, 40, 70, NULL, NULL);
INSERT INTO s_inventory VALUES
    (40422, 301, 65, 40, 70, NULL, NULL);
INSERT INTO s_inventory VALUES
    (41010, 301, 59, 40, 70, NULL, NULL);
INSERT INTO s_inventory VALUES
    (41020, 301, 61, 40, 70, NULL, NULL);
INSERT INTO s_inventory VALUES
    (41050, 301, 49, 40, 70, NULL, NULL);
INSERT INTO s_inventory VALUES
    (41080, 301, 50, 40, 70, NULL, NULL);
```

plsqlobj.sql

```
INSERT INTO s_inventory VALUES
    (41100, 301, 42, 40, 70, NULL, NULL);
INSERT INTO s_inventory VALUES
    (20510, 401, 88, 50, 100, NULL, NULL);
INSERT INTO s_inventory VALUES
    (20512, 401, 75, 75, 140, NULL, NULL);
INSERT INTO s_inventory VALUES
    (30321, 401, 102, 80, 140, NULL, NULL);
INSERT INTO s_inventory VALUES
    (30326, 401, 113, 80, 140, NULL, NULL);
INSERT INTO s_inventory VALUES
    (30421, 401, 85, 80, 140, NULL, NULL);
INSERT INTO s_inventory VALUES
    (30426, 401, 135, 80, 140, NULL, NULL);
INSERT INTO s_inventory VALUES
    (30433, 401, 0, 100, 175, 'A defective shipment was  sent ' ||
    'to Hong Kong and needed to be returned. The soonest ACME ' ||
    'can turn this around is early February.', '07-SEP-92');
INSERT INTO s_inventory VALUES
    (32779, 401, 135, 100, 175, NULL, NULL);
INSERT INTO s_inventory VALUES
    (32861, 401, 250, 150, 250, NULL, NULL);
INSERT INTO s_inventory VALUES
    (40421, 401, 47, 40, 70, NULL, NULL);
INSERT INTO s_inventory VALUES
    (40422, 401, 50, 40, 70, NULL, NULL);
INSERT INTO s_inventory VALUES
    (41010, 401, 80, 70, 220, NULL, NULL);
INSERT INTO s_inventory VALUES
    (41020, 401, 91, 70, 220, NULL, NULL);
INSERT INTO s_inventory VALUES
    (41050, 401, 169, 70, 220, NULL, NULL);
INSERT INTO s_inventory VALUES
    (41080, 401, 100, 70, 220, NULL, NULL);
INSERT INTO s_inventory VALUES
    (41100, 401, 75, 70, 220, NULL, NULL);
INSERT INTO s_inventory VALUES
    (50169, 401, 240, 200, 350, NULL, NULL);
INSERT INTO s_inventory VALUES
    (50273, 401, 224, 150, 280, NULL, NULL);
INSERT INTO s_inventory VALUES
    (50417, 401, 130, 120, 210, NULL, NULL);
INSERT INTO s_inventory VALUES
    (50418, 401, 156, 100, 175, NULL, NULL);
INSERT INTO s_inventory VALUES
    (50419, 401, 151, 150, 280, NULL, NULL);
INSERT INTO s_inventory VALUES
    (50530, 401, 119, 100, 175, NULL, NULL);
```

```
INSERT INTO s_inventory VALUES
   (50532, 401, 233, 200, 350, NULL, NULL);
INSERT INTO s_inventory VALUES
   (50536, 401, 138, 100, 175, NULL, NULL);
INSERT INTO s_inventory VALUES
   (10012, 10501, 300, 300, 525, NULL, NULL);
INSERT INTO s_inventory VALUES
   (10013, 10501, 314, 300, 525, NULL, NULL);
INSERT INTO s_inventory VALUES
   (10022, 10501, 502, 300, 525, NULL, NULL);
INSERT INTO s_inventory VALUES
   (10023, 10501, 500, 300, 525, NULL, NULL);
INSERT INTO s_inventory VALUES
   (20106, 10501, 150, 100, 175, NULL, NULL);
INSERT INTO s_inventory VALUES
   (20108, 10501, 222, 200, 350, NULL, NULL);
INSERT INTO s_inventory VALUES
   (20201, 10501, 275, 200, 350, NULL, NULL);
INSERT INTO s_inventory VALUES
   (20510, 10501, 57, 50, 87, NULL, NULL);
INSERT INTO s_inventory VALUES
   (20512, 10501, 62, 50, 87, NULL, NULL);
INSERT INTO s_inventory VALUES
   (30321, 10501, 194, 150, 275, NULL, NULL);
INSERT INTO s_inventory VALUES
   (30326, 10501, 277, 250, 440, NULL, NULL);
INSERT INTO s_inventory VALUES
   (30421, 10501, 190, 150, 275, NULL, NULL);
INSERT INTO s_inventory VALUES
   (30426, 10501, 423, 250, 450, NULL, NULL);
INSERT INTO s_inventory VALUES
   (30433, 10501, 273, 200, 350, NULL, NULL);
INSERT INTO s_inventory VALUES
   (32779, 10501, 280, 200, 350, NULL, NULL);
INSERT INTO s_inventory VALUES
   (32861, 10501, 288, 200, 350, NULL, NULL);
INSERT INTO s_inventory VALUES
   (40421, 10501, 97, 80, 140, NULL, NULL);
INSERT INTO s_inventory VALUES
   (40422, 10501, 90, 80, 140, NULL, NULL);
INSERT INTO s_inventory VALUES
   (41010, 10501, 151, 140, 245, NULL, NULL);
INSERT INTO s_inventory VALUES
   (41020, 10501, 224, 140, 245, NULL, NULL);
INSERT INTO s_inventory VALUES
   (41050, 10501, 157, 140, 245, NULL, NULL);
INSERT INTO s_inventory VALUES
   (41080, 10501, 159, 140, 245, NULL, NULL);
```

```
INSERT INTO s_inventory VALUES
   (41100, 10501, 141, 140, 245, NULL, NULL);

-- Item Table
INSERT INTO s_item VALUES (100, 1, 10011, 135, 500, 500);
INSERT INTO s_item VALUES (100, 2, 10013, 380, 400, 400);
INSERT INTO s_item VALUES (100, 3, 10021, 14, 500, 500);
INSERT INTO s_item VALUES (100, 5, 30326, 582, 600, 600);
INSERT INTO s_item VALUES (100, 7, 41010, 8, 250, 250);
INSERT INTO s_item VALUES (100, 6, 30433, 20, 450, 450);
INSERT INTO s_item VALUES (100, 4, 10023, 36, 400, 400);
INSERT INTO s_item VALUES (101, 1, 30421, 16, 15, 15);
INSERT INTO s_item VALUES (101, 3, 41010, 8, 20, 20);
INSERT INTO s_item VALUES (101, 5, 50169, 4.29, 40, 40);
INSERT INTO s_item VALUES (101, 6, 50417, 80, 27, 27);
INSERT INTO s_item VALUES (101, 7, 50530, 45, 50, 50);
INSERT INTO s_item VALUES (101, 4, 41100, 45, 35, 35);
INSERT INTO s_item VALUES (101, 2, 40422, 50, 30, 30);
INSERT INTO s_item VALUES (102, 1, 20108, 28, 100, 100);
INSERT INTO s_item VALUES (102, 2, 20201, 123, 45, 45);
INSERT INTO s_item VALUES (103, 1, 30433, 20, 15, 15);
INSERT INTO s_item VALUES (103, 2, 32779, 7, 11, 11);
INSERT INTO s_item VALUES (104, 1, 20510, 9, 7, 7);
INSERT INTO s_item VALUES (104, 4, 30421, 16, 35, 35);
INSERT INTO s_item VALUES (104, 2, 20512, 8, 12, 12);
INSERT INTO s_item VALUES (104, 3, 30321, 1669, 19, 19);
INSERT INTO s_item VALUES (105, 1, 50273, 22.89, 16, 16);
INSERT INTO s_item VALUES (105, 3, 50532, 47, 28, 28);
INSERT INTO s_item VALUES (105, 2, 50419, 80, 13, 13);
INSERT INTO s_item VALUES (106, 1, 20108, 28, 46, 46);
INSERT INTO s_item VALUES (106, 4, 50273, 22.89, 75, 75);
INSERT INTO s_item VALUES (106, 5, 50418, 75, 98, 98);
INSERT INTO s_item VALUES (106, 6, 50419, 80, 27, 27);
INSERT INTO s_item VALUES (106, 2, 20201, 123, 21, 21);
INSERT INTO s_item VALUES (106, 3, 50169, 4.29, 125, 125);
INSERT INTO s_item VALUES (107, 1, 20106, 11, 50, 50);
INSERT INTO s_item VALUES (107, 3, 20201, 115, 130, 130);
INSERT INTO s_item VALUES (107, 5, 30421, 16, 55, 55);
INSERT INTO s_item VALUES (107, 4, 30321, 1669, 75, 75);
INSERT INTO s_item VALUES (107, 2, 20108, 28, 22, 22);
INSERT INTO s_item VALUES (108, 1, 20510, 9, 9, 9);
INSERT INTO s_item VALUES (108, 6, 41080, 35, 50, 50);
INSERT INTO s_item VALUES (108, 7, 41100, 45, 42, 42);
INSERT INTO s_item VALUES (108, 5, 32861, 60, 57, 57);
INSERT INTO s_item VALUES (108, 2, 20512, 8, 18, 18);
INSERT INTO s_item VALUES (108, 4, 32779, 7, 60, 60);
INSERT INTO s_item VALUES (108, 3, 30321, 1669, 85, 85);
INSERT INTO s_item VALUES (109, 1, 10011, 140, 150, 150);
```

```
INSERT INTO s_item VALUES (109, 5, 30426, 18.25, 500, 500);
INSERT INTO s_item VALUES (109, 7, 50418, 75, 43, 43);
INSERT INTO s_item VALUES (109, 6, 32861, 60, 50, 50);
INSERT INTO s_item VALUES (109, 4, 30326, 582, 1500, 1500);
INSERT INTO s_item VALUES (109, 2, 10012, 175, 600, 600);
INSERT INTO s_item VALUES (109, 3, 10022, 21.95, 300, 300);
INSERT INTO s_item VALUES (110, 1, 50273, 22.89, 17, 17);
INSERT INTO s_item VALUES (110, 2, 50536, 50, 23, 23);
INSERT INTO s_item VALUES (111, 1, 40421, 65, 27, 27);
INSERT INTO s_item VALUES (111, 2, 41080, 35, 29, 29);
INSERT INTO s_item VALUES (97, 1, 20106, 9, 1000, 1000);
INSERT INTO s_item VALUES (97, 2, 30321, 1500, 50, 50);
INSERT INTO s_item VALUES (98, 1, 40421, 85, 7, 7);
INSERT INTO s_item VALUES (99, 1, 20510, 9, 18, 18);
INSERT INTO s_item VALUES (99, 2, 20512, 8, 25, 25);
INSERT INTO s_item VALUES (99, 3, 50417, 80, 53, 53);
INSERT INTO s_item VALUES (99, 4, 50530, 45, 69, 69);
INSERT INTO s_item VALUES (112, 1, 20106, 11, 50, 50);

-- Longtext Table
INSERT INTO s_longtext VALUES (1017, 'N', NULL,
    'Protective knee pads for any number of physical ' ||
    'activities including bicycling and skating (4-wheel, ' ||
    'in-line, and ice).  Also provide support for stress ' ||
    'activities such as weight-lifting.  Velcro belts ' ||
    'allow easy adjustment for any size and snugness of ' ||
    'fit.  Hardened plastic shell comes in a variety of ' ||
    'colors, so you can buy a pair to match every outfit. Can ' ||
    'also be worn at the beach to cover particularly ugly knees.');
INSERT INTO s_longtext VALUES (1019, 'N', NULL,
    'Protective elbow pads for any number of physical ' ||
    'activities including bicycling and skating (4-wheel, ' ||
    'in-line, and ice).  Also provide support for stress ' ||
    'activities such as weight-lifting.  Velcro belts ' ||
    'allow easy adjustment for any size and snugness of fit. ' ||
    'Hardened plastic shell comes in a variety of colors, so ' ||
    'you can buy a pair to match every outfit.');
INSERT INTO s_longtext VALUES (1037, NULL, NULL, NULL);
INSERT INTO s_longtext VALUES (1039, NULL, NULL, NULL);
INSERT INTO s_longtext VALUES (1043, NULL, NULL, NULL);
INSERT INTO s_longtext VALUES (1286, 'N', NULL,
    'Don''t slack off—try the Slaker Water Bottle.  With its ' ||
    '1 quart capacity, this is the only water bottle you''ll ' ||
    'need.  It''s lightweight, durable, and guaranteed for ' ||
    'life to be leak proof.  It comes with a convenient ' ||
    'velcro strap so it can be conveniently attached to your ' ||
    'bike or other sports equipment.');
INSERT INTO s_longtext VALUES (1368, NULL, NULL, NULL);
```

```
INSERT INTO s_longtext VALUES (517, NULL, NULL, NULL);
INSERT INTO s_longtext VALUES (518, 'N', NULL,
    'Perfect for the beginner.  Rear entry (easy to put on ' ||
    'with only one buckle), weight control adjustment on side ' ||
    'of boot for easy access, comes in a wide variety of ' ||
    'colors to match every outfit.');
INSERT INTO s_longtext VALUES (519, 'N', NULL,
    'If you have mastered the basic techniques you are ready ' ||
    'for the Ace Ski Boot.  This intermediate boot comes as a ' ||
    'package with self adjustable bindings that will adapt to ' ||
    'your skill and speed. The boot is designed for extra grip ' ||
    'on slopes and jumps.');
INSERT INTO s_longtext VALUES (520, 'N', NULL,
    'The Pro ski boot is an advanced boot that combines high ' ||
    'tech and comfort.  It''s made of fiber that will mold to ' ||
    'your foot with body heat.  If you''re after perfection, ' ||
    'don''t look any further: this is it!');
INSERT INTO s_longtext VALUES (527, NULL, NULL, NULL);
INSERT INTO s_longtext VALUES (528, 'N', NULL,
    'Lightweight aluminum pole, comes in a variety of sizes ' ||
    'and neon colors.  Comfortable adjustable straps.');
INSERT INTO s_longtext VALUES (529, NULL, NULL, NULL);
INSERT INTO s_longtext VALUES (530, NULL, NULL, NULL);
INSERT INTO s_longtext VALUES (557, NULL, NULL, NULL);
INSERT INTO s_longtext VALUES (587, NULL, NULL, NULL);
INSERT INTO s_longtext VALUES (607, NULL, NULL, NULL);
INSERT INTO s_longtext VALUES (613, NULL, NULL, NULL);
INSERT INTO s_longtext VALUES (615, NULL, NULL, NULL);
INSERT INTO s_longtext VALUES (676, NULL, NULL, NULL);
INSERT INTO s_longtext VALUES (708, NULL, NULL, NULL);
INSERT INTO s_longtext VALUES (780, NULL, NULL, NULL);
INSERT INTO s_longtext VALUES (828, NULL, NULL, NULL);
INSERT INTO s_longtext VALUES (833, NULL, NULL, NULL);
INSERT INTO s_longtext VALUES (924, NULL, NULL, NULL);
INSERT INTO s_longtext VALUES (925, NULL, NULL, NULL);
INSERT INTO s_longtext VALUES (926, NULL, NULL, NULL);
INSERT INTO s_longtext VALUES (927, NULL, NULL, NULL);
INSERT INTO s_longtext VALUES (928, NULL, NULL, NULL);
INSERT INTO s_longtext VALUES (929, NULL, NULL, NULL);
INSERT INTO s_longtext VALUES (933, 'N', NULL,
    'The widest, strongest, and knobbiest tires for mountain ' ||
    'bike enthusiasts.  Guaranteed to withstand pummelling ' ||
    'that will reduce most bicycles (except for the Himalayan) ' ||
    'to scrap iron.  These tires can carry you to places where ' ||
    'nobody would want to bicycle.  Sizes to fit all makes of ' ||
    'mountain bike including wide and super wide rims.  ' ||
    'Steel-banded radial models are also available by direct ' ||
    ' factory order.');
```

```
INSERT INTO s_longtext VALUES (940, NULL, NULL, NULL);

-- Order Table
INSERT INTO s_order VALUES
    (100, 204, '31-AUG-92', '10-SEP-92', 11, 601100, 'CREDIT', 'Y');
INSERT INTO s_order VALUES
    (101, 205, '31-AUG-92', '15-SEP-92', 14, 8056.6, 'CREDIT', 'Y');
INSERT INTO s_order VALUES
    (102, 206, '01-SEP-92', '08-SEP-92', 15, 8335, 'CREDIT', 'Y');
INSERT INTO s_order VALUES
    (103, 208, '02-SEP-92', '22-SEP-92', 15, 377, 'CASH', 'Y');
INSERT INTO s_order VALUES
    (104, 208, '03-SEP-92', '23-SEP-92', 15, 32430, 'CREDIT', 'Y');
INSERT INTO s_order VALUES
    (105, 209, '04-SEP-92', '18-SEP-92', 11, 2722.24, 'CREDIT','Y');
INSERT INTO s_order VALUES
    (106, 210, '07-SEP-92', '15-SEP-92', 12, 15634, 'CREDIT', 'Y');
INSERT INTO s_order VALUES
    (107, 211, '07-SEP-92', '21-SEP-92', 15, 142171, 'CREDIT', 'Y');
INSERT INTO s_order VALUES
    (108, 212, '07-SEP-92', '10-SEP-92', 13, 149570, 'CREDIT','Y');
INSERT INTO s_order VALUES
    (109, 213, '08-SEP-92', '28-SEP-92', 11, 1020935, 'CREDIT','Y');
INSERT INTO s_order VALUES
    (110, 214, '09-SEP-92', '21-SEP-92', 11, 1539.13, 'CASH', 'Y');
INSERT INTO s_order VALUES
    (111, 204, '09-SEP-92', '21-SEP-92', 11, 2770, 'CASH', 'Y');
INSERT INTO s_order VALUES
    (97, 201, '28-AUG-92', '17-SEP-92', 12, 84000, 'CREDIT', 'Y');
INSERT INTO s_order VALUES
    (98, 202, '31-AUG-92', '10-SEP-92', 14, 595, 'CASH', 'Y');
INSERT INTO s_order VALUES
    (99, 203, '31-AUG-92', '18-SEP-92', 14, 7707, 'CREDIT', 'Y');
INSERT INTO s_order VALUES
    (112, 210, '31-AUG-92', '10-SEP-92', 12, 550, 'CREDIT', 'Y');

-- Product Table
INSERT INTO s_product VALUES (10011, 'BUNNY BOOT',
    'BEGINNER''S SKI BOOT', 518, 1001, 150, NULL);
INSERT INTO s_product VALUES (10012, 'ACE SKI BOOT',
    'INTERMEDIATE SKI BOOT', 519, 1002, 200, NULL);
INSERT INTO s_product VALUES (10013, 'PRO SKI BOOT',
    'ADVANCED SKI BOOT', 520, 1003, 410, NULL);
INSERT INTO s_product VALUES (10021, 'BUNNY SKI POLE',
    'BEGINNER''S SKI POLE', 528, 1011, 16.25, NULL);
INSERT INTO s_product VALUES (10022, 'ACE SKI POLE',
    'INTERMEDIATE SKI POLE', 529, 1012, 21.95, NULL);
INSERT INTO s_product VALUES (10023, 'PRO SKI POLE',
```

```
                    'ADVANCED SKI POLE', 530, 1013, 40.95, NULL);
INSERT INTO s_product VALUES (20106, 'JUNIOR SOCCER BALL',
    'JUNIOR SOCCER BALL', 613, NULL, 11, NULL);
INSERT INTO s_product VALUES (20108, 'WORLD CUP SOCCER BALL',
    'WORLD CUP SOCCER BALL', 615, NULL, 28, NULL);
INSERT INTO s_product VALUES (20201, 'WORLD CUP NET',
    'WORLD CUP NET', 708, NULL, 123, NULL);
INSERT INTO s_product VALUES (20510, 'BLACK HAWK KNEE PADS',
    'KNEE PADS, PAIR', 1017, NULL, 9, NULL);
INSERT INTO s_product VALUES (20512, 'BLACK HAWK ELBOW PADS',
    'ELBOW PADS, PAIR', 1019, NULL, 8, NULL);
INSERT INTO s_product VALUES (30321, 'GRAND PRIX BICYCLE',
    'ROAD BICYCLE', 828, 1291, 1669, NULL);
INSERT INTO s_product VALUES (30326, 'HIMALAYA BICYCLE',
    'MOUNTAIN BICYCLE', 833, 1296, 582, NULL);
INSERT INTO s_product VALUES (30421, 'GRAND PRIX BICYCLE TIRES',
    'ROAD BICYCLE TIRES', 927, NULL, 16, NULL);
INSERT INTO s_product VALUES (30426, 'HIMALAYA TIRES',
    'MOUNTAIN BICYCLE TIRES', 933, NULL, 18.25, NULL);
INSERT INTO s_product VALUES (30433, 'NEW AIR PUMP',
    'TIRE PUMP', 940, NULL, 20, NULL);
INSERT INTO s_product VALUES (32779, 'SLAKER WATER BOTTLE',
    'WATER BOTTLE', 1286, NULL, 7, NULL);
INSERT INTO s_product VALUES (32861, 'SAFE-T HELMET',
    'BICYCLE HELMET', 1368, 1829, 60, NULL);
INSERT INTO s_product VALUES (40421, 'ALEXEYER PRO LIFTING BAR',
    'STRAIGHT BAR', 928, 1381, 65, NULL);
INSERT INTO s_product VALUES (40422, 'PRO CURLING BAR',
    'CURLING BAR', 929, 1382, 50, NULL);
INSERT INTO s_product VALUES (41010, 'PROSTAR 10 POUND WEIGHT',
    'TEN POUND WEIGHT', 517, NULL, 8, NULL);
INSERT INTO s_product VALUES (41020, 'PROSTAR 20 POUND WEIGHT',
    'TWENTY POUND WEIGHT', 527, NULL, 12, NULL);
INSERT INTO s_product VALUES (41050, 'PROSTAR 50 POUND WEIGHT',
    'FIFTY POUND WEIGHT', 557, NULL, 25, NULL);
INSERT INTO s_product VALUES (41080, 'PROSTAR 80 POUND WEIGHT',
    'EIGHTY POUND WEIGHT', 587, NULL, 35, NULL);
INSERT INTO s_product VALUES (41100, 'PROSTAR 100 POUND WEIGHT',
    'ONE HUNDRED POUND WEIGHT', 607, NULL, 45, NULL);
INSERT INTO s_product VALUES (50169, 'MAJOR LEAGUE BASEBALL',
    'BASEBALL', 676, 1119, 4.29, NULL);
INSERT INTO s_product VALUES (50273, 'CHAPMAN HELMET',
    'BATTING HELMET', 780, 1223, 22.89, NULL);
INSERT INTO s_product VALUES (50417, 'GRIFFEY GLOVE',
    'OUTFIELDER''S GLOVE', 924, 1367, 80, NULL);
INSERT INTO s_product VALUES (50418, 'ALOMAR GLOVE',
    'INFIELDER''S GLOVE', 925, 1368, 75, NULL);
INSERT INTO s_product VALUES (50419, 'STEINBACH GLOVE',
```

```
      'CATCHER''S GLOVE', 926, 1369, 80, NULL);
INSERT INTO s_product VALUES (50530, 'CABRERA BAT',
   'THIRTY INCH BAT', 1037, 1480, 45, NULL);
INSERT INTO s_product VALUES (50532, 'PUCKETT BAT',
   'THIRTY-TWO INCH BAT', 1039, 1482, 47, NULL);
INSERT INTO s_product VALUES (50536, 'WINFIELD BAT',
   'THIRTY-SIX INCH BAT', 1043, 1486, 50, NULL);

-- Region Table
INSERT INTO S_REGION VALUES (1, 'NORTH AMERICA');
INSERT INTO S_REGION VALUES (2, 'SOUTH AMERICA');
INSERT INTO S_REGION VALUES (3, 'AFRICA / MIDDLE EAST');
INSERT INTO S_REGION VALUES (4, 'ASIA');
INSERT INTO S_REGION VALUES (5, 'EUROPE');

-- Title Table
INSERT INTO S_TITLE VALUES ('PRESIDENT');
INSERT INTO S_TITLE VALUES ('SALES REPRESENTATIVE');
INSERT INTO S_TITLE VALUES ('STOCK CLERK');
INSERT INTO S_TITLE VALUES ('VP, ADMINISTRATION');
INSERT INTO S_TITLE VALUES ('VP, FINANCE');
INSERT INTO S_TITLE VALUES ('VP, OPERATIONS');
INSERT INTO S_TITLE VALUES ('VP, SALES');
INSERT INTO S_TITLE VALUES ('WAREHOUSE MANAGER');

-- Warehouse Table
INSERT INTO s_warehouse VALUES (101, 1, '283 King Street',
   'Seattle', 'WA', 'USA', NULL, NULL, 6);
INSERT INTO s_warehouse VALUES (10501, 5, '5 Modrany',
   'Bratislava', NULL, 'Czechozlovakia', NULL, NULL, 10);
INSERT INTO s_warehouse VALUES (201, 2, '68 Via Centrale',
   'Sao Paolo', NULL, 'Brazil', NULL, NULL, 7);
INSERT INTO s_warehouse VALUES (301, 3, '6921 King Way',
   'Lagos', NULL, 'Nigeria', NULL, NULL, 8);
INSERT INTO s_warehouse VALUES (401, 4, '86 Chu Street',
   'Hong Kong', NULL, NULL, NULL, NULL, 9);
-- ***************************************************************

-- ***************************************************************
-- Alters tables and adds foreign key constraints for use in
-- example database.
--
-- Foreign Key Table/Column   Primary Key Table/Column Referenced
-- -----------------------------------------------------------
-- s_department/region_id      s_region/region_id
-- s_employee/manager_id       s_employee/employee_id
-- s_employee/department_id    s_department/department_id
-- s_employee/title            s_title/title
```

```
-- s_customer/sales_rep_id      s_employee/employee_id
-- s_customer/region_id         s_region/region_id
-- s_order/customer_id          s_customer/customer_id
-- s_order/sales_rep_id         s_employee/employee_id
-- s_product/image_id           s_image/image_id
-- s_product/longtext_id        s_longtext/longtext_id
-- s_item/order_id              s_order/order_id
-- s_item/product_id            s_product/product_id
-- s_warehouse/manager_id       s_employee/employee_id
-- s_warehouse/region_id        s_region/region_id
-- s_inventory/product_id       s_product/product_id
-- s_inventory/warehouse_id     s_warehouse/warehouse_id
-- ***************************************************************

-- Department Table
ALTER TABLE s_department
ADD    CONSTRAINT s_department_region_id_fk
FOREIGN KEY (region_id) REFERENCES s_region (region_id);

-- Employee Table
ALTER TABLE s_employee
ADD    CONSTRAINT s_employee_manager_id_fk
FOREIGN KEY (manager_id) REFERENCES s_employee (employee_id);

ALTER TABLE s_employee
ADD    CONSTRAINT s_employee_department_id_fk
FOREIGN KEY (department_id) REFERENCES
   s_department (department_id);

ALTER TABLE s_employee
ADD    CONSTRAINT s_employee_title_fk
FOREIGN KEY (title) REFERENCES s_title (title);

-- Customer Table
ALTER TABLE s_customer
ADD    CONSTRAINT s_customer_sales_rep_id_fk
FOREIGN KEY (sales_rep_id) REFERENCES s_employee (employee_id);

ALTER TABLE s_customer
ADD    CONSTRAINT s_customer_region_id_fk
FOREIGN KEY (region_id) REFERENCES s_region (region_id);

-- Order Table
ALTER TABLE s_order
ADD    CONSTRAINT s_order_customer_id_fk
```

```
FOREIGN KEY (customer_id) REFERENCES s_customer (customer_id);

ALTER TABLE s_order
ADD   CONSTRAINT s_order_sales_rep_id_fk
FOREIGN KEY (sales_rep_id) REFERENCES s_employee (employee_id);

-- Product Table
ALTER TABLE s_product
ADD   CONSTRAINT s_product_image_id_fk
FOREIGN KEY (image_id) REFERENCES s_image (image_id);


ALTER TABLE s_product
ADD   CONSTRAINT s_product_longtext_id_fk
FOREIGN KEY (longtext_id) REFERENCES s_longtext (longtext_id);

-- Item Table
ALTER TABLE s_item
ADD   CONSTRAINT s_item_order_id_fk
FOREIGN KEY (order_id) REFERENCES s_order (order_id);

ALTER TABLE s_item
ADD   CONSTRAINT s_item_product_id_fk
FOREIGN KEY (product_id) REFERENCES s_product (product_id);

-- Warehouse Table
ALTER TABLE s_warehouse
ADD   CONSTRAINT s_warehouse_manager_id_fk
FOREIGN KEY (manager_id) REFERENCES s_employee (employee_id);

ALTER TABLE s_warehouse
ADD   CONSTRAINT s_warehouse_region_id_fk
FOREIGN KEY (region_id) REFERENCES s_region (region_id);

-- Inventory Table
ALTER TABLE s_inventory
ADD   CONSTRAINT s_inventory_product_id_fk
FOREIGN KEY (product_id) REFERENCES s_product (product_id);

ALTER TABLE s_inventory
ADD   CONSTRAINT s_inventory_warehouse_id_fk
FOREIGN KEY (warehouse_id) REFERENCES s_warehouse (warehouse_id);
-- ***********************************************************

COMMIT;

SPOOL OFF
```

plsqlobj.sql

File: plsqlsyn.sql

```
-- Program:     plsqlsyn.sql
-- Creation:    01/01/99
-- Created By:  TUSC
-- Description: Creates the synonyms for the example tables
-- for the PL/SQL Tips and Techniques Book.

SET ECHO OFF
SET FEEDBACK 1
SET TERMOUT ON

SPOOL plsqlsyn.log

-- ****************************************************************
-- Creates public synonyms for use in example database.
--
--      Public Synonym    Table
--      ----------------------------------------
--      s_customer        s_customer
--      s_department      s_department
--      s_employee        s_employee
--      s_image           s_image
--      s_inventory       s_inventory
--      s_item            s_item
--      s_longtext        s_longtext
--      s_order           s_order
--      s_product         s_product
--      s_region          s_region
--      s_title           s_title
--      s_warehouse       s_warehouse
-- ****************************************************************
CREATE PUBLIC SYNONYM s_customer    FOR s_customer;
CREATE PUBLIC SYNONYM s_department  FOR s_department;
CREATE PUBLIC SYNONYM s_employee    FOR s_employee;
CREATE PUBLIC SYNONYM s_image       FOR s_image;
CREATE PUBLIC SYNONYM s_inventory   FOR s_inventory;
CREATE PUBLIC SYNONYM s_item        FOR s_item;
CREATE PUBLIC SYNONYM s_longtext    FOR s_longtext;
CREATE PUBLIC SYNONYM s_order       FOR s_order;
CREATE PUBLIC SYNONYM s_product     FOR s_product;
CREATE PUBLIC SYNONYM s_region      FOR s_region;
CREATE PUBLIC SYNONYM s_title       FOR s_title;
CREATE PUBLIC SYNONYM s_warehouse   FOR s_warehouse;
SPOOL OFF
```

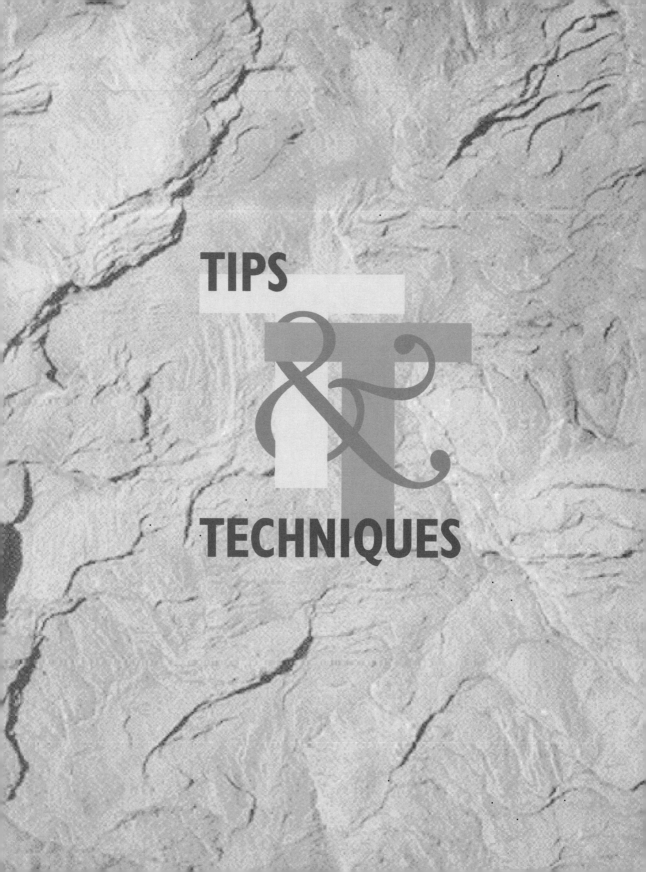

TIPS

&

TECHNIQUES

APPENDIX

B

PL/SQL
Quick Reference
(Developer and DBA)

```
KEY

New feature found in:
  Oracle 8.0 (bold)
  Oracle 8.1 (shaded)
  [ ] optional syntax element
  |  separates list of items
```

SCHEMA-LEVEL UNITS

ANONYMOUS BLOCK

```
[DECLARE
    declarations;]
BEGIN
    statements;
[EXCEPTION
    WHEN exception THEN
          statements;]
END;
```

PACKAGES

```
CREATE [OR REPLACE] PACKAGE pkg_name
[AUTHID CURRENT_USER | DEFINER] IS | AS
    [public_declarations];
    [subprogram_specifications];
END [pkg_name];

CREATE [OR REPLACE] PACKAGE BODY pkg_name IS | AS
    [package_body_specific_declarations];
    [subprograms];
[BEGIN statements;]
END [pkg_name];
```

SUBPROGRAMS

```
PROCEDURE procedure_name [(parameter_list)]
    [subprogram_properties] IS | AS
    [declarations];
```

```
BEGIN
   statements;
[EXCEPTION exceptions;]
END [procedure_name];

FUNCTION function_name [(parameter_list)]
   RETURN datatype [subprogram_properties] IS | AS
   [declarations];
BEGIN
   statements;
   RETURN value; -- constant, expression, or variable
[EXCEPTION exceptions];
END [function_name];
```

PARAMETER LIST

```
(variable_1  [direction] datatype[,. . .
 variable_n  [direction] datatype])

Direction: IN  | OUT [NOCOPY]  |  IN OUT [NOCOPY]
```

SUBPROGRAM PROPERTIES

```
DETERMINISTIC
PARALLEL_ENABLE
AUTHID CURRENT_USER | DEFINER
```

INDIVIDUAL STORED PROCEDURES AND FUNCTIONS
(Use same structure as SUBPROGRAMS)

```
CREATE [OR REPLACE] PROCEDURE
CREATE [OR REPLACE] FUNCTION
```

DATABASE TRIGGERS

```
CREATE [OR REPLACE] TRIGGER trigger_name
   event_timing action ON table_name
[FOR EACH ROW [WHEN [expression]]]
[DECLARE
   declarations;]
BEGIN
   statements;
[EXCEPTION exceptions];
```

```
END [trigger_name];
Event_timing: BEFORE, AFTER, INSTEAD OF
Action: DELETE, INSERT, UPDATE, CREATE, ALTER, DROP,
        SERVERERROR, LOGON, LOGOFF, STARTUP, SHUTDOWN
```

OBJECT TYPES

```
CREATE [OR REPLACE] TYPE type_name AS OBJECT
(attribute_declaration, ...
    [[MAP | ORDER] MEMBER subprogram_specification,...]
    [STATIC subprogram_specification, ...]);

CREATE [OR REPLACE] TYPE BODY type_name AS
[[MAP | ORDER] MEMBER subprogram; ...]
    [STATIC subprogram; ...]
END [type_name];
```

TYPES

PREDEFINED TYPES
Boolean
 BOOLEAN

Character

CHAR(length)	CHARACTER(length)	LONG
NCHAR (length)	**NVARCHAR2 (length)**	STRING
VARCHAR(length)	VARCHAR2(max_length)	

Date
 DATE

Exception
 EXCEPTION

Numeric

BINARY_INTEGER	DEC	DECIMAL
DOUBLE PRECISION	FLOAT	INT
INTEGER	NATURAL	NATURALN
NUMBER[(precision[, scale])]	NUMERIC	PLS_INTEGER
POSITIVE	POSITIVEN	REAL
SMALLINT		

Objects

BFILE	**BLOB**	**CLOB**	**NCLOB**

Raw

LONG RAW	RAW

ROWID

ROWID	UROWID

USER-DEFINED TYPES

```
tablename%ROWTYPE
tablename.columnname%TYPE
Cursors:          (see CURSORS)
PL/SQL Tables:    TABLE OF datatype INDEX BY
                  BINARY_INTEGER
Nested Tables:    TABLE OF datatype
Varrays:          VARRAY (max_size) OF datatype
                  VARYING ARRAY (max_size) OF
                  datatype
Records:          RECORD (field_declaration; ...)
Ref Cursors:      REF CURSOR [RETURN datatype]
Object types:     (see SCHEMA-LEVEL UNITS)
Object Refs:      REF object_type
```

DECLARATIONS

```
DECLARE
    variable_name [CONSTANT] datatype [:= value | DEFAULT value];
    SUBTYPE subtype_name IS datatype;
    TYPE type_name IS user_defined_type;
```

CURSORS

DECLARATION

```
CURSOR cursor_name [(variable_1 IN datatype[,
    variable_n IN datatype]) IS select_statement;
```

EXPLICIT

```
OPEN cursor_name [FOR select_statement];
OPEN cursor_name [FOR query_string [USING
    [direction] expression_list]]
FETCH cursor_name INTO [variable(s) or record];
FETCH cursor_name BULK COLLECT INTO [variable(s) or
    record];
CLOSE cursor_name;
```

IMPLICIT (SELECT INTO, INSERT, UPDATE, DELETE)

```
FOR inrec_name IN cursor_name LOOP
    statements;
END LOOP;
```

CONDITIONS

```
%found          %isopen
%notfound       %rowcount         %bulk_rowcount
```

EXAMPLES
Cursor Declaration

```
DECLARE
    lv_emp_num          emp.empno%TYPE;
    lv_ename_txt        emp.ename%TYPE;
    lv_dept_num         emp.deptno%TYPE;
    CURSOR cur_emp IS
```

```
SELECT empno, ename
FROM   emp
WHERE  deptno = lv_dept_num;
```

Explicit Cursor

```
BEGIN
   lv_dept_num := 10;
   OPEN cur_emp;
   LOOP
      FETCH cur_emp INTO lv_emp_num, lv_ename_txt;
      EXIT WHEN cur_emp%NOTFOUND;
   END LOOP;
   CLOSE cur_emp;
END;
```

Implicit Cursor (Cursor FOR LOOP)

```
BEGIN
   lv_dept_num := 10;
   FOR cur_emp_rec IN cur_emp LOOP
      lv_emp_num := cur_emp_rec.empno;
      lv_ename_txt := cur_emp_rec.ename;
   END LOOP;
END;
```

BUILT-INS

OPERATORS

Arithmetic	* / + - ** MOD REM
Assignment	:=
Attribute declare	%
Comparison	= != <> < > <= >= IS NULL LIKE BETWEEN IN
Concatenation	||
Boolean	AND OR XOR NOT
Delimiters	( ) . , " ; : ' @
Labels	<< >>

FUNCTIONS
Number

ABS	ACOS	ASIN	ATAN
CEIL	COS	COSH	EXP
FLOOR	LN	LOG	MOD
POWER	ROUND	SIGN	SIN
SINH	SQRT	TAN	TANH
TRUNC			

Character String

CONCAT	INITCAP	INSTR
INSTRB	LENGTH	LENGTHB
LOWER	LPAD	LTRIM
NLS_INITCAP	NLS_LOWER	NLS_UPPER
NLSSORT	REPLACE	RPAD
RTRIM	SOUNDEX	SUBSTR
SUBSTRB	TRANSLATE	UPPER

Conversion

ASCII	CHR	CHARTOROWID
CONVERT	HEXTORAW	NVL
RAWTOHEX	ROWIDTOCHAR	TO_CHAR
TO_DATE	TO_LABEL	TO_MULTI_BYTE
TO_NUMBER	TO_SINGLE_BYTE	

Date

ADD_MONTHS	NEW_TIME	ROUND
LAST_DAY	NEXT_DAY	SYSDATE
MONTHS_BETWEEN	TRUNC	

Error

SQLCODE	SQLERRM	RAISE_APPLICATION_ ERROR

Exceptions

ACCESS_INTO_NULL	**COLLECTION_IS_NULL**
CURSOR_ALREADY_OPEN	DUP_VAL_ON_INDEX
INVALID_CURSOR	INVALID_NUMBER
LOGIN_DENIED	NO_DATA_FOUND
NOT_LOGGED_ON	OTHERS
PROGRAM_ERROR	ROWTYPE_MISMATCH
SELF_IS_NULL	STORAGE_ERROR
SUBSCRIPT_BEYOND_COUNT	**SUBSCRIPT_OUTSIDE_LIMIT**
SYS_INVALID_ROWID	TIMEOUT_ON_RESOURCE
TOO_MANY_ROWS	VALUE_ERROR
ZERO_DIVIDE	

Miscellaneous

LEAST	USER	LEAST_LB
USERENV	GREATEST	NVL
VSIZE	GREATEST_LB	UID

STATEMENTS

CONDITIONAL ITERATION WITH EXIT

```
<<loop_name>>
LOOP
    statements;
    EXIT [loop_name] [WHEN expression];
    [statements;]
END LOOP;
```

CONDITIONAL ITERATION WITH WHILE LOOP

```
WHILE expression LOOP
    statements;
END LOOP;
```

ITERATION WITHIN LIMITS

```
FOR counter IN [REVERSE] lower_bound .. higher_bound LOOP
    statements;
END LOOP;
```

RAISE

```
RAISE [exception_name];
```

NULL

```
NULL;
```

ASSIGNMENT

```
variable := expression;
```

PROCEDURE CALLS

```
procedure_name [(arguments)];
```

UNCONDITIONAL BRANCHING

```
<<label_1>>
statements;
GOTO label_2;
statements;
<<label_2>>
statements;
GOTO label_1;
```

CONDITIONAL BRANCHING

```
IF expression_1 THEN
   statements;
[ELSIF expression_2 THEN
   statements;]
[ELSIF expression_n THEN
   statements;]
[ELSE
   statements;]
END IF;
```

RETURN STATEMENT

```
RETURN [expression];
```

DML AND QUERIES

(The syntax is meant only as a guideline.)

SIMPLE DML STATEMENT

```
SELECT expression_list
[BULK COLLECT] INTO variable_list
FROM   table_list
[WHERE condition_list];

UPDATE table_name
SET    column=value
[WHERE condition_list]
[return_clause];
```

```
INSERT INTO table_name
VALUES
(value_list)
[return_clause];

DELETE [FROM] table_name
[WHERE condition_list]
[return_clause];

return_clause: RETURNING expression_list
```

BULK SQL

```
FORALL name IN  lower_bound .. upper_bound
simple_dml_statement;
```

DYNAMIC SQL

```
EXECUTE IMMEDIATE statement_string
    [INTO variable_list]
    [USING [direction] expression,
          [direction] expression, ...]
direction: IN  |  OUT  |  IN OUT
```

DDL

(The sample syntax here is meant only as a guideline.)

```
COMMIT [WORK] [COMMENT distributed_transaction_comment];
ROLLBACK [WORK] [COMMENT distributed_transaction_comment];
ROLLBACK [WORK] TO [SAVEPOINT] savepoint_name;
SAVEPOINT savepoint_name;

LOCK TABLE table_name_list IN lock_mode_list [NOWAIT];

  lock_mode: ROW    SHARE     EXCLUSIVE

SET TRANSACTION READ ONLY;
SET TRANSACTION READ WRITE;
SET TRANSACTION USE ROLLBACK SEGMENT name;
SET TRANSACTION ISOLATION LEVEL SERIALIZABLE;
SET TRANSACTION ISOLATION LEVEL READ COMMITTED;
```

INVOCATION FROM SQL*PLUS

SQL*PLUS

```
SQL> SET SERVEROUTPUT ON SIZE 1000000
SQL> EXECUTE procedure_name[(parameters)];
```

or

```
SQL> VARIABLE n NUMBER;
SQL> EXECUTE :n := function_name [(parameters)];
SQL> PRINT n;
```

PL/SQL

```
BEGIN
   statements;
   DBMS_OUTPUT.PUT_LINE(char_value);
   statements;
END;
```

QUICK TROUBLESHOOTING

```
SET SERVEROUTPUT ON SIZE 1000000

DECLARE
   lv_error_num        NUMBER;
   lv_error_message_txt VARCHAR2(255);
BEGIN
   [statements];
EXCEPTION
   WHEN OTHERS THEN
      lv_error_num        := SQLCODE;
      lv_error_message_txt := SUBSTR(SQLERRM, 1, 255);
      DBMS_OUTPUT.PUT_LINE(lv_error_message_txt);
END;
/
```

LITERALS

CHARACTER LITERALS

```
'Z'       '%'
```

STRING LITERALS

```
'Hello, Mrs. Robinson'

'XYZ Corporation'
```

REAL LITERALS

```
6.6667     0.0      -12.0
```

NUMERIC LITERALS

```
1.0E-7     3.14159e0
```

NULL LITERAL

```
NULL
```

MISCELLANEOUS

COMMENTS
Multiple line

```
/* This is an example of a
multiple line comment   */
```

Single line

```
[statement]; -- Single line comment
-- Another single line comment
```

STORED OBJECT ADMINISTRATION
Allow Users to Execute Stored PL/SQL Objects

```
GRANT EXECUTE ON stored_object TO user;
```

Object Source Views

USER_SOURCE	ALL_SOURCE	DBA_SOURCE
USER_TRIGGERS	ALL_TRIGGERS	DBA_TRIGGERS

Object Information Views

USER_OBJECTS	ALL_OBJECTS	DBA_OBJECTS
USER_OBJECT_SIZE		DBA_OBJECT_SIZE
USER_DEPENDENCIES	ALL_DEPENDENCIES	DBA_DEPENDENCIES

EXTERNAL PROCEDURES

CREATING THE WRAPPER PROCEDURE OR FUNCTION

```
PROCEDURE procedure_name [(parameter_list)] AS EXTERNAL
LANGUAGE C
LIBRARY library_name
[NAME external_name]
[CALLING STANDARD {C | PASCAL}]
[WITH CONTEXT]
[PARAMETERS (external_parameter_list)];

FUNCTION function_name [(parameter_list)] RETURN
datatype AS
LANGUAGE JAVA
NAME java_signature_string;
```

PRAGMAS

```
PRAGMA AUTONOMOUS_TRANSACTION;
PRAGMA EXCEPTION_INIT(exception_name, exception_number);
PRAGMA RESTRICT_REFERENCES(function_name, [RNDS, RNPS,
    WNDS, WNPS, TRUST]);
PRAGMA SERIALLY_REUSABLE;
```

Many thanks to Herbert H. Rea, Guhan Viswanathan, and Usha Sangam of Oracle Corporation.

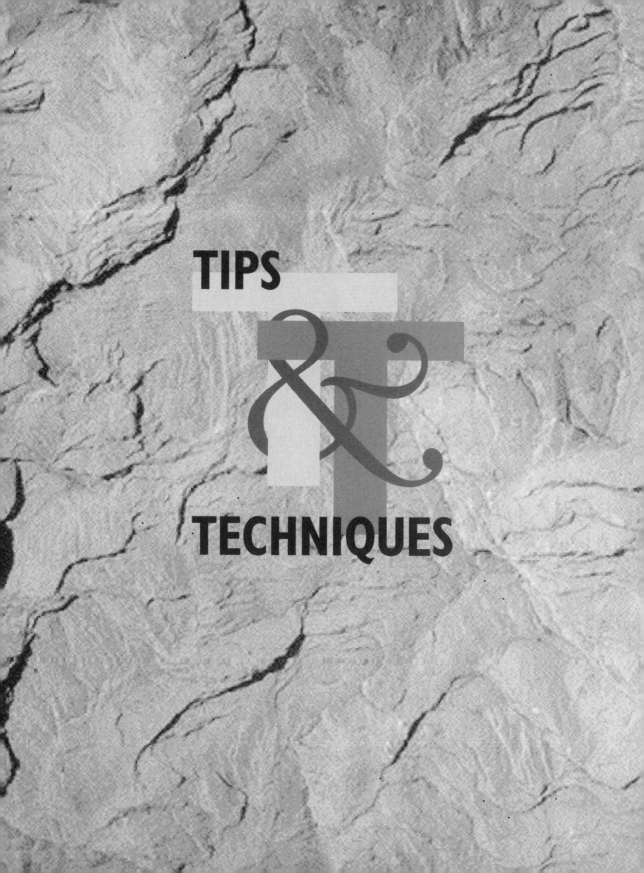

TIPS & TECHNIQUES

APPENDIX C

PL/SQL Data Dictionary Reference
(Developer and DBA)

The data dictionary provides a powerful mechanism as outlined in Chapter 13. The main PL/SQL data dictionary views are provided in this appendix for reference. It contains a brief description of each view, followed by a listing of the columns, the primary use for each view, and the differences between Oracle 7.3, 8.0, and 8.1.

Main PL/SQL Data Dictionary Views

The following is a list of the main PL/SQL data dictionary views contained in this appendix.

```
USER_ARGUMENTS          ALL_ARGUMENTS
USER_DEPENDENCIES       ALL_DEPENDENCIES    DBA_DEPENDENCIES
USER_ERRORS             ALL_ERRORS          DBA_ERRORS
USER_JOBS                                   DBA_JOBS
                                            DBA_JOBS_RUNNING
USER_OBJECTS            ALL_OBJECTS         DBA_OBJECTS
USER_OBJECT_SIZE                            DBA_OBJECT_SIZE
USER_SOURCE             ALL_SOURCE          DBA_SOURCE
USER_TRIGGERS           ALL_TRIGGERS        DBA_TRIGGERS
USER_TRIGGER_COLS       ALL_TRIGGER_COLS    DBA_TRIGGER_COLS
```

For most of the views, there are corresponding USER_*, ALL_*, and DBA_* views, noted in parentheses for each view. Each column list is from Oracle 8.1.5.

View Name: USER_ARGUMENTS (ALL_ARGUMENTS)

Stores the parameter list for all stored PL/SQL program units.

Name	Null?	Type
OBJECT_NAME		VARCHAR2(30)
PACKAGE_NAME		VARCHAR2(30)
OBJECT_ID	NOT NULL	NUMBER
OVERLOAD		VARCHAR2(40)
ARGUMENT_NAME		VARCHAR2(30)
POSITION	NOT NULL	NUMBER
SEQUENCE	NOT NULL	NUMBER
DATA_LEVEL	NOT NULL	NUMBER
DATA_TYPE		VARCHAR2(14)
DEFAULT_VALUE		LONG

```
DEFAULT_LENGTH                          NUMBER
IN_OUT                                  VARCHAR2(9)
DATA_LENGTH                             NUMBER
DATA_PRECISION                          NUMBER
DATA_SCALE                              NUMBER
RADIX                                   NUMBER
CHARACTER_SET_NAME                      VARCHAR2(44)
TYPE_OWNER                              VARCHAR2(30)
TYPE_NAME                               VARCHAR2(30)
TYPE_SUBNAME                            VARCHAR2(30)
TYPE_LINK                               VARCHAR2(128)
```

Version Differences: The last five columns are new as of Oracle 8.0.
View Usage: Primary use for this PL/SQL view is to identify all parameters for a stored PL/SQL program unit. An example of this is shown in Chapter 11.

View Name: USER_DEPENDENCIES (ALL_DEPENDENCIES, DBA_DEPENDENCIES)

Stores information about PL/SQL object dependencies, which is used by Oracle to determine the dependencies and INVALIDate objects when necessary.

```
Name                            Null?      Type
------------------------------- --------   ---------------
NAME                            NOT NULL   VARCHAR2(30)
TYPE                                       VARCHAR2(12)
REFERENCED_OWNER                          VARCHAR2(30)
REFERENCED_NAME                           VARCHAR2(64)
REFERENCED_TYPE                           VARCHAR2(12)
REFERENCED_LINK_NAME                      VARCHAR2(128)
SCHEMAID                                  NUMBER
DEPENDENCY_TYPE                           VARCHAR2(4)
```

Version Differences: The last two columns are new as of Oracle 8.0. Column referenced_name was increased to 64 from 30 in Oracle 8.0.
View Usage: Primary use for this PL/SQL view is to list all the dependencies of PL/SQL objects to determine impact analysis. A basic example of this is shown in Chapter 13; a more detailed dependency map is shown in Chapter 9.

View Name: **USER_ERRORS (ALL_ERRORS, DBA_ERRORS)**

Stores error information related to the creation of PL/SQL program units in the database. These errors occur for procedures, functions, packages, and triggers.

Name	Null?	Type
NAME	NOT NULL	VARCHAR2(30)
TYPE		VARCHAR2(12)
SEQUENCE	NOT NULL	NUMBER
LINE	NOT NULL	NUMBER
POSITION	NOT NULL	NUMBER
TEXT	NOT NULL	VARCHAR2(4000)

Version Differences: The text column increased to 4,000 from 2,000 in Oracle 8.0.
View Usage: Primary use for this PL/SQL view is to list all the errors encountered during PL/SQL object creation.

View Name: **USER_JOBS (DBA_JOBS)**

Stores the jobs submitted through DBMS_JOB; further detail on this view is provided in Chapter 12 in the DBMS_JOB package section.

Name	Null?	Type
JOB	NOT NULL	NUMBER
LOG_USER	NOT NULL	VARCHAR2(30)
PRIV_USER	NOT NULL	VARCHAR2(30)
SCHEMA_USER	NOT NULL	VARCHAR2(30)
LAST_DATE		DATE
LAST_SEC		VARCHAR2(8)
THIS_DATE		DATE
THIS_SEC		VARCHAR2(8)
NEXT_DATE	NOT NULL	DATE
NEXT_SEC		VARCHAR2(8)
TOTAL_TIME		NUMBER
BROKEN		VARCHAR2(1)
INTERVAL	NOT NULL	VARCHAR2(200)
FAILURES		NUMBER
WHAT		VARCHAR2(4000)
NLS_ENV		VARCHAR2(4000)

MISC_ENV	RAW(32)
INSTANCE	NUMBER

Version Differences: The what and nls_env columns increased to 4,000 from 2,000 in Oracle 8.0. The current_session_label, clearance_hi, and clearance_lo columns were eliminated in Oracle 8.1; the instance column was added in Oracle 8.1.
View Usage: Primary use for this PL/SQL view is to list all the processes (jobs) currently in the queue and retrieve detailed information of what each process is, the interval of execution, if it is enabled, the next time it will execute, and the last time it executed.

View Name: DBA_JOBS_RUNNING

Stores the jobs currently executing in the job queue. Further detail on this view is provided in Chapter 12 in the DBMS_JOB package section.

Name	Null?	Type
SID		NUMBER
JOB		NUMBER
FAILURES		NUMBER
LAST_DATE		DATE
LAST_SEC		VARCHAR2(8)
THIS_DATE		DATE
THIS_SEC		VARCHAR2(8)
INSTANCE		NUMBER

Version Differences: The instance column was added in Oracle 8.1.
View Usage: Primary use for this PL/SQL view is to list all processes currently executing in the job queue and the time the process started.

View Name: USER_OBJECTS (ALL_OBJECTS, DBA_OBJECTS)

Stores the name of each object in the database, as well as the status, creation date, and last modified date.

Name	Null?	Type
OBJECT_NAME		VARCHAR2(128)
SUBOBJECT_NAME		VARCHAR2(30)

OBJECT_ID	NUMBER
DATA_OBJECT_ID	NUMBER
OBJECT_TYPE	VARCHAR2(18)
CREATED	DATE
LAST_DDL_TIME	DATE
TIMESTAMP	VARCHAR2(19)
STATUS	VARCHAR2(7)
TEMPORARY	VARCHAR2(1)
GENERATED	VARCHAR2(1)
SECONDARY	VARCHAR2(1)

Version Differences: The subobject_name, data_object_id, temporary, and generated columns were added in Oracle 8.0. The timestamp column changed from 75 to 19 in Oracle 8.0. The object_type column changed from 13 to 15 to 18 in Oracle 8.0 and 8.1, respectively.

View Usage: Primary use for this PL/SQL view is to list all objects that are INVALID. This identifies all objects that need to be recompiled. It also provides a method of determining when the object was created and the last time the object was compiled (last_ddl_time column). Examples of the use of this view are shown in Chapters 3 and 13.

View Name: USER_OBJECT_SIZE (DBA_OBJECT_SIZE)

Stores the size of the object components, which are necessary to reside in memory for different compilations and executions of PL/SQL objects.

Name	Null?	Type
NAME	NOT NULL	VARCHAR2(30)
TYPE		VARCHAR2(13)
SOURCE_SIZE		NUMBER
PARSED_SIZE		NUMBER
CODE_SIZE		NUMBER
ERROR_SIZE		NUMBER

Version Differences: The type column changed from 12 to 13 in Oracle 8.1.

View Usage: Primary use for this PL/SQL view is to determine the size loaded into memory for PL/SQL object compilation and execution. The source code is the size of the actual source code of the object. The parsed code is the size loaded into memory when another object that references the object is being compiled. The code_size is the compiled p-code size, and the error_size is the size of the error text for the object (if successful object creation, error_size is 0).

View Name: USER_SOURCE (ALL_SOURCE, DBA_SOURCE)

Stores the source code for all PL/SQL procedures, functions, and packages. PL/SQL packages are stored as two separate objects, namely package and package body.

Name	Null?	Type
NAME	NOT NULL	VARCHAR2(30)
TYPE		VARCHAR2(12)
LINE	NOT NULL	NUMBER
TEXT		VARCHAR2(4000)

Version Differences: The text column changed from 2,000 to 4,000 in Oracle 8.0. **View Usage:** Primary use for this PL/SQL view is to list the source code of the PL/SQL object. PL/SQL objects that have been created from WRAPped files are stored in this view in hexadecimal format. This view can also be used to re-create source code of an object or to search for a specified string to determine the location(s). An example of this is shown in Chapter 13.

View Name: USER_TRIGGERS (ALL_TRIGGERS, DBA_TRIGGERS)

Stores information related to database triggers, including the type of trigger and entire PL/SQL source code.

Name	Null?	Type
TRIGGER_NAME		VARCHAR2(30)
TRIGGER_TYPE		VARCHAR2(16)
TRIGGERING_EVENT		VARCHAR2(75)
TABLE_OWNER		VARCHAR2(30)
BASE_OBJECT_TYPE		VARCHAR2(16)
TABLE_NAME		VARCHAR2(30)
COLUMN_NAME		VARCHAR2(4000)
REFERENCING_NAMES		VARCHAR2(128)
WHEN_CLAUSE		VARCHAR2(4000)

```
STATUS                          VARCHAR2(8)
DESCRIPTION                     VARCHAR2(4000)
ACTION_TYPE                     VARCHAR2(11)
TRIGGER_BODY                    LONG
```

Version Differences: The when_clause and description columns changed from 2,000 to 4,000 in Oracle 8.0. The base_object_type, column_name, and action_type columns were added in Oracle 8.1. The triggering_event column was changed from 26 to 75 and the referencing_names column changed from 87 to 128 in Oracle 8.1.

View Usage: Primary use for this PL/SQL view is to list all trigger source code and attributes. This view can also be used to determine if disabled database triggers exist. An example of this is shown in Chapters 9 and 13.

View Name: USER_TRIGGER_COLS (ALL_TRIGGER_COLS, DBA_TRIGGER_COLS)

Stores the column information associated with database triggers.

```
Name                             Null?      Type
-------------------------------- ---------- ----------------
TRIGGER_OWNER                               VARCHAR2(30)
TRIGGER_NAME                                VARCHAR2(30)
TABLE_OWNER                                 VARCHAR2(30)
TABLE_NAME                                  VARCHAR2(30)
COLUMN_NAME                                 VARCHAR2(4000)
COLUMN_LIST                                 VARCHAR2(3)
COLUMN_USAGE                                VARCHAR2(17)
```

Version Differences: The column_name column changed from 30 to 4,000 in Oracle 8.0.

View Usage: Primary use for this PL/SQL view is to identify the column use in database triggers.

Index

! = or <> (NOT EQUAL) operators,
 371–372
/ character, placing at the end of source
 code files, 89
! command, branching to the UNIX
 operating system, 65
— (single line comment command), 88,
 281, 282
— (two hyphen) comment method,
 367–368
$ command, 65
% wildcard
     with the LIKE function, 287–289
     in SQL statements, 371
&& (double ampersand), 52
/* and */
     for multiline comments, 88, 281, 282
_ wildcard, with the LIKE function,
 287–289
5111 error message, 783

A

ABS function, 295–296
Absolute value of a number, 295–296
Access
     for developers, 484–487
     to the PL/SQL data dictionary,
      678–680

on stored PL/SQL program units,
 681–682
Active Server Pages (ASP), 192
Active sessions, logging to a database
 table, 393
ADD_MONTHS function, 52–53
Address, of a cursor, 484
ADMIN_TABLES procedure, in
 DBMS_REPAIR, 817–818
Advanced queuing, in Oracle8, 814–815
Alert message, 562
Alert system, 561–566
Alerting, scheduling, 478
Alerts, waiting for, 562–563
Alias, creating for a column, 270
ALL_* level data dictionary views, 665
ALL_* views, 92, 680
ALL_ARGUMENTS view, 537–538
ALL_DEPENDENCIES view, 680. See also
     USER_DEPENDENCIES view
ALL_ERRORS view, 680. See also
     USER_ERRORS view
ALL_OBJECT_SIZE view, 680. See also
     USER_OBJECT_SIZE view
ALL_OBJECTS view, 680. See also
     USER_OBJECTS view
ALL_ROWS hint, 368
ALL_SOURCE view, 680. See also
     USER_SOURCE view

ALL_TRIGGER_COLS view, 680. *See also*
USER_TRIGGER_COLS view
ALL_TRIGGERS view, 680. *See also*
USER_TRIGGERS view
ALTER command, 454
ALTER ROLLBACK SEGMENT
command, 632
ALTER SESSION command, 545, 577, 810
ALTER SESSION system privilege, 501
ALTER SYSTEM command
flushing the Shared Pool, 482–483
modifying init.ora parameters,
576–577
modifying init.ora parameters in real
time, 810
ALTER SYSTEM FLUSH command,
482–483
ALTER SYSTEM FLUSH SHARED_POOL
command, 385, 612, 713
ALTER SYSTEM KILL SESSION
command, 477
ALTER SYSTEM option, 847
ALTER trigger, 808
ALTER TRIGGER command, 692
ALTER USER command, 831
ALTER_COMPILER procedure, 573–574
ANALYZE_DATABASE procedure, 635
ANALYZE_ERROR procedure, 744–746
ANALYZE_OBJECT procedure, 574–575
ANALYZE_SCHEMA procedure, 635–636
Anchor, including sound as a, 773
Anonymous blocks. *See* PL/SQL
anonymous block
APPEND argument, with SAVE command,
65–66
Append (A) mode, in UTL.FILE, 645
Application design, DBA role in, 459–460
Application development and deployment
environment, 105–107, 495
Application development schema, 99–105
Application errors, 788, 789–790
Application indexes, creating a listing of,
324–325
Application information registration, 566
Application level, 318
Application object grants, scripts for
providing lists of, 514–515

Application object privileges, 496,
502–504
Application objects, order of creation, 496
Application threshold alerting, 561
application_control table, 153–154
Applications
adding a control table for each, 154
adding indexes to, 355–359
ensuring portability through the use
of PUBLIC synonyms, 511–512
locking in postproduction, 517–518
registering information in V$
views, 540
stress testing, 640
AQ_TM_PROCESS parameter set, 815
Arithmetic operations, 32, 36–38
Arithmetic operators, 887
Array index, 135
Arrays, 724
ASCII equivalents, of control characters, 54
ASP, 766
Assignment operators, 887
Assignment statement, 890
Asynchronous message facility, 586–597
Attribute declare operator, 887
Attributes, listing about stored PL/SQL
objects, 63–64
Audit logs, 225–227
AUTHID option, 825, 827
AUTOCOMMIT option, 69
Automatic method, for executing SQL files
at database creation, 667
AUTONOMOUS_TRANSACTION pragma,
805–806
AUTOTRACE tool, 338–344

B

Background sound, 773
Batch processing routines, 163
Batch-oriented environments, 324
BEFORE INSERT trigger, 223
Begin Transaction URI, 770, 771
BETWEEN operator, 283–286
BFILE data type, 832
BFILE objects, 833, 834

BFILENAME function, 834
Bind variable references, 466
Bind variables
    finding similar SQL statements and
        SQL NOT, 420–422
    handling by the PL/SQL engine,
        415–418
    updating salaries, 800
BIND_VARIABLE procedure, in
    DBMS_SQL, 617
Blank lines
    in PL/SQL code, 85
    standards in this book, 94
Blank spaces, in PL/SQL code, 85–86
_bln suffix, 83
BLOB data type, 832
Block labels, implementing in nested
    blocks, 238–239
Block local variables, 82
Block repair facility, 817–819
Body section part, of an Oracle supplied
    package, 528
Boolean data type, 114, 119–121, 884
Boolean logic, extending the basics of the
    IF statement, 274–275
Boolean operator, 887
Boolean variables
    in conditional commands, 276
    defaulting in the declaration, 111
    suffix for, 83
BROKEN procedure, in DBMS_JOB, 582
Browsers, directing to the correct scripting
    language, 775
buffer_gets, returning SQL statements
    by, 331
Built-ins, 887–889
Bulk binds, with the FORALL statement,
    801–802
Bulk SQL statement, 892
Business logic, performing in PL/SQL, 30

C

C functions, providing an interface for
    calling, 723
Caching, small tables in memory, 372–373

Call stack, returning at the point in time of
    the error, 640
CALL_FORM built-in procedure, 732
Cartridges, 758
CASCADE CONSTRAINTS option, in
    DROP COLUMN, 844
Case, increasing visual distinction in
    PL/SQL code, 80–82
Case-sensitivity, of hints, 369
cat prefix, with data dictionary related
    files, 669
catalog.sql file, 665
catoctk.sql script, 816
catproc.sql file, 531–533, 665, 812
CEIL function, 292–293
CHANGE procedure, in DBMS_JOB, 581
Character column, suppressing, 351
Character data type, simulating a Boolean
    variable, 119–120
Character functions, 54–61, 296–303
Character literals, 894
Character sets, searching character strings
    for, 58–59
Character string functions, 888
Character strings
    comparing with the LIKE
        operator, 287
    formatting and converting, 297–300
    manipulating with functions, 54–61
    modifying with
        INITCAP/LOWER/UPPER,
        296–297
    processing, 300–301
    searching data files for, 648–654
    searching for character sets, 58–59
    sending to the message buffer, 170
    stripping characters from, 59–60
    transforming and masking, 301–303
Character types, 884
Character values
    comparing to a numeric data type,
        408–409
    comparing with the BETWEEN
        operator, 284–285
Character variables
    defaulting in the declaration, 111
    suffix for, 83

CHAR(length) type, 884
CHECK_OBJECT procedure, in
    DBMS_REPAIR, 818–819
CHOOSE setting, for the init.ora optimizer
    parameter, 321
CHR function, 54, 297–298
Class, 835
client_info parameter, in
    DBMS_APPLICATION_INFO, 572
Client-side PL/SQL Engine, 415
CLOB data type, 832, 833
CLOSE command, 139
CLOSE_CURSOR procedure, in
    DBMS_SQL, 618
Code. *See also* Source code
        centralizing with KEY-triggers,
            746–748
        commenting, 87–88
Code generation, 765–766
Code regression, 196
CODE_SIZE, for PL/SQL-related
    objects, 438
Coding standards, 76, 77
COL$ data dictionary table, 670
Collections, 836–838
Column aliases, 270–271
COLUMN command, 695
Column names, duplicating as variable
    names in PL/SQL, 148–149
COLUMN_VALUE procedure, in
    DBMS_SQL, 621
Columns
        dropping, 843–844
        hidden interval conversion of, 353
        specifying all allowing NULL values,
            32–33
        specifying as attributes in FOR
            UPDATE, 162
Command prompt, changing in SQL*Plus,
    70–71
Command types, for statements, 330
Comments
        in code, 87–88
        multiple line, 281–282
        in PL/SQL, 894
        providing for views, 682–684
Commit point information, 169
Commit Transaction URI, 770

Commits, 169
Comparison operations, ensuring the same
    data types in, 408–410
Comparison operator, 887
Compilation, of stored PL/SQL program
    units, 207–215
COMPILE_SCHEMA procedure, in
    DBMS_UTILITY, 636–637
'COMPUTE' literal, 636
Concatenated indexes, 322–323, 353–355
Concatenation operator, 887
Concurrent database user count, 770
Conditional branching statements, 891
Conditional iteration with exit, 890
Conditional iteration with while loop, 890
Conditions, 886
CONNECT role, 498, 499, 501
Connection issue, PL/SQL cartridge and,
    767–768
Consistent format, verifying for converted
    values, 57–58
Consistent gets (memory reads), reviewing
    in Explain Plan, 339
Constant connection, versus a stateless
    connection, 845
Constant values, comparing, 408
Constants, 262–263
Constrained cursor variables, 142
Constraint definition script, 101–102
Constraints, 847–848
Control characters, embedding into SQL
    commands, 54
Control Structures, in the Shared Pool, 463
Control table, 153–154
Conventions, in PL/SQL development, 89
Conversion functions, 306–310, 888
Cookies, 761, 771
Correlated subqueries, 359, 360
Cost-based optimization, 320
        compared to rule-based, 361–363
        computing statistics for, 634–636
        example of using, 327
        versus RULE-based, 325–327
Cost-based optimizer, 366
Countering, text dynamically, 300
Counters
        defaulting to 0 in the
            declaration, 270

providing for records, 45–46
using to limit size of transaction per commit, 166–169
CREATE ANY PROCEDURE system privilege, 505
CREATE ANY TRIGGER system privilege, 505
CREATE CLUSTER system privilege, 501
CREATE command, 89
CREATE DATABASE LINK system privilege, 501
CREATE DIRECTORY command, 834
CREATE OR REPLACE command, 89
CREATE PROCEDURE system privilege, 501, 505
CREATE PUBLIC SYNONYM system privilege, 499, 501
CREATE SEQUENCE system privilege, 501
CREATE SESSION system privilege, 501, 517–518
CREATE SYNONYM system privilege, 501
CREATE TABLE system privilege, 501
CREATE trigger, 808
CREATE TRIGGER system privilege, 501, 505
CREATE VIEW system privilege, 501
CREATE_PIPE function, 587–588
Creation files, 669
Creation scripts, 436
cur_ prefix, for variables, 83
CURSOR FOR LOOP statements, 128–131
Cursor name variables, 83
Cursor parameters, 139–140
Cursor variables
    implementing for similar queries with different data sources, 141–145
    opening, 142
    referencing, 265
cursor_space_for_time init.ora parameter, 455, 467
Cursors
    closing, 128, 618, 627
    implementing package specifications as repositories for reusable, 198–199
    opening, 166, 616
    pinning, 484, 609–610
    in PL/SQL, 886–887

reusing, 627
specifying the maximum number of, 455
using rollback segments during the processing of, 165–166

D

DAD (Database Access Descriptor), 760
Data block wizard, 751
Data dictionary, 664. *See also* PL/SQL data dictionary
    changes in Oracle8, 806–807
    defragmenting, 437
    reducing fragmentation, 425
    storing tables in PL/SQL program units, 670
Data dictionary cache, 463
Data dictionary related files, 669
Data dictionary views, 900–906
    containing columns defined as LONG data type, 146
    for information on privileges, users, and roles, 512
    levels of, 665
Data files. *See* files
Data integrity, enforcing with database triggers, 221–225
Data type conversion, 305–310
Data types
    ensuring the same, in comparison operations, 408–410
    implementing package specifications as repositories for reusable, 198–199
Database Access Descriptor (DAD), 760
Database buffer blocks, 848
Database columns
    changing from a NUMBER data type to a VARCHAR2 data type, 109
    forcing to uppercase, 297
    using type casting with, 110
Database creation, automating SQL files executed upon, 667–669
Database events, 539
Database fragmentation. *See also* Space fragmentation
    eliminating, 670

Database level
  building security logic at, 520
  optimizing performance, 318
Database links, 369
Database objects, 474–475, 698–700
Database recreation, 668
Database source code log table, 90–93
Database statistics, 848
Database tables. *See also* Tables
  logging information to, 171–172
  logging timing information in,
    391–393
  making program units dynamically
    adjustable, 152–154
  storage approach for constants,
    262–263
  using temporary for increased
    performance, 425–426
Database testing environments, used for
  this book, 14–15
Database triggers, 190
  avoiding mutating tables, 227–232
  creating audit logs for data
    manipulation, 225–227
  creating on tables containing DATE
    columns, 45
  enforcing with data integrity,
    221–225
  identifying all, 694
  identifying disabled, 452–453
  implementing with DBMS_PIPE,
    593–594
  implicit execution of, 677
  new in Oracle 8.1, 807–810
  Oracle system tables and, 94
  performance of, 222
  in PL/SQL, 883–884
  privileges required for, 503
  providing additional security
    with, 520
  providing the capability to
    enable/disable, 692–694
  reduced overhead of, 694
  searching text stored in the data
    dictionary, 146–148
  source code for, 676–677

storing column information
    associated with, 906
  storing information related to,
    905–906
  versioning the source code for, 94
Database trigger source code, 698
Databases
  changing during off-hours, 109
  expanded upper limits of, 839–840
  recreating, 665
  recreating PL/SQL source code from,
    687–692
  reviewing the example for this book,
    15–22
  storing PL/SQL program units,
    422–423
Date and time, retrieving the current, 405
DATE columns
  guidelines for using in applications,
    44–45
  stripping time values from, 45
DATE data type, 40, 52, 113, 117–119
DATE defined columns, 40
Date format, 62, 601–602
DATE functions, 51–54, 303–305, 889
_date suffix, 83
Date type, 884
DATE values, 40, 285–286
Date variables, suffix for, 83
Dates, truncating, 117
db block gets, reviewing in Explain
  Plan, 339
DBA
  building a monitoring system,
    477–478
  versus developer in the PL/SQL
    world, 22–24
  knowledge of PL/SQL, 434
  learning PL/SQL, 487–488
  monitoring and eliminating
    fragmentation, 673
  Oracle supplied packages, 441–442
  resource monitoring, 561
  role, 459–460, 498, 499
DBA_* level data dictionary views, 665
DBA_* views, 92

DBA_DEPENDENCIES view, 680. *See also* USER_DEPENDENCIES view

DBA_ERRORS view, 680. *See also* USER_ERRORS view

DBA_JOBS view, 577, 578, 579

DBA_JOBS_RUNNING view, 903, 577, 579

DBA_KEEPSIZES view, 546

DBA_OBJECT_SIZE view, 680. *See also* USER_OBJECT_SIZE view

DBA_OBJECTS view, 680. *See also* USER_OBJECTS view

DBA_ROLE_PRIVS data dictionary view, 512, 515

DBA_ROLLBACK_SEGS data dictionary view, 165

dba_source database view, 90

DBA_SOURCE view, 680. *See also* USER_SOURCE view
  backing up on a regular interval, 443
  recreating source code, 687, 692

DBA_SYS_PRIVS data dictionary view, 512, 513

DBA_TAB_PRIVS data dictionary view, 512, 514

DBA_TRIGGER_COLS view, 680. *See also* USER_TRIGGER_COLS view

DBA_TRIGGERS view, 680, 687, 692. *See also* USER_TRIGGERS view

dblink_encrypt_login init.ora parameter, 827–828

DBMS, prefixing Oracle supplied packages, 528

dbms prefix, with package specification related files, 669

DBMS_ALERT package, 478, 539–540, 561–566

DBMS_APPLICATION_INFO package, 540–541, 566–572
  logging the current point in time, 387
  logging the location of processing logic execution, 426
  uniquely identifying cursors, 484
  using for real time package monitoring, 388–391

DBMS_APPLICATION_INFO.SET_MODULE procedure, 426, 567–568

DBMS_AQ package, 814–815

DBMS_AQADM package, 814–815

DBMS_DDL package, 541, 573–575

DBMS_DEBUG package, 821–822

DBMS_ERROR_CODE variable, 738

DBMS_ERROR_TEXT variable, 738

DBMS_JOB package, 90, 93, 478, 541–542, 575–584
  specifying the time interval for, 455
  storing the jobs submitted through, 902–903

DBMS_LOCK package, 655–656

DBMS_LOCK.SLEEP procedure, 386

DBMS_LOG package, 815

DBMS_OUTPUT package, 170–171, 542–543, 584–586
  features of, 121–122
  flushing the message buffer, 594

DBMS_OUTPUT.ENABLE command, 122

DBMS_OUTPUT.GET_LINE(S) procedure, 122

DBMS_OUTPUT.PUT_LINE procedure, 170, 292
  displaying information, 387
  displaying to the screen, 584–585
  keeping in PL/SQL program units, 586
  methods for handling calls for code deployed into production, 123
  mixing values to pass to, 113
  in the stop_watch package, 387
  using effectively, 121–125
  using for message or screen display, 124

DBMS_PIPE package, 478, 543–545, 586–597
  compared to DBMS_DEBUG, 822
  implementing in a database trigger, 593–594
  monitoring long running processes, 594–596
  sending results to a pipe, 387

DBMS_PROFILER package, 821, 822–823

DBMS_RANDOM package, 816–817

DBMS_REPAIR package, 817

DBMS_ROWID package, 819–821, 840

DBMS_SESSION package, 545, 597–607

DBMS_SESSION.SET_ROLE
procedure, 520
DBMS_SESSION.SET_SQL_TRACE
procedure, 427
DBMS_SHARED_POOL package, 424,
545–546, 608, 612
DBMS_SHARED_POOL.SIZES package
procedure, 462
DBMS_SPACE package, 546–547, 613–615
DBMS_SQL package, 164, 427, 428,
547–551, 615–628, 732
compared to EXECUTE
IMMEDIATE, 799
putting a rollback segment
online, 165
DBMS_SQL.INCONSISTENT_TYPES
exception, 624
DBMS_SQL.NATIVE language flag
parameter, 617
DBMS_SQL.PARSE, 213
DBMS_STANDARD package, 525,
527–528
DBMS_SYSTEM package, 551–552,
628–631
DBMS_TRACE package, 821, 823–824
DBMS_TRANSACTION package, 164,
552–553, 631–634
DBMS_TRANSACTION.USE_ROLLBACK_
SEGMENT, 164
DBMS_UTILITY package, 554–555,
634–642
DBMS_UTILITY.GET TIME function,
385–386
dbmsrepr.sql file, 817
dbmsstdx.sql file, 525–527
dbmsutil.sql file, 528
DCL statements, 615–616
DDE package, 722
DDL commands
performing with PL/SQL, 634
in SQL*Plus, 69
DDL scripts, 701–703
DDL SET ROLE procedure, 520
DDL statements, 616–619, 892
DEBUG command, 824
Debug mode, switching on, 822
DEBUG package, 723

Debugging facility, for PL/SQL program
units, 584–586
Declaration attributes, 264–265
Declaration section of a PL/SQL program
unit, 261–267
Declarations, 886
DECODE function, 54–57, 270, 282
DECODE statements, nesting, 55–56
Default optimization mode, 456
Default parameters, identifying with
DESCRIBE, 536–537
Default parameter values, 233
Default values
expanding by using PL/SQL
functions, 263–264
testing procedures with, 768–769
DEFINE_COLUMN procedure, in
DBMS_SQL, 620
DELETE statement
changing to a SELECT statement,
106, 107
optimizing, 363–364
DELETES, performing ad hoc in
SQL*Plus, 69
DELETING keyword, 222
Delimiters, 887
Dependency mapping, 699, 700
DEPENDENCY$ data dictionary table, 670
dependency_tree package, 445–450
Dependency-mapping tree, 444–450
Dependent contents, of PL/SQL
packages, 560
Dependent object recompilation, 451, 686
Deployment environment, 105–107
DESCRIBE command, 536–537
DESCribe command in SQL*Plus, 63–64
Developer group, of Oracle system
privileges, 496
Developers
versus DBAs in the PL/SQL world,
22–24
providing with additional access,
484–487
SQL tuning for, 316
Development Foundation, 76, 173
Development schema/account, 500–501
Dictionary cache, 469–470

DICTIONARY view, 684
Direct role grants, 515–516
Directories, enabling in either UNIX or
    Windows NT, 643
DISABLE script, 452, 453
DISABLED database triggers, 692
Disk sorts, 848
Distinct keys, 372
Distributed transactions, 771
Distribution of data, 361–363
dlbmssql.sql file, 529–531
DML (Data Manipulation Language)
    statements, 163
        performing, 616–618
        RETURNING clause of, 802–803
        sample, 891–892
        using %ROWCOUNT with, 271
DML operations, 374, 477, 692
DO_KEY command, 748
Documentation, 87
Domain, 759
Double ampersand (&&), 52
Driving table, forcing, 364–366
DROP COLUMN command, 843–844
DROP PUBLIC SYNONYM system
    privilege, 499, 501
DROP trigger, 808
DROP USER command, 15
Dynamic configuration information,
    152–154
Dynamic PL/SQL routines, 615
Dynamic SQL, 427–428, 701
Dynamic SQL statements, 369–371, 892

E

Early binding, 509–510
Editor, changing the default, 62
ELSIF component, of the IF statement,
    277–278
EMPTY_BLOB function, 832
EMPTY_CLOB function, 832
ENABLE procedure, in
    DBMS_OUTPUT, 585
ENABLED database triggers, 692
Encapsulation, 835

Encrypted files, naming conventions for
    supporting, 79–80
END command, 89
END statements, providing labels for all,
    238–239
Enhancements, reviewing for PL/SQL
    versions, 8–12
Entity relationship (ER) diagram, for the
    example database, 15, 16
Environment variables, PL/SQL Agent usage
    of, 780
Environments, used for testing examples in
    this book, 14–15
Error function, 889
Error handler, 250–252
Error handling, 193–195, 244–245
Error information, writing to a log file,
    740–744
Error pages, 791–792
Error procedure, handling exceptions with
    a generic catchall, 789–790
Error stacks
        providing an interface to, 723
        returning at the point in time of the
            error, 640
ERROR$ data dictionary table, 670
ERROR_CODE variable, 738
error_log_dir global variable, 740
ERROR_TEXT variable, 738
ERROR_TYPE variable, 738
Error-handling routines, 734–738
Error-logging table, 250–251
Errors
        communicating between client-side
            and server-side PL/SQL, 734–738
        creating a generic error handler to
            log, 250–252
        processing unaccounted, 637
        storing for unsuccessful object
            compilation, 677–678
Example database, 15–22, 854–878
_excep suffix, 83
EXCEPTION handler
        encapsulating PL/SQL source code in
            a nested PL/SQL block with, 195
        infrastructure, 245
        for PL/SQL applications, 789

EXCEPTION sections, including in PL/SQL blocks, 244–245
Exception type, 884
Exception variables, suffix for, 83
EXCEPTION_INIT PRAGMA, 249–250
EXCEPTION_QUEUE, 814
Exceptions, 889
    handling in UTL_FILE, 647–648
    implementing package specifications as repositories for reusable, 198–199
exec_ddl procedure, 618–619
EXECPU parameter, in TKPROF, 333
EXECU parameter, in TKPROF, 333
execute command, testing procedures with default values, 768–769
EXECUTE functions, in DBMS_SQL, 617–618
EXECUTE IMMEDIATE command, 215, 428, 799–801, 811
EXECUTE privilege, 508–509, 681–682
EXECUTE_AND_FETCH function, in DBMS_SQL, 620–621
Execution map, of files executed by catalog.sql and catproc.sql, 665–666, 667
Execution, pausing for a specified amount of time, 655–656
Execution plan, 319, 344–345
EXEDSK (disk reads during execution) parameter, in TKPROF, 333
EXEQRY (memory reads during execution) parameter, in TKPROF, 333
EXEROW (row processed during execution) parameter, in TKPROF, 333
EXISTS operator, using with subqueries, 359, 360
EXIT condition, for FETCH_ROWS, 620
EXPLAIN option, of AUTOTRACE, 342
Explain Plan, 344–346
    displaying AUTOTRACE, 340
    displaying the output of, 338
    performing on SQL statements, 345
    reading output, 341–342
    using natively, 346
Explicit cursors
    versus implicit, 125–128, 419–420, 732–734

parameters in, 139–140
    in PL/SQL, 886, 887
    using CURSOR FOR LOOPs to process multiple records, 128–129
Extensibility, 835
Extensions
    length of, 79
    for PL/SQL program units, 78–79
External procedure calls, 803
External procedures, 811, 895

F

FAILED_LOGIN_ATTEMPTS option, 829
Fatal system errors, 247
FCHCPU (CPU time of fetch) parameter, in TKPROF, 333
FCHCU parameter, in TKPROF, 333
FCHDSK (disk reads of fetch) parameter, in TKPROF, 333
FCHQRY (memory reads for fetch) parameter, in TKPROF, 333
FCHROW (number of rows fetched) parameter, in TKPROF, 333
FCLOSE procedure, in UTL_FILE, 647
FCLOSE_ALL procedure, in UTL_FILE, 647
Feedback from users, about performance problems, 328
FETCH_ROWS function, in DBMS_SQL, 620
Fetching, performed by explicit and implicit cursors, 420
FFLUSH procedure, in UTL_FILE, 646
File handles, declaring in UTL_FILE, 645
FILE_TYPE variable type, in UTL_FILE, 644–645
Filename extensions, removing from strings, 58
Filenames
    developing descriptive for PL/SQL code, 77–80
    length of, 79
    naming standards in this book, 94
Files
    closing, 647, 653–654
    loading and searching for character strings, 648–654

naming, 651
opening, 645–646
reading from, 646
writing to, 646
find_dep procedure, 444
FIRST_ROWS hint, 368
Fixed length records, processing in a data
file, 652
Flat files, storing source code for stored
program units in, 195–196
FLOOR function, for forced rounding,
292–293
fn extension, 80
fnc extension, 79
FOPEN function, in UTL_FILE, 645
FOR UPDATE clause
to LOCK records for transaction
processing, 157–163
specifying columns as attributes, 162
wait states and, 159–160
FORALL command, 801–802, 811
Forced rounding, PL/SQL functions for,
292–293
Foreign key references, filling descriptions
for, 732–734
Form block, basing on a stored procedure,
748–751
Form Builder Help/About Form Builder
menu, 7
Form fields, 415
Form modules, 734–737
Form objects, 775–779
Format masks
displaying date and time, 41
setting for PL/SQL program units,
262–263
FORMAT_CALL_STACK function, in
DBMS_UTILITY, 637–640
FORMAT_ERROR_STACK function, in
DBMS_UTILITY, 637–640
Form-level error handling, 739
Forms Builder, 724
Forms module of Oracle Developer. *See*
Oracle Developer Forms module
Forms PL/SQL Library unit, locating PL/SQL
source code in, 725

Forms PL/SQL program unit, locating
PL/SQL source code in, 725
Forms PL/SQL version, 7
Forms security, 519–520
Forms, sharing variables between, 728
%FOUND cursor attribute, 139, 272–274
Fragmentation. *See also* Database
fragmentation; Space fragmentation
eliminating, 437
script for monitoring, 671–672, 673
Free memory value, in the V$SGASTAT
result set, 461
FREE_BLOCKS procedure, in
DBMS_SPACE, 613–615
FREE_UNUSED_USER_MEMORY
procedure, in DBMS_SESSION,
605–607
Free-form languages, indentation and word
spacing in, 84
Frequency of the condition, ordering IF
conditions based on, 410–411
FULL hint, 368
Full table scan, 324, 368
Function keys, associated with KEY-
triggers, 746, 747
Function key triggers, 746
Function parameter variables, prefix for, 83
Functional based indexes, 297
Functional objects, 772–779
Function-based indexes, 189, 841–842
Functions
expanding default values by using
PL/SQL, 263–264
extension standard for, 79
identifying, 539
making the logic available in
PL/SQL, 30–31
overloading to make calls more
flexible, 232–233
parameterizing, 233
in PL/SQL, 189, 883, 888–889
purity levels for, 217
simplifying SQL statement logic,
216–219
in SQL, 51–61

G

Generic error handler, 250–252
GET method, 780, 781
GET_LINE procedure
    with DBMS_OUTPUT, 585
    reading all currently stored
      output, 596
    in UTL.FILE, 646
GET_LINES procedure, with
    DBMS_OUTPUT, 585
GET_TIME function, in DBMS_UTILITY,
    640–641
Global session objects, 198
Global variables
    creating session-wide, 198
    creating with package
      specifications, 728
    fixed length of, 728
glogin.sql file, 61–62, 69
GRANT ROLE command, 600
GRANT SELECT command, 92
GRANT_TYPE_ACCESS procedure, in
    DBMS_AQADM, 815
Graphics, including on the Web, 773
Graphics module of Oracle Developer. *See*
    Oracle Developer Graphics module
GROUP BY functions, 38–39, 56–57
Group function, 32
GROUP functions, %FOUND with,
    273–274
Groups, breaking users into, 502, 503

H

Hardcoding ROWIDs, 840
Hardware and operating system level, 318
hash_value, of a cursor, 484
Hints, 366
    case-sensitivity of, 369
    referencing table names only, 369
    specifying more than one, 368
    using with the second comment
      command, 367–368
History log table, 673–675
Hit ratios, monitoring for the library cache,
    468–469

HOST command, 65
Hostname, 759
HTF (HyperText Functions), 761
HTML form, passing parameters using,
    781–782
HTML output, viewing from SQL*Plus, 768
HTML package, writing, 763
HTML pages, converting to PL/SQL using
    Web Alchemy, 766
HTML tags, 763
HTML variables, 784–787
HTP (HyperText Procedures), 761
HTP.APPLET procedure, 774
HTP.BGSOUND procedure, 773
HTP.IMG procedure, 773
HTP.PARAM procedure, 774
HTP.PRINT procedure
    embedding JavaScript code, 775
    embedding Java tags, 774
    generating functional objects, 772
    with the PL/SQL cartridge, 763–764
HTP.SCRIPT procedure, 775
HTTP (HyperText Transfer Protocol),
    759, 769
Hyperlink, including sound as a, 773
HyperText Functions. *See* HTF
HyperText Procedures. *See* HTP
HyperText Transfer Protocol. *See* HTTP

I

IDL_CHAR$ data dictionary table, 670
IDL_SB4$ data dictionary table, 670
IDL_UB1$ data dictionary table, 670
IDL_UB2$ data dictionary table, 670
IF conditions, ordering, 410–411
IF statements
    ELSIF components of, 277–278
    using to the fullest, 274–276
Impact analysis, evaluating, 444–450
Impact analysis facility, 698–700
Impact Rating, for PL/SQL tuning, 382–383
Implicit cursors
    versus explicit, 125–128, 419–420,
      732–734
    in PL/SQL, 886, 887

IN operator
  compared to the EXISTS operator, 359
  setting a Boolean variable, 289–290
Indentation, in PL/SQL code, 84–86
Index definition script, 103
INDEX hint, 368
Indexes
  adding to applications, 355–359
  adjusting the storage of, 672–673
  analyzing in an already analyzed table, 355
  determining appropriate, 323–324
  expanding to contain columns satisfying queries, 358, 359
  forcing the use of, 368, 373
  function-based, 841–842
  limiting in transaction-oriented environments, 323
  listing in applications, 324–325
  multiple on a table, 322
  NOT EQUAL operators and, 371–372
  suppressing unintentionally, 348–353
  suppressing with NO_INDEX hint, 842–843
  understanding the Oracle use of, 319–327
  using the most selective, 373
Index-organized tables, 843
Inheritance, 835
_init_sql_file parameter, 668
init_sql_file parameter, changing to _init_sql_file, 668
INITCAP function, 296–297
INITIAL extent, 437, 670–671
init.ora parameters
  in different Oracle versions, 458
  displaying, 458–459
  listing PL/SQL-related, 455–457
  modifying for DBMS_JOB, 576–577
  modifying in real-time, 455, 810
  reviewing PL/SQL related, 453–459
  setting for TRACE, 332
  setting NLS parameters, 601

Inline documentation, 87, 88
Inline functions, 189, 217, 628
input_trace_file, in TKPROF, 333
INSERT statements, specifying table columns, 149–150
insert_product procedure, 806
INSERTING keyword, 222
Instance startup script, 484
Instances, working with multiple, 71
INSTR function, 58–59, 300–301
Integer operations, 411–412
Intentional index suppression, 351
Interface errors, capturing in forms, 739–746
INTERNAL_ERROR exception, in UTL.FILE, 647
Intersession communication processes, 814
Intervals, specifying in DBMS_JOB.SUBMIT, 581
INVALID objects, 695
  checking and recompiling, 109
INVALID PL/SQL objects, 450–451, 686
INVALID program units, 78, 207–215
INVALID script, 452
INVALID_FILEHANDLE exception, 647
INVALID_MODE exception, 647
INVALID_OPERATION exception, 646, 647
INVALID_PATH exception, 647
Inventory, raising an alert at the reorder point, 563–565
Invocation, from SQL*PLUS, 893
Invoker's privilege, 825–826
I/O, evaluating per user, 470–471
IP address, mapping to a specific, 759
IS NULL, OR condition with, 35
IS_OPEN function, 626, 627, 645
IS_ROLE_ENABLED function, in DBMS_SESSION, 598–599
ISOPEN cursor attribute, 128
%ISOPEN cursor attribute, 139
Iteration logic, 394–396
Iteration within limits statement, 890
Iterative processing, 403–405

J

Java, 774–775
> integration into the Oracle core
> > foundation, 12, 13
> integration with SQL, 846
Java Database Connectivity. *See* JDBC
Java VM (Virtual Machine), 13
JavaScript, 775
JBuilder, 844–845
JDBC, 846
JDeveloper, 13, 844, 845
Job numbers, 579
Job queue
> disabling submitted jobs, 582
> executing submitted jobs
> > immediately, 583
> monitoring, 577–579
> removing submitted jobs from,
> > 581–582
> scheduling stored PL/SQL procedure
> > execution in, 541
> scheduling the execution of PL/SQL
> > program units in, 575
> storing the jobs currently
> > executing, 903
job_queue_interval init.ora parameter, 455,
576–577
job_queue_processes init.ora parameter,
455, 576–577
Jobs, 579–581

K

KEEP procedure, in
DBMS_SHARED_POOL, 609
KEY- triggers, centralizing code with,
746–748
KEY-EXIT trigger, 746, 747, 748
KEY-OTHERS trigger, 746
ksppinm column, of the x$ksppi table, 669

L

Label identifiers, adding to PL/SQL
blocks, 116
LABEL usage, expanding for loops,
269–270

Labels
> in PL/SQL, 887
> providing for all END statements,
> > 238–239
language_flag parameter values, 617
Large Object (LOG) data types, support for,
831–834
Large object support, 815–816
LAST_DAY function, 52–53
LAST_ERROR_POSITION function,
626, 627
LAST_ROW_COUNT function, 626, 627
LAST_ROW_ID function, 626, 627
LAST_SQL_FUNCTION_CODE
function, 627
last_update_date column locking strategy,
771–772
Leading column, using for concatenated
indexes, 353–355
LENGTH function, 300–301
Less than (<) operator, with ROWNUM, 47
Less than and equal to (<=) operator, with
ROWNUM, 47
Less than optimistic locking strategy, 771
Library cache, 467–469
Library cache component, of the Shared
Pool, 463–468
LIKE operator
> setting a Boolean variable, 286–289
> in SQL statements, 371
Line breaks, 695
Line length maximum, of the UTL_FILE
package, 654
Line numbers, for source code errors, 676
LINK$ data dictionary table, 670
LIST package, 724
Literal single quotes, enabling in literal
strings, 280–281
Literal strings, enabling literal single quotes
in, 280–281
Literals, 894
LOB data types, 815
Local variables, 131–134, 215–216
Lock Contention, 475–476
Locked records, 162
Locked user(s), 475
Locking
> creating a less than optimistic
> > strategy, 771

reviewing in a Web environment, 769–772
Locking user(s), 476
Log file, writing error information to, 740–744
Log timing information, in a database table, 391–393
log_error procedure, 247, 251–252, 739–744
log_source procedure, 90, 576
Logins, using captive, 60
login.sql file, 61–63, 69
LOGOFF trigger, 808
Logon statistics table, 809–810
LOGON trigger, 808
LONG database columns, 145–148
LONG data type
    in Oracle8, 676
    replacing, 832
LONG RAW data type, 832
Loops, creating labels for, 269–270
LOWER function, 296–297
LPAD function, 297–298
LTRIM function, 59–60, 300–301, 652
lv_ prefix, for variables, 82
lv_test_date variable declaration, 286

M

Main production account, 517
Maintainability, of PL/SQL code, 108
Manual method, for executing SQL files at database creation, 667
Materialized views, 847
math_calc function, 624–626
Maxwait default, in the DBMS_ALERT package, 563
Memory
    allocating to PL/SQL tables, 400–403
    caching small tables in, 372–373
    freeing unused session, 605–607
    improvements in PL/SQL, 811
    viewing requirements for stored objects, 700–701
Message buffer
    enabling, 121–122
    flushing the contents of the current, 591

logging information in, 542–543
sending character strings to, 170
Messages, sending between sessions asynchronously, 543
Metadata, 835
Methods, 667, 835
Microsoft Active Server Pages (ASP), 766
MIDI sound files, 773
MOD function, 290–292, 413–415
Modular code, 197
Module calls, 232, 236
Module comments, 88
Module documentation, 87
Monitoring, scheduling, 478
Monitoring facility, 169–173
Monitoring system. *See* Alert system
MONTHS_BETWEEN function, 53–54
Multiline comments, 88
Multiple indexes, 322, 373
Multiple line comment command, 281, 282
Multiple line comments, 281–282, 894
Multitable joins, analyzing all tables in, 363
Multivalued parameters, 784–787
Mutating error-avoidance technique, 230
Mutating tables, avoiding in database triggers, 227–232

N

name_pkg.get_name function, 143–144
Named-notation, using for parameters, 235–236
Naming conventions
    for Oracle files, 669
    for PL/SQL code, 77–80
NCHAR type, 884
NCLOB data type, 832
Nested blocks, implementing block labels in, 238–239
Nested PL/SQL functions, 274
NESTED TABLE, 835, 837–838
NESTED_TABLE_ID column, 837, 838
Net8, replacing SQL*Net, 847
NEW_FORM built-in procedure, 732
NEXT EXTENT value, 437
NEXT (incremental) extent, 670–671

NEXT_ITEM_TYPE function, 590, 591
Nightly process, executing during the day,
160–163
NLS parameters, modifying via SET_NLS,
601–602
NO_DATA_FOUND exception error,
247, 787
NO_INDEX hint, 842–843
NOCOPY modifier, passing large
parameters, 198
NOCOPY parameter option, 803, 811
Non-correlated subqueries, 359–360
Non-PUBLIC synonyms, 151
Non-query DMS statements, 615
Nontransactions, preventing, 771
NORMAL_QUEUE, 814
NOT EQUAL (!=) condition, retrieving all
records including NULL values, 34–35
not equal operands (! = or <>), using with
NULL values in a predicate clause,
31–32
NOT EQUAL operators, modifying to use
an index, 371–372
NOT NULL attribute, 266–267
NOT NULL constraint, 39
%NOTFOUND cursor attribute, 139,
272–274
NOWAIT argument, 160
NULL command, 278–279
NULL literals, 894
NULL statement, 890
NULL value columns, 35–36
NULL values
in arithmetic operations, 32, 36–38
changing the order of retrieval of,
33–34
defaulting to zero (0), 36, 37–38
in a group function, 32
in Oracle, 31
in PL/SQL, 113, 114–117
in a predicate clause containing a
"not equal" operand (!= or <>),
31–32
rules applying to, 31–32
using columns in GROUP BY
functions, 38–39
using columns with in a predicate
clause, 32–36

_num suffix, 83
NUMBER data type
changing a database column to a
VARCHAR2, 109
compared to PLS_INTEGER, 411
Number functions, 888
Number variables, defaulting in the
declaration, 111
Numbers
manipulating with
ROUND/TRUNC/SIGN/ABS,
293–296
returning the absolute value of,
295–296
Numeric column, suppressing, 351
Numeric data type, comparing to a
character value, 408–409
Numeric functions, provided with PL/SQL,
290–296
Numeric literals, 894
Numeric or value error, 783–784
Numeric types, 885
Numeric unique key, loading as the array
index for index searches, 135
Numeric variables, suffix for, 83
NVL function, 35, 36, 117, 310
treating NULL values as zero (0), 38
using on columns with arithmetic
operations, 36, 37–38

O

OBJ$ data dictionary table, 670
OBJAUTH$ data dictionary table, 670
Object cache, statement for
examining, 468
Object data types, 838–839
Object dependencies, 901
Object information views, 895
Object privileges. *See also* Application
object privileges
granting for the creation of PL/SQL
stored objects, 506–508
reviewing, 512–517
roles and, 506–507
Object references, parsing precedence
for, 500

Object source views, 895
Object storage fragmentation, 437
Object types, 884, 885
Object View, 835
Object-oriented programming, 839
Objects, 835
    compiling, 636–637
    compiling and analyzing, 541,
       573–575
    listing free blocks for, 613–615
    listing of all in the database, 675
    listing space not used for, 613
    new types and concepts in Oracle8,
       834–839
    privileges required for, 502–503
    storing the names of, 903–904
    storing the size of components,
       904–905
    viewing creation and modification
       dates, 684–685
    viewing dependencies between, 677
    viewing the sizes of, 678
oerr utility, 791
OLE2 package, 723
On-error trigger, 739–746
Online help, building for PL/SQL data
    dictionary information, 682–684
Open cursors, 472–473
OPEN_CURSOR function, in
    DBMS_SQL, 616
open_cursors init.ora parameter, 128, 455
OPEN_FORM built-in procedure, 732
Operands, expanding the standard
    capabilities, 283–290
Operating system
    specifying the maximum amount of
       memory, 457
    viewing script files at, 528–531
Operating system files
    reading and writing, 555,
       642–655, 723
    saving SQL*Plus attributes to, 66
    searching line by line, 233–234
Operators, 887
OPS$ accounts, 59–61
Optimistic locking, maintaining state with,
    770–771

Optimization
    levels of, 318
    methods, 320
    in SQL*Plus, 337–338
Optimizer, forcing to perform a full table
    scan, 368
optimizer_mode init.ora parameter, 456
OR condition
    with IS NULL, 35
    replacing a NOT EQUAL operator
       with, 372
ORA: 04091 mutating table error, 232
ORA_DE package, 724
ORA_FFI package, 723
ORA_NLS package, 723
ORA_PROF package, 723
ORA-00001 error, 738
ORA-00054: resource busy and acquire
    with NOWAIT specified error, 160
ORA-0653 Subscript beyond count
    error, 836
ORA-00947: not enough values error, 150
ORA-01001: invalid cursor error, 128
ORA-01002: fetch out of sequence
    error, 157
ORA-01400 error, 738
ORA-01401 error, 738
ORA-01562: failed to extend rollback
    segment number 7 error, 163
ORA-01598: rollback segment is not online
    error, 165
ORA-01628: max # extents (2) reached for
    rollback segment RB_1 error, 163
ORA-2800: the account is locked
    error, 831
ORA-4031: unable to allocate XXX bytes of
    shared memory error, 612
ORA-06502: PL/SQL: numeric or value
    error, 235
ORA-06556: the pipe is empty error, 592
ORA-6562: type of OUT argument must
    match type of column or bind variable
    error, 624
ORA-010301, 738
ORA-20101: Defined exception occurred
    error, 245

ORA-28001: the account has expired
error, 831
Oracle
allocating memory to PL/SQL tables,
400–403
early versions of, 2–3
index use by, 319–327
init.ora parameters in different
versions, 458
NULL values in, 31–39
upgrading versions of, 4–5
version 4, 3
versions with corresponding PL/SQL
versions, 3
Oracle 8.0, 796–848
Oracle 8i. *See* Oracle 8.1
Oracle 8.1, 796–848
Oracle Application Server, role of PL/SQL
in, 756
Oracle Call Intercase (OCI) cursor
manager, 847
Oracle creation files, 667
Oracle Designer
PL/SQL Engine in, 709, 710
PL/SQL program unit execution
in, 711
SQL statement execution in, 712
Oracle Developer
built-in packages available in,
721–724
component modules of, 719
enabling the sharing of library
data, 732
PL/SQL Engine for each module, 711
PL/SQL Engine in, 4, 709, 710
PL/SQL packages in, 719–724
PL/SQL program unit execution
in, 711
SQL statement execution in, 712
Web-enabling and, 845
Oracle Developer Forms module, 719
built-in packages available in, 720
internally creating cursors, 418
Oracle Developer Forms product. *See*
Forms security
Oracle Developer Graphics module, 719,
721, 722
Oracle Developer Reports module, 719,
720–721

Oracle Discoverer
PL/SQL Engine in, 4, 709, 710
PL/SQL program unit execution
in, 711
SQL statement execution in, 712
Oracle environment, establishing security
for, 495
Oracle error numbers, 249, 791
Oracle Forms
executing a PL/SQL anonymous
block, 713–714
executing a PL/SQL program unit,
714–715
Oracle Forms error (FRM-40508),
determining the cause of, 738
Oracle Forms error variables, 738,
739–744
Oracle Forms form modules, 739
Oracle Government site, 765–766
Oracle kernel, PL/SQL engine in, 4
Oracle PL/SQL. *See* PL/SQL
Oracle PL/SQL Agent. *See* PL/SQL Agent
Oracle production environment, 451
Oracle Product User Profile, eliminating
SQL*Plus access, 519
Oracle Security Server, single sign-on
environment in, 827
Oracle supplied packages, 709
added in Oracle8, 812–824
creating, 531–533
for the DBA, 441–442
detailed reference of, 538–556
executing, 440, 533–534
exploring the structure of, 525–528
identifying, 534–538
parts of, 528
script files with information about,
528–531
storage of source code for, 533
understanding the scope of, 525
viewing those installed in your
database, 813–814
Oracle system privileges. *See also* System
privileges
providing, 496–502
scripts for providing a list of,
513–514
Oracle Web Agent. *See* OWA
Oracle Web Application Server, 756

Oracle Web Server, 756
Oracle Webserver, PL/SQL engine in, 4
Oracle*Terminal module, 723
Oracle7, expanded role of PL/SQL, 3
Oracle8, defining differences in Oracle
    supplied packages, 538
Oracle8i, new PL/SQL security feature
    in, 520
Oracle-supplied packages, 511
ORDER BY clause
    referencing number position in the
        SELECT line of columns, 682
    removing, 343–344
'os_authent_prefix', setting init.ora
    parameter, 61
Osborne McGraw-Hill Web site, 15, 854
Output, placing into pipes, 596
Output variables
    defining, 620
    retrieving values of, 624
Overhead, associated with large
    transactions, 374
Overloaded procedures, 539, 787–788
Overloading, modules, 232–233
OWA, 761, 762
OWA_COOKIE, 761, 762
OWA_IMAGE, 761, 762
OWA_OPT_LOCK package, 761, 772
OWA_SEC, 761
OWA_TEXT, 762
OWA_UTIL, 761, 762
OWA_UTIL.GET_CGI_ENV procedure, 781
OWA_UTIL.SHOWSOURCE
    procedure, 768
OWA_UTIL.SIGNATURE procedure, 768
OWA_UTL.SHOWPAGE procedure, 768

P

p_ prefix for variables, 83
PACK_MESSAGE procedure, in
    DBMS_PIPE, 589–590
Package body, 187–188, 197
    adding a versioning variable to, 202
    comments in, 88
    defining PUBLIC procedures and
        functions, 185–186
    documenting, 88–89

extension for, 78
    naming conventions for related
        files, 669
    recompiling after modification, 78
    separating from the package
        specification, 204–207
    WRAPping, 80
Package creation files, 669
Package global variables, 83, 198
Package references, 206–207
Package specifications, 185–187, 197
    comments in, 88
    creating session-wide global
        variables and elements, 198–201
    documenting, 88
    elements, 186
    extension for, 78
    naming conventions for related
        files, 669
    recompiling, 207
    segregating from package bodies,
        196, 197
    separating from the package body,
        78, 204–207
    using to create global variables, 728
Package values, 603–605
Package variables
    prefix for, 82
    setting and retrieving server-side,
        728–732
    setting for dates, 117
Packaged inline functions, 219–221
Packages
    commenting, 88
    in PL/SQL, 882
Pageclose procedure, 766
Pageopen procedure, 766–767
Parameter list, 883
Parameter passing options, 803
Parameter values, 233
Parameters
    altering for a session, 454
    displaying those passed into PL/SQL
        procedures, 765
    in explicit cursors, 139–140
    handling multivalued, 784–787
    named-notation for, 235–236
    passing to PL/SQL, 780–782

passing using an HTML form,
781–782
providing default values for,
782–784
Parent/child integrity, with NESTED
TABLE, 838
PARSE procedure, in DBMS_SQL, 616–617
PARSED_SIZE, for PL/SQL-related
objects, 438
Parsing precedence, for object
references, 500
Password management facility, 831
PASSWORD_* options, 829
Passwords
checking, 830
encrypting, 828
expiring, 831
pb extension, 79
PECS package, 724
Performance
improvements in Oracle 8, 811
monitoring continuously, 391
Performance testing environment, creating
a PL/SQL, 384–388
Persistent areas, in private SQL Areas, 464
PFE (Programmer's File Editor), 62
PGA memory, 605–607
PGA (Program Global Area), 401–402
ph extension, 79
Phone number format, 58
Physical reads (disk reads), reviewing in
Explain Plan, 339
pin_objects procedure, 478–481
Pinned cursors, 609–610
Pinning
identifying candidates for, 611–612
PL/SQL objects, 608
Piped messages, 589–593
Pipes
creating, 587–588
managing, 593
removing, 588–589
pkb extension, 78
pkh extension, 78
Place holders, associating with
variables, 617
PLAN_TABLE, 342, 345

.plb extension, 80, 241, 669
plb suffix, 528
PLITBLM package, 724
.PLL file extension, 725
PLS_INTEGER PL/SQL data type, 411–412
PLS-00201 error, 507
PLS-00382: expression is of wrong type
error, 134
PL/SQL Agent
calling transaction procedures, 770
error handling by, 788–792
getting parameters from the Web
browser to, 780–781
logging into the database, 760
parsing the SCRIPT_NAME, 760
passing parameters to PL/SQL
tables, 786
restriction on overloading
procedures, 788
setting the error level for, 790
using environment variables, 780
PL/SQL anonymous block
creating with an explicit cursor in the
POST-QUERY trigger, 416
executing in Oracle Forms, 713–714
executing in SQL*Plus, 716–717
locating PL/SQL source code in, 725
naming to enable unique variable
naming, 268–269
in PL/SQL, 882
PL/SQL API support, for OLE2, 723
PL/SQL blocks
dynamically creating with
DBMS_SQL, 623
including EXCEPTION sections,
244–245
labeling, 116
method of execution for, 4
naming, 268
PL/SQL cartridge, 758, 767–768
PL/SQL CGI (Common Gateway Interface)
program, 761
PL/SQL code
commenting, 281–282
debugging techniques for, 594–595
developing an audit trail/version
control of stored, 89–94

executing through the Web, 758
expanding SQL*Plus variables
    into, 64
getting maximum readability
    from, 85
naming variables, 82–84
shielding from schema changes,
    108–111
using synonyms for portability,
    150–152
PL/SQL code segments, 184, 727
PL/SQL coding standards, 76, 77–94
PL/SQL components, 435–436
PL/SQL cursors, 270–274
PL/SQL data dictionary
    building online help for, 682–684
    knowing the contents of, 675–678
    providing correct access to the,
        678–680
    storage allocation of tables, 671–672
PL/SQL Development Foundation, 76, 173
PL/SQL Engines
    compared to the SQL engine, 444
    embedded in Oracle products, 709
    examples of execution and order of
        events, 712–718
    execution of the client-side and
        server-side, 711–712
    handling of bind variables, 415–418
    placing the resource load on, 282
    upgrading of, 710
    for various products, 4, 5
PL/SQL functions, limiting to a single
    RETURN statement, 215–216
PL/SQL IF statements, realizing the
    functionality of DECODE, 54–55
PL/SQL language
    applying to SQL scripts, 487–488
    areas affecting the DBA's
        responsibilities, 434
    backward compatibility of, 810
    conventions to aid development, 89
    core function support of, 723
    data dictionary views, 900–906
    defining standard coding
        techniques, 98
    developing in, 30

differences with SQL, 282–283
extended set of data dictionary tables
    and views for, 664
extending by dynamically creating
    SQL and PL/SQL, 615–628
future of, 12–13
general processing and execution
    flow, 710
history of, 2–4, 435
identifying the version of, 4–7
importance of, 31
integral role in Oracle Application
    Server, 756
integration in the product set,
    711–719
integration into development
    products, 708
integration into Oracle products,
    709–711
internal performance
    improvements, 811
monitoring routine processing,
    594–595
new commands and concepts, in
    Oracle8, 798–810
new features in 2.3, 138
passing parameters to, 780–782
past versions of, 3–4
performance related considerations,
    423–428
performance tuning, 380
programming logic flexibility of, 471
providing information during a long
    executing program, 171
ranking the impact of tuning different
    areas, 381–383
reducing code volume, 130
reviewing major version
    enhancements, 8–12
role of SQL in, 29–31
setting standards when writing for the
    Web, 766–767
standard commands, 526
troubleshooting, 893
turning tracing on and off, 823–824
utilities for expanding, 634–642
writing for the Web, 765–767

PL/SQL logic
 encapsulating for error handling,
  193–195
 turning into stored PL/SQL functions,
  216–217
PL/SQL logic flow, using %ROWCOUNT
 attribute as part of, 271
PL/SQL LONG data type, 145
PL/SQL object errors, 694–696
PL/SQL objects
 becoming INVALID, 109
 controlling the caching of, 608–612
 identifying those needing
  pinning, 424
 pinning, 478, 608–610
 pinpointing invalid, 450–452
 security for the creation of stored,
  504–510
 unpinning, 610–611
 verifying the validity of, 685–686
PL/SQL object source code, developing
 search engines for, 696–698
PL/SQL packages. *See also* Oracle supplied
 packages
 building Web pages with, 763–765
 features of, 196–197
 implementing version reporting
  in, 202
 modularizing code with, 197
 in Oracle Developer, 719–724
 Oracle supplied, 560
 SERIALLY_REUSABLE pragma for,
  803–805
 storing source code for, 905
PL/SQL procedure creation script, within
 the WRAP.SQL file, 240–241
PL/SQL procedure execution, 541
PL/SQL procedures
 calling in response to user
  actions, 761
 debugging parameters passed
  into, 765
PL/SQL program units. *See also* Stored
 PL/SQL program units
 advantages of storing, 184–185
 allowing for dynamic and
  flexible, 547

AUTONOMOUS_TRANSACTION
 pragma, 805–806
 building communication with Form
  modules, 734–737
 closing transactions prior to the
  completion of, 279
 controlling the interface for
  Web-based applications, 518
 debugging, 584–586
 declaring within program units,
  190–191
 determining access on stored,
  681–682
 evaluating memory requirements,
  464–465
 executing in Oracle Forms, 714–715
 executing in SQL*Plus, 717–718
 executing more than once, 387
 executing on the client, 710
 executing on the server side, 425
 execution by the PL/SQL Engine,
  711–712
 identifying by file type, 78
 length of parameters, 235
 moving from the client side to the
  server side, 417–418
 name resolution, 727–728
 optimizing, 380
 parameter list for all stored, 900–901
 pausing execution, 655–656
 pinning, 424
 recompiling, 209–215
 recompiling stored, 78
 reducing iterations and iteration
  time, 394–396
 storage of, 533
 storing error information relating to
  the creation of, 902
 storing in the database, 8, 182,
  422–423
 testing for potential performance
  improvements, 384–388
PL/SQL program unit source code,
 encrypting, 442–443
PL/SQL quick reference, 882–896
PL/SQL record, 131–134
PL/SQL record types, 133–134

PL/SQL REF CURSORs. *See* Cursor variables

PL/SQL security model, 439–441

PL/SQL source code. *See also* Source code
creating backup versions, 91–93
expansion of database storage to include, 670
locating, 725–727
message buffer for use in debugging, 542–543
methods for locating files, 79
realizing the location transformation, 8
re-creating from the database, 687–692
relocating, 726
reviewing the storage size of, 437–438
storing files, 79
types with extension standards, 78–79

PL/SQL stored objects
creating as PLSQL_USER, 495
granting the object privilege to create, 506–508
granting the privilege for users to execute, 508–509
granting the system privilege to create, 505–506

PL/SQL table attributes, 135

PL/SQL tables
%ROWTYPE and, 400
building a custom stack error, 242–243
improving performance, 134–139, 396–403
as parameters to pass data to program units, 237–238
providing support for, 724

PL/SQL toolkit, 764, 772

PL/SQL variables, 111–113

PL/SQL Web Agent, 767

PL/SQL Web toolkit, 761
components of, 761–763
creating HTML tags not located in the, 763
support of form objects, 775–779

PLSQL_DEBUG, 822

PLSQL_USER, providing SELECT privilege, 93

PLSQL_USER schema, 495, 826

PLSQL_USER UNIX account, 60

PLSQL_V2_COMPATIBILITY init.ora parameter, 810

plsqlobj.sql file, 854–877

plsqlobj.sql script, 15, 17–22

plsqlsyn.sql file, 878

plsqlsyn.sql script, 15

plsqlusr.sql file, 854

plsqlusr.sql script, 15, 16

PLUSTRACE role, granting to users, 343

plustrce.sql script, 343

Point in time information, communicating about execution, 388

Polymorphism, 835

POPULATE_PROD_TABLE procedure, in PROCESS_PRODUCTS, 607

Port number, 759

Positional notation, combining with named notation, 236

POST method, 780, 781

Postproduction period, for applications, 517

pr extension, 79

Pragmas, 896

prc extension, 78

Precedence order, for PL/SQL program unit resolution, 727–728

Predefined types, in PL/SQL, 884–885

Predicate clauses, index suppression and, 353

Predicate columns, building indexes encompassing, 324

PRIVATE components, in the package body, 187–188

Private pipes, 587

Private SQL Areas, in the Shared Pool, 464

Privileges
for application development and deployment, 496
extending granting ability to others, 679
reviewing at all levels, 512

Pro Languages, 712

Probe facility, 821–824
Procedure Builder, 384
Procedure calls, 890
Procedure, extension for, 78
Procedure variables, prefix for, 83
Procedures, 189
  overloading, 232–233, 787–788
  parameterizing, 233
  testing with default values, 768–769
process_products procedure, 648–652
process_timing_log table, creating and
  logging timing information into,
  391–393
Processes
  committing once at the end of, 163
  developing a monitoring facility for
    long running, 169–173
  monitoring long running, with
    DBMS_PIPE, 594–596
Processing, pausing for a specified amount
  of seconds, 386–387
Product versions, 107–108
Production code, keeping the
  DBMS_OUTPUT.PUT_LINE calls
  in, 123
Production environment, 451
profrep.sql script, 823
profsum.sql script, 823
proftab.sql script, 823
Program Global Area. See PGA (Program
  Global Area); PGA memory
Program unit levels, integrating with inline
  documentation, 87–89
Program unit resolution, performed by the
  PL/SQL Engine, 727–728
Program units
  communicating failure via
    user-defined exceptions, 245–250
  creating in form called from a
    POST-QUERY trigger, 416–417
  prefix for variables, 82
  segmentation for PL/SQL source
    code, 726
Protocol, 759
PRVT, prefixing the body filename, 528
prvt prefix, with package body related
  files, 669

prvtutil.plb file, 528
Pseudo column, 48
Public (global) packages, 78
Public pipes, 586, 587
PUBLIC procedures and functions,
  185–186
PUBLIC role, 498
PUBLIC synonyms
  creating, 390, 495
  determining for objects in
    applications, 104–105
  ensuring application portability
    through, 511–512
  examples of creating, 151
  implementing, 152
pupbld.sql script, 519
PURGE procedure, in DBMS_PIPE, 593
Purity levels, 217, 219
PUT_LINE procedure
  in DBMS_OUTPUT, 585
  in UTL.FILE, 646
pv_ prefix for variables, 82
pvg_ prefix for variables, 83

Q

Quality Assurance (QA) team, 77
Quarter, returning date information for a
  given, 52–53
Queries, running multiple times in
  succession, 348
Query string, 759
query_rewrite_enabled init.ora
  parameter, 842
Queue process, in Advanced Queuing, 814

R

RAISE statement, 890
RAISE_APPLICATION_ERROR procedure,
  in EXCEPTION sections, 244–245
RANDOM function, 816
Random number generator, 816–817
Raw types, 885

READ privilege, avoiding to developers, 485

READ_CLIENT_INFO procedure, in DBMS_APPLICATION_INFO, 571

READ_ERROR exception, in UTL.FILE, 646, 647

READ_MODULE procedure, in DBMS_APPLICATION_INFO, 570–571

Readability, in PL/SQL code, 84–86

Read (R) mode, in UTL.FILE, 645

Reads No Database State purity level, 217

Reads No Package State purity level, 217, 218

Real literals, 894

Real time monitoring, 388–391

Real-time activity, monitoring in databases, 468

_rec suffix, 83

RECEIVE_MESSAGE function, in DBMS_PIPE, 591–592

recompile_all_objects procedure, 211–215

Recompiling, INVALID program units, 207–215

Record variables, suffix for, 83

Records
  adding sequential numbers to, 47–48
  counting in all tables of the current schema, 799–800
  deleting duplicate using the ROWID, 49–51
  limiting the number returned with ROWNUM, 46–47
  locking optimistically, 761
  processing fixed length, in a data file, 652
  providing counters for, 45–46
  re-querying through a SQL statement in SQL*Plus, 37
  storing the before image of, 631
  time stamping with SYSDATE, 42–44
  uniquely identifying, 48

Recursive calls, reviewing in Explain Plan, 339

REGISTER procedure, in DBMS_ALERT, 561–562

Releases, learning new features of, 798

REMOVE procedure, in DBMS_ALERT, 563

REMOVE_PIPE function, 588–589

REMOVEALL procedure, in DBMS_ALERT, 563

REPLACE argument, with the SAVE command, 65

REPLACE function, 60, 301–303

Reports module of Oracle Developer, 719, 720–721

REQUEST_METHOD, 780

Reserved words, 80–82

RESET_BUFFER procedure, in DBMS_PIPE, 591

RESET_PACKAGE procedure, in DBMS session, 603–605

Resource consumption, evaluating for each user, 471–472

Resource files, manipulating for Oracle*Terminal, 723

RESOURCE role, 498, 499, 500
  changing to include CONNECT role privileges, 499
  system privileges modified for, 501
  UNLIMITED TABLESPACE system privilege and, 500

RESTRICT_REFERENCES PRAGMA, 219–221

Result set, creating without locking records, 162

RESUME keyword, 847

RETURN statement
  limiting PL/SQL functions to a single, 215–216
  in PL/SQL, 891

RETURNING clause, of DML statements, 802–803

Reusability, of PL/SQL code segments, 727

RMAN recovery manager, 847

RNDS (Reads No Database State) purity level, 217

RNPS (Reads No Package State) purity level, 217, 218

Role Responsibility, for PL/SQL tuning, 382–383

Roles
  assigning, 503–504, 599
  changing, 507

identifying and revoking from
users, 518
new in Oracle 8.0, 828–829
object privileges and, 506–507
for Oracle databases, 497–500
setting, 600
Rollback segments
checking the size of, 165
choosing large, 163–166
displaying the current, 631–632
flushing and switching, 167
listing active, 632–633
monitoring use, 476–477
processing large transaction sets, 427
specifying, 631–634
using during the processing of
cursors, 165–166
Rollback Transaction URI, 770
Rollbacks, controlling, 169
ROUND function, 293–294
Roundtrip time, to the database, 726
Row level triggers, 221
%ROWCOUNT cursor attribute,
271–272, 274
ROWID
changes to the format of, 840–841
content of, 49
deleting duplicate records, 49–51
displaying, 48
format of, 49
improving transaction processing
performance, 155–157
processing, 819–821
returning for the last row
processed, 626
using for iterative processing,
403–405
ROWID pseudo column, 48–51, 418
Rowid types, 885
ROWID_BLOCK_NUMBER function, in
DBMS_ROWID, 820–821
ROWID_ROW_NUMBER function, in
DBMS_ROWID, 820–821
ROWID_TO_RESTRICTED function, in
DBMS_ROWID, 819–820
Row-level database triggers, overcoming
mutating table errors, 230

ROWNUM pseudo column, 45–48
Rows, fetching, 620–621
%ROWTYPE declaration attribute, 108,
109–111, 264–265
PL/SQL tables and, 400
using for creating local
variables, 131
using with NOT NULL, 266–267
RPAD function, 297–298
RTRIM function, 59–60, 300–301, 652
RULE hint, 366–367, 368
Rule-based optimization, 320, 325–327,
361–363
Rule-based optimizer, 326–327, 366
RUN procedure, in DBMS_JOB, 583
Runaway processes, 477
Runtime areas, in private SQL Areas, 464
Runtime error information, 738
Runtime errors, 739

S

SAVE command, 65
Schema changes, shielding PL/SQL code
from, 108–111
Schema level units, 882–884
Schema name, in COMPILE_SCHEMA, 636
Schema profiles, added in Oracle8,
829–830
Schema role assignments, displaying a list
of current, 598–599
Schemas, executing Oracle supplied
packages, 440
Script files
PL/SQL-related, 436
viewing at the operating system, for
Oracle supplied packages,
528–531
Script method, for executing SQL files at
database creation, 667
Scripts. *See also* V$ scripts
creating public synonyms for all
stored PL/SQL objects under a
schema, 703
determining free memory, 461
disabling all triggers, 693

displaying detailed information on
Oracle supplied packages,
535–536

displaying memory requirements for
stored objects, 700–701

dropping all stored PL/SQL objects
under a schema, 701–702

examining object cache, 468

exemplifying dynamic SQL, 701–703

granting access to all stored PL/SQL
objects under a schema, 702–703

identifying all triggers, 694

identifying disabled database
triggers, 452

identifying invalid PL/SQL objects,
450–451

listing all Oracle supplied
packages, 534

locating stored PL/SQL object
dependencies, 698–700

monitoring fragmentation,
671–672, 673

for the pin_objects procedure,
478–481

querying contents of a data
dictionary view or column in a
view, 682–684

recompiling all stored PL/SQL
objects under a schema, 702

recreating source code, 688–692

retrieving information on current
privileges, 512–517

returning the errors in the
USER_ERRORS view, 695

searching USER_SOURCE view,
696–698

for Shared Pool sizing, 467–468

viewing init.ora parameters, 453–454

Search engines, developing for the PL/SQL
object source code, 696–698

Search key, using as a PL/SQL
table index, 399

Security

establishing for an Oracle
environment, 495–504

new features in Oracle8, 824–831

providing additional with database
triggers, 520

Seed number, 816

Segment space information, 546

Segmentation of program units, for PL/SQL
source code, 726

SELECT INTO statement, creating directly
into a POST-QUERY trigger, 416

SELECT privilege, on selected
V$ views, 485

SELECT statements

%ROWCOUNT cursor attribute,
271–272

changing UPDATE or DELETE
statements to, 106, 107

constructing dynamically, 621–623

creating dynamically with
DBMS_SQL, 619–623

creating using an explicit or implicit
cursor, 419

executing in SQL*Plus, 715–716

extending performance tuning
beyond, 364

in PL/SQL program units using a
cursor record type, 466

retrieving timing of the execution of,
337–338

Selectivity, determining for SQL
statements, 372

Semantics, checking for wrapped
code, 241

SEND_MESSAGE function, in DBMS_PIPE,
590–591

SEND_MESSAGE procedure, 587

Sequence definition script, 103–104

Sequential numbers, adding to records,
47–48

Sequential orders, of IF conditions,
410–411

SERIALLY_REUSABLE pragma, for PL/SQL
packages, 803–805

Server side, executing PL/SQL program
units on, 425

SERVERERROR trigger, 808

serveroutput buffer, enabling, 124

SERVEROUTPUT ON, turning on in
SQL*Plus, 585

Server-side, storing PL/SQL objects on, 422

Session information, registering or logging, 566–569

Session TRACE statistics, 332–335

session_cached_cursors init.ora parameter, 456

SESSION_MAX_OPEN_FILES init.ora parameter, 833

Sessions
    enhancing control and identification, 597–607
    modifying the operation of, 545
    setting TRACE in, 629
    tracing with SID and SERIAL#, 552
    viewing to analyze physical disk and memory activity, 470–471

SET AUTOTRACE command, 70

SET AUTOTRACE ON SQL*Plus command, 338

SET command
    allowing rollback segments to be specified in SQL*Plus, 164
    placing in the glogin.sql file, 69
    placing in the login.sql file, 69

SET options, 66–67, 69–71

SET ROLE command, 507–508

SET SERVEROUTPUT command
    with RESET-PACKAGE, 604–605
    using the FORMAT WORD_WRAPPED attribute, 124

SET SERVEROUTPUT ON command, 122

SET SQLPROMPT command, 70–71

SET TIME command, 70

SET TIMING command, 70, 384

SET TRANSACTION command, 427

SET_ACTION procedure, in DBMS_APPLICATION_INFO, 569–570

SET_CLIENT_INFO procedure, in DBMS_APPLICATION_INFO, 571

SET_MODULE procedure, in DBMS_APPLICATION_INFO, 566

SET_NLS procedure, in DBMS_SESSION, 601–602

SET_PIPEOUTPUT_ON procedure, 596

SET_ROLE procedure, 598, 599–600

SET_SQL_TRACE procedure, in DBMS_SESSION, 602–603

SET_SQL_TRACE_IN_SESSION, 629

set_sql_trace_in_session procedure, 552

SGA memory, 605

SGA (System Global Area), 461

Sharable memory, 481

SHARE_LIBRARY_DATA parameter, in built-in procedures, 732

Shared areas, flushing from the Shared Pool, 467

Shared Pool
    areas comprising, 463
    caching stored PL/SQL objects in, 700
    compiled PL/SQL code within, 463
    flushing, 385, 713
    flushing shared areas from, 467
    flushing shared memory, 612
    increasing the size of, 424, 460
    monitoring use to determine optimization, 459–463
    pinning objects in, 608
    providing access to, 545–546
    sizing script, 467–468
    specifying the size of, 456–457
    viewing allocation within, 462
    viewing the contents of, 460

Shared Pool SQL Area, caching SQL statements, 328

Shared SQL Areas, 464, 466–467

shared_pool_reserved_min_alloc init.ora parameter, 456, 457

shared_pool_reserved_size init.ora parameter, 456, 457

shared_pool_size init.ora parameter, 424, 456

SHOW ERRORS command, 696

SHOW_ORDERS procedure, 621–623

SHUTDOWN trigger, 808

SIGNAL procedure, in DBMS_ALERT, 562

Single line comment command, 281, 282

Single-line comments, 88, 894

SIZES procedure, in DBMS_SHARED_POOL, 611–612

SLEEP procedure, in DBMS_LOCK, 655–656

sort_area_size init.ora parameter, 457

Sorting order, ROWNUM and, 47

Sound, including on the Web, 773

Source code. *See also* PL/SQL source code
breaking down into smaller
segments, 106
encrypting, 518
line numbers for errors, 676
locating PL/SQL, 725–727
storing for all PL/SQL procedures,
functions, and packages, 905
storing for PL/SQL stored
objects, 239
storing in flat files for stored program
units, 195–196
view containing the current version
of, 676

Source code database storage, database
fragmentation and, 670

Source code log table, 90–93

Source code segments, programming in the
same manner, 76

Source code version control, 89–94

source directory, for PL/SQL source code
files, 79

SOURCE$ data dictionary table, 670

SOURCE_SIZE, for PL/SQL-related
objects, 438

Space, retrieving information about free,
613–615

Space fragmentation, automating the
process of checking, 673–675

Space management, 436–437

Spaces, in the SET SQLPROMPT
command, 71

Specification part, of an Oracle supplied
package, 528

Spyglass listener, GET method and, 781

SQL Area, 330, 422

SQL buffer, 65–67

SQL commands, 54

SQL DATE functions. *See* DATE functions

SQL engine
compared to the PL/SQL engine, 444
placing the resource load on, 282

.sql extension, 79, 80, 241
with data dictionary related files, 669
with package specification related
files, 669

SQL files, automating the execution of at
database creation, 667–669

SQL functions, performing in PL/SQL,
30–31

SQL language
creating dynamic, 547
differences with PL/SQL, 282–283
enhancements to, 840–843
functions in, 51–61
importance of, 28
integration with Java, 846
reviewing critical concepts, 31–51
role in PL/SQL, 29–31

SQL scripts
applying the PL/SQL language to,
487–488
extension standard for, 79

SQL SELECT statements, 619–623

SQL statements
caching, 328
command types for, 330
conversion to uppercase by the
PL/SQL Engine, 711, 719
determining the selectivity of, 372
displaying those currently being
executed, 473–474
executing more than once, 384–385
executing twice to get true timing,
347–348
execution of, 712
finding similar, 420
fine-tuning Web-based
application, 371
limiting dynamic, 369–371
optimizing, 134, 316
pinpointing problem, 327–335
in PL/SQL program units, 380
processing of, 716
returning resource-intensive, 331
techniques for improving, 347
testing in SQL*Plus, 337
using functions to simplify logic,
216–219
writing with intentional index
suppression, 351
writing with unintentional index
suppression, 350

SQL transaction commands, 552
SQL tuning
    establishing the process, 335–337
    responsibility for, 316
    value of, 318–319
SQL*Forms 3.0, 708
SQL*Navigator, 384
SQL*Plus, 61
    changing the command prompt,
      70–71
    committing transactions in, 69
    executing a PL/SQL anonymous
      block, 716–717
    executing a PL/SQL program unit,
      717–718
    executing PL/SQL program unit
      creation or modification, 89
    executing SELECT statements in,
      715–716
    executing stored PL/SQL objects, 63
    execution of PL/SQL program units
      and SQL statements, 712
    expanding the DESCribe command,
      63–64
    expanding variables into PL/SQL, 64
    limiting access to, 519
    logging in and noting the version of
      PL/SQL, 5–6
    optimizing in, 337–338
    performance enhancement
      techniques, 384–385
    performing ad hoc UPDATES or
      DELETES, 69
    retrieving information outside of, 65
    SET options, 69–71
    startup files, 61–63
    testing environment provided
      by, 384
    testing procedures with default
      values, 768–769
    timing function, 343
    using for development, debugging,
      and testing, 106
    verifying dates in, 52–53
    viewing HTML output from, 768
SQL*Station, 384
sql.bsq file, 437, 665, 666

executing at database creation, 667
modifying for optimal storage and
    speed, 670–673
modifying storage parameters in, 673
modifying to reduce data dictionary
    fragmentation, 425
SQLJ, 846
SRW package, 724
Standalone contents, of PL/SQL
    packages, 560
Standard exceptions, 247
STANDARD Extensions package, 724
STANDARD package, 525–527, 527–528,
    719, 723
Standards, setting for writing code for the
    Web, 766–767
standard.sql file, 525–527
START or @ command, executing the
    operating system file with, 66
START_TIME_MANAGER procedure, in
    DBMS.AQADM, 815
Starting time, logging for testing, 385–386
Startup files, in SQL*Plus, 61–63
STARTUP trigger, 808
State, 770–771
Stateless interface, versus a constant
    connection, 845
Stateless protocol, 769
Statement cursors, explicitly opening and
    closing, 465
Statement-level database triggers, 230
Statements
    executing, 617–618
    parsing, 616–617
    in PL/SQL, 890–891
Statistics, computing for cost-based
    optimization, 634–636
STATISTICS options, of AUTOTRACE, 342
Statistics output file, connecting to a
    readable formatted file, 332
Stop watch timer, 70
STORAGE clause, adding to data dictionary
    tables, 672
Storage space, allocating for data
    dictionary tables, 670–673
STORE SET command, 66, 67
Stored object administration, 895

Stored PL/SQL functions, 189
Stored PL/SQL object errors, 694–696
Stored PL/SQL objects
    compiling, 509–510
    executing in SQL*Plus, 63
    executing with the invokers
        privilege, 520
    security for the creation of, 504–510
    verifying the validity of, 685–686
Stored PL/SQL packages, 196–207, 560
Stored PL/SQL procedure, 189
Stored PL/SQL program units. *See also*
    PL/SQL program units
    advantages of, 184–185
    coding techniques using, 182
    creating, 439, 440
    determining access on, 681–682
    encrypting source code, 239–242
    executing, 439, 825–827
    locating components correctly,
        185–195
    locating PL/SQL source code in, 726
    making compilation easy, 207–215
    maximum size of, 840
    memory components of, 437–438
    passing records to, 237
    referencing, 440
    showing the source code of, 768
    space management of, 436–437
Stored procedures
    accessing, 767–769
    basing form blocks on, 748–751
    in PL/SQL, 883
STPROC package, 724
Stress testing, applications, 640
String literals, 894
string_line procedure, 233–234
Strong-type declaration, 142
Stub, using the NULL command as a, 279
SUBMIT procedure, in DBMS_JOB,
    579–581
Submitted jobs, 581–583
Subprogram properties, 883
Subprograms, 882–883
Subqueries, improving execution of,
    359–360
SUBSTRing function, 58–59
Subtypes, 410

Supplied packages. *See* Oracle supplied
    packages
Suppression, of indexes, 348–353
SUSPEND keyword, 847
Synonym definition script, 104–105
SYNONYM privileges, adding to the
    RESOURCE role, 499
Synonyms
    overhead of using, 152
    for portability of PL/SQL code,
        150–152
    as underlying objects, 105
SYS user, Oracle-supplied packages
    created under, 511
SYSAUTH$ data dictionary table, 670
SYSDATE variable, 40
    reducing calls to, 405–407
    referencing, 734
    setting the date and time, 42
    time stamping records, 42–44
    using TRUNC with, 44
SYSTEM default storage, 670–671
System errors, 788, 790–791
System Global Area (SGA), 461
System level utilities, 552
System privileges. *See also* Oracle system
    privileges
    displaying for the current session,
        505–506
    executing Oracle-supplied
        packages, 511
    granting for the creation of PL/SQL
        stored objects, 505–506
    modified for the CONNECT and
        RESOURCE roles, 501
    reviewing, 512–517
System tables, database triggers and, 94
SYSTEM user, assigning to the DBA role,
    498–499
system_errors table, 250–251

T

Table and view definition script, 100–101
Table columns, specifying with INSERT
    statements, 149–150
_table suffix, 83

Table variables, suffix for, 83
Tables. *See also* Database tables
    analyzing all in a multitable
      join, 363
    caching small, in memory, 372–373
TCP/IP port, 759
Template generator, 765
Templates, using for code generation,
  765–766
Temporary database tables, 425–426
test_if procedure, 408–410
Testing, logging the starting time, 385–386
Text
    countering dynamically, 300
    reading from specified files, 646
TEXT_IO package, 642, 723
Time
    included with SYSDATE, 40
    never storing in DATE columns, 44
    storing in an additional column, 45
    storing in a separate column, 41
Time value, setting to 00:00:00, 42, 43–44
Timer Manager, monitoring the status of
  the queued messages, 815
Timers
    setting multiple, 68
    for testing, 385–386
Timestamps, viewing for object creation
  and modification, 684–685
Timing and tracing mechanism, 426–427
TIMING command, 68
Timing functions
    enabling, 343
    providing support for, 723
    in SQL*Plus, 384
Timing logic, deploying with TRACE, 427
Timing routines, integrating to monitor
  PL/SQL performance, 640–641
Timing statistics
    inserting into a database table, 391
    returning, 292
TKPROF operating system command, 332,
  333–334, 334–335
TO_CHAR function, 53–54, 297–298
    converting number data types to
      character strings, 306–308

displaying the date and time portion
    of a column, 41
    indexing and, 44
TO_DATE function, 53–54, 308
TO_NUMBER function, 308–310
TOAD, 384
TOO_MANY_ROWS exception, 733
TOOL_ENV package, 723
TOOL_ERR package, 723
TOOL_INT package, 724
TOOL_RES package, 723
TRACE facility
    compared to DBMS_TRACE,
      823, 824
    conditionally turning on, 602–603
    turning on conditionally, 427
    turning on for any session, 628–631
    turning ON for resource-intensive
      processes, 487–488
trace_all_calls, 823
trace_all_exceptions, 824
trace_enabled_calls, 824
trace_enabled_exceptions, 824
TRACEONLY option, of AUTOTRACE, 342
TRACE/TKPROF facility, 344
Tracing facility, turning on an
  automatic, 70
Transaction life, 767–768
Transaction logic, controlling in PL/SQL
  program units, 279–280
Transaction processing, using FOR
  UPDATE to LOCK records, 157–163
Transaction Services
    automating application state
      management, 769–770
    best uses of, 770
    implementing distributes
      transactions, 771
Transaction sets, 163–166, 427
Transaction state, 805–806
Transactional trigger, 221
Transaction-oriented environments,
  limiting indexes in, 323
Transactions
    assigning to rollback segments, 427
    committing at time intervals, 166
    committing in SQL*Plus, 69

implementing a counter to commit a specified number of, 167
improving processing performance using ROWID, 155–157
processing large, 631
understanding the overhead associated with large, 374
TRANSLATE function, 57–58, 301–303
Transportable tablespaces, 848
trg extension, 79
TRIGGER$ data dictionary table, 670
TRIGGERCOL$ data dictionary table, 670
Triggering DML events, 222
Triggers, extension standard for, 79
TRIM functions, 59–60
Troubleshooting, in PL/SQL, 893
TRUNC function, 294
    eliminating the time portion of the DATE column, 41–42
    indexing and, 44
    truncating the time portion of SYSDATE, 405–406
    using with SYSDATE, 44
Tuning checklist, 346–360
Tuning methodology, 335–337
TUSC Web site, 15, 854
Two hyphen (—) comment method, 367–368
_txt suffix, 83
Type casting, using with database columns, 110
%TYPE declaration attribute, 108–109, 110, 264–265
    specifying the parameter data type, 140
    using with NOT NULL, 266–267
type_ prefix, for variables, 83
Types, 884–885

U

UGA memory, 605–607
UGA (User Global Area), 401–402
Unconditional branching statements, 891
Unconstrained cursor variables, 142

Underscore "_", avoiding in PL/SQL filenames, 78
Undocumented init.ora parameters, 459
Unexplained exceptions, 647–648
Universal Resource Locators. See URLs
UNIX operating system, 65
UNKEEP procedure, in DBMS_SHARED_POOL, 610–611
UNLIMITED TABLESPACE system privilege, RESOURCE role and, 500
UNPACK_MESSAGE procedure, in DBMS_PIPE, 592–593
Unpinning
    objects, 482
    PL/SQL objects, 610–611
Unused space, 613
UNUSED_SPACE procedure, in DBMS_SPACE, 613
UPDATE statement
    changing to a SELECT statement, 106, 107
    optimizing, 363–364
UPDATES, performing ad hoc in SQL*Plus, 69
UPDATING keyword, 222
UPPER function, 296–297
URLs (Universal Resource Locators)
    calling procedures or packaged procedures with, 767
    executing applications, 758–760
    identifying underlying operations when referencing, 760–761
    parts of, 758–759
    processing, 760
    providing the capability to display, 724
USE_ROLLBACK_SEGMENT procedure, in DBMS_TRANSACTION, 631–633
User accounts, locking, 831
User defined data type variables, prefix for, 83
User Global Area. See UGA (User Global Area)
User group, of Oracle system privileges, 496
User information/feedback, about performance problems, 328

User privileges, script for providing a list of, 516–517
User schemas/accounts, 501
User statistics, 471–472
User tracking mechanism, integrating to pinpoint execution location, 426
USER variable, 71
USER$ data dictionary table, 670
USER_* level data dictionary views, 665
USER_* views, 92, 675
USER_ARGUMENTS view, 900–901
USER_COL_COMMENTS, 682–684
USER_DEPENDENCIES view, 901, 206–207, 677, 680, 698
USER_DEPENDENCY views, 444
USER_ERRORS view, 902, 677–678, 680, 694–696
USER_INDEXES view, 372
USER_INTERNAL_TRIGGERS view, 807
USER_JOBS view, 902–903, 577
USER_OBJECT_SIZE view, 904–905, 437–438, 678, 680, 700
USER_OBJECTS view, 903–904, 675–676, 680
    accessing creation date and last modification date, 684–685
    reviewing for INVALID objects, 215
USER_SOURCE data dictionary view, 768
USER_SOURCE view, 905, 676, 680
    querying to determine a package version, 202
    recreating source code, 687
    searching, 696–698
USER_TAB_COMMENTS, 682–684
USER_TRIGGER_COLS view, 906, 677, 680
USER_TRIGGERS view, 905–906, 676–677, 680, 687
User-defined exceptions
    creating standard, 245–250
    implementing in triggers, 224
    propagating between program units, 249
User-defined record types, 132–133
User-defined types, 885
Users
    assigning to roles, 503–504
    breaking into groups, 502, 503

granting the privilege for executing PL/SQL stored objects, 508–509
highlighting open cursors for, 472–473
identifying locked, 475
logging into Oracle immediately upon UNIX login, 60
Utilities, versions provided in DBMS_UTILITY, 554
UTL_FILE package, 107, 555–556, 642–655
    logging results to an operating system file, 387
    possible uses of, 654–655
    raising pre-defined exceptions, 647–648
    specifying operating system directories for, 457
utl_file_dir init.ora parameter, 457, 643–644
UTL_FILE.FCLOSE_ALL procedure call, 645
UTL_RAW package, 815
utlxplan.sql script, 342, 345

V

V$ scripts, 468–477
V$ views
    monitoring PL/SQL related information, 468–477
    providing developers with SELECT privilege on selected, 485–487
    of value to developers, 486–487
V$ACCESS view, 474–475
V$DB_OBJECT_CACHE view, 424
    identifying objects in, 611
    viewing pinned PL/SQL objects, 608–609
V$DB_PIPES view, 588, 589
V$LIBRARY_CACHE view, 468–469
V$LOCK view, 475–476
V$OPEN_CURSOR view, 472–473
V$PARAMETER query, 576
V$PARAMETER view, 486
    displaying all init.ora parameters, 458, 459
    querying, 325–326

V$ROLLSTAT view, 476–477
V$ROWCACHE view, 469–470
V$SESS_IO view, 470–471, 486
V$SESSION view, 486
    determining sid and serial #,
      552, 629
    limiting retrieval to only the
      executing users session
      information, 390
    monitoring progress, 389–390
    monitoring record logging in, 361
    registering application information
      in, 540
    setting and reading client_info,
      571–572
    updating, 567–568
V$SESSTAT view, 471–472, 486, 487
V$SGA view, 461
V$SGASTAT view
    mappings of V$SGA to, 461
    viewing the contents of the Shared
      Pool, 460
V$SHARED_POOL_RESERVED view, 463
V$SQL view, retrieving the amount of, 465
V$SQLAREA script
    displaying PL/SQL and SQL
      statements, 712–713
    executing the server side, 418
V$SQLAREA view, 328–331, 486
    accessing the current contents of the
      Shared SQL Area, 420
    identifying objects in, 611
    registering application information
      in, 540
    retrieving the amount of, 465
    searching, 637
    updating, 568–569
V$SQLTEXT view, 330, 473–474, 486
V$STATNAME view, 487
V$TRANSACTION view, 476–477
V_$PARAMETER view, 644
V_$SQLAREA, 328
Valid language flag parameter values, 617
VALID PL/SQL objects, 450, 686
Validation errors, 242–243
VALUE_ERROR exception, in
    UTL.FILE, 646

Values, retrieving from output
    variables, 623
VARCHAR type, 884
VARCHAR2 data type, 145–148, 786
Variable names, 82–84, 148–149
Variable scope, 191–193
Variable type casting, 108–111
VARIABLE_VALUE procedure, in
    DBMS_SQL, 623, 624
Variables
    binding any input, 617
    comparing, 408
    creating composite, 131
    expanding SQL*Plus into PL/SQL, 64
    making lowercase, 83
    returning results into, 621
    scope of, 191–193
    setting with &&, 52
    sharing between forms, 728–732
Variables content, providing an interface
    to, 723
VARRAY, 835, 836–837
VBX package, 724
VERIFY_FUNCTION function script, 830
Version control mechanism, 239, 443
Version control system, 89, 687
Version function, 202–203
Version reporting, implementing in PL/SQL
    packages, 202–204
Versions
    developing source code for different,
      107–108
    reviewing enhancements for PL/SQL,
      8–12
Very large databases (VLDBs), 840
Views, creating to access the PL/SQL data
    dictionary, 678–680
Virtual Path, 759
Visual distinction, differentiating case to
    increase in PL/SQL code, 80–82
VMS operating system, 65

W

WAITANY procedure, in DBMS_ALERT,
    562–563

WAITONE procedure, in DBMS_ALERT, 562–563
Weak-type declaration, 142
Web
    executing PL/SQL code through, 758
    writing PL/SQL for, 765–767
Web browser, getting parameters to the PL/SQL Agent, 780–781
Web environment, locking in, 769–772
Web integration, expanded in Oracle8, 844–846
WEB package, 724
Web pages, building with PL/SQL packages, 763–765
Web Request Broker. *See* WRB
Web Request Broker Executable Engine (WRBX), 760
Web servers, 756
Web toolkit. *See* PL/SQL Web toolkit
WebAlchemy, 766
Web-based applications
    fine-tuning SQL statements in, 371
    permission for, 518
WebView set of packages, 766
WHEN CURRENT OF clause, 159
WHEN-VALIDATE_ITEM trigger, 735–737
Whitespace
    integrating to increase readability in PL/SQL code, 84–86
    standards in this book, 94

WIIFM principle, 484
with grant option, 679
WNDS (Writes No Database State) purity level, 217, 218
WNPS (Writes No Package State) purity level, 217, 218
Word spacing, in PL/SQL code, 84–86
word_wrapped attribute, 695
WRAP utility, 79–80, 239–240, 443, 518
Wrapped code, 241
WRAPped files, standard filenaming convention for, 79–80
WRAPped PL/SQL program units, 718
Wrapped source files, 240
Wrapper procedure or function, 895
WRB (Web Request Broker), 759
wrb.log file, 765
WRITE_ERROR exception, 647
Writes No Database State purity level (WNDS), 217, 218
Writes No Package State purity level (WNPS), 217, 218
Write (W) mode, in UTL.FILE, 645

X

X$ tables, 485–486
x$ksppi table, v$parameter view and, 668–669

Get Your FREE Subscription to Oracle Magazine

Stay informed and increase your productivity with every issue of *Oracle Magazine.* Inside each FREE, bimonthly issue you'll get:

- Up-to-date information on Oracle Data Server, Oracle Applications, Network Computing Architecture, and tools
- Third-party news and announcements
- Technical articles on Oracle products and operating environments
- Software tuning tips
- Oracle customer application stories

Three easy ways to subscribe:

1 MAIL Cut out this page, complete the questionnaire on the back, and mail it to: *Oracle Magazine,* P.O. Box 1263, Skokie, IL 60076-8263.

2 FAX Cut out this page, complete the questionnaire on the back, and fax it to **+ 847.647.9735.**

3 WEB Visit our Web site at **www.oramag.com.** You'll find a subscription form there, plus much more!

If there are other Oracle users at your location who would like to receive their own subscription to *Oracle Magazine,* please photocopy the form and pass it along.

☐ **YES! Please send me a FREE subscription to Oracle Magazine.** ☐ NO, I am not interested at this time.

If you wish to receive your free bimonthly subscription to *Oracle Magazine,* you must fill out the entire form, sign it, and date it (incomplete forms cannot be processed or acknowledged). You can also subscribe at our Web site at **www.oramag.com/html/subform.html** or fax your application to *Oracle Magazine* at **+847.647.9735.**

SIGNATURE (REQUIRED) ✓ _____ **DATE** _____

NAME _____ TITLE _____

COMPANY _____ E-MAIL ADDRESS _____

STREET/P.O. BOX _____

CITY/STATE/ZIP _____

COUNTRY _____ TELEPHONE _____

You must answer all eight questions below.

1 What is the primary business activity of your firm at this location?
(circle only one)
- ○ 01 Agriculture, Mining, Natural Resources
- ○ 02 Architecture, Construction
- ○ 03 Communications
- ○ 04 Consulting, Training
- ○ 05 Consumer Packaged Goods
- ○ 06 Data Processing
- ○ 07 Education
- ○ 08 Engineering
- ○ 09 Financial Services
- ○ 10 Government—Federal, Local, State, Other
- ○ 11 Government—Military
- ○ 12 Health Care
- ○ 13 Manufacturing—Aerospace, Defense
- ○ 14 Manufacturing—Computer Hardware
- ○ 15 Manufacturing—Noncomputer Products
- ○ 16 Real Estate, Insurance
- ○ 17 Research & Development
- ○ 18 Human Resources
- ○ 19 Retailing, Wholesaling, Distribution
- ○ 20 Software Development
- ○ 21 Systems Integration, VAR, VAD, OEM
- ○ 22 Transportation
- ○ 23 Utilities (Electric, Gas, Sanitation)
- ○ 24 Other Business and Services _____

2 Which of the following best describes your job function? *(circle only one)*
CORPORATE MANAGEMENT/STAFF
- ○ 01 Executive Management (President, Chair, CEO, CFO, Owner, Partner, Principal)
- ○ 02 Finance/Administrative Management (VP/Director/Manager/Controller, Purchasing, Administration)
- ○ 03 Sales/Marketing Management (VP/Director/Manager)
- ○ 04 Computer Systems/Operations Management (CIO/VP/Director/Manager MIS, Operations)
- ○ 05 Other Finance/Administration Staff
- ○ 06 Other Sales/Marketing Staff

IS/IT Staff
- ○ 07 Systems Development/Programming Management
- ○ 08 Systems Development/Programming Staff
- ○ 09 Consulting
- ○ 10 DBA/Systems Administrator
- ○ 11 Education/Training
- ○ 12 Engineering/R&D/Science Management
- ○ 13 Engineering/R&D/Science Staff
- ○ 14 Technical Support Director/Manager
- ○ 15 Webmaster/Internet Specialist
- ○ 16 Other Technical Management/Staff

3 What is your current primary operating platform? *(circle all that apply)*
- ○ 01 DEC UNIX
- ○ 02 DEC VAX VMS
- ○ 03 Java
- ○ 04 HP UNIX
- ○ 05 IBM AIX
- ○ 06 IBM UNIX
- ○ 07 Macintosh
- ○ 08 MPE-ix
- ○ 09 MS-DOS
- ○ 10 MVS
- ○ 11 NetWare
- ○ 12 Network Computing
- ○ 13 OpenVMS
- ○ 14 SCO UNIX
- ○ 15 Sun Solaris/SunOS
- ○ 16 SVR4
- ○ 17 Ultrix
- ○ 18 UnixWare
- ○ 19 VM
- ○ 20 Windows
- ○ 21 Windows NT
- ○ 22 Other _____
- ○ 23 Other UNIX _____

4 Do you evaluate, specify, recommend, or authorize the purchase of any of the following? *(circle all that apply)*
- ○ 01 Hardware
- ○ 02 Software
- ○ 03 Application Development Tools
- ○ 04 Database Products
- ○ 05 Internet or Intranet Products

5 In your job, do you use or plan to purchase any of the following products or services?
(check all that apply)

SOFTWARE

	Use	Plan to buy
01 Business Graphics	☐	☐
02 CAD/CAE/CAM	☐	☐
03 CASE	☐	☐
04 CIM	☐	☐
05 Communications	☐	☐
06 Database Management	☐	☐
07 File Management	☐	☐
08 Finance	☐	☐
09 Java	☐	☐
10 Materials Resource Planning	☐	☐
11 Multimedia Authoring	☐	☐
12 Networking	☐	☐
13 Office Automation	☐	☐
14 Order Entry/Inventory Control	☐	☐
15 Programming	☐	☐
16 Project Management	☐	☐
17 Scientific and Engineering	☐	☐
18 Spreadsheets	☐	☐
19 Systems Management	☐	☐
20 Workflow	☐	☐

HARDWARE

	Use	Plan to buy
21 Macintosh	☐	☐
22 Mainframe	☐	☐
23 Massively Parallel Processing	☐	☐
24 Minicomputer	☐	☐
25 PC	☐	☐
26 Network Computer	☐	☐
27 Supercomputer	☐	☐
28 Symmetric Multiprocessing	☐	☐
29 Workstation	☐	☐

PERIPHERALS

	Use	Plan to buy
30 Bridges/Routers/Hubs/Gateways	☐	☐
31 CD-ROM Drives	☐	☐
32 Disk Drives/Subsystems	☐	☐
33 Modems	☐	☐
34 Tape Drives/Subsystems	☐	☐
35 Video Boards/Multimedia	☐	☐

SERVICES

	Use	Plan to buy
36 Computer-Based Training	☐	☐
37 Consulting	☐	☐
38 Education/Training	☐	☐
39 Maintenance	☐	☐
40 Online Database Services	☐	☐
41 Support	☐	☐
42 None of the above	☐	☐

6 What Oracle products are in use at your site? *(circle all that apply)*
SERVER/SOFTWARE
- ○ 01 Oracle8
- ○ 02 Oracle7
- ○ 03 Oracle Application Server
- ○ 04 Oracle Data Mart Suites
- ○ 05 Oracle Internet Commerce Server
- ○ 06 Oracle InterOffice
- ○ 07 Oracle Lite
- ○ 08 Oracle Payment Server
- ○ 09 Oracle Rdb
- ○ 10 Oracle Security Server
- ○ 11 Oracle Video Server
- ○ 12 Oracle Workgroup Server

TOOLS
- ○ 13 Designer/2000
- ○ 14 Developer/2000 (Forms, Reports, Graphics)
- ○ 15 Oracle OLAP Tools
- ○ 16 Oracle Power Object

ORACLE APPLICATIONS
- ○ 17 Oracle Automotive
- ○ 18 Oracle Energy
- ○ 19 Oracle Consumer Packaged Goods
- ○ 20 Oracle Financials
- ○ 21 Oracle Human Resources
- ○ 22 Oracle Manufacturing
- ○ 23 Oracle Projects
- ○ 24 Oracle Sales Force Automation
- ○ 25 Oracle Supply Chain Management
- ○ 26 Other _____
- ○ 27 **None of the above**

7 What other database products are in use at your site? *(circle all that apply)*
- ○ 01 Access
- ○ 02 BAAN
- ○ 03 dbase
- ○ 04 Gupta
- ○ 05 IBM DB2
- ○ 06 Informix
- ○ 07 Ingres
- ○ 08 Microsoft Access
- ○ 09 Microsoft SQL Server
- ○ 10 Peoplesoft
- ○ 11 Progress
- ○ 12 SAP
- ○ 13 Sybase
- ○ 14 VSAM
- ○ 15 **None of the above**

8 During the next 12 months, how much do you anticipate your organization will spend on computer hardware, software, peripherals, and services for your location? *(circle only one)*
- ○ 01 Less than $10,000
- ○ 02 $10,000 to $49,999
- ○ 03 $50,000 to $99,999
- ○ 04 $100,000 to $499,999
- ○ 05 $500,000 to $999,999
- ○ 06 $1,000,000 and over

OMG

Think you're
smart?

You're an Oracle DBA. You're implementing a backup and recovery plan. Which component stores the synchronization information needed for database recovery?

a. *redo log files*

b. *control file*

c. *parameter file*

d. *trace file*

Think you're ready to wear this badge?

The time is right to become an Oracle Certified Professional (OCP) and we're here to help you do it. Oracle's cutting edge Instructor-Led Training, Interactive Courseware, and this exam guide can prepare you for certification faster than ever. OCP status is one of the top honors in your profession. Now is the time to take credit for what you know. *Call 800.441.3541 (Outside the U.S. call +1.310.335.2403)* for an OCP training solution that meets your time, budget, and learning needs. Or visit us at *http://education.oracle.com/certification* for more information.

ORACLE®
Education